CAT

TRAIL OF THE CATWOMAN

WOMAN

VOLUME **1**

Darwyn Cooke
Ed Brubaker
Writers

Darwyn Cooke
Cameron Stewart
Mike Allred
Brad Rader
Rick Burchett
Artists

Sean Konot
Willie Schubert
Letters

Matt Hollingsworth
Lee Loughridge
Giulia Brusco
Colors and Separations

Darwyn Cooke
Paul Pope
Covers

Darwyn Cooke
Collection Cover

CAT

TRAIL OF THE CATWOMAN

WOMAN

VOLUME 1

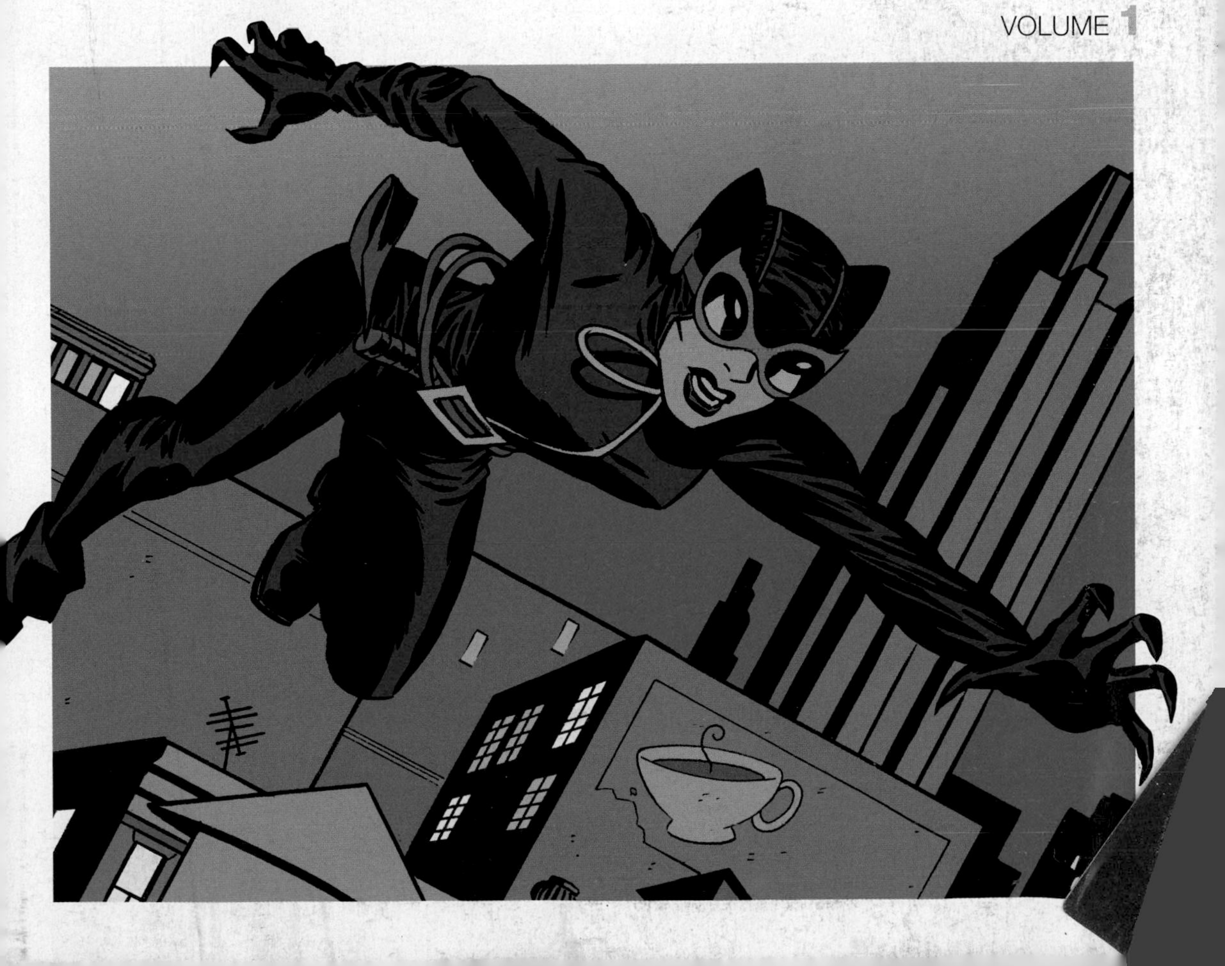

Mark Chiarello **Matt Idelson** Editors – Original Series
Lysa Hawkins Associate Editor – Original Series
Valerie D'Orazio **Nachie Castro** Assistant Editors – Original Series
Ian Sattler Director – Editorial, Special Projects and Archival Editions
Robbin Brosterman Design Director – Books

Eddie Berganza Executive Editor
Bob Harras VP – Editor-in-Chief

Diane Nelson President
Dan DiDio and **Jim Lee** Co-Publishers
Geoff Johns Chief Creative Officer
John Rood Executive VP – Sales, Marketing and Business Development
Amy Genkins Senior VP – Business and Legal Affairs
Nairi Gardiner Senior VP – Finance
Jeff Boison VP – Publishing Operations
Mark Chiarello VP – Art Direction and Design
John Cunningham VP – Marketing
Terri Cunningham VP – Talent Relations and Services
Alison Gill Senior VP – Manufacturing and Operations
David Hyde VP – Publicity
Hank Kanalz Senior VP – Digital
Jay Kogan VP – Business and Legal Affairs, Publishing
Jack Mahan VP – Business Affairs, Talent
Nick Napolitano VP – Manufacturing Administration
Sue Pohja VP – Book Sales
Courtney Simmons Senior VP – Publicity
Bob Wayne Senior VP – Sales

Catwoman Volume 1: Trail of the Catwoman

DC Comics, 1700 Broadway, New York, NY 10019
A Warner Bros. Entertainment Company.
Printed by RR Donnelley, Salem, VA, USA. 12/20/11. First Printing.
ISBN: 978-1-4012-3384-6

SUSTAINABLE FORESTRY INITIATIVE
Certified Chain of Custody
Promoting Sustainable Forest Management

Fiber used in this product line meets the sourcing requirements of the SFI program.
www.sfiprogram.org SGS-SFI/COC-US10/81072

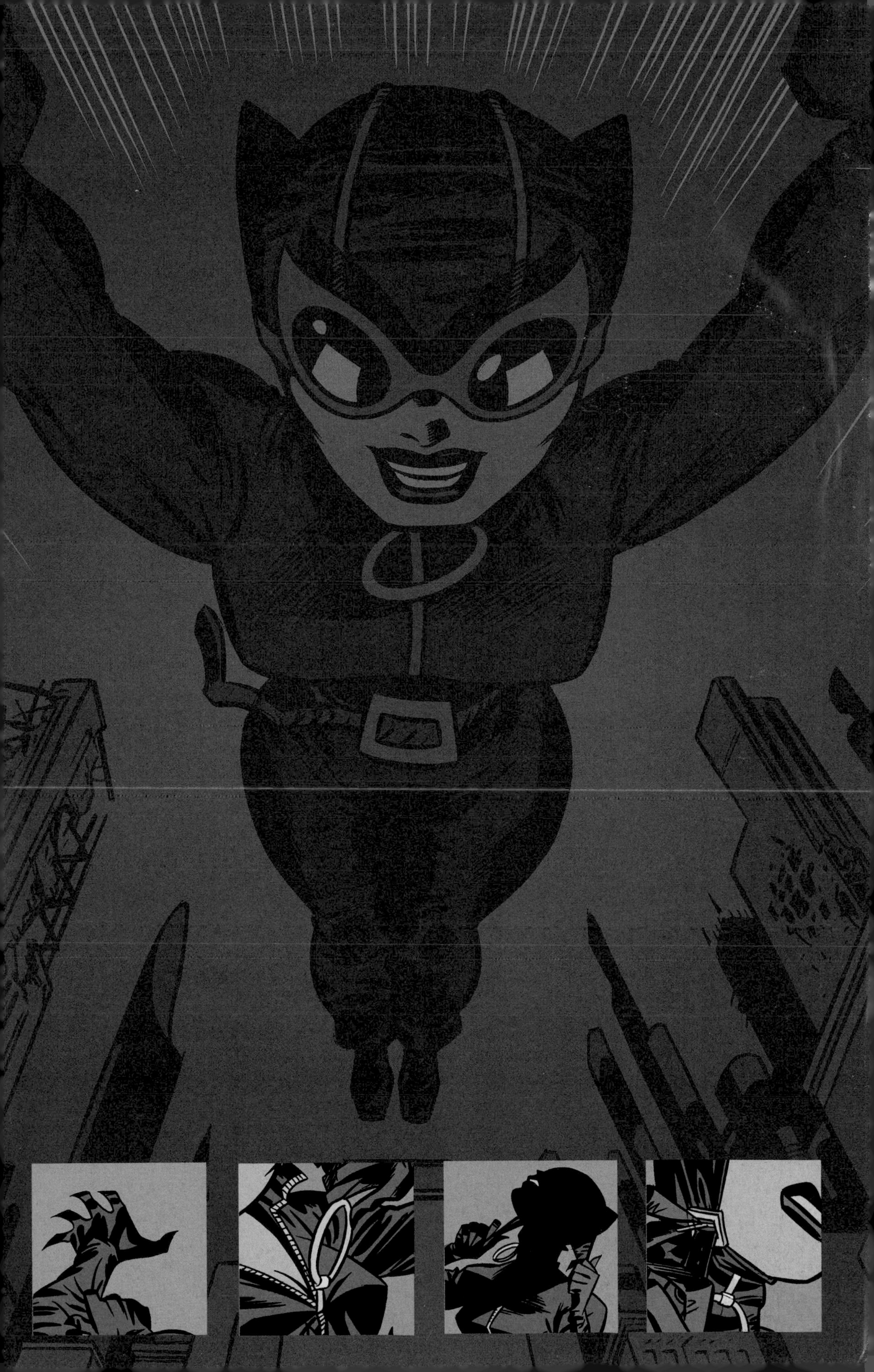

Catwoman: Selina's Big Score
Cover and Art by Darwyn Cooke with Matt Hollingsworth
Written by Darwyn Cooke

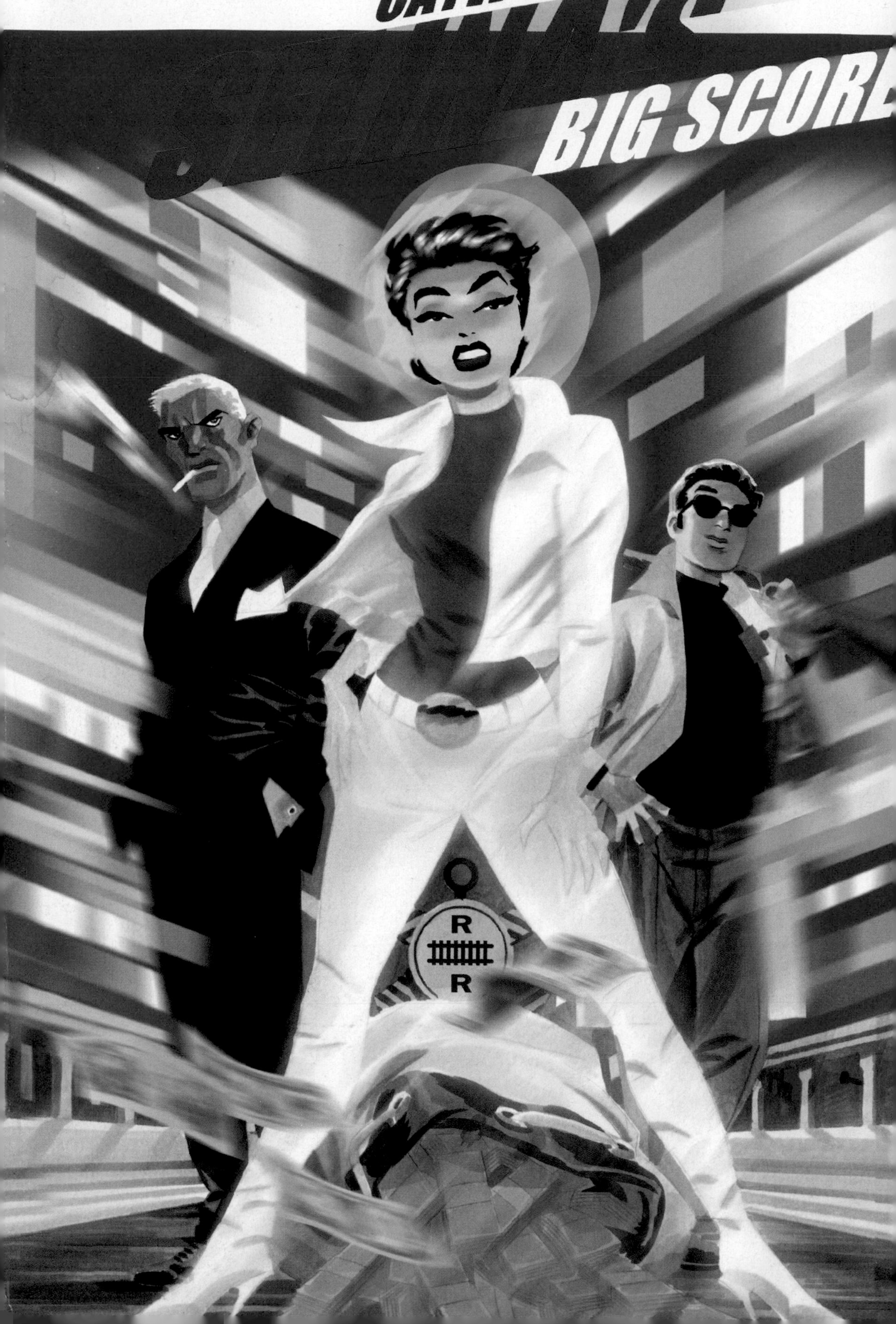
CATWOMAN
BIG SCORE
R
R

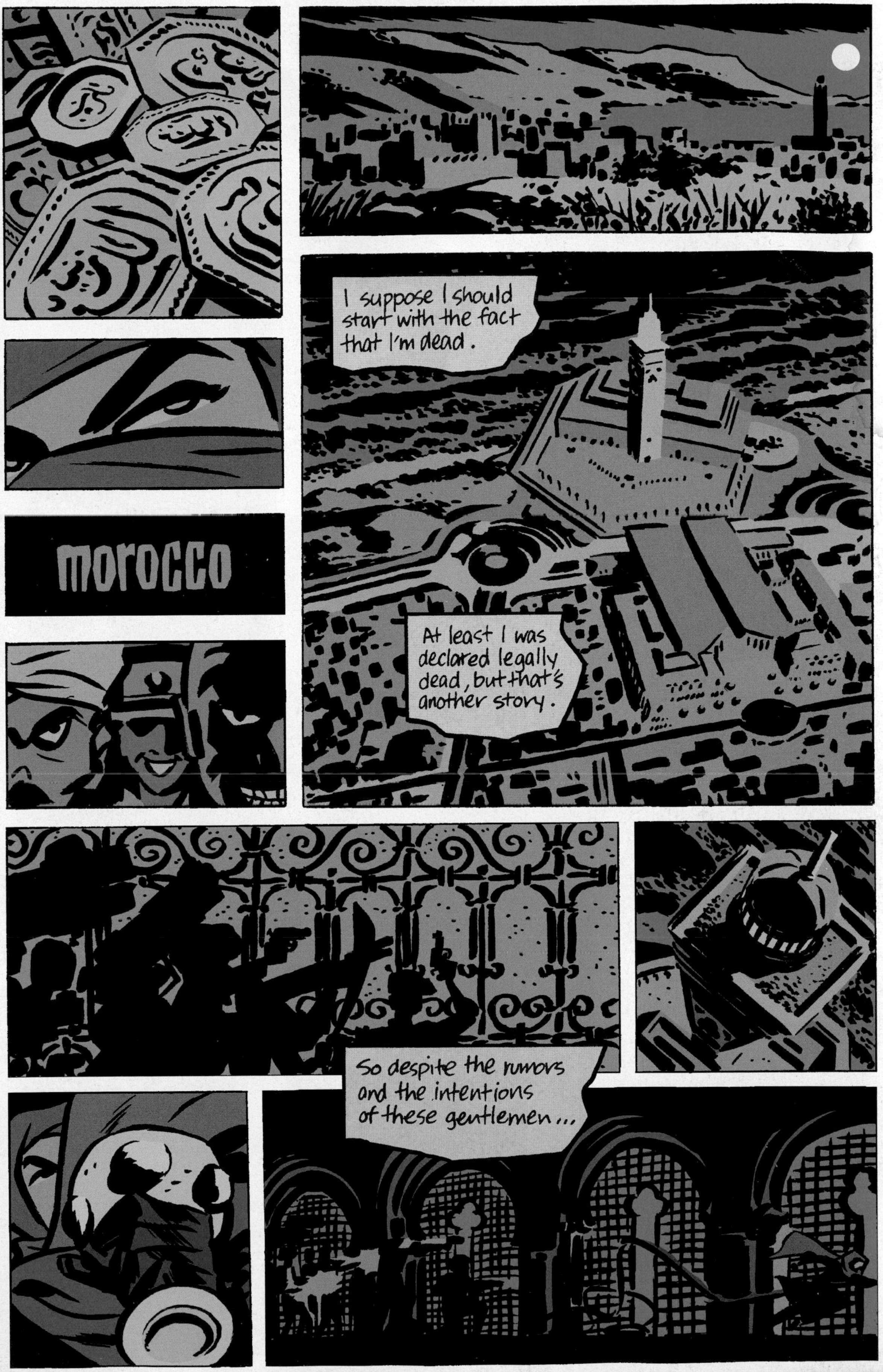
MOROCCO
I suppose I should start with the fact that I'm dead.
At least I was declared legally dead, but that's another story.
So despite the rumors and the intentions of these gentlemen...

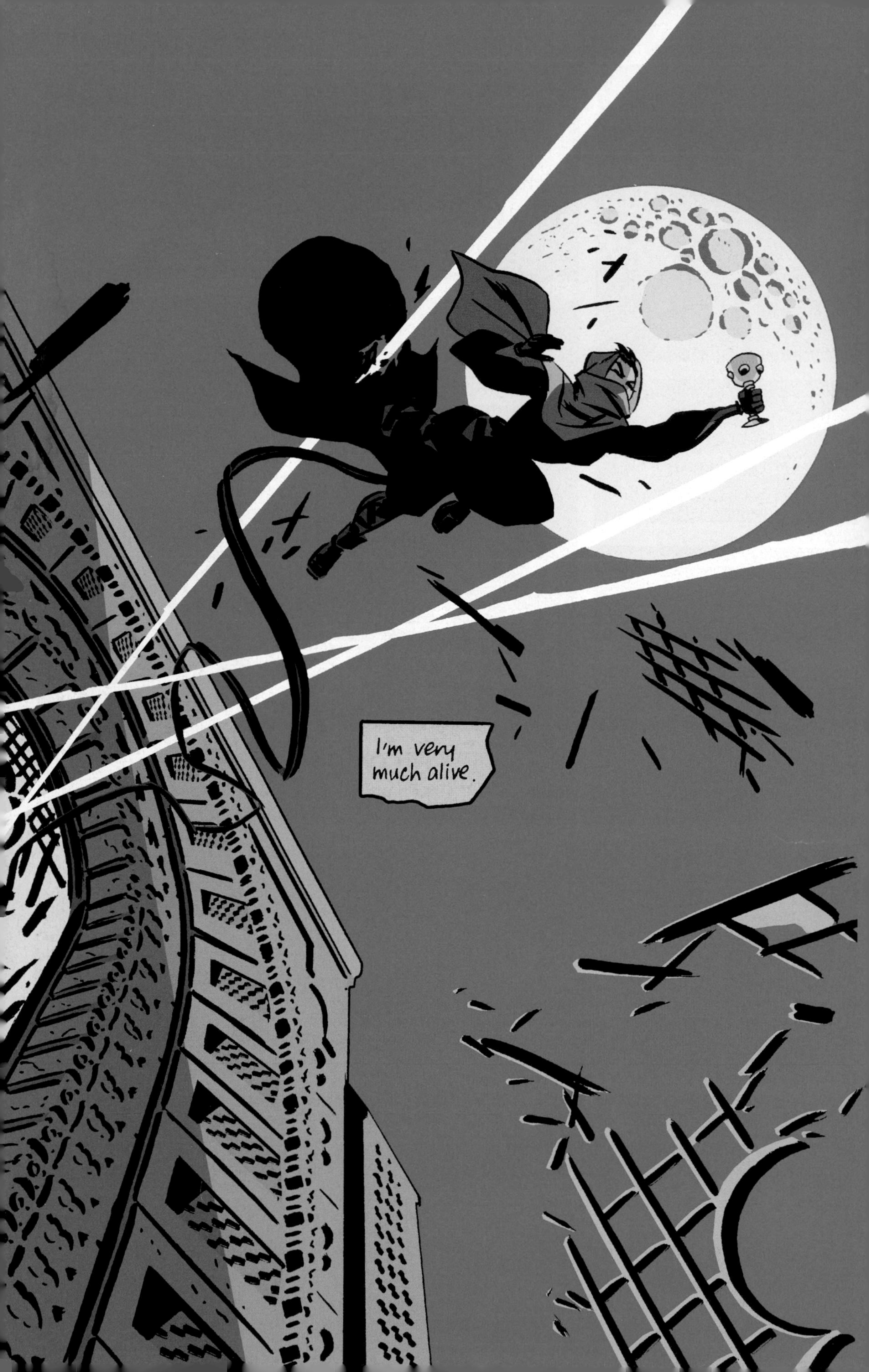
I'm very much alive.

BOOK ONE
SELINA

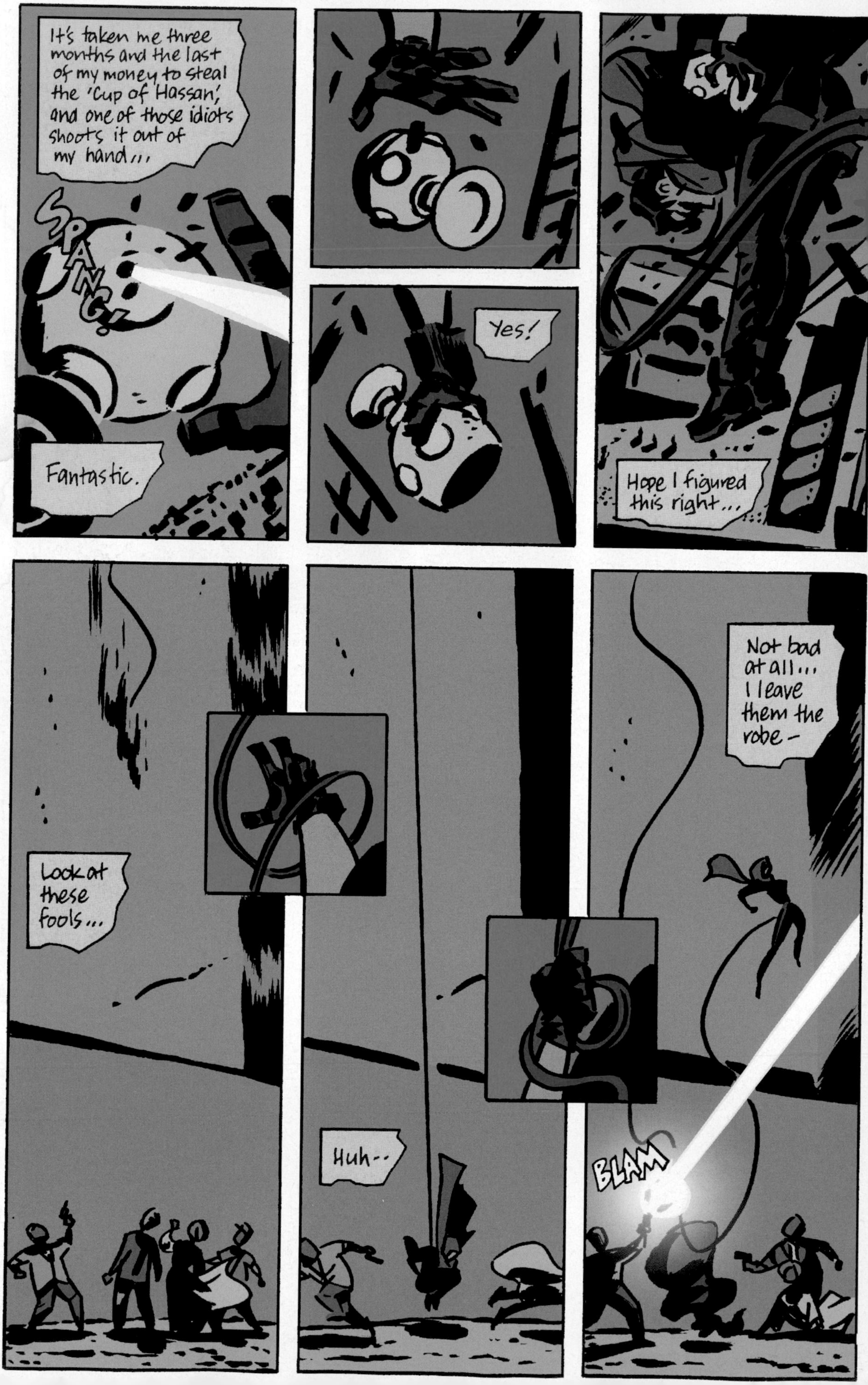
It's taken me three months and the last of my money to steal the 'Cup of Hassan,' and one of those idiots shoots it out of my hand...
SPANG!
Fantastic.
Yes!
Hope I figured this right...
Look at these fools...
Huh--
Not bad at all... I leave them the robe -
BLAM

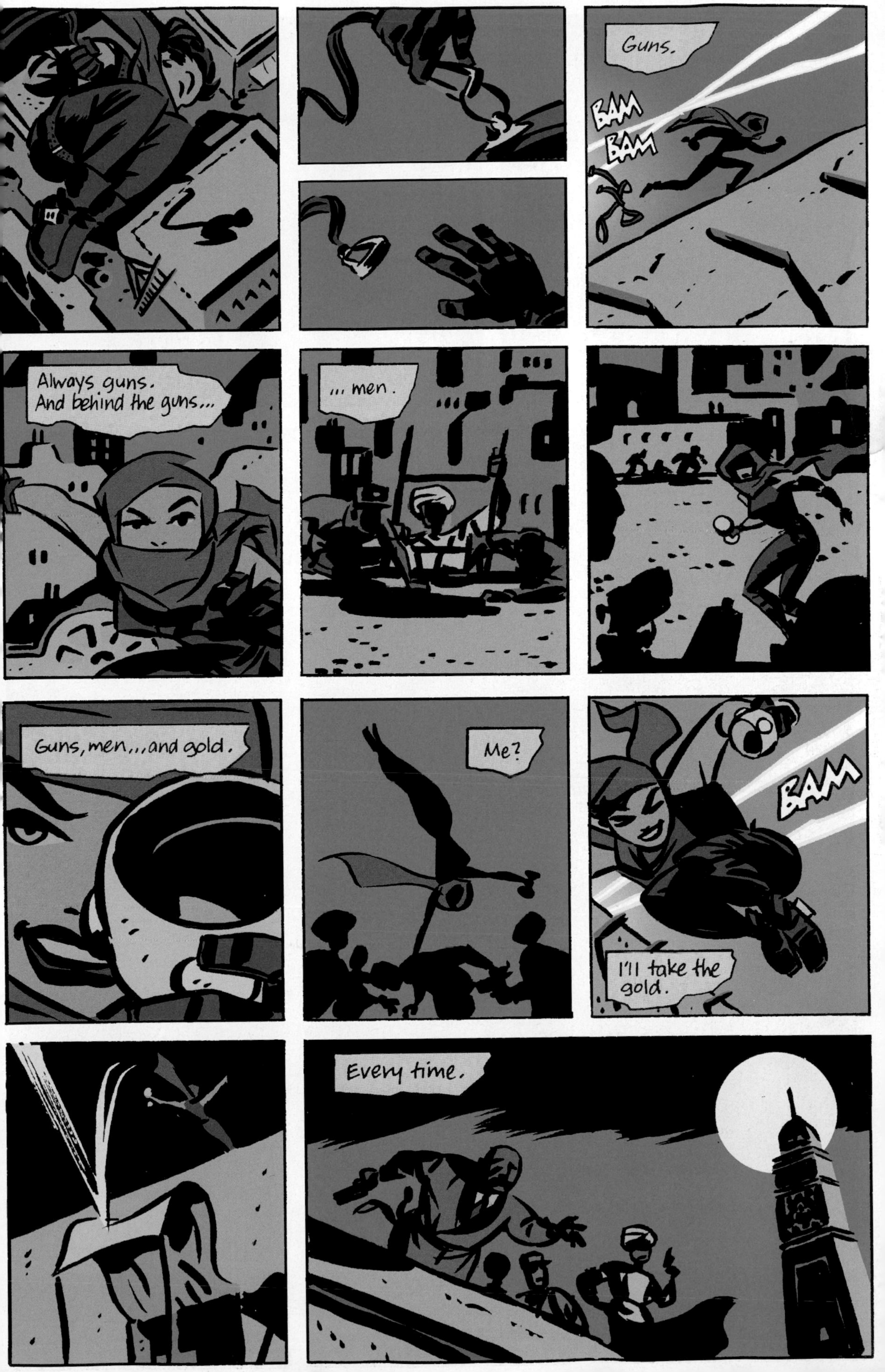
Guns.
BAM
BAM
Always guns.
And behind the guns...
... men.
Guns, men... and gold.
Me?
BAM
I'll take the gold.
Every time.

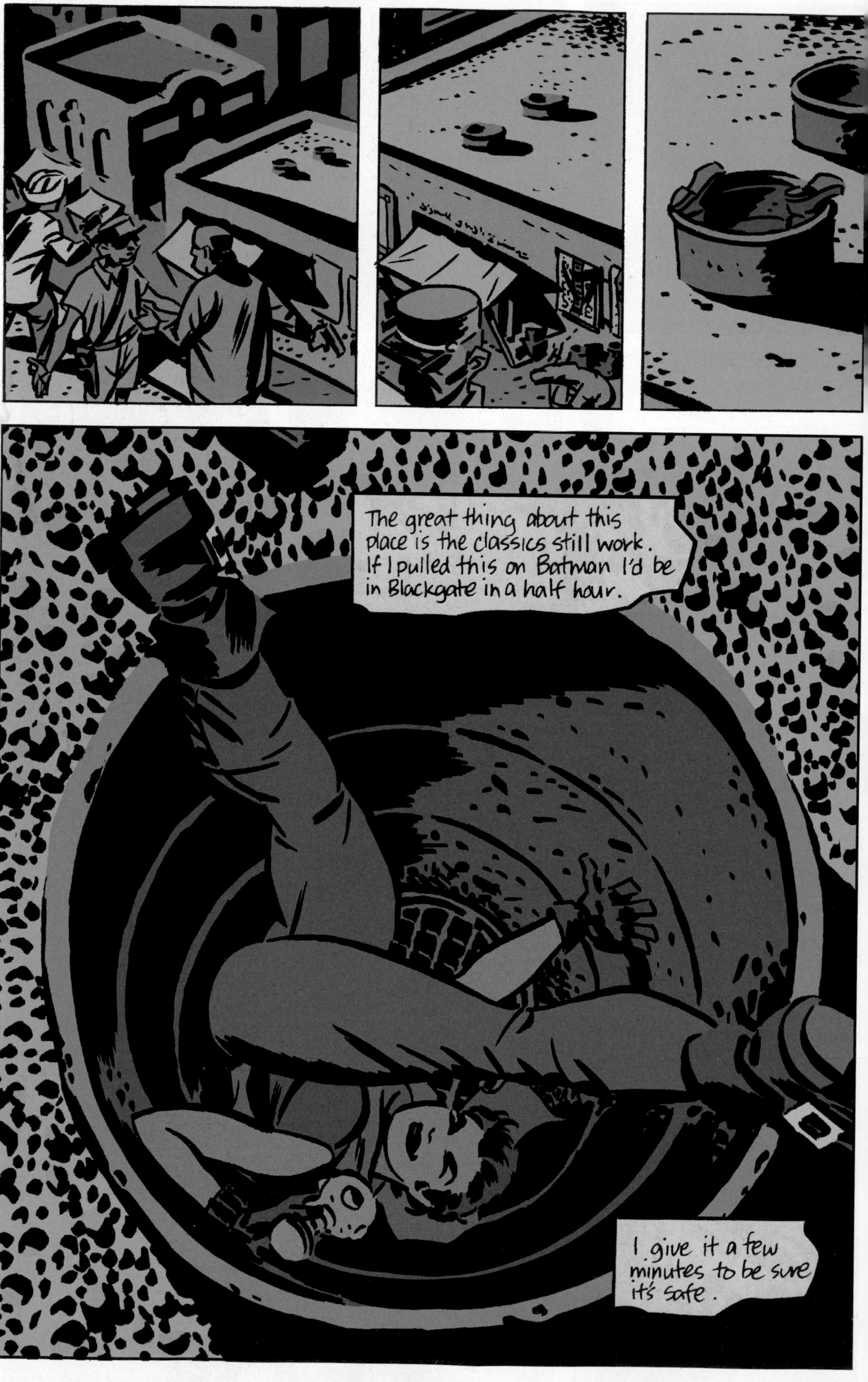
The great thing about this place is the classics still work. If I pulled this on Batman I'd be in Blackgate in a half hour.
I give it a few minutes to be sure it's safe.

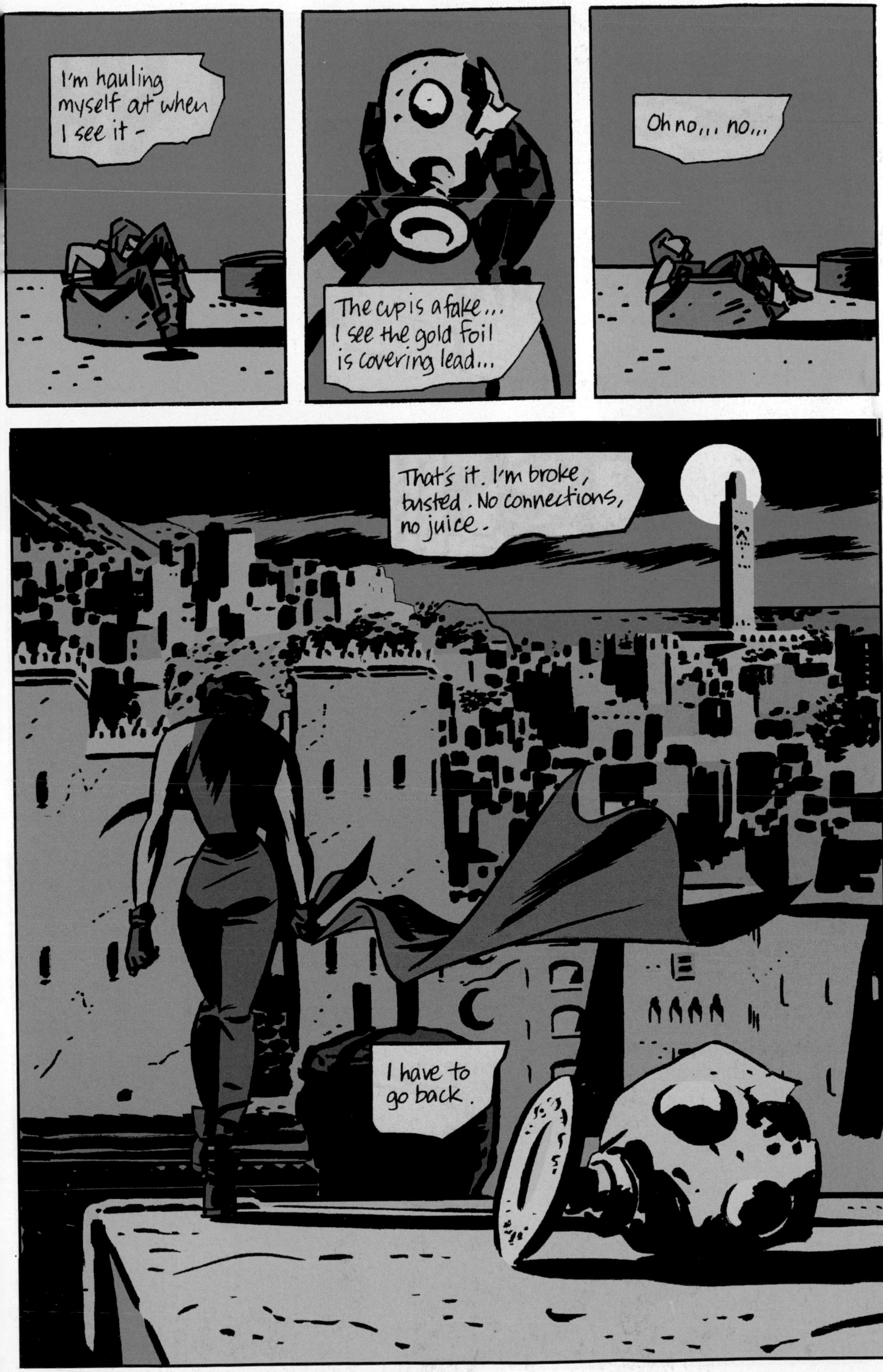

I'm hauling myself out when I see it -
The cup is a fake... I see the gold foil is covering lead...
Oh no... no...
That's it. I'm broke, busted. No connections, no juice.
I have to go back.

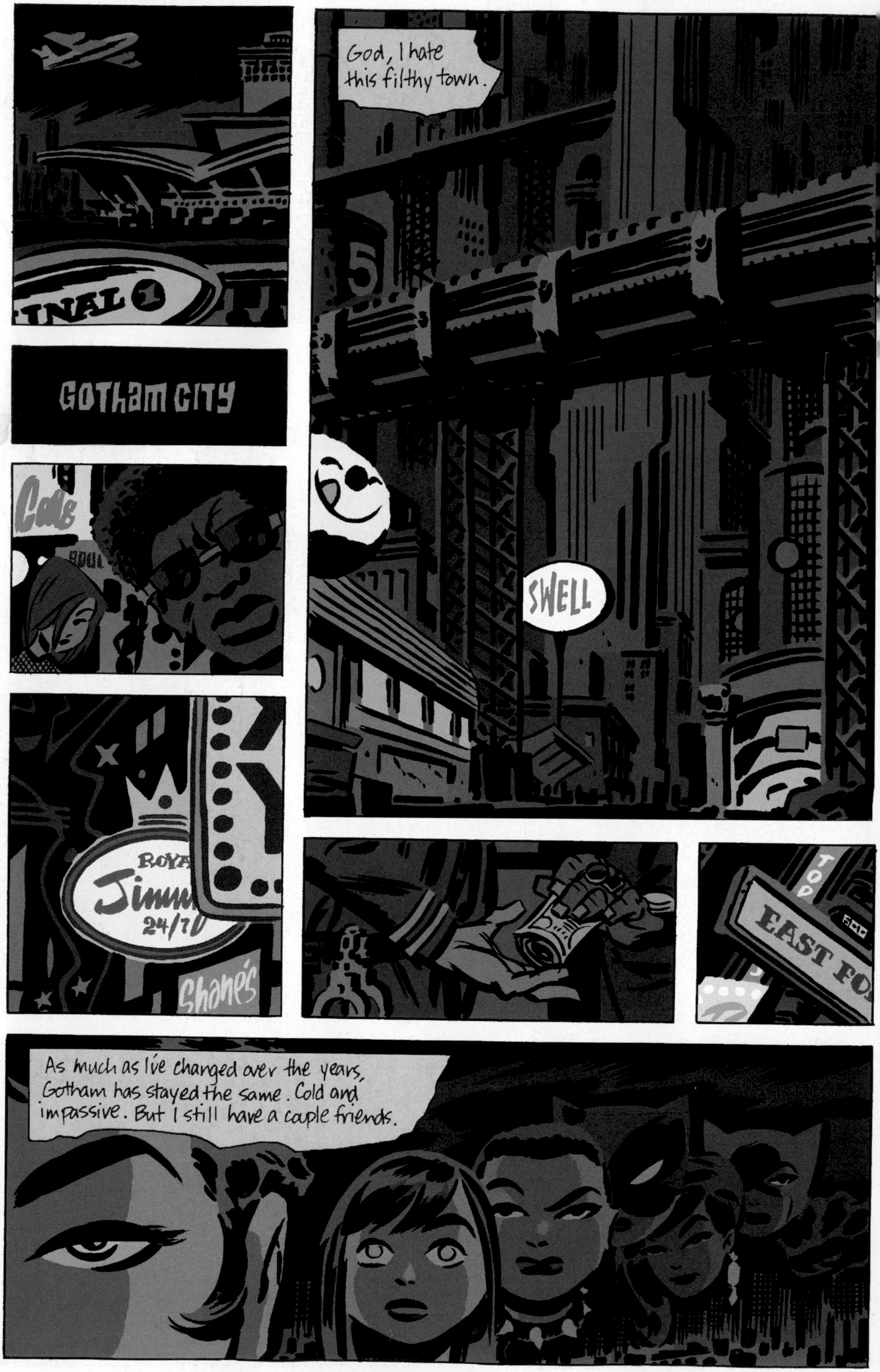
God, I hate this filthy town.
INAL 1
GOTHAM CITY
SWELL
ROYA
24/7
Shane's
EAST FO
As much as I've changed over the years, Gotham has stayed the same. Cold and impassive. But I still have a couple friends.

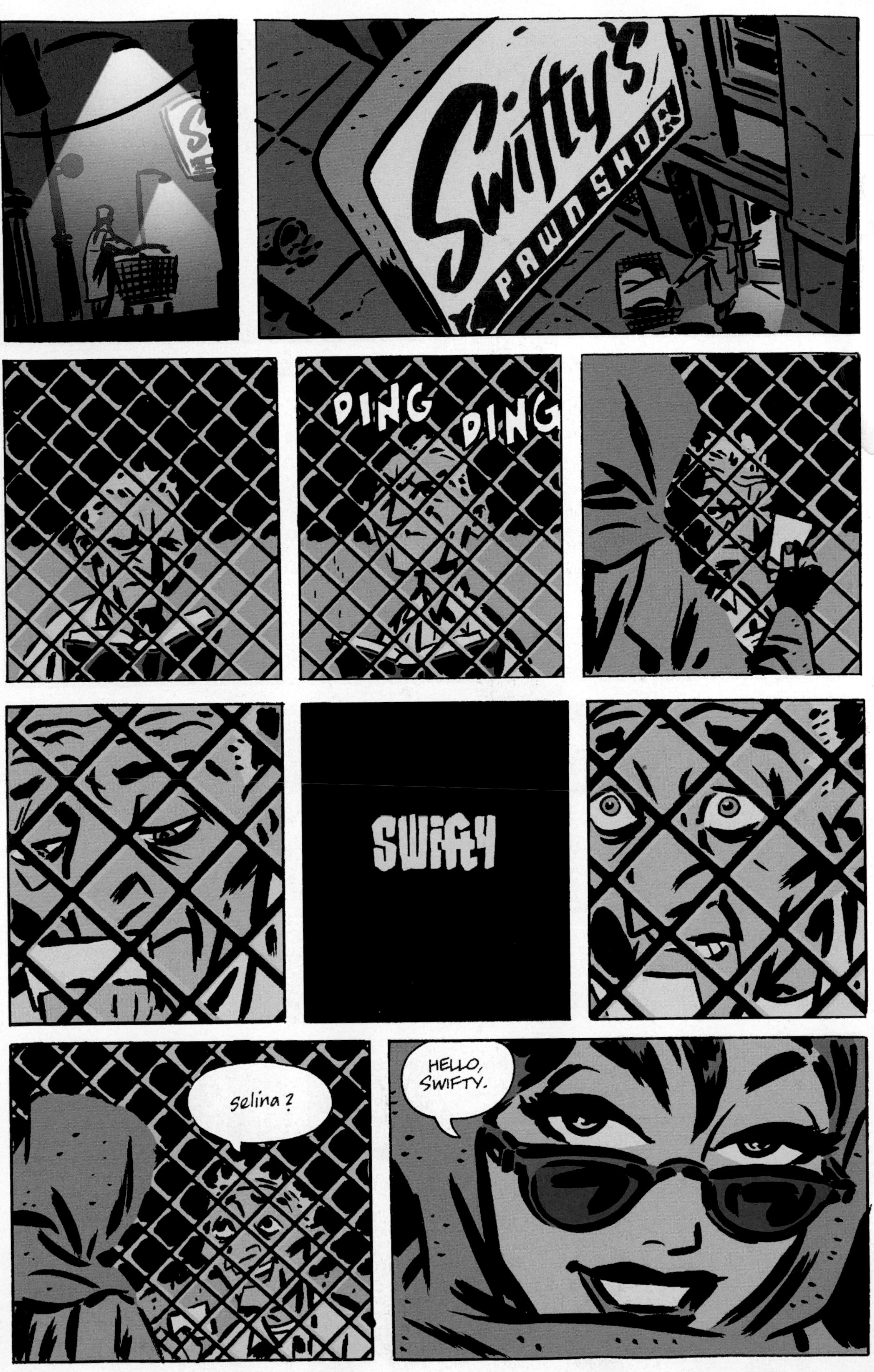
Swifty's
PAWN SHOP
DING DING
SWIFTY
selina ?
HELLO, SWIFTY.

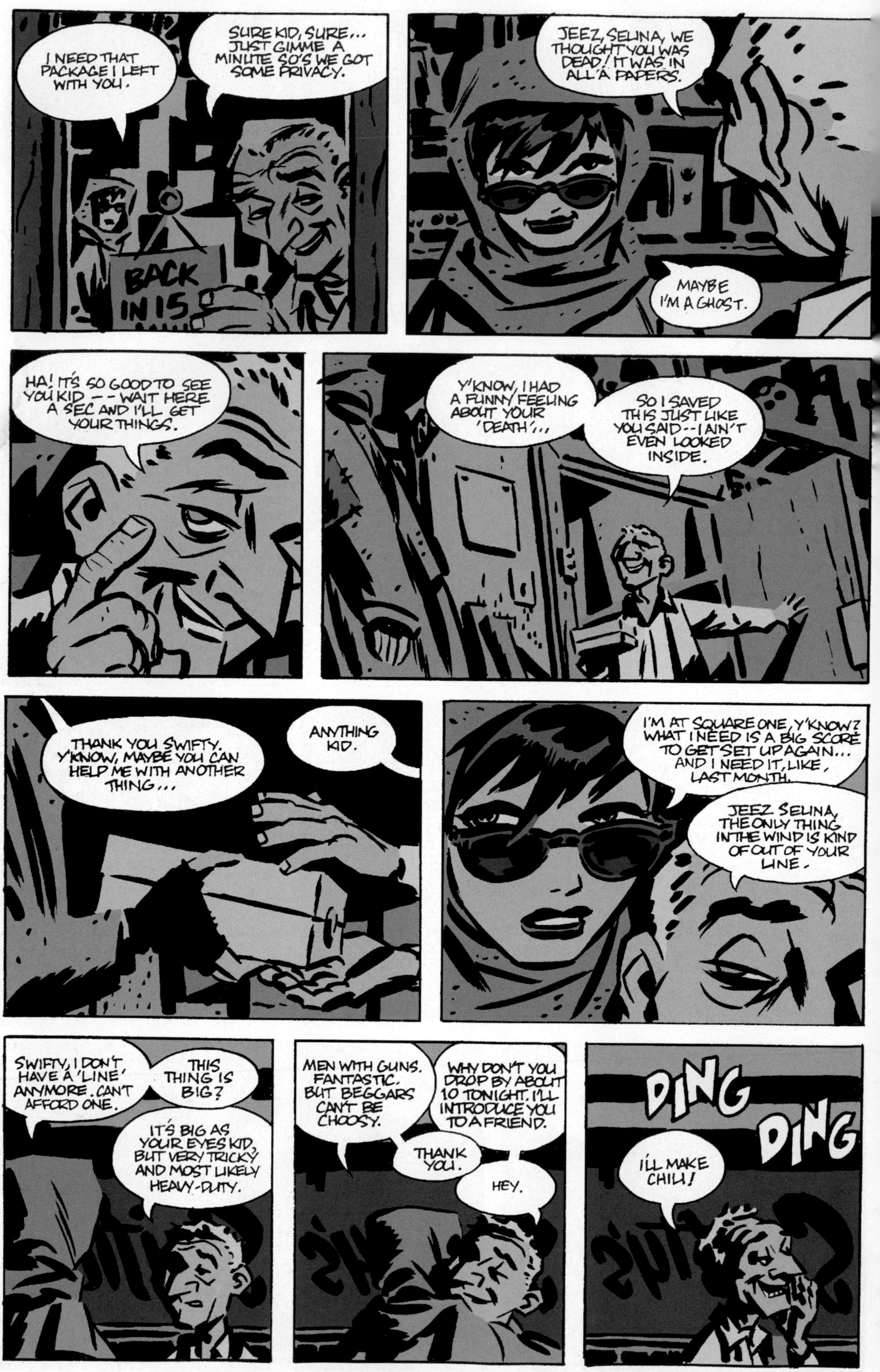
I NEED THAT PACKAGE I LEFT WITH YOU.
SURE KID, SURE... JUST GIMME A MINUTE SO'S WE GOT SOME PRIVACY.
BACK IN 15
JEEZ, SELINA, WE THOUGHT YOU WAS DEAD! IT WAS IN ALL'A PAPERS.
MAYBE I'M A GHOST.
HA! IT'S SO GOOD TO SEE YOU KID -- WAIT HERE A SEC AND I'LL GET YOUR THINGS.
Y'KNOW, I HAD A FUNNY FEELING ABOUT YOUR 'DEATH'...
SO I SAVED THIS JUST LIKE YOU SAID--I AIN'T EVEN LOOKED INSIDE.
THANK YOU SWIFTY. Y'KNOW, MAYBE YOU CAN HELP ME WITH ANOTHER THING...
ANYTHING KID.
I'M AT SQUARE ONE, Y'KNOW? WHAT I NEED IS A BIG SCORE TO GET SET UP AGAIN... AND I NEED IT, LIKE, LAST MONTH.
JEEZ SELINA, THE ONLY THING IN THE WIND IS KIND OF OUT OF YOUR LINE.
SWIFTY, I DON'T HAVE A 'LINE' ANYMORE. CAN'T AFFORD ONE.
THIS THING IS BIG?
IT'S BIG AS YOUR EYES KID, BUT VERY TRICKY AND MOST LIKELY HEAVY-DUTY.
MEN WITH GUNS. FANTASTIC. BUT BEGGARS CAN'T BE CHOOSY.
WHY DON'T YOU DROP BY ABOUT 10 TONIGHT. I'LL INTRODUCE YOU TO A FRIEND.
THANK YOU.
HEY.
DING
DING
I'LL MAKE CHILI!

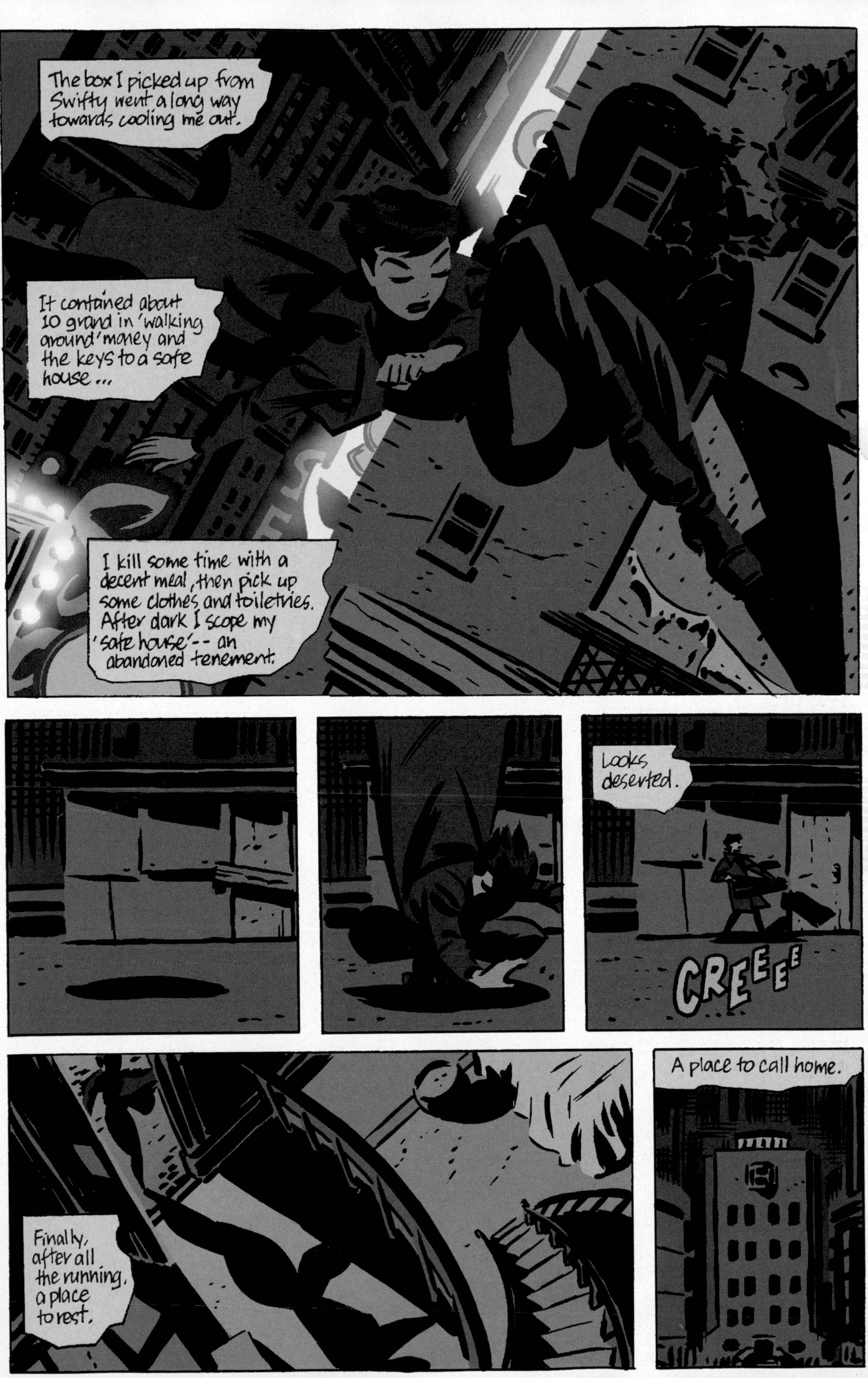
The box I picked up from Swifty went a long way towards cooling me out.
It contained about 10 grand in 'walking around' money and the keys to a safe house...
I kill some time with a decent meal, then pick up some clothes and toiletries. After dark I scope my 'safe house'-- an abandoned tenement.
Looks deserted.
CREEEE
Finally, after all the running, a place to rest.
A place to call home.

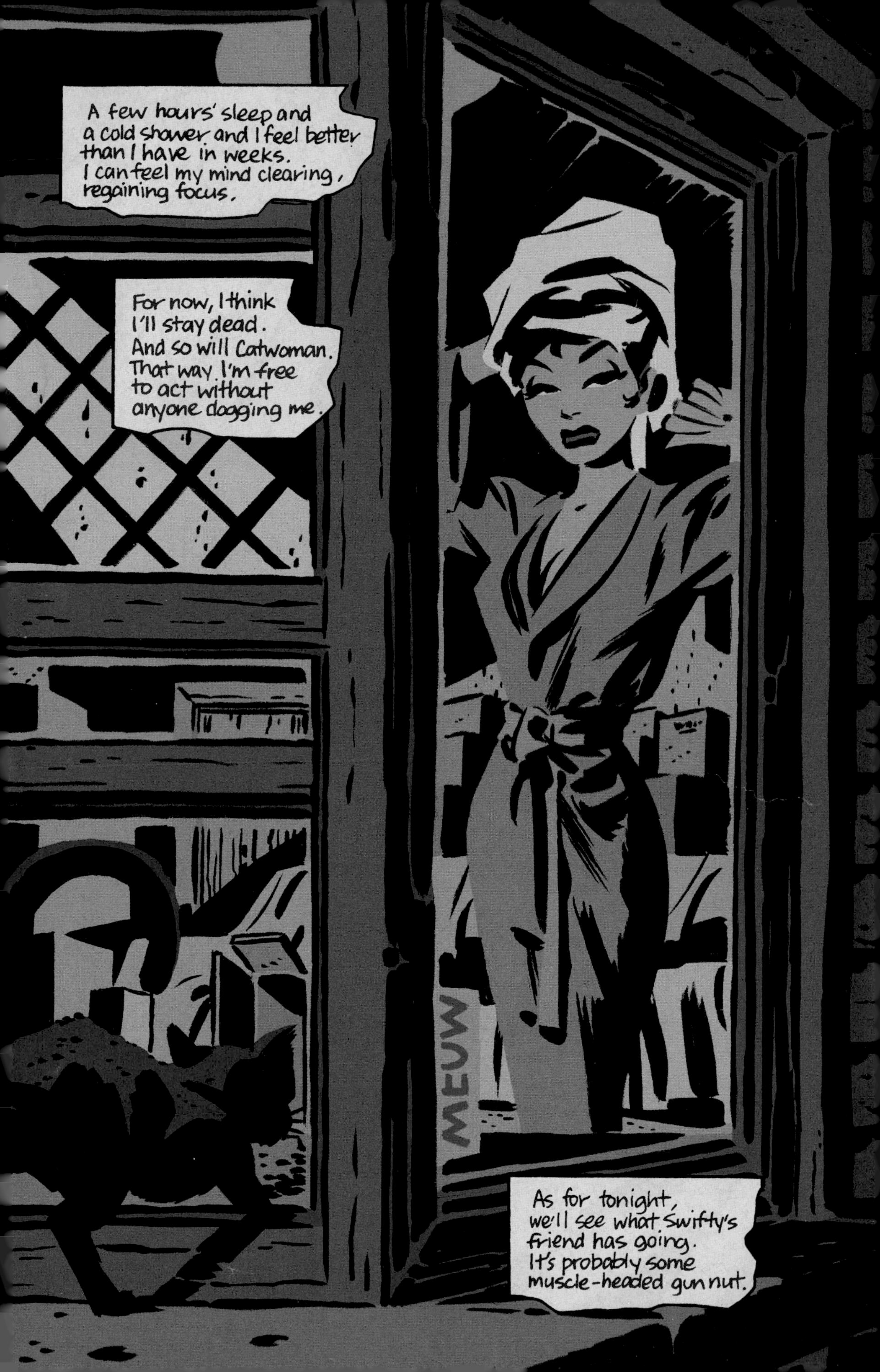
A few hours' sleep and a cold shower and I feel better than I have in weeks. I can feel my mind clearing, regaining focus.
For now, I think I'll stay dead. And so will Catwoman. That way, I'm free to act without anyone dogging me.
MEUW
As for tonight, we'll see what Swifty's friend has going. It's probably some muscle-headed gun nut.

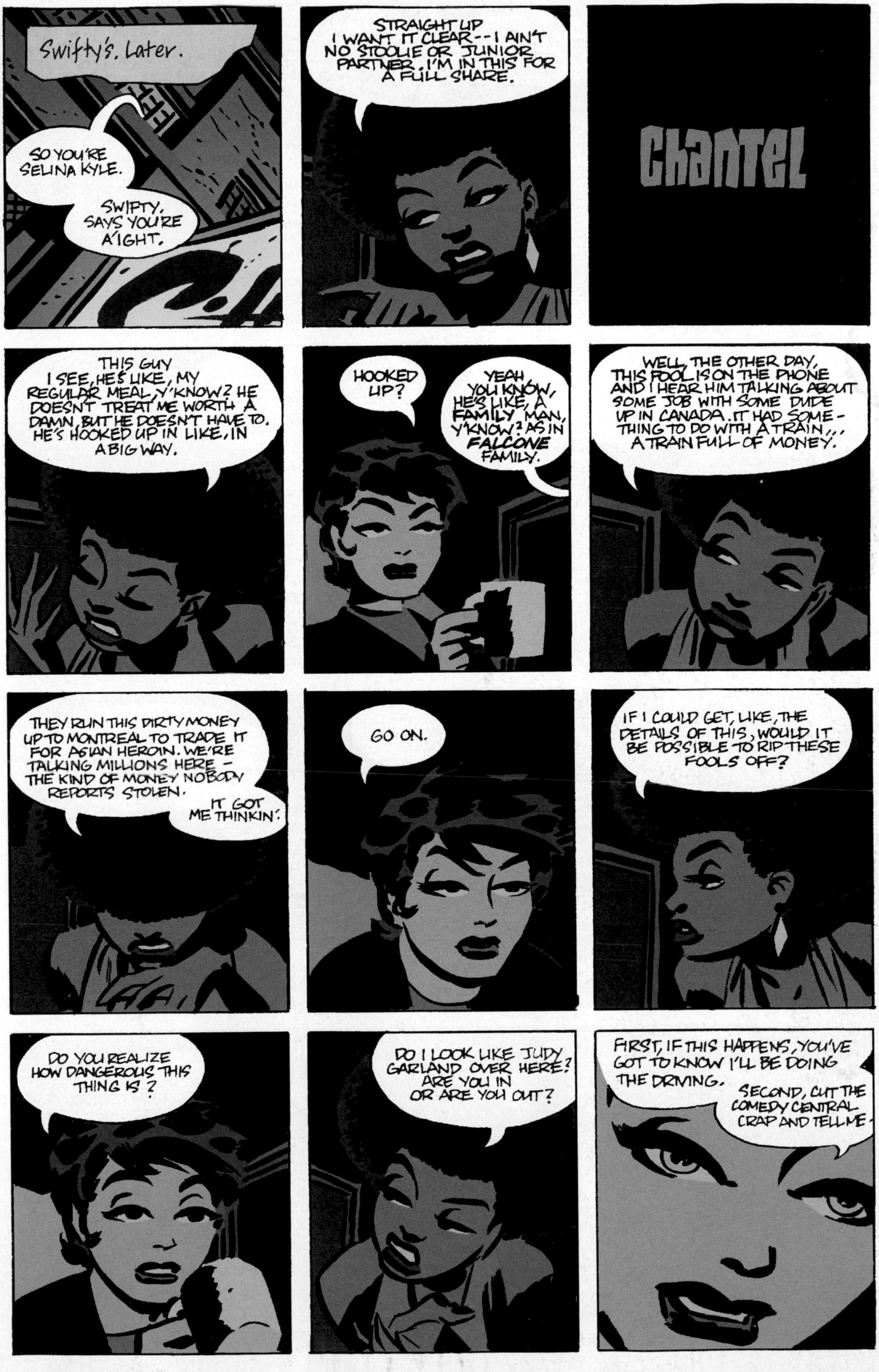

Swifty's. Later.
SO YOU'RE SELINA KYLE.
SWIFTY SAYS YOU'RE A'IGHT.
STRAIGHT UP I WANT IT CLEAR--I AIN'T NO STOOLIE OR JUNIOR PARTNER. I'M IN THIS FOR A FULL SHARE.
Chantel
THIS GUY I SEE, HE'S LIKE, MY REGULAR MEAL, Y'KNOW? HE DOESN'T TREAT ME WORTH A DAMN, BUT HE DOESN'T HAVE TO. HE'S HOOKED UP IN LIKE, IN A BIG WAY.
HOOKED UP?
YEAH YOU KNOW, HE'S LIKE, A FAMILY MAN, Y'KNOW? AS IN FALCONE FAMILY.
WELL, THE OTHER DAY, THIS FOOL IS ON THE PHONE AND I HEAR HIM TALKING ABOUT SOME JOB WITH SOME DUDE UP IN CANADA. IT HAD SOMETHING TO DO WITH A TRAIN... A TRAIN FULL OF MONEY.
THEY RUN THIS DIRTY MONEY UP TO MONTREAL TO TRADE IT FOR ASIAN HEROIN. WE'RE TALKING MILLIONS HERE - THE KIND OF MONEY NOBODY REPORTS STOLEN.
IT GOT ME THINKIN'.
GO ON.
IF I COULD GET, LIKE, THE DETAILS OF THIS, WOULD IT BE POSSIBLE TO RIP THESE FOOLS OFF?
DO YOU REALIZE HOW DANGEROUS THIS THING IS?
DO I LOOK LIKE JUDY GARLAND OVER HERE? ARE YOU IN OR ARE YOU OUT?
FIRST, IF THIS HAPPENS, YOU'VE GOT TO KNOW I'LL BE DOING THE DRIVING.
SECOND, CUT THE COMEDY CENTRAL CRAP AND TELL ME-

I DON'T HAVE NO FREE AND EASY TIME OF IT LIKE YOU THERE... I GOT RESPONSIBILITIES TO CONSIDER... MY MAMA, MY BABY GIRL--

Y'SEE, THEY DON'T KNOW ABOUT ME, NOT THAT WAY.

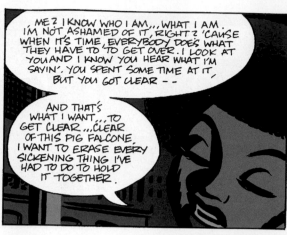

, ME? I KNOW WHO I AM... WHAT I AM. I'M NOT ASHAMED OF IT, RIGHT? 'CAUSE WHEN IT'S TIME, EVERYBODY DOES WHAT THEY HAVE TO TO GET OVER. I LOOK AT YOU AND I KNOW YOU HEAR WHAT I'M SAYIN'. YOU SPENT SOME TIME AT IT, BUT YOU GOT CLEAR--

AND THAT'S WHAT I WANT... TO GET CLEAR... CLEAR OF THIS PIG FALCONE. I WANT TO ERASE EVERY SICKENING THING I'VE HAD TO DO TO HOLD IT TOGETHER.

I COULD FEED YOU A PILE ABOUT MY KID, BUT THAT'S NONE OF YOUR NEVERMIND. I COULD BLUBBER ABOUT MY SICK OLD MAMA AND GET ALL COUNTRY AND WESTERN ON YOUR ASS, BUT THE STONE TRUTH IS...

IT'S ME. I'M SICK OF IT. LIKE I'D RATHER DIE, RIGHT?

SO MAYBE BY DOING ONE MORE REALLY BAD THING I CAN MAKE SOMETHING GOOD HAPPEN. FOR ME, FOR MY LITTLE GIRL.

I'M NOT TALKING ABOUT RIGHT OR WRONG...

I'M TALKING ABOUT BASIC HUMAN DIGNITY.

My God -- those words -

COME SIT DOWN CHANTEL. DINNER'S GETTING COLD.

AND WE'VE GOT A LOT TO TALK ABOUT IF WE'RE GOING TO DO THIS THING.

SUPPOSE? CHANTEL, DEAR CHILD, PREPARE FOR THE BEST MEAL YOU'VE HAD ALL NIGHT!

SUPPOSE I COULD EAT.

And so it starts -- We talk into the small of the evening, feeling eachother out.

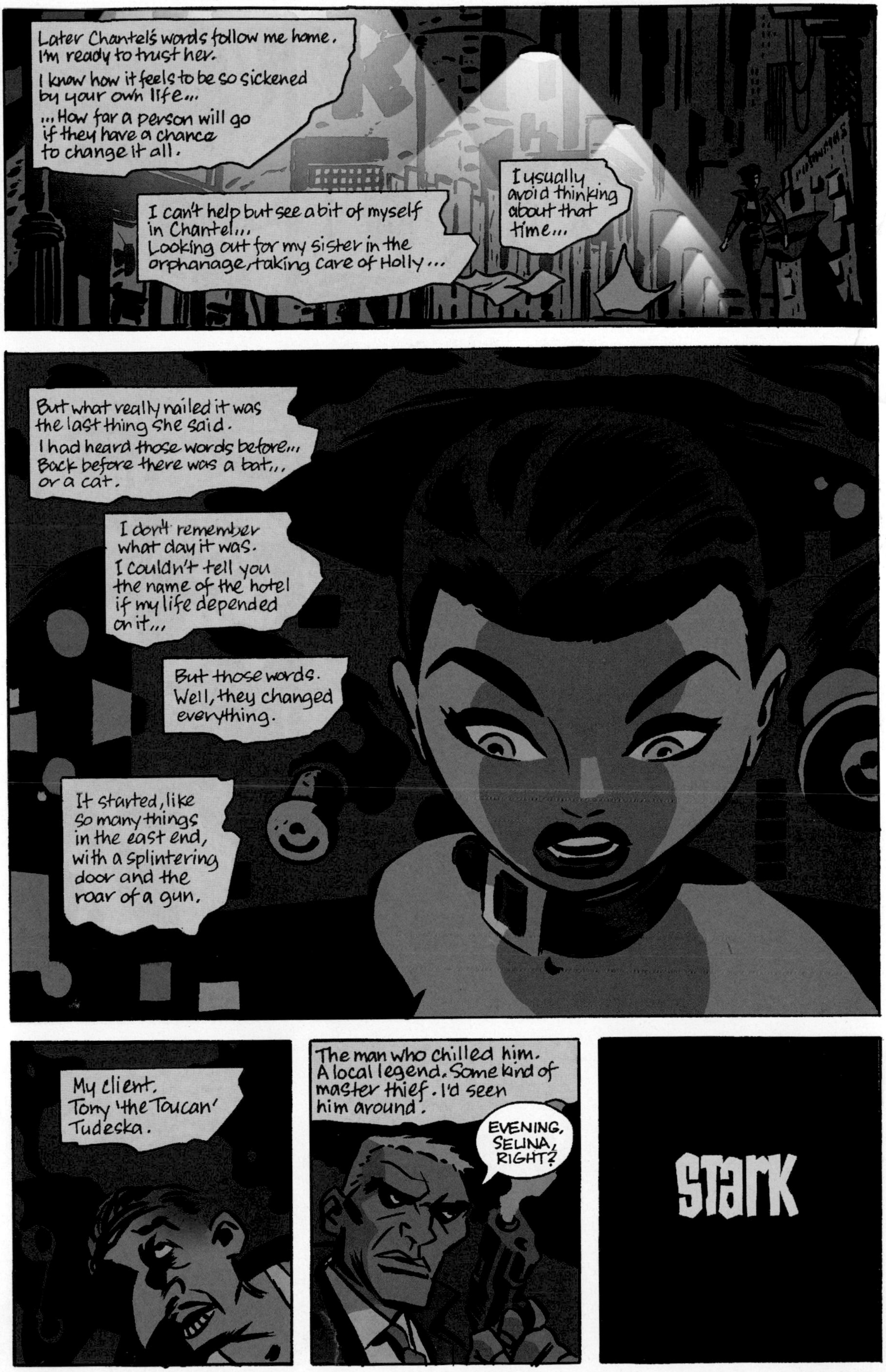
Later Chantel's words follow me home. I'm ready to trust her.
I know how it feels to be so sickened by your own life...
...How far a person will go if they have a chance to change it all.
I can't help but see a bit of myself in Chantel... Looking out for my sister in the orphanage, taking care of Holly...
I usually avoid thinking about that time...
But what really nailed it was the last thing she said.
I had heard those words before... Back before there was a bat... or a cat.
I don't remember what day it was. I couldn't tell you the name of the hotel if my life depended on it...
But those words. Well, they changed everything.
It started, like so many things in the east end, with a splintering door and the roar of a gun.
My client. Tony 'the Toucan' Tudeska.
The man who chilled him. A local legend. Some kind of master thief. I'd seen him around.
EVENING, SELINA, RIGHT?
STARK

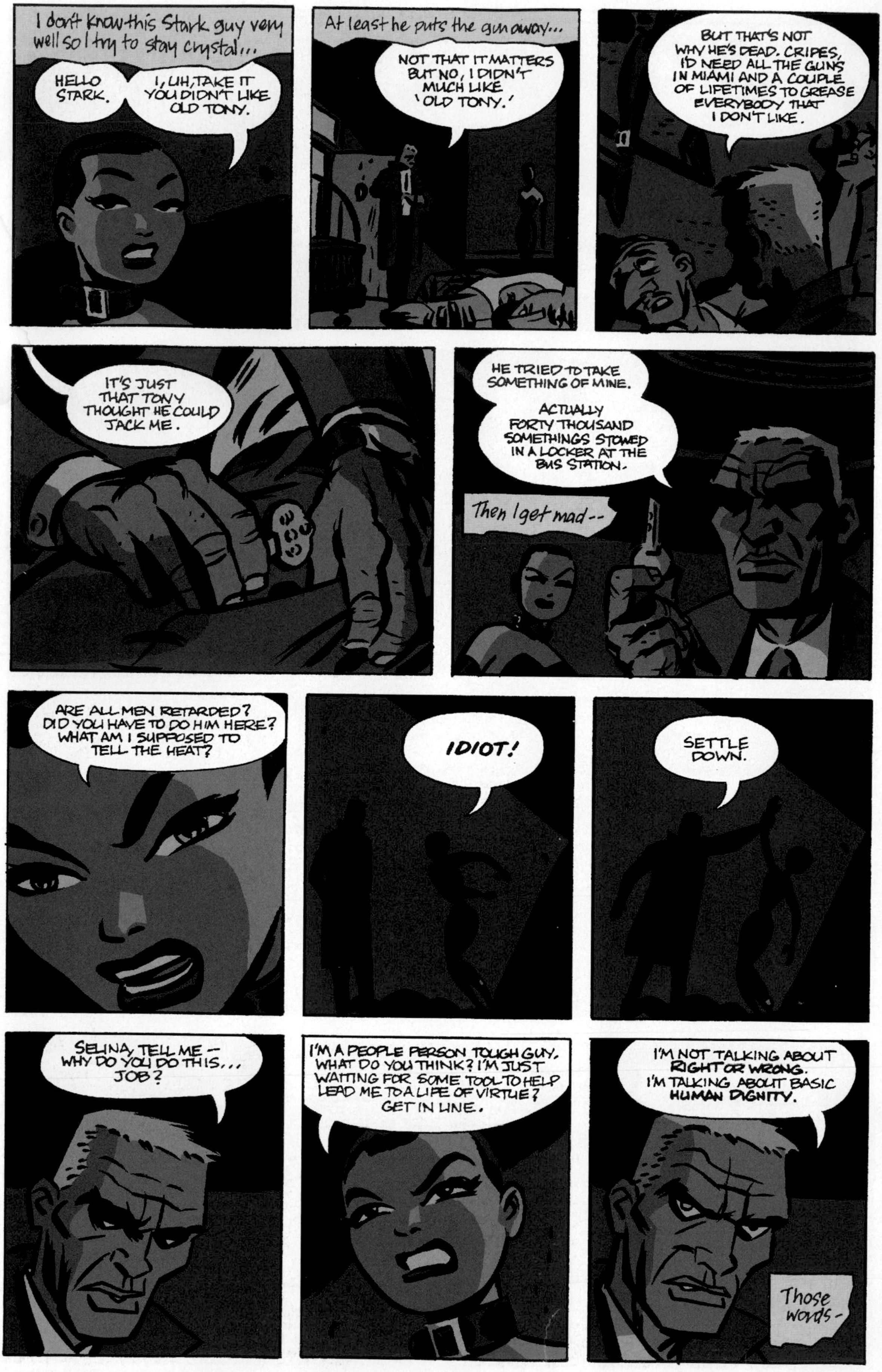
I don't know this Stark guy very well so I try to stay crystal...
HELLO STARK.
I, UH, TAKE IT YOU DIDN'T LIKE OLD TONY.
At least he puts the gun away...
NOT THAT IT MATTERS BUT NO, I DIDN'T MUCH LIKE 'OLD TONY.'
BUT THAT'S NOT WHY HE'S DEAD. CRIPES, I'D NEED ALL THE GUNS IN MIAMI AND A COUPLE OF LIFETIMES TO GREASE EVERYBODY THAT I DON'T LIKE.
IT'S JUST THAT TONY THOUGHT HE COULD JACK ME.
HE TRIED TO TAKE SOMETHING OF MINE.
ACTUALLY FORTY THOUSAND SOMETHINGS STOWED IN A LOCKER AT THE BUS STATION.
Then I get mad--
ARE ALL MEN RETARDED? DID YOU HAVE TO DO HIM HERE? WHAT AM I SUPPOSED TO TELL THE HEAT?
IDIOT!
SETTLE DOWN.
SELINA, TELL ME-- WHY DO YOU DO THIS... JOB?
I'M A PEOPLE PERSON TOUGH GUY. WHAT DO YOU THINK? I'M JUST WAITING FOR SOME TOOL TO HELP LEAD ME TO A LIFE OF VIRTUE? GET IN LINE.
I'M NOT TALKING ABOUT RIGHT OR WRONG. I'M TALKING ABOUT BASIC HUMAN DIGNITY.
Those words-

YOU KNOW YOU'RE BETTER THAN THIS BUT THERE'S NOTHING TO BELIEVE IN. NO ONE TO TRUST.

LET ME GUESS. I COULD TRUST YOU, RIGHT?

HEH. GOOD ONE.

NO.

TRUST YOURSELF. IF YOU'RE GOING TO SPEND YOUR LIFE ON THIS SIDE OF THE LAW, AND YOU WANT TO SURVIVE...

YOU HAVE TO CARE ABOUT YOURSELF. LET ME SHOW YOU.

His touch... as cold and sure as... my own.

I could feel the strength coming off of him in a steady, quiet current.

All those years of being in control, looking after Maggie, Holly -- Those years had made me hard ...but Stark --

Stark was like living granite.

Back then I had a joke I used. 'The reason I don't like men is I've never met one.' Ha. Stark laid that joke to rest.

I left with him that night. I could never tell Holly or others about him. It was a world of two. There were other men who taught me, like Ted Grant. But none of them were as frankly amoral as Stark.

He promised to teach me, and was good as his word -- Which is more than I can say for myself.

And now here I am with the biggest payoff since Lufthansa and I screwed over the one man who could help me.

In other words, karmic par for my course.

SWIFTY? YES. TELL CHANTEL WE ARE ON. I'LL GET YOU SPECS FOR SOME LISTENING HARDWARE I'LL NEED...

WELL NOW, THAT'S JUST IT. WE NEED A PRO -- SOMEONE WITH THE KNOW-HOW AND THE JUICE TO PULL THIS TOGETHER.

I WANT YOU TO CALL STARK.

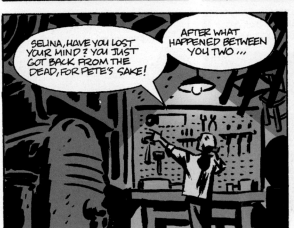

SELINA, HAVE YOU LOST YOUR MIND? YOU JUST GOT BACK FROM THE DEAD, FOR PETE'S SAKE!

AFTER WHAT HAPPENED BETWEEN YOU TWO ...

SWIFTY, IF STARK WAS GOING TO ACE ME HE'D HAVE DONE IT YEARS AGO.

JUST MAKE THE CALL, NO, I DO NOT WANT TO THINK ABOUT IT. RIGHT. SEE YOU THURSDAY.

Here I go again.

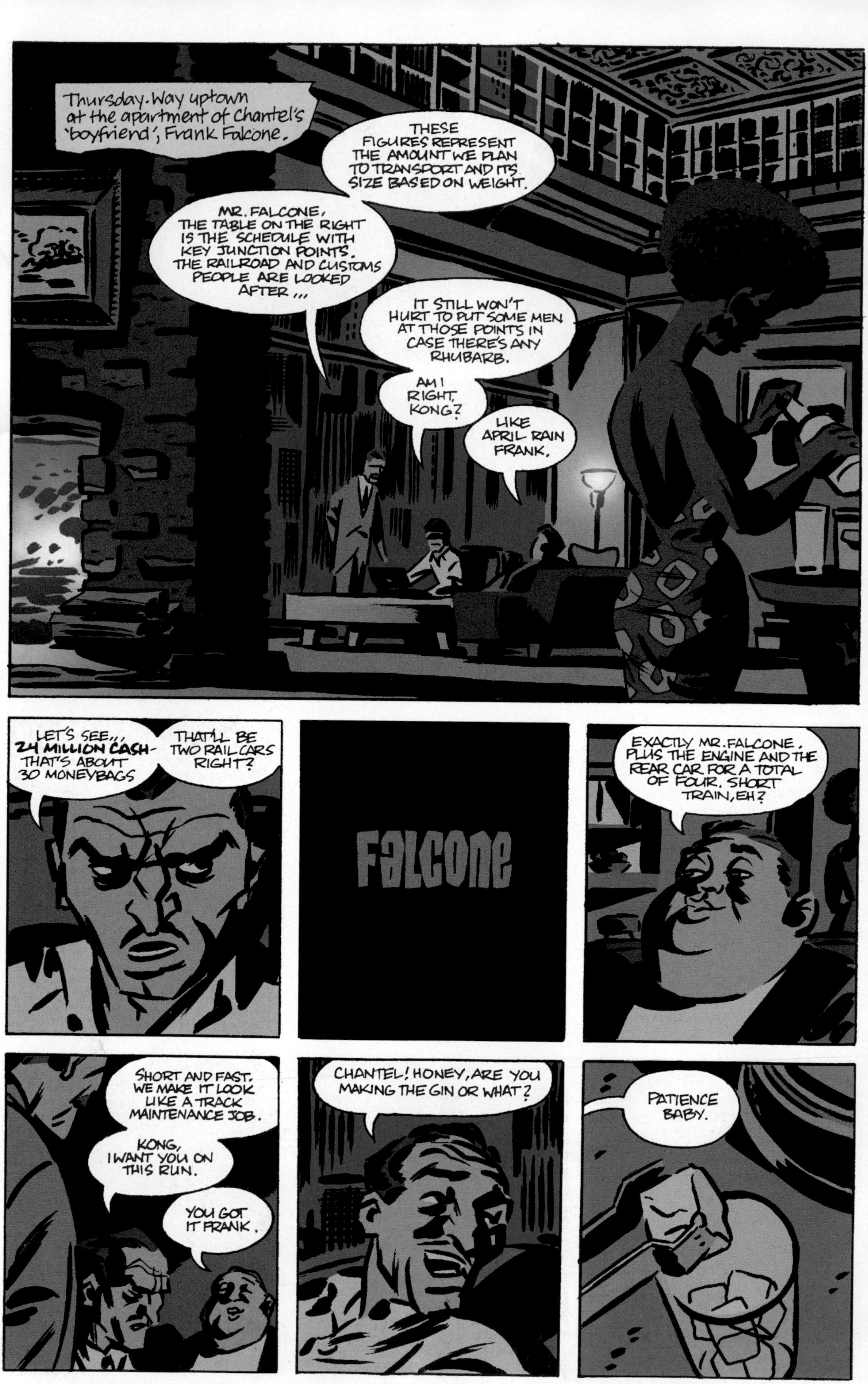
Thursday. Way uptown at the apartment of Chantel's 'boyfriend', Frank Falcone.
THESE FIGURES REPRESENT THE AMOUNT WE PLAN TO TRANSPORT AND ITS SIZE BASED ON WEIGHT.
MR. FALCONE, THE TABLE ON THE RIGHT IS THE SCHEDULE WITH KEY JUNCTION POINTS. THE RAILROAD AND CUSTOMS PEOPLE ARE LOOKED AFTER...
IT STILL WON'T HURT TO PUT SOME MEN AT THOSE POINTS IN CASE THERE'S ANY RHUBARB.
AM I RIGHT, KONG?
LIKE APRIL RAIN FRANK.
LET'S SEE... 24 MILLION CASH- THAT'S ABOUT 30 MONEYBAGS
THAT'LL BE TWO RAIL CARS RIGHT?
FALCONE
EXACTLY MR. FALCONE. PLUS THE ENGINE AND THE REAR CAR FOR A TOTAL OF FOUR. SHORT TRAIN, EH?
SHORT AND FAST. WE MAKE IT LOOK LIKE A TRACK MAINTENANCE JOB.
KONG, I WANT YOU ON THIS RUN.
YOU GOT IT FRANK.
CHANTEL! HONEY, ARE YOU MAKING THE GIN OR WHAT?
PATIENCE BABY.

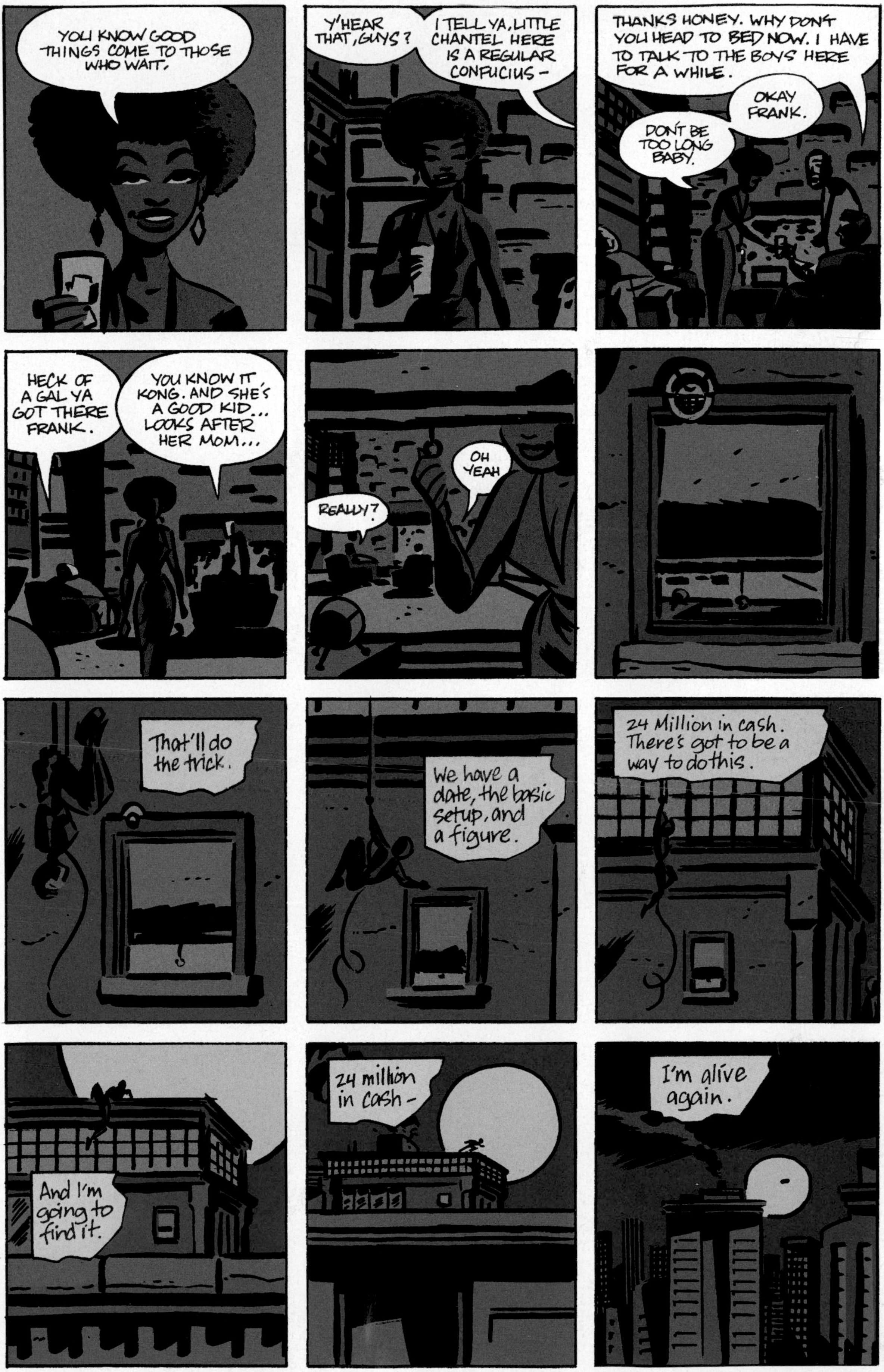
YOU KNOW GOOD THINGS COME TO THOSE WHO WAIT.
Y'HEAR THAT, GUYS?
I TELL YA, LITTLE CHANTEL HERE IS A REGULAR CONFUCIUS -
THANKS HONEY. WHY DON'T YOU HEAD TO BED NOW. I HAVE TO TALK TO THE BOYS HERE FOR A WHILE.
OKAY FRANK.
DON'T BE TOO LONG BABY.
HECK OF A GAL YA GOT THERE FRANK.
YOU KNOW IT, KONG. AND SHE'S A GOOD KID... LOOKS AFTER HER MOM...
OH YEAH
REALLY?
That'll do the trick.
We have a date, the basic setup, and a figure.
24 Million in cash. There's got to be a way to do this.
And I'm going to find it.
24 million in cash -
I'm alive again.

BOOK TWO

STARK

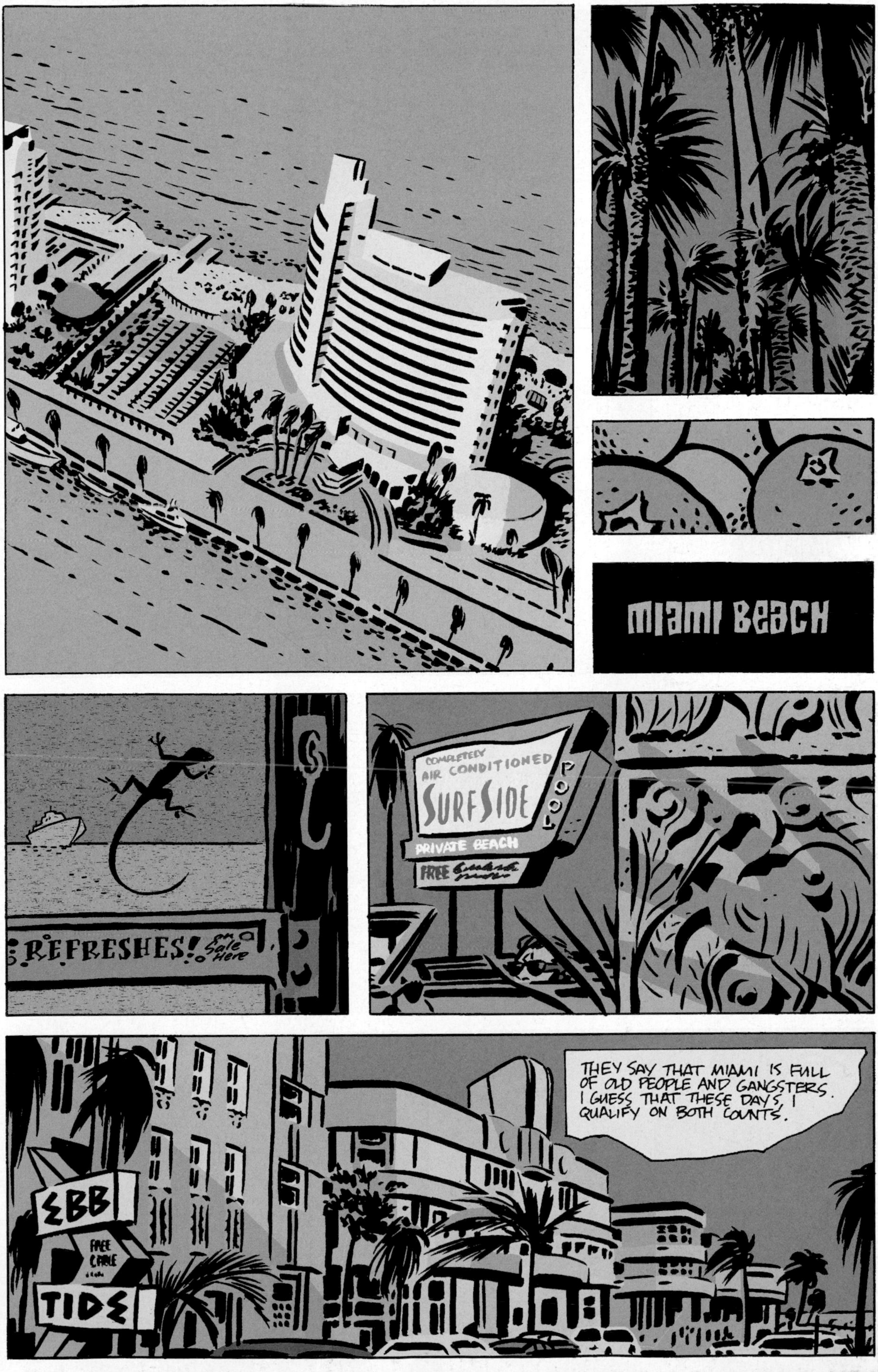
MIAMI BEACH
REFRESHES! on Sale Here
COMPLETELY AIR CONDITIONED
SURFSIDE
POOL
PRIVATE BEACH
FREE
THEY SAY THAT MIAMI IS FULL OF OLD PEOPLE AND GANGSTERS. I GUESS THAT THESE DAYS, I QUALIFY ON BOTH COUNTS.
EBB
FREE CABLE
TIDE

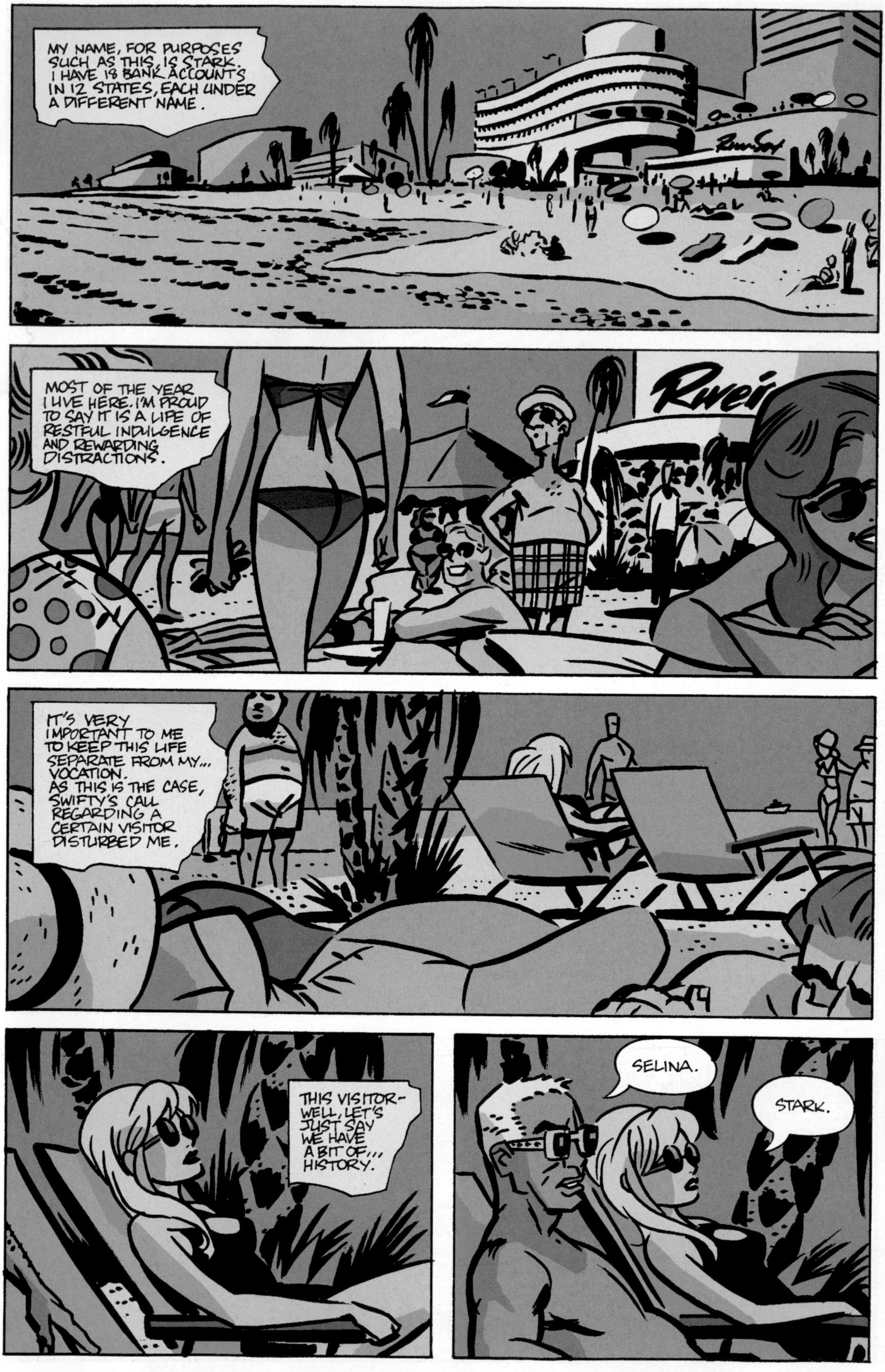

MY NAME, FOR PURPOSES SUCH AS THIS, IS STARK. I HAVE 18 BANK ACCOUNTS IN 12 STATES, EACH UNDER A DIFFERENT NAME.
MOST OF THE YEAR I LIVE HERE. I'M PROUD TO SAY IT IS A LIFE OF RESTFUL INDULGENCE AND REWARDING DISTRACTIONS.
IT'S VERY IMPORTANT TO ME TO KEEP THIS LIFE SEPARATE FROM MY... VOCATION. AS THIS IS THE CASE, SWIFTY'S CALL REGARDING A CERTAIN VISITOR DISTURBED ME.
THIS VISITOR-WELL, LET'S JUST SAY WE HAVE A BIT OF... HISTORY.
SELINA.
STARK.

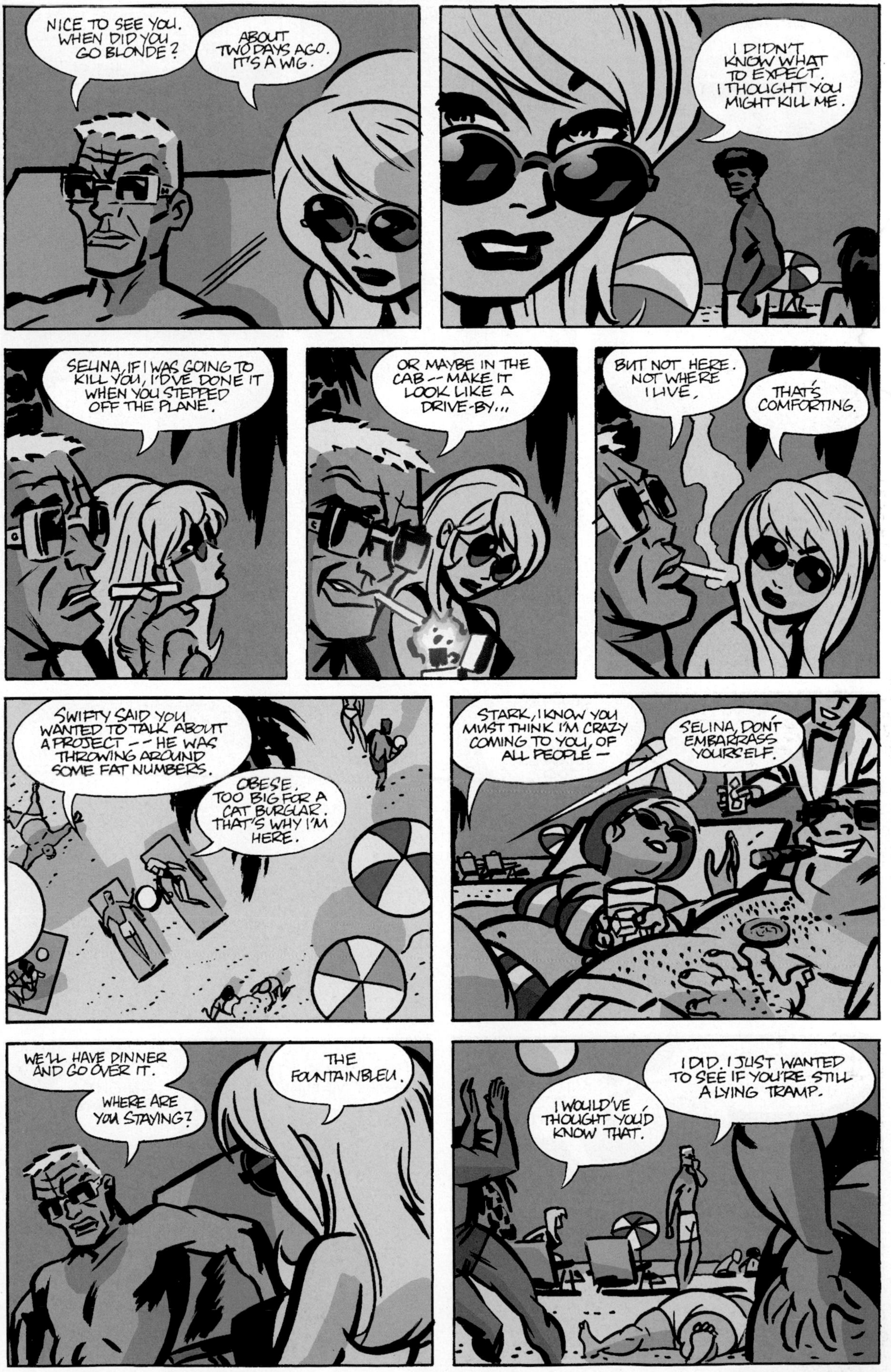
NICE TO SEE YOU. WHEN DID YOU GO BLONDE?
ABOUT TWO DAYS AGO. IT'S A WIG.
I DIDN'T KNOW WHAT TO EXPECT. I THOUGHT YOU MIGHT KILL ME.
SELINA, IF I WAS GOING TO KILL YOU, I'D'VE DONE IT WHEN YOU STEPPED OFF THE PLANE.
OR MAYBE IN THE CAB -- MAKE IT LOOK LIKE A DRIVE-BY...
BUT NOT HERE. NOT WHERE I LIVE.
THAT'S COMFORTING.
SWIFTY SAID YOU WANTED TO TALK ABOUT A PROJECT -- HE WAS THROWING AROUND SOME FAT NUMBERS.
OBESE. TOO BIG FOR A CAT BURGLAR. THAT'S WHY I'M HERE.
STARK, I KNOW YOU MUST THINK I'M CRAZY COMING TO YOU, OF ALL PEOPLE --
SELINA, DON'T EMBARRASS YOURSELF.
WE'LL HAVE DINNER AND GO OVER IT.
WHERE ARE YOU STAYING?
THE FOUNTAINBLEU.
I WOULD'VE THOUGHT YOU'D KNOW THAT.
I DID. I JUST WANTED TO SEE IF YOU'RE STILL A LYING TRAMP.

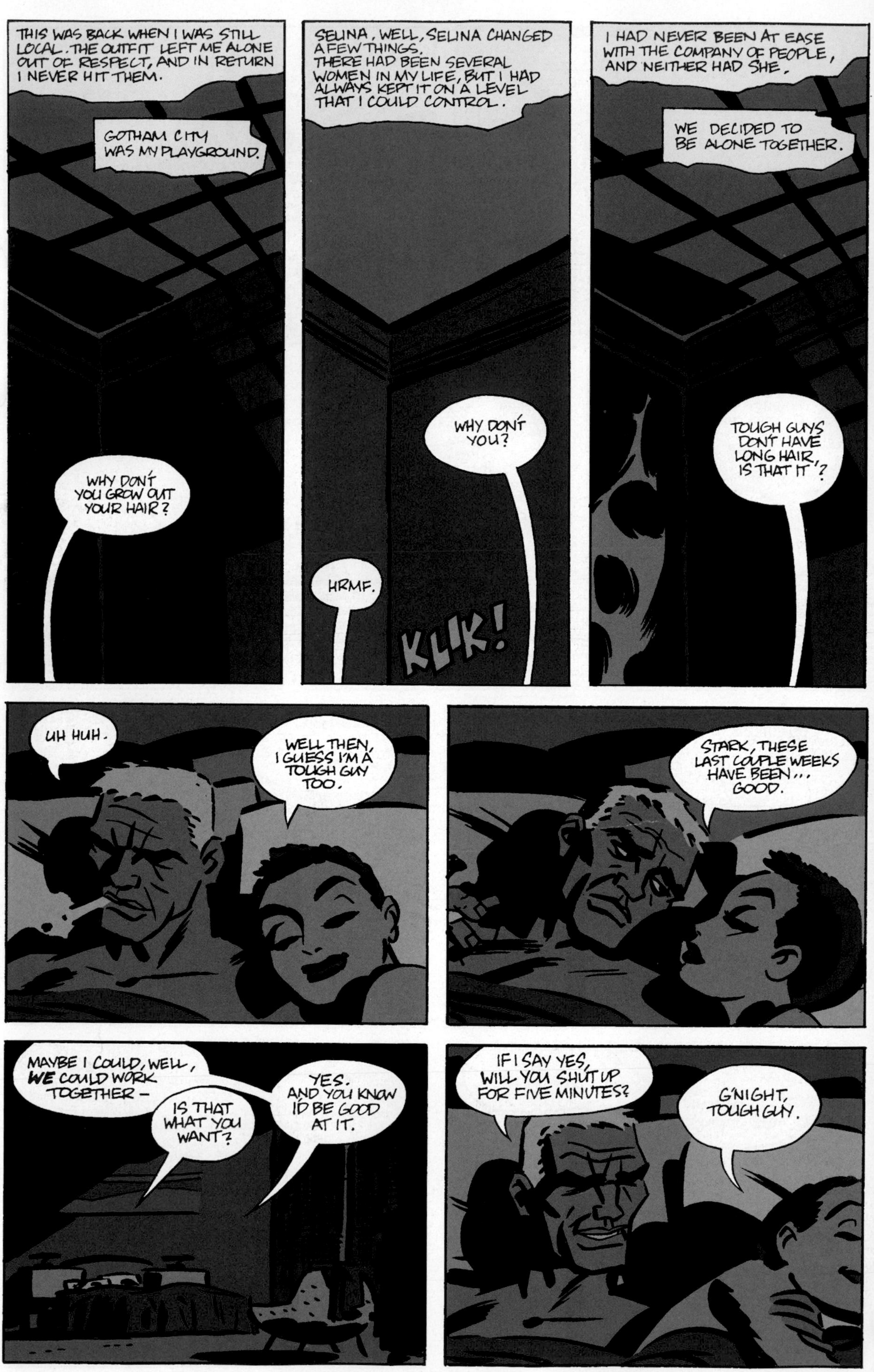
THIS WAS BACK WHEN I WAS STILL LOCAL. THE OUTFIT LEFT ME ALONE OUT OF RESPECT, AND IN RETURN I NEVER HIT THEM.
GOTHAM CITY WAS MY PLAYGROUND.
WHY DON'T YOU GROW OUT YOUR HAIR?
SELINA, WELL, SELINA CHANGED A FEW THINGS. THERE HAD BEEN SEVERAL WOMEN IN MY LIFE, BUT I HAD ALWAYS KEPT IT ON A LEVEL THAT I COULD CONTROL.
WHY DON'T YOU?
HRMF.
KLIK!
I HAD NEVER BEEN AT EASE WITH THE COMPANY OF PEOPLE, AND NEITHER HAD SHE.
WE DECIDED TO BE ALONE TOGETHER.
TOUGH GUYS DON'T HAVE LONG HAIR, IS THAT IT?
UH HUH.
WELL THEN, I GUESS I'M A TOUGH GUY TOO.
STARK, THESE LAST COUPLE WEEKS HAVE BEEN... GOOD.
MAYBE I COULD, WELL, WE COULD WORK TOGETHER -
IS THAT WHAT YOU WANT?
YES. AND YOU KNOW I'D BE GOOD AT IT.
IF I SAY YES, WILL YOU SHUT UP FOR FIVE MINUTES?
G'NIGHT, TOUGH GUY.

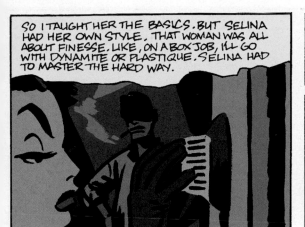

SO I TAUGHT HER THE BASICS. BUT SELINA HAD HER OWN STYLE. THAT WOMAN WAS ALL ABOUT FINESSE. LIKE, ON A BOX JOB, I'LL GO WITH DYNAMITE OR PLASTIQUE. SELINA HAD TO MASTER THE HARD WAY.

I TAUGHT HER ABOUT WHAT WAS WORTH STEALING, BUT MORE IMPORTANTLY, WHAT NOT TO STEAL. HOW TO SPOT TROUBLE BEFORE IT HAPPENS AND HOW TO COVER YOUR TRACKS. SHE SOAKED IT IN....

SHE HAD A JOB IN MIND. IT WAS A SIMPLE HEIST WITH MILLIONS IN UNCUT DIAMONDS.... IT WAS A GREAT SET-UP...

...EXCEPT THE DIAMONDS BELONGED TO THE MOB.

I KNOW ABOUT THE MOB, BUT THIS IS MILLIONS IN UNCUT DIAMONDS JUST WAITING TO BE SNATCHED—

IT COULD BE OUR WAY OUT. Y'KNOW, DISAPPEAR. YOU AND I, ALONE TOGETHER.

OKAY. WE'LL LOOK AT IT.

AND THAT WAS MY FIRST MISTAKE. I LET THE POTENTIAL PAYOFF ON A JOB COMPROMISE MY GOLDEN RULE—DON'T SCREW WITH THE ITALIANS.

THAT WAS THEN.

STARK?

AND THAT IS THE NOW.

EARTH TO STARK!

SO THE QUESTION BECOMES WHETHER I'M JUST LISTENING TO HER PLAY ME ALL OVER AGAIN. I LET HER TALK, GET HER HOPES UP...

AND THERE ISN'T THAT MUCH TIME. IT GOES DOWN IN THREE WEEKS.

WHO'S THE INSIDE PERSON?

IT'S A WORKING GIRL. HER NAME'S NONE OF YOUR BUSINESS, BUT I TRUST HER. SHE'LL STAND UP.

TRUST. FORTUNATELY FOR YOU, IT DOESN'T COME DOWN TO TRUST.

LET'S STICK TO SOMETHING MORE CONCRETE -- LIKE COMMON SENSE.

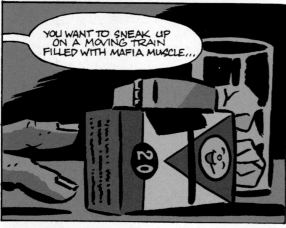

YOU WANT TO SNEAK UP ON A MOVING TRAIN FILLED WITH MAFIA MUSCLE...

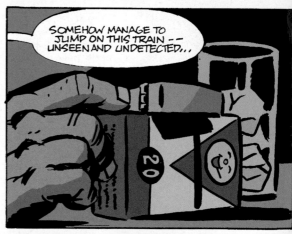

SOMEHOW MANAGE TO JUMP ON THIS TRAIN -- UNSEEN AND UNDETECTED...

AND WHAT DO WE DO THEN? DO WE FLY AWAY WITH THE MONEY IN OUR POCKETS?

BABY, YOU WERE GOOD, BUT YOU WERE NEVER THAT GOOD.

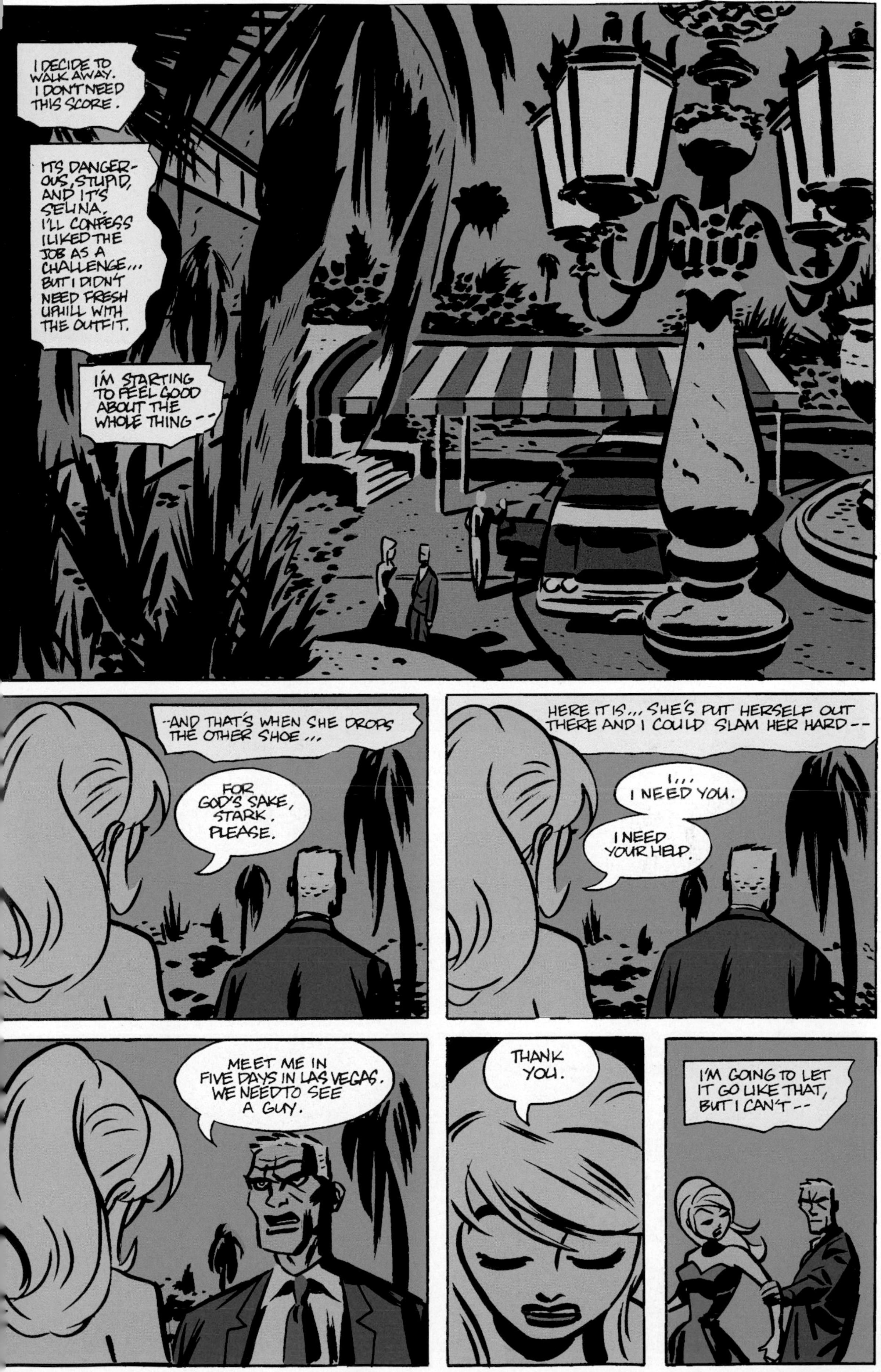
I DECIDE TO WALK AWAY. I DON'T NEED THIS SCORE.
ITS DANGEROUS, STUPID, AND IT'S SELINA. I'LL CONFESS I LIKED THE JOB AS A CHALLENGE... BUT I DIDN'T NEED FRESH UPHILL WITH THE OUTFIT.
I'M STARTING TO FEEL GOOD ABOUT THE WHOLE THING--
--AND THAT'S WHEN SHE DROPS THE OTHER SHOE...
FOR GOD'S SAKE, STARK. PLEASE.
HERE IT IS... SHE'S PUT HERSELF OUT THERE AND I COULD SLAM HER HARD--
I... I NEED YOU.
I NEED YOUR HELP.
MEET ME IN FIVE DAYS IN LAS VEGAS. WE NEED TO SEE A GUY.
THANK YOU.
I'M GOING TO LET IT GO LIKE THAT, BUT I CAN'T--

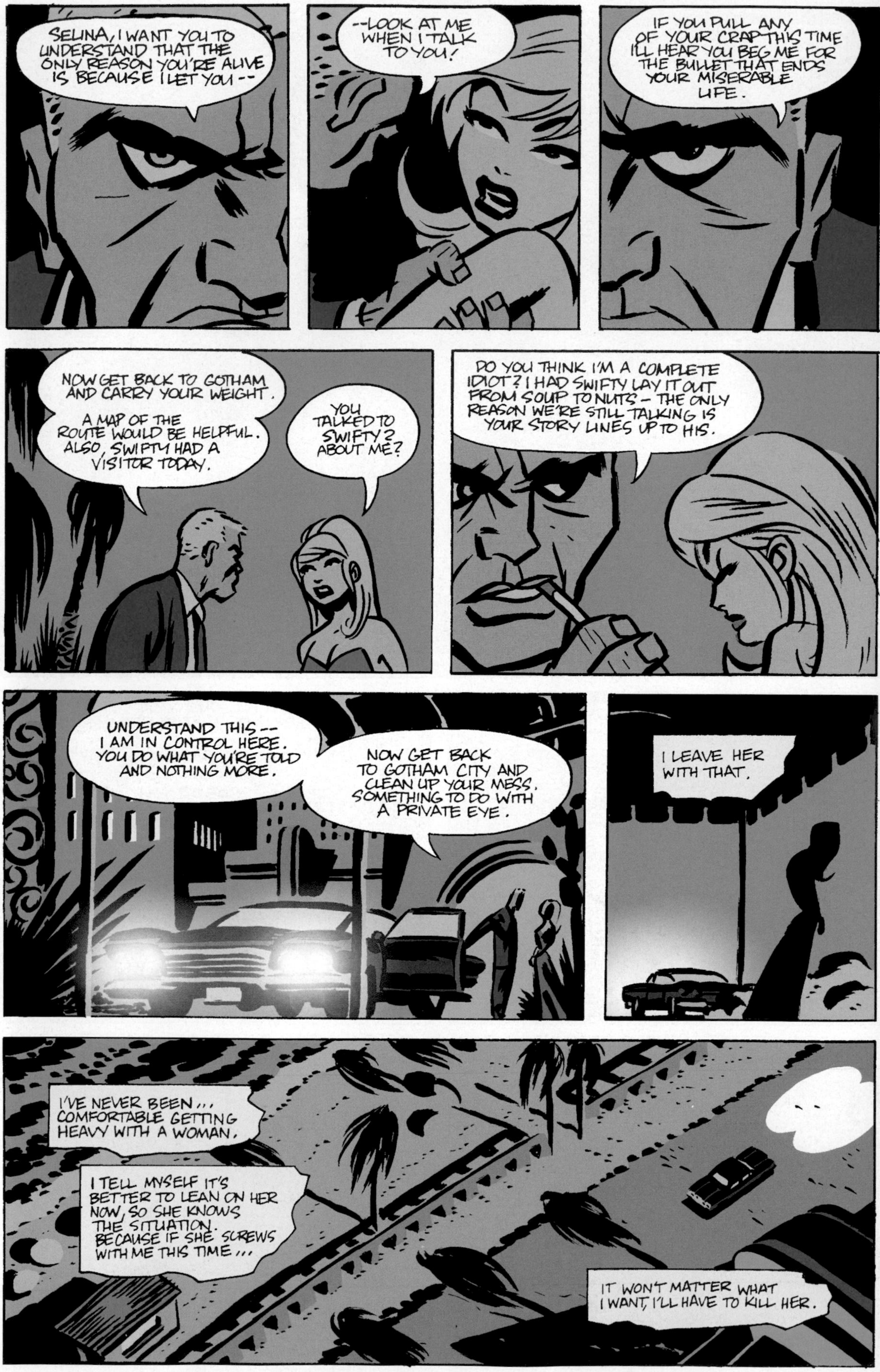
SELINA, I WANT YOU TO UNDERSTAND THAT THE ONLY REASON YOU'RE ALIVE IS BECAUSE I LET YOU --
--LOOK AT ME WHEN I TALK TO YOU!
IF YOU PULL ANY OF YOUR CRAP THIS TIME I'LL HEAR YOU BEG ME FOR THE BULLET THAT ENDS YOUR MISERABLE LIFE.
NOW GET BACK TO GOTHAM AND CARRY YOUR WEIGHT.
A MAP OF THE ROUTE WOULD BE HELPFUL. ALSO, SWIFTY HAD A VISITOR TODAY.
YOU TALKED TO SWIFTY? ABOUT ME?
DO YOU THINK I'M A COMPLETE IDIOT? I HAD SWIFTY LAY IT OUT FROM SOUP TO NUTS -- THE ONLY REASON WE'RE STILL TALKING IS YOUR STORY LINES UP TO HIS.
UNDERSTAND THIS -- I AM IN CONTROL HERE. YOU DO WHAT YOU'RE TOLD AND NOTHING MORE.
NOW GET BACK TO GOTHAM CITY AND CLEAN UP YOUR MESS. SOMETHING TO DO WITH A PRIVATE EYE.
I LEAVE HER WITH THAT.
I'VE NEVER BEEN... COMFORTABLE GETTING HEAVY WITH A WOMAN.
I TELL MYSELF IT'S BETTER TO LEAN ON HER NOW, SO SHE KNOWS THE SITUATION. BECAUSE IF SHE SCREWS WITH ME THIS TIME...
IT WON'T MATTER WHAT I WANT, I'LL HAVE TO KILL HER.

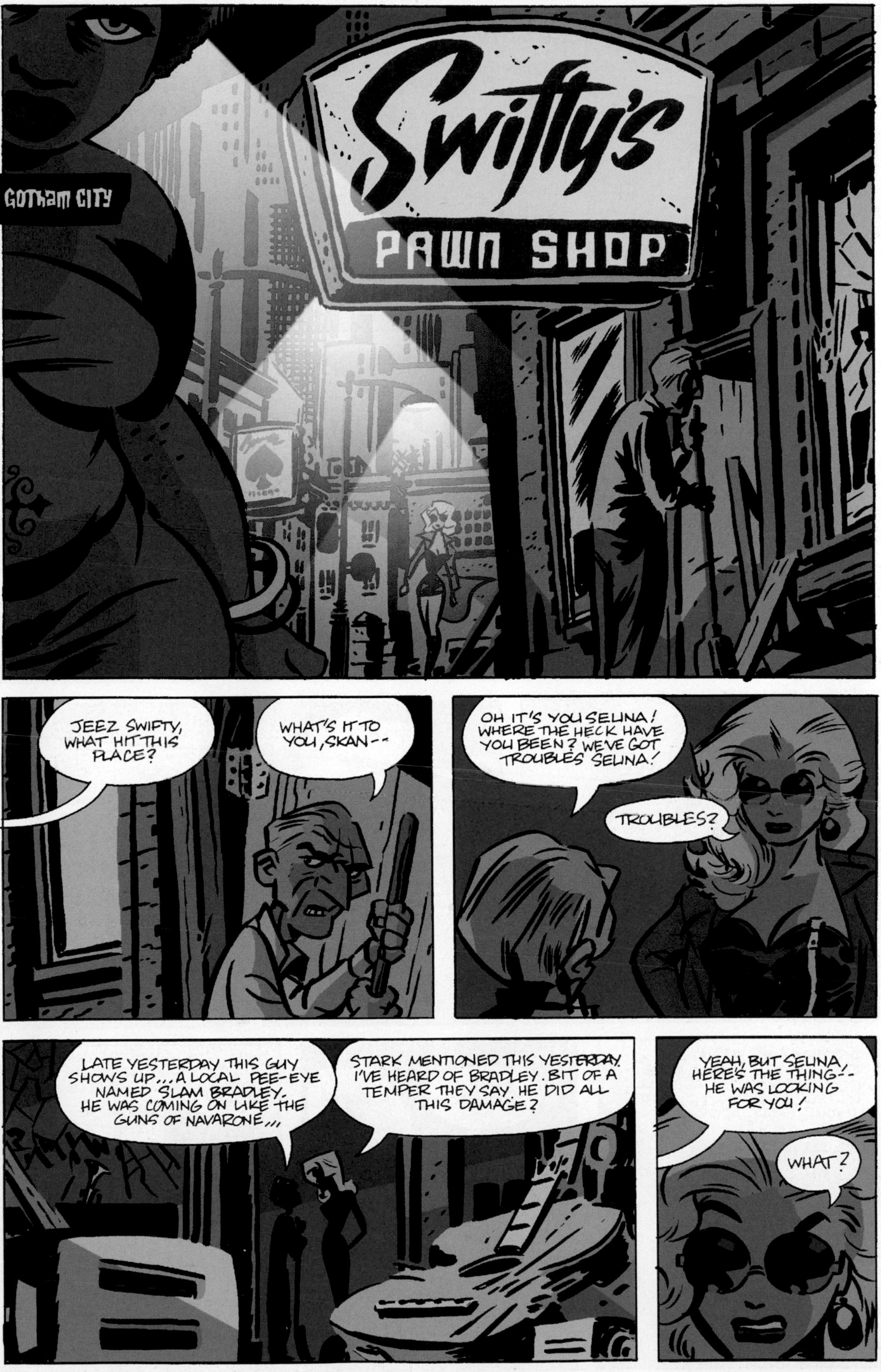
Swifty's
PAWN SHOP
GOTHAM CITY
JEEZ SWIFTY, WHAT HIT THIS PLACE?
WHAT'S IT TO YOU, SKAN--
OH IT'S YOU SELINA! WHERE THE HECK HAVE YOU BEEN? WE'VE GOT TROUBLES SELINA!
TROUBLES?
LATE YESTERDAY THIS GUY SHOWS UP... A LOCAL PEE-EYE NAMED SLAM BRADLEY. HE WAS COMING ON LIKE THE GUNS OF NAVARONE...
STARK MENTIONED THIS YESTERDAY. I'VE HEARD OF BRADLEY. BIT OF A TEMPER THEY SAY. HE DID ALL THIS DAMAGE?
YEAH, BUT SELINA, HERE'S THE THING-- HE WAS LOOKING FOR YOU!
WHAT?

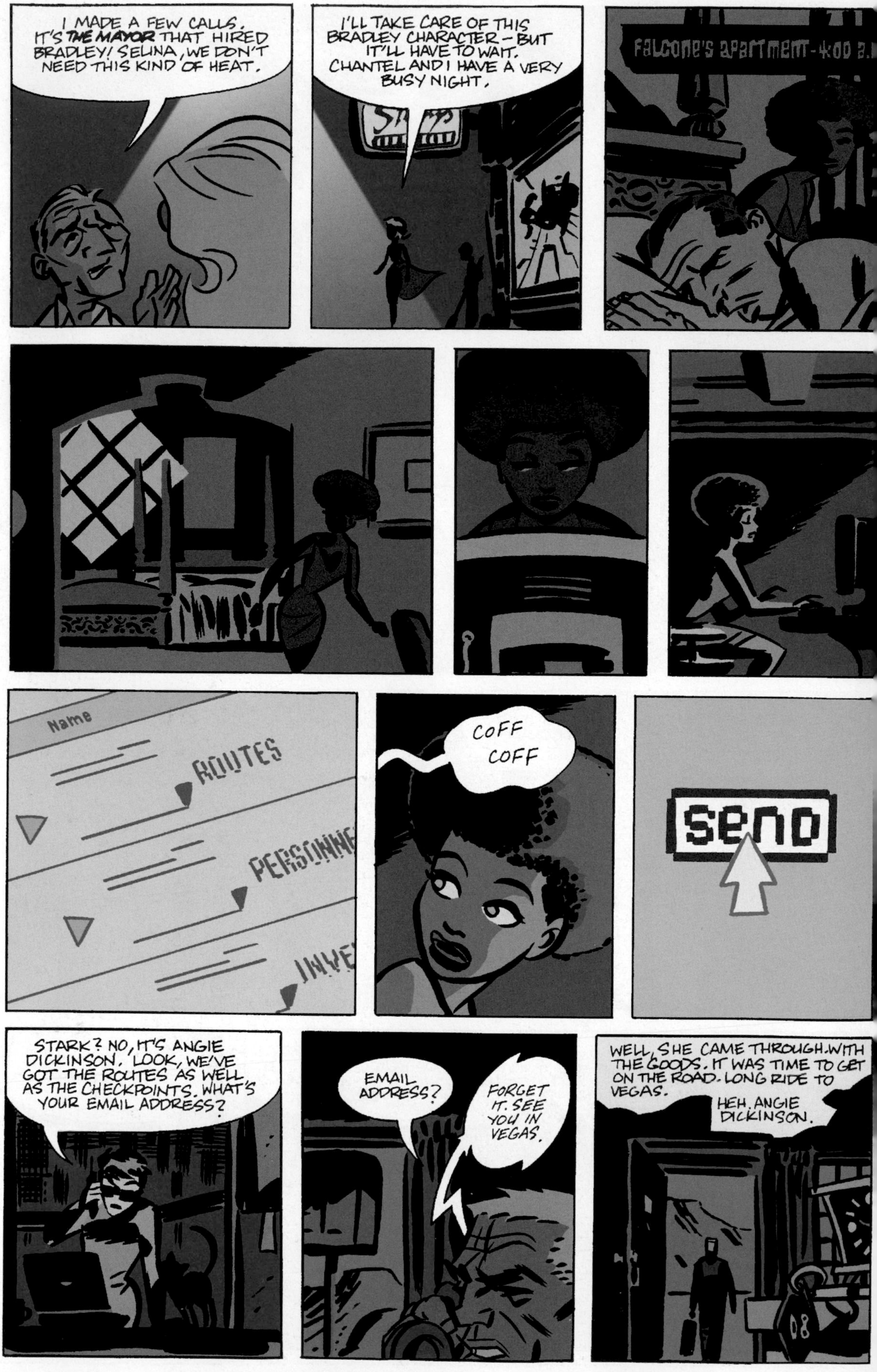

I MADE A FEW CALLS. IT'S THE MAYOR THAT HIRED BRADLEY! SELINA, WE DON'T NEED THIS KIND OF HEAT.
I'LL TAKE CARE OF THIS BRADLEY CHARACTER — BUT IT'LL HAVE TO WAIT. CHANTEL AND I HAVE A VERY BUSY NIGHT.
Falcone's apartment - 4:00 a.
Name
ROUTES
PERSONNE
INVE
COFF COFF
SEND
STARK? NO, IT'S ANGIE DICKINSON. LOOK, WE'VE GOT THE ROUTES AS WELL AS THE CHECKPOINTS. WHAT'S YOUR EMAIL ADDRESS?
EMAIL ADDRESS?
FORGET IT. SEE YOU IN VEGAS.
WELL, SHE CAME THROUGH WITH THE GOODS. IT WAS TIME TO GET ON THE ROAD. LONG RIDE TO VEGAS.
HEH. ANGIE DICKINSON.

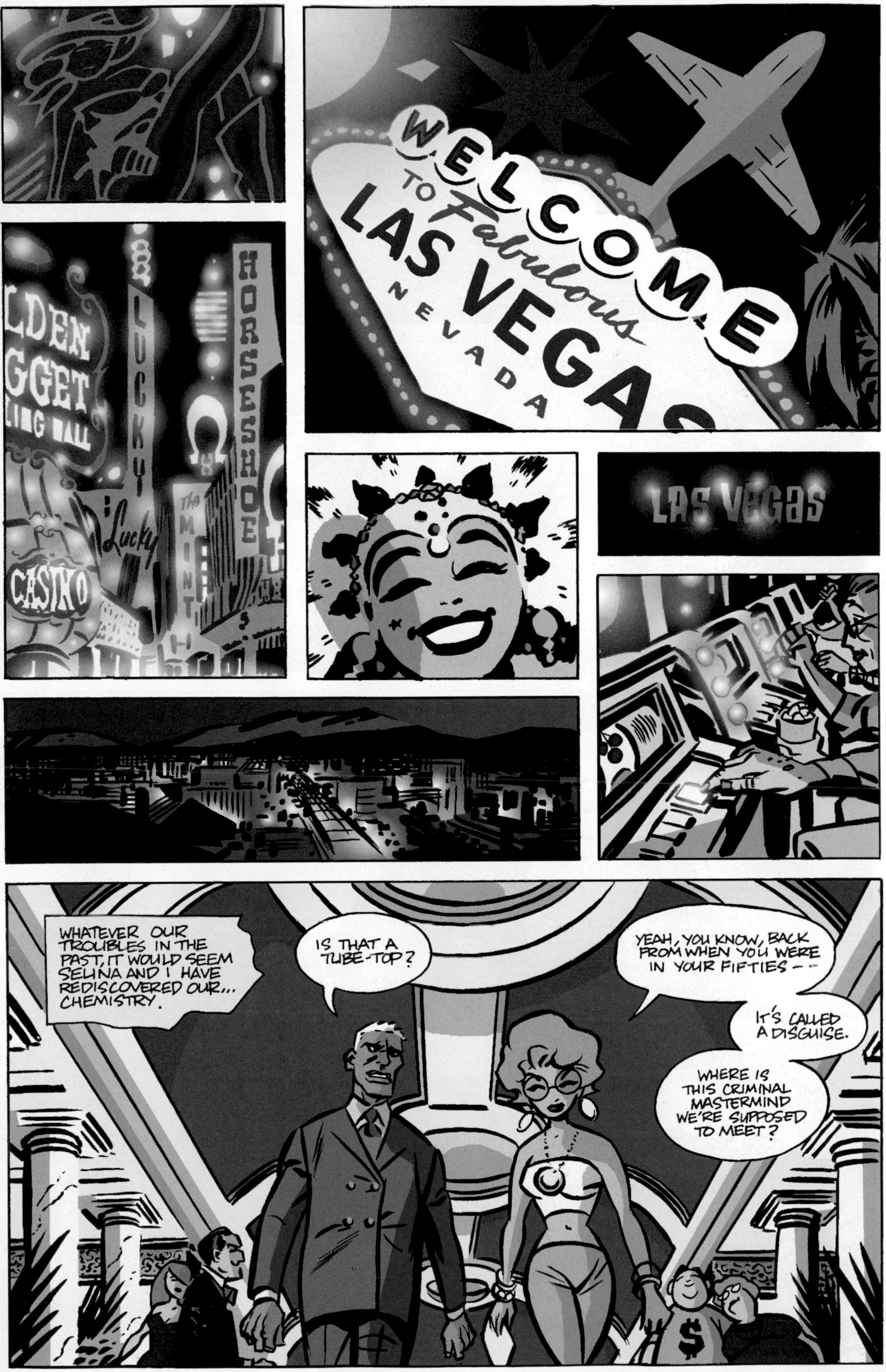
WELCOME
TO Fabulous
LAS VEGAS
NEVADA
HORSESHOE
LUCKY
Lucky
The MINT
CASINO
LAS VEGAS
WHATEVER OUR TROUBLES IN THE PAST, IT WOULD SEEM SELINA AND I HAVE REDISCOVERED OUR... CHEMISTRY.
IS THAT A TUBE-TOP?
YEAH, YOU KNOW, BACK FROM WHEN YOU WERE IN YOUR FIFTIES --
IT'S CALLED A DISGUISE.
WHERE IS THIS CRIMINAL MASTERMIND WE'RE SUPPOSED TO MEET?

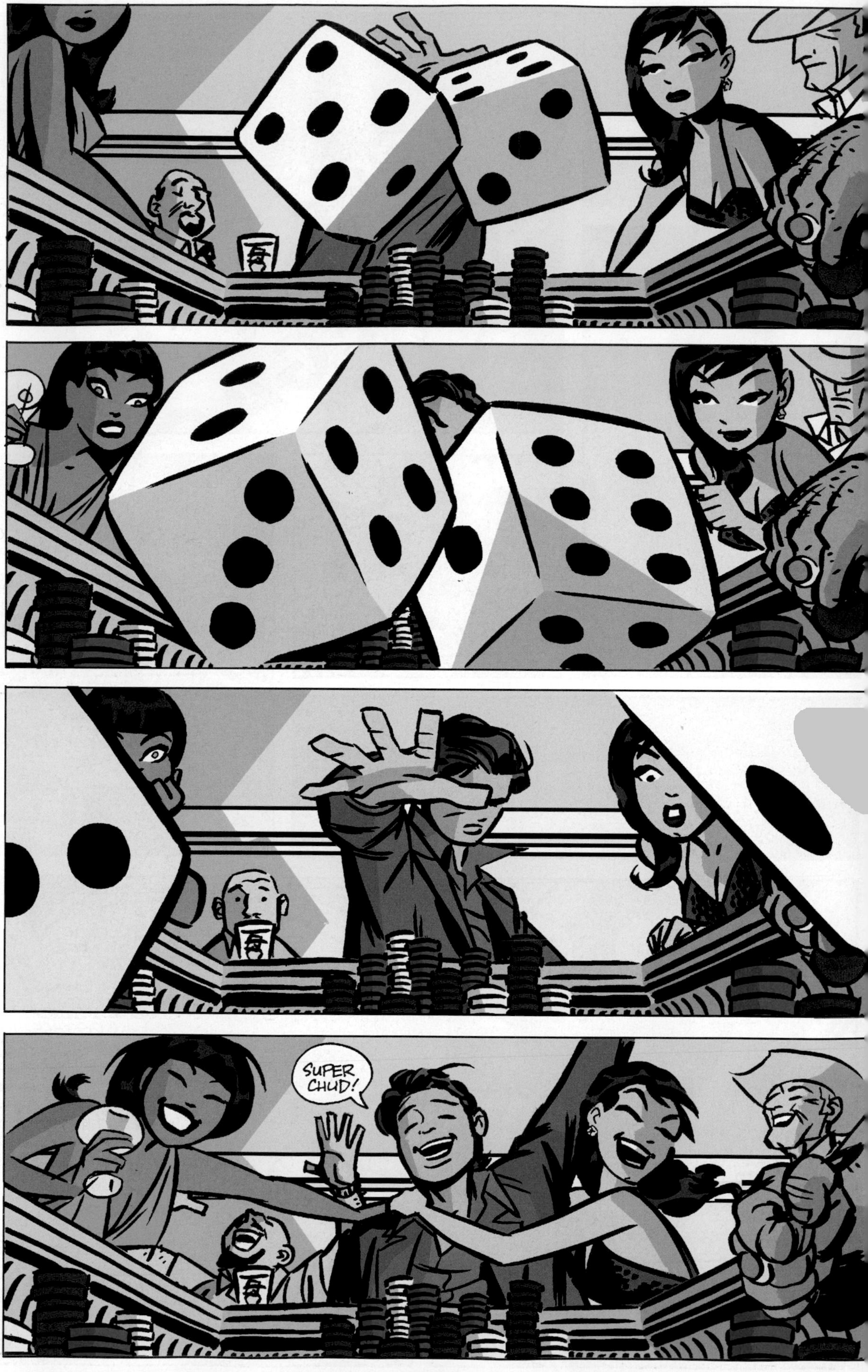
SUPER CHUD!

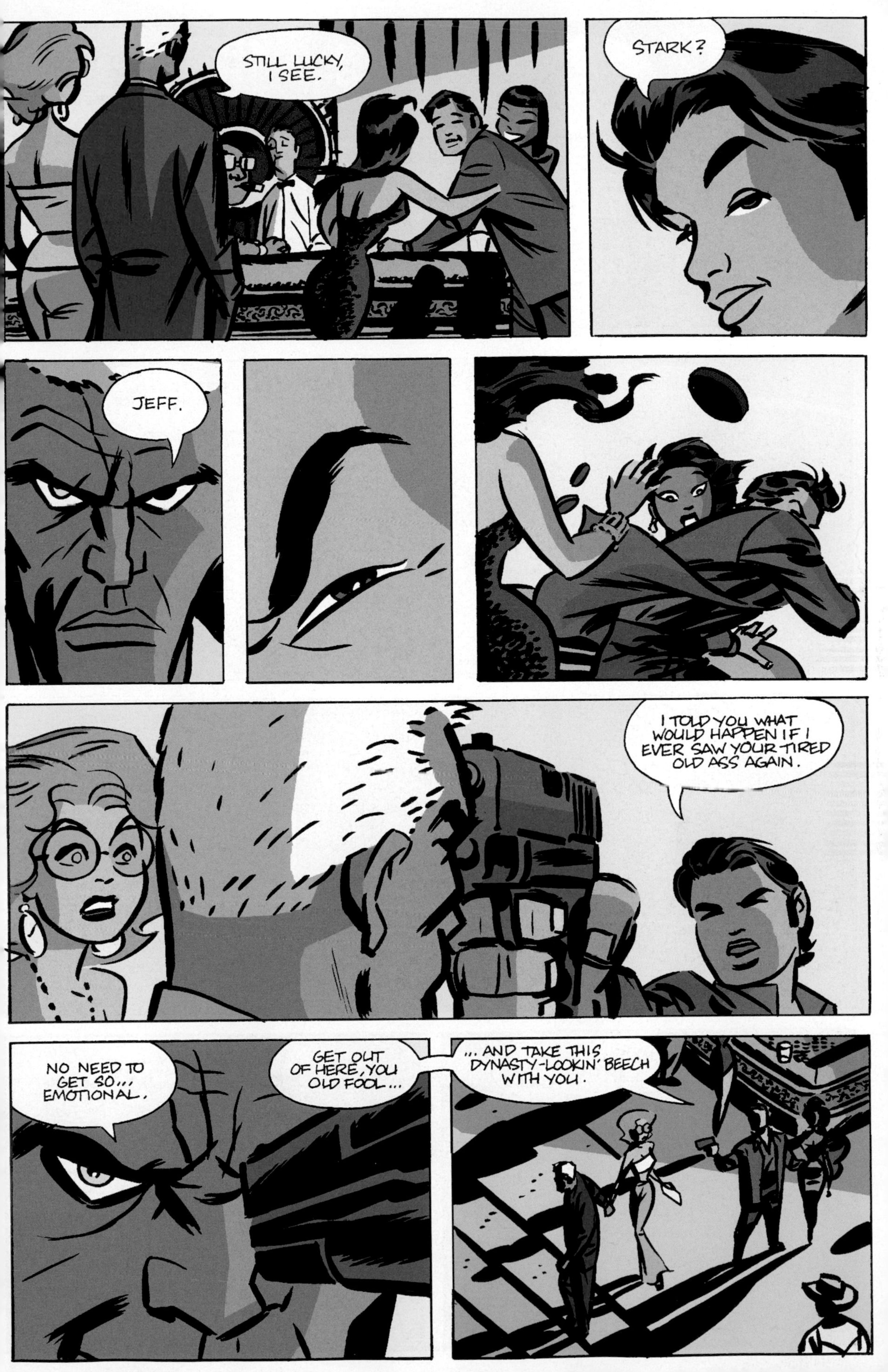
STILL LUCKY, I SEE.
STARK?
JEFF.
I TOLD YOU WHAT WOULD HAPPEN IF I EVER SAW YOUR TIRED OLD ASS AGAIN.
NO NEED TO GET SO... EMOTIONAL.
GET OUT OF HERE, YOU OLD FOOL...
...AND TAKE THIS DYNASTY-LOOKIN' BEECH WITH YOU.

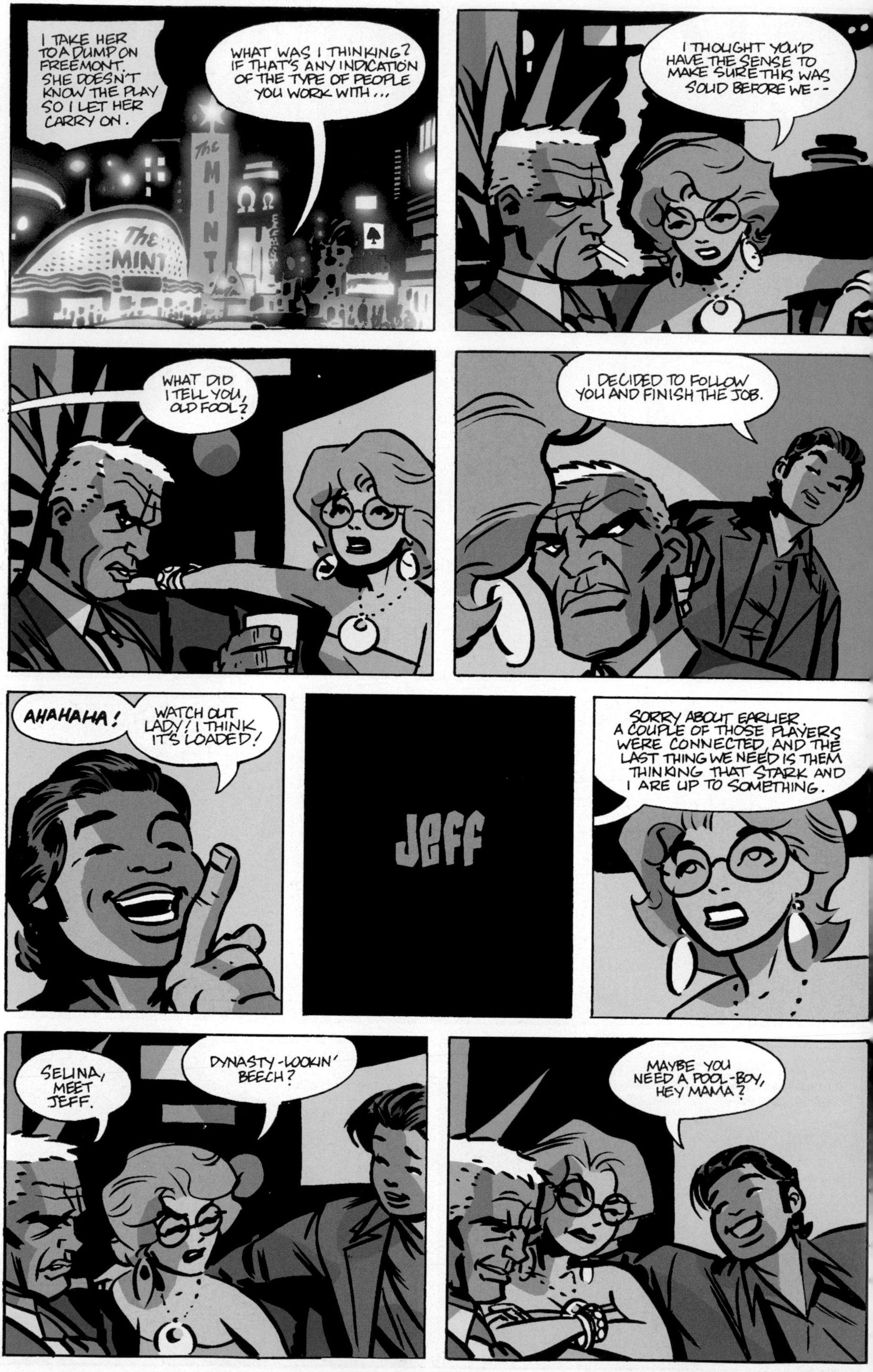
I TAKE HER TO A DUMP ON FREEMONT. SHE DOESN'T KNOW THE PLAY SO I LET HER CARRY ON.
WHAT WAS I THINKING? IF THAT'S ANY INDICATION OF THE TYPE OF PEOPLE YOU WORK WITH...
The MINT
The MINT
I THOUGHT YOU'D HAVE THE SENSE TO MAKE SURE THIS WAS SOLID BEFORE WE--
WHAT DID I TELL YOU, OLD FOOL?
I DECIDED TO FOLLOW YOU AND FINISH THE JOB.
AHAHAHA!
WATCH OUT LADY! I THINK IT'S LOADED!
JEFF
SORRY ABOUT EARLIER. A COUPLE OF THOSE PLAYERS WERE CONNECTED, AND THE LAST THING WE NEED IS THEM THINKING THAT STARK AND I ARE UP TO SOMETHING.
SELINA, MEET JEFF.
DYNASTY-LOOKIN' BEECH?
MAYBE YOU NEED A POOL-BOY, HEY MAMA?

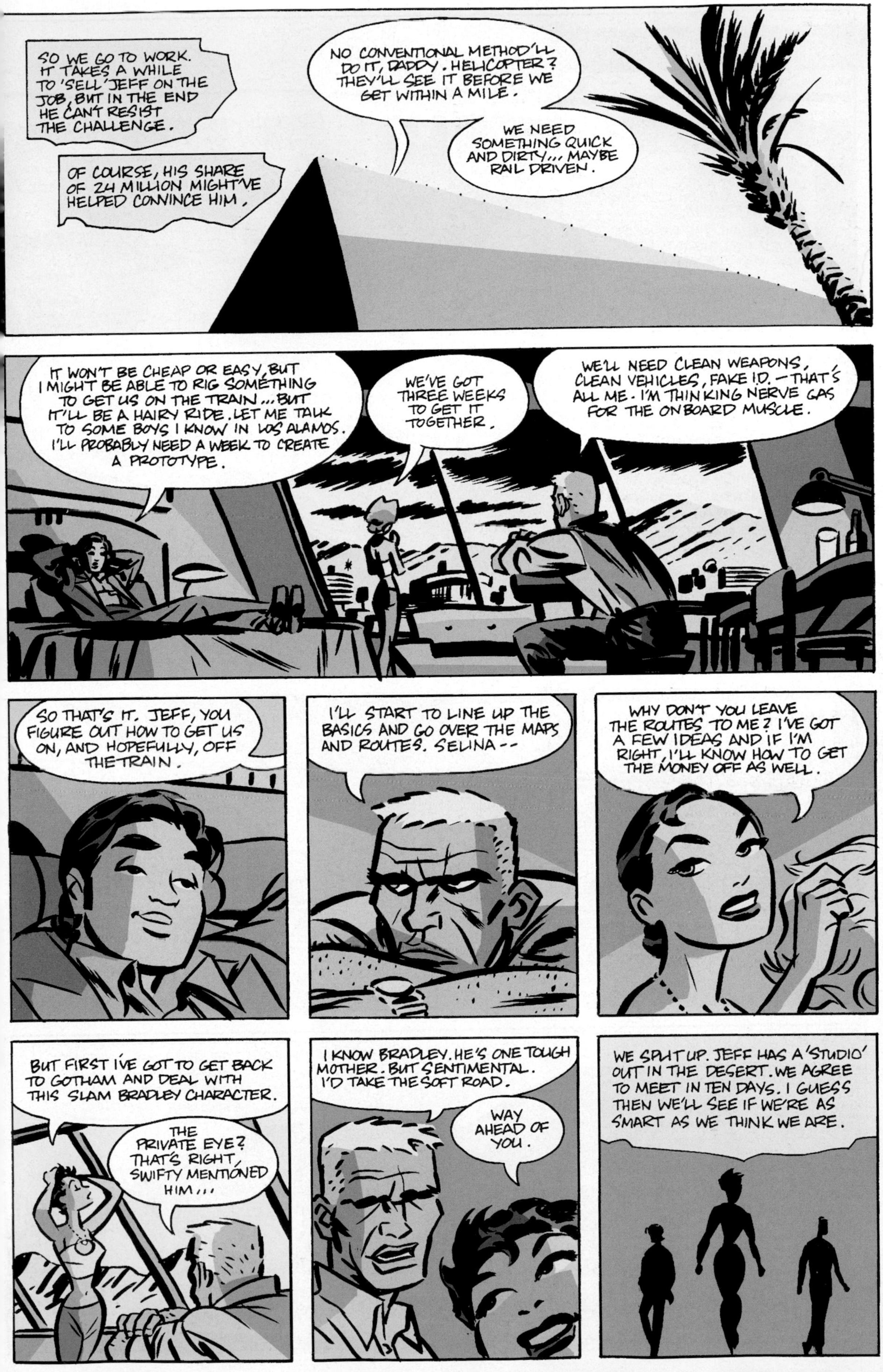
SO WE GO TO WORK. IT TAKES A WHILE TO 'SELL' JEFF ON THE JOB, BUT IN THE END HE CAN'T RESIST THE CHALLENGE.
OF COURSE, HIS SHARE OF 24 MILLION MIGHT'VE HELPED CONVINCE HIM.
NO CONVENTIONAL METHOD'LL DO IT, DADDY. HELICOPTER? THEY'LL SEE IT BEFORE WE GET WITHIN A MILE.
WE NEED SOMETHING QUICK AND DIRTY... MAYBE RAIL DRIVEN.
IT WON'T BE CHEAP OR EASY, BUT I MIGHT BE ABLE TO RIG SOMETHING TO GET US ON THE TRAIN... BUT IT'LL BE A HAIRY RIDE. LET ME TALK TO SOME BOYS I KNOW IN LOS ALAMOS. I'LL PROBABLY NEED A WEEK TO CREATE A PROTOTYPE.
WE'VE GOT THREE WEEKS TO GET IT TOGETHER.
WE'LL NEED CLEAN WEAPONS, CLEAN VEHICLES, FAKE I.D. -- THAT'S ALL ME. I'M THINKING NERVE GAS FOR THE ONBOARD MUSCLE.
SO THAT'S IT. JEFF, YOU FIGURE OUT HOW TO GET US ON, AND HOPEFULLY, OFF THE TRAIN.
I'LL START TO LINE UP THE BASICS AND GO OVER THE MAPS AND ROUTES. SELINA--
WHY DON'T YOU LEAVE THE ROUTES TO ME? I'VE GOT A FEW IDEAS AND IF I'M RIGHT, I'LL KNOW HOW TO GET THE MONEY OFF AS WELL.
BUT FIRST I'VE GOT TO GET BACK TO GOTHAM AND DEAL WITH THIS SLAM BRADLEY CHARACTER.
THE PRIVATE EYE? THAT'S RIGHT, SWIFTY MENTIONED HIM...
I KNOW BRADLEY. HE'S ONE TOUGH MOTHER. BUT SENTIMENTAL. I'D TAKE THE SOFT ROAD.
WAY AHEAD OF YOU.
WE SPLIT UP. JEFF HAS A 'STUDIO' OUT IN THE DESERT. WE AGREE TO MEET IN TEN DAYS. I GUESS THEN WE'LL SEE IF WE'RE AS SMART AS WE THINK WE ARE.

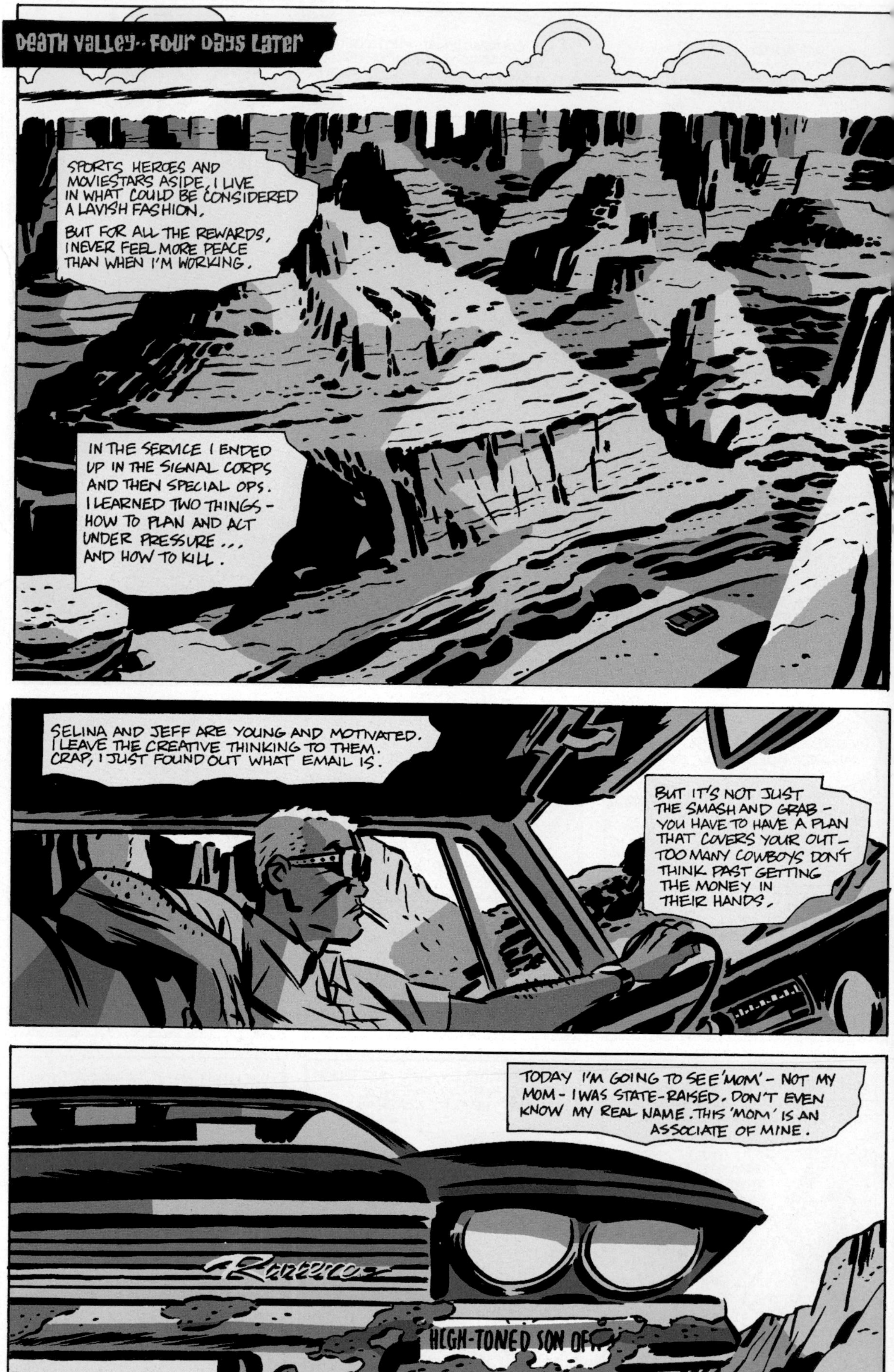
DEATH VALLEY-- FOUR DAYS LATER
SPORTS HEROES AND MOVIESTARS ASIDE, I LIVE IN WHAT COULD BE CONSIDERED A LAVISH FASHION.
BUT FOR ALL THE REWARDS, I NEVER FEEL MORE PEACE THAN WHEN I'M WORKING.
IN THE SERVICE I ENDED UP IN THE SIGNAL CORPS AND THEN SPECIAL OPS. I LEARNED TWO THINGS - HOW TO PLAN AND ACT UNDER PRESSURE... AND HOW TO KILL.
SELINA AND JEFF ARE YOUNG AND MOTIVATED. I LEAVE THE CREATIVE THINKING TO THEM. CRAP, I JUST FOUND OUT WHAT EMAIL IS.
BUT IT'S NOT JUST THE SMASH AND GRAB - YOU HAVE TO HAVE A PLAN THAT COVERS YOUR OUT- TOO MANY COWBOYS DON'T THINK PAST GETTING THE MONEY IN THEIR HANDS.
TODAY I'M GOING TO SEE 'MOM' - NOT MY MOM - I WAS STATE-RAISED. DON'T EVEN KNOW MY REAL NAME. THIS 'MOM' IS AN ASSOCIATE OF MINE.
HIGH-TONED SON OF A

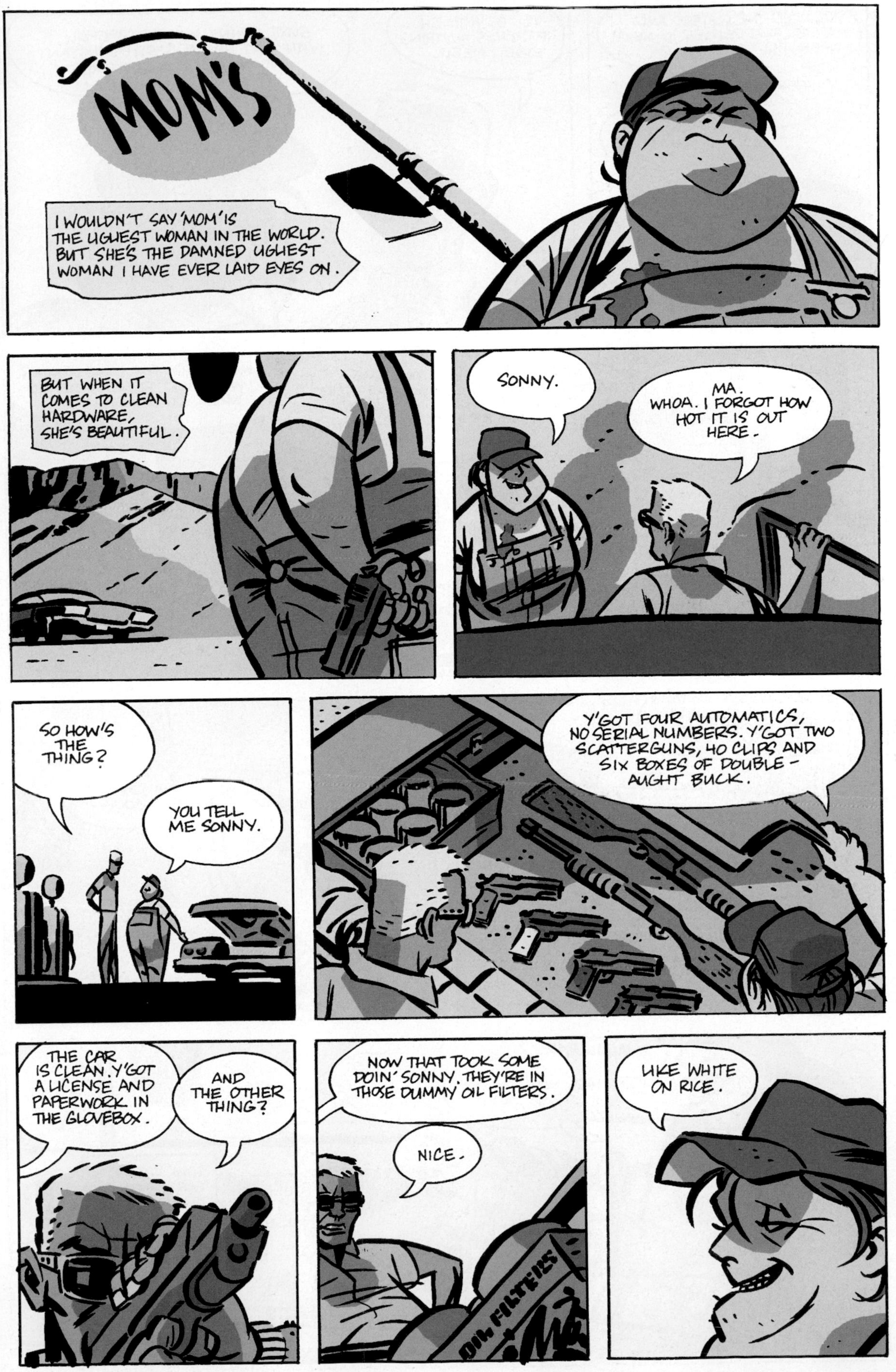
MOM'S
I WOULDN'T SAY 'MOM' IS THE UGLIEST WOMAN IN THE WORLD. BUT SHE'S THE DAMNED UGLIEST WOMAN I HAVE EVER LAID EYES ON.
BUT WHEN IT COMES TO CLEAN HARDWARE, SHE'S BEAUTIFUL.
SONNY.
MA. WHOA. I FORGOT HOW HOT IT IS OUT HERE.
SO HOW'S THE THING?
YOU TELL ME SONNY.
Y'GOT FOUR AUTOMATICS, NO SERIAL NUMBERS. Y'GOT TWO SCATTERGUNS, 40 CLIPS AND SIX BOXES OF DOUBLE-AUGHT BUCK.
THE CAR IS CLEAN. Y'GOT A LICENSE AND PAPERWORK IN THE GLOVEBOX.
AND THE OTHER THING?
NOW THAT TOOK SOME DOIN' SONNY. THEY'RE IN THOSE DUMMY OIL FILTERS.
NICE.
OIL FILTERS
LIKE WHITE ON RICE.

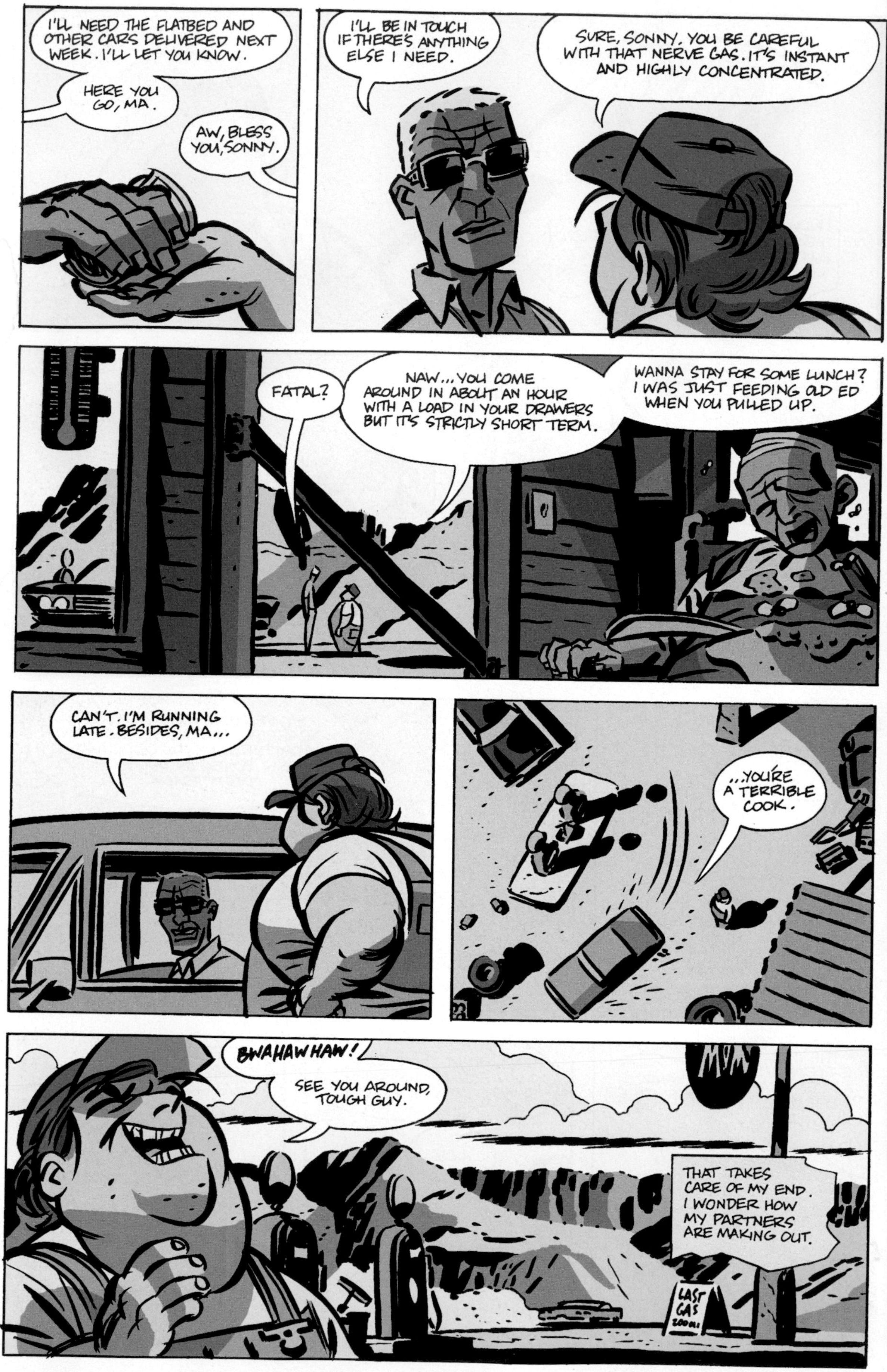
I'LL NEED THE FLATBED AND OTHER CARS DELIVERED NEXT WEEK. I'LL LET YOU KNOW.
HERE YOU GO, MA.
AW, BLESS YOU, SONNY.
I'LL BE IN TOUCH IF THERE'S ANYTHING ELSE I NEED.
SURE, SONNY. YOU BE CAREFUL WITH THAT NERVE GAS. IT'S INSTANT AND HIGHLY CONCENTRATED.
FATAL?
NAW... YOU COME AROUND IN ABOUT AN HOUR WITH A LOAD IN YOUR DRAWERS BUT IT'S STRICTLY SHORT TERM.
WANNA STAY FOR SOME LUNCH? I WAS JUST FEEDING OLD ED WHEN YOU PULLED UP.
CAN'T. I'M RUNNING LATE. BESIDES, MA...
...YOU'RE A TERRIBLE COOK.
BWAHAWHAW!
SEE YOU AROUND, TOUGH GUY.
THAT TAKES CARE OF MY END. I WONDER HOW MY PARTNERS ARE MAKING OUT.
LAST GAS

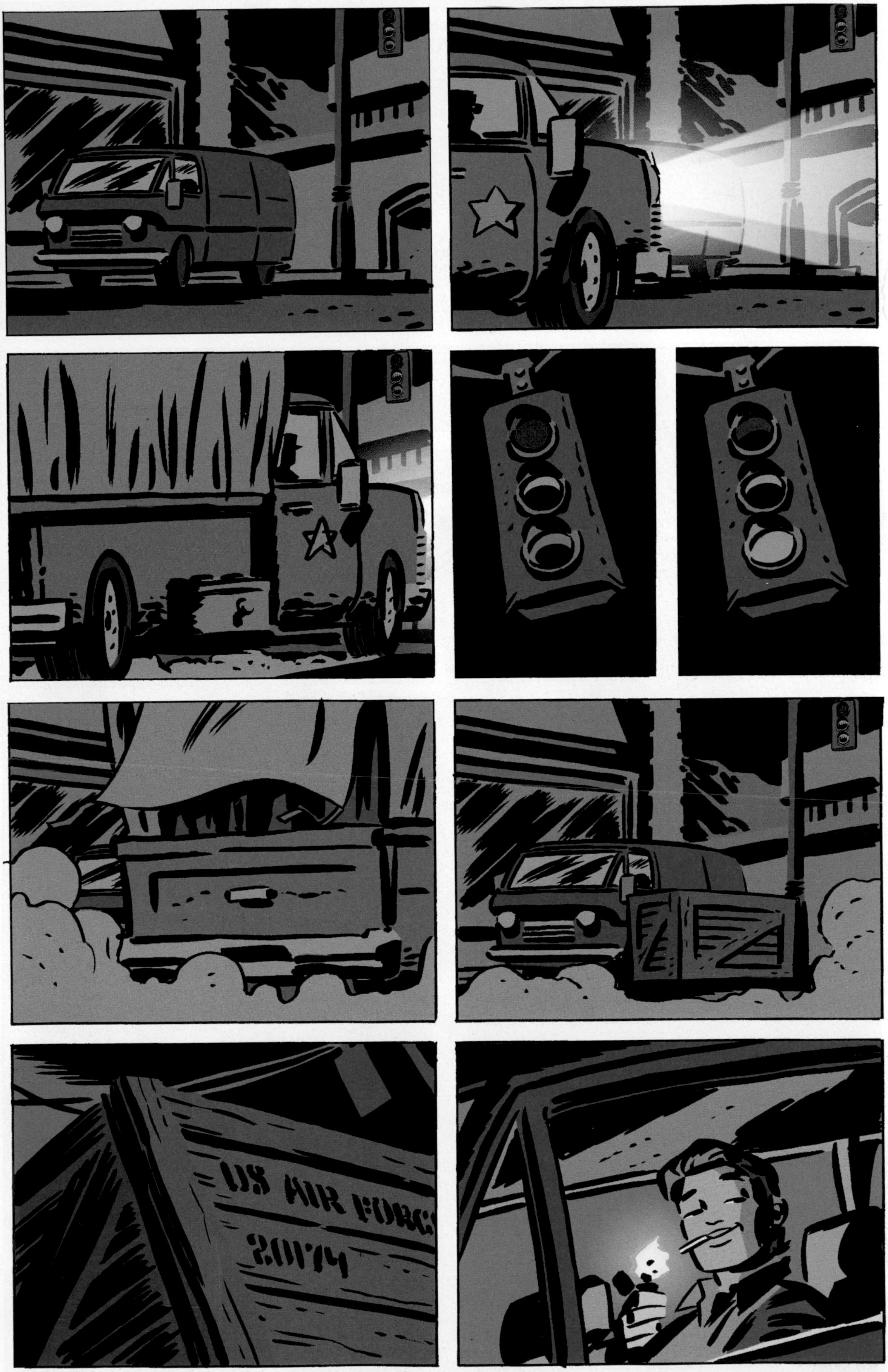
US AIR FORC
20774

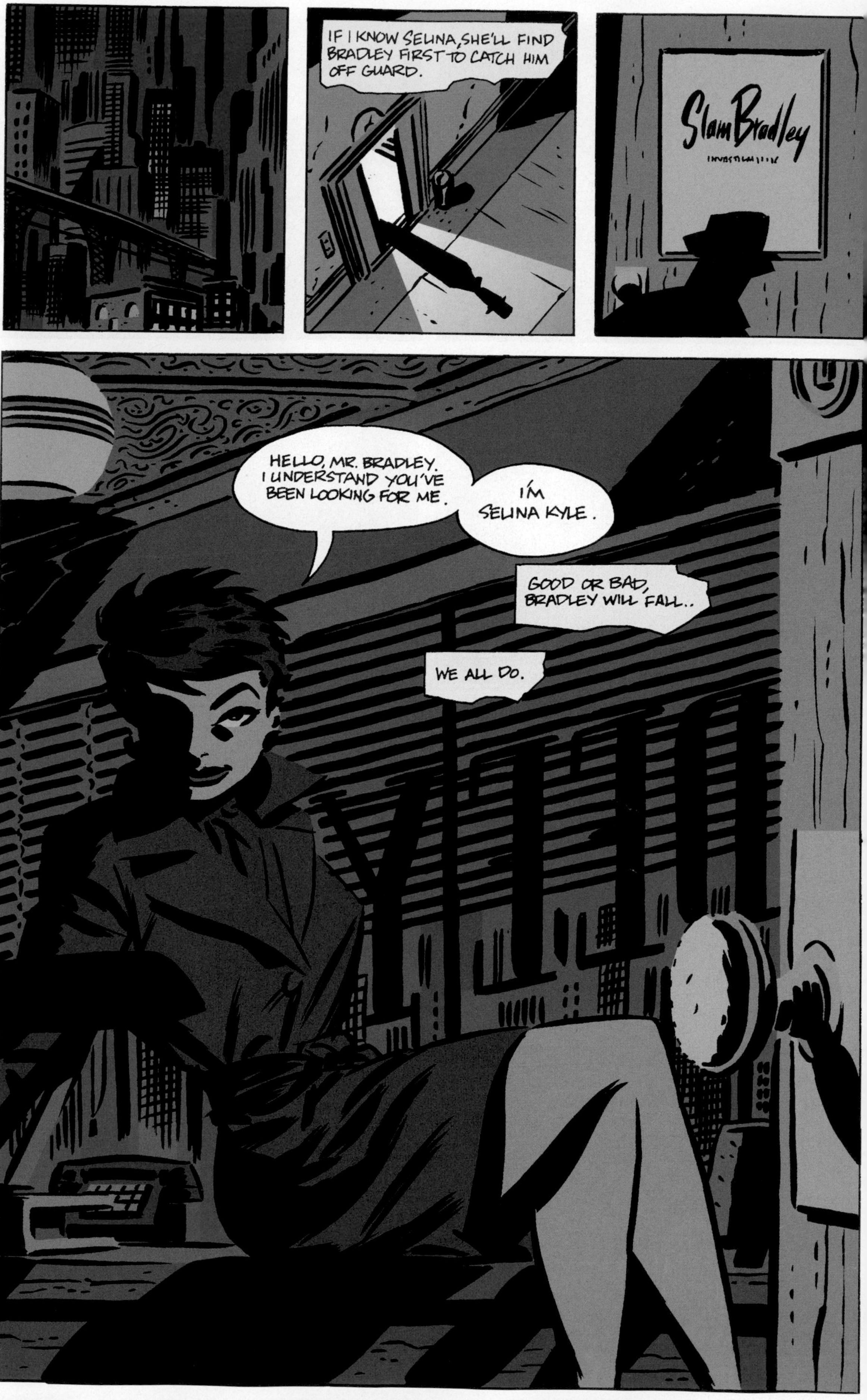
IF I KNOW SELINA, SHE'LL FIND BRADLEY FIRST TO CATCH HIM OFF GUARD.
Slam Bradley
HELLO, MR. BRADLEY. I UNDERSTAND YOU'VE BEEN LOOKING FOR ME.
I'M SELINA KYLE.
GOOD OR BAD, BRADLEY WILL FALL..
WE ALL DO.

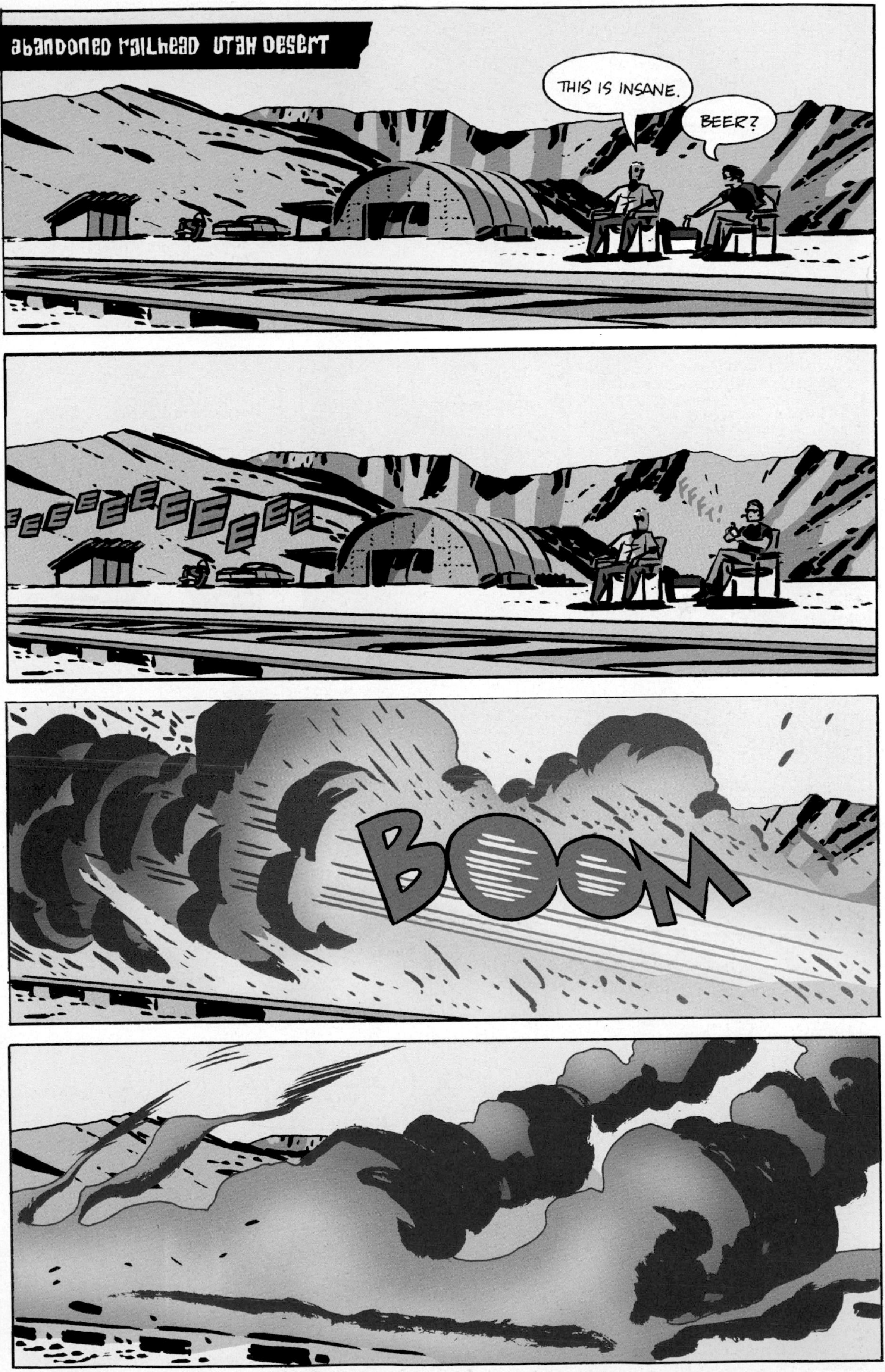
abandoned railhead utah desert
THIS IS INSANE.
BEER?
EEEEEEEEEEEEE
FFFT!
BOOM

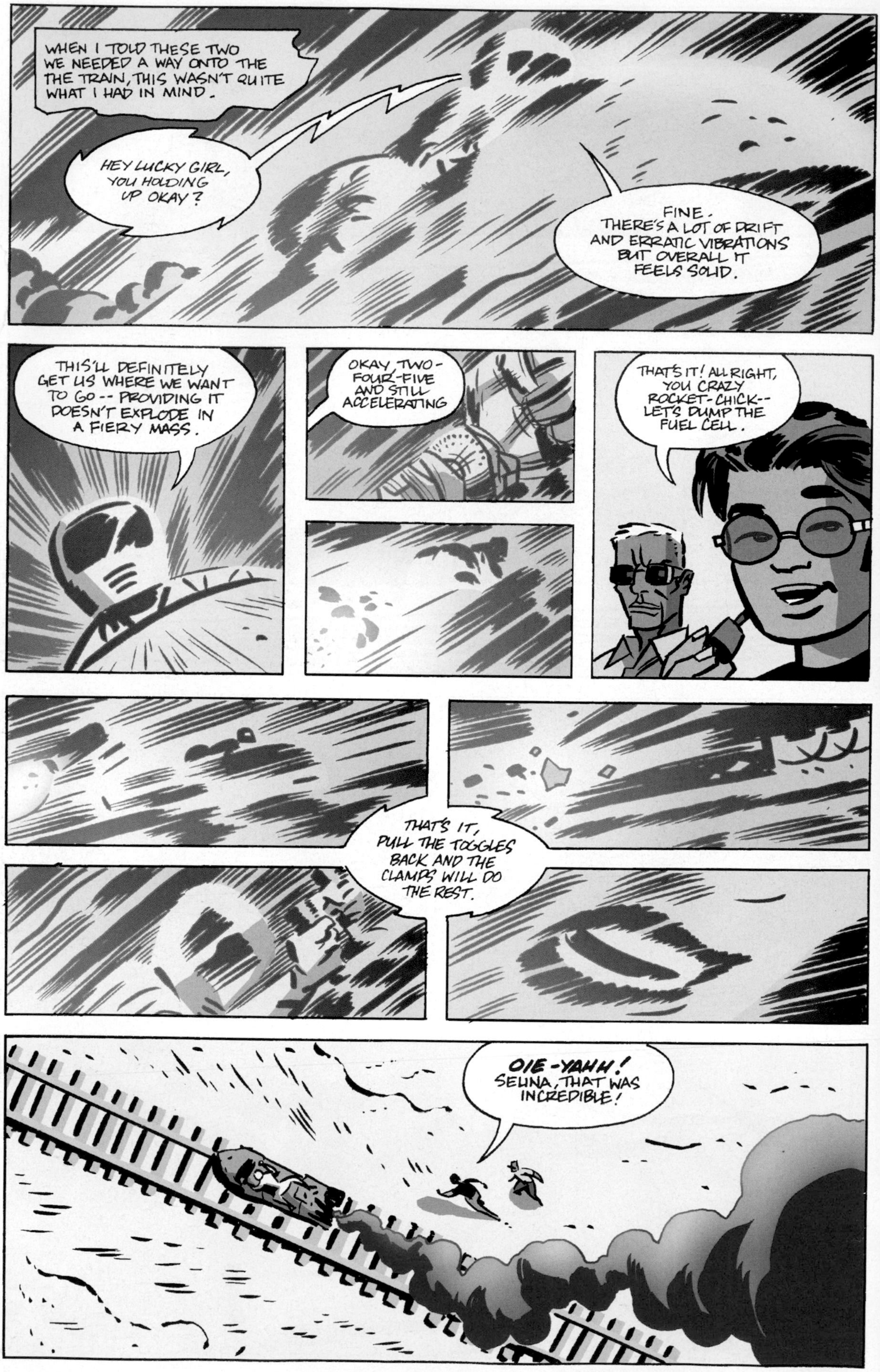
WHEN I TOLD THESE TWO WE NEEDED A WAY ONTO THE THE TRAIN, THIS WASN'T QUITE WHAT I HAD IN MIND.
HEY LUCKY GIRL, YOU HOLDING UP OKAY?
FINE. THERE'S A LOT OF DRIFT AND ERRATIC VIBRATIONS BUT OVERALL IT FEELS SOLID.
THIS'LL DEFINITELY GET US WHERE WE WANT TO GO -- PROVIDING IT DOESN'T EXPLODE IN A FIERY MASS.
OKAY, TWO-FOUR-FIVE AND STILL ACCELERATING
THAT'S IT! ALL RIGHT, YOU CRAZY ROCKET-CHICK-- LET'S DUMP THE FUEL CELL.
THAT'S IT, PULL THE TOGGLES BACK AND THE CLAMPS WILL DO THE REST.
OIE-YAHH! SELINA, THAT WAS INCREDIBLE!

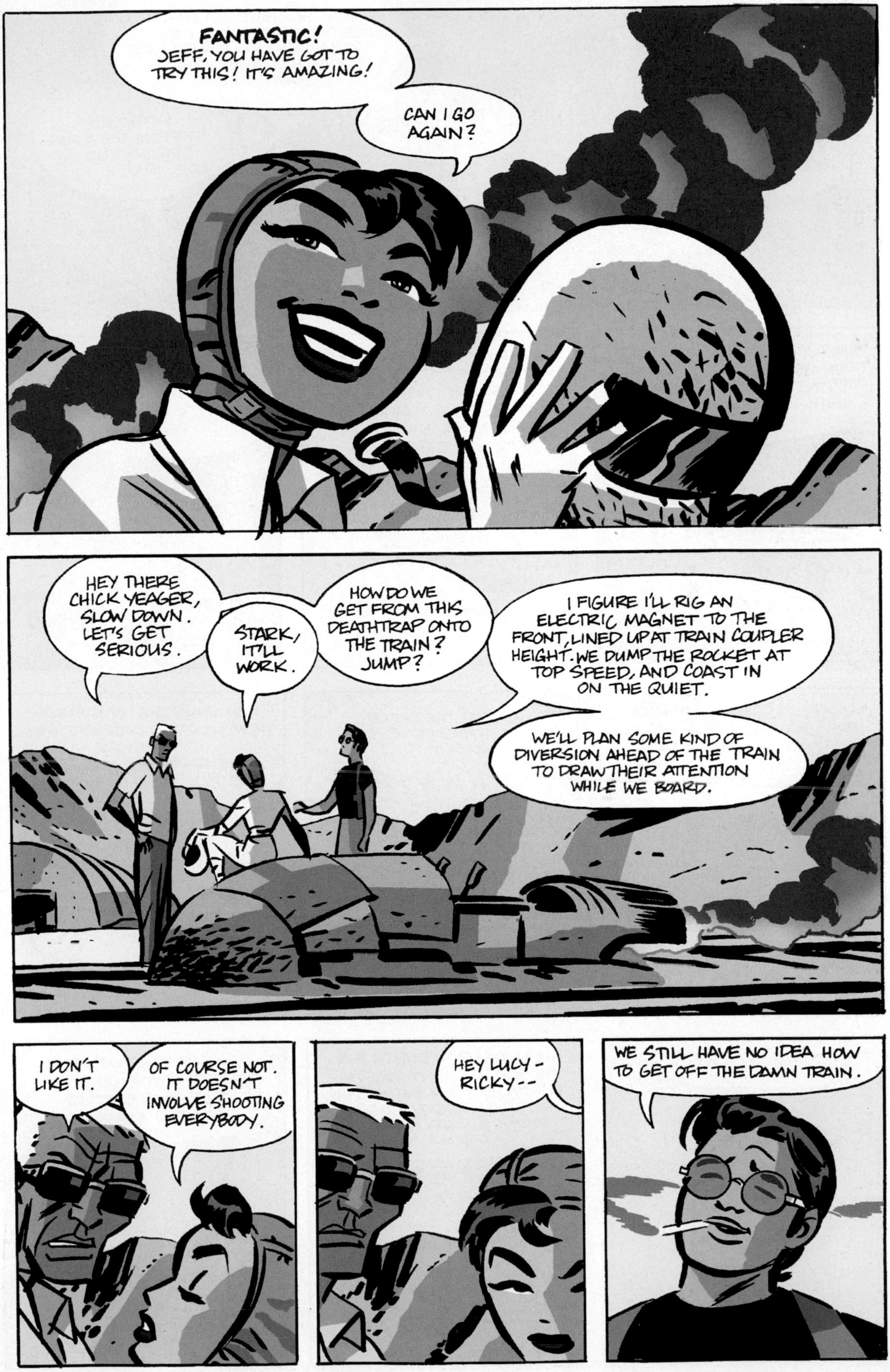
FANTASTIC! JEFF, YOU HAVE GOT TO TRY THIS! IT'S AMAZING!
CAN I GO AGAIN?
HEY THERE CHICK YEAGER, SLOW DOWN. LET'S GET SERIOUS.
STARK, IT'LL WORK.
HOW DO WE GET FROM THIS DEATHTRAP ONTO THE TRAIN? JUMP?
I FIGURE I'LL RIG AN ELECTRIC MAGNET TO THE FRONT, LINED UP AT TRAIN COUPLER HEIGHT. WE DUMP THE ROCKET AT TOP SPEED, AND COAST IN ON THE QUIET.
WE'LL PLAN SOME KIND OF DIVERSION AHEAD OF THE TRAIN TO DRAW THEIR ATTENTION WHILE WE BOARD.
I DON'T LIKE IT.
OF COURSE NOT. IT DOESN'T INVOLVE SHOOTING EVERYBODY.
HEY LUCY - RICKY --
WE STILL HAVE NO IDEA HOW TO GET OFF THE DAMN TRAIN.

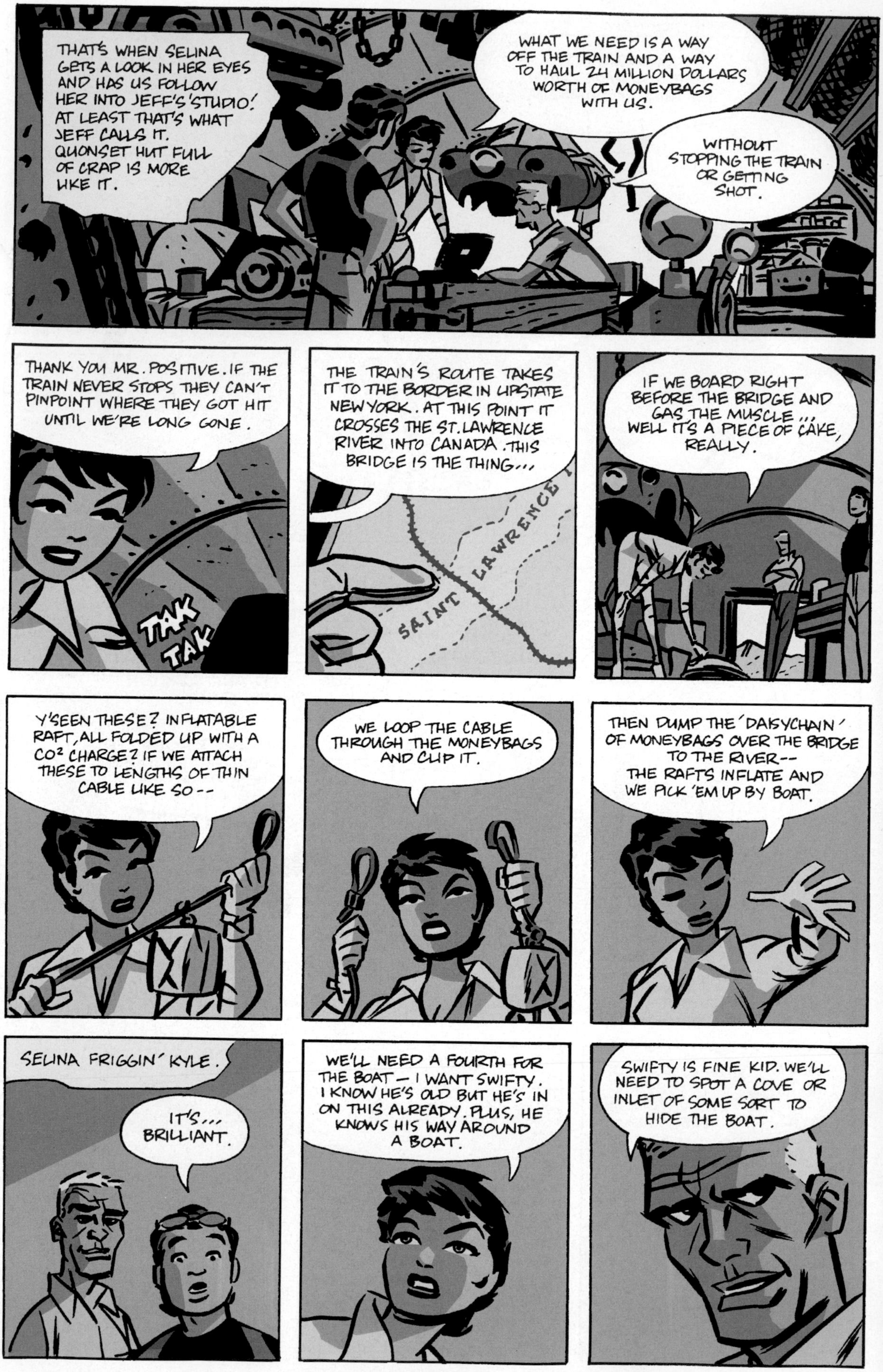
THAT'S WHEN SELINA GETS A LOOK IN HER EYES AND HAS US FOLLOW HER INTO JEFF'S 'STUDIO.' AT LEAST THAT'S WHAT JEFF CALLS IT. QUONSET HUT FULL OF CRAP IS MORE LIKE IT.
WHAT WE NEED IS A WAY OFF THE TRAIN AND A WAY TO HAUL 24 MILLION DOLLARS WORTH OF MONEYBAGS WITH US.
WITHOUT STOPPING THE TRAIN OR GETTING SHOT.
THANK YOU MR. POSITIVE. IF THE TRAIN NEVER STOPS THEY CAN'T PINPOINT WHERE THEY GOT HIT UNTIL WE'RE LONG GONE.
TAK
TAK
THE TRAIN'S ROUTE TAKES IT TO THE BORDER IN UPSTATE NEW YORK. AT THIS POINT IT CROSSES THE ST. LAWRENCE RIVER INTO CANADA. THIS BRIDGE IS THE THING...
SAINT LAWRENCE
IF WE BOARD RIGHT BEFORE THE BRIDGE AND GAS THE MUSCLE... WELL IT'S A PIECE OF CAKE, REALLY.
Y'SEEN THESE? INFLATABLE RAFT, ALL FOLDED UP WITH A CO2 CHARGE? IF WE ATTACH THESE TO LENGTHS OF THIN CABLE LIKE SO--
WE LOOP THE CABLE THROUGH THE MONEYBAGS AND CLIP IT.
THEN DUMP THE 'DAISYCHAIN' OF MONEYBAGS OVER THE BRIDGE TO THE RIVER-- THE RAFTS INFLATE AND WE PICK 'EM UP BY BOAT.
SELINA FRIGGIN' KYLE.
IT'S... BRILLIANT.
WE'LL NEED A FOURTH FOR THE BOAT— I WANT SWIFTY. I KNOW HE'S OLD BUT HE'S IN ON THIS ALREADY. PLUS, HE KNOWS HIS WAY AROUND A BOAT.
SWIFTY IS FINE KID. WE'LL NEED TO SPOT A COVE OR INLET OF SOME SORT TO HIDE THE BOAT.

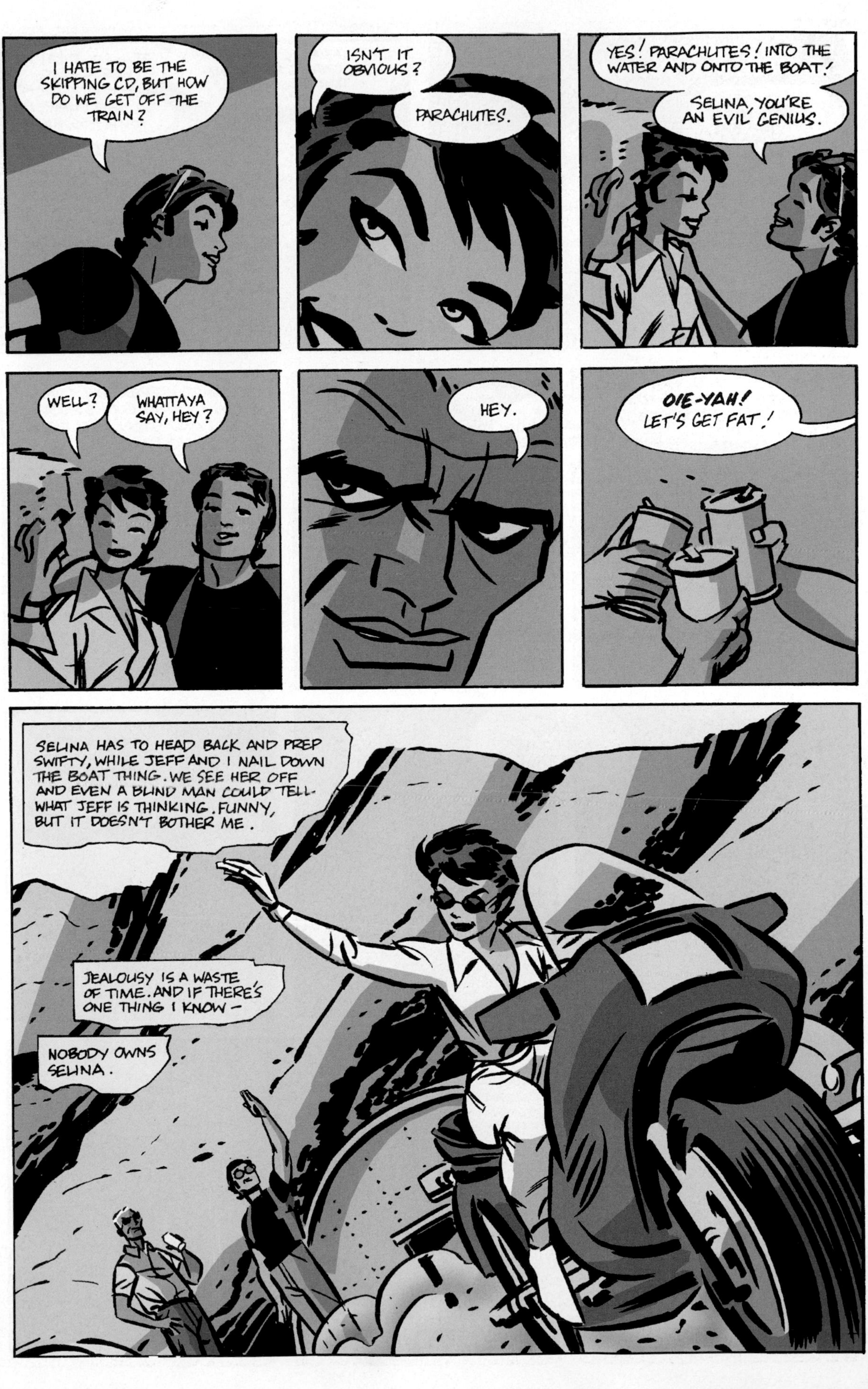
I HATE TO BE THE SKIPPING CD, BUT HOW DO WE GET OFF THE TRAIN?
ISN'T IT OBVIOUS?
PARACHUTES.
YES! PARACHUTES! INTO THE WATER AND ONTO THE BOAT!
SELINA, YOU'RE AN EVIL GENIUS.
WELL?
WHATTAYA SAY, HEY?
HEY.
OIE-YAH! LET'S GET FAT!
SELINA HAS TO HEAD BACK AND PREP SWIFTY, WHILE JEFF AND I NAIL DOWN THE BOAT THING. WE SEE HER OFF AND EVEN A BLIND MAN COULD TELL WHAT JEFF IS THINKING. FUNNY, BUT IT DOESN'T BOTHER ME.
JEALOUSY IS A WASTE OF TIME. AND IF THERE'S ONE THING I KNOW -
NOBODY OWNS SELINA.

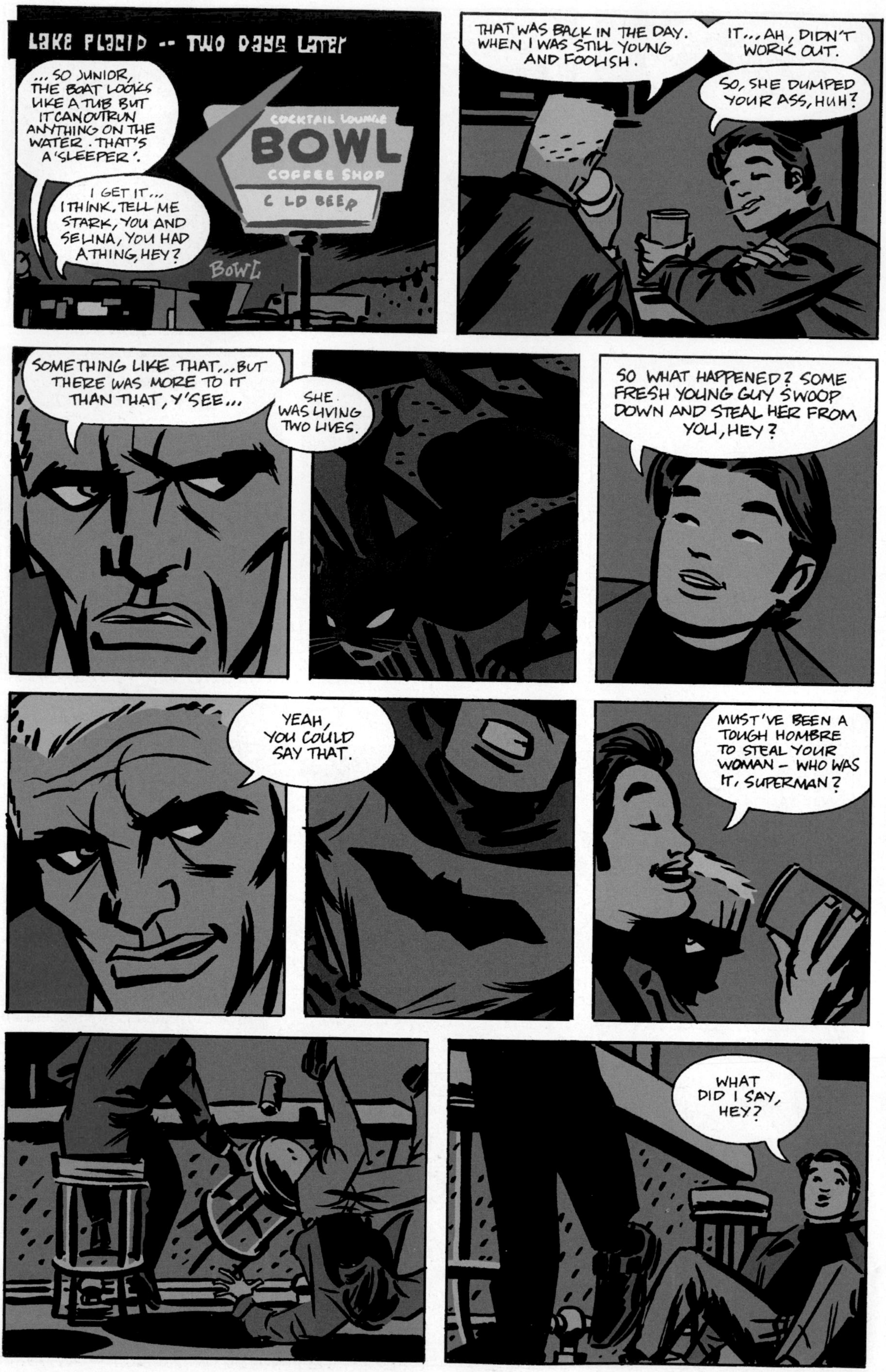
Lake Placid -- Two Days Later
...SO JUNIOR, THE BOAT LOOKS LIKE A TUB BUT IT CAN OUTRUN ANYTHING ON THE WATER. THAT'S A 'SLEEPER'.
COCKTAIL LOUNGE
BOWL
COFFEE SHOP
C LD BEER
I GET IT... I THINK. TELL ME STARK, YOU AND SELINA, YOU HAD A THING, HEY?
BOWL
THAT WAS BACK IN THE DAY. WHEN I WAS STILL YOUNG AND FOOLISH.
IT... AH, DIDN'T WORK OUT.
SO, SHE DUMPED YOUR ASS, HUH?
SOMETHING LIKE THAT... BUT THERE WAS MORE TO IT THAN THAT, Y'SEE...
SHE WAS LIVING TWO LIVES.
SO WHAT HAPPENED? SOME FRESH YOUNG GUY SWOOP DOWN AND STEAL HER FROM YOU, HEY?
YEAH, YOU COULD SAY THAT.
MUST'VE BEEN A TOUGH HOMBRE TO STEAL YOUR WOMAN - WHO WAS IT, SUPERMAN?
WHAT DID I SAY, HEY?

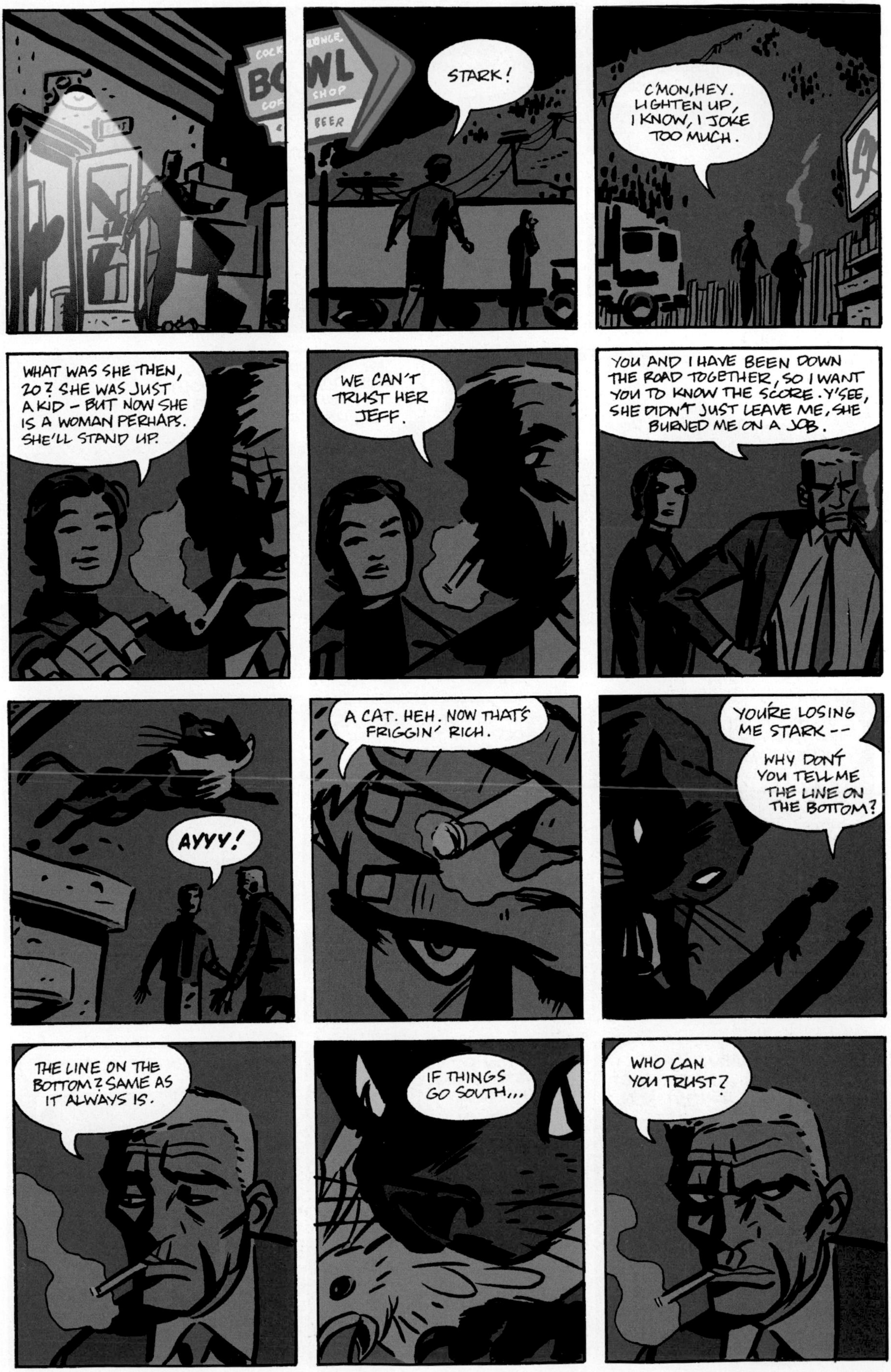
COCK LOUNGE
BOWL
COFFEE SHOP
BEER
STARK!
C'MON, HEY. LIGHTEN UP, I KNOW, I JOKE TOO MUCH.
WHAT WAS SHE THEN, 20? SHE WAS JUST A KID - BUT NOW SHE IS A WOMAN PERHAPS. SHE'LL STAND UP.
WE CAN'T TRUST HER JEFF.
YOU AND I HAVE BEEN DOWN THE ROAD TOGETHER, SO I WANT YOU TO KNOW THE SCORE. Y'SEE, SHE DIDN'T JUST LEAVE ME, SHE BURNED ME ON A JOB.
AYYY!
A CAT. HEH. NOW THAT'S FRIGGIN' RICH.
YOU'RE LOSING ME STARK --
WHY DON'T YOU TELL ME THE LINE ON THE BOTTOM?
THE LINE ON THE BOTTOM? SAME AS IT ALWAYS IS.
IF THINGS GO SOUTH...
WHO CAN YOU TRUST?

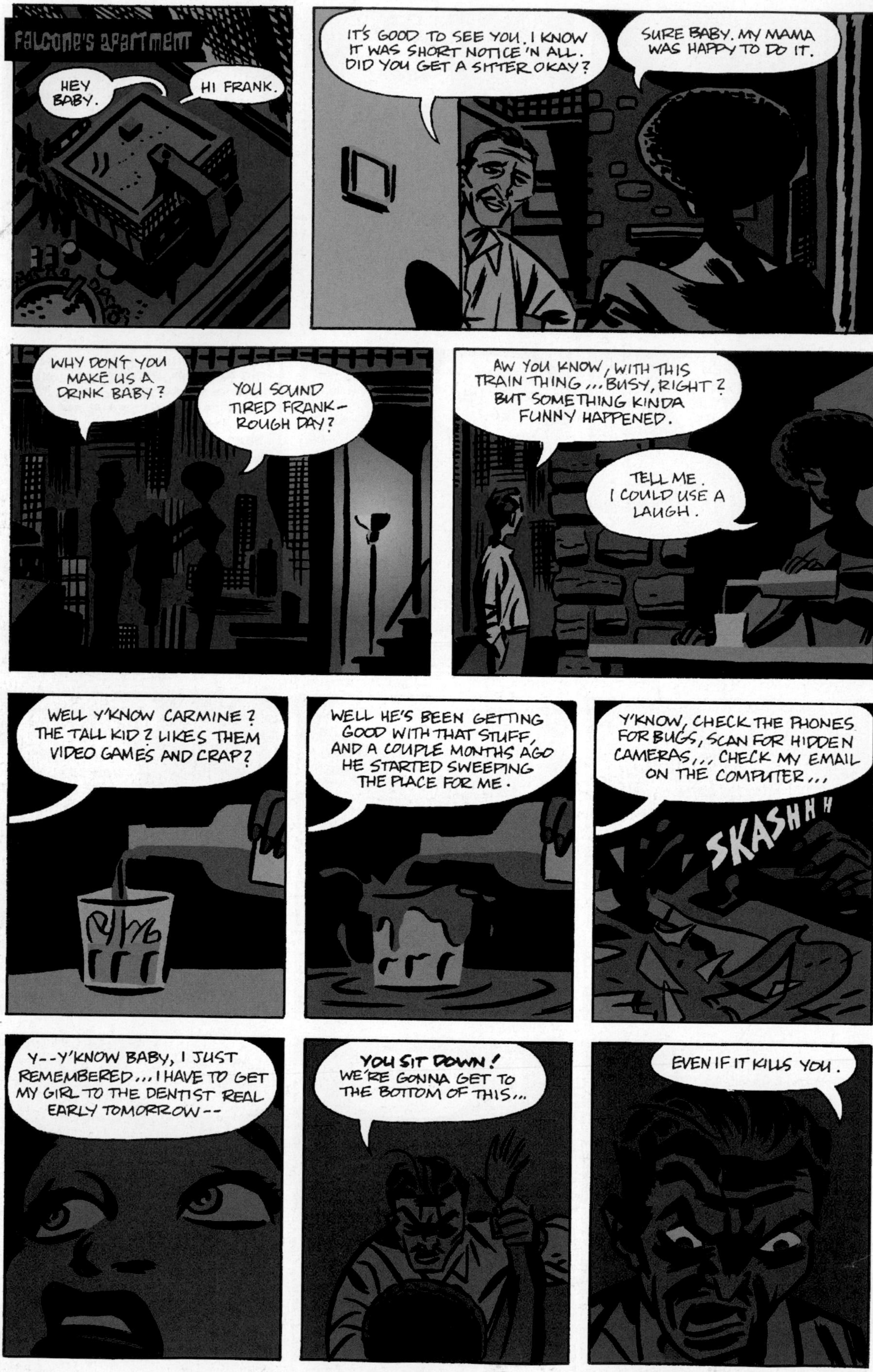
Falcone's apartment
HEY BABY.
HI FRANK.
IT'S GOOD TO SEE YOU. I KNOW IT WAS SHORT NOTICE 'N ALL. DID YOU GET A SITTER OKAY?
SURE BABY. MY MAMA WAS HAPPY TO DO IT.
WHY DON'T YOU MAKE US A DRINK BABY?
YOU SOUND TIRED FRANK-- ROUGH DAY?
AW YOU KNOW, WITH THIS TRAIN THING... BUSY, RIGHT? BUT SOMETHING KINDA FUNNY HAPPENED.
TELL ME. I COULD USE A LAUGH.
WELL Y'KNOW CARMINE? THE TALL KID? LIKES THEM VIDEO GAMES AND CRAP?
WELL HE'S BEEN GETTING GOOD WITH THAT STUFF, AND A COUPLE MONTHS AGO HE STARTED SWEEPING THE PLACE FOR ME.
Y'KNOW, CHECK THE PHONES FOR BUGS, SCAN FOR HIDDEN CAMERAS... CHECK MY EMAIL ON THE COMPUTER...
SKASHHH
Y--Y'KNOW BABY, I JUST REMEMBERED... I HAVE TO GET MY GIRL TO THE DENTIST REAL EARLY TOMORROW--
YOU SIT DOWN! WE'RE GONNA GET TO THE BOTTOM OF THIS...
EVEN IF IT KILLS YOU.

BOOK THREE
SLAM

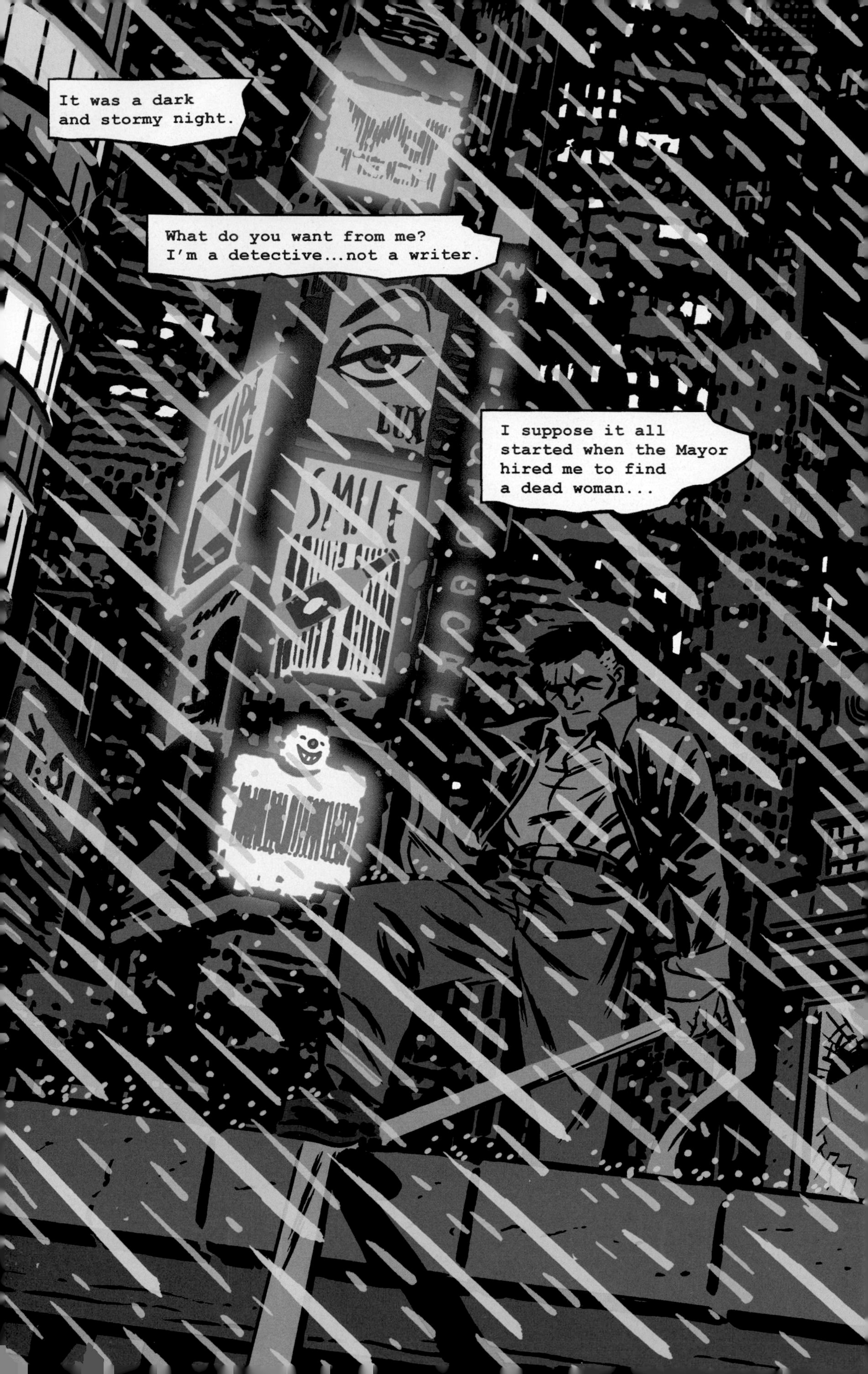
It was a dark and stormy night.
What do you want from me? I'm a detective...not a writer.
I suppose it all started when the Mayor hired me to find a dead woman...

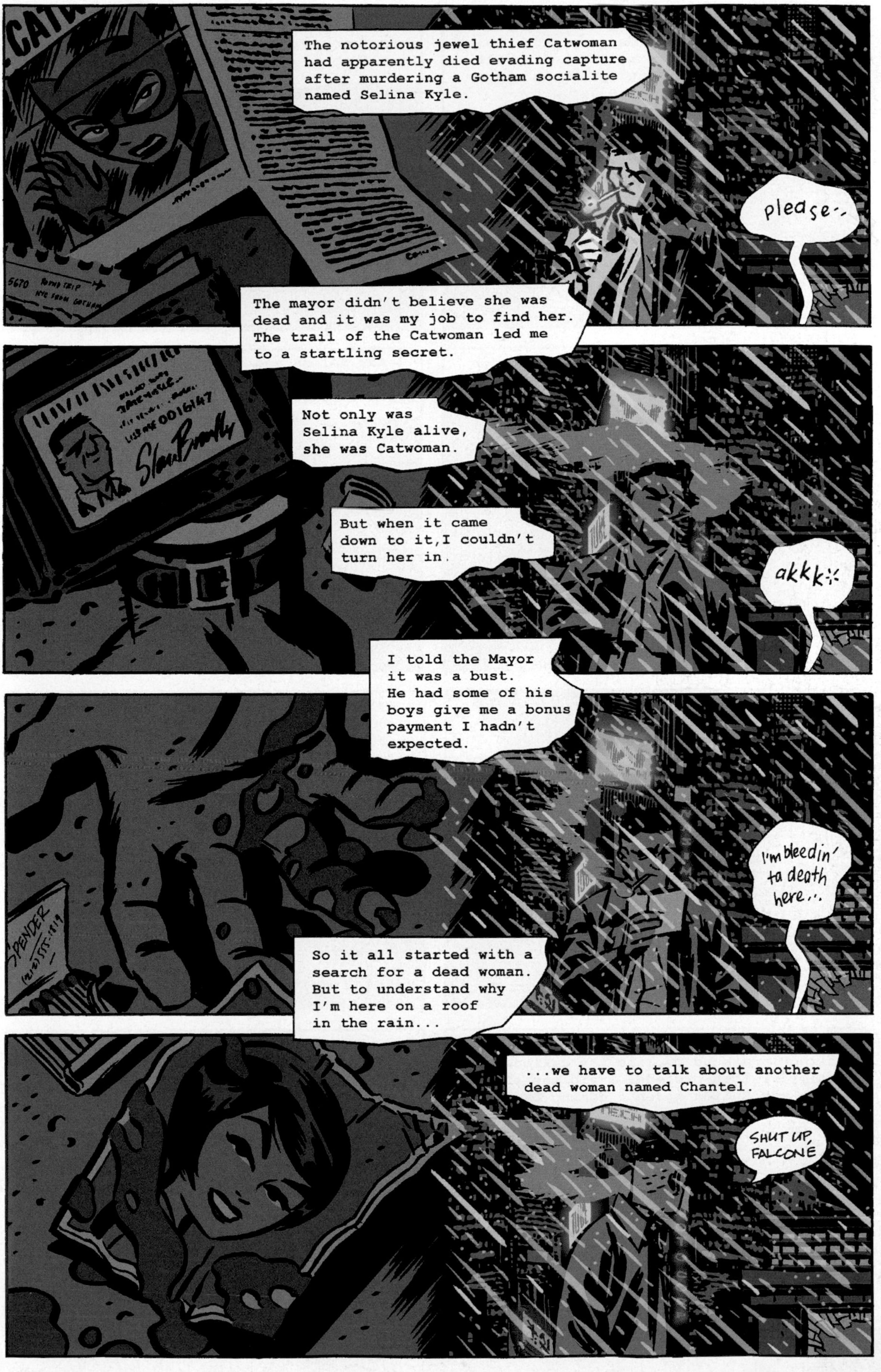

The notorious jewel thief Catwoman had apparently died evading capture after murdering a Gotham socialite named Selina Kyle.
please...
The mayor didn't believe she was dead and it was my job to find her. The trail of the Catwoman led me to a startling secret.
Not only was Selina Kyle alive, she was Catwoman.
But when it came down to it, I couldn't turn her in.
akkk
I told the Mayor it was a bust. He had some of his boys give me a bonus payment I hadn't expected.
I'm bleedin' ta death here...
So it all started with a search for a dead woman. But to understand why I'm here on a roof in the rain...
...we have to talk about another dead woman named Chantel.
SHUT UP, FALCONE

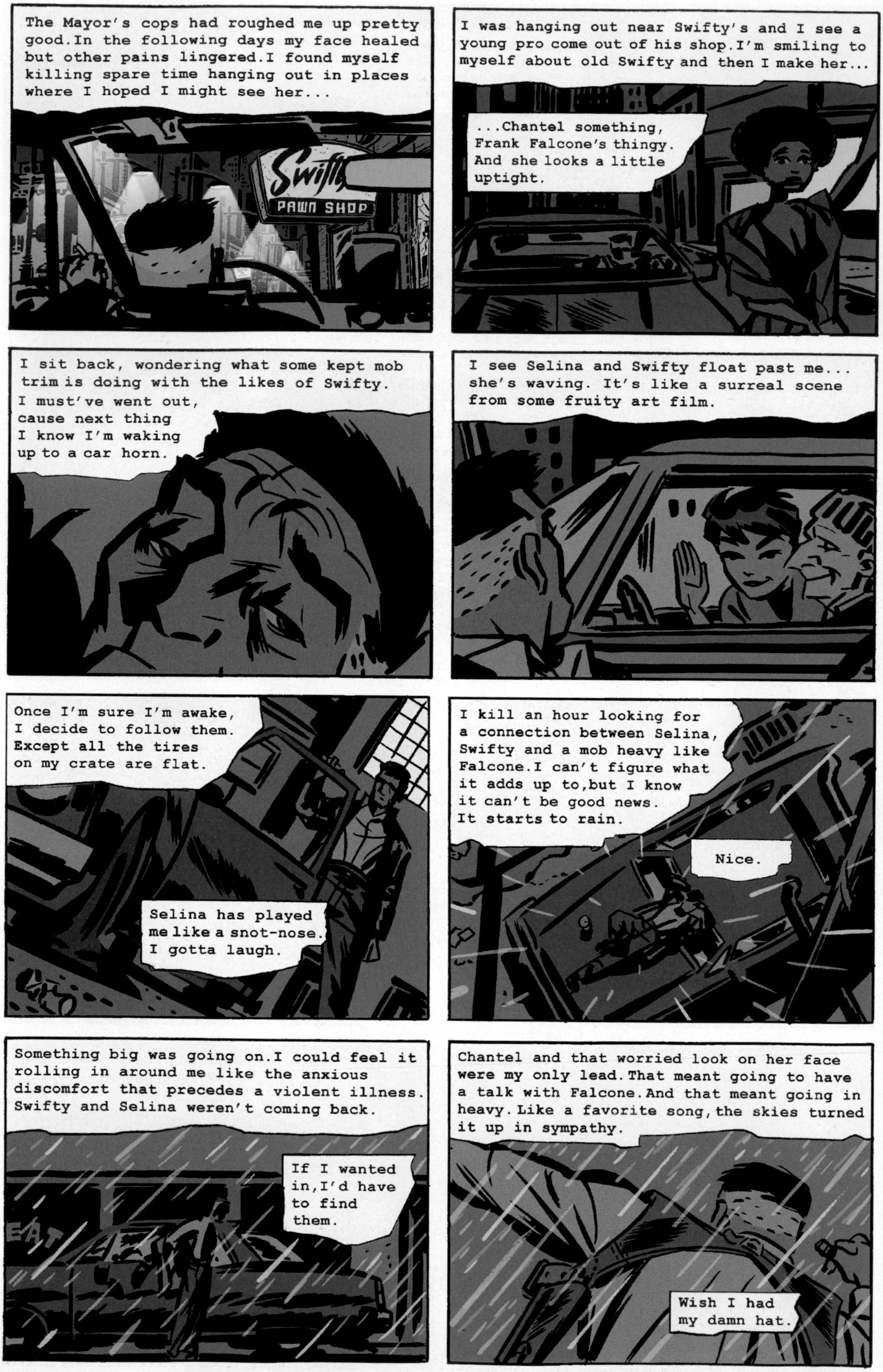
The Mayor's cops had roughed me up pretty good. In the following days my face healed but other pains lingered. I found myself killing spare time hanging out in places where I hoped I might see her...
Swifty
PAWN SHOP
I was hanging out near Swifty's and I see a young pro come out of his shop. I'm smiling to myself about old Swifty and then I make her...
...Chantel something, Frank Falcone's thingy. And she looks a little uptight.
I sit back, wondering what some kept mob trim is doing with the likes of Swifty.
I must've went out, cause next thing I know I'm waking up to a car horn.
I see Selina and Swifty float past me... she's waving. It's like a surreal scene from some fruity art film.
Once I'm sure I'm awake, I decide to follow them. Except all the tires on my crate are flat.
Selina has played me like a snot-nose. I gotta laugh.
I kill an hour looking for a connection between Selina, Swifty and a mob heavy like Falcone. I can't figure what it adds up to, but I know it can't be good news. It starts to rain.
Nice.
Something big was going on. I could feel it rolling in around me like the anxious discomfort that precedes a violent illness. Swifty and Selina weren't coming back.
If I wanted in, I'd have to find them.
EAT
Chantel and that worried look on her face were my only lead. That meant going to have a talk with Falcone. And that meant going in heavy. Like a favorite song, the skies turned it up in sympathy.
Wish I had my damn hat.

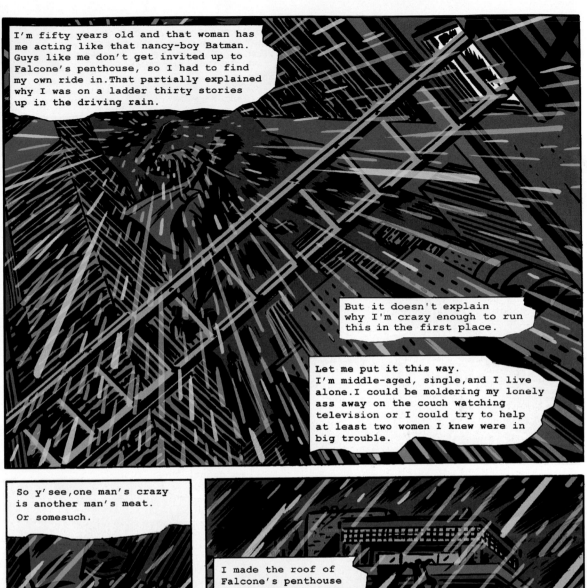

I'm fifty years old and that woman has me acting like that nancy-boy Batman. Guys like me don't get invited up to Falcone's penthouse, so I had to find my own ride in. That partially explained why I was on a ladder thirty stories up in the driving rain.

But it doesn't explain why I'm crazy enough to run this in the first place.

Let me put it this way. I'm middle-aged, single, and I live alone. I could be moldering my lonely ass away on the couch watching television or I could try to help at least two women I knew were in big trouble.

So y'see, one man's crazy is another man's meat. Or somesuch.

I made the roof of Falcone's penthouse just as the screaming starts.

The goon guarding the terrace was a nice warm-up.

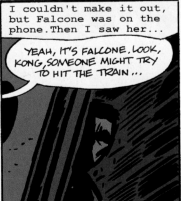

I couldn't make it out, but Falcone was on the phone. Then I saw her...

YEAH, IT'S FALCONE. LOOK, KONG, SOMEONE MIGHT TRY TO HIT THE TRAIN...

I knew it was Chantel from her dress, but sweet mother--her face.

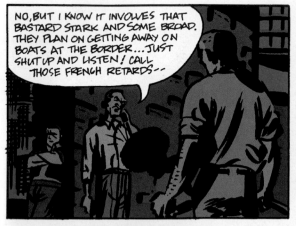

NO, BUT I KNOW IT INVOLVES THAT BASTARD STARK AND SOME BROAD. THEY PLAN ON GETTING AWAY ON BOATS AT THE BORDER...JUST SHUT UP AND LISTEN! CALL THOSE FRENCH RETARDS--

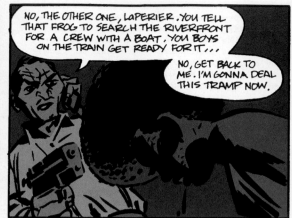

NO, THE OTHER ONE, LAPERIER. YOU TELL THAT FROG TO SEARCH THE RIVERFRONT FOR A CREW WITH A BOAT, YOU BOYS ON THE TRAIN GET READY FOR IT...

NO, GET BACK TO ME. I'M GONNA DEAL THIS TRAMP NOW.

My whole Irish life it's been the same. I need something to fight about. Something to fight for.

No fear, no doubt, no choice...

BAM

Just the righteous anger of the killer inside me.

BAM BAM BAM BAM BAM

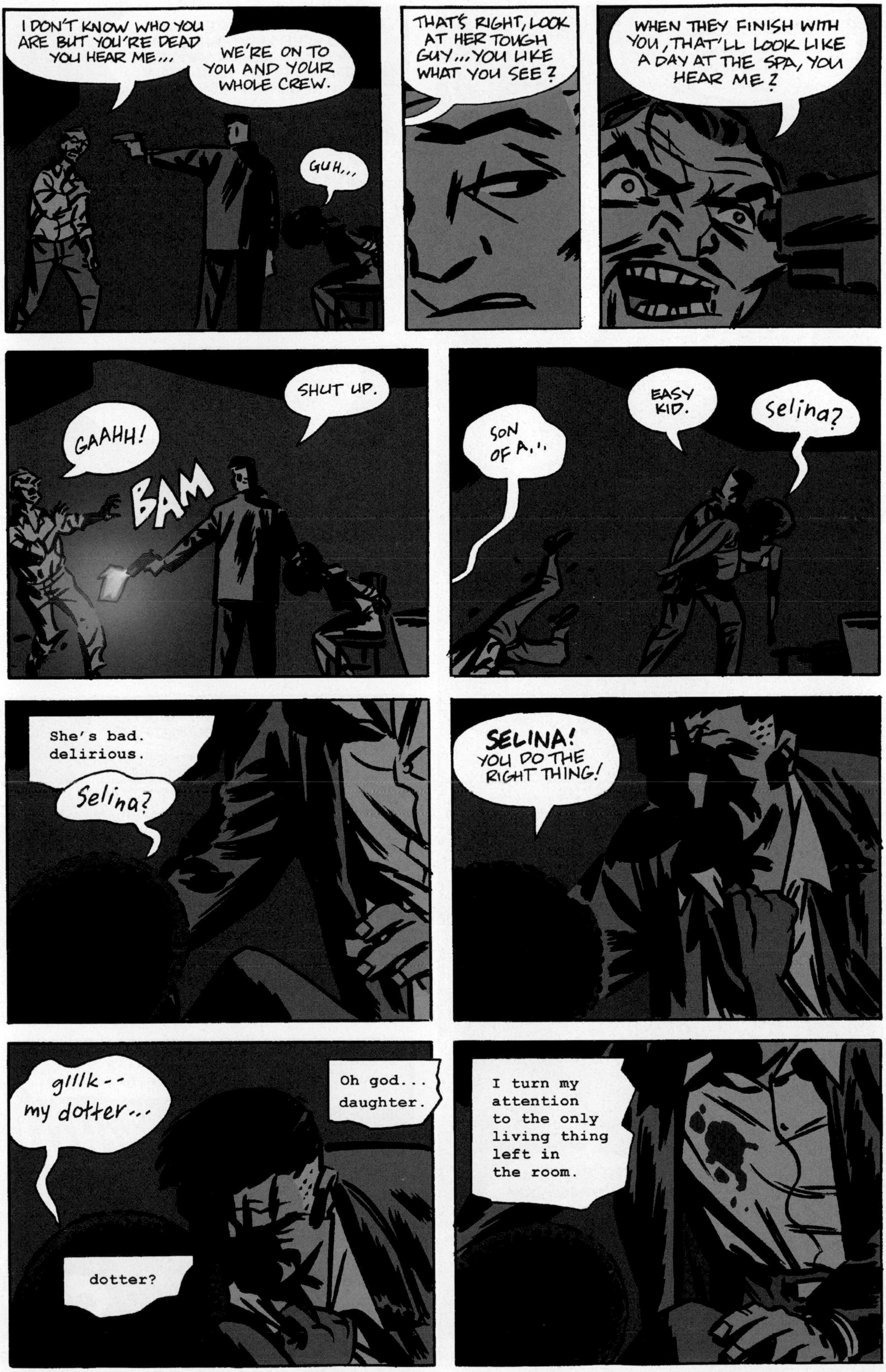
I DON'T KNOW WHO YOU ARE BUT YOU'RE DEAD YOU HEAR ME...
WE'RE ON TO YOU AND YOUR WHOLE CREW.
GUH...
THAT'S RIGHT, LOOK AT HER TOUGH GUY... YOU LIKE WHAT YOU SEE?
WHEN THEY FINISH WITH YOU, THAT'LL LOOK LIKE A DAY AT THE SPA, YOU HEAR ME?
GAAHH!
SHUT UP.
BAM
SON OF A...
EASY KID.
Selina?
She's bad. delirious.
Selina?
SELINA! YOU DO THE RIGHT THING!
glllk-- my dotter...
Oh god... daughter.
dotter?
I turn my attention to the only living thing left in the room.

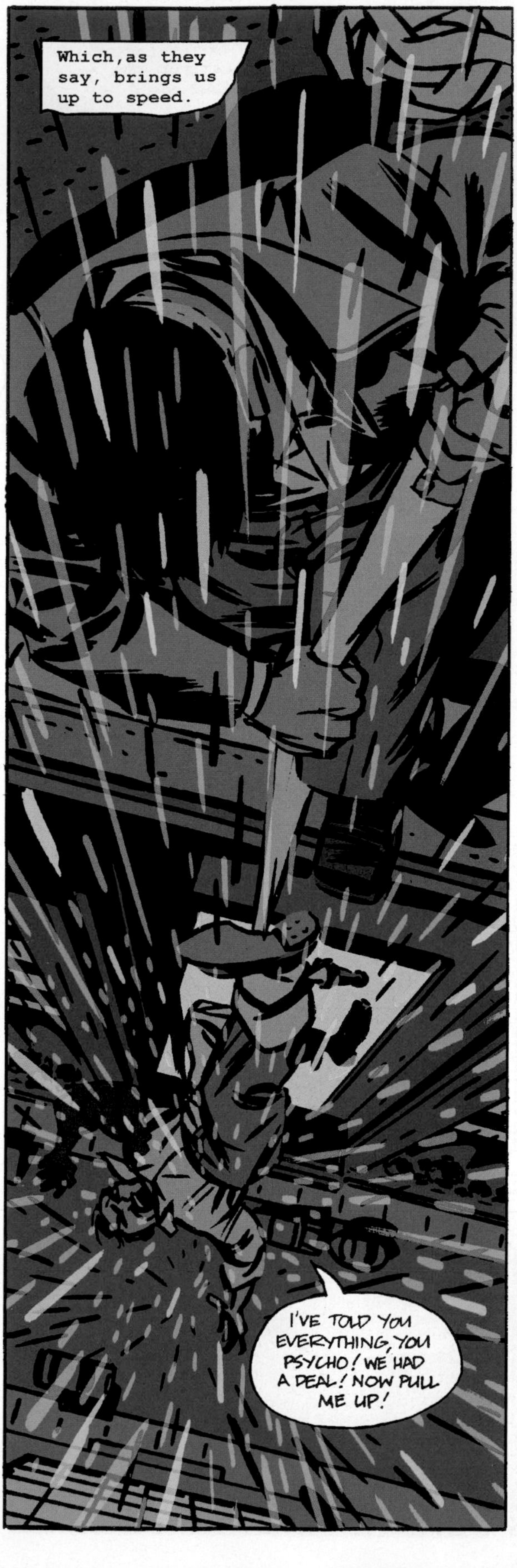
Which, as they say, brings us up to speed.
I'VE TOLD YOU EVERYTHING, YOU PSYCHO! WE HAD A DEAL! NOW PULL ME UP!

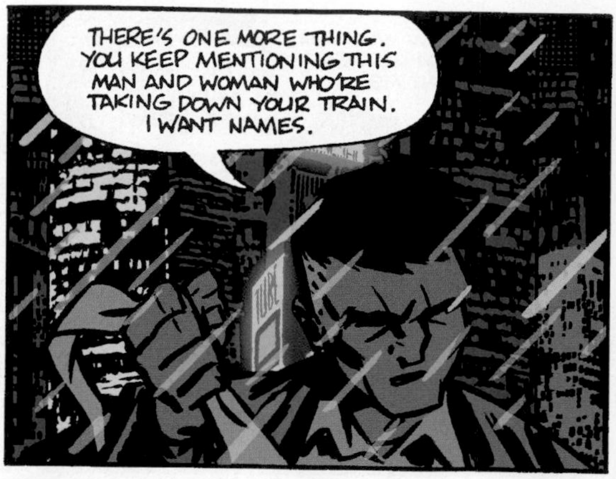
THERE'S ONE MORE THING. YOU KEEP MENTIONING THIS MAN AND WOMAN WHO'RE TAKING DOWN YOUR TRAIN. I WANT NAMES.

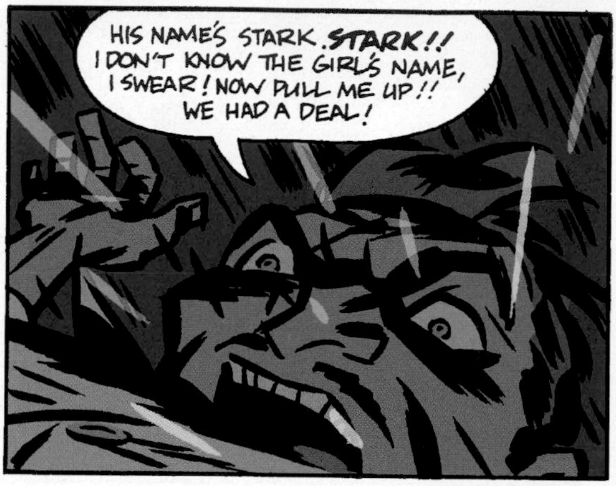
HIS NAME'S STARK. STARK!! I DON'T KNOW THE GIRL'S NAME, I SWEAR! NOW PULL ME UP!! WE HAD A DEAL!

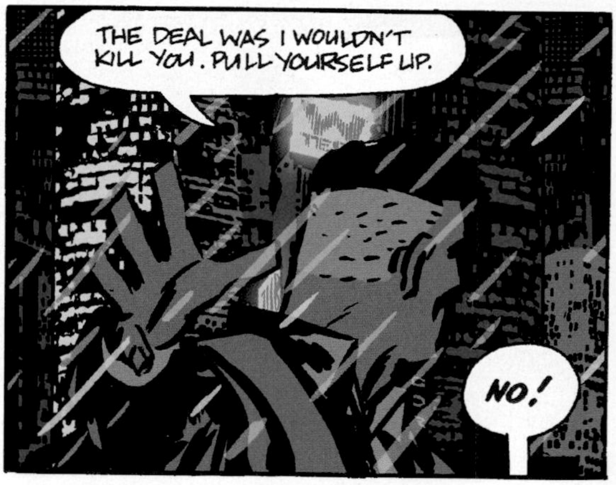
THE DEAL WAS I WOULDN'T KILL YOU. PULL YOURSELF UP.
NO!

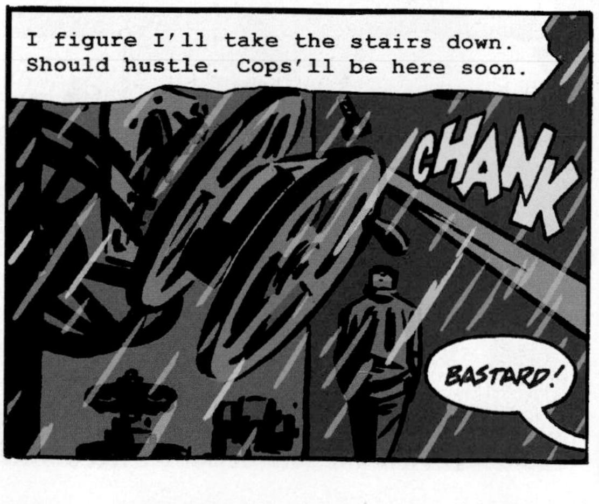
I figure I'll take the stairs down. Should hustle. Cops'll be here soon.
CHANK
BASTARD!

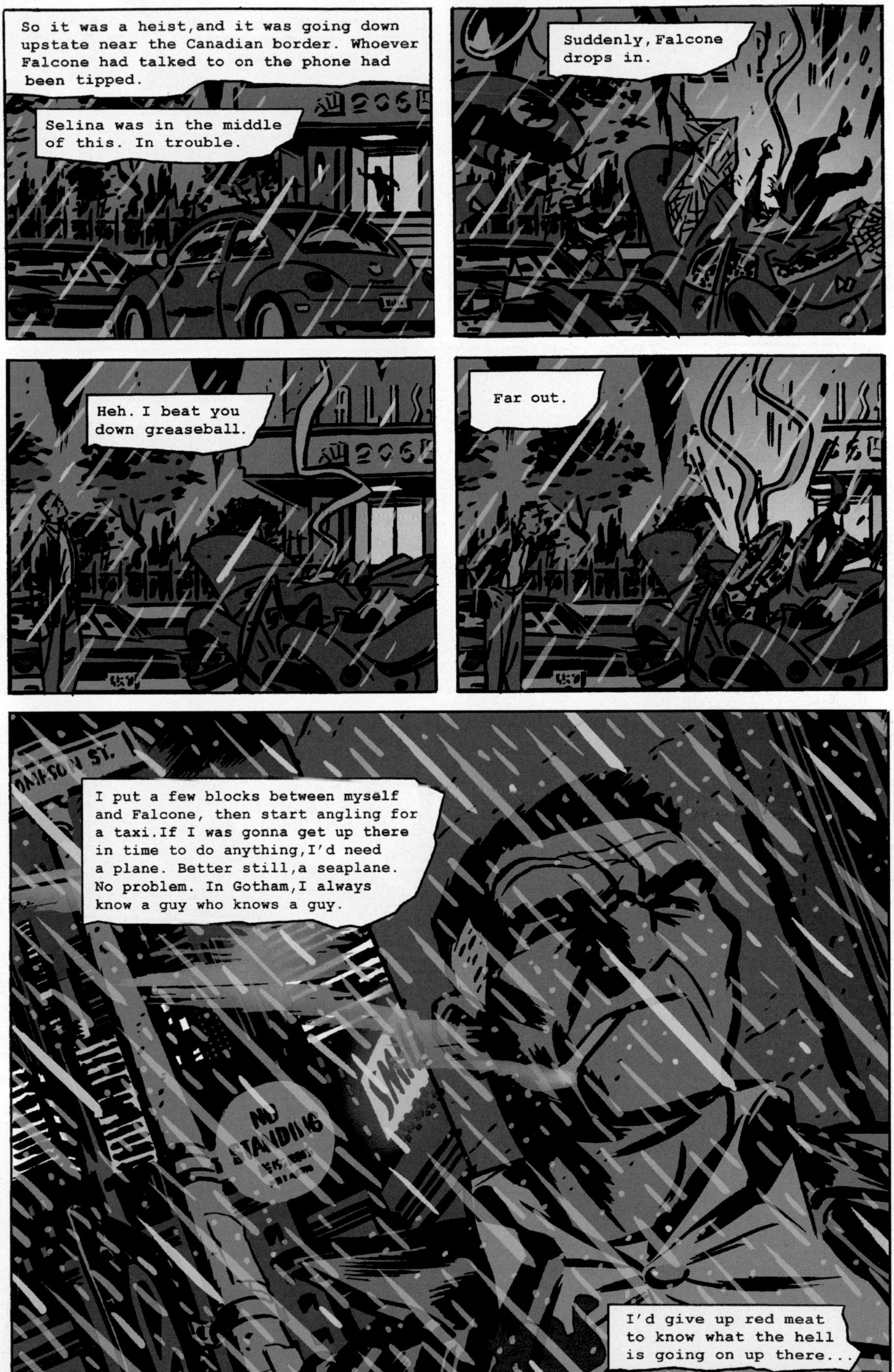
So it was a heist, and it was going down upstate near the Canadian border. Whoever Falcone had talked to on the phone had been tipped.
Selina was in the middle of this. In trouble.
Suddenly, Falcone drops in.
Heh. I beat you down greaseball.
Far out.
I put a few blocks between myself and Falcone, then start angling for a taxi. If I was gonna get up there in time to do anything, I'd need a plane. Better still, a seaplane. No problem. In Gotham, I always know a guy who knows a guy.
NO STANDING
I'd give up red meat to know what the hell is going on up there...

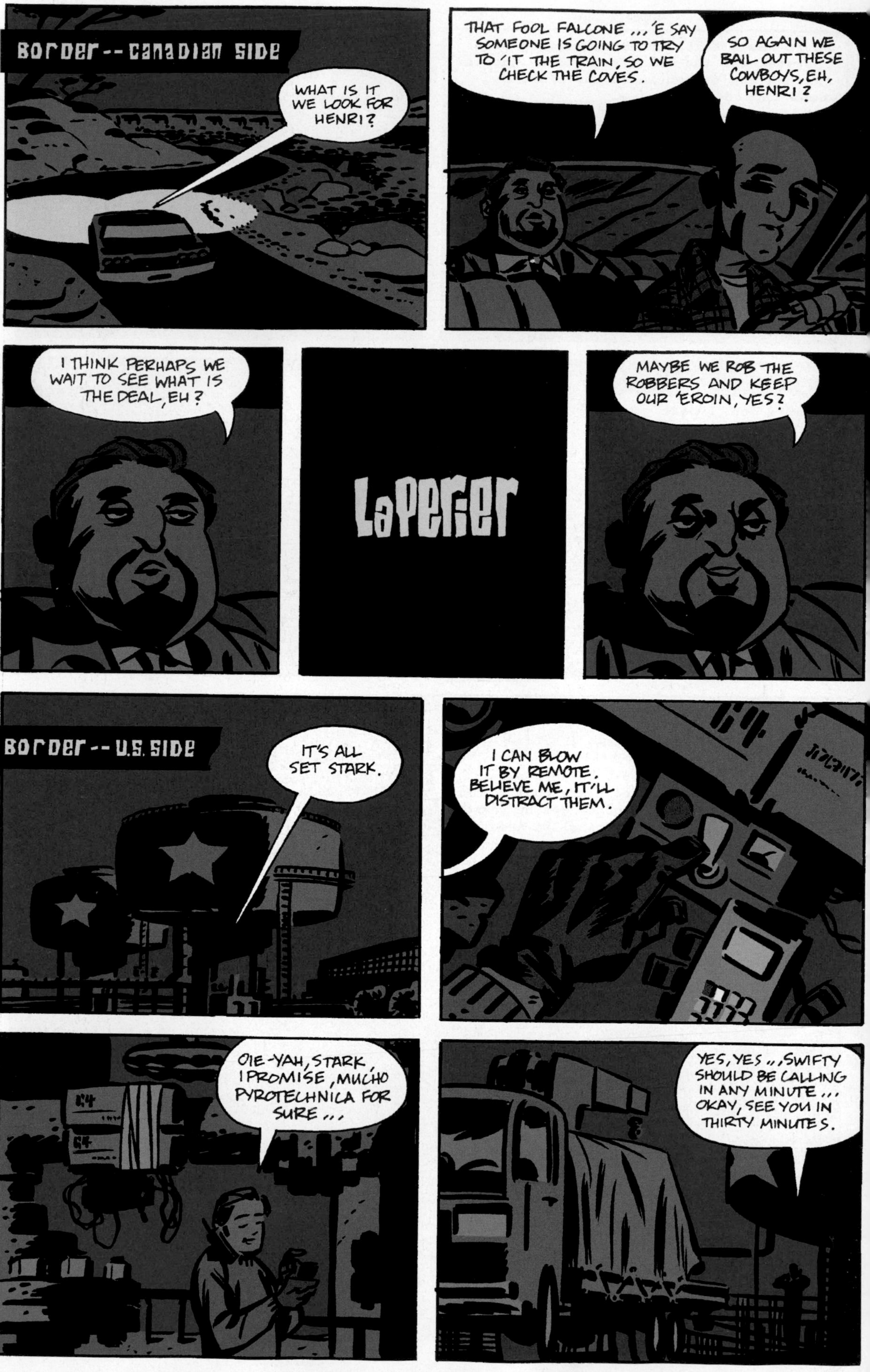
BORDER -- CANADIAN SIDE
WHAT IS IT WE LOOK FOR HENRI?
THAT FOOL FALCONE ... 'E SAY SOMEONE IS GOING TO TRY TO 'IT THE TRAIN, SO WE CHECK THE COVES.
SO AGAIN WE BAIL OUT THESE COWBOYS, EH, HENRI?
I THINK PERHAPS WE WAIT TO SEE WHAT IS THE DEAL, EH?
LaPERIER
MAYBE WE ROB THE ROBBERS AND KEEP OUR 'EROIN, YES?
BORDER -- U.S. SIDE
IT'S ALL SET STARK.
I CAN BLOW IT BY REMOTE. BELIEVE ME, IT'LL DISTRACT THEM.
OIE-YAH, STARK, I PROMISE, MUCHO PYROTECHNICA FOR SURE ...
YES, YES ... SWIFTY SHOULD BE CALLING IN ANY MINUTE ... OKAY, SEE YOU IN THIRTY MINUTES.

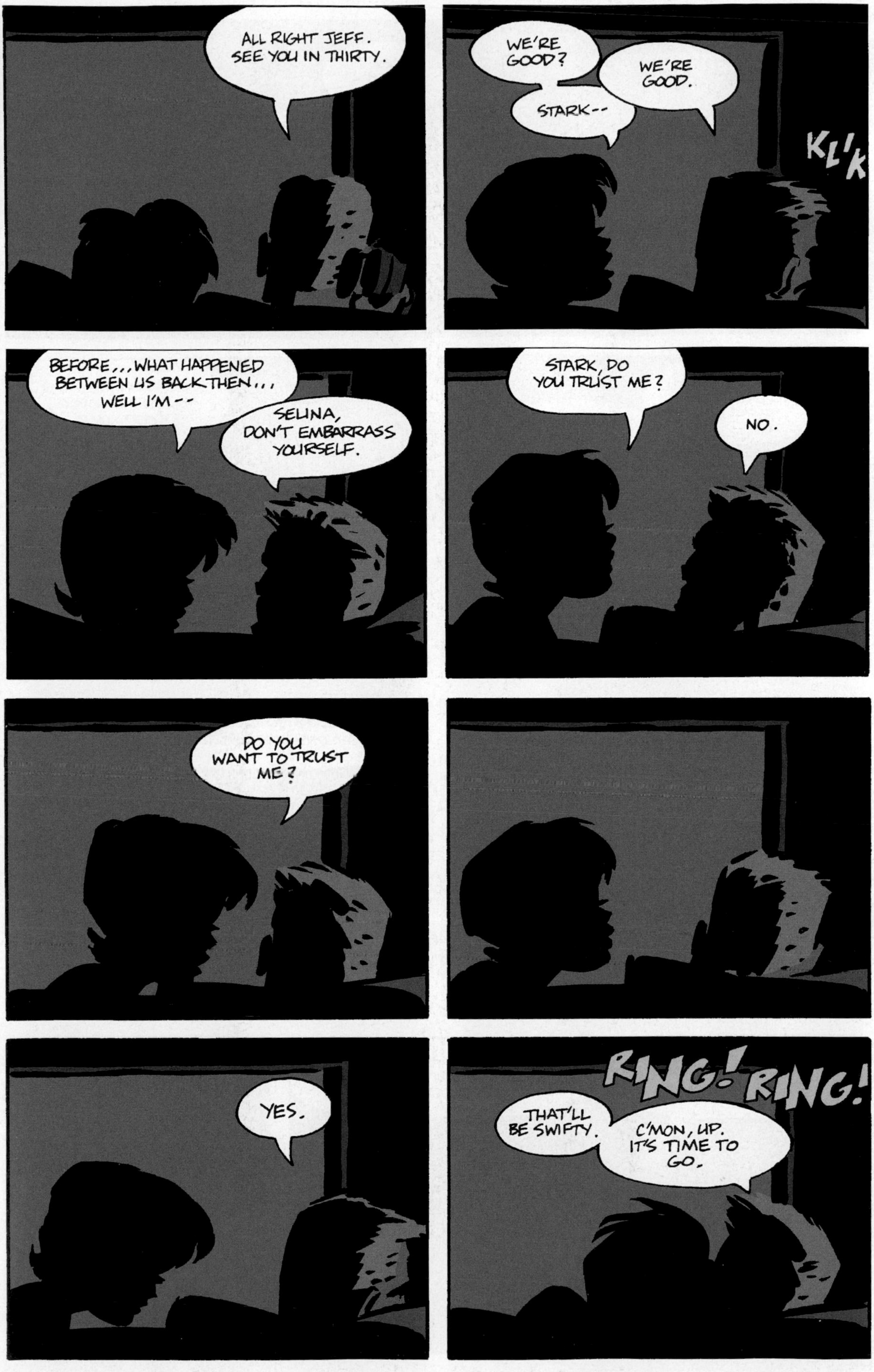
ALL RIGHT JEFF. SEE YOU IN THIRTY.
WE'RE GOOD?
WE'RE GOOD.
STARK--
KLIK
BEFORE,,, WHAT HAPPENED BETWEEN US BACK THEN,,, WELL I'M--
SELINA, DON'T EMBARRASS YOURSELF.
STARK, DO YOU TRUST ME?
NO.
DO YOU WANT TO TRUST ME?
YES.
RING! RING!
THAT'LL BE SWIFTY.
C'MON, UP. IT'S TIME TO GO.

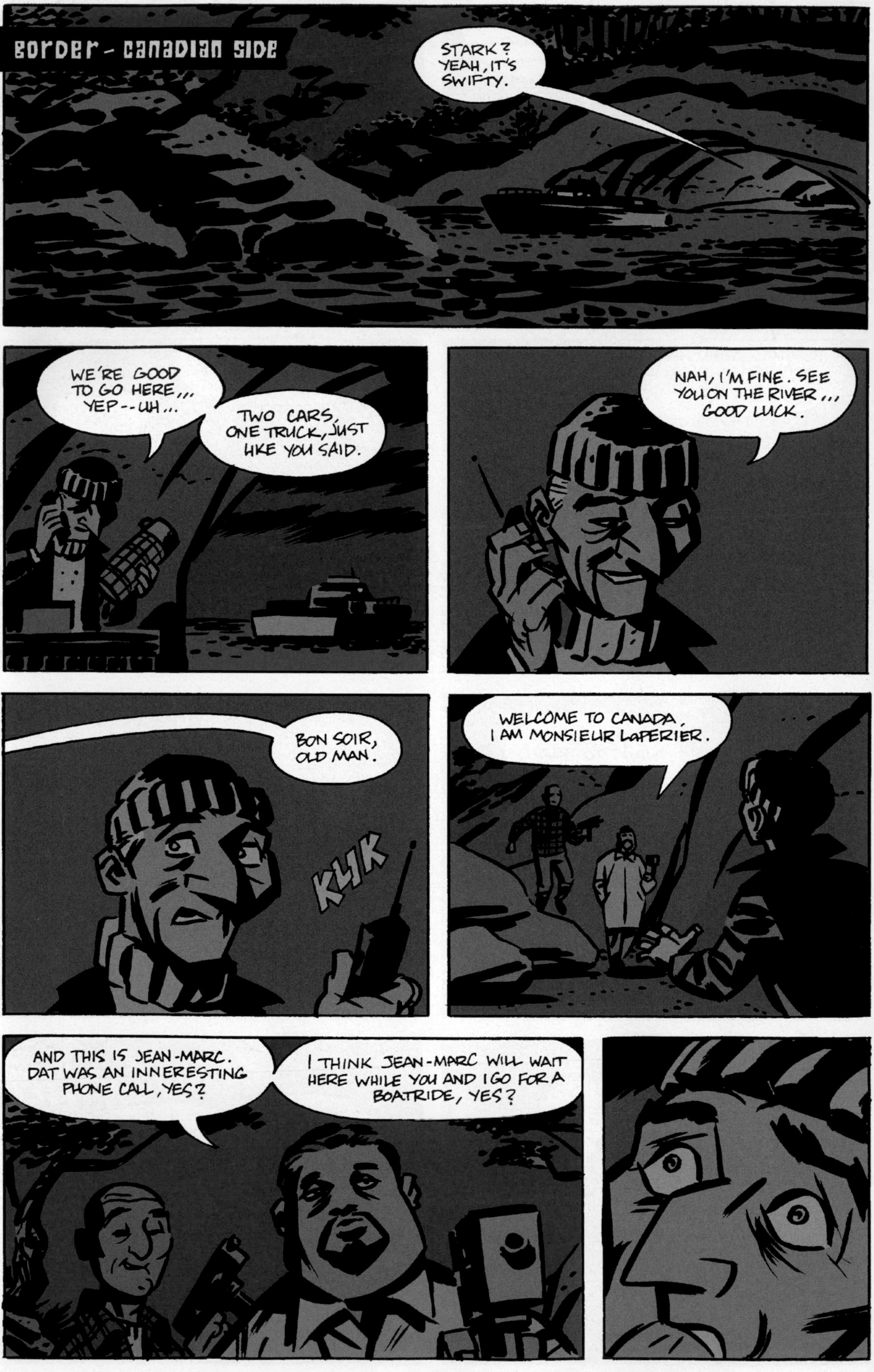

BORDER - CANADIAN SIDE
STARK? YEAH, IT'S SWIFTY.
WE'RE GOOD TO GO HERE,,, YEP--UH...
TWO CARS, ONE TRUCK, JUST LIKE YOU SAID.
NAH, I'M FINE. SEE YOU ON THE RIVER,,, GOOD LUCK.
BON SOIR, OLD MAN.
KLIK
WELCOME TO CANADA. I AM MONSIEUR LaPERIER.
AND THIS IS JEAN-MARC. DAT WAS AN INNERESTING PHONE CALL, YES?
I THINK JEAN-MARC WILL WAIT HERE WHILE YOU AND I GO FOR A BOATRIDE, YES?

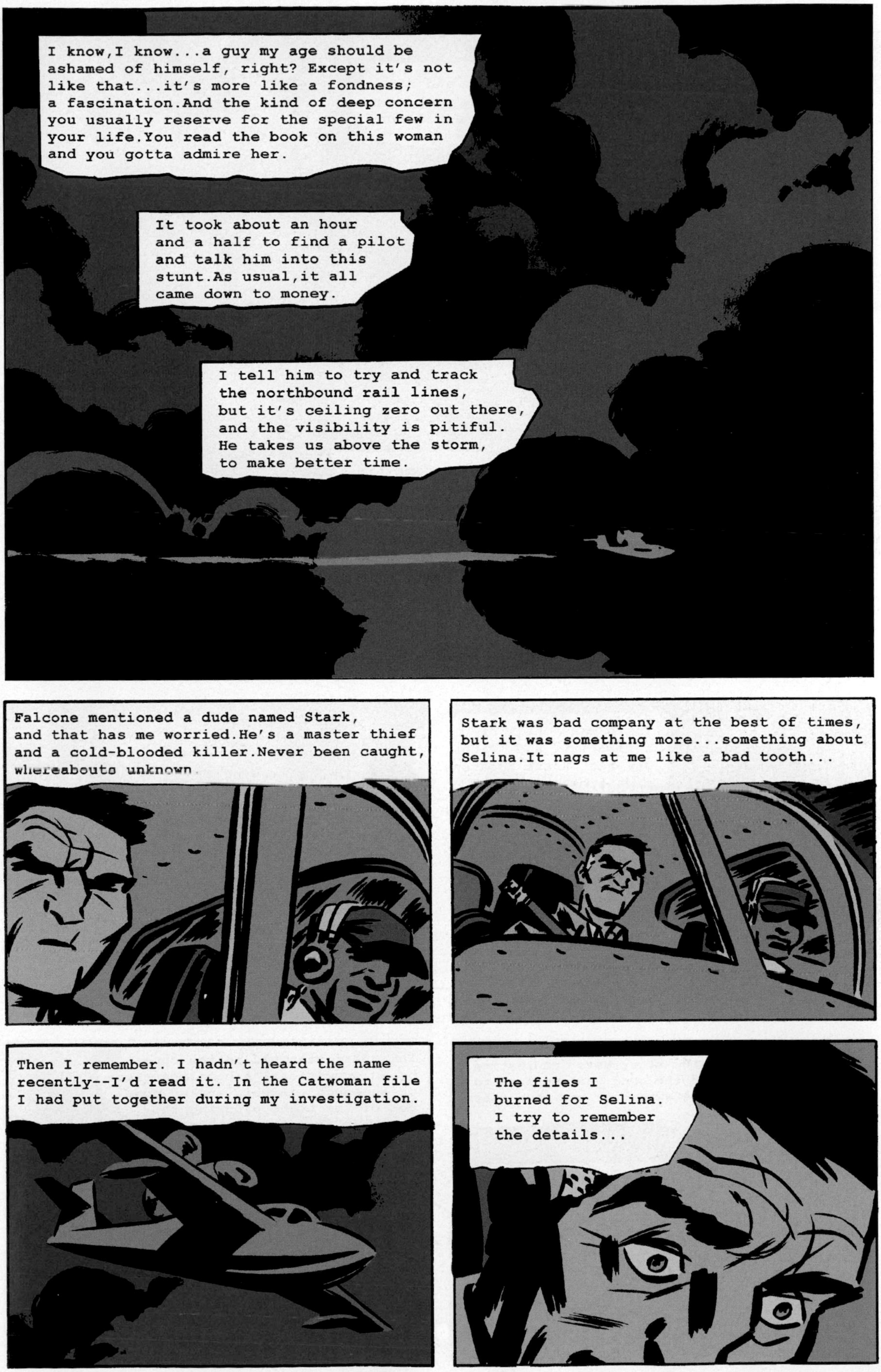

I know,I know...a guy my age should be ashamed of himself, right? Except it's not like that...it's more like a fondness; a fascination.And the kind of deep concern you usually reserve for the special few in your life.You read the book on this woman and you gotta admire her.
It took about an hour and a half to find a pilot and talk him into this stunt.As usual,it all came down to money.
I tell him to try and track the northbound rail lines, but it's ceiling zero out there, and the visibility is pitiful. He takes us above the storm, to make better time.
Falcone mentioned a dude named Stark, and that has me worried.He's a master thief and a cold-blooded killer.Never been caught, whereabouts unknown.
Stark was bad company at the best of times, but it was something more...something about Selina.It nags at me like a bad tooth...
Then I remember. I hadn't heard the name recently--I'd read it. In the Catwoman file I had put together during my investigation.
The files I burned for Selina. I try to remember the details...

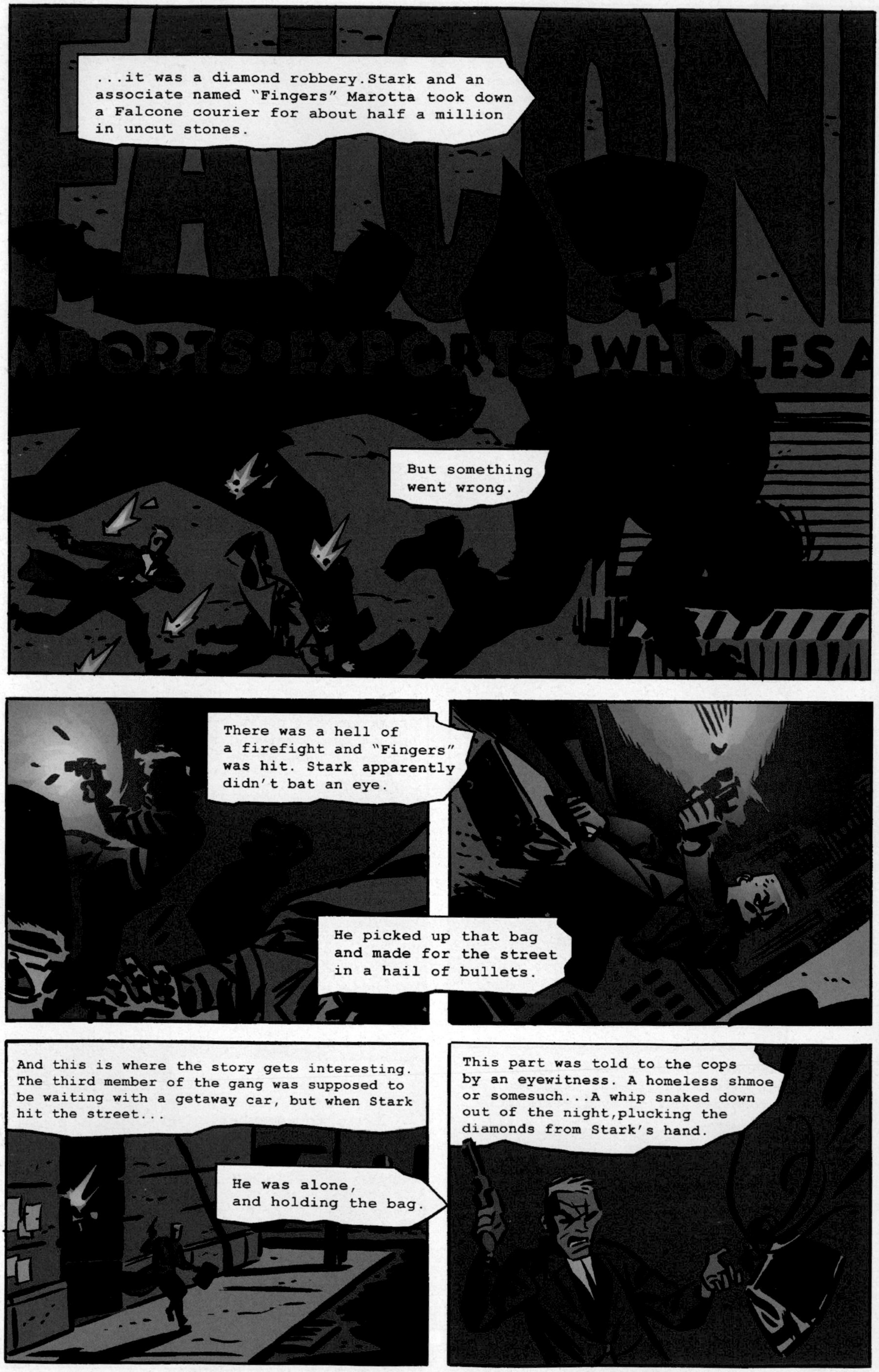
...it was a diamond robbery.Stark and an associate named "Fingers" Marotta took down a Falcone courier for about half a million in uncut stones.
MPORTS•EXPORTS•WHOLESA
But something went wrong.
There was a hell of a firefight and "Fingers" was hit. Stark apparently didn't bat an eye.
He picked up that bag and made for the street in a hail of bullets.
And this is where the story gets interesting. The third member of the gang was supposed to be waiting with a getaway car, but when Stark hit the street...
He was alone, and holding the bag.
This part was told to the cops by an eyewitness. A homeless shmoe or somesuch...A whip snaked down out of the night,plucking the diamonds from Stark's hand.

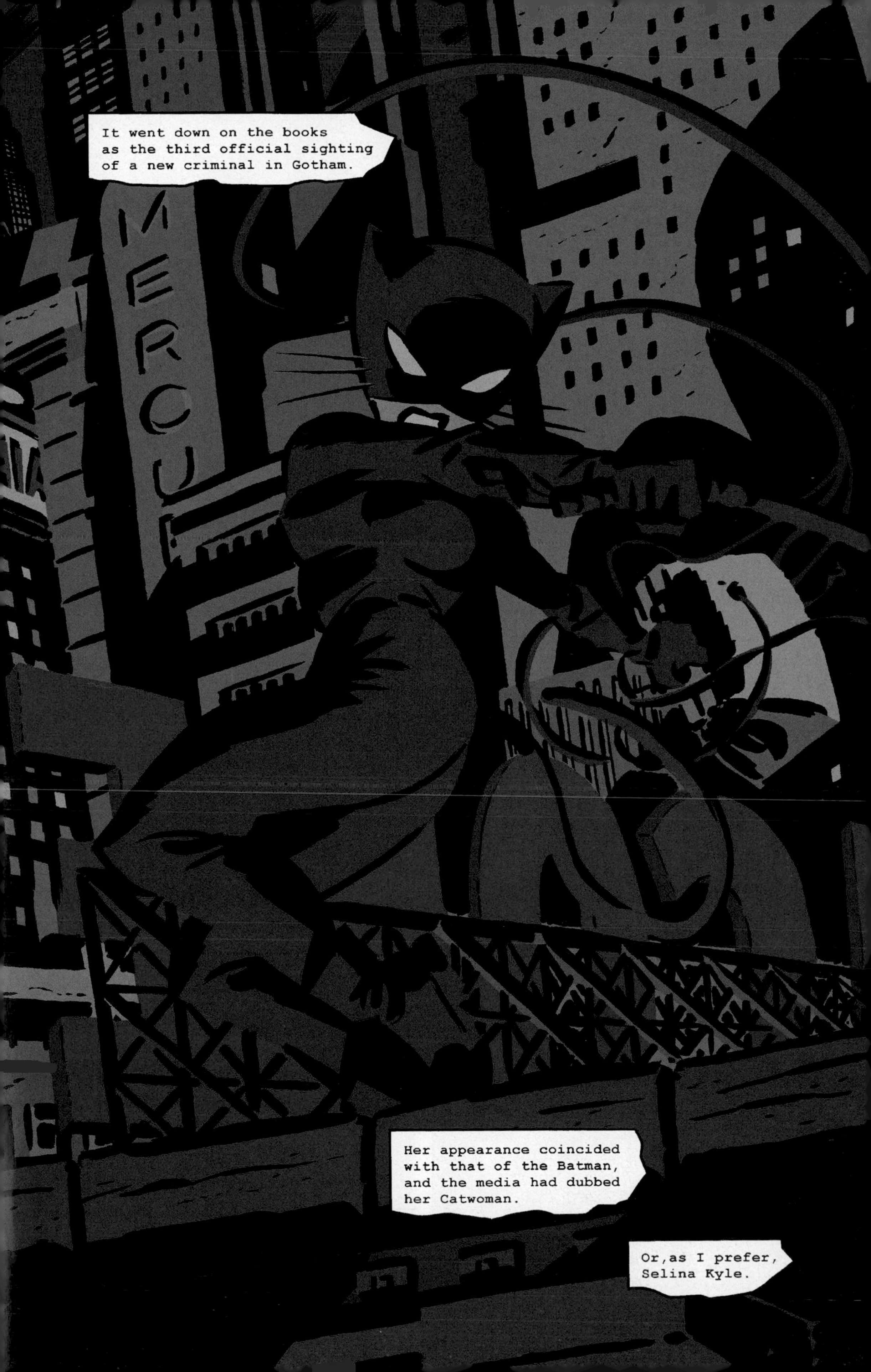
It went down on the books as the third official sighting of a new criminal in Gotham.
Her appearance coincided with that of the Batman, and the media had dubbed her Catwoman.
Or, as I prefer, Selina Kyle.

It's hard to imagine what went through Stark's mind. Did he know who was behind the mask?

What happened to the driver of the getaway car?

According to the witness, Stark just stood there without firing a shot, as the sound of a cracking whip took her away into the night.

The boys got hold of "Fingers" before he checked out. He gave up Stark and "some girl" before he died on them.

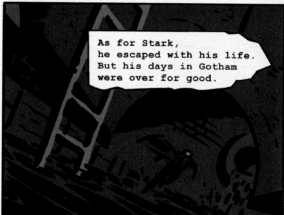

As for Stark, he escaped with his life. But his days in Gotham were over for good.

The clouds pull open in front of us and below us is the border. We've flown clear of the storm.

Tonight I killed three men and held a twenty-year-old girl in my arms while she died. But God help me, it felt like the worst was yet to come.

BOOK Four

score

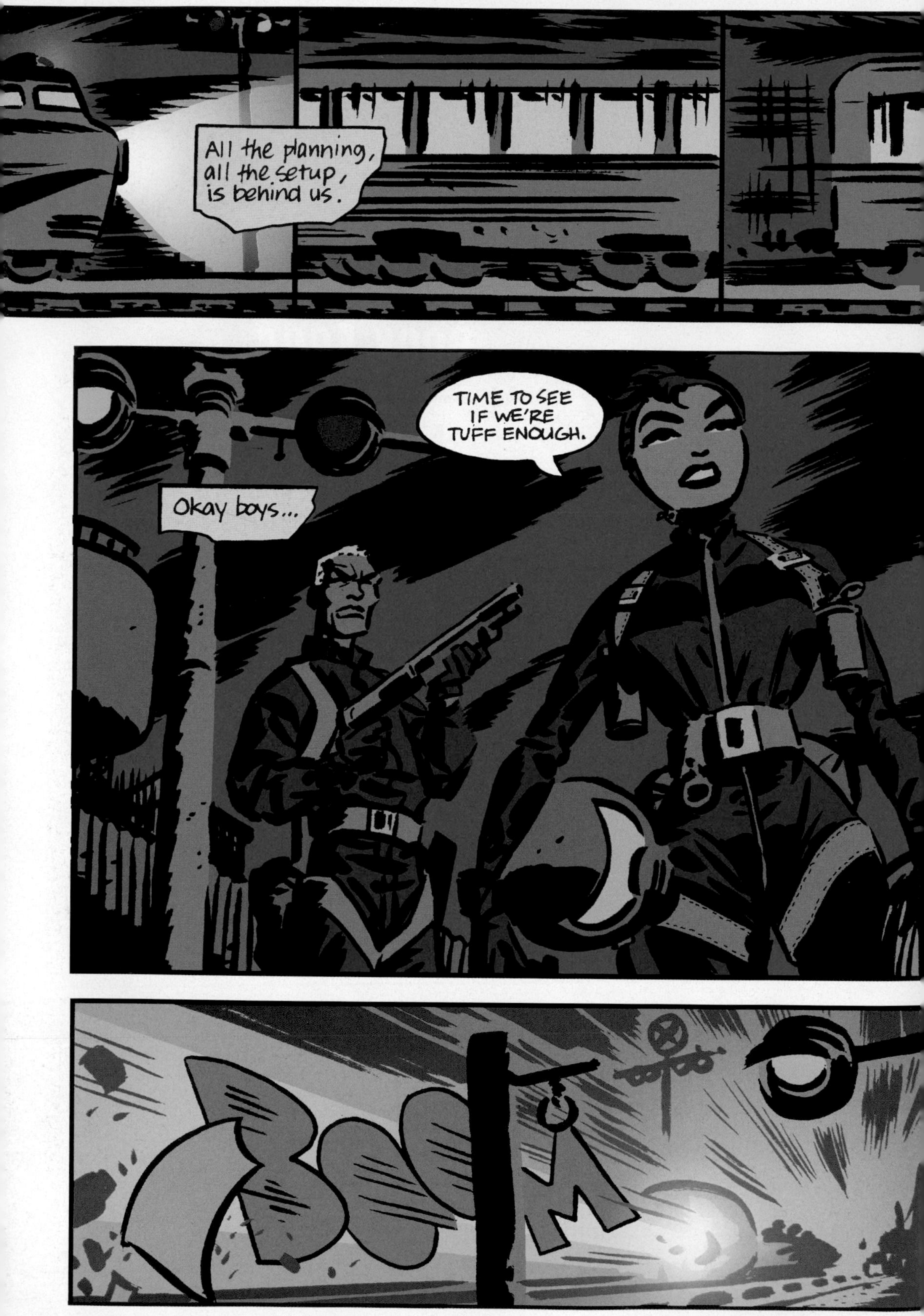
All the planning, all the setup, is behind us.
Okay boys...
TIME TO SEE IF WE'RE TUFF ENOUGH.
BOOM

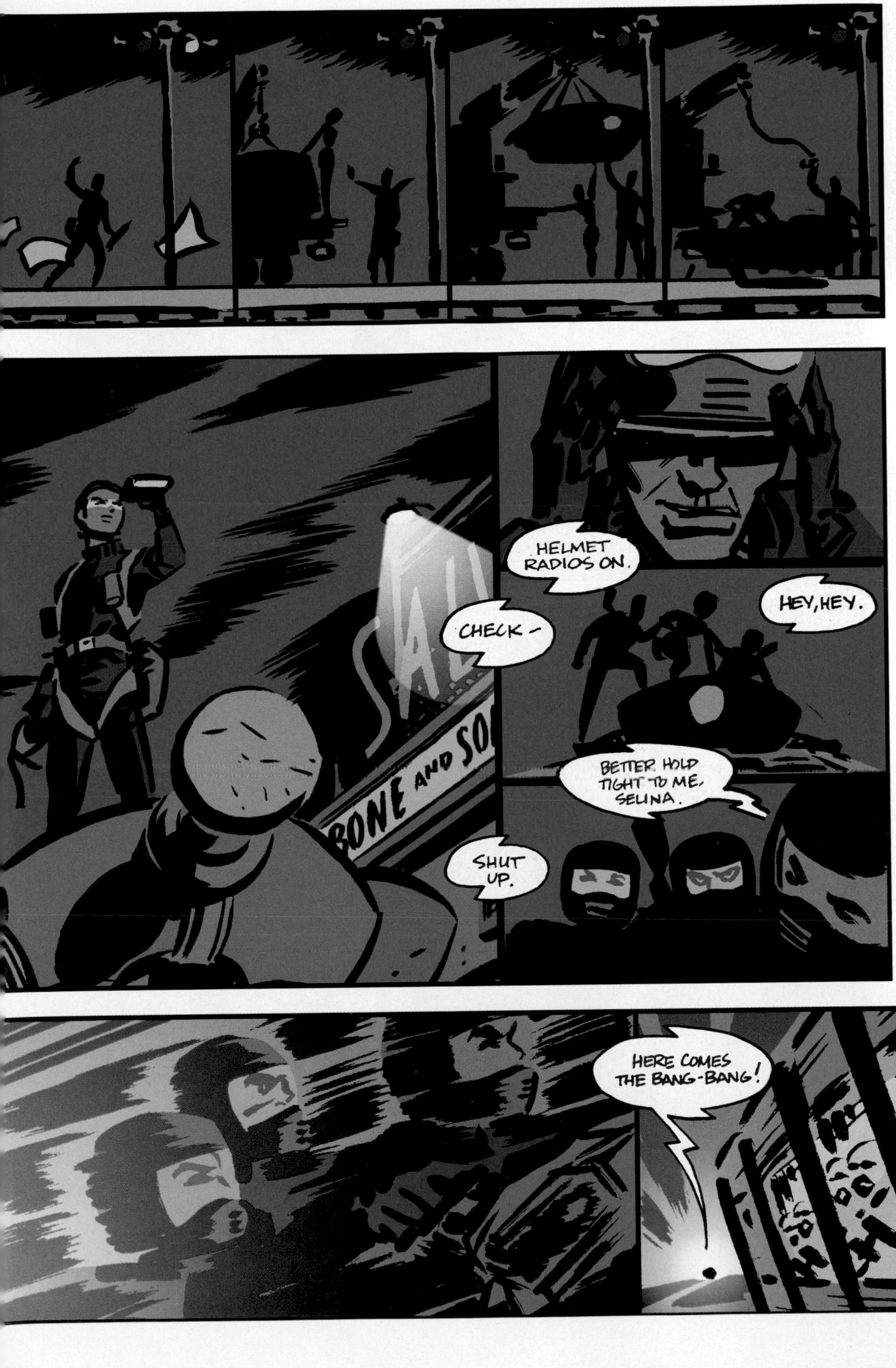
BONE AND SO
HELMET RADIOS ON.
CHECK -
HEY, HEY.
BETTER HOLD TIGHT TO ME, SELINA.
SHUT UP.
HERE COMES THE BANG-BANG!

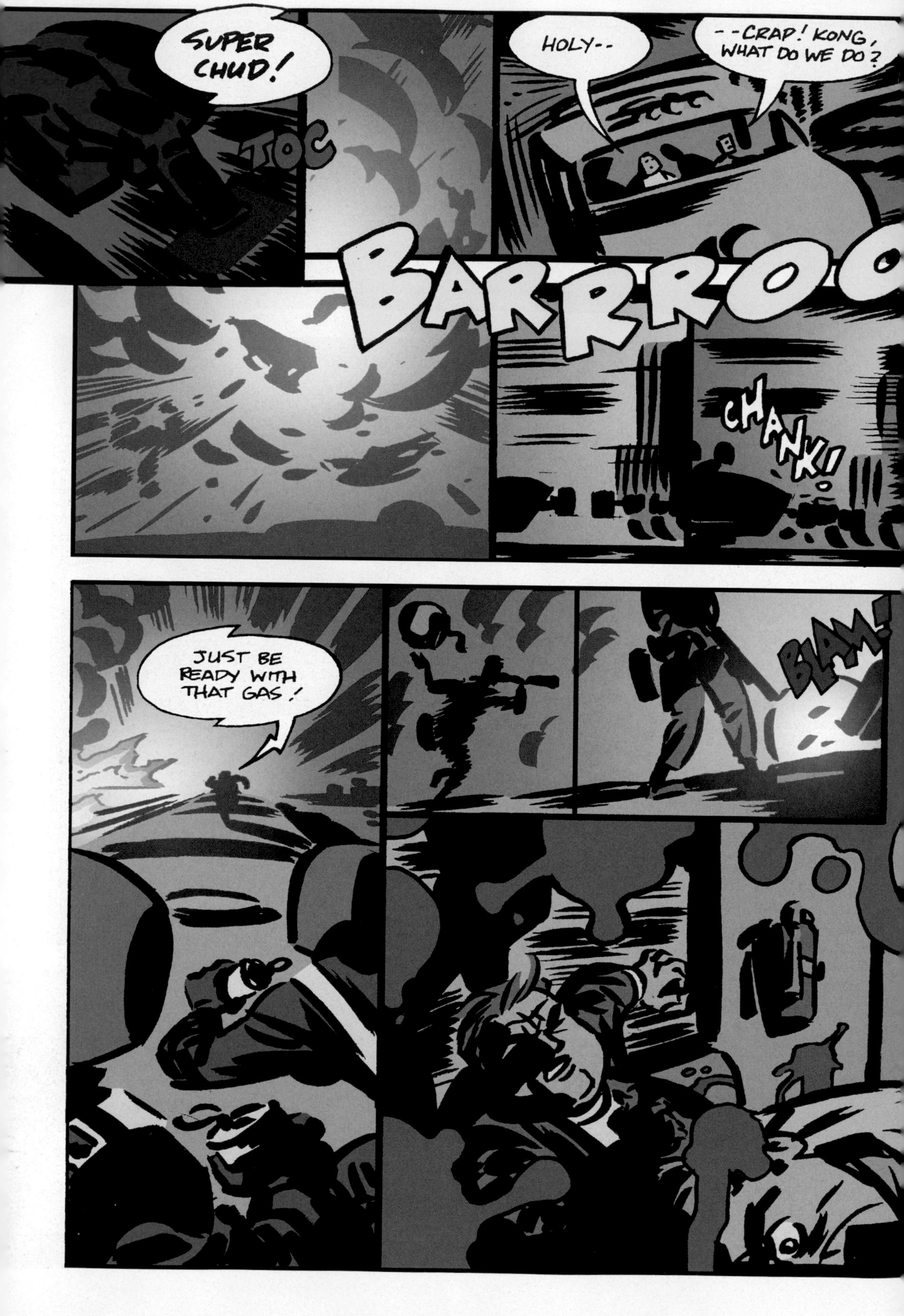
SUPER CHUD!
TOC
HOLY--
--CRAP! KONG, WHAT DO WE DO?
BARROO
CHANK!
JUST BE READY WITH THAT GAS!
BLAM!

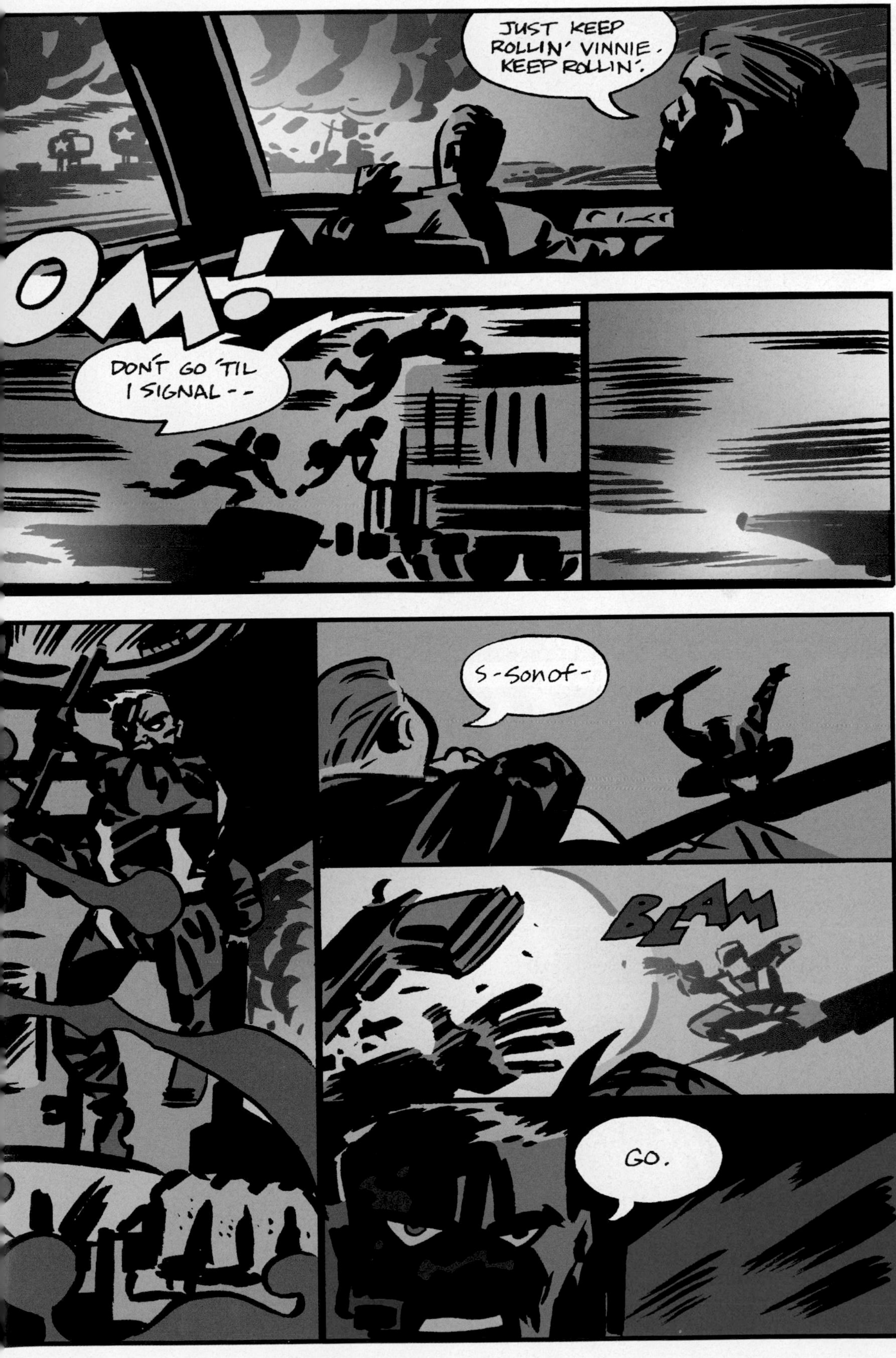
JUST KEEP ROLLIN' VINNIE. KEEP ROLLIN'.
OM!
DON'T GO 'TIL I SIGNAL--
S-SONOF-
BLAM
GO.

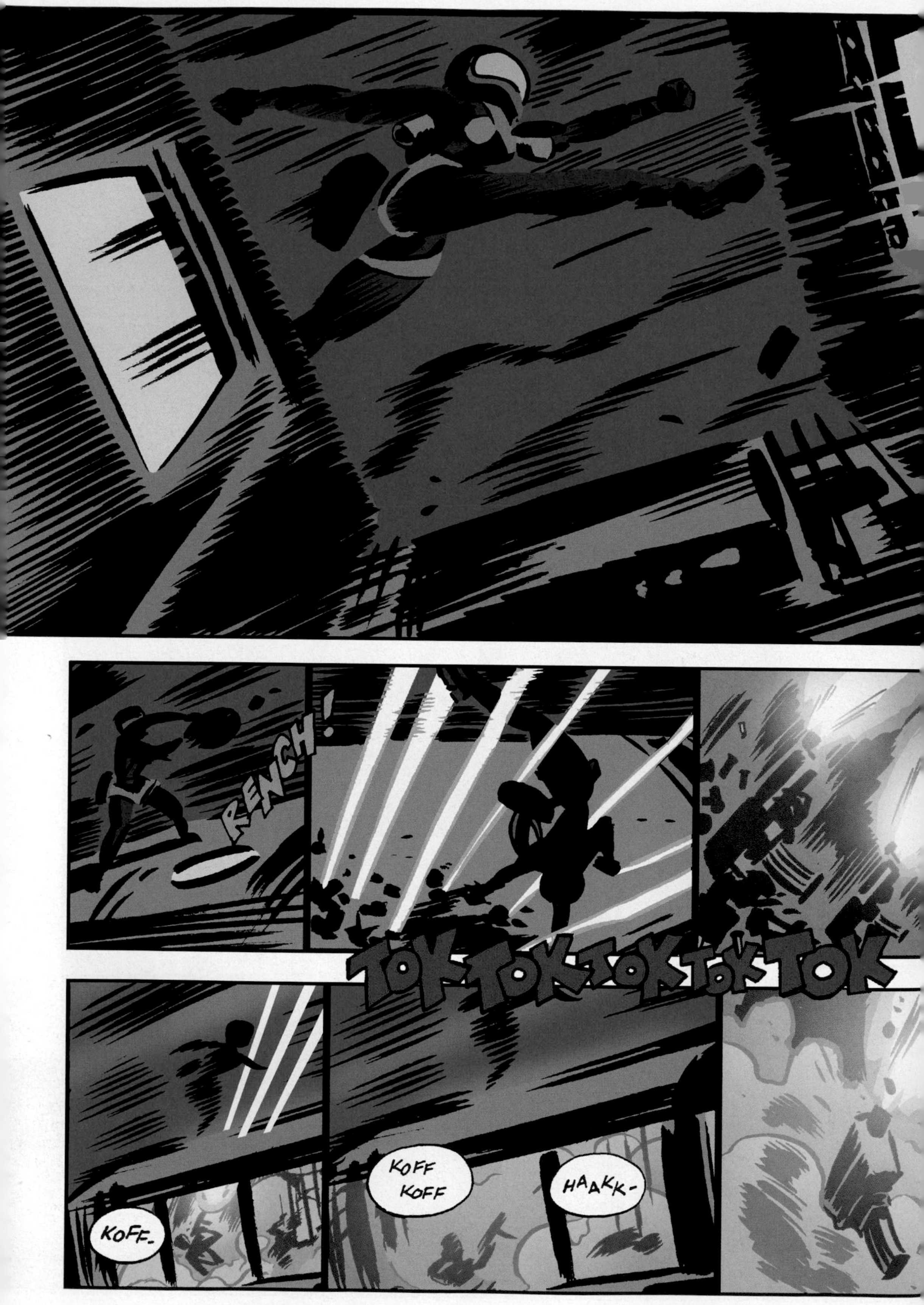
RENCH!
TOK TOK TOK TOK TOK TOK
KOFF-
KOFF KOFF
HAAKK-

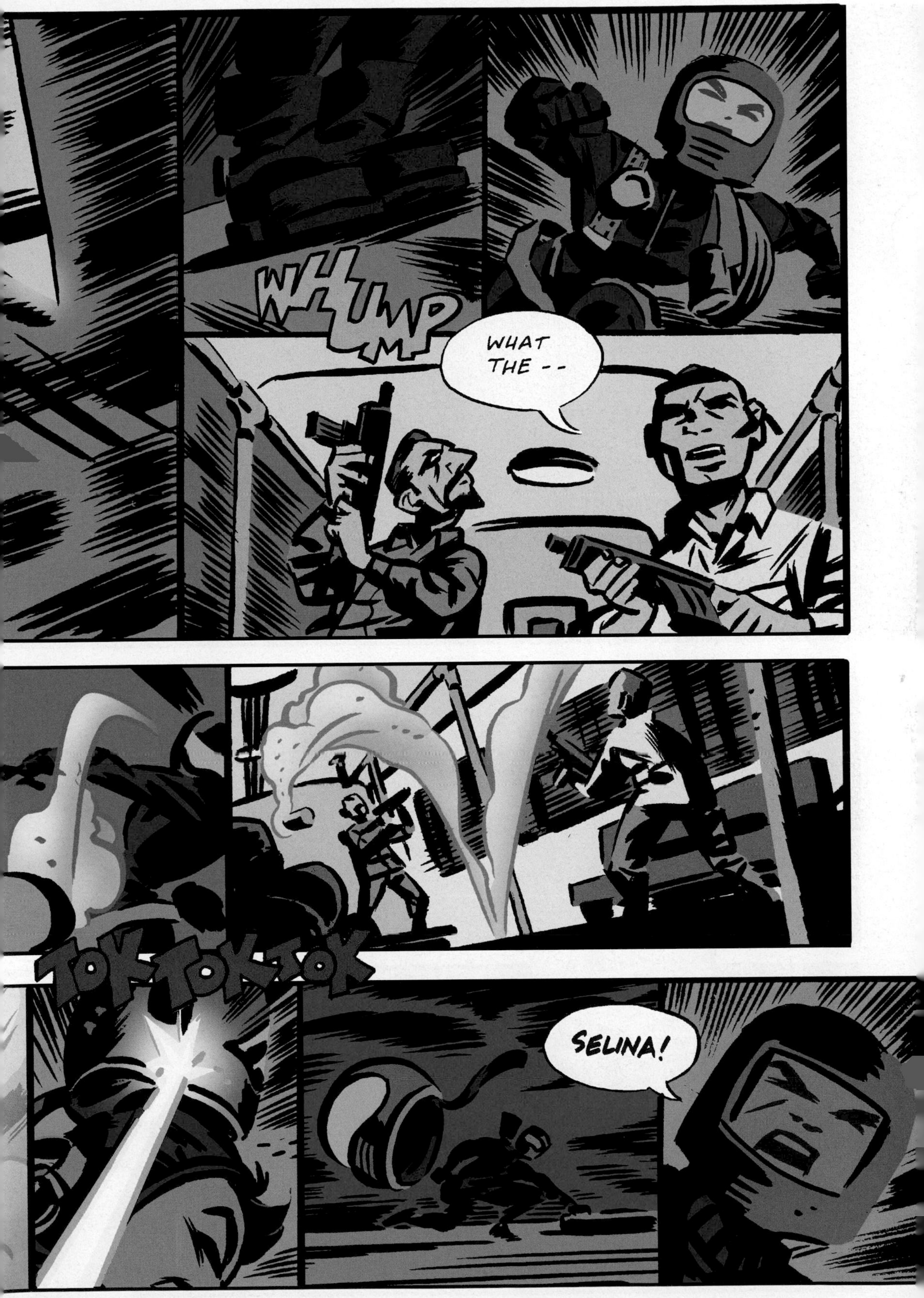
WHUMP
WHAT THE --
TOK TOK TOK
SELINA!

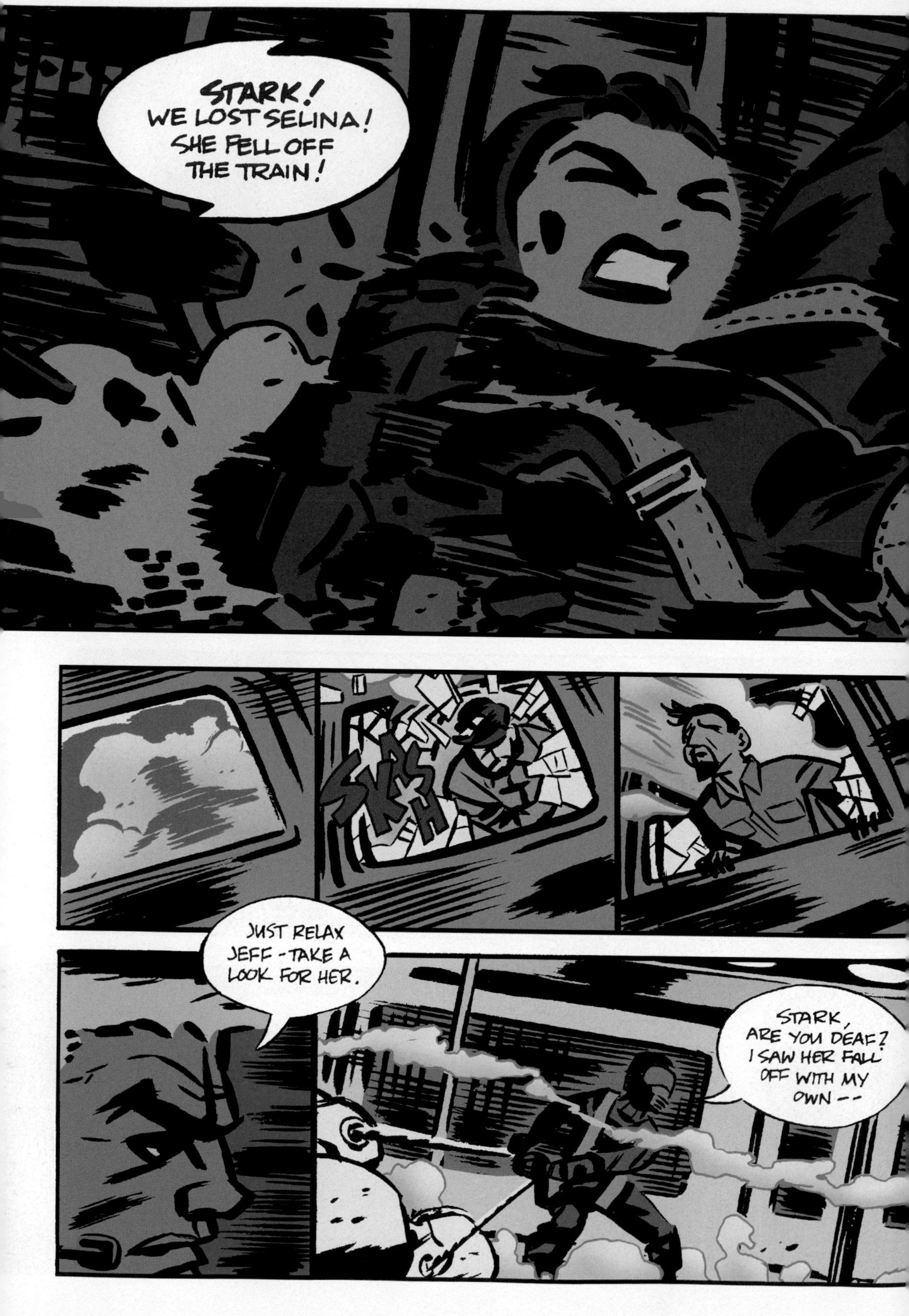
STARK! WE LOST SELINA! SHE FELL OFF THE TRAIN!
SKRASH
JUST RELAX JEFF - TAKE A LOOK FOR HER.
STARK, ARE YOU DEAF? I SAW HER FALL OFF WITH MY OWN --

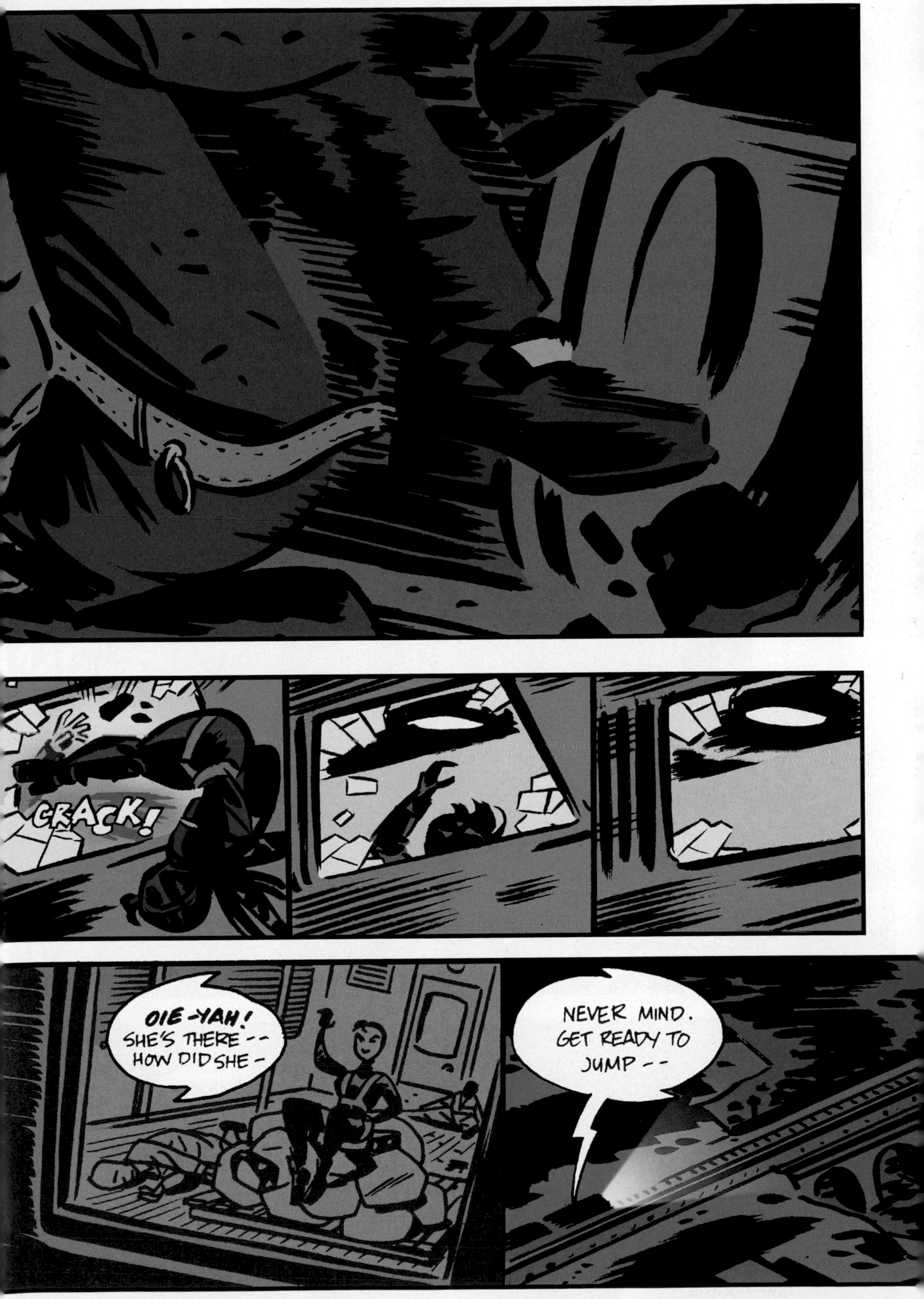
CRACK!
OIE-YAH! SHE'S THERE-- HOW DID SHE-
NEVER MIND. GET READY TO JUMP--

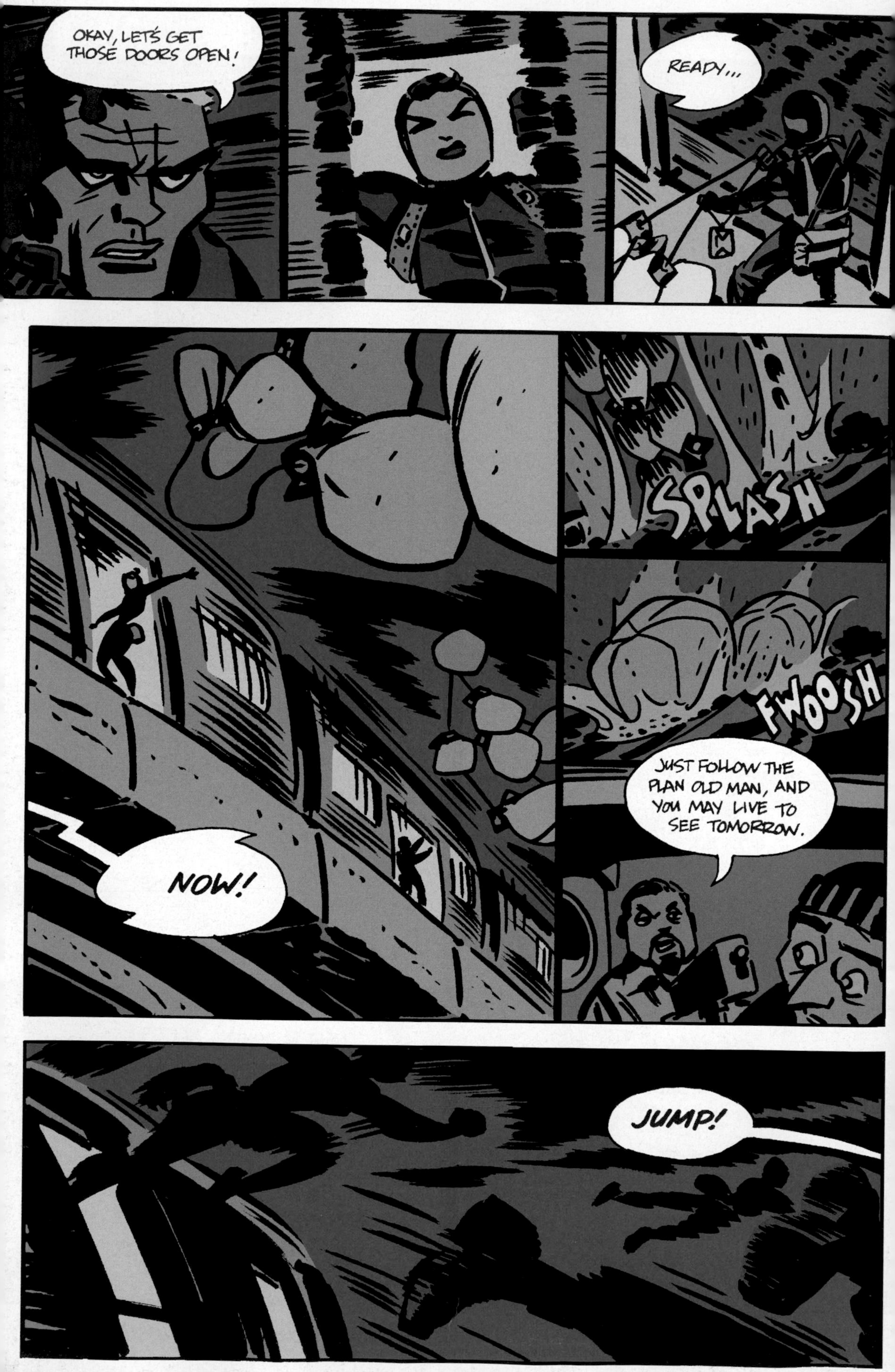
OKAY, LET'S GET THOSE DOORS OPEN!
READY...
SPLASH
FWOOSH
JUST FOLLOW THE PLAN OLD MAN, AND YOU MAY LIVE TO SEE TOMORROW.
NOW!
JUMP!

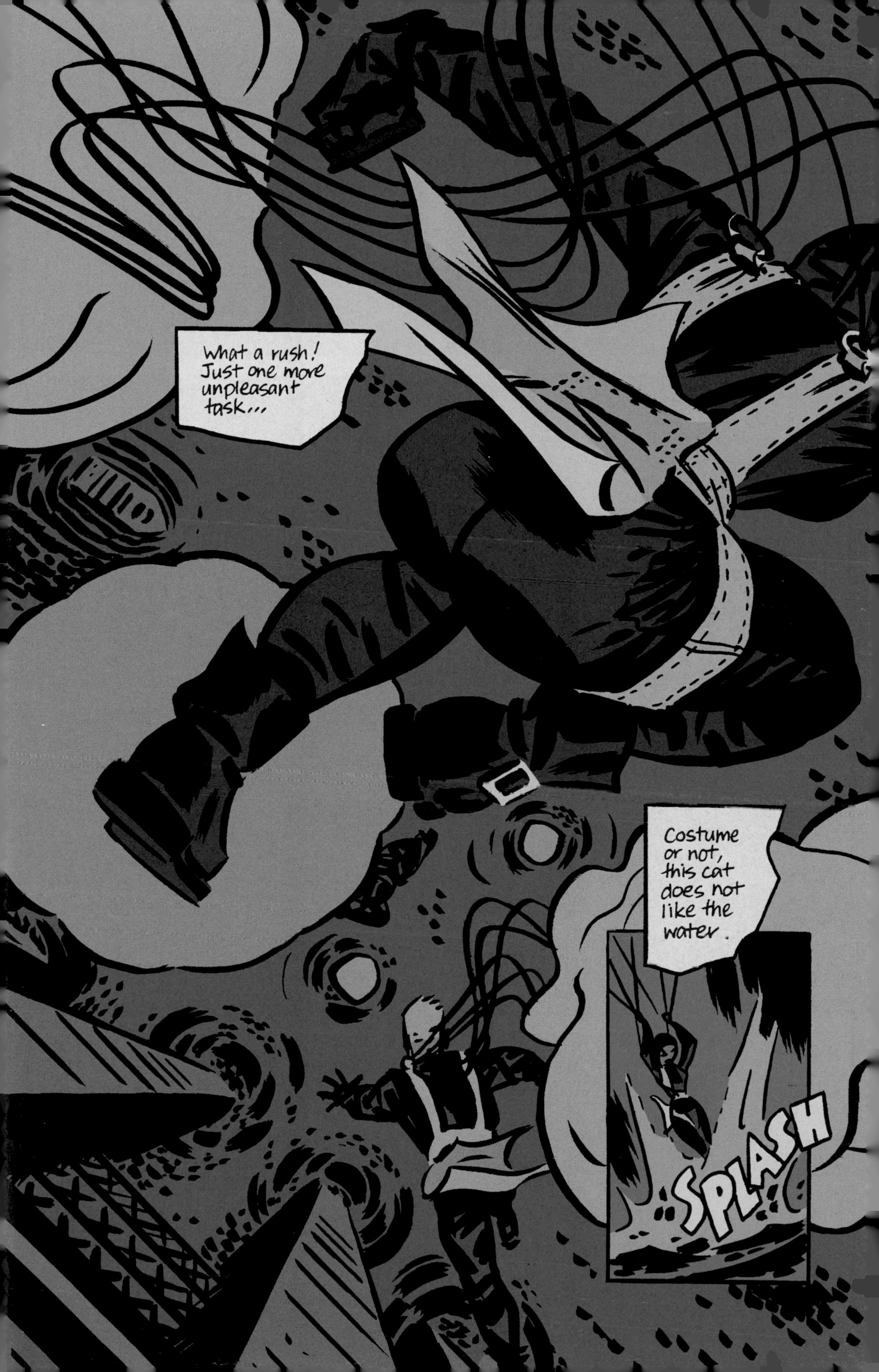
What a rush! Just one more unpleasant task...
Costume or not, this cat does not like the water.
SPLASH

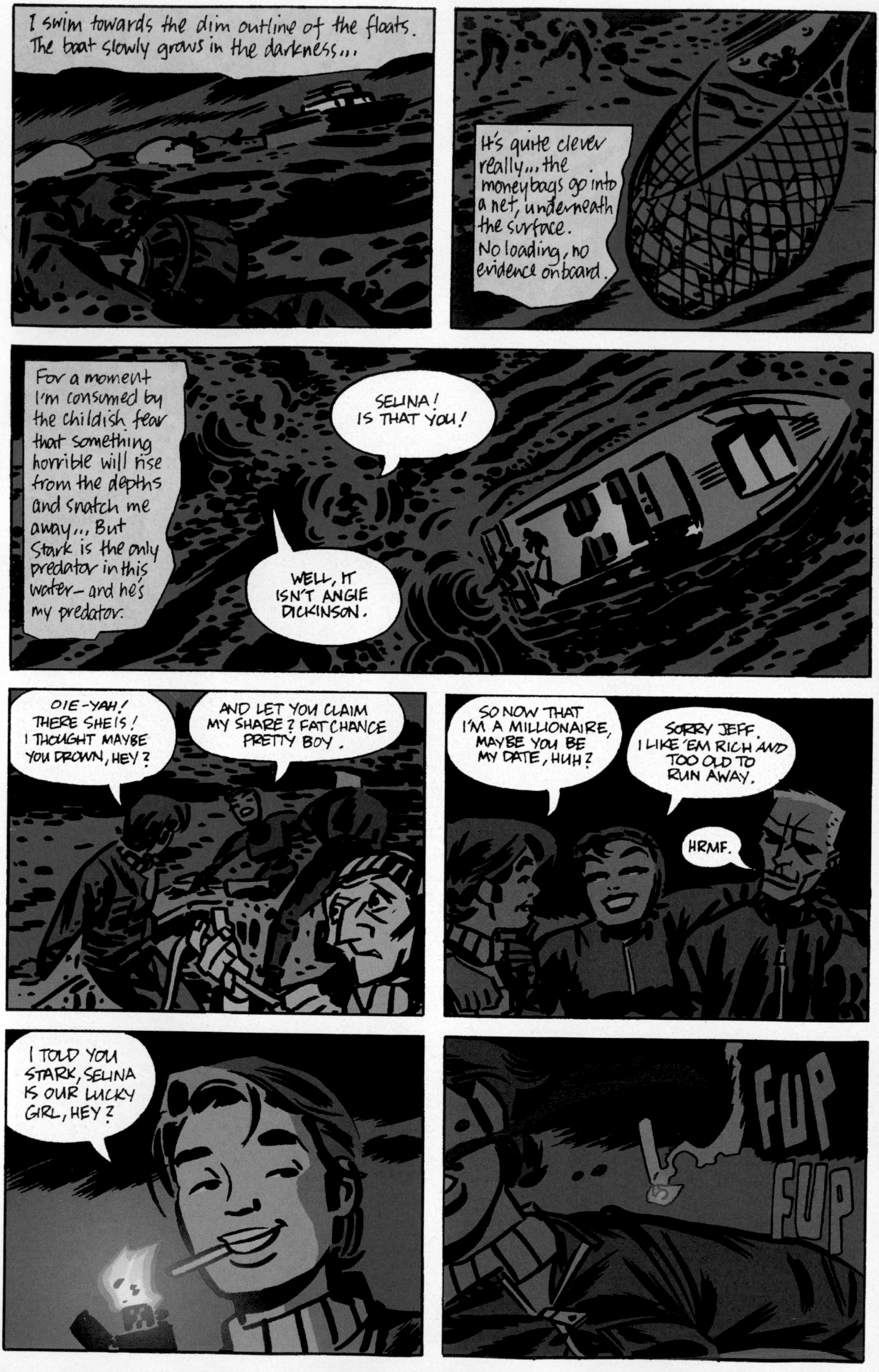
I swim towards the dim outline of the floats. The boat slowly grows in the darkness...
It's quite clever really... the moneybags go into a net, underneath the surface. No loading, no evidence onboard.
For a moment I'm consumed by the childish fear that something horrible will rise from the depths and snatch me away... But Stark is the only predator in this water—and he's my predator.
SELINA! IS THAT YOU!
WELL, IT ISN'T ANGIE DICKINSON.
OIE-YAH! THERE SHE IS! I THOUGHT MAYBE YOU DROWN, HEY?
AND LET YOU CLAIM MY SHARE? FAT CHANCE PRETTY BOY.
SO NOW THAT I'M A MILLIONAIRE, MAYBE YOU BE MY DATE, HUH?
SORRY JEFF. I LIKE 'EM RICH AND TOO OLD TO RUN AWAY.
HRMF.
I TOLD YOU STARK, SELINA IS OUR LUCKY GIRL, HEY?
FUP
FUP

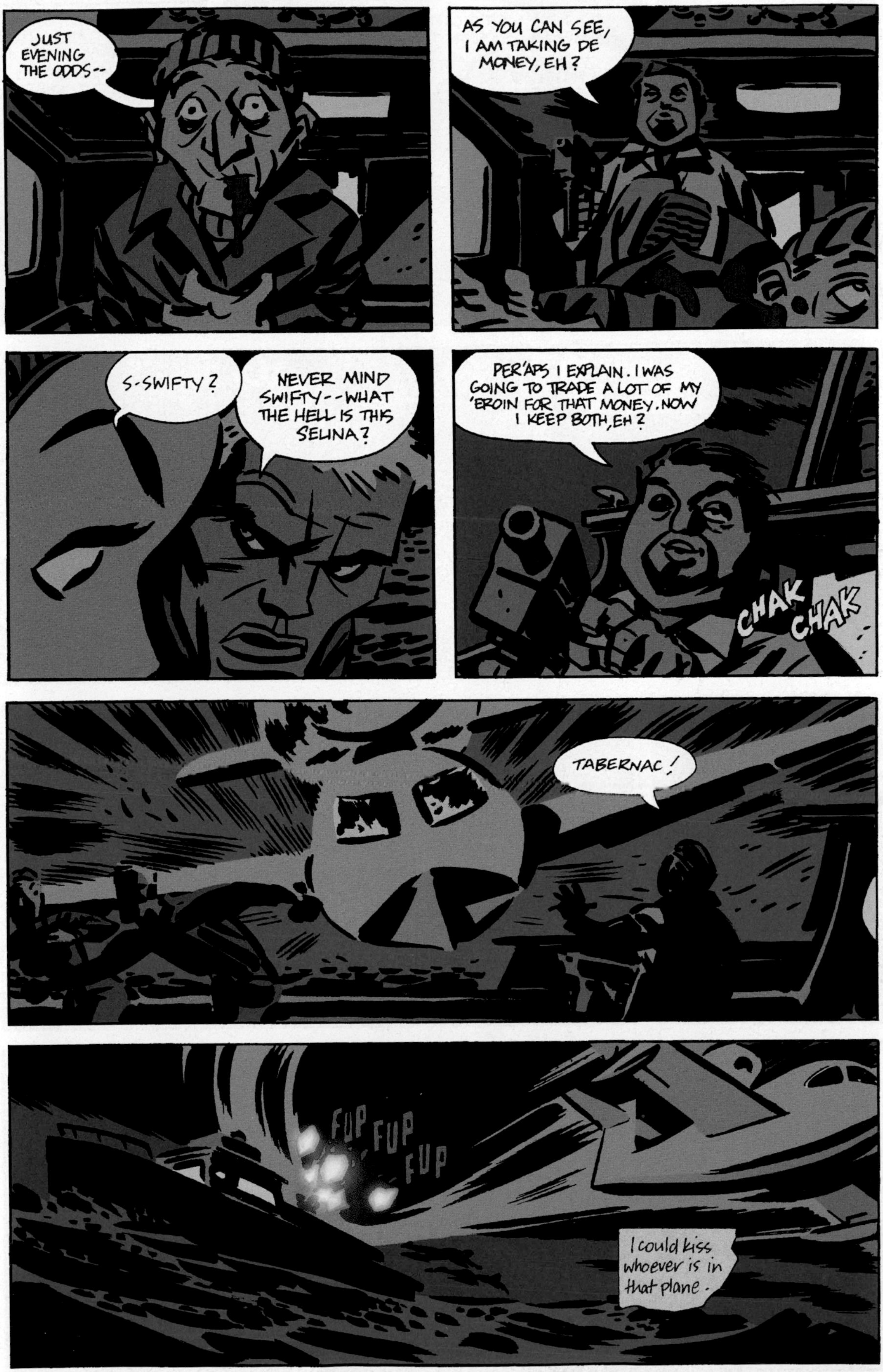
JUST EVENING THE ODDS--
AS YOU CAN SEE, I AM TAKING DE MONEY, EH?
S-SWIFTY?
NEVER MIND SWIFTY--WHAT THE HELL IS THIS SELINA?
PER'APS I EXPLAIN. I WAS GOING TO TRADE A LOT OF MY 'EROIN FOR THAT MONEY. NOW I KEEP BOTH, EH?
CHAK CHAK
TABERNAC!
FUP FUP FUP
I could kiss whoever is in that plane.

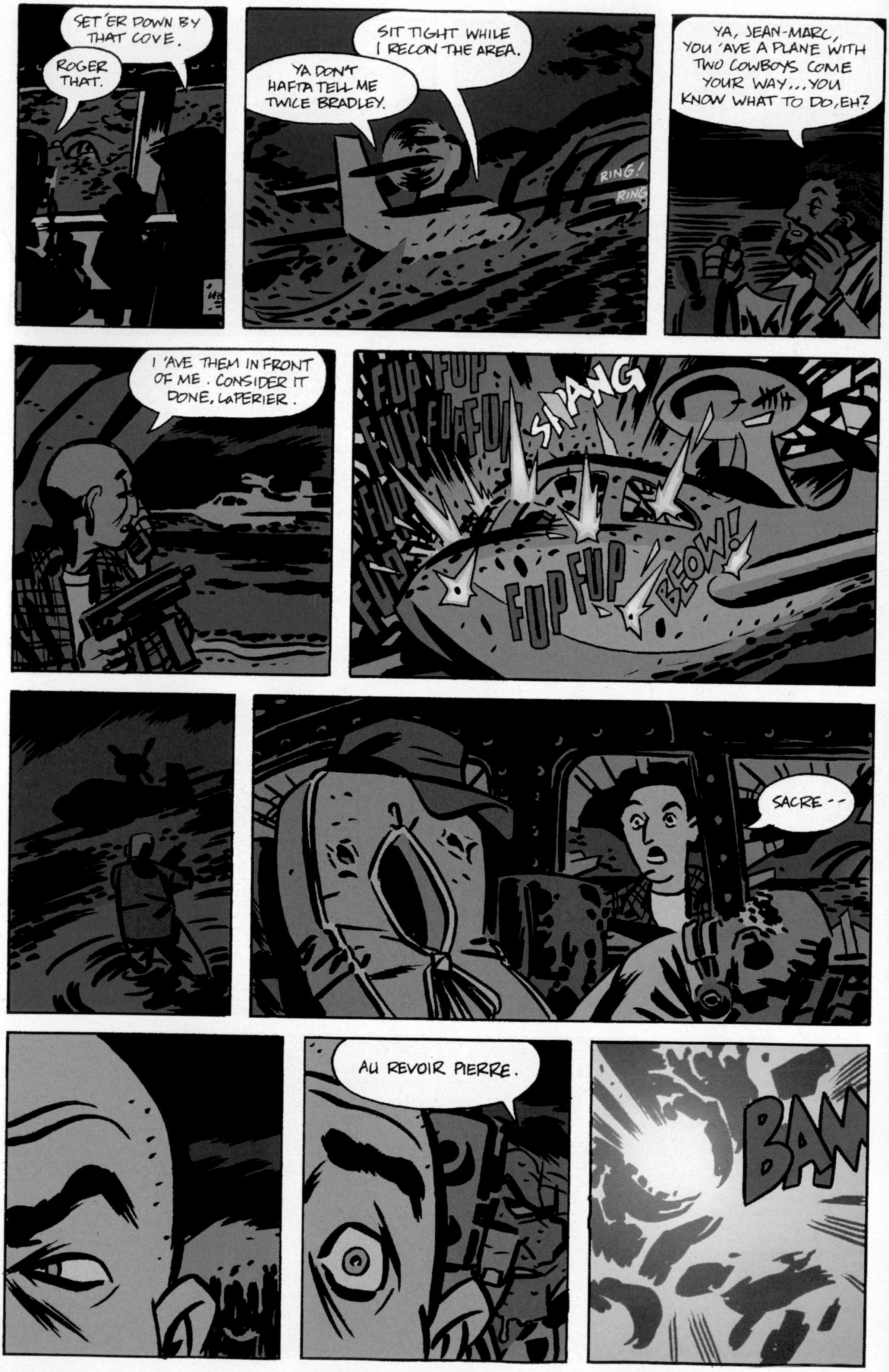
SET 'ER DOWN BY THAT COVE.
ROGER THAT.
SIT TIGHT WHILE I RECON THE AREA.
YA DON'T HAFTA TELL ME TWICE BRADLEY.
RING!
RING
YA, JEAN-MARC, YOU 'AVE A PLANE WITH TWO COWBOYS COME YOUR WAY... YOU KNOW WHAT TO DO, EH?
I 'AVE THEM IN FRONT OF ME. CONSIDER IT DONE, LAPERIER.
FUP FUP FUP FUP FUP
SPANG
FUP FUP
BLOW!
SACRE --
AU REVOIR PIERRE.
BAN

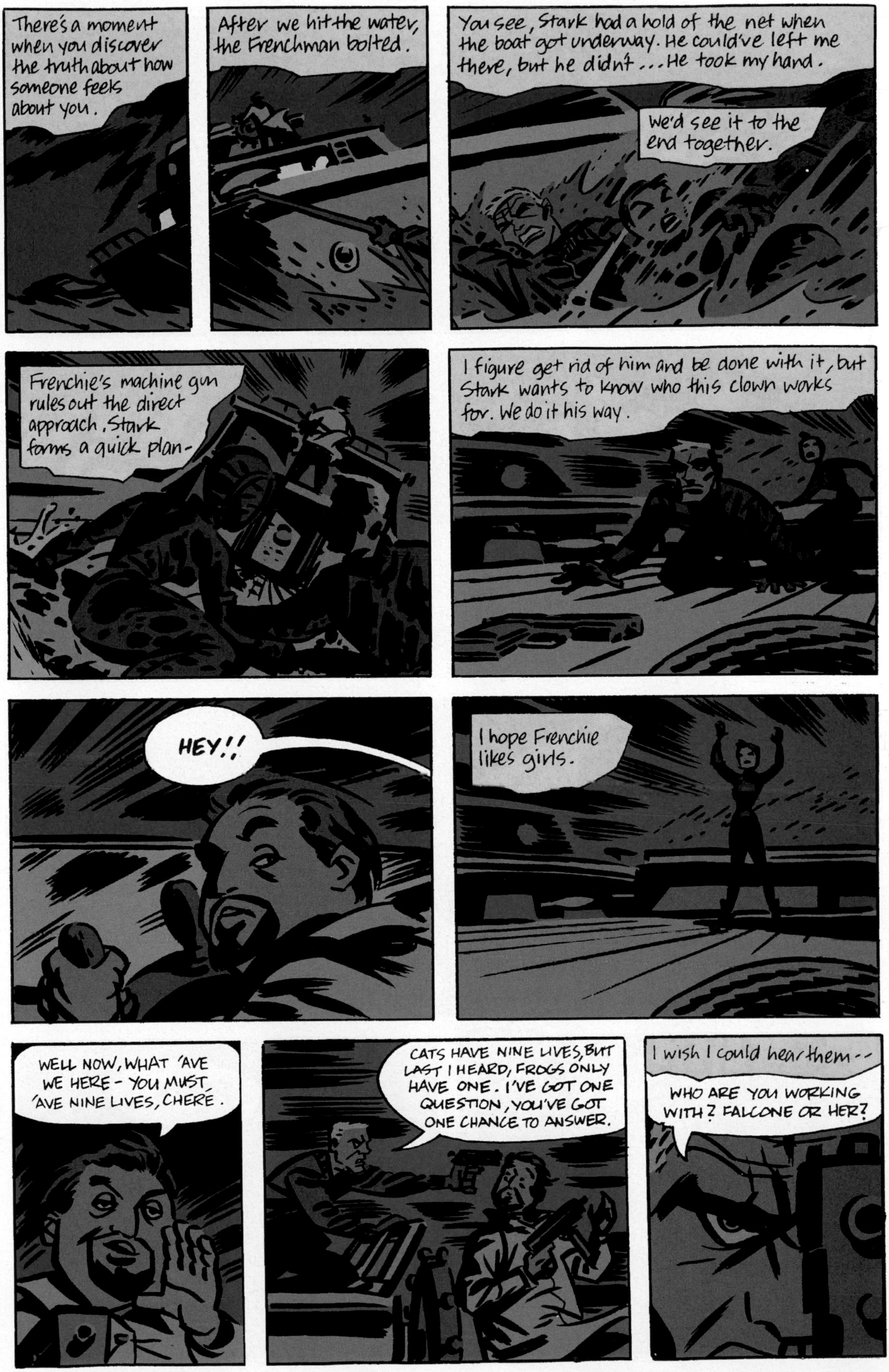
There's a moment when you discover the truth about how someone feels about you.
After we hit the water, the Frenchman bolted.
You see, Stark had a hold of the net when the boat got underway. He could've left me there, but he didn't... He took my hand.
We'd see it to the end together.
Frenchie's machine gun rules out the direct approach. Stark forms a quick plan-
I figure get rid of him and be done with it, but Stark wants to know who this clown works for. We do it his way.
HEY!!
I hope Frenchie likes girls.
WELL NOW, WHAT 'AVE WE HERE - YOU MUST 'AVE NINE LIVES, CHERE.
CATS HAVE NINE LIVES, BUT LAST I HEARD, FROGS ONLY HAVE ONE. I'VE GOT ONE QUESTION, YOU'VE GOT ONE CHANCE TO ANSWER.
I wish I could hear them--
WHO ARE YOU WORKING WITH? FALCONE OR HER?

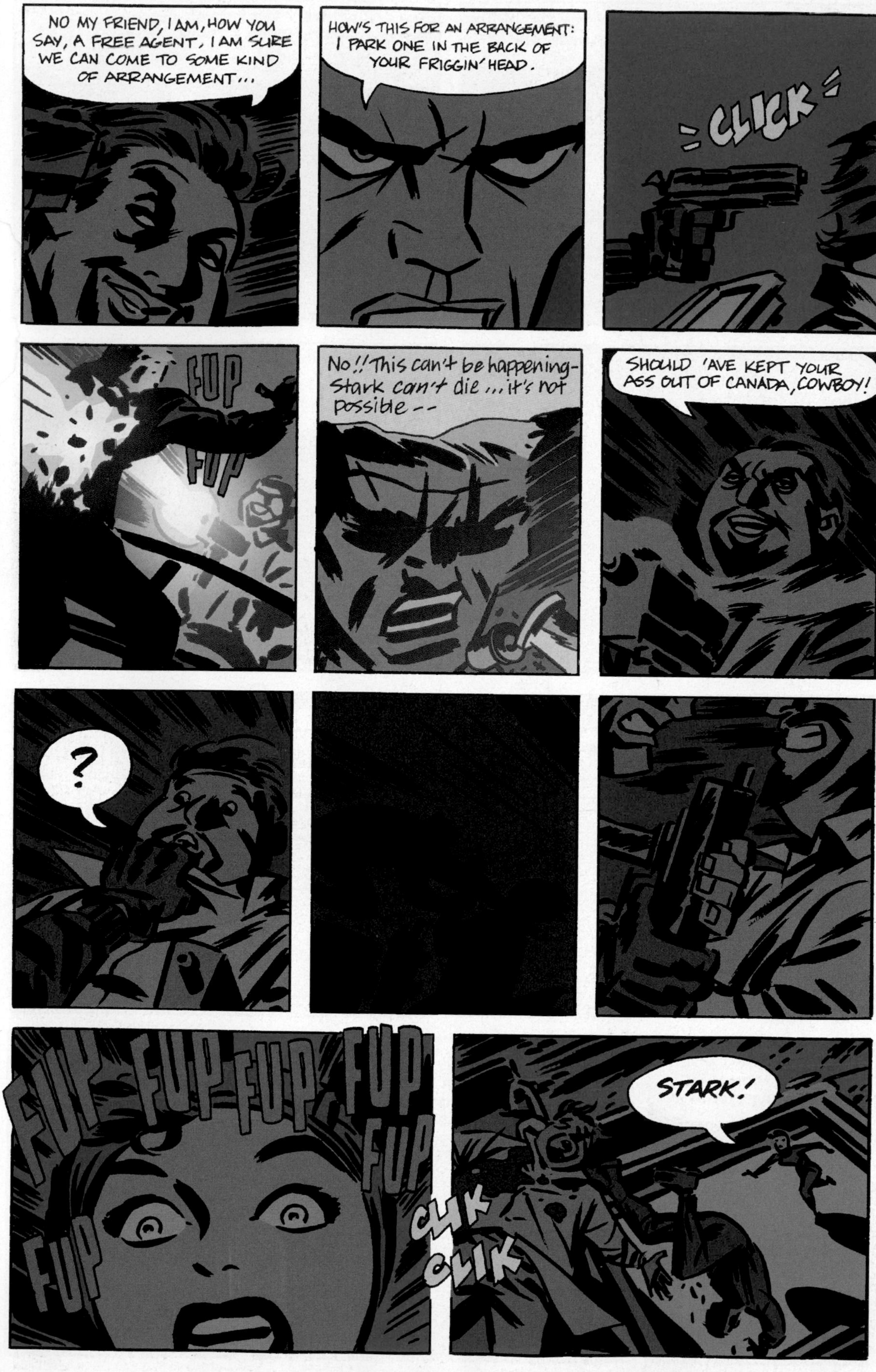
NO MY FRIEND, I AM, HOW YOU SAY, A FREE AGENT. I AM SURE WE CAN COME TO SOME KIND OF ARRANGEMENT...
HOW'S THIS FOR AN ARRANGEMENT: I PARK ONE IN THE BACK OF YOUR FRIGGIN' HEAD.
CLICK
FUP
FUP
No!! This can't be happening-- Stark can't die... it's not possible--
SHOULD 'AVE KEPT YOUR ASS OUT OF CANADA, COWBOY!
?
FUP FUP FUP FUP FUP FUP
CLIK
CLIK
STARK!

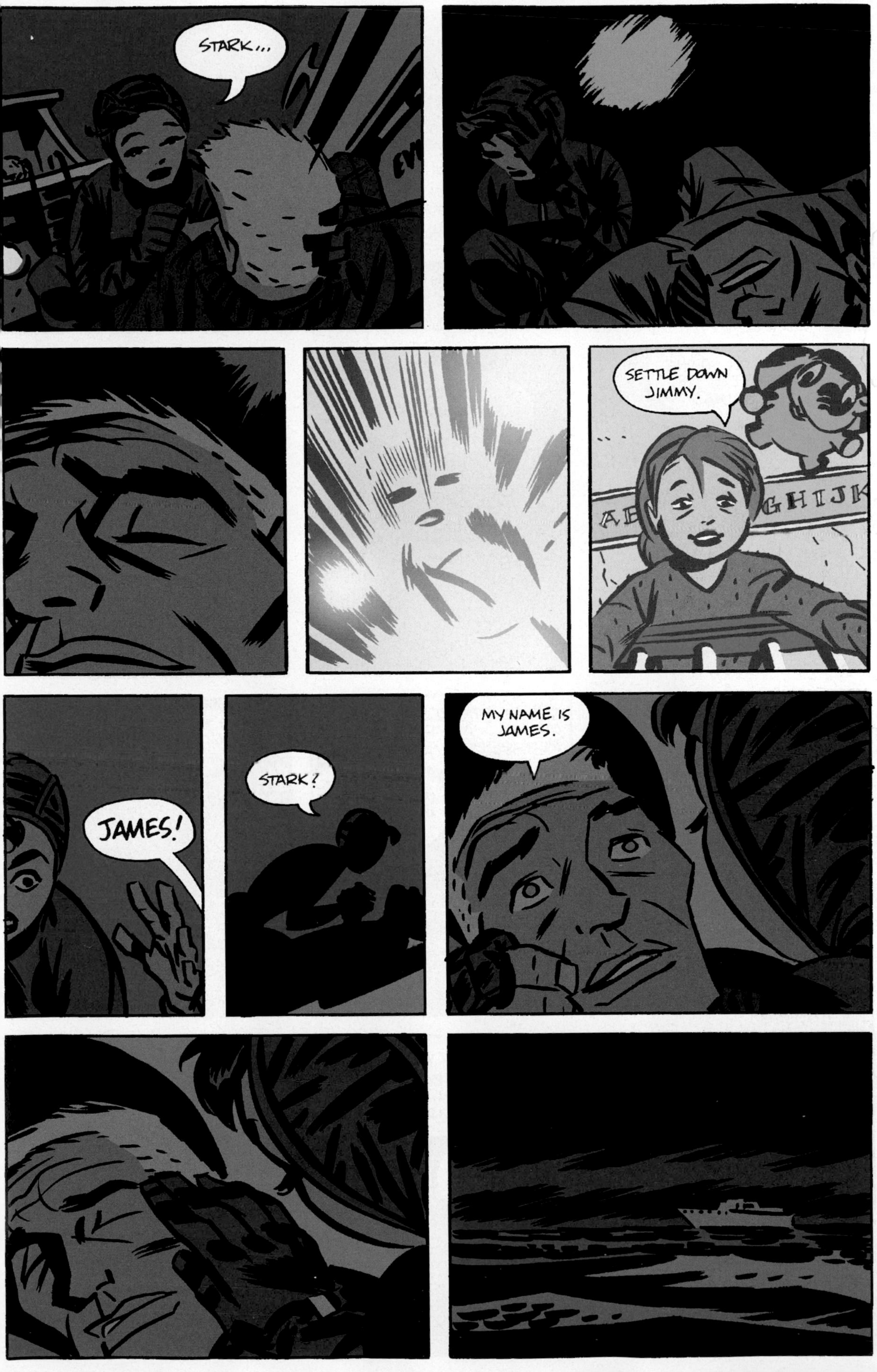
STARK...
SETTLE DOWN JIMMY.
JAMES!
STARK?
MY NAME IS JAMES.

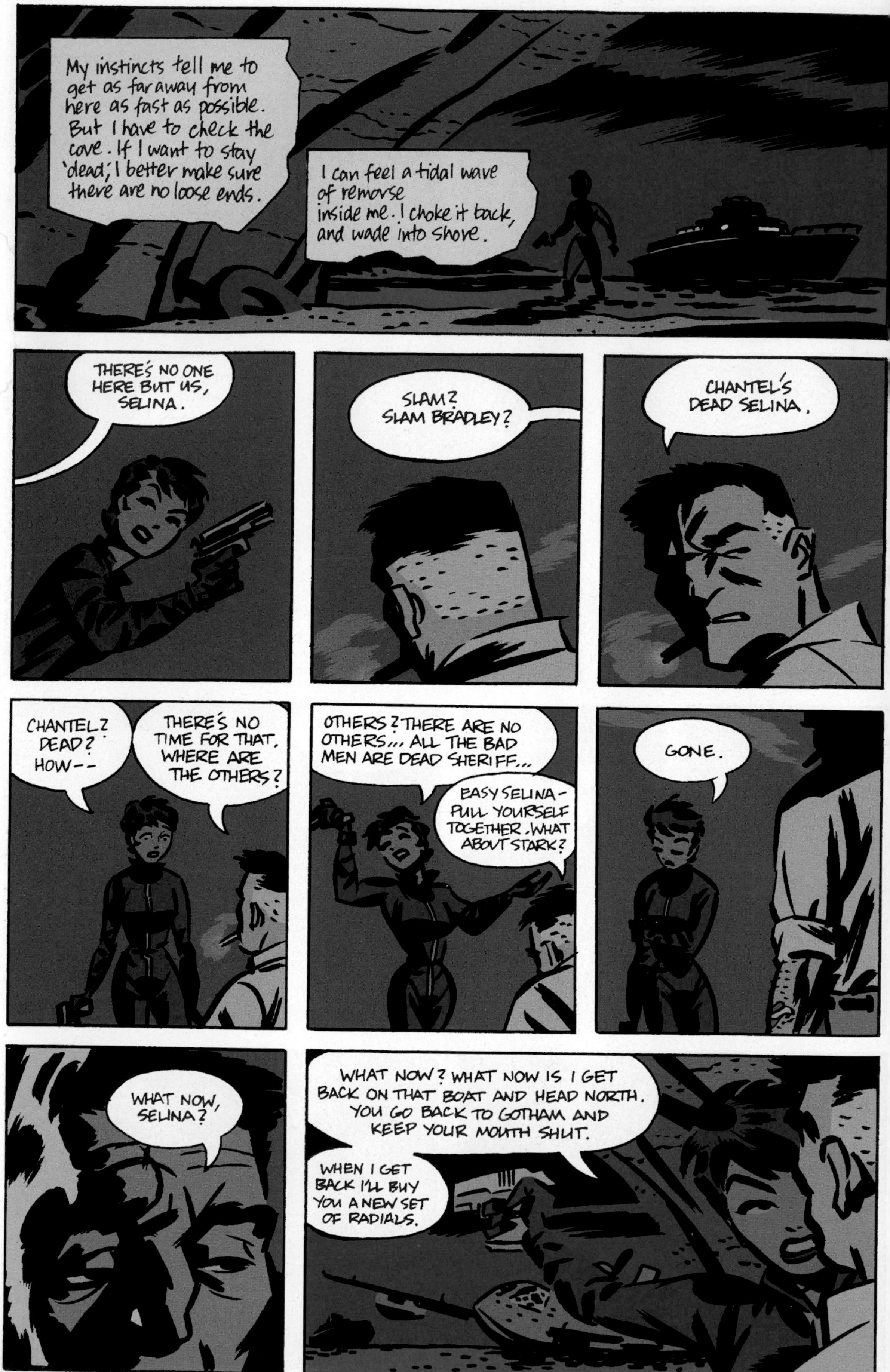
My instincts tell me to get as far away from here as fast as possible. But I have to check the cove. If I want to stay 'dead,' I better make sure there are no loose ends.
I can feel a tidal wave of remorse inside me. I choke it back, and wade into shore.
THERE'S NO ONE HERE BUT US, SELINA.
SLAM? SLAM BRADLEY?
CHANTEL'S DEAD SELINA.
CHANTEL? DEAD? HOW--
THERE'S NO TIME FOR THAT. WHERE ARE THE OTHERS?
OTHERS? THERE ARE NO OTHERS... ALL THE BAD MEN ARE DEAD SHERIFF...
EASY SELINA-PULL YOURSELF TOGETHER. WHAT ABOUT STARK?
GONE.
WHAT NOW, SELINA?
WHAT NOW? WHAT NOW IS I GET BACK ON THAT BOAT AND HEAD NORTH. YOU GO BACK TO GOTHAM AND KEEP YOUR MOUTH SHUT.
WHEN I GET BACK I'LL BUY YOU A NEW SET OF RADIALS.

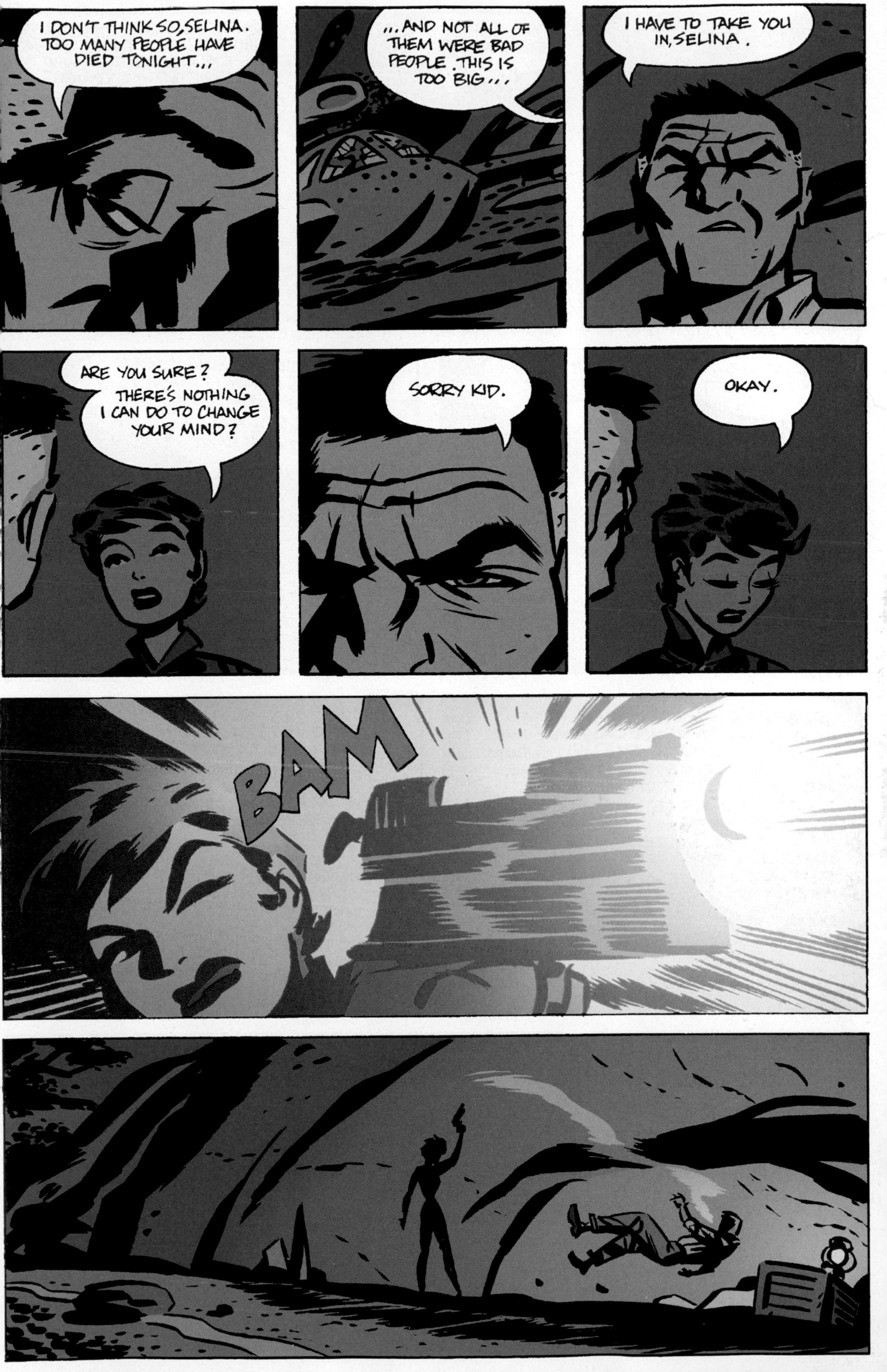
I DON'T THINK SO, SELINA. TOO MANY PEOPLE HAVE DIED TONIGHT...
...AND NOT ALL OF THEM WERE BAD PEOPLE. THIS IS TOO BIG...
I HAVE TO TAKE YOU IN, SELINA.
ARE YOU SURE?
THERE'S NOTHING I CAN DO TO CHANGE YOUR MIND?
SORRY KID.
OKAY.
BAM

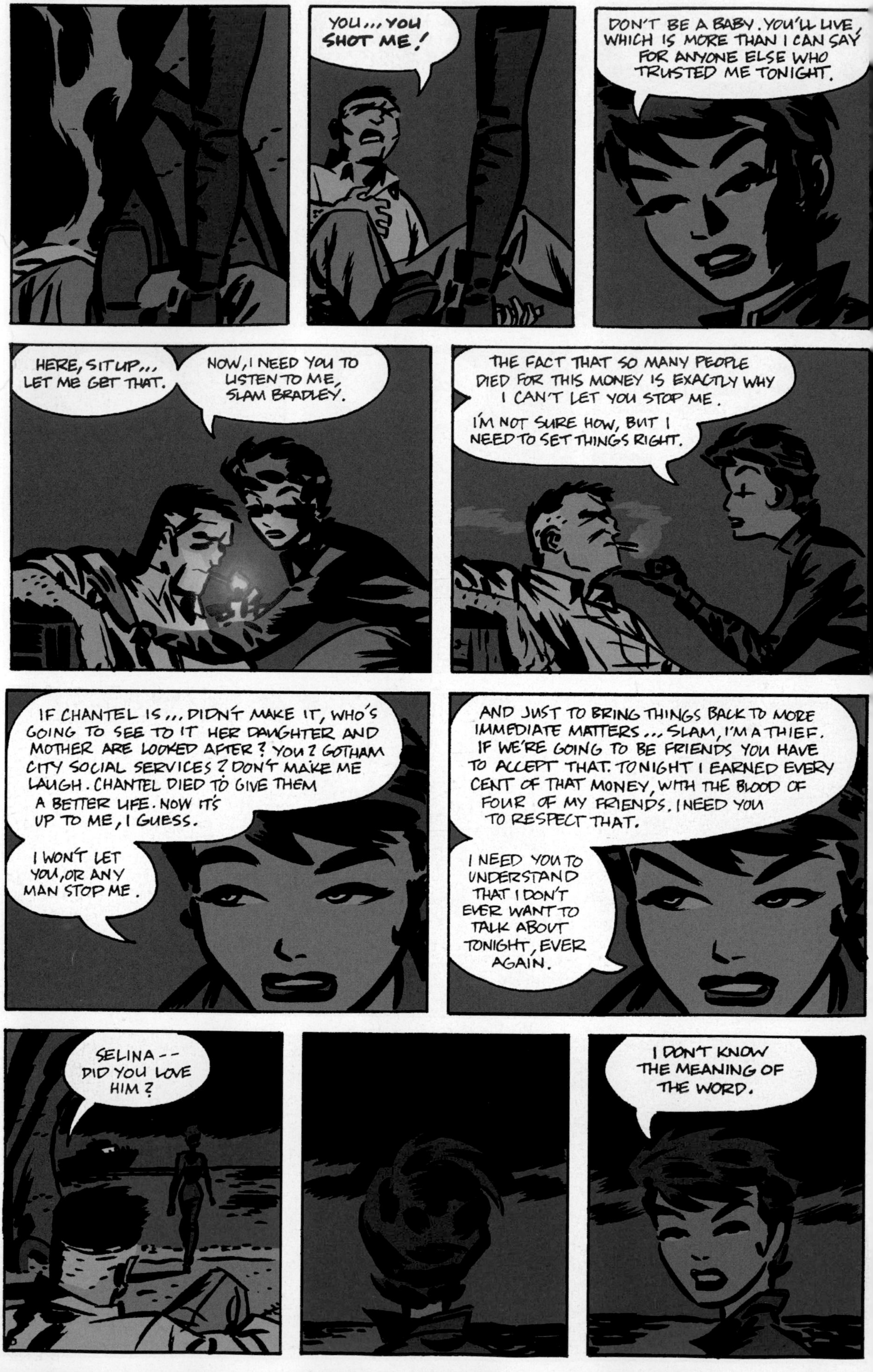
YOU... YOU SHOT ME!
DON'T BE A BABY. YOU'LL LIVE, WHICH IS MORE THAN I CAN SAY FOR ANYONE ELSE WHO TRUSTED ME TONIGHT.
HERE, SIT UP... LET ME GET THAT.
NOW, I NEED YOU TO LISTEN TO ME, SLAM BRADLEY.
THE FACT THAT SO MANY PEOPLE DIED FOR THIS MONEY IS EXACTLY WHY I CAN'T LET YOU STOP ME.
I'M NOT SURE HOW, BUT I NEED TO SET THINGS RIGHT.
IF CHANTEL IS... DIDN'T MAKE IT, WHO'S GOING TO SEE TO IT HER DAUGHTER AND MOTHER ARE LOOKED AFTER? YOU? GOTHAM CITY SOCIAL SERVICES? DON'T MAKE ME LAUGH. CHANTEL DIED TO GIVE THEM A BETTER LIFE. NOW IT'S UP TO ME, I GUESS.
I WON'T LET YOU, OR ANY MAN STOP ME.
AND JUST TO BRING THINGS BACK TO MORE IMMEDIATE MATTERS... SLAM, I'M A THIEF. IF WE'RE GOING TO BE FRIENDS YOU HAVE TO ACCEPT THAT. TONIGHT I EARNED EVERY CENT OF THAT MONEY, WITH THE BLOOD OF FOUR OF MY FRIENDS. I NEED YOU TO RESPECT THAT.
I NEED YOU TO UNDERSTAND THAT I DON'T EVER WANT TO TALK ABOUT TONIGHT, EVER AGAIN.
SELINA-- DID YOU LOVE HIM?
I DON'T KNOW THE MEANING OF THE WORD.

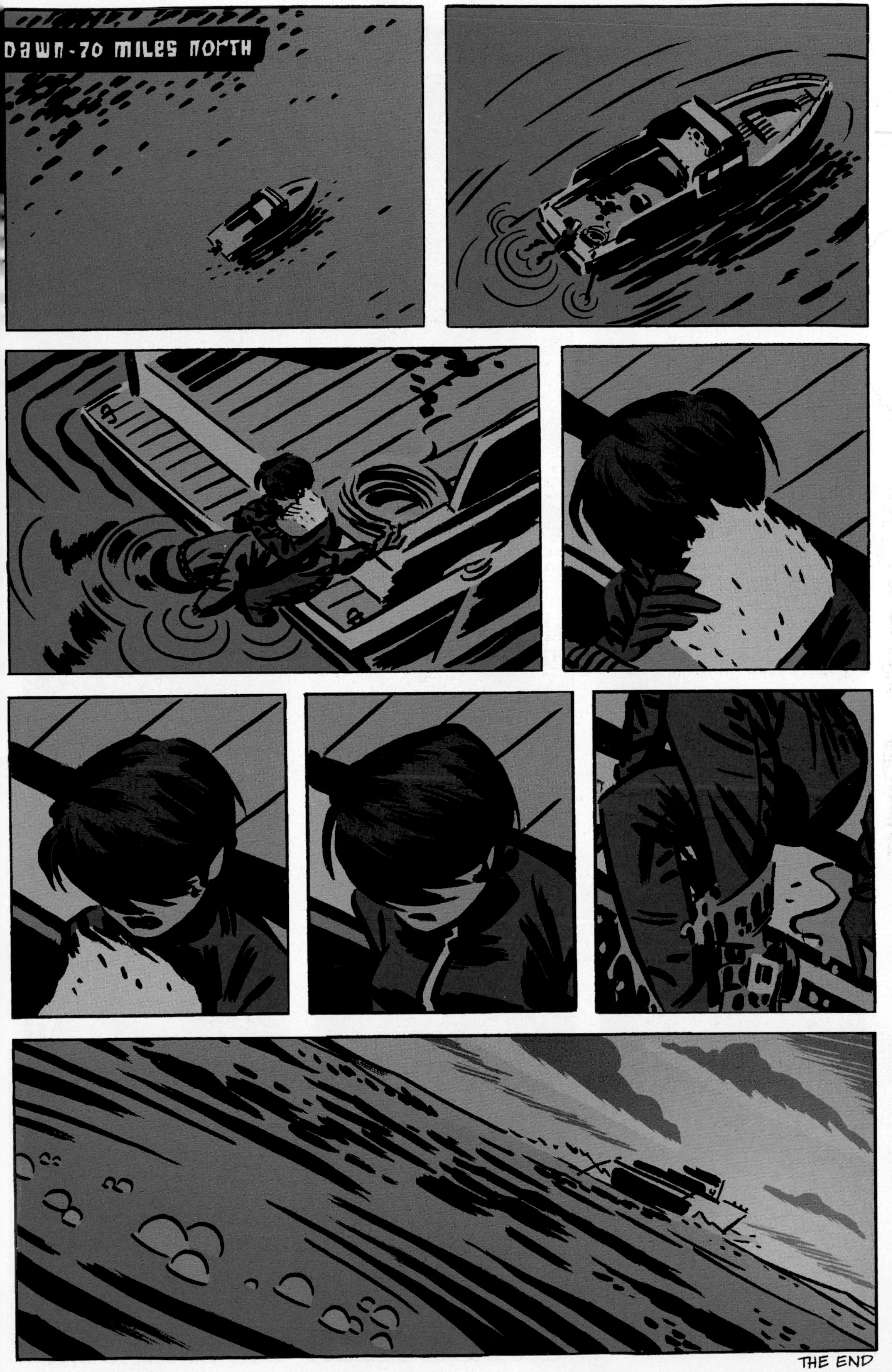
DAWN-70 MILES NORTH

THE END

I'm back in Gotham for two weeks, and it already feels like I'm home again...

... in all the wrong ways.

Now I'm starting to remember the screwed-up parts of this city instead of just thinking about all those great restaurants in Chinatown.

It takes a while for Gotham to really soak into you, I guess.

And as much as this city's changed over the years, some things seem to just stay the same no matter what.

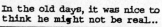

Like the class division. The harsh split between the Haves and Have-Nots that has, if anything, gotten worse in recent times.

NO CREDIT

Then of course, there's the Batman. Gotham's own vigilante hero, who for some reason likes to pretend he's a myth.

In the old days, it was nice to think he might not be real..

FNAP!

... but I know better now.

CRUNCH

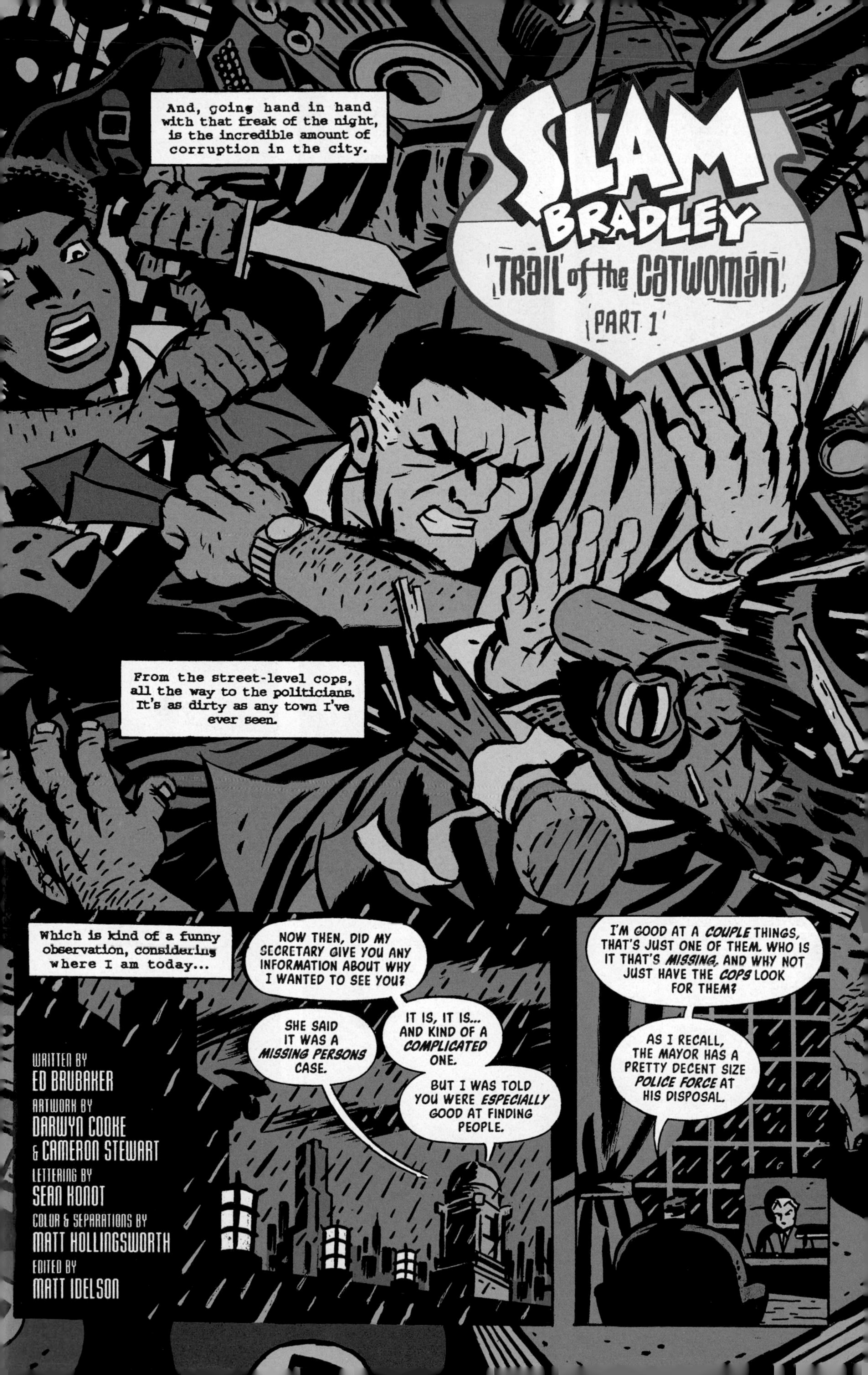
And, going hand in hand with that freak of the night, is the incredible amount of corruption in the city.
SLAM BRADLEY
TRAIL of the CATWOMAN
PART 1
From the street-level cops, all the way to the politicians. It's as dirty as any town I've ever seen.
Which is kind of a funny observation, considering where I am today...
NOW THEN, DID MY SECRETARY GIVE YOU ANY INFORMATION ABOUT WHY I WANTED TO SEE YOU?
SHE SAID IT WAS A MISSING PERSONS CASE.
IT IS, IT IS... AND KIND OF A COMPLICATED ONE.
BUT I WAS TOLD YOU WERE ESPECIALLY GOOD AT FINDING PEOPLE.
I'M GOOD AT A COUPLE THINGS, THAT'S JUST ONE OF THEM. WHO IS IT THAT'S MISSING, AND WHY NOT JUST HAVE THE COPS LOOK FOR THEM?
AS I RECALL, THE MAYOR HAS A PRETTY DECENT SIZE POLICE FORCE AT HIS DISPOSAL.
WRITTEN BY
ED BRUBAKER
ARTWORK BY
DARWYN COOKE
& CAMERON STEWART
LETTERING BY
SEAN KONOT
COLOR & SEPARATIONS BY
MATT HOLLINGSWORTH
EDITED BY
MATT IDELSON

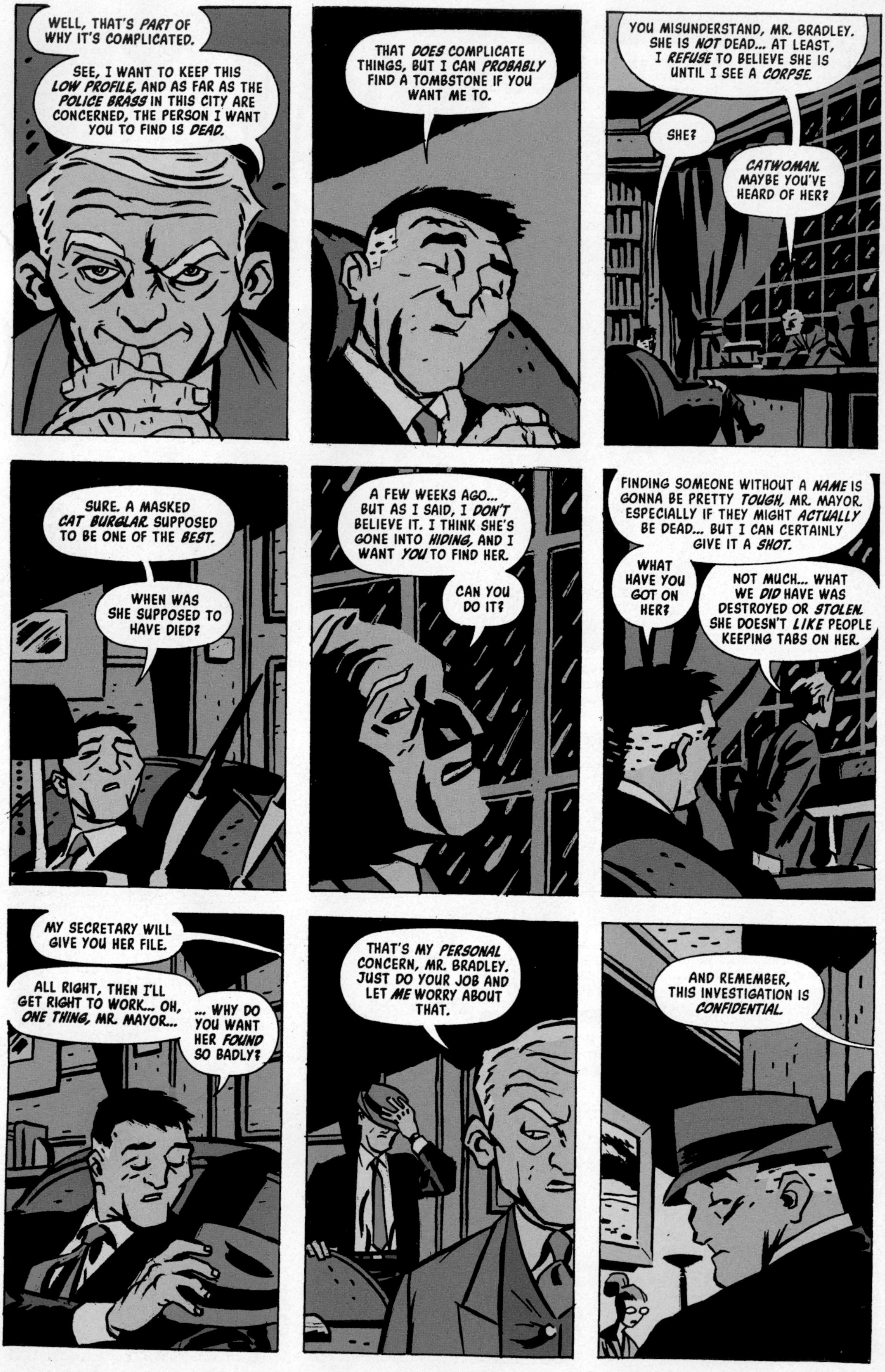
WELL, THAT'S PART OF WHY IT'S COMPLICATED.
SEE, I WANT TO KEEP THIS LOW PROFILE, AND AS FAR AS THE POLICE BRASS IN THIS CITY ARE CONCERNED, THE PERSON I WANT YOU TO FIND IS DEAD.
THAT DOES COMPLICATE THINGS, BUT I CAN PROBABLY FIND A TOMBSTONE IF YOU WANT ME TO.
YOU MISUNDERSTAND, MR. BRADLEY. SHE IS NOT DEAD... AT LEAST, I REFUSE TO BELIEVE SHE IS UNTIL I SEE A CORPSE.
SHE?
CATWOMAN. MAYBE YOU'VE HEARD OF HER?
SURE. A MASKED CAT BURGLAR. SUPPOSED TO BE ONE OF THE BEST.
WHEN WAS SHE SUPPOSED TO HAVE DIED?
A FEW WEEKS AGO... BUT AS I SAID, I DON'T BELIEVE IT. I THINK SHE'S GONE INTO HIDING, AND I WANT YOU TO FIND HER.
CAN YOU DO IT?
FINDING SOMEONE WITHOUT A NAME IS GONNA BE PRETTY TOUGH, MR. MAYOR. ESPECIALLY IF THEY MIGHT ACTUALLY BE DEAD... BUT I CAN CERTAINLY GIVE IT A SHOT.
WHAT HAVE YOU GOT ON HER?
NOT MUCH... WHAT WE DID HAVE WAS DESTROYED OR STOLEN. SHE DOESN'T LIKE PEOPLE KEEPING TABS ON HER.
MY SECRETARY WILL GIVE YOU HER FILE.
ALL RIGHT, THEN I'LL GET RIGHT TO WORK... OH, ONE THING, MR. MAYOR...
... WHY DO YOU WANT HER FOUND SO BADLY?
THAT'S MY PERSONAL CONCERN, MR. BRADLEY. JUST DO YOUR JOB AND LET ME WORRY ABOUT THAT.
AND REMEMBER, THIS INVESTIGATION IS CONFIDENTIAL.

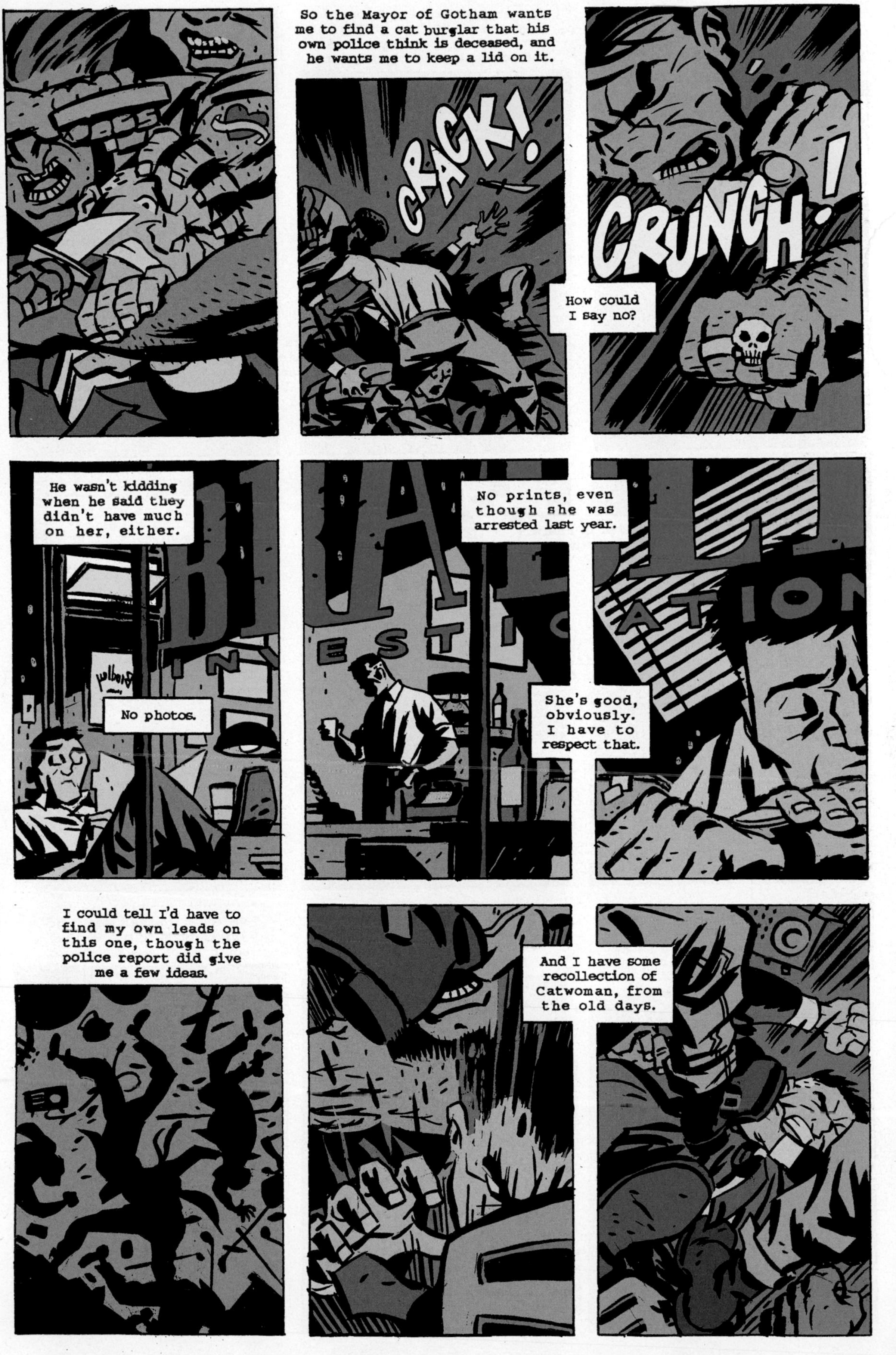
So the Mayor of Gotham wants me to find a cat burglar that his own police think is deceased, and he wants me to keep a lid on it.
CRACK!
CRUNCH!
How could I say no?
He wasn't kidding when he said they didn't have much on her, either.
No photos.
No prints, even though she was arrested last year.
She's good, obviously. I have to respect that.
I could tell I'd have to find my own leads on this one, though the police report did give me a few ideas.
And I have some recollection of Catwoman, from the old days.

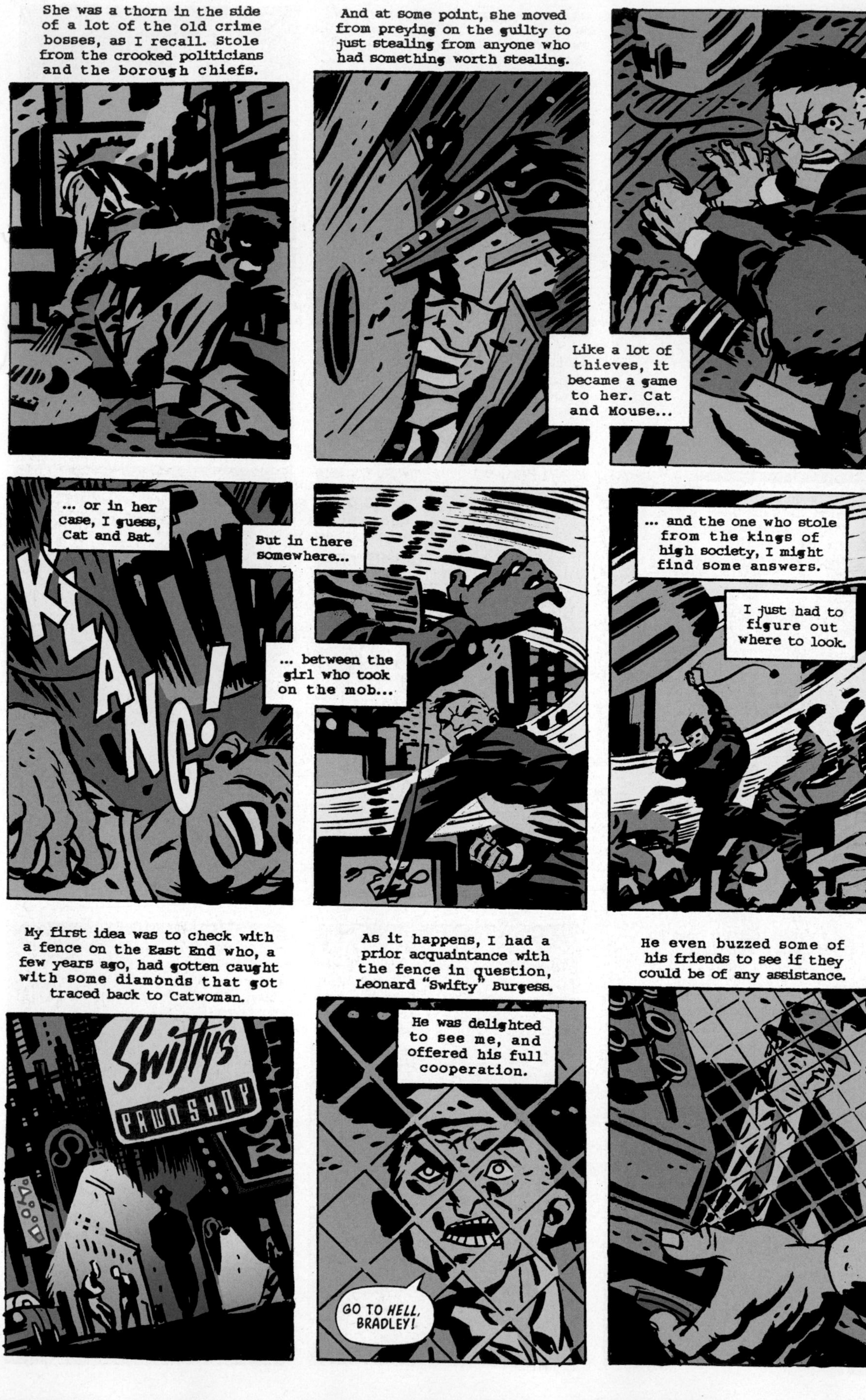
She was a thorn in the side of a lot of the old crime bosses, as I recall. Stole from the crooked politicians and the borough chiefs.
And at some point, she moved from preying on the guilty to just stealing from anyone who had something worth stealing.
Like a lot of thieves, it became a game to her. Cat and Mouse...
... or in her case, I guess, Cat and Bat.
KLANG!
But in there somewhere...
... between the girl who took on the mob...
... and the one who stole from the kings of high society, I might find some answers.
I just had to figure out where to look.
My first idea was to check with a fence on the East End who, a few years ago, had gotten caught with some diamonds that got traced back to Catwoman.
Swifty's
PAWNSHOP
As it happens, I had a prior acquaintance with the fence in question, Leonard "Swifty" Burgess.
He was delighted to see me, and offered his full cooperation.
GO TO HELL, BRADLEY!
He even buzzed some of his friends to see if they could be of any assistance.

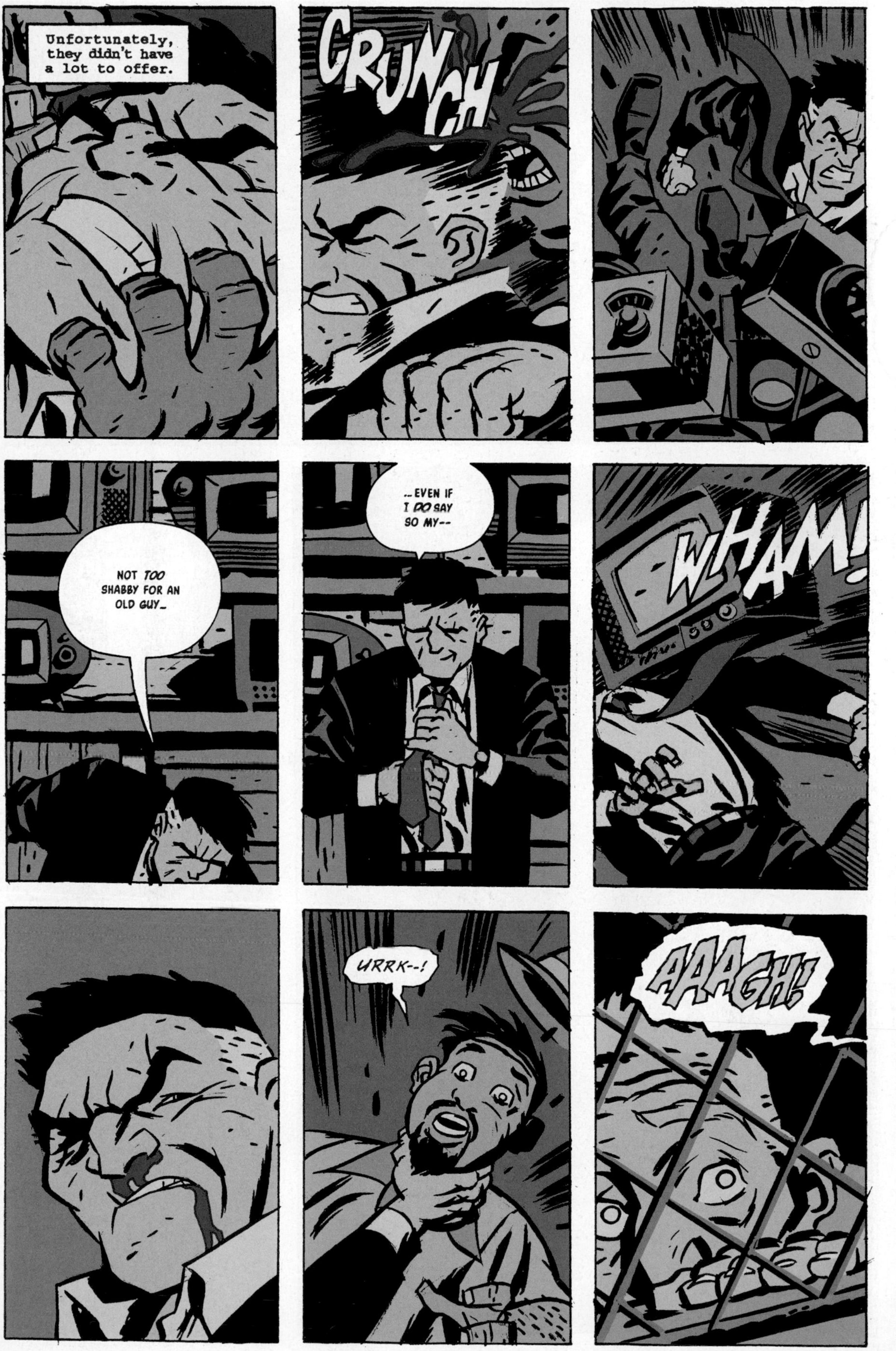
Unfortunately, they didn't have a lot to offer.
CRUNCH
NOT TOO SHABBY FOR AN OLD GUY_
...EVEN IF I DO SAY SO MY--
WHAM!
URRK--!
AAAGH!

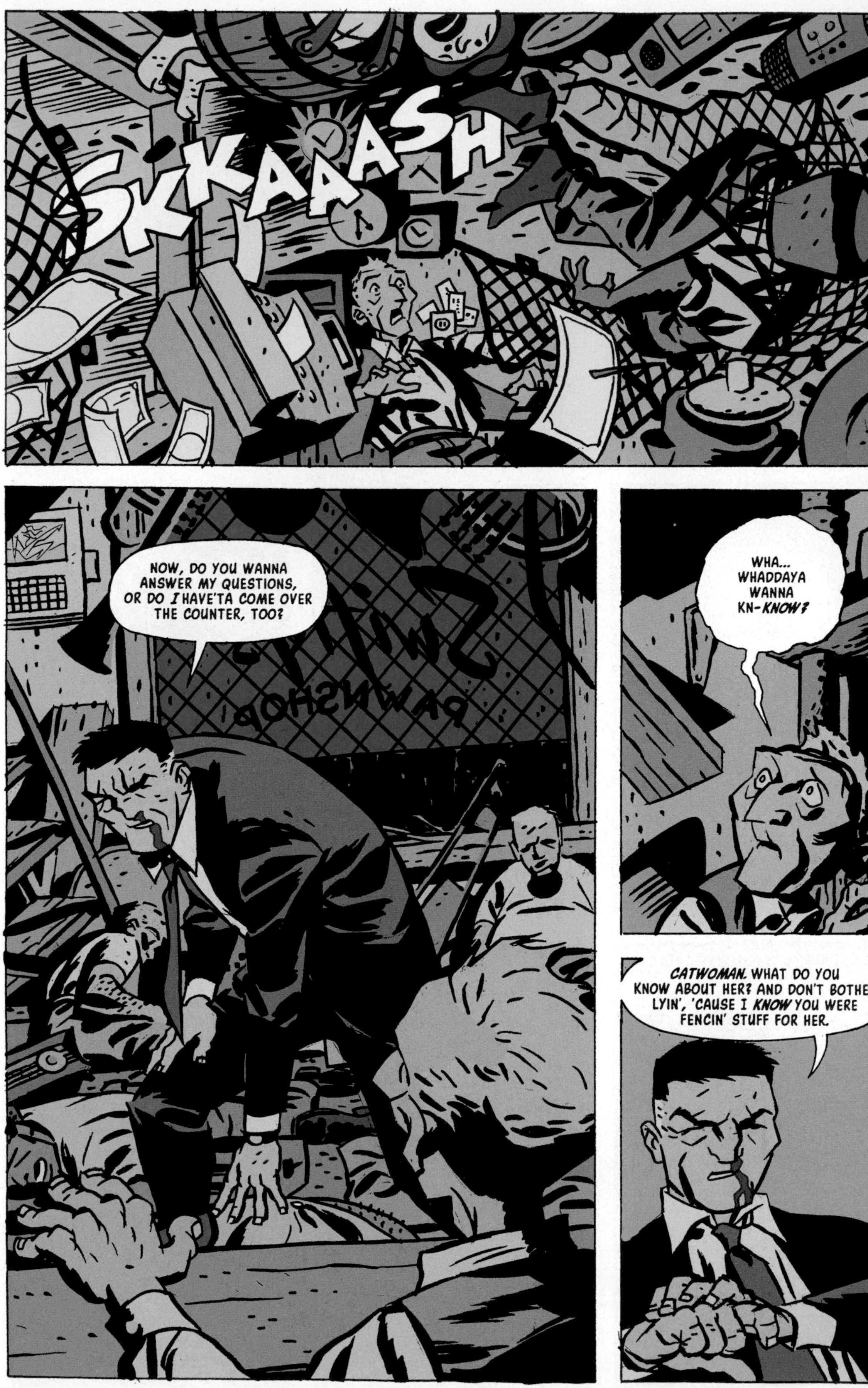
SKKAAASH
NOW, DO YOU WANNA ANSWER MY QUESTIONS, OR DO I HAVE'TA COME OVER THE COUNTER, TOO?
PAWNSHOP
WHA... WHADDAYA WANNA KN-KNOW?
CATWOMAN. WHAT DO YOU KNOW ABOUT HER? AND DON'T BOTHER LYIN', 'CAUSE I KNOW YOU WERE FENCIN' STUFF FOR HER.

AW, JEEZ... DAT'S WHA'CHER AFTER?
WORD ON'NA STREET IS SHE'S DEAD, SLAM.
SO I HEAR.
WHO WAS SHE?
YOU KIDDIN' ME? I MET HER ONCE 'R TWICE, MOVED SOME ICE. SHE DIDN'T FLASH ME HER FACE 'R NUTHIN'... WASN'T LIKE WE WUZ BEST FRIENDS.
DON'T HOLD OUT ON ME, SWIFTY...
I AIN'T, SLAM, I SWEAR... I DON'T KNOW NUTHIN'...
OKAY, MAYBE YOU DON'T... WHAT DO YOU HEAR ABOUT HER DEATH, THEN?
ASK THE COPPERS.
WORD IS THERE WUZ A FEW PIGGIES WITH A SERIOUS MAD-ON FOR HER...
... SHE WUZ CRUISIN' FOR A BRUISIN' EVER SINCE SHE S'POSEDLY KAKKED THAT SELINA KYLE BROAD OVER IN NEW YORK.
ALL RIGHT, SWIFTY, LET'S SEE IF THE COPS AGREE WITH YOU ON THAT...
... AND NEXT TIME TRY LETTING ME FINISH A SENTENCE. YOU MIGHT SAVE YOURSELF SOME REPAIR BILLS.
PERSONAL CHECKS
A lot of trouble, but at least I got my lead. I knew it had to be here somewhere.
Of course, who knew I'd have to dig into the life of one dead woman to try to find another?
But right now, Selina Kyle is all I've got.
ADULTS ONLY
I just hope she leads me somewhere.

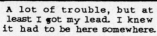

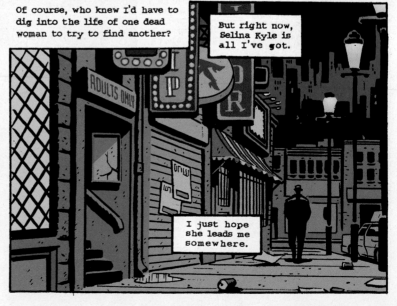

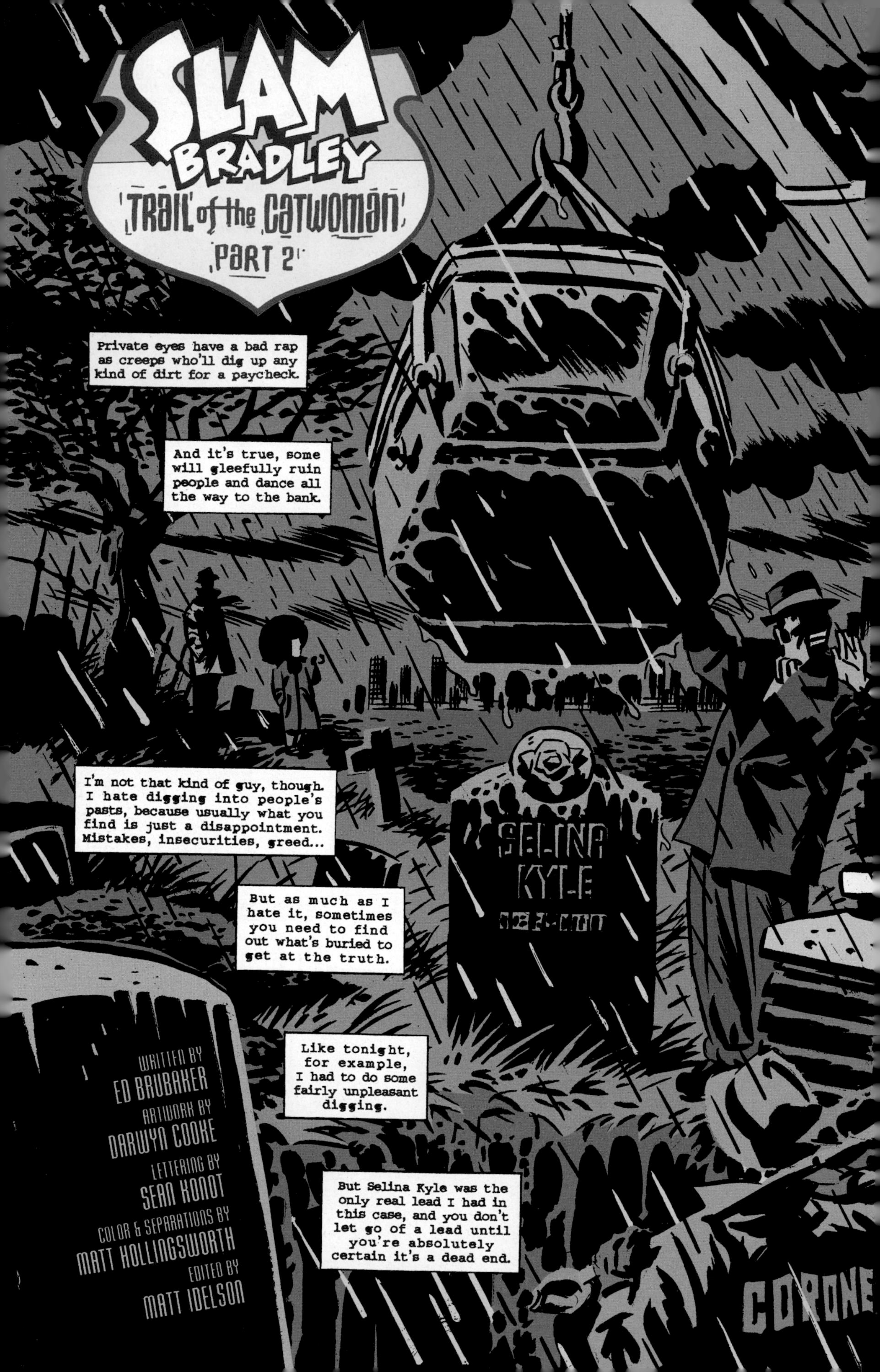
SLAM BRADLEY
TRAIL of the CATWOMAN
PART 2
Private eyes have a bad rap as creeps who'll dig up any kind of dirt for a paycheck.
And it's true, some will gleefully ruin people and dance all the way to the bank.
I'm not that kind of guy, though. I hate digging into people's pasts, because usually what you find is just a disappointment. Mistakes, insecurities, greed...
But as much as I hate it, sometimes you need to find out what's buried to get at the truth.
Like tonight, for example, I had to do some fairly unpleasant digging.
But Selina Kyle was the only real lead I had in this case, and you don't let go of a lead until you're absolutely certain it's a dead end.
SELINA KYLE
WRITTEN BY ED BRUBAKER
ARTWORK BY DARWYN COOKE
LETTERING BY SEAN KONOT
COLOR & SEPARATIONS BY MATT HOLLINGSWORTH
EDITED BY MATT IDELSON
CORONE

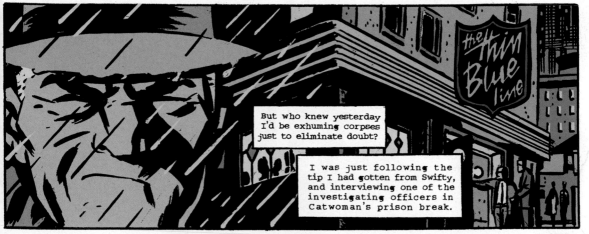

But who knew yesterday I'd be exhuming corpses just to eliminate doubt?

I was just following the tip I had gotten from Swifty, and interviewing one of the investigating officers in Catwoman's prison break.

THE MAYOR TOLD ME TO *COOPERATE,* BRADLEY... BUT I DON'T KNOW WHAT YOU WANT ME TO SAY...

I'M INTERESTED IN WHAT ANGLE YOU AND YOUR PARTNER WERE PURSUING...

ANGLE? WASN'T MANY TO CHOOSE FROM... WE GOT A WOMAN WHO'S NOT IN THE SYSTEM *ANYWHERE.*

ONLY THING WE *DO* HAVE IS SHE LOOKS A LOT LIKE A LADY WHO WAS RECENTLY KILLED WHILE RUNNING FOR MAYOR OF *NEW YORK.*

SELINA KYLE, RIGHT? I HEARD THE COPS HAD CATWOMAN UNDER THE MICROSCOPE ON THAT ONE, TOO.

YEAH, BUT THAT WAS *N.Y.P.D.,* NOT GOTHAM. STILL, WE FOLLOW THIS *KYLE* CONNECTION AS FAR AS IT LEADS...

... AND WE COME UP WITH *MAGGIE* KYLE, YOUNGER SISTER OF THE DECEASED...

... THING *IS,* WE CAN'T TRACK HER DOWN.

HEARD SHE JOINED A *CONVENT* OR SOMETHIN' TEN YEARS AGO...

AND FROM THERE IT WAS JUST *BUBKISS.* THEN CATWOMAN GETS *KILLED,* SO WHO CARES?

I GUESS YOUR *MAYOR* DOES, FOR ONE.

WHATEVER. MY OPINION, HE'S WASTING *YOUR* TIME AND *HIS* MONEY.

WELL, LUCKILY, THERE'S PLENTY OF *BOTH* TO GO AROUND...

... THANKS FOR THE *COOPERATION,* DETECTIVE.

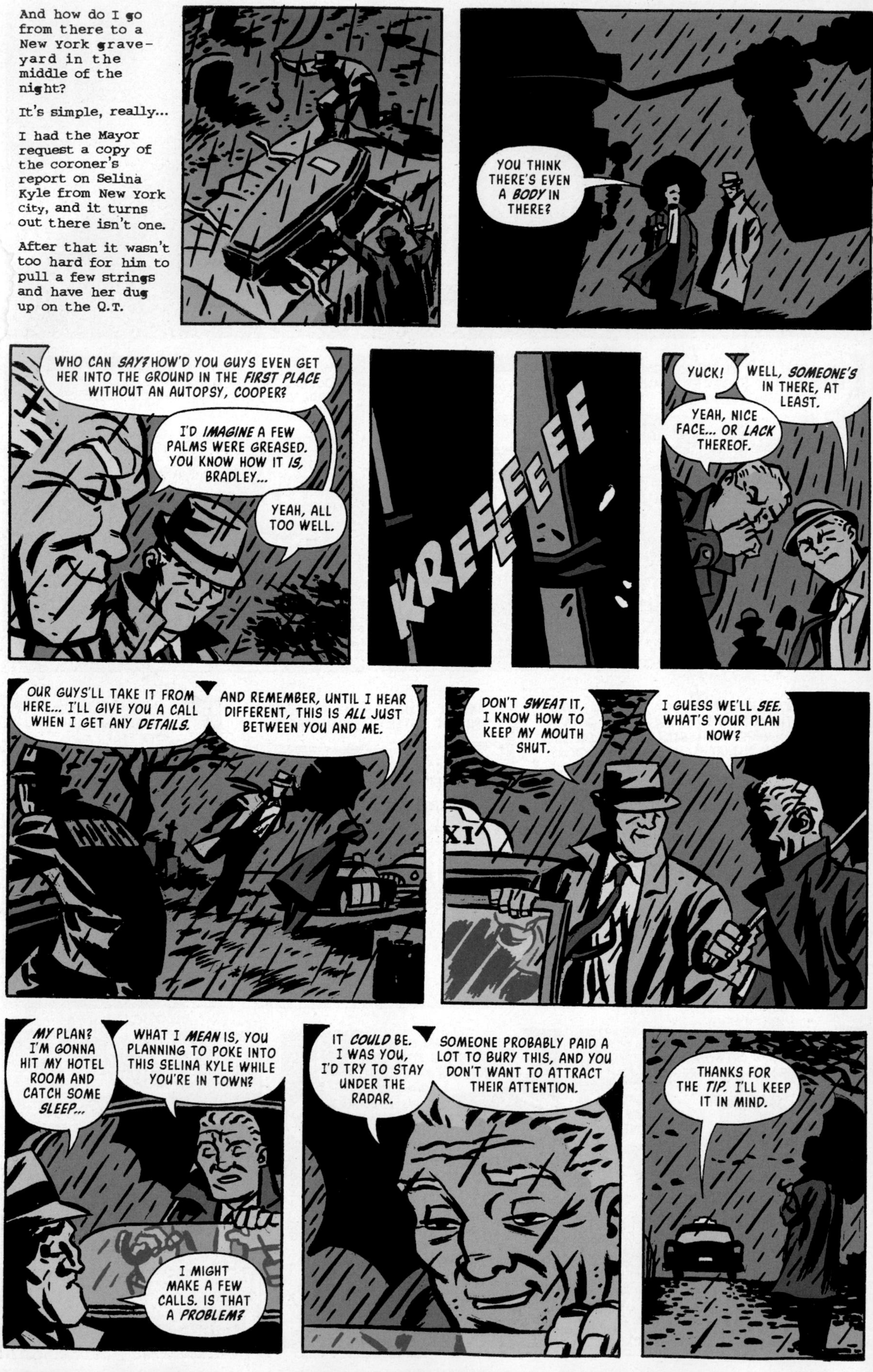
And how do I go from there to a New York grave-yard in the middle of the night?
It's simple, really...
I had the Mayor request a copy of the coroner's report on Selina Kyle from New York city, and it turns out there isn't one.
After that it wasn't too hard for him to pull a few strings and have her dug up on the Q.T.
YOU THINK THERE'S EVEN A BODY IN THERE?
WHO CAN SAY? HOW'D YOU GUYS EVEN GET HER INTO THE GROUND IN THE FIRST PLACE WITHOUT AN AUTOPSY, COOPER?
I'D IMAGINE A FEW PALMS WERE GREASED. YOU KNOW HOW IT IS, BRADLEY...
YEAH, ALL TOO WELL.
KREEEEEEEEE
YUCK!
WELL, SOMEONE'S IN THERE, AT LEAST.
YEAH, NICE FACE... OR LACK THEREOF.
OUR GUYS'LL TAKE IT FROM HERE... I'LL GIVE YOU A CALL WHEN I GET ANY DETAILS.
AND REMEMBER, UNTIL I HEAR DIFFERENT, THIS IS ALL JUST BETWEEN YOU AND ME.
DON'T SWEAT IT, I KNOW HOW TO KEEP MY MOUTH SHUT.
I GUESS WE'LL SEE. WHAT'S YOUR PLAN NOW?
MY PLAN? I'M GONNA HIT MY HOTEL ROOM AND CATCH SOME SLEEP...
WHAT I MEAN IS, YOU PLANNING TO POKE INTO THIS SELINA KYLE WHILE YOU'RE IN TOWN?
I MIGHT MAKE A FEW CALLS. IS THAT A PROBLEM?
IT COULD BE. I WAS YOU, I'D TRY TO STAY UNDER THE RADAR.
SOMEONE PROBABLY PAID A LOT TO BURY THIS, AND YOU DON'T WANT TO ATTRACT THEIR ATTENTION.
THANKS FOR THE TIP. I'LL KEEP IT IN MIND.

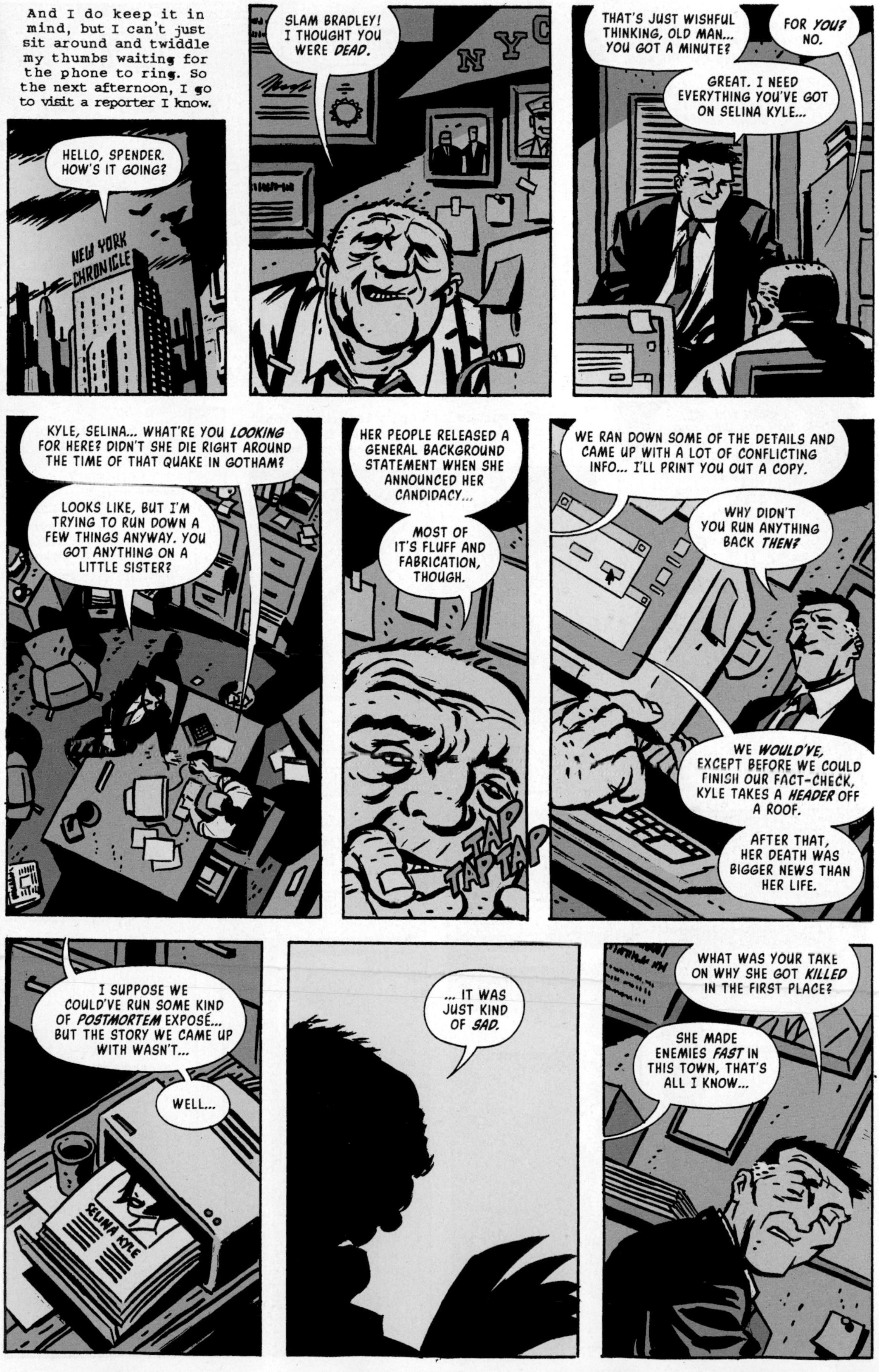

And I do keep it in mind, but I can't just sit around and twiddle my thumbs waiting for the phone to ring. So the next afternoon, I go to visit a reporter I know.
HELLO, SPENDER. HOW'S IT GOING?
NEW YORK CHRONICLE
SLAM BRADLEY! I THOUGHT YOU WERE *DEAD*.
NYC
THAT'S JUST WISHFUL THINKING, OLD MAN... YOU GOT A MINUTE?
FOR *YOU?* NO.
GREAT. I NEED EVERYTHING YOU'VE GOT ON SELINA KYLE...
KYLE, SELINA... WHAT'RE YOU *LOOKING* FOR HERE? DIDN'T SHE DIE RIGHT AROUND THE TIME OF THAT QUAKE IN GOTHAM?
LOOKS LIKE, BUT I'M TRYING TO RUN DOWN A FEW THINGS ANYWAY. YOU GOT ANYTHING ON A LITTLE SISTER?
HER PEOPLE RELEASED A GENERAL BACKGROUND STATEMENT WHEN SHE ANNOUNCED HER CANDIDACY...
MOST OF IT'S FLUFF AND FABRICATION, THOUGH.
TAP TAP TAP
WE RAN DOWN SOME OF THE DETAILS AND CAME UP WITH A LOT OF CONFLICTING INFO... I'LL PRINT YOU OUT A COPY.
WHY DIDN'T YOU RUN ANYTHING BACK *THEN?*
WE *WOULD'VE*, EXCEPT BEFORE WE COULD FINISH OUR FACT-CHECK, KYLE TAKES A *HEADER* OFF A ROOF.
AFTER THAT, HER DEATH WAS BIGGER NEWS THAN HER LIFE.
I SUPPOSE WE COULD'VE RUN SOME KIND OF *POSTMORTEM* EXPOSÉ... BUT THE STORY WE CAME UP WITH WASN'T...
WELL...
SELINA KYLE
... IT WAS JUST KIND OF *SAD*.
WHAT WAS YOUR TAKE ON WHY SHE GOT *KILLED* IN THE FIRST PLACE?
SHE MADE ENEMIES *FAST* IN THIS TOWN, THAT'S ALL I KNOW...

SHE'S HERE A *WEEK* AND SHE'S MANIPULATED HERSELF INTO A *POWERFUL* POSTION BETWEEN THE MONEYMEN AND THE MOB.

THAT KIND OF LIFE TENDS TO HAVE A PRETTY *SHORT* EXPIRATION DATE.

I'LL TELL YOU *ONE THING*, THOUGH, I MET HER ONCE, AND SHE HAD *GUTS*... AND *CLASS* TO SPARE.

SOUNDS LIKE YOU LIKED HER. A *LOT*.

HEY, *C'MON, SLAM*... I'M A *MARRIED MAN*...

SURE YOU ARE, YOU OLD *BIRD DOG*...

GIVE MY BEST TO MARIE.

So, between the coroner's report, which I'd probably get later, and the file from Spender, I had enough to keep me busy.

But was I just following a smoke trail?

Was there really a connection between Selina Kyle and Catwoman?

Or maybe her sister Maggie?

DING

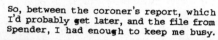

As I pondered all of this, I got a surprise that told me my instincts were right on the money.

CRACK

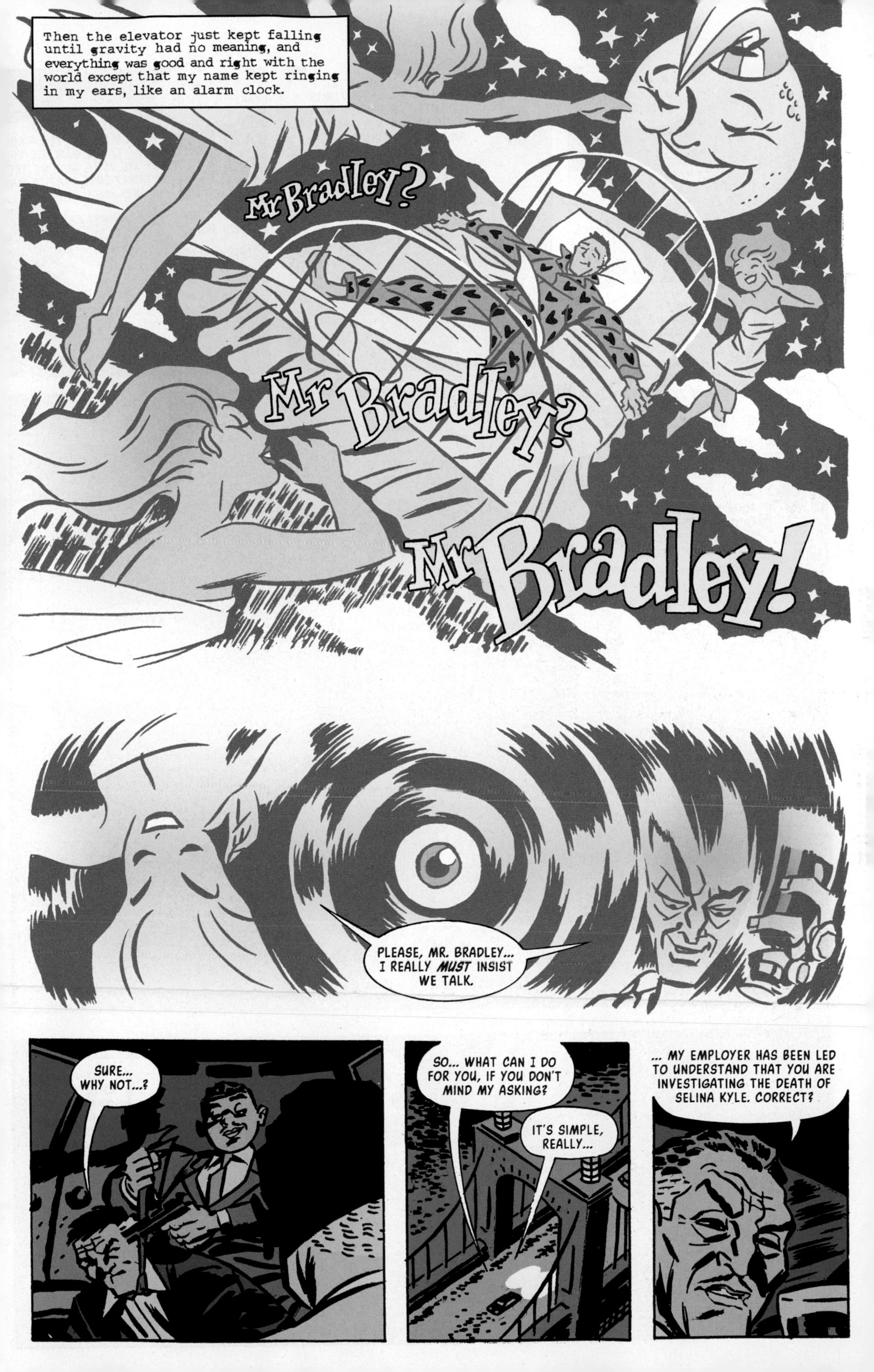
Then the elevator just kept falling until gravity had no meaning, and everything was good and right with the world except that my name kept ringing in my ears, like an alarm clock.
Mr Bradley?
Mr Bradley?
Mr Bradley!
PLEASE, MR. BRADLEY... I REALLY MUST INSIST WE TALK.
SURE... WHY NOT...?
SO... WHAT CAN I DO FOR YOU, IF YOU DON'T MIND MY ASKING?
IT'S SIMPLE, REALLY...
... MY EMPLOYER HAS BEEN LED TO UNDERSTAND THAT YOU ARE INVESTIGATING THE DEATH OF SELINA KYLE. CORRECT?

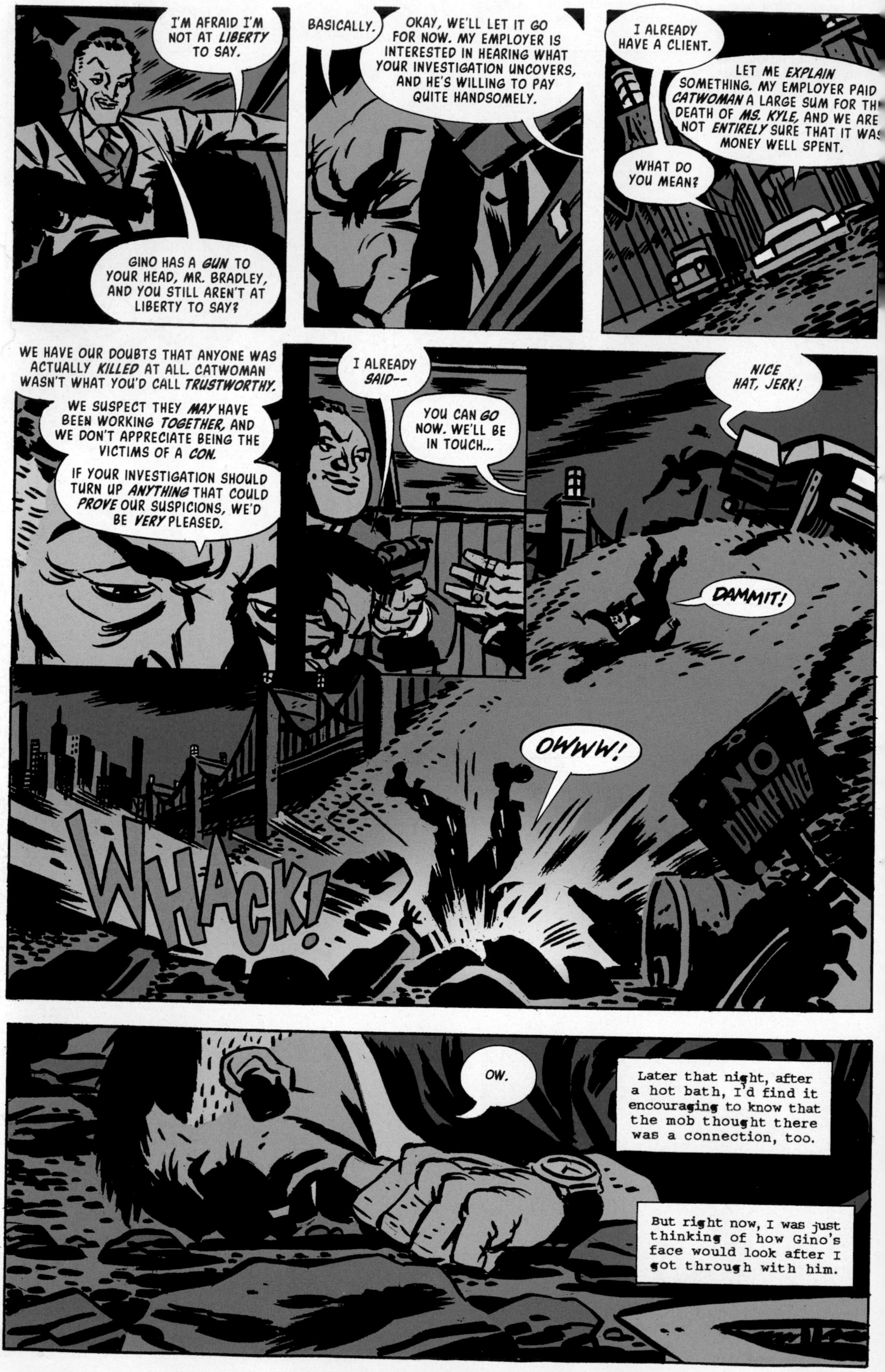

I'M AFRAID I'M NOT AT LIBERTY TO SAY.
GINO HAS A GUN TO YOUR HEAD, MR. BRADLEY, AND YOU STILL AREN'T AT LIBERTY TO SAY?
BASICALLY.
OKAY, WE'LL LET IT GO FOR NOW. MY EMPLOYER IS INTERESTED IN HEARING WHAT YOUR INVESTIGATION UNCOVERS, AND HE'S WILLING TO PAY QUITE HANDSOMELY.
I ALREADY HAVE A CLIENT.
LET ME EXPLAIN SOMETHING. MY EMPLOYER PAID CATWOMAN A LARGE SUM FOR THE DEATH OF MS. KYLE, AND WE ARE NOT ENTIRELY SURE THAT IT WAS MONEY WELL SPENT.
WHAT DO YOU MEAN?
WE HAVE OUR DOUBTS THAT ANYONE WAS ACTUALLY KILLED AT ALL. CATWOMAN WASN'T WHAT YOU'D CALL TRUSTWORTHY.
WE SUSPECT THEY MAY HAVE BEEN WORKING TOGETHER, AND WE DON'T APPRECIATE BEING THE VICTIMS OF A CON.
IF YOUR INVESTIGATION SHOULD TURN UP ANYTHING THAT COULD PROVE OUR SUSPICIONS, WE'D BE VERY PLEASED.
I ALREADY SAID--
YOU CAN GO NOW. WE'LL BE IN TOUCH...
NICE HAT, JERK!
DAMMIT!
OWWW!
WHACK!
NO DUMPING
OW.
Later that night, after a hot bath, I'd find it encouraging to know that the mob thought there was a connection, too.
But right now, I was just thinking of how Gino's face would look after I got through with him.

I had to give credit to Spender. His people did good work, and he was right about Selina Kyle. She did have guts and class, which was even rarer after what she'd gone through growing up.

She and her little sister had been knocked around from orphanages to foster homes since she was about ten years old.

Most of the records on this have disappeared, but Spender managed to find a few people from the youth authority who remembered her.

They told him of a shy girl who became tough over the years, and who was especially protective of her sister, Maggie.

KYLE, S

Then she and Maggie ran away when she was fifteen, and she dropped off the face of the earth, only to resurface six years later in Gotham's high society.

WAYNE AND SELINA KYL
...ie that benefit...
...Clinic a...

Reading with an eye on the Catwoman connection, it's so obvious. Young Selina Kyle, out on the streets surviving by her wits, and Catwoman's early days of stealing from the local mobsters.

RRRIING!

Then she becomes high society Selina Kyle, just around the same time that Catwoman starts to rob from the rich.

BRADLEY HERE.

IT'S COOPER. THE AUTOPSY GOT SHUT DOWN, AND THE BOSSES JUST TORE MY HEAD OFF, SO FORGET ABOUT ANY OF THIS COMING OUT TO THE WORLD.

WHO CARES ABOUT THE *WORLD*-- DID THEY FIND ANYTHING?

YEAH... BUT JUST BETWEEN YOU AND ME AND THE LAMPPOST... THE CORPSE'S PRINTS MATCHED A D.O.A. FROM THREE DAYS BEFORE SELINA KYLE WAS KILLED.

IT *WASN'T* HER.

5'6"

5'D"

SELINA KYLE 70.11.0

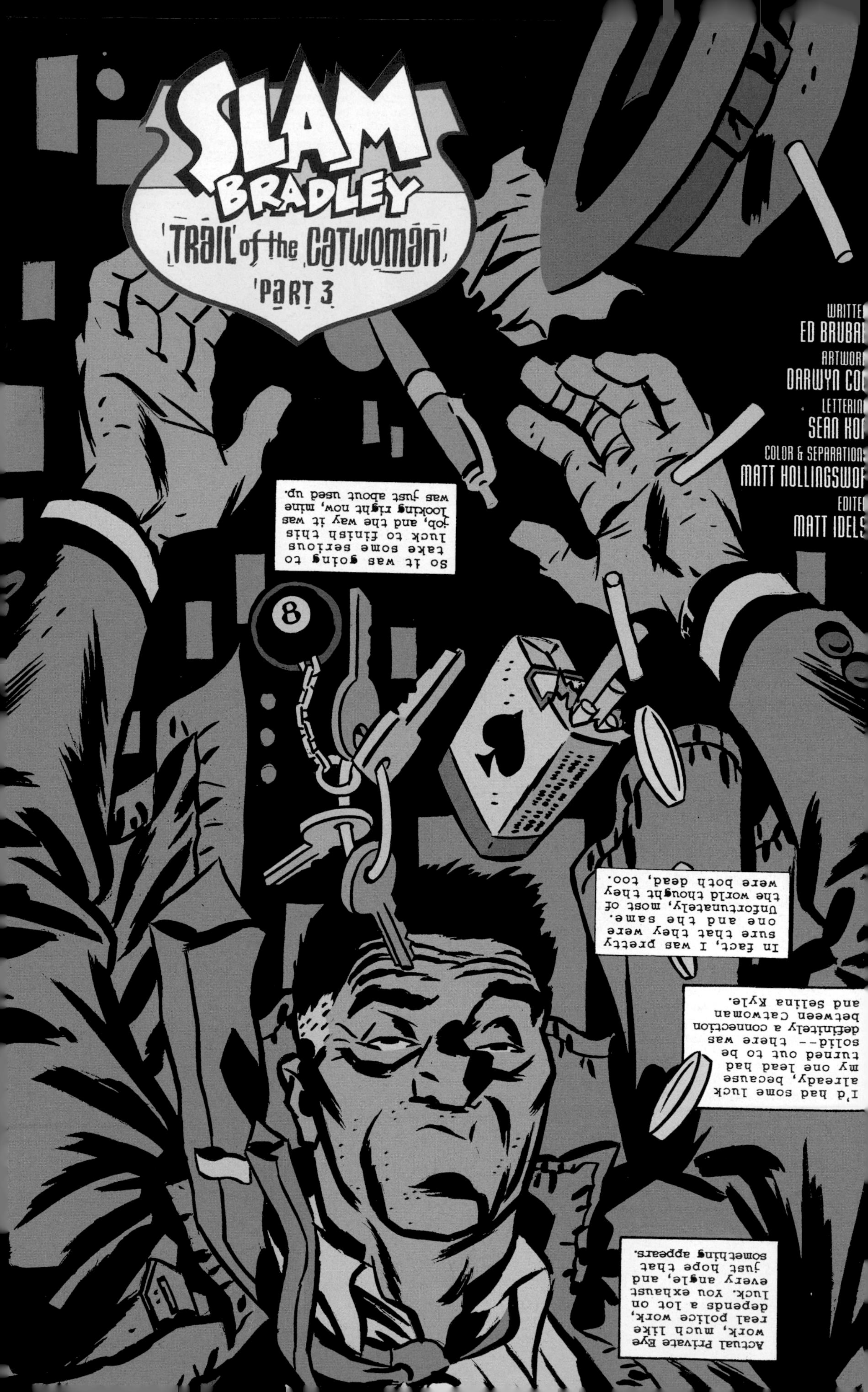
SLAM BRADLEY
TRAIL of the CATWOMAN
PART 3
WRITTE
ED BRUBA
ARTWOR
DARWYN CO
LETTERIN
SEAN KO
COLOR & SEPARATION:
MATT HOLLINGSWO
EDITE
MATT IDELS
Actual private Eye work, much like real police work, depends a lot on luck. you exhaust every angle, and just hope that something appears.
I'd had some luck already, because my one lead had turned out to be solid-- there was definitely a connection between Catwoman and Selina Kyle.
In fact, I was pretty sure that they were one and the same. Unfortunately, most of the world thought they were both dead, too.
So it was going to take some serious luck to finish this job, and the way it was looking right now, mine was just about used up.

Just that morning I had been in the plush offices of one of Gotham's finest citizens.

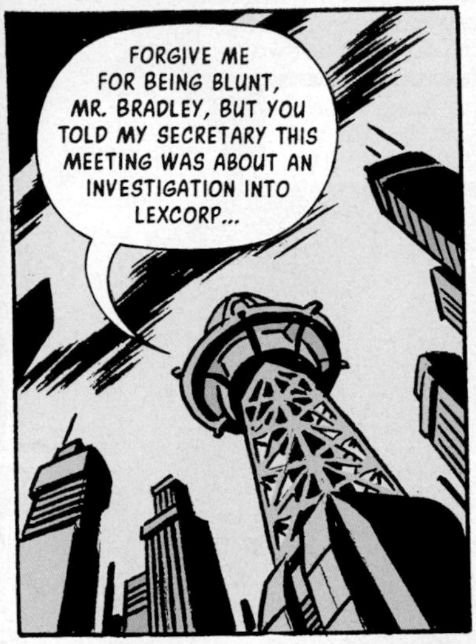
FORGIVE ME FOR BEING BLUNT, MR. BRADLEY, BUT YOU TOLD MY SECRETARY THIS MEETING WAS ABOUT AN INVESTIGATION INTO LEXCORP...

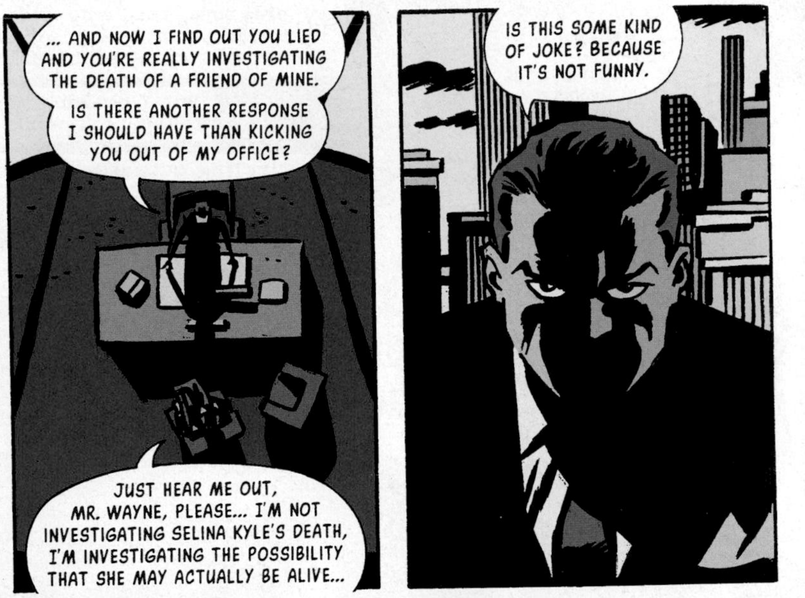
... AND NOW I FIND OUT YOU LIED AND YOU'RE REALLY INVESTIGATING THE DEATH OF A FRIEND OF MINE.
IS THERE ANOTHER RESPONSE I SHOULD HAVE THAN KICKING YOU OUT OF MY OFFICE?
JUST HEAR ME OUT, MR. WAYNE, PLEASE... I'M NOT INVESTIGATING SELINA KYLE'S DEATH, I'M INVESTIGATING THE POSSIBILITY THAT SHE MAY ACTUALLY BE ALIVE...
IS THIS SOME KIND OF JOKE? BECAUSE IT'S NOT FUNNY.

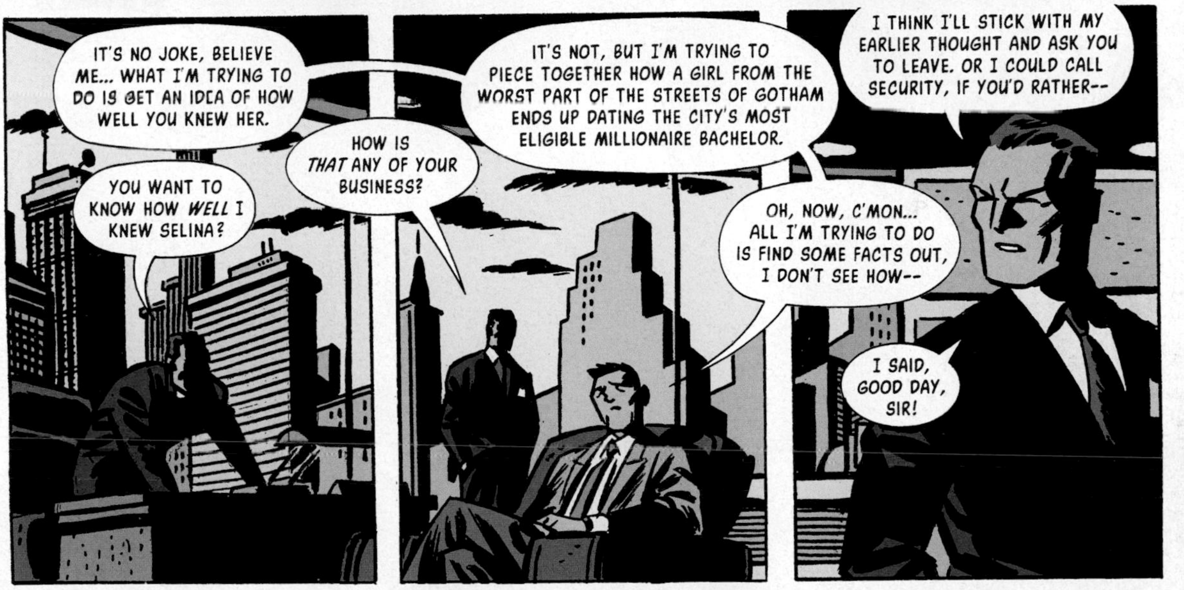
IT'S NO JOKE, BELIEVE ME... WHAT I'M TRYING TO DO IS GET AN IDEA OF HOW WELL YOU KNEW HER.
YOU WANT TO KNOW HOW *WELL* I KNEW SELINA?
HOW IS *THAT* ANY OF YOUR BUSINESS?
IT'S NOT, BUT I'M TRYING TO PIECE TOGETHER HOW A GIRL FROM THE WORST PART OF THE STREETS OF GOTHAM ENDS UP DATING THE CITY'S MOST ELIGIBLE MILLIONAIRE BACHELOR.
I THINK I'LL STICK WITH MY EARLIER THOUGHT AND ASK YOU TO LEAVE. OR I COULD CALL SECURITY, IF YOU'D RATHER--
OH, NOW, C'MON... ALL I'M TRYING TO DO IS FIND SOME FACTS OUT, I DON'T SEE HOW--
I SAID, GOOD DAY, SIR!

I wasn't expecting Wayne to clam up like that, it didn't fit in with the laid-back playboy image I was so used to with him. Maybe he'd been closer to Selina than I thought.

And while my mind was on Wayne, I bumped into a friend.

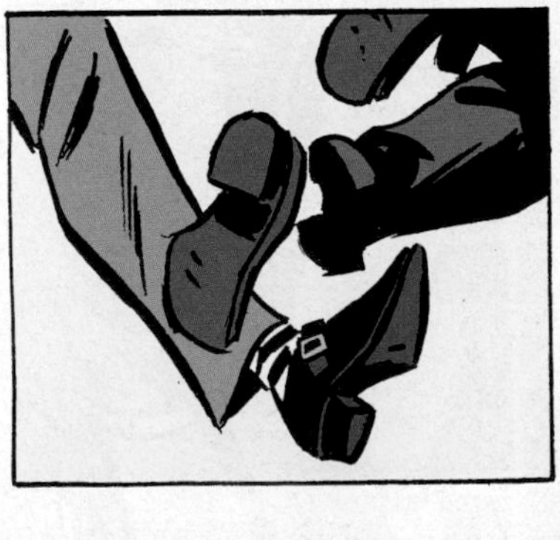

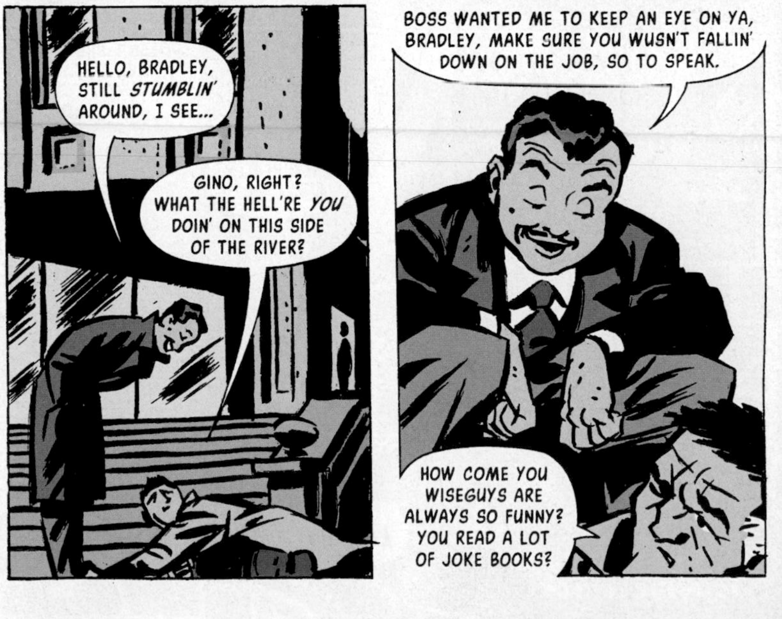
HELLO, BRADLEY, STILL *STUMBLIN'* AROUND, I SEE...
GINO, RIGHT? WHAT THE HELL'RE *YOU* DOIN' ON THIS SIDE OF THE RIVER?
BOSS WANTED ME TO KEEP AN EYE ON YA, BRADLEY, MAKE SURE YOU WUSN'T FALLIN' DOWN ON THE JOB, SO TO SPEAK.
HOW COME YOU WISEGUYS ARE ALWAYS SO FUNNY? YOU READ A LOT OF JOKE BOOKS?

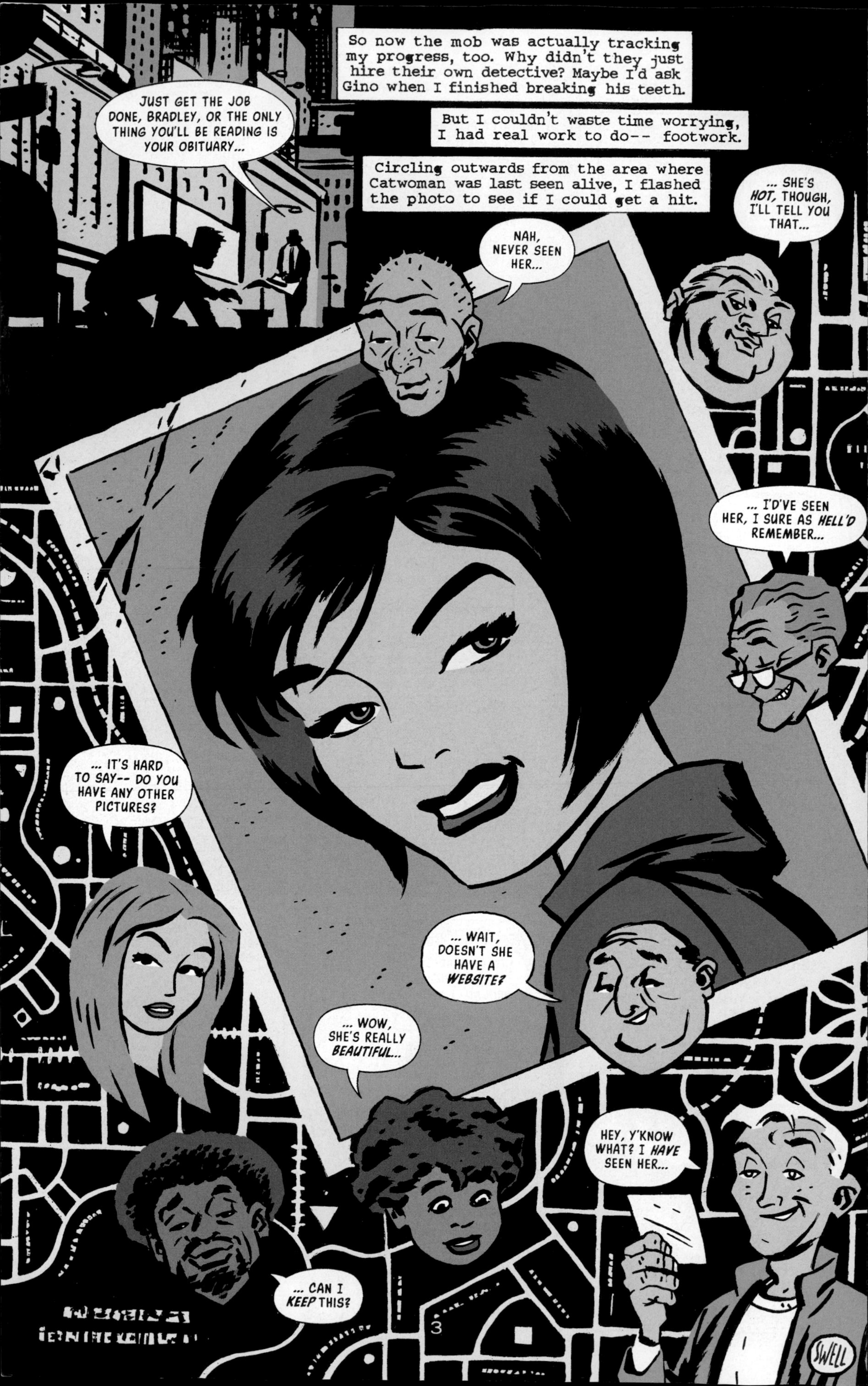
So now the mob was actually tracking my progress, too. Why didn't they just hire their own detective? Maybe I'd ask Gino when I finished breaking his teeth.
JUST GET THE JOB DONE, BRADLEY, OR THE ONLY THING YOU'LL BE READING IS YOUR OBITUARY...
But I couldn't waste time worrying, I had real work to do-- footwork.
Circling outwards from the area where Catwoman was last seen alive, I flashed the photo to see if I could get a hit.
NAH, NEVER SEEN HER...
... SHE'S HOT, THOUGH, I'LL TELL YOU THAT...
... I'D'VE SEEN HER, I SURE AS HELL'D REMEMBER...
... IT'S HARD TO SAY-- DO YOU HAVE ANY OTHER PICTURES?
... WAIT, DOESN'T SHE HAVE A WEBSITE?
... WOW, SHE'S REALLY BEAUTIFUL...
HEY, Y'KNOW WHAT? I HAVE SEEN HER...
... CAN I KEEP THIS?
SWELL

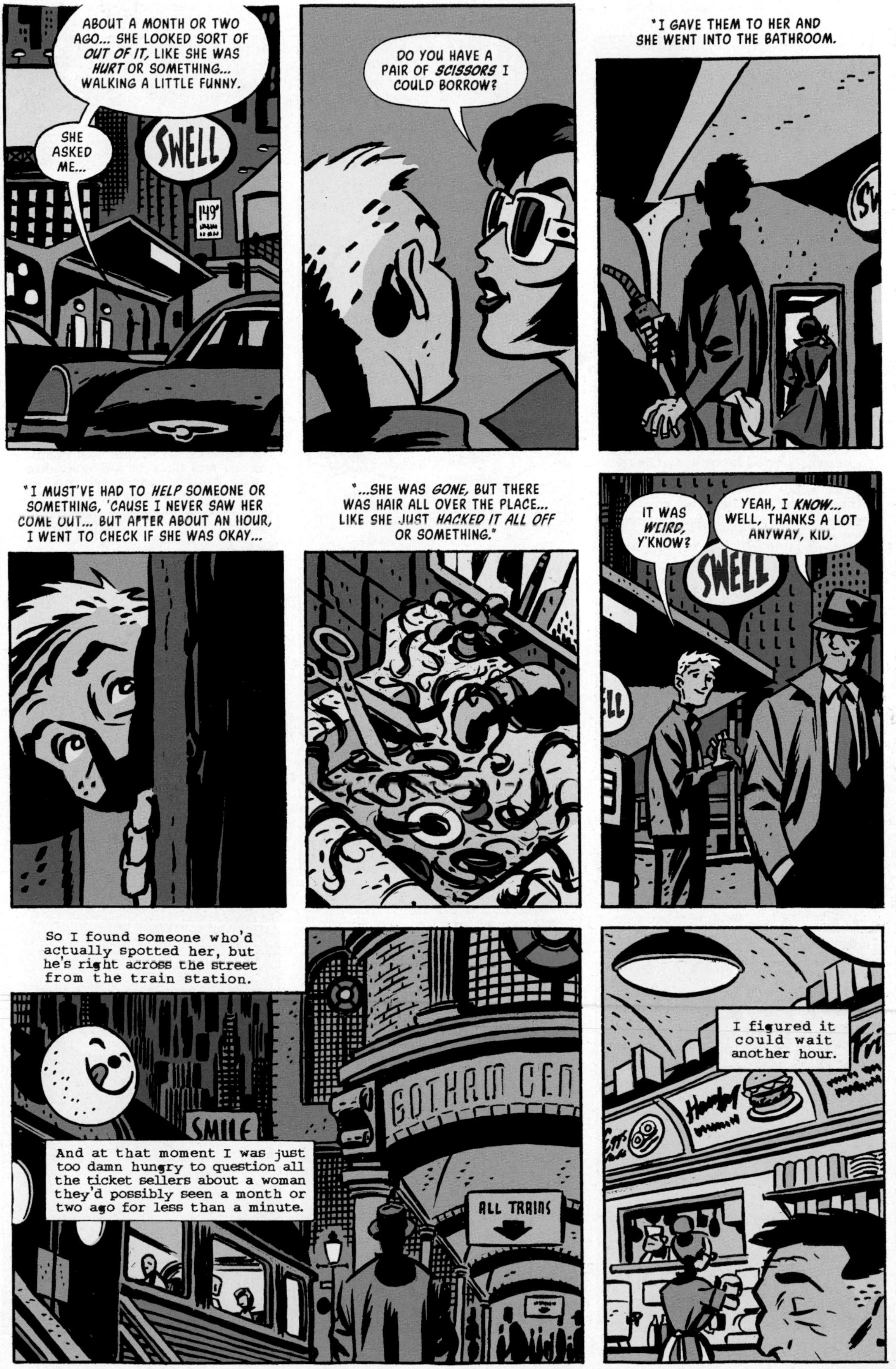

ABOUT A MONTH OR TWO AGO... SHE LOOKED SORT OF *OUT OF IT,* LIKE SHE WAS *HURT* OR SOMETHING... WALKING A LITTLE FUNNY.
SHE ASKED ME...
SWELL
149⁹
DO YOU HAVE A PAIR OF *SCISSORS* I COULD BORROW?
"I GAVE THEM TO HER AND SHE WENT INTO THE BATHROOM.
"I MUST'VE HAD TO *HELP* SOMEONE OR SOMETHING, 'CAUSE I NEVER SAW HER COME OUT... BUT AFTER ABOUT AN HOUR, I WENT TO CHECK IF SHE WAS OKAY...
"...SHE WAS *GONE,* BUT THERE WAS HAIR ALL OVER THE PLACE... LIKE SHE JUST *HACKED IT ALL OFF* OR SOMETHING."
IT WAS *WEIRD,* Y'KNOW?
SWELL
YEAH, I *KNOW*... WELL, THANKS A LOT ANYWAY, KID.
So I found someone who'd actually spotted her, but he's right across the street from the train station.
SMILE
And at that moment I was just too damn hungry to question all the ticket sellers about a woman they'd possibly seen a month or two ago for less than a minute.
GOTHAM CEN
ALL TRAINS
I figured it could wait another hour.

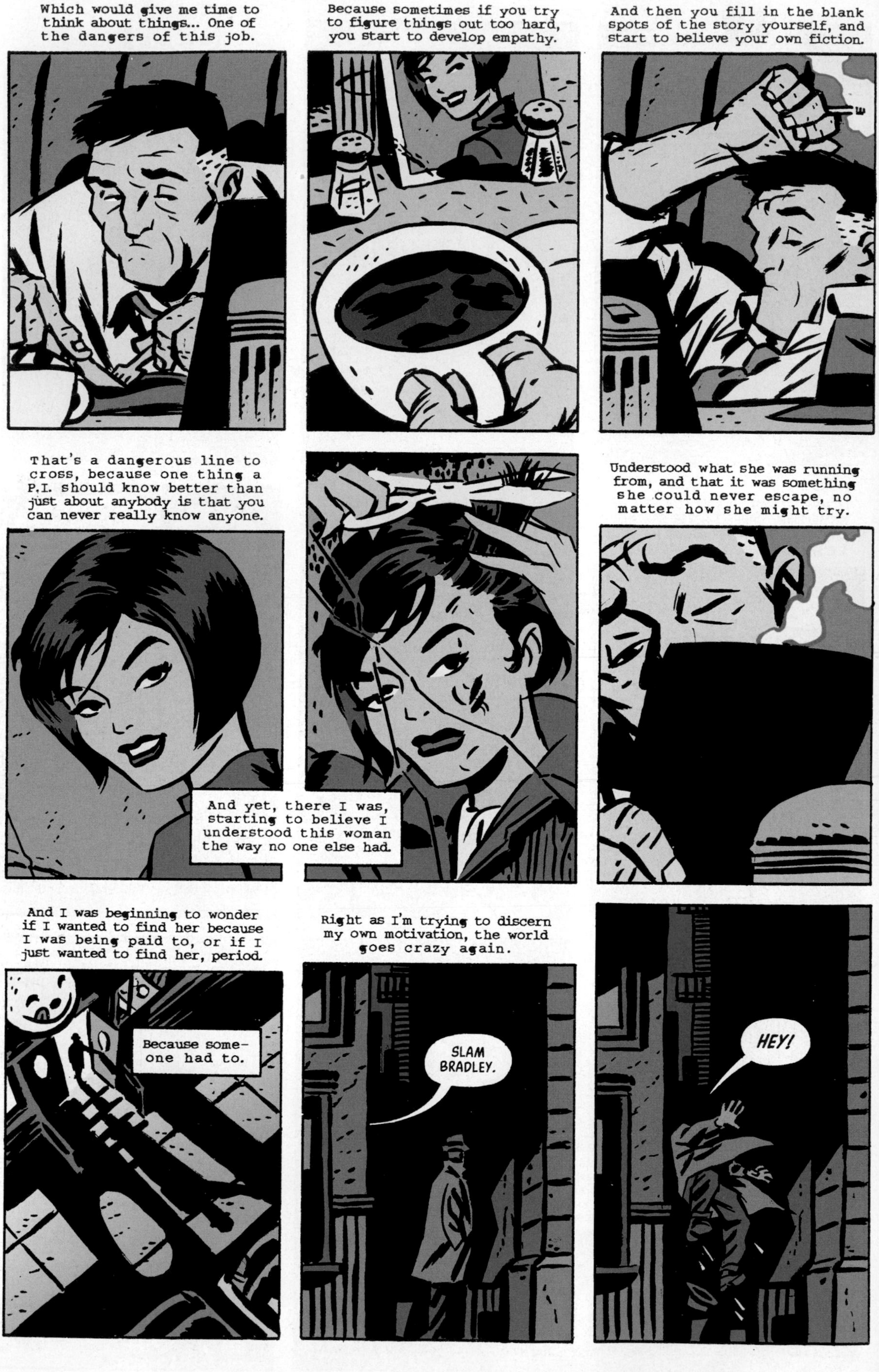
Which would give me time to think about things... One of the dangers of this job.
Because sometimes if you try to figure things out too hard, you start to develop empathy.
And then you fill in the blank spots of the story yourself, and start to believe your own fiction.
That's a dangerous line to cross, because one thing a P.I. should know better than just about anybody is that you can never really know anyone.
And yet, there I was, starting to believe I understood this woman the way no one else had.
Understood what she was running from, and that it was something she could never escape, no matter how she might try.
And I was beginning to wonder if I wanted to find her because I was being paid to, or if I just wanted to find her, period.
Because someone had to.
Right as I'm trying to discern my own motivation, the world goes crazy again.
SLAM BRADLEY.
HEY!

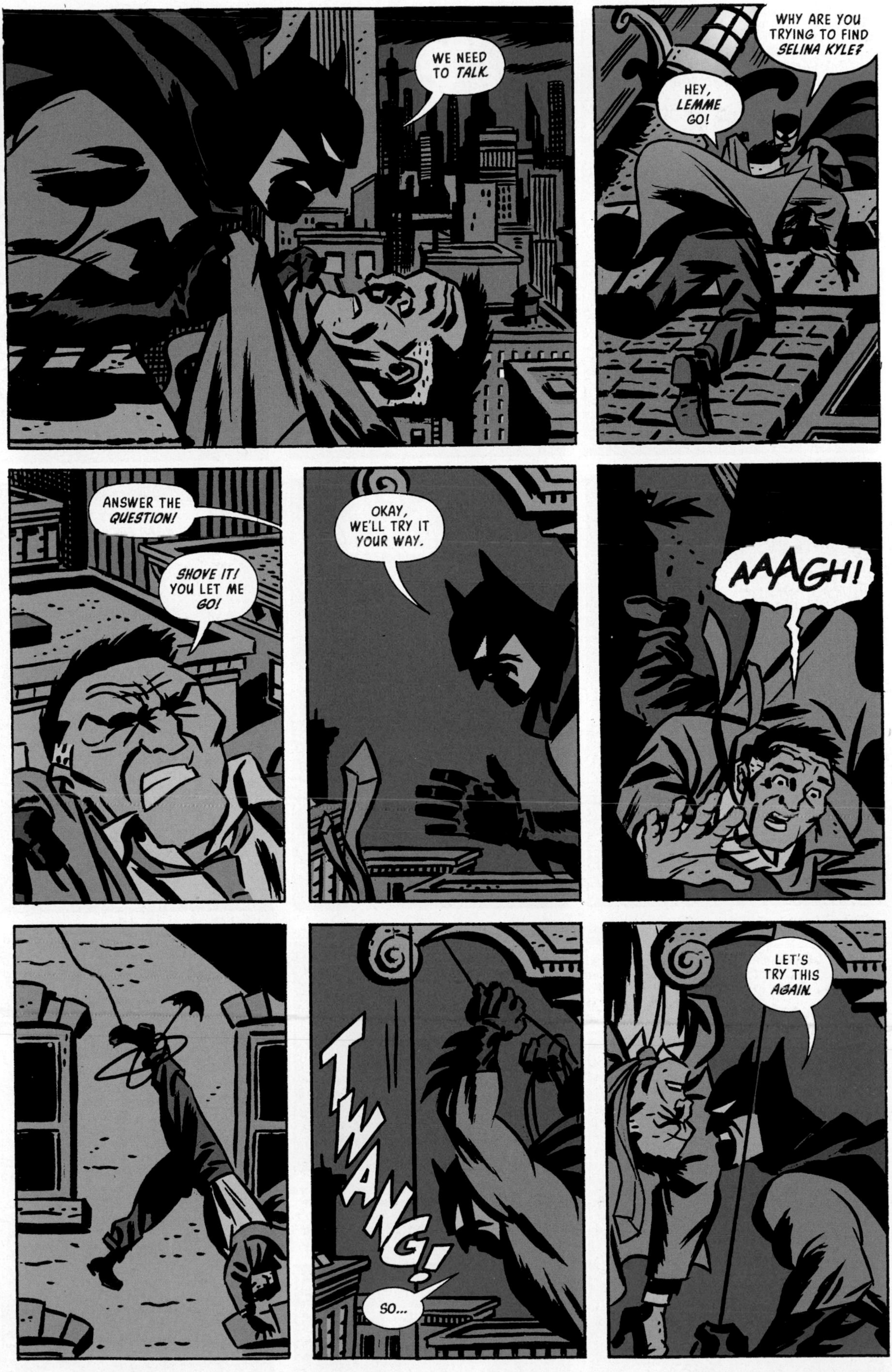
WE NEED TO TALK.
HEY, LEMME GO!
WHY ARE YOU TRYING TO FIND SELINA KYLE?
ANSWER THE QUESTION!
SHOVE IT! YOU LET ME GO!
OKAY, WE'LL TRY IT YOUR WAY.
AAAGH!
TWANG!
SO...
LET'S TRY THIS AGAIN.

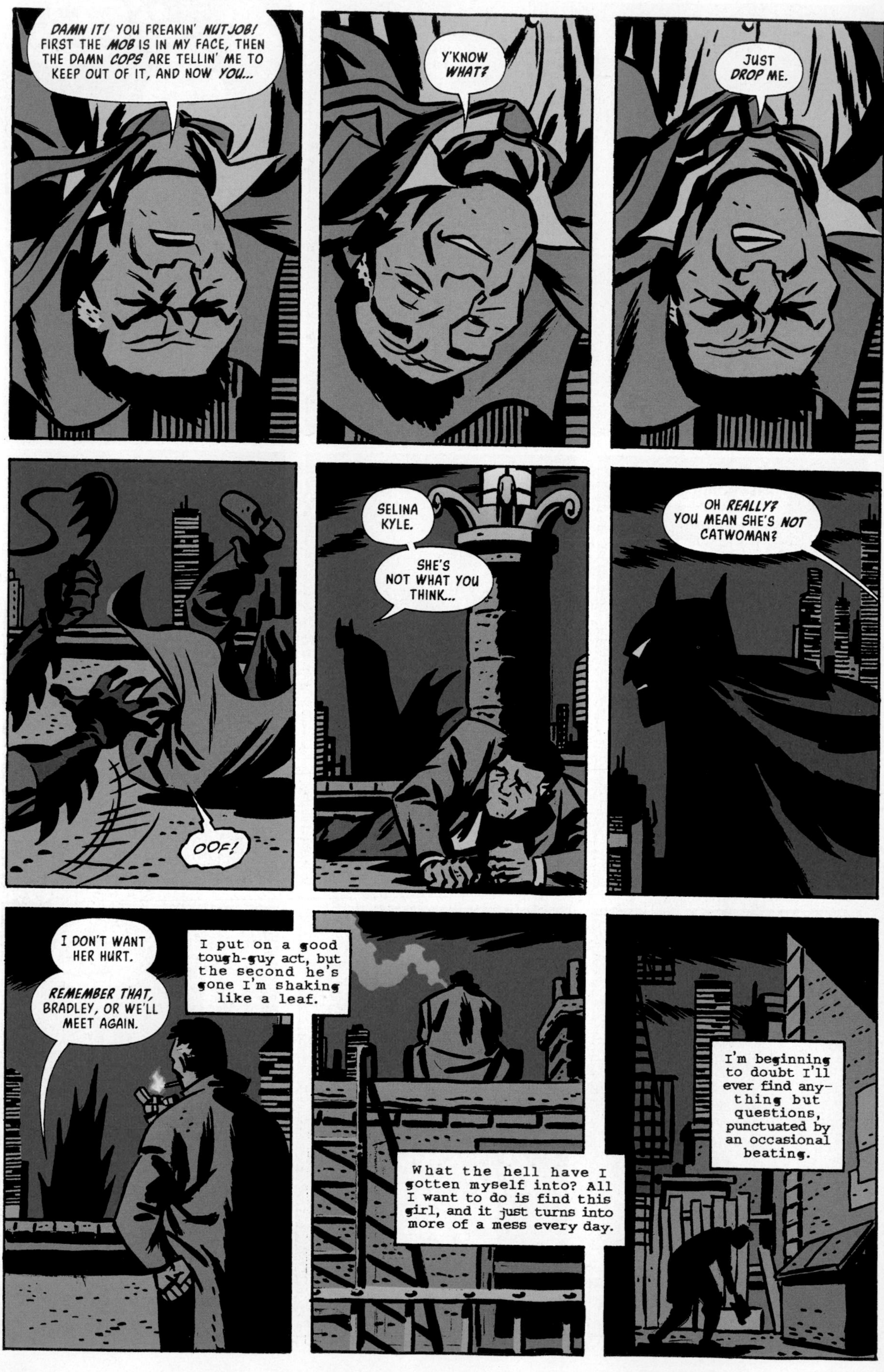
DAMN IT! YOU FREAKIN' NUTJOB! FIRST THE MOB IS IN MY FACE, THEN THE DAMN COPS ARE TELLIN' ME TO KEEP OUT OF IT, AND NOW YOU...
Y'KNOW WHAT?
JUST DROP ME.
OOF!
SELINA KYLE.
SHE'S NOT WHAT YOU THINK...
OH REALLY? YOU MEAN SHE'S NOT CATWOMAN?
I DON'T WANT HER HURT.
REMEMBER THAT, BRADLEY, OR WE'LL MEET AGAIN.
I put on a good tough-guy act, but the second he's gone I'm shaking like a leaf.
What the hell have I gotten myself into? All I want to do is find this girl, and it just turns into more of a mess every day.
I'm beginning to doubt I'll ever find anything but questions, punctuated by an occasional beating.

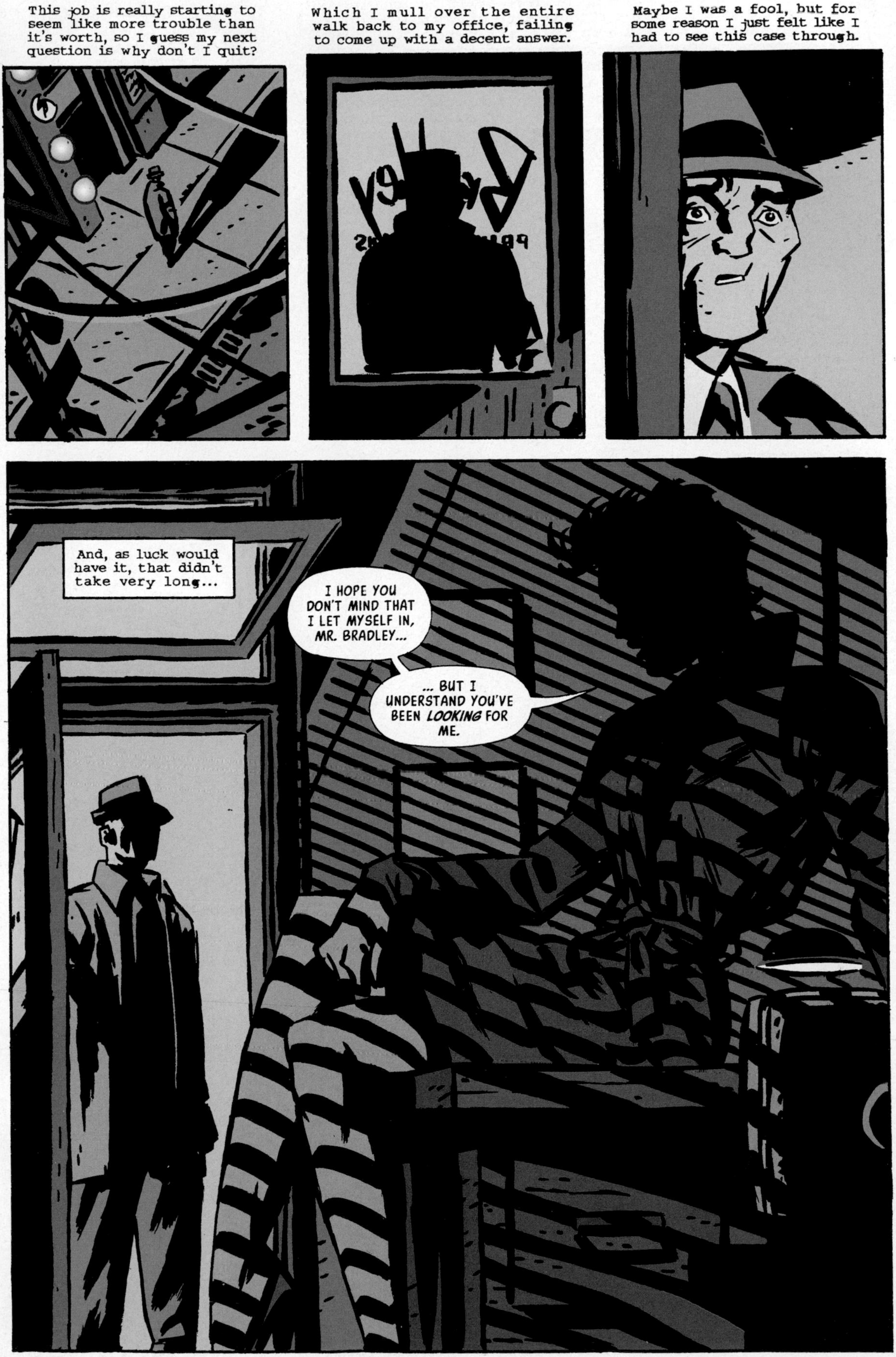
This job is really starting to seem like more trouble than it's worth, so I guess my next question is why don't I quit?
Which I mull over the entire walk back to my office, failing to come up with a decent answer.
Maybe I was a fool, but for some reason I just felt like I had to see this case through.
And, as luck would have it, that didn't take very long...
I HOPE YOU DON'T MIND THAT I LET MYSELF IN, MR. BRADLEY...
... BUT I UNDERSTAND YOU'VE BEEN *LOOKING* FOR ME.

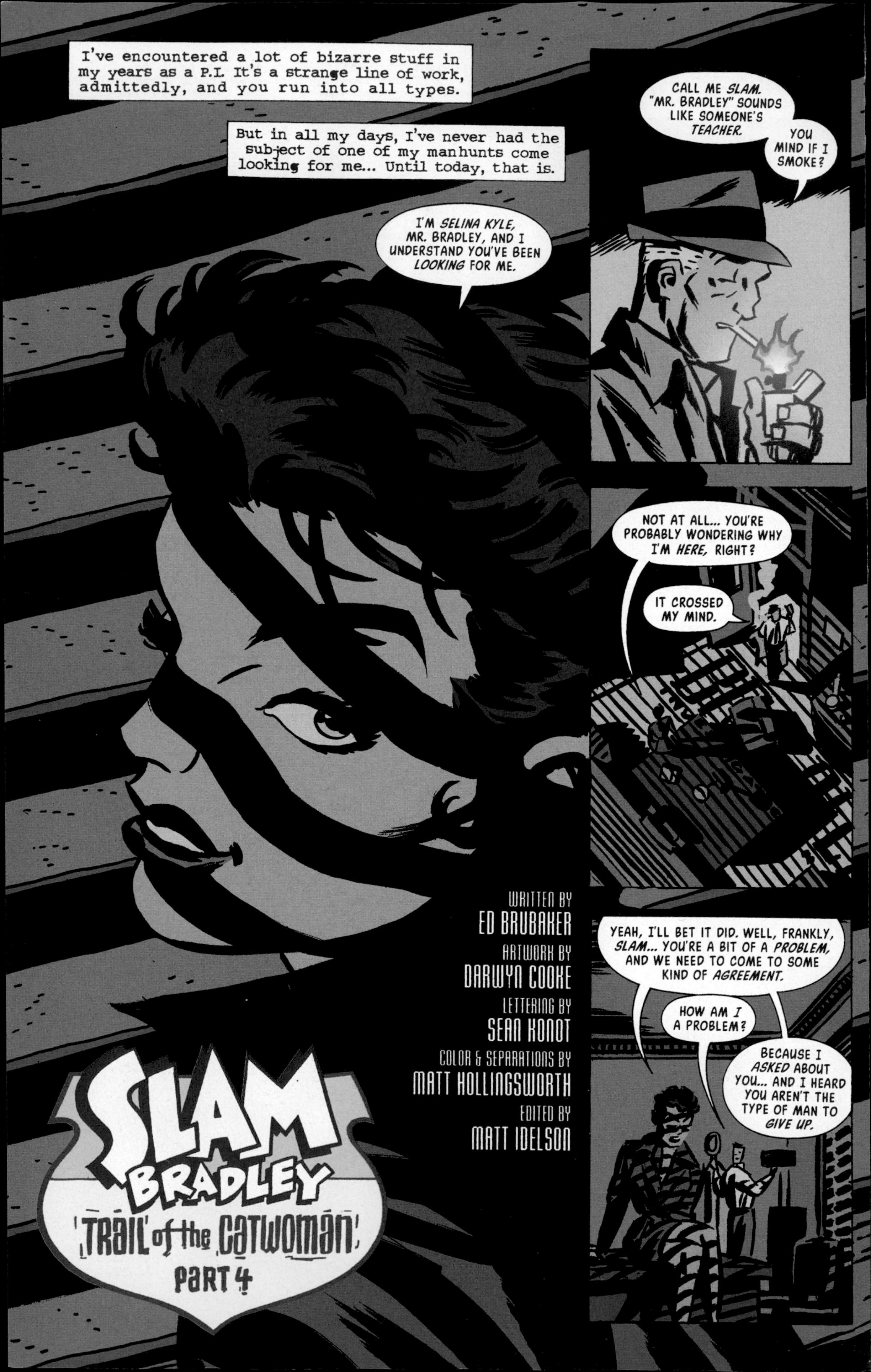

I've encountered a lot of bizarre stuff in my years as a P.I. It's a strange line of work, admittedly, and you run into all types.
But in all my days, I've never had the subject of one of my manhunts come looking for me... Until today, that is.
I'M SELINA KYLE, MR. BRADLEY, AND I UNDERSTAND YOU'VE BEEN LOOKING FOR ME.
CALL ME SLAM. "MR. BRADLEY" SOUNDS LIKE SOMEONE'S TEACHER.
YOU MIND IF I SMOKE?
NOT AT ALL... YOU'RE PROBABLY WONDERING WHY I'M HERE, RIGHT?
IT CROSSED MY MIND.
WRITTEN BY ED BRUBAKER
ARTWORK BY DARWYN COOKE
LETTERING BY SEAN KONOT
COLOR & SEPARATIONS BY MATT HOLLINGSWORTH
EDITED BY MATT IDELSON
SLAM BRADLEY
TRAIL of the CATWOMAN
PART 4
YEAH, I'LL BET IT DID. WELL, FRANKLY, SLAM... YOU'RE A BIT OF A PROBLEM, AND WE NEED TO COME TO SOME KIND OF AGREEMENT.
HOW AM I A PROBLEM?
BECAUSE I ASKED ABOUT YOU... AND I HEARD YOU AREN'T THE TYPE OF MAN TO GIVE UP.

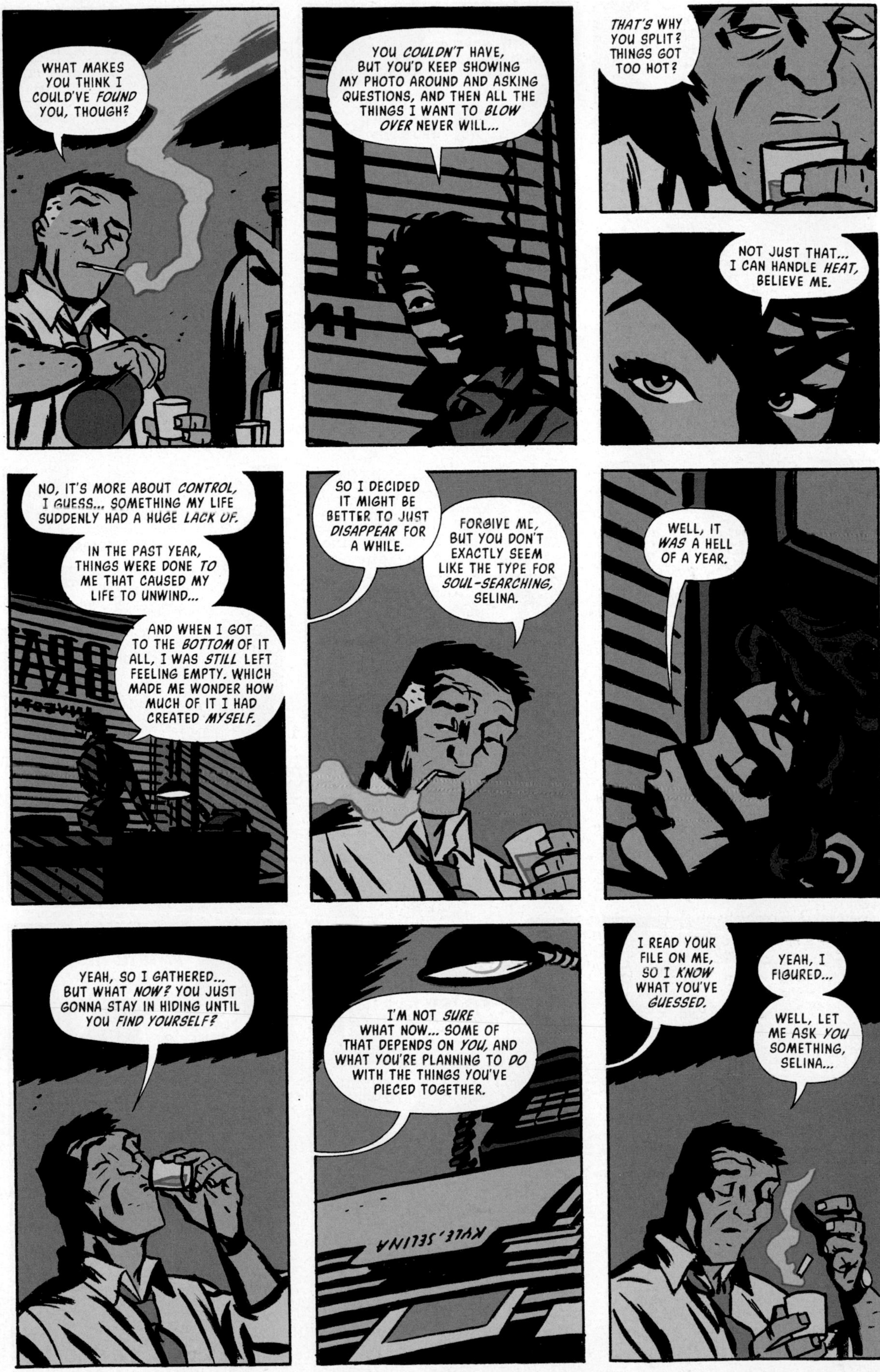
WHAT MAKES YOU THINK I COULD'VE *FOUND* YOU, THOUGH?
YOU *COULDN'T* HAVE, BUT YOU'D KEEP SHOWING MY PHOTO AROUND AND ASKING QUESTIONS, AND THEN ALL THE THINGS I WANT TO *BLOW OVER* NEVER WILL...
THAT'S WHY YOU SPLIT? THINGS GOT TOO HOT?
NOT JUST THAT... I CAN HANDLE *HEAT,* BELIEVE ME.
NO, IT'S MORE ABOUT *CONTROL,* I GUESS... SOMETHING MY LIFE SUDDENLY HAD A HUGE *LACK OF.*
IN THE PAST YEAR, THINGS WERE DONE *TO* ME THAT CAUSED MY LIFE TO UNWIND...
AND WHEN I GOT TO THE *BOTTOM* OF IT ALL, I WAS *STILL* LEFT FEELING EMPTY. WHICH MADE ME WONDER HOW MUCH OF IT I HAD CREATED *MYSELF.*
SO I DECIDED IT MIGHT BE BETTER TO JUST *DISAPPEAR* FOR A WHILE.
FORGIVE ME, BUT YOU DON'T EXACTLY SEEM LIKE THE TYPE FOR *SOUL-SEARCHING,* SELINA.
WELL, IT *WAS* A HELL OF A YEAR.
YEAH, SO I GATHERED... BUT WHAT *NOW?* YOU JUST GONNA STAY IN HIDING UNTIL YOU *FIND YOURSELF?*
I'M NOT *SURE* WHAT NOW... SOME OF THAT DEPENDS ON *YOU,* AND WHAT YOU'RE PLANNING TO *DO* WITH THE THINGS YOU'VE PIECED TOGETHER.
KYLE, SELINA
I READ YOUR FILE ON ME, SO I *KNOW* WHAT YOU'VE *GUESSED.*
YEAH, I FIGURED...
WELL, LET ME ASK *YOU* SOMETHING, SELINA...

YOU SAY YOU'RE TRYING TO FIGURE THINGS OUT, AND AFTER ALL I KNOW ABOUT YOU, YOU DESERVE THE *CHANCE,* PROBABLY...

... BUT A WHILE BACK, YOU *KILLED OFF* SELINA KYLE...

... AND A FEW *MONTHS* AGO, YOU KILLED CATWOMAN, TOO...

... SO, THE *QUESTION* IS-- WHO'S LEFT FOR YOU TO *FIND?*

I DON'T *KNOW.* HOPEFULLY SOMEONE WHO CAN LOOK IN THE MIRROR WITHOUT ANY PAIN.

BUT, AS I SAID, SOME OF IT'S UP TO *YOU,* SLAM-- AND WHAT YOU INTEND TO TELL THE *MAYOR.*

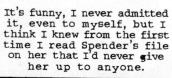

It's funny, I never admitted it, even to myself, but I think I knew from the first time I read Spender's file on her that I'd never give her up to anyone.

THEN I GUESS YOU SHOULD *KNOW* THAT I'M *RESIGNING* FROM THIS CASE TOMORROW. IT'S TOO MUCH *TROUBLE* TRYING TO FIND SOMEONE WHO'S *CLEARLY* DECEASED.

AND THE *FILE?*

WHAT FILE?

YOU'RE A VERY UNPREDICTABLE MAN, SLAM BRADLEY...

WHAT? DID'JA THINK YOU'D HAVE'TA *ROUGH* ME UP?

IT CROSSED MY MIND.

MAYBE I'LL SEE YOU AROUND SOMETIME.

YEAH, *MAYBE.* I'D LIKE THAT.

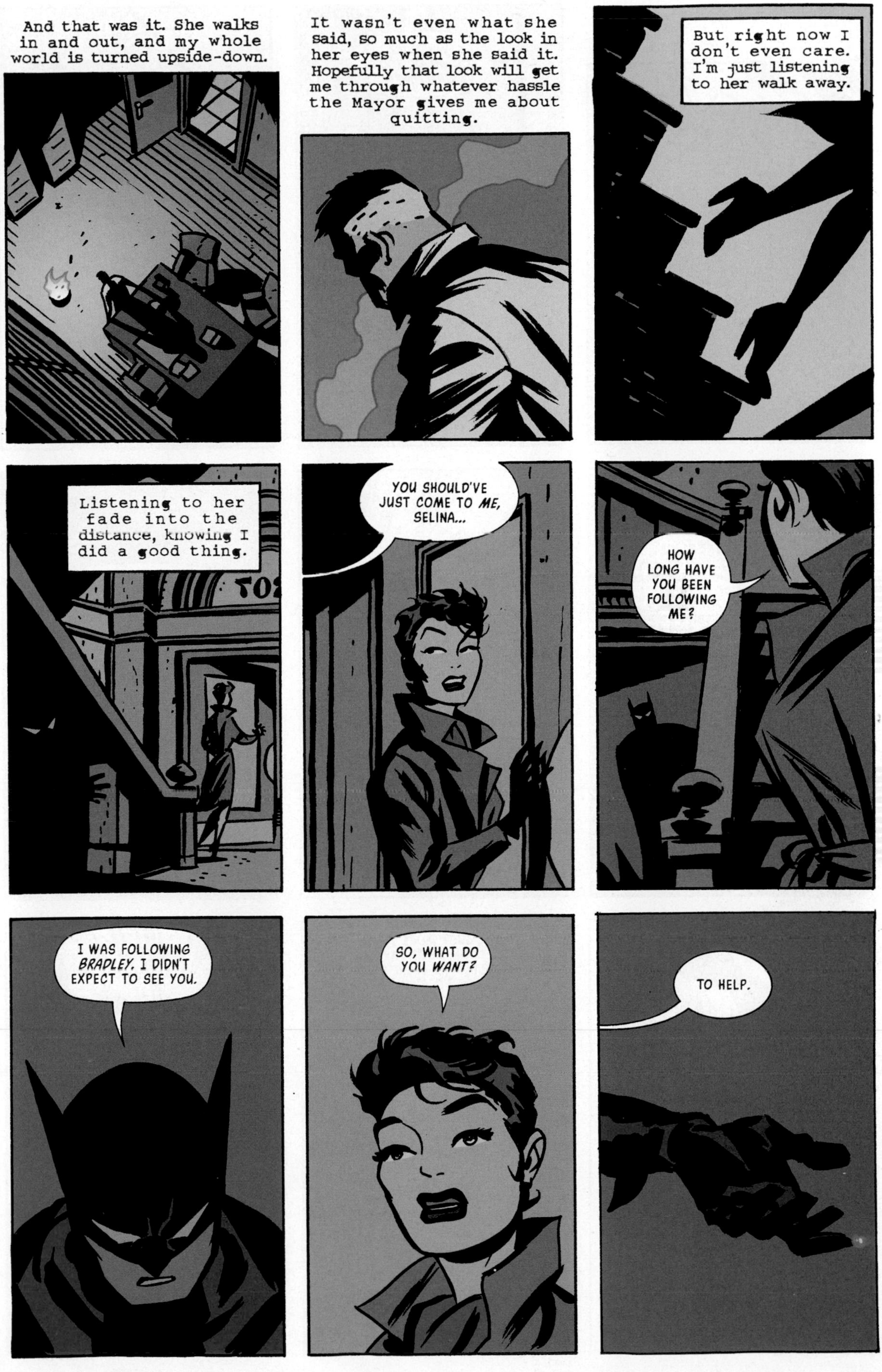
And that was it. She walks in and out, and my whole world is turned upside-down.
It wasn't even what she said, so much as the look in her eyes when she said it. Hopefully that look will get me through whatever hassle the Mayor gives me about quitting.
But right now I don't even care. I'm just listening to her walk away.
Listening to her fade into the distance, knowing I did a good thing.
YOU SHOULD'VE JUST COME TO ME, SELINA...
HOW LONG HAVE YOU BEEN FOLLOWING ME?
I WAS FOLLOWING BRADLEY. I DIDN'T EXPECT TO SEE YOU.
SO, WHAT DO YOU WANT?
TO HELP.

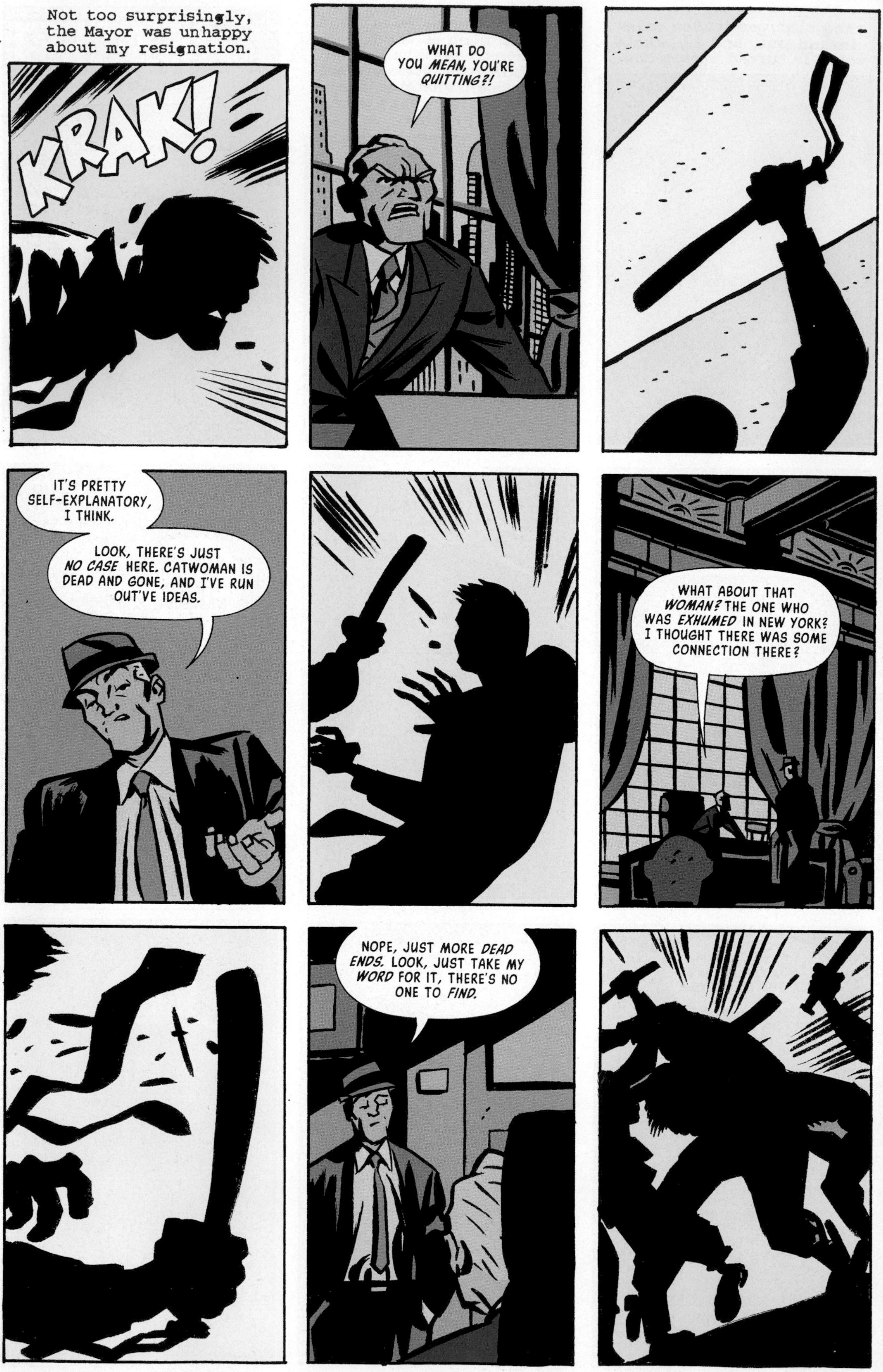
Not too surprisingly, the Mayor was unhappy about my resignation.
KRAK!
WHAT DO YOU MEAN, YOU'RE QUITTING?!
IT'S PRETTY SELF-EXPLANATORY, I THINK.
LOOK, THERE'S JUST NO CASE HERE. CATWOMAN IS DEAD AND GONE, AND I'VE RUN OUT'VE IDEAS.
WHAT ABOUT THAT WOMAN? THE ONE WHO WAS EXHUMED IN NEW YORK? I THOUGHT THERE WAS SOME CONNECTION THERE?
NOPE, JUST MORE DEAD ENDS. LOOK, JUST TAKE MY WORD FOR IT, THERE'S NO ONE TO FIND.

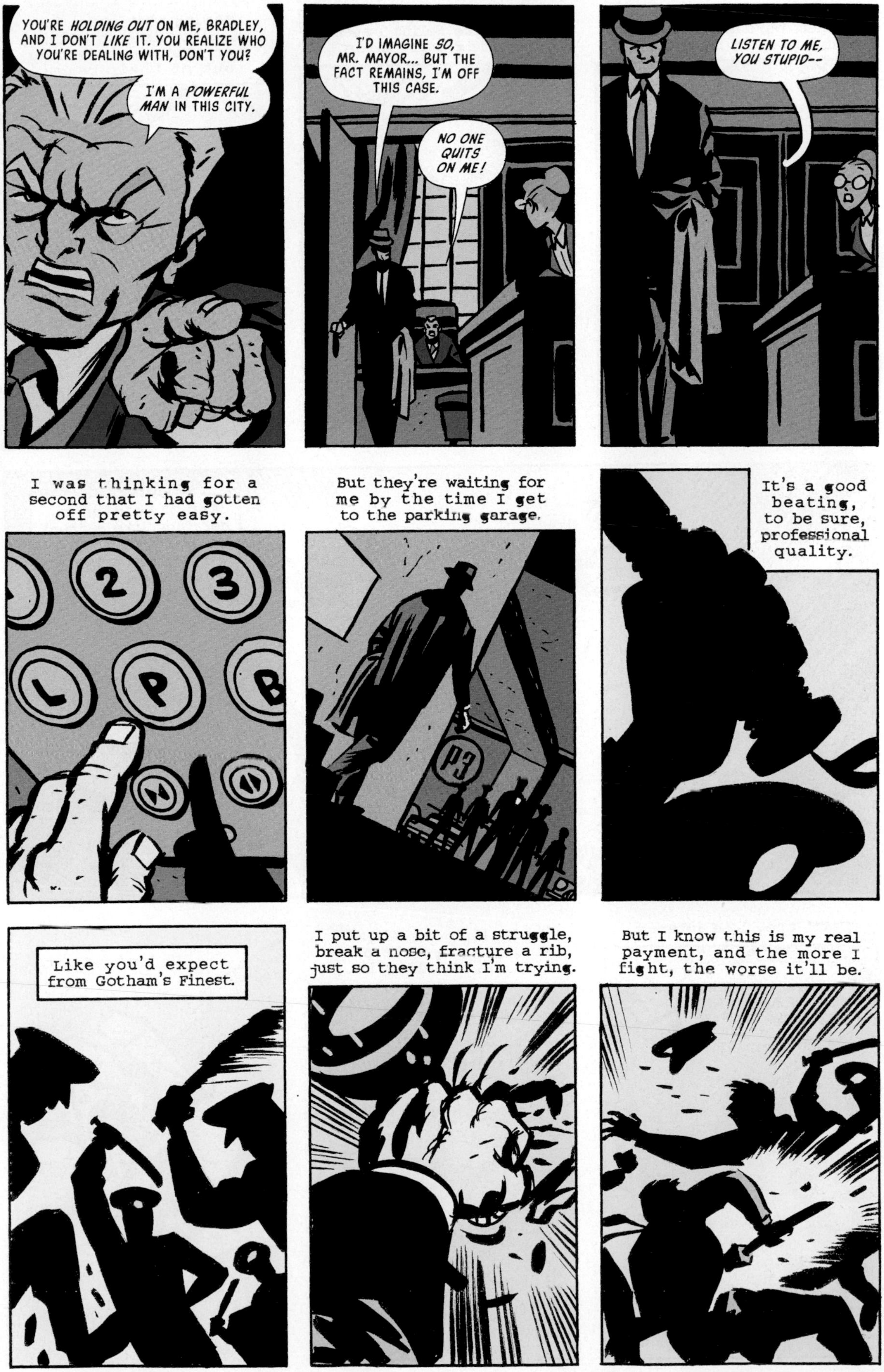
YOU'RE HOLDING OUT ON ME, BRADLEY, AND I DON'T LIKE IT. YOU REALIZE WHO YOU'RE DEALING WITH, DON'T YOU?
I'M A POWERFUL MAN IN THIS CITY.
I'D IMAGINE SO, MR. MAYOR... BUT THE FACT REMAINS, I'M OFF THIS CASE.
NO ONE QUITS ON ME!
LISTEN TO ME, YOU STUPID--
I was thinking for a second that I had gotten off pretty easy.
2
3
L
P
B
But they're waiting for me by the time I get to the parking garage.
P3
It's a good beating, to be sure, professional quality.
Like you'd expect from Gotham's Finest.
I put up a bit of a struggle, break a nose, fracture a rib, just so they think I'm trying.
But I know this is my real payment, and the more I fight, the worse it'll be.

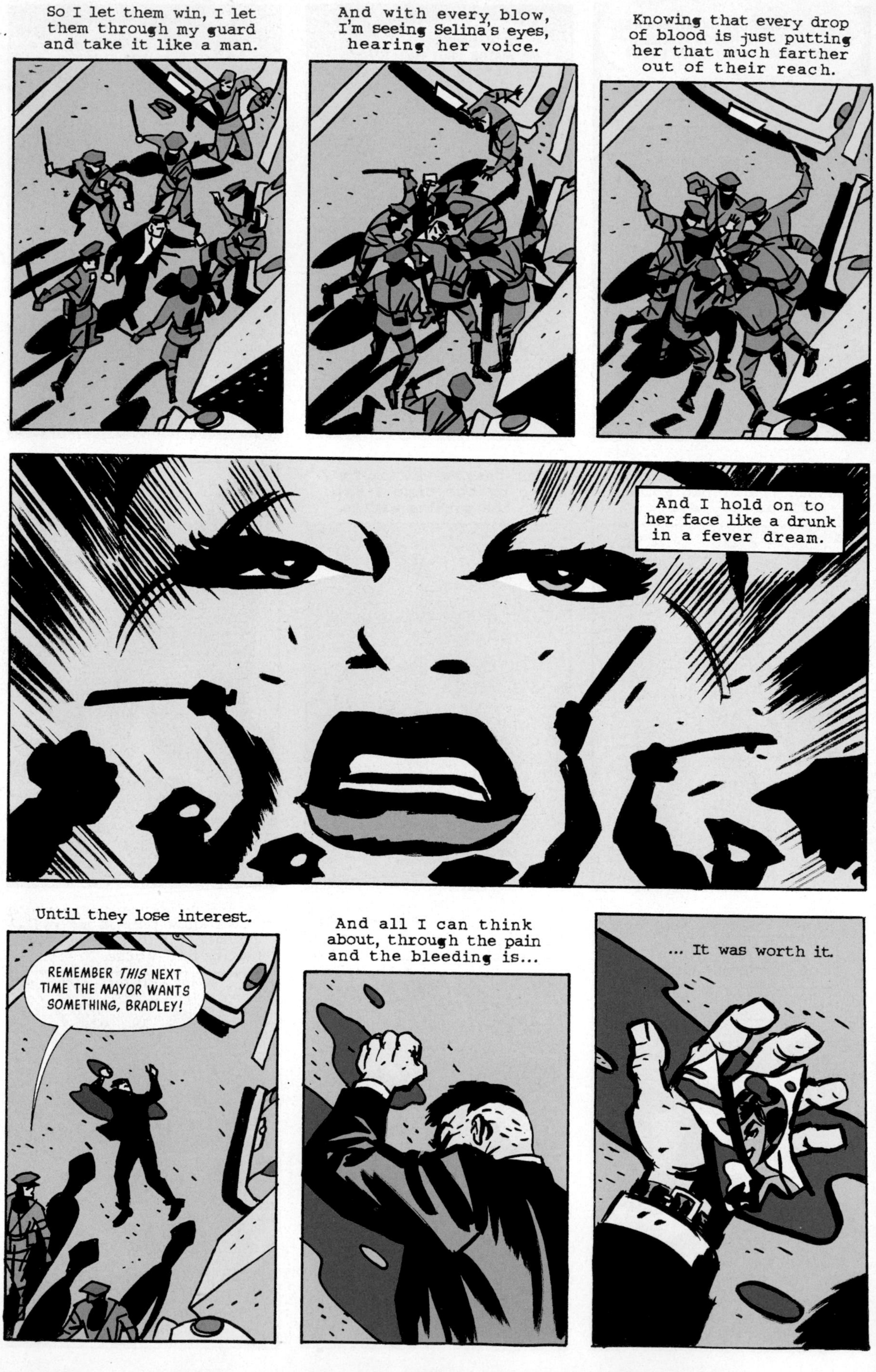
So I let them win, I let them through my guard and take it like a man.
And with every blow, I'm seeing Selina's eyes, hearing her voice.
Knowing that every drop of blood is just putting her that much farther out of their reach.
And I hold on to her face like a drunk in a fever dream.
Until they lose interest.
REMEMBER THIS NEXT TIME THE MAYOR WANTS SOMETHING, BRADLEY!
And all I can think about, through the pain and the bleeding is...
... It was worth it.

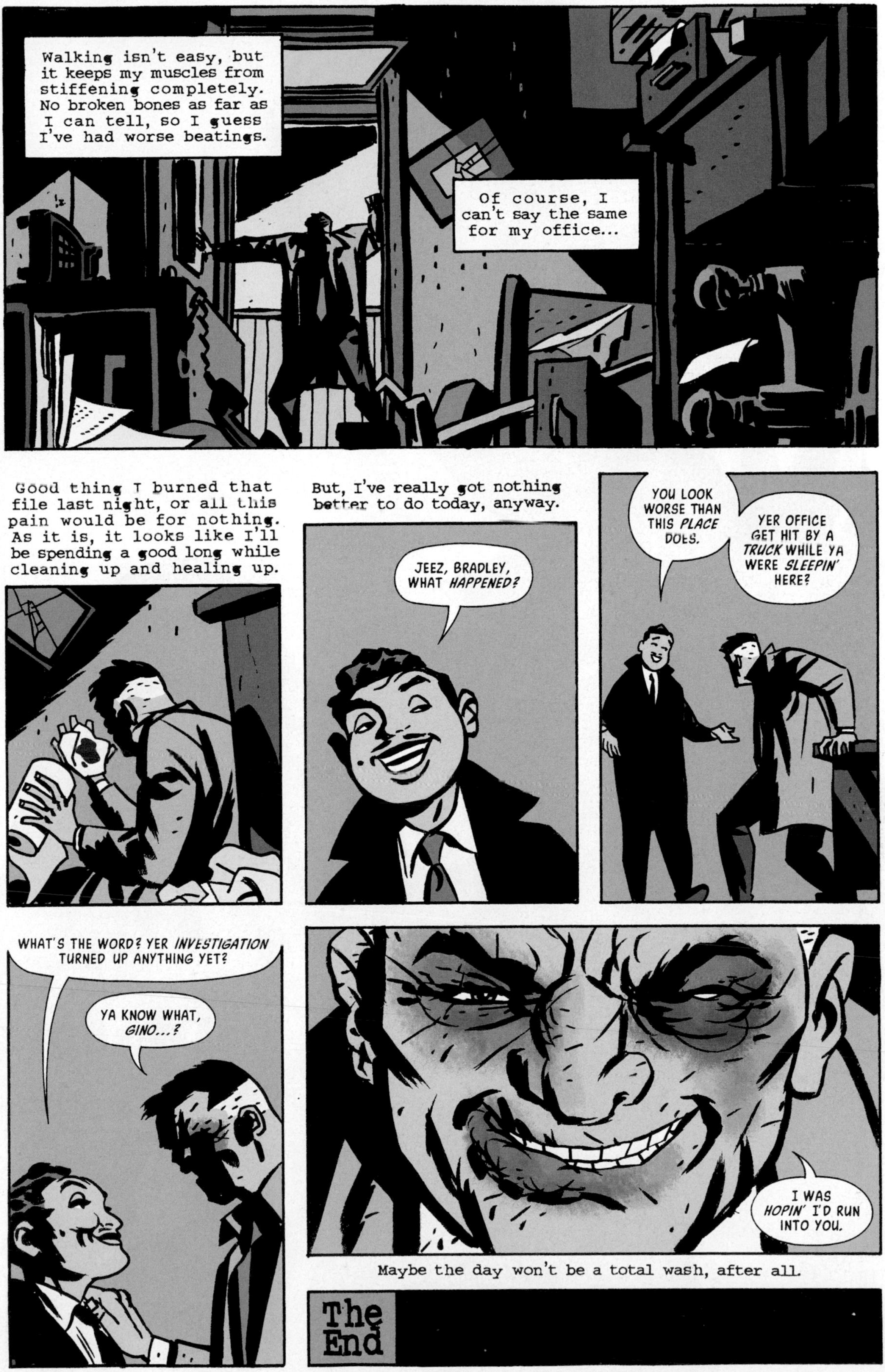
Walking isn't easy, but it keeps my muscles from stiffening completely. No broken bones as far as I can tell, so I guess I've had worse beatings.
Of course, I can't say the same for my office...
Good thing I burned that file last night, or all this pain would be for nothing. As it is, it looks like I'll be spending a good long while cleaning up and healing up.
But, I've really got nothing better to do today, anyway.
JEEZ, BRADLEY, WHAT HAPPENED?
YOU LOOK WORSE THAN THIS PLACE DOES.
YER OFFICE GET HIT BY A TRUCK WHILE YA WERE SLEEPIN' HERE?
WHAT'S THE WORD? YER INVESTIGATION TURNED UP ANYTHING YET?
YA KNOW WHAT, GINO...?
I WAS HOPIN' I'D RUN INTO YOU.
Maybe the day won't be a total wash, after all.
The End

Catwoman 1 Cover by Darwyn Cooke

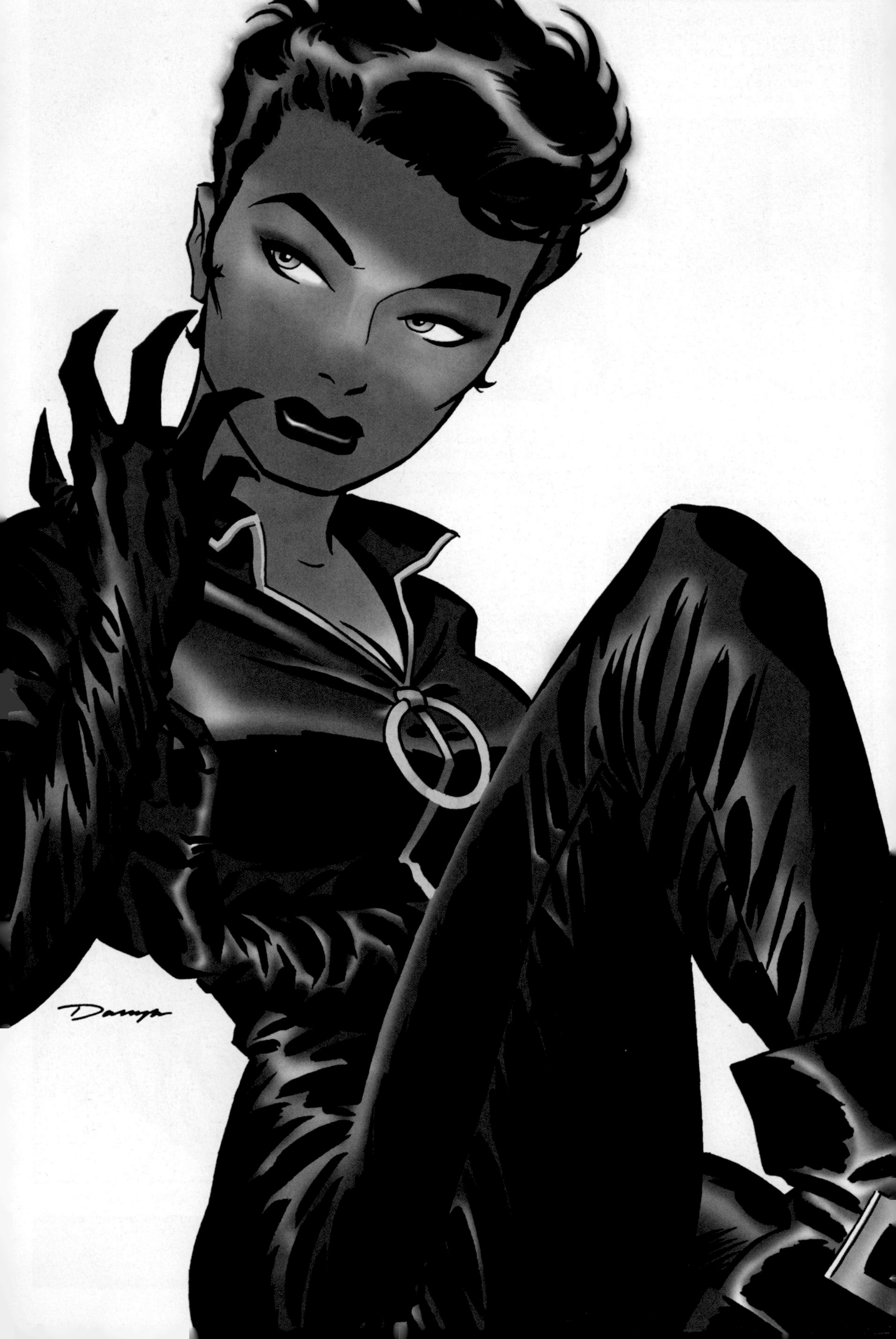
Darwyn

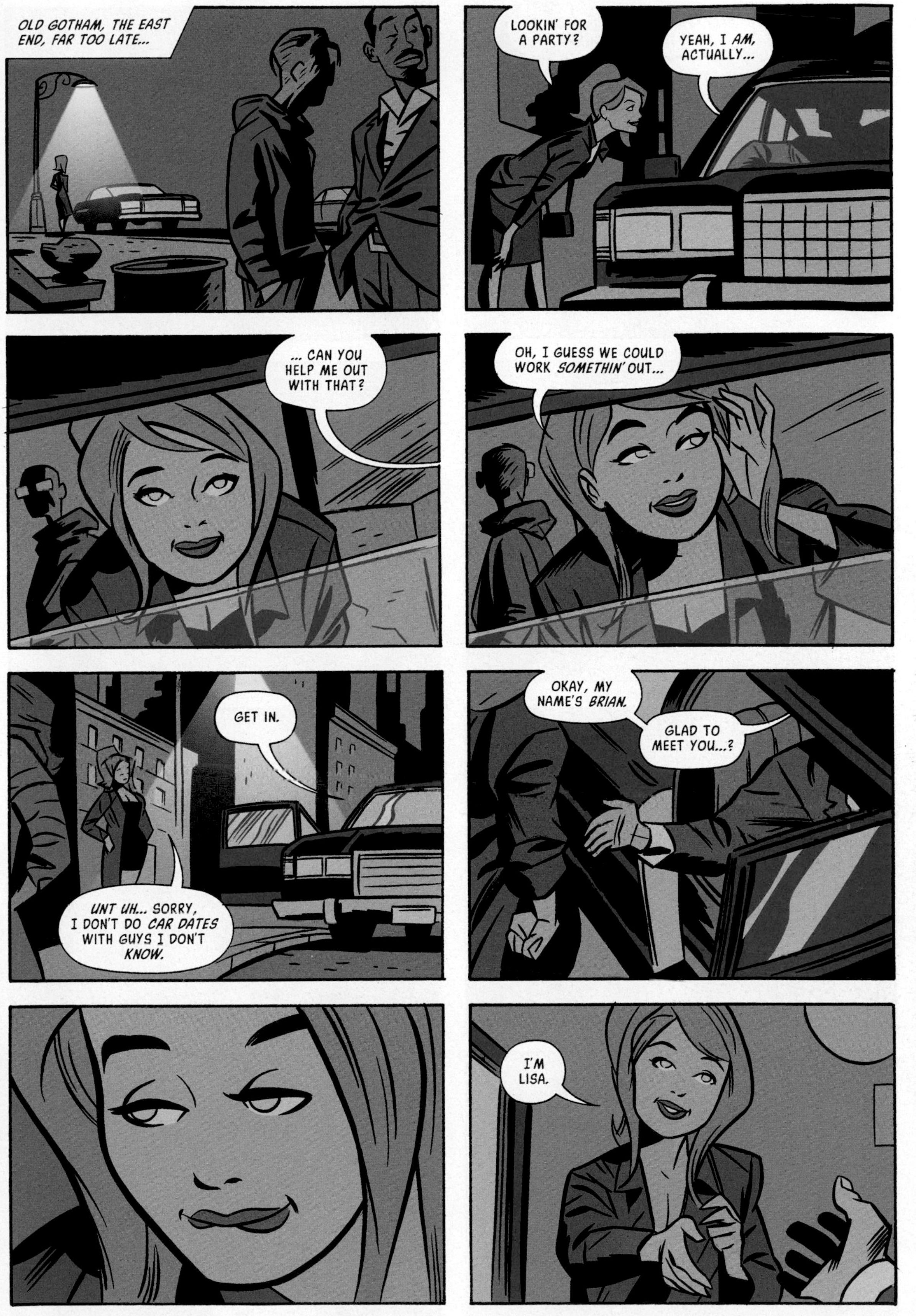
OLD GOTHAM, THE EAST END, FAR TOO LATE...
LOOKIN' FOR A PARTY?
YEAH, I AM, ACTUALLY...
... CAN YOU HELP ME OUT WITH THAT?
OH, I GUESS WE COULD WORK SOMETHIN' OUT...
GET IN.
UNT UH... SORRY, I DON'T DO CAR DATES WITH GUYS I DON'T KNOW.
OKAY, MY NAME'S BRIAN.
GLAD TO MEET YOU...?
I'M LISA.

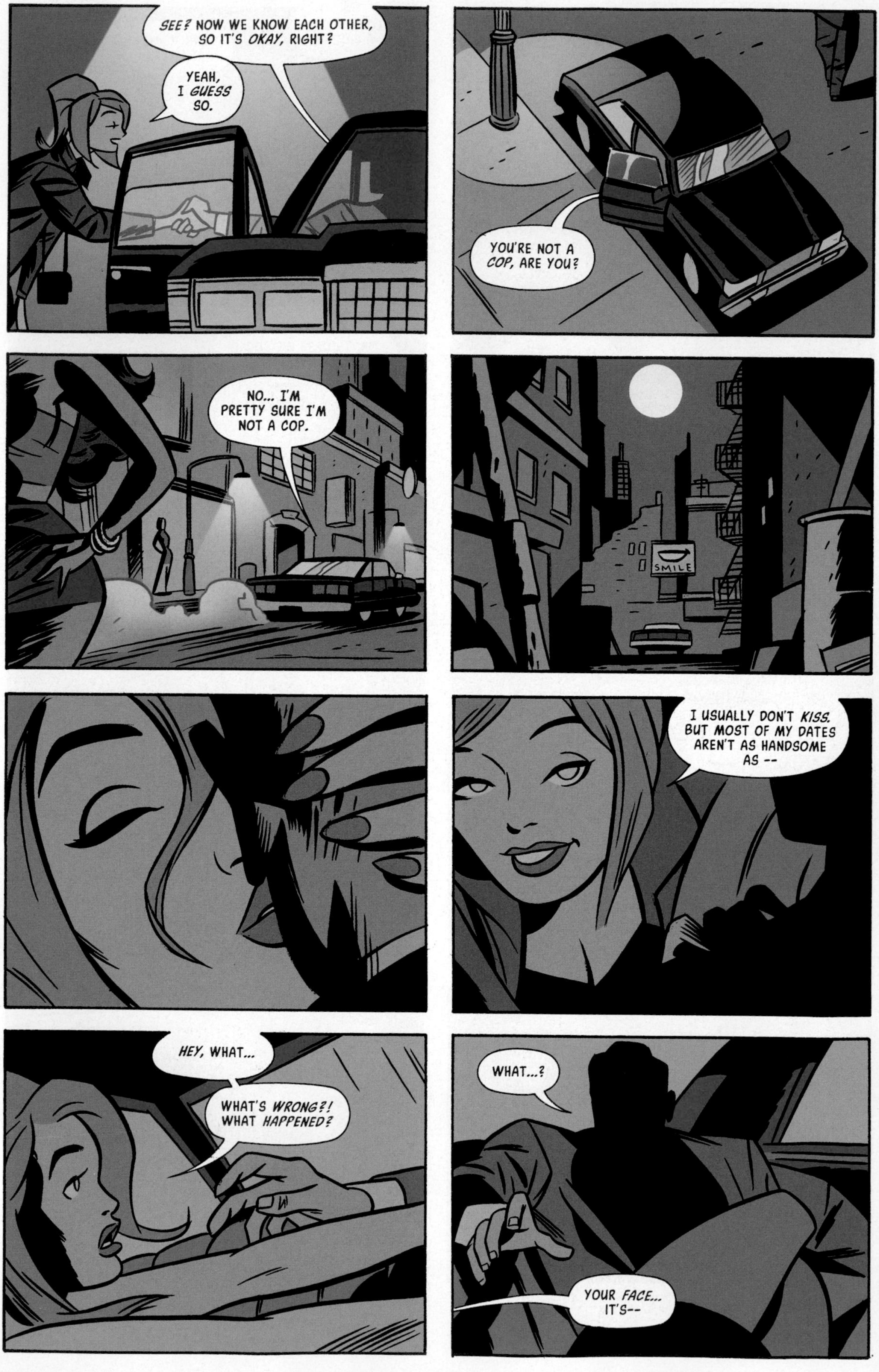
SEE? NOW WE KNOW EACH OTHER, SO IT'S OKAY, RIGHT?
YEAH, I GUESS SO.
YOU'RE NOT A COP, ARE YOU?
NO... I'M PRETTY SURE I'M NOT A COP.
SMILE
I USUALLY DON'T KISS. BUT MOST OF MY DATES AREN'T AS HANDSOME AS --
HEY, WHAT...
WHAT'S WRONG?! WHAT HAPPENED?
WHAT...?
YOUR FACE... IT'S--

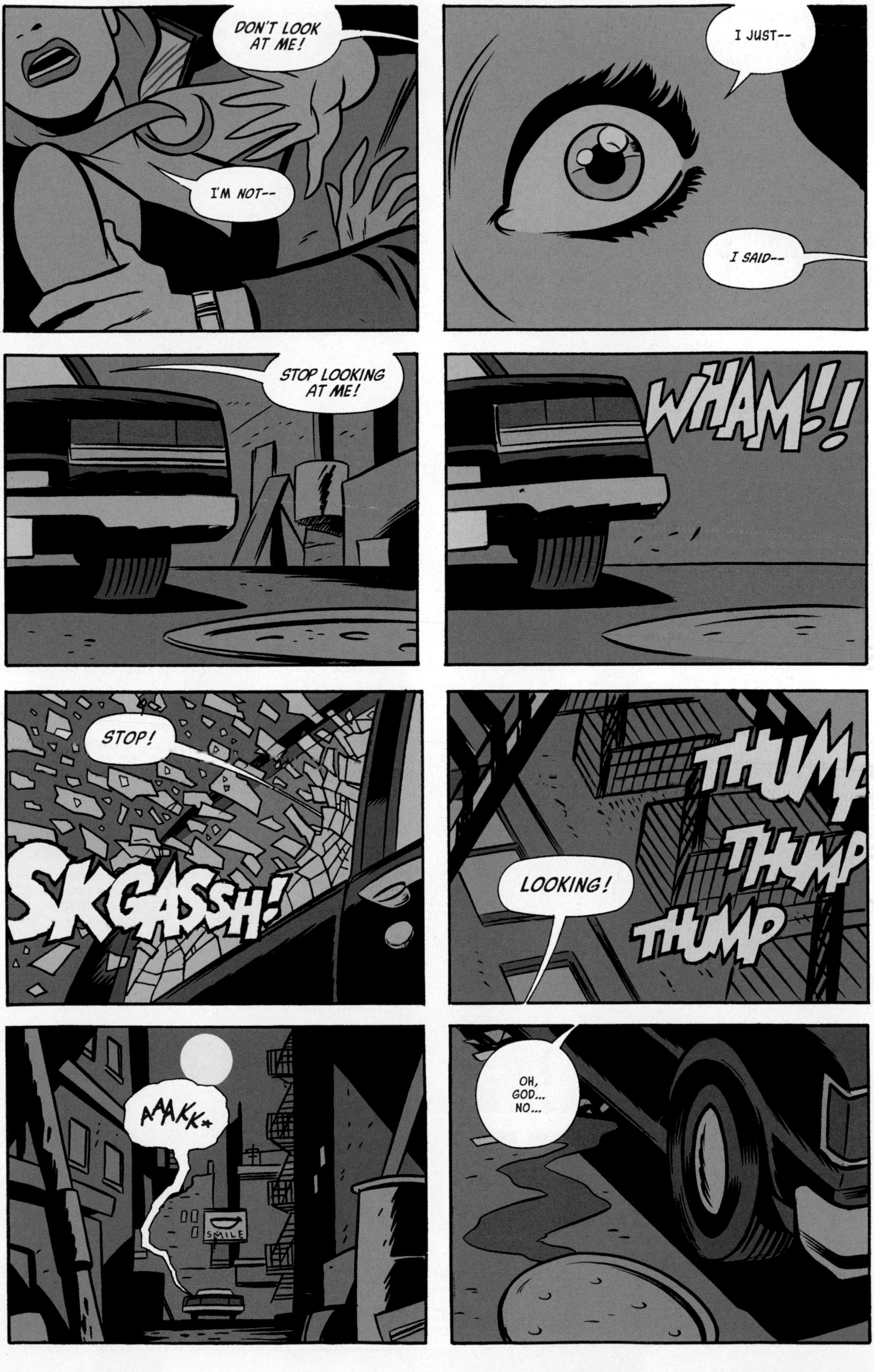
DON'T LOOK AT ME!
I'M NOT--
I JUST--
I SAID--
STOP LOOKING AT ME!
WHAM!!
STOP!
SKGASSH!
LOOKING!
THUMP
THUMP
THUMP
AAAKK
SMILE
OH, GOD... NO...

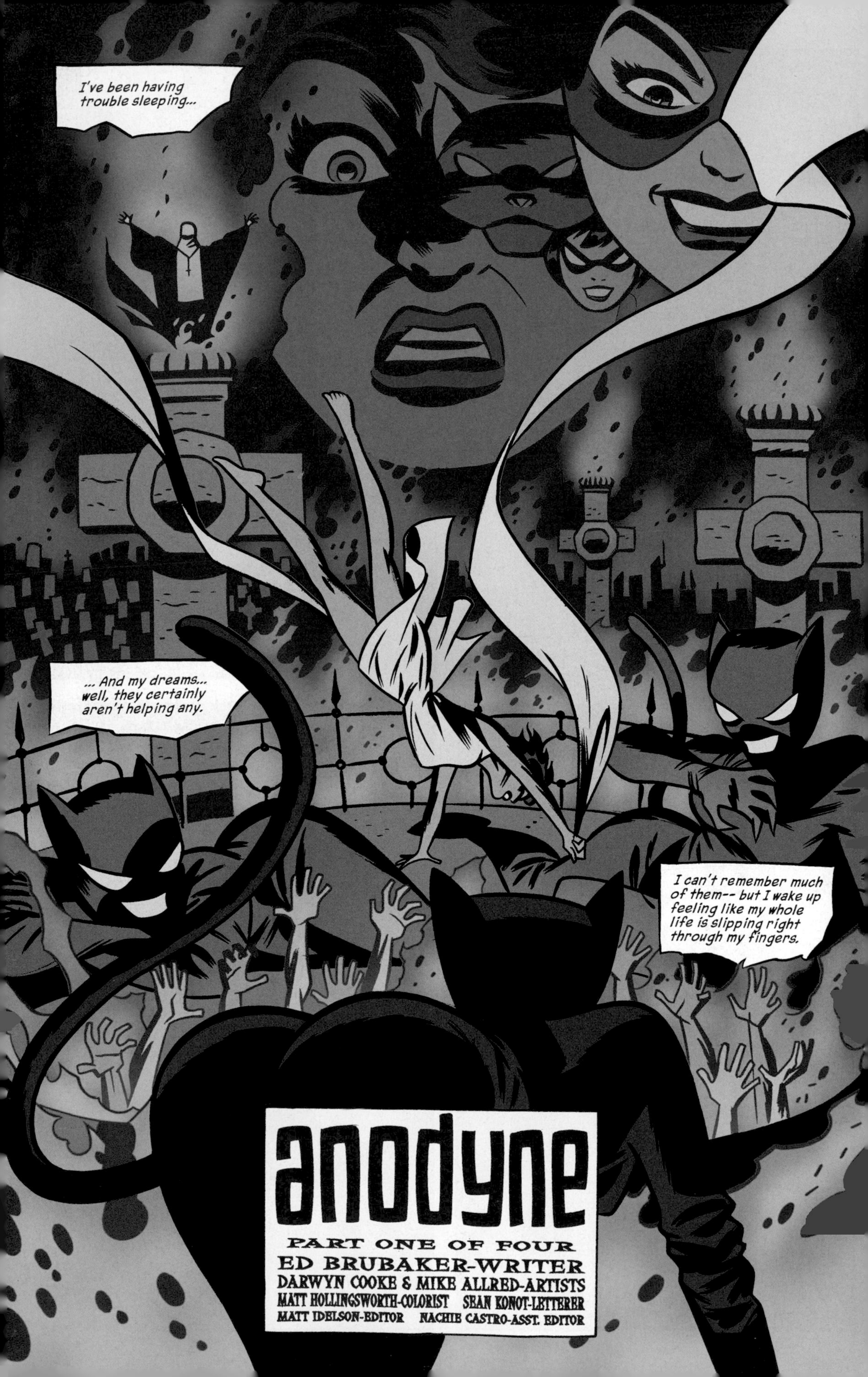
I've been having trouble sleeping...
... And my dreams... well, they certainly aren't helping any.
I can't remember much of them-- but I wake up feeling like my whole life is slipping right through my fingers.
anodyne
PART ONE OF FOUR
ED BRUBAKER-WRITER
DARWYN COOKE & MIKE ALLRED-ARTISTS
MATT HOLLINGSWORTH-COLORIST SEAN KONOT-LETTERER
MATT IDELSON-EDITOR NACHIE CASTRO-ASST. EDITOR

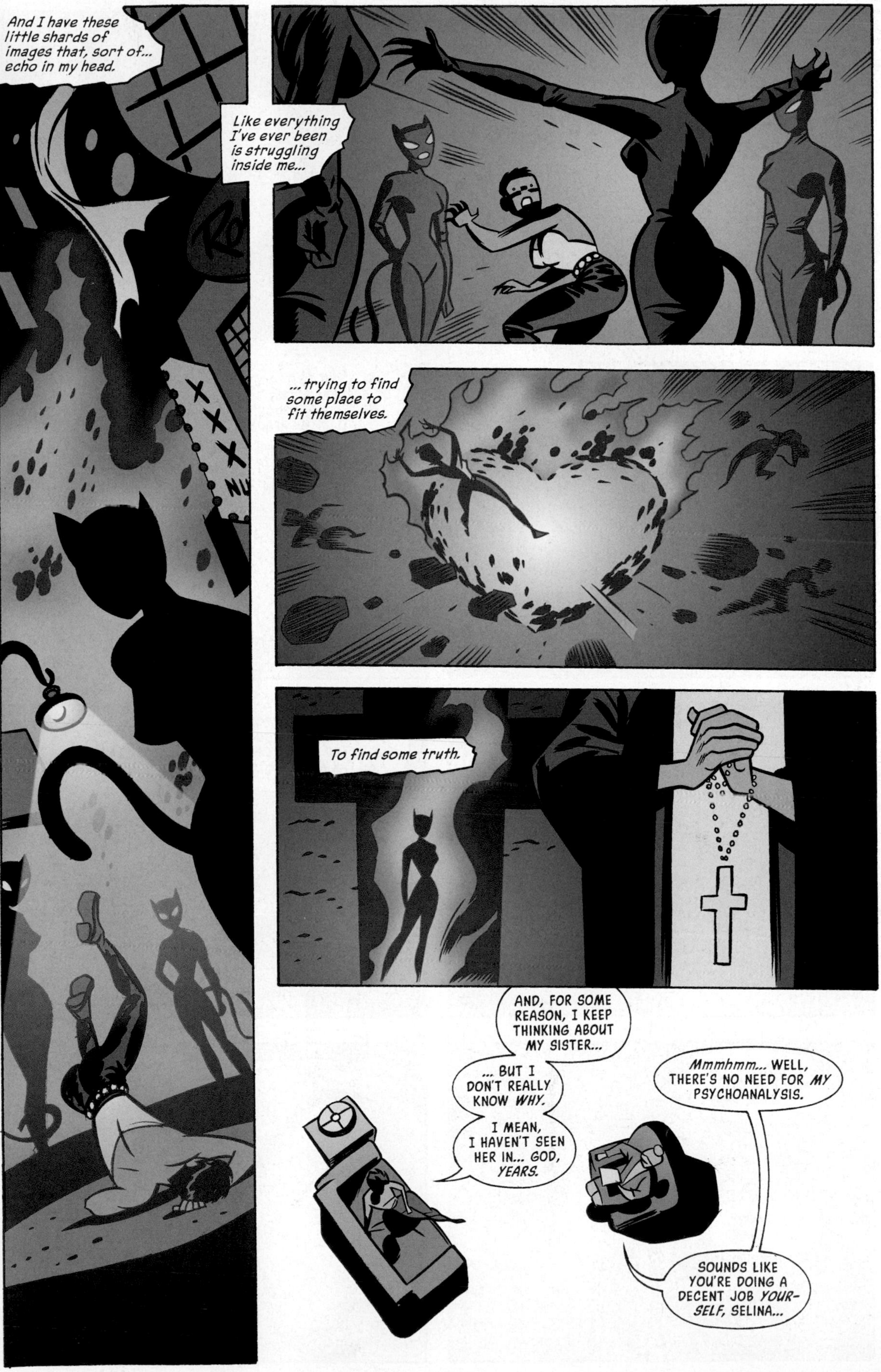
And I have these little shards of images that, sort of... echo in my head.
Like everything I've ever been is struggling inside me...
...trying to find some place to fit themselves.
To find some truth.
AND, FOR SOME REASON, I KEEP THINKING ABOUT MY SISTER...
... BUT I DON'T REALLY KNOW WHY.
I MEAN, I HAVEN'T SEEN HER IN... GOD, YEARS.
Mmmhmm... WELL, THERE'S NO NEED FOR MY PSYCHOANALYSIS.
SOUNDS LIKE YOU'RE DOING A DECENT JOB YOURSELF, SELINA...

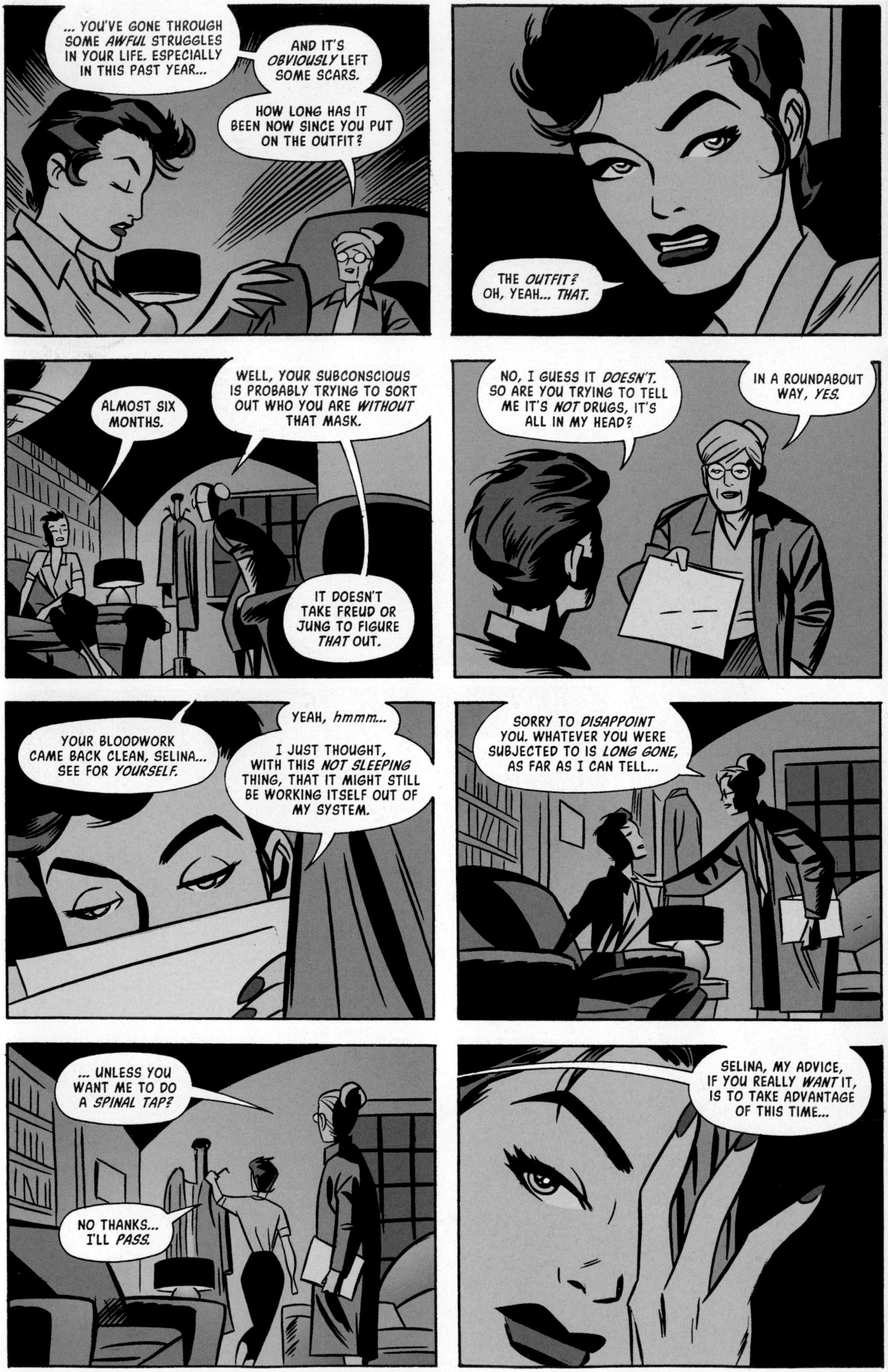
... YOU'VE GONE THROUGH SOME AWFUL STRUGGLES IN YOUR LIFE. ESPECIALLY IN THIS PAST YEAR...
AND IT'S OBVIOUSLY LEFT SOME SCARS.
HOW LONG HAS IT BEEN NOW SINCE YOU PUT ON THE OUTFIT?
THE OUTFIT? OH, YEAH... THAT.
ALMOST SIX MONTHS.
WELL, YOUR SUBCONSCIOUS IS PROBABLY TRYING TO SORT OUT WHO YOU ARE WITHOUT THAT MASK.
IT DOESN'T TAKE FREUD OR JUNG TO FIGURE THAT OUT.
NO, I GUESS IT DOESN'T. SO ARE YOU TRYING TO TELL ME IT'S NOT DRUGS, IT'S ALL IN MY HEAD?
IN A ROUNDABOUT WAY, YES.
YOUR BLOODWORK CAME BACK CLEAN, SELINA... SEE FOR YOURSELF.
YEAH, hmmm...
I JUST THOUGHT, WITH THIS NOT SLEEPING THING, THAT IT MIGHT STILL BE WORKING ITSELF OUT OF MY SYSTEM.
SORRY TO DISAPPOINT YOU. WHATEVER YOU WERE SUBJECTED TO IS LONG GONE, AS FAR AS I CAN TELL...
... UNLESS YOU WANT ME TO DO A SPINAL TAP?
NO THANKS... I'LL PASS.
SELINA, MY ADVICE, IF YOU REALLY WANT IT, IS TO TAKE ADVANTAGE OF THIS TIME...

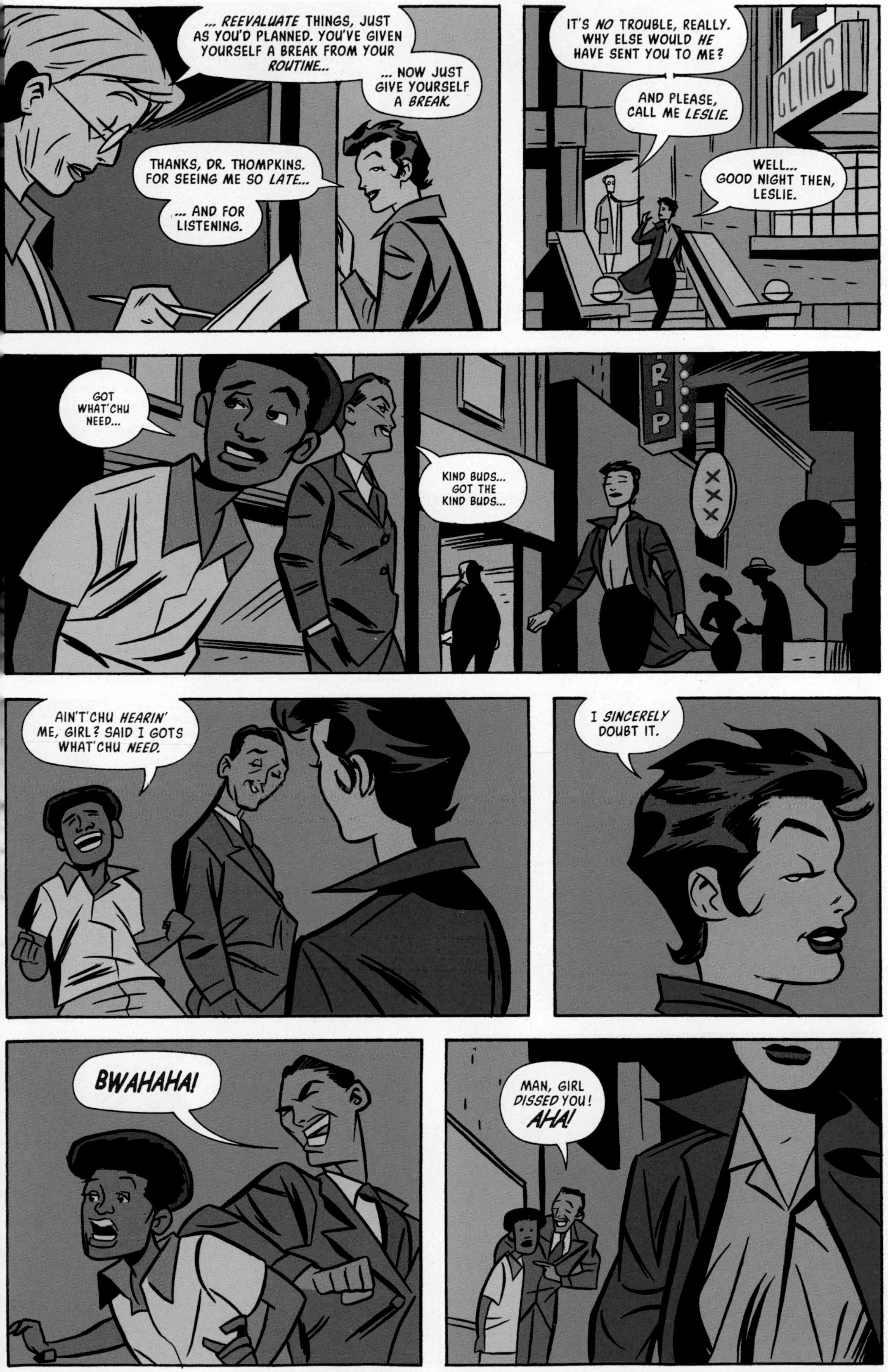
... REEVALUATE THINGS, JUST AS YOU'D PLANNED. YOU'VE GIVEN YOURSELF A BREAK FROM YOUR ROUTINE...
... NOW JUST GIVE YOURSELF A BREAK.
THANKS, DR. THOMPKINS. FOR SEEING ME SO LATE...
... AND FOR LISTENING.
IT'S NO TROUBLE, REALLY. WHY ELSE WOULD HE HAVE SENT YOU TO ME?
AND PLEASE, CALL ME LESLIE.
CLINIC
WELL... GOOD NIGHT THEN, LESLIE.
GOT WHAT'CHU NEED...
KIND BUDS... GOT THE KIND BUDS...
XXX
AIN'T'CHU HEARIN' ME, GIRL? SAID I GOTS WHAT'CHU NEED.
I SINCERELY DOUBT IT.
BWAHAHA!
MAN, GIRL DISSED YOU! AHA!

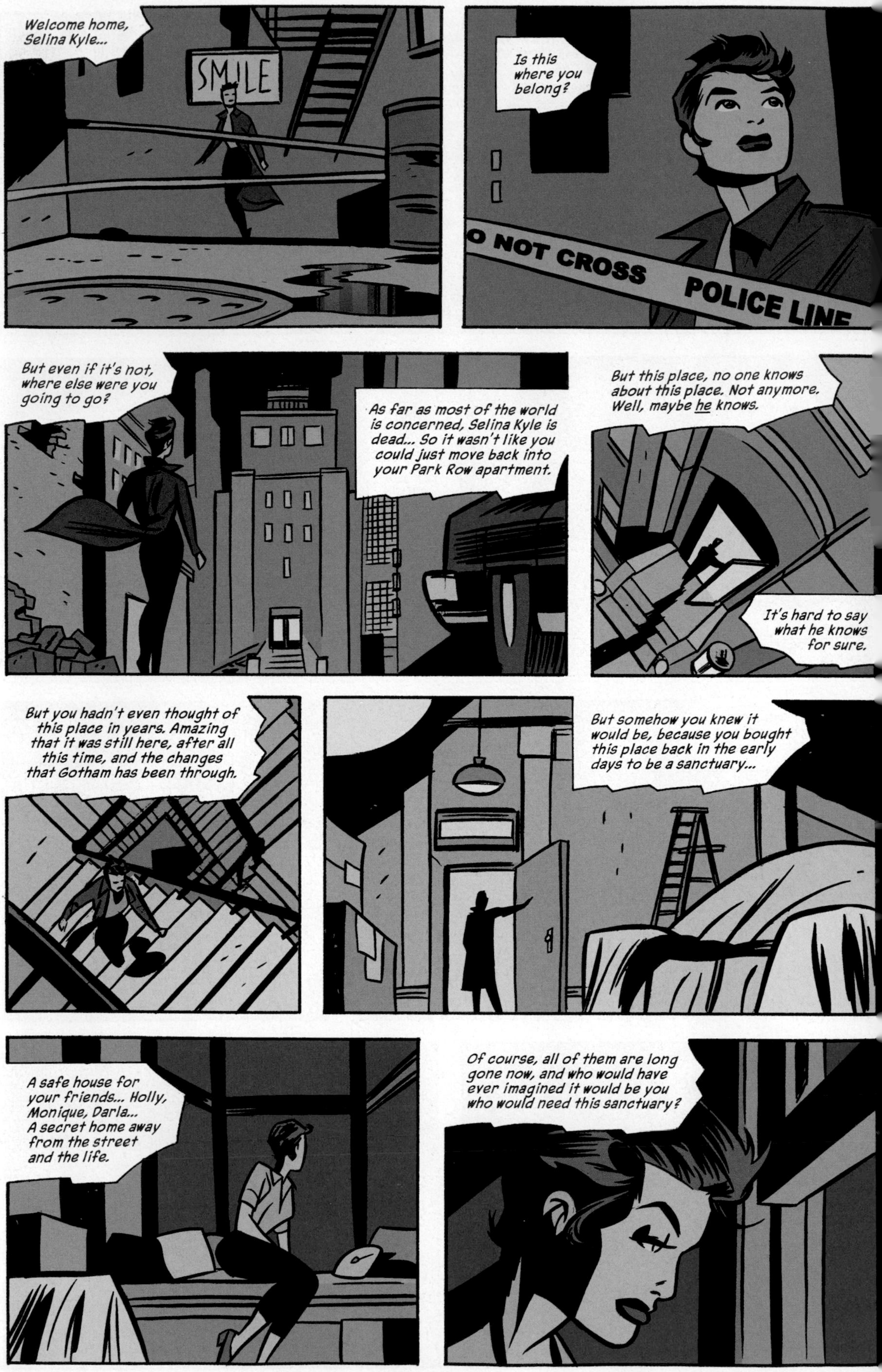
Welcome home, Selina Kyle...
SMILE
Is this where you belong?
O NOT CROSS
POLICE LINE
But even if it's not, where else were you going to go?
As far as most of the world is concerned, Selina Kyle is dead... So it wasn't like you could just move back into your Park Row apartment.
But this place, no one knows about this place. Not anymore. Well, maybe he knows.
It's hard to say what he knows for sure.
But you hadn't even thought of this place in years. Amazing that it was still here, after all this time, and the changes that Gotham has been through.
But somehow you knew it would be, because you bought this place back in the early days to be a sanctuary...
A safe house for your friends... Holly, Monique, Darla... A secret home away from the street and the life.
Of course, all of them are long gone now, and who would have ever imagined it would be you who would need this sanctuary?

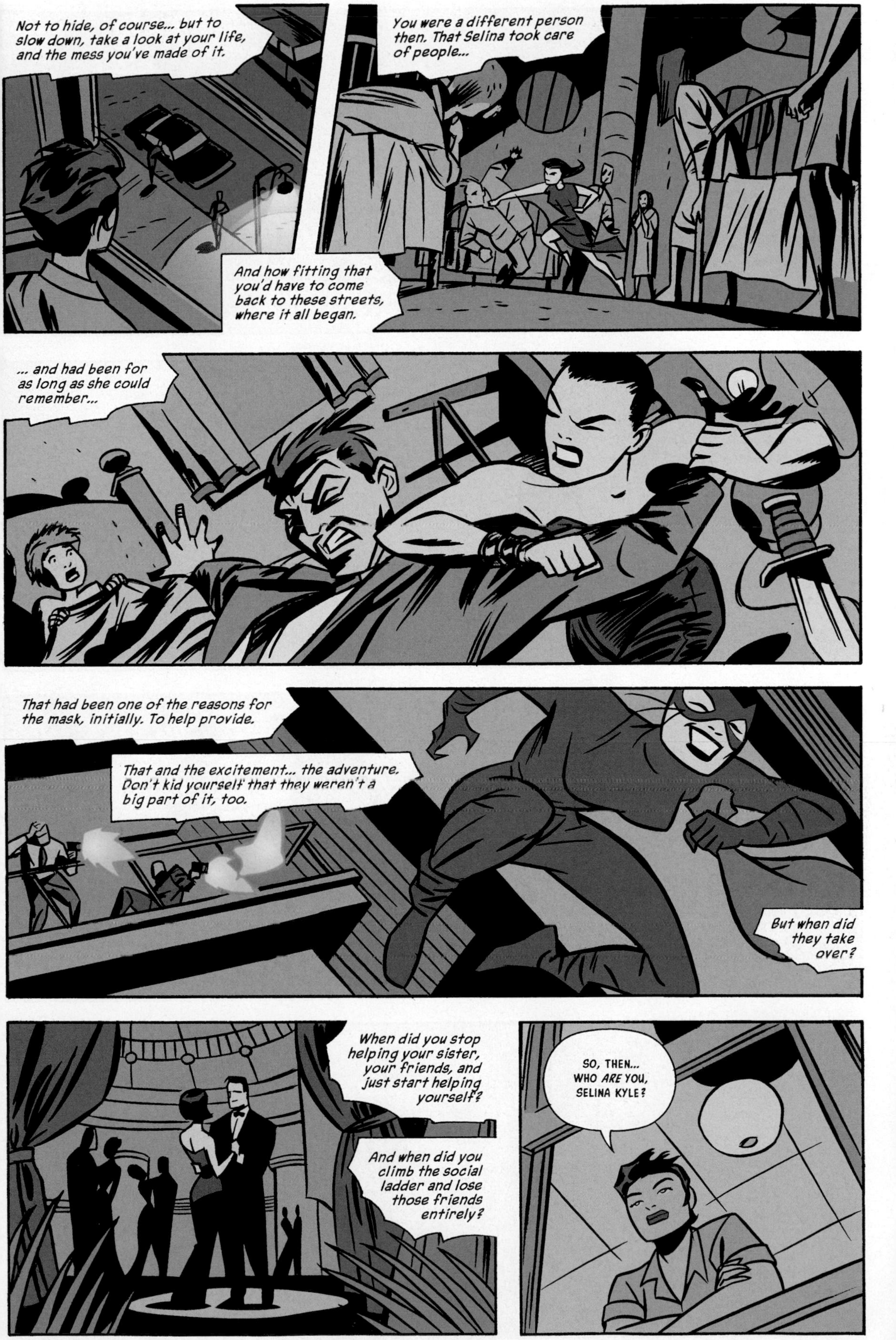
Not to hide, of course... but to slow down, take a look at your life, and the mess you've made of it.
You were a different person then. That Selina took care of people...
And how fitting that you'd have to come back to these streets, where it all began.
... and had been for as long as she could remember...
That had been one of the reasons for the mask, initially. To help provide.
That and the excitement... the adventure. Don't kid yourself that they weren't a big part of it, too.
But when did they take over?
When did you stop helping your sister, your friends, and just start helping yourself?
And when did you climb the social ladder and lose those friends entirely?
SO, THEN... WHO ARE YOU, SELINA KYLE?

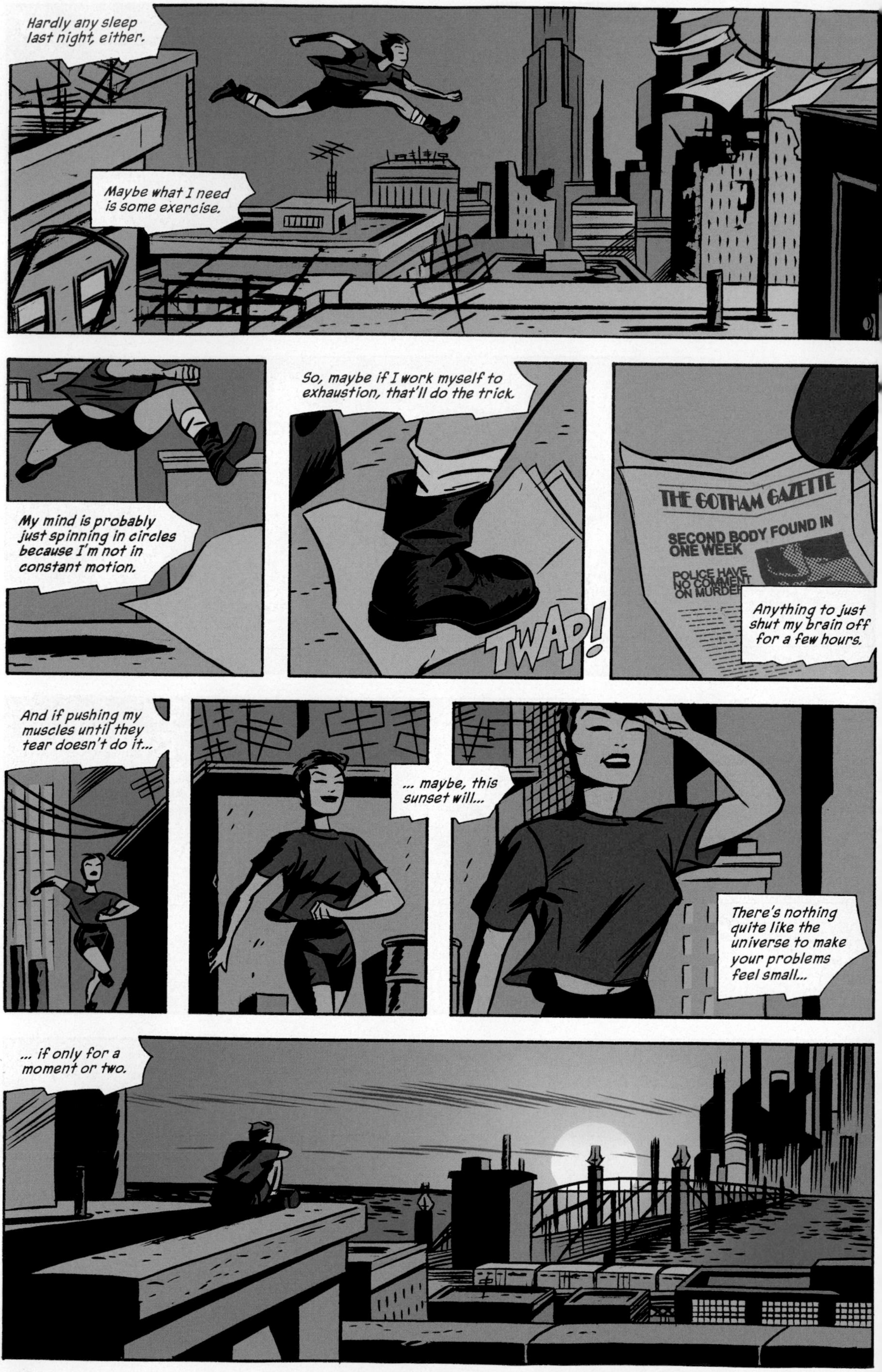
Hardly any sleep last night, either.
Maybe what I need is some exercise.
My mind is probably just spinning in circles because I'm not in constant motion.
So, maybe if I work myself to exhaustion, that'll do the trick.
TWAP!
THE GOTHAM GAZETTE
SECOND BODY FOUND IN ONE WEEK
POLICE HAVE NO COMMENT ON MURDER
Anything to just shut my brain off for a few hours.
And if pushing my muscles until they tear doesn't do it...
... maybe, this sunset will...
There's nothing quite like the universe to make your problems feel small...
... if only for a moment or two.

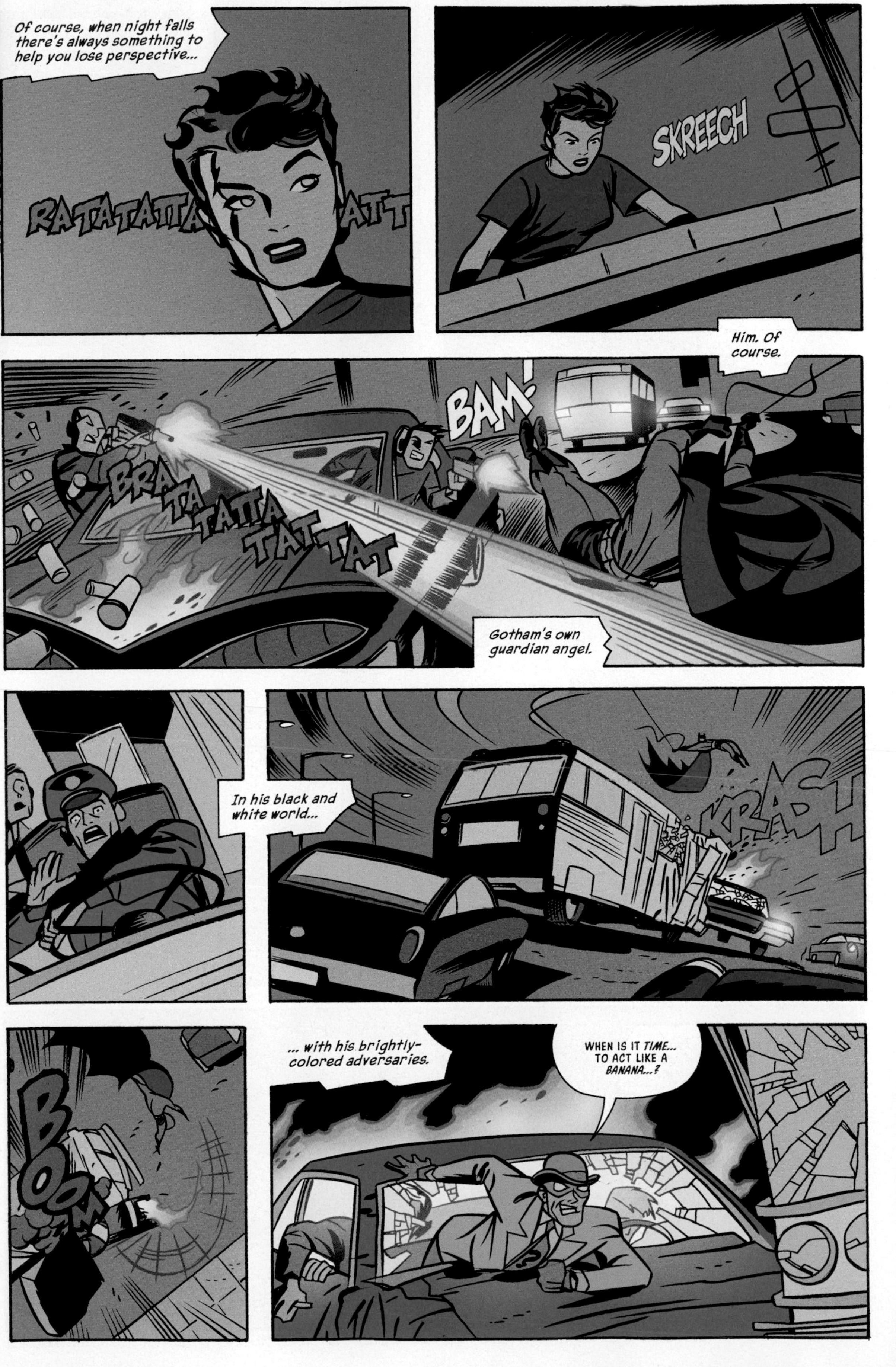

Of course, when night falls there's always something to help you lose perspective...
RATATATTA ATT
SKREECH
Him. Of course.
BAM!
BRATATATTA TAT TAT
Gotham's own guardian angel.
In his black and white world...
KRASH
BOOM
... with his brightly-colored adversaries.
WHEN IS IT *TIME*... TO ACT LIKE A *BANANA*...?

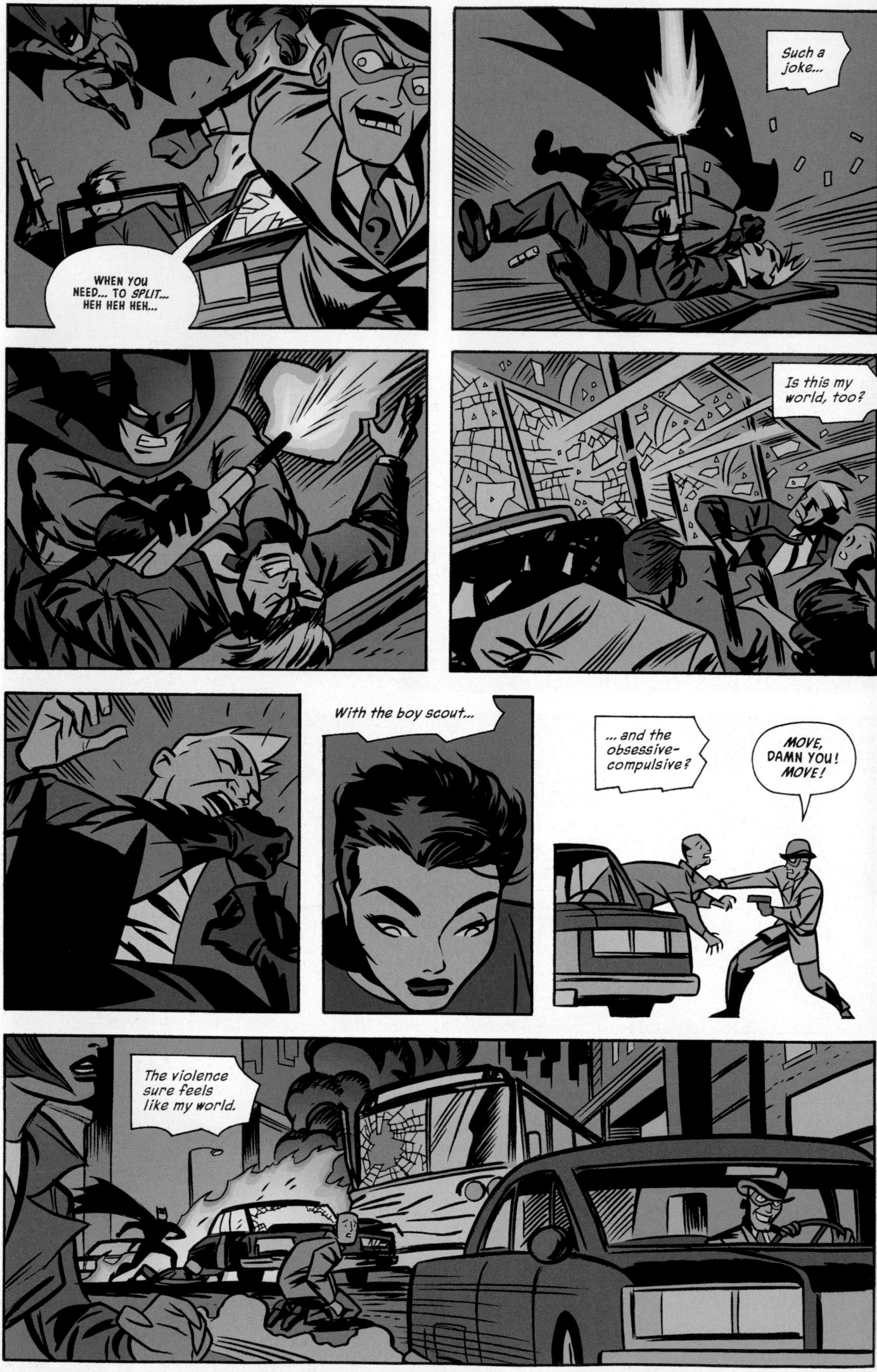
WHEN YOU NEED... TO SPLIT... HEH HEH HEH...
Such a joke...
Is this my world, too?
With the boy scout...
...and the obsessive-compulsive?
MOVE, DAMN YOU! MOVE!
The violence sure feels like my world.

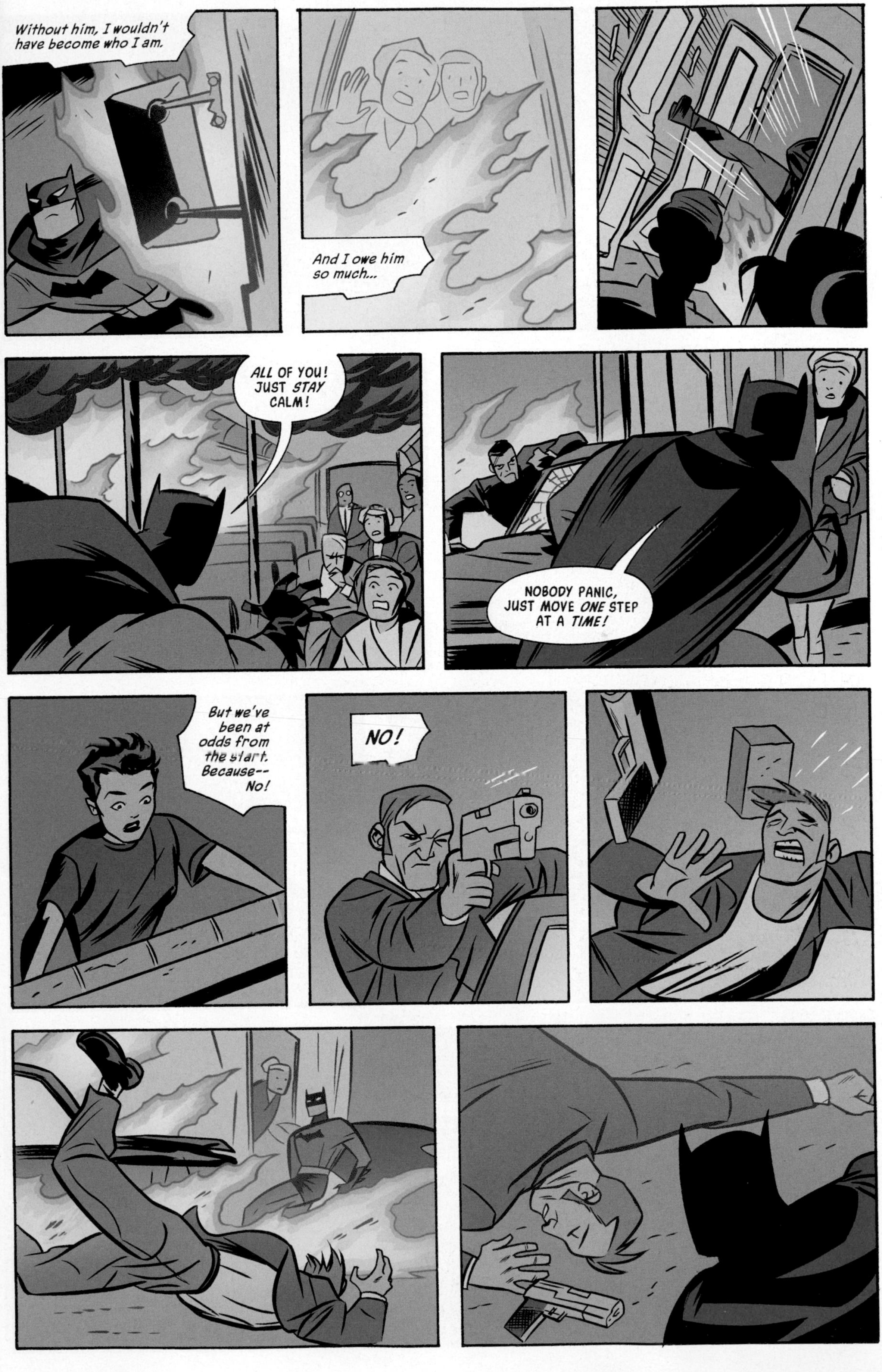

Without him, I wouldn't have become who I am.
And I owe him so much...
ALL OF YOU! JUST STAY CALM!
NOBODY PANIC, JUST MOVE ONE STEP AT A TIME!
But we've been at odds from the start. Because-- No!
NO!

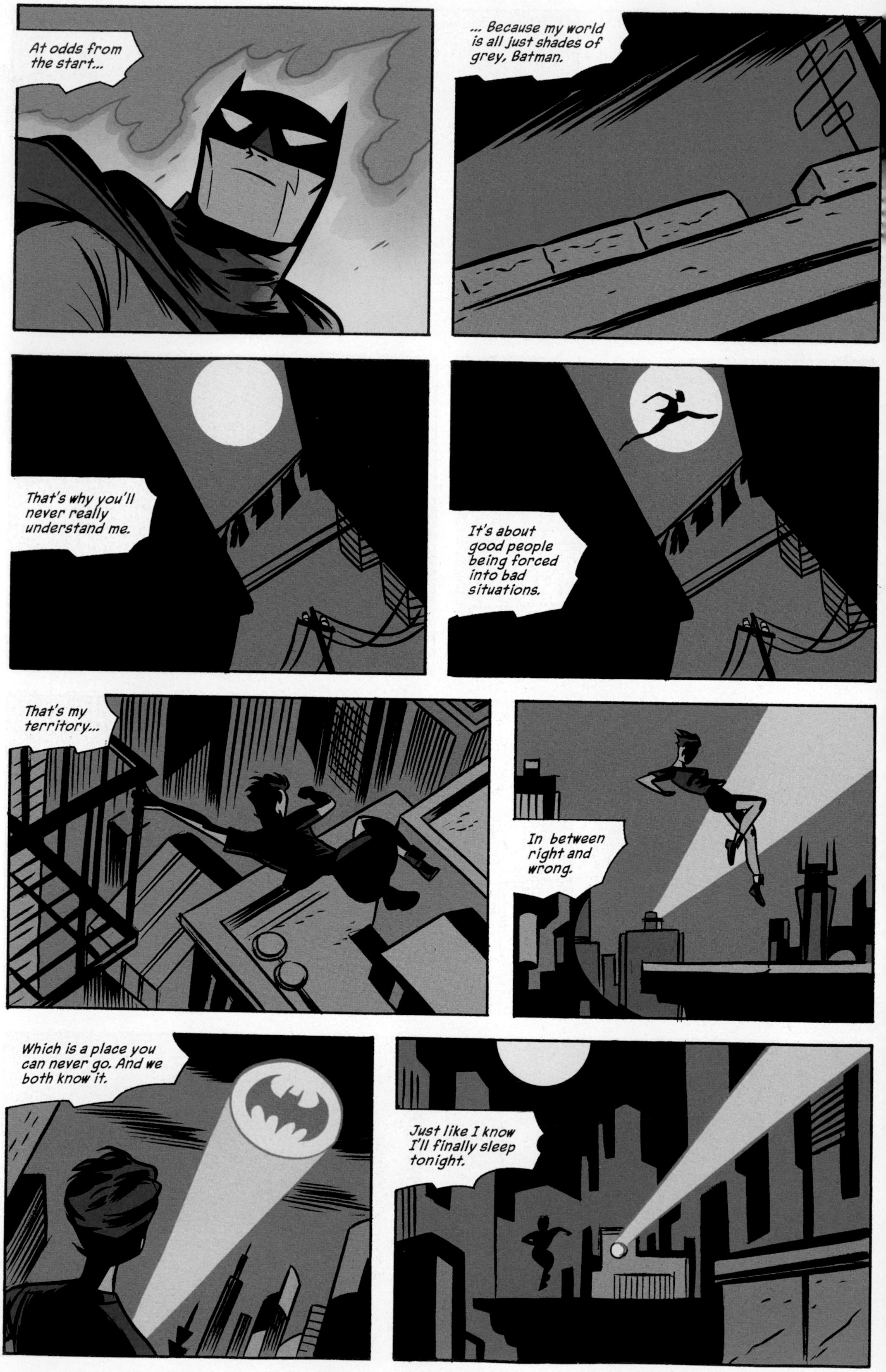
At odds from the start...
... Because my world is all just shades of grey, Batman.
That's why you'll never really understand me.
It's about good people being forced into bad situations.
That's my territory...
In between right and wrong.
Which is a place you can never go. And we both know it.
Just like I know I'll finally sleep tonight.

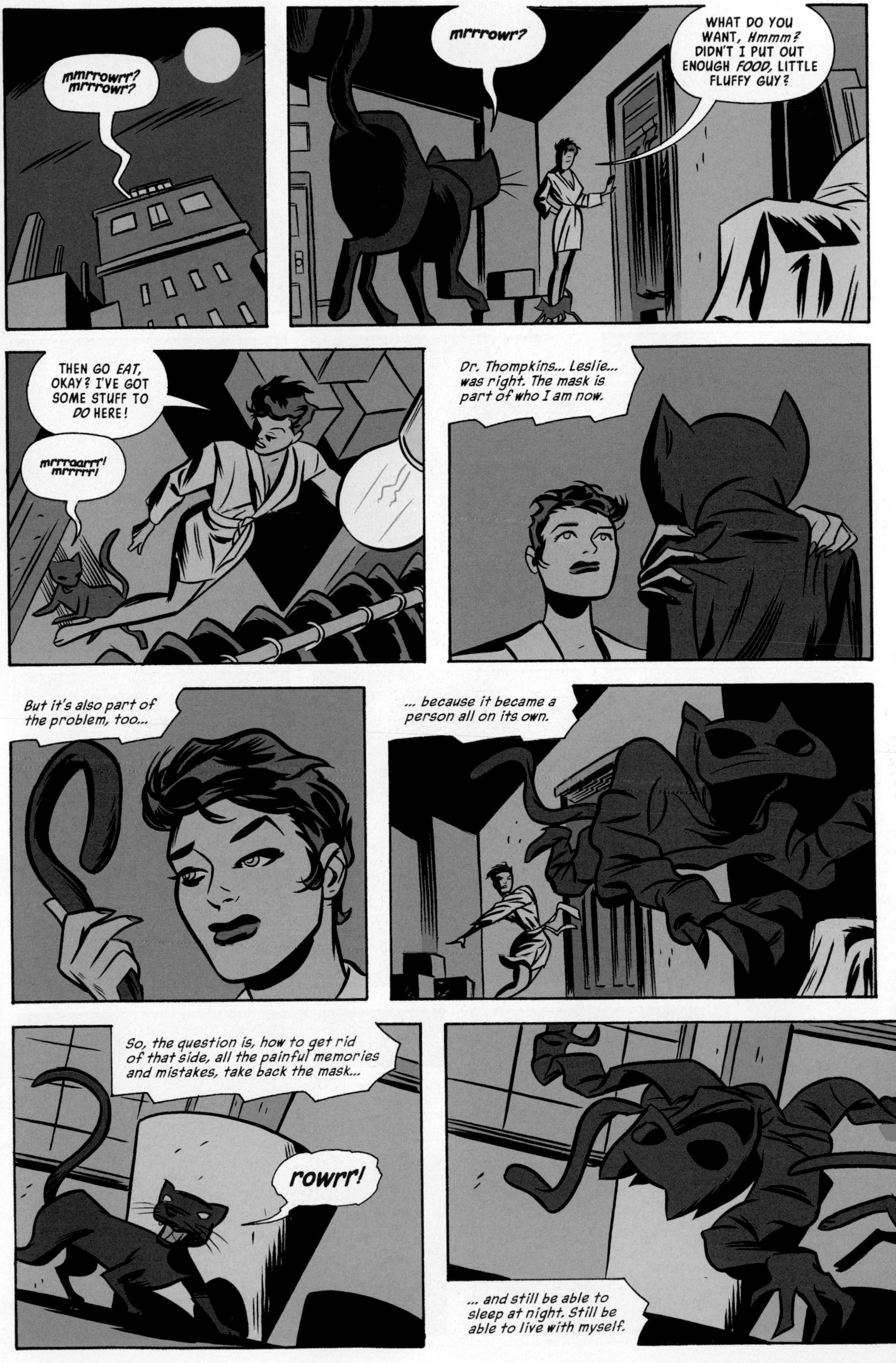
mmrrowrr? mrrrowr?
mrrrowr?
WHAT DO YOU WANT, *Hmmm?* DIDN'T I PUT OUT ENOUGH *FOOD*, LITTLE FLUFFY GUY?
THEN GO *EAT*, OKAY? I'VE GOT SOME STUFF TO *DO* HERE!
mrrraarrr! mrrrrrr!
Dr. Thompkins... Leslie... was right. The mask is part of who I am now.
But it's also part of the problem, too...
... because it became a person all on its own.
So, the question is, how to get rid of that side, all the painful memories and mistakes, take back the mask...
rowrr!
... and still be able to sleep at night. Still be able to live with myself.

I'm not sure if I can do all that, really...

... but I think I know how to try...

SURPLUS

GOV. CODE # 173
PART # H 155 AA

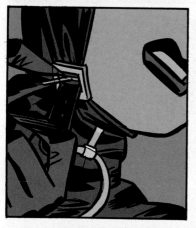

We can skip the tail for now...

And figure out what else to skip as time goes on.

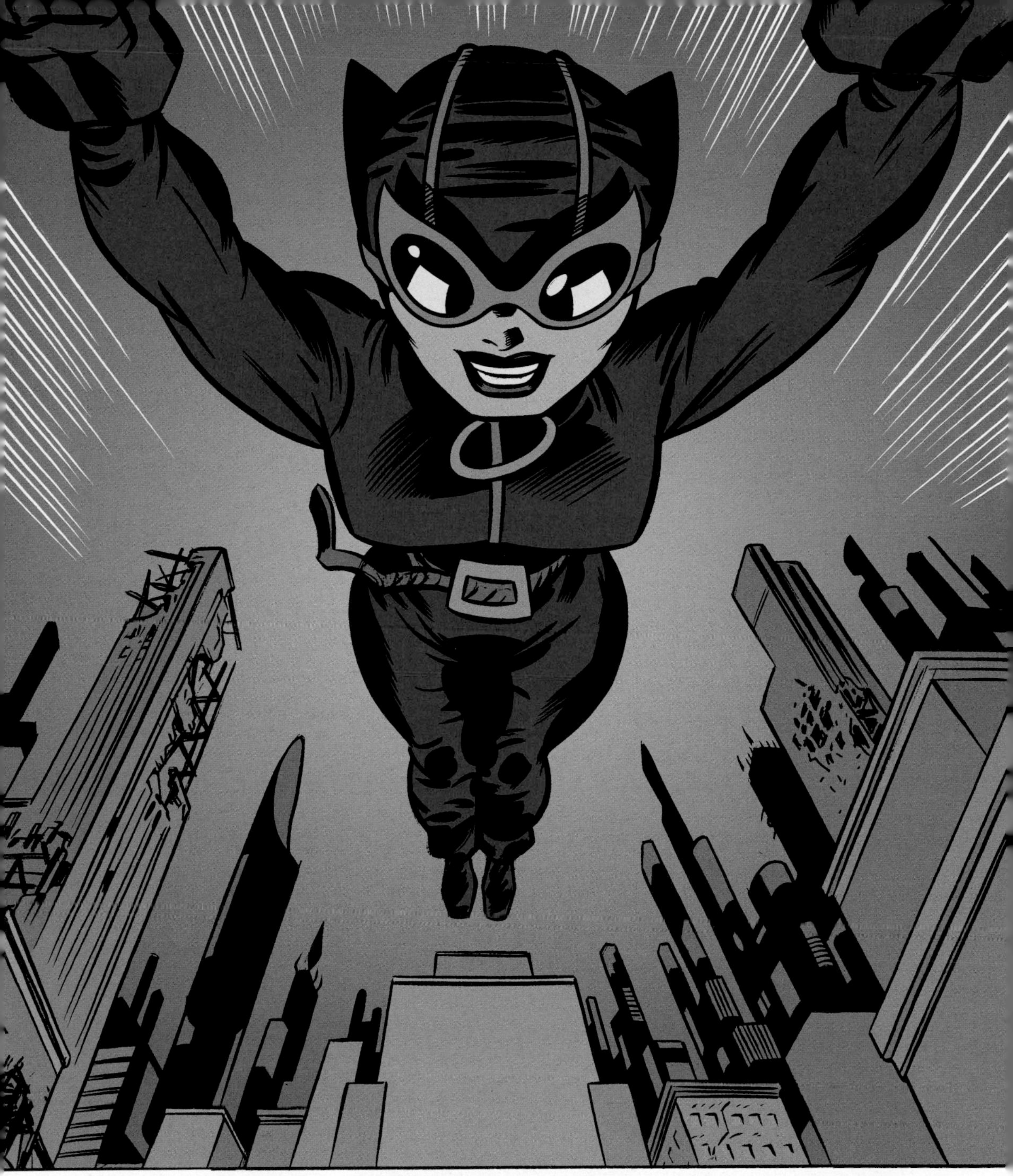

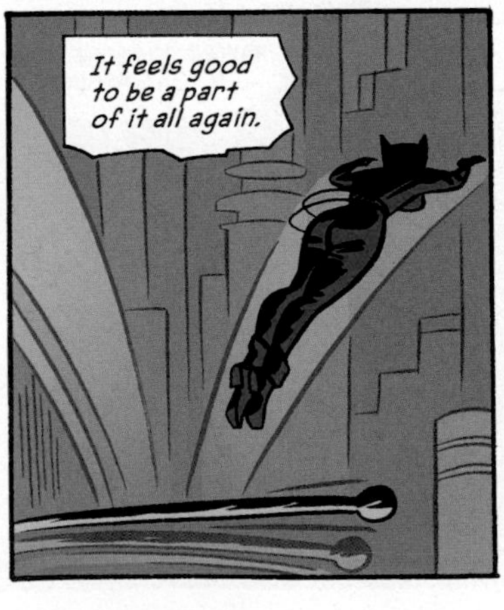
It feels good
to be a part
of it all again.

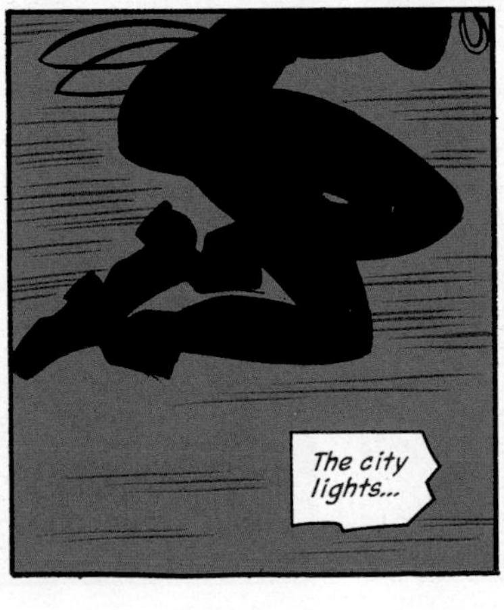
The city
lights...

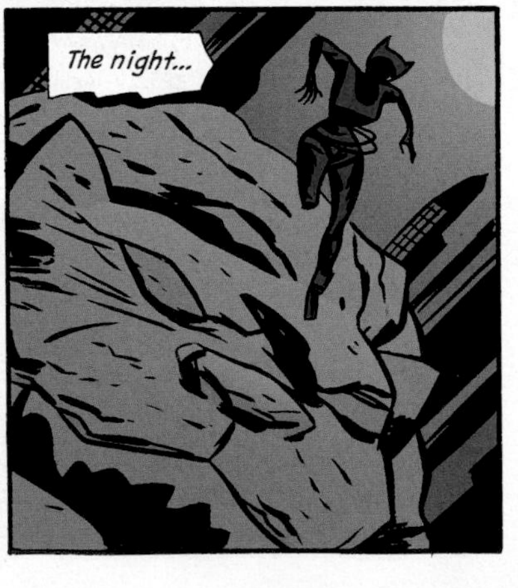
The night...

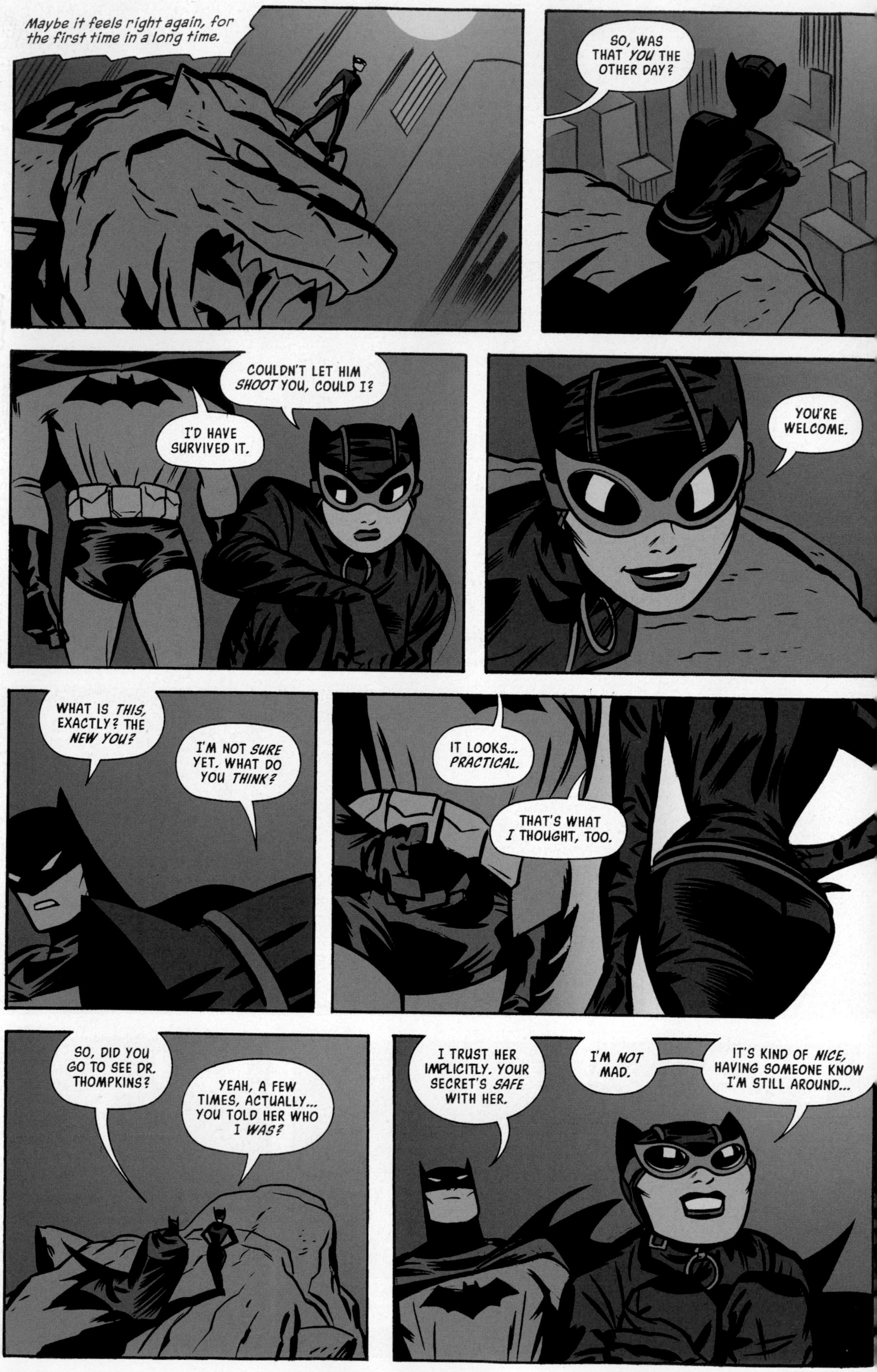
Maybe it feels right again, for the first time in a long time.
SO, WAS THAT YOU THE OTHER DAY?
COULDN'T LET HIM SHOOT YOU, COULD I?
I'D HAVE SURVIVED IT.
YOU'RE WELCOME.
WHAT IS THIS, EXACTLY? THE NEW YOU?
I'M NOT SURE YET. WHAT DO YOU THINK?
IT LOOKS... PRACTICAL.
THAT'S WHAT I THOUGHT, TOO.
SO, DID YOU GO TO SEE DR. THOMPKINS?
YEAH, A FEW TIMES, ACTUALLY... YOU TOLD HER WHO I WAS?
I TRUST HER IMPLICITLY. YOUR SECRET'S SAFE WITH HER.
I'M NOT MAD.
IT'S KIND OF NICE, HAVING SOMEONE KNOW I'M STILL AROUND...

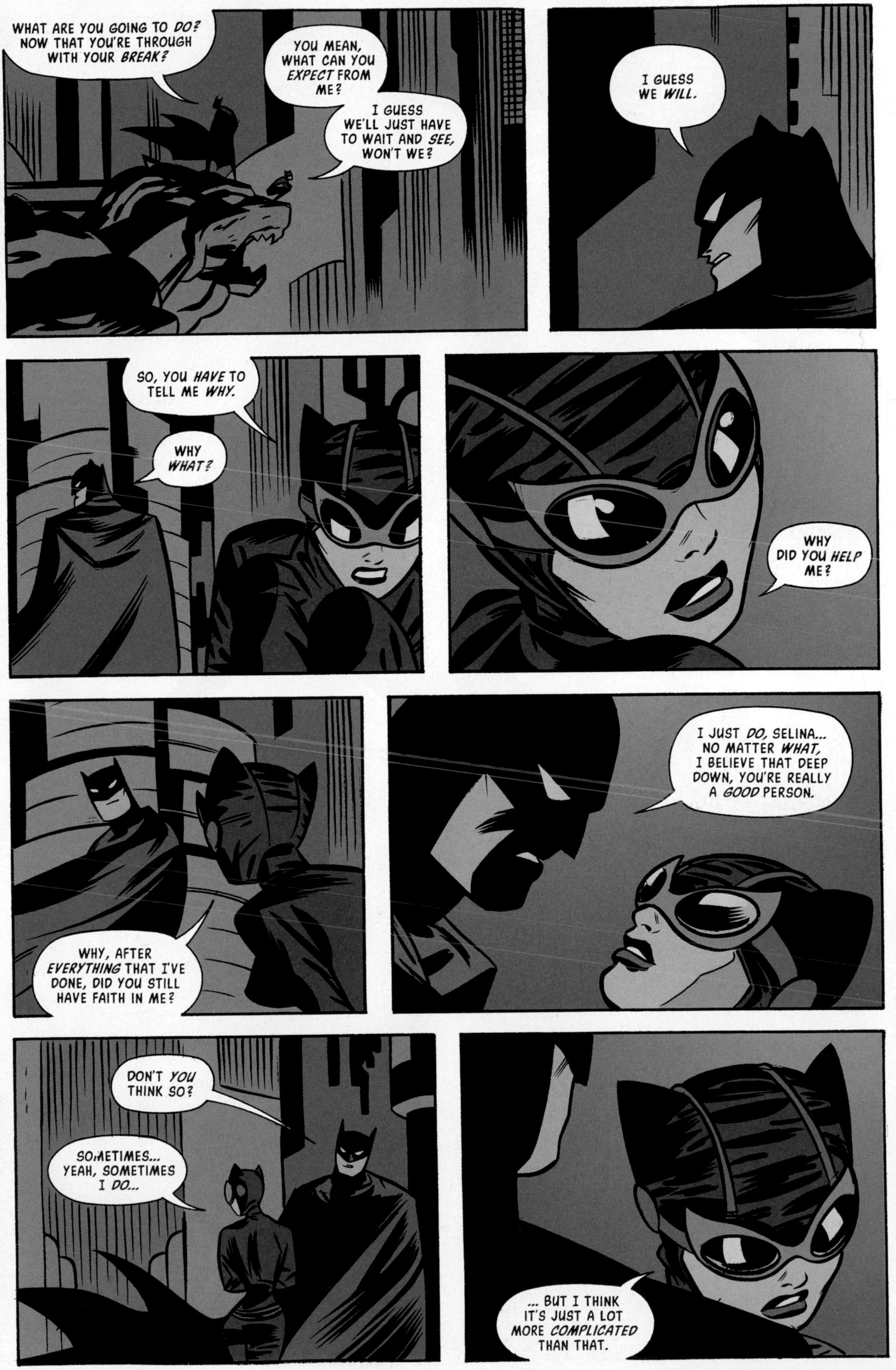
WHAT ARE YOU GOING TO DO? NOW THAT YOU'RE THROUGH WITH YOUR BREAK?
YOU MEAN, WHAT CAN YOU EXPECT FROM ME?
I GUESS WE'LL JUST HAVE TO WAIT AND SEE, WON'T WE?
I GUESS WE WILL.
SO, YOU HAVE TO TELL ME WHY.
WHY WHAT?
WHY DID YOU HELP ME?
WHY, AFTER EVERYTHING THAT I'VE DONE, DID YOU STILL HAVE FAITH IN ME?
I JUST DO, SELINA... NO MATTER WHAT, I BELIEVE THAT DEEP DOWN, YOU'RE REALLY A GOOD PERSON.
DON'T YOU THINK SO?
SOMETIMES... YEAH, SOMETIMES I DO...
... BUT I THINK IT'S JUST A LOT MORE COMPLICATED THAN THAT.

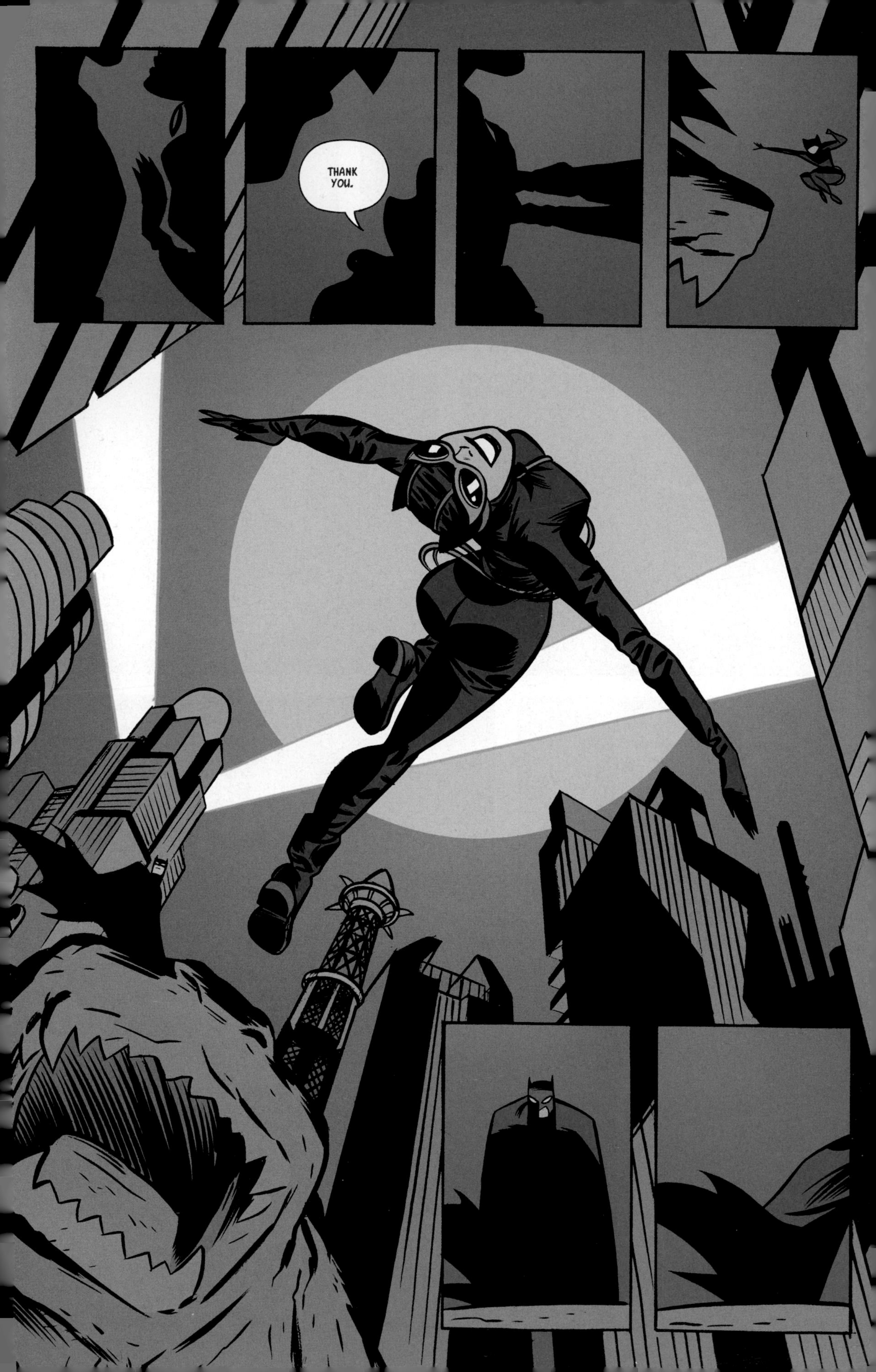
THANK YOU.

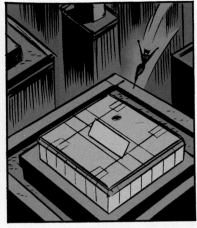

Maybe this will actually work. I'll have to give it time.

But the mask felt good again... It felt like me.

Whoever *that* is --

CHK
CHK
CHK

CHK
CHK

-- WHAT THE HELL?

CHK

SOMEONE TRYING TO PICK MY LOCK?

CHK
CHK
CHK

AHH! WAIT!

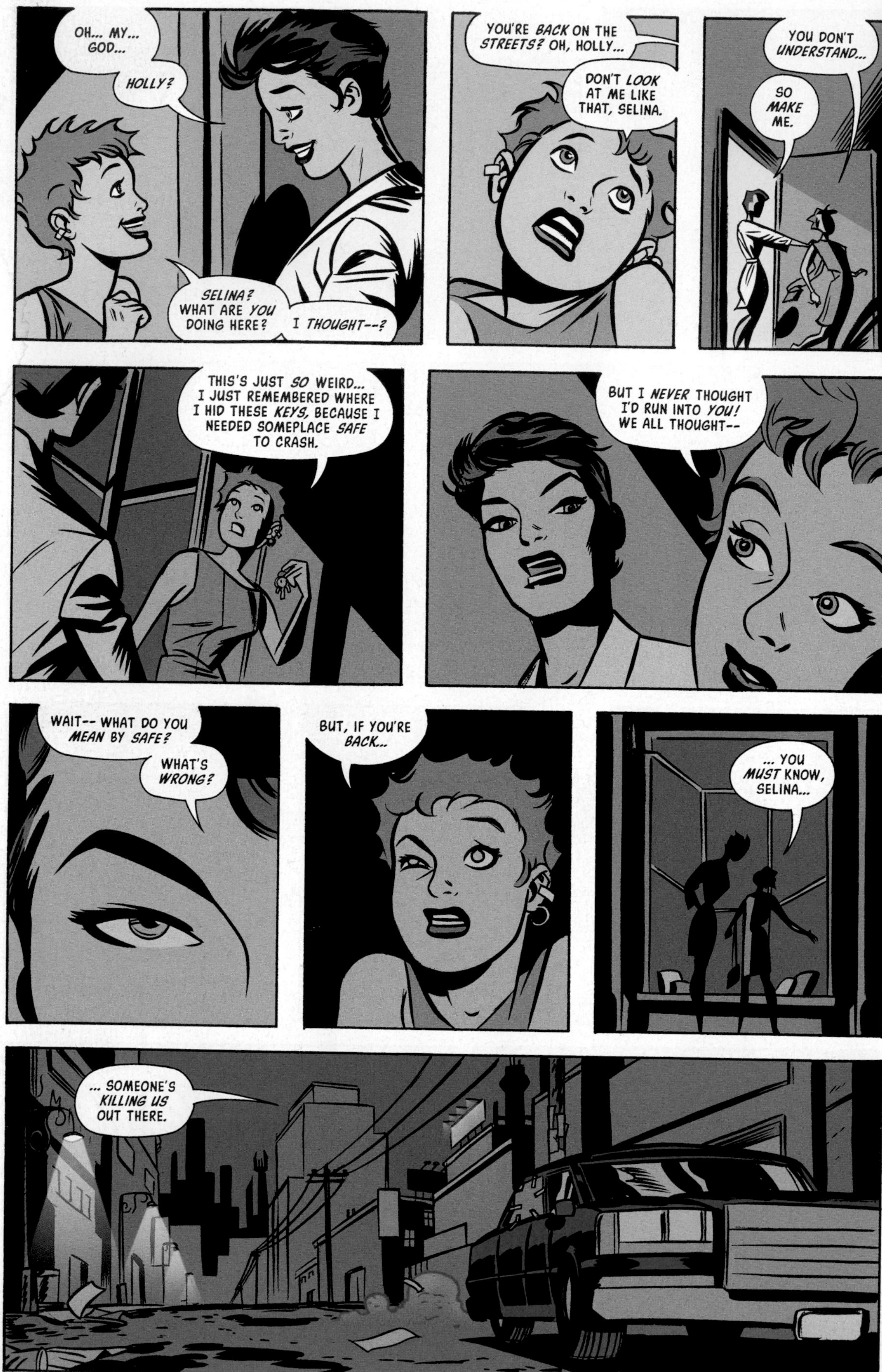
OH... MY... GOD...
HOLLY?
SELINA? WHAT ARE YOU DOING HERE?
I THOUGHT--?
YOU'RE BACK ON THE STREETS? OH, HOLLY...
DON'T LOOK AT ME LIKE THAT, SELINA.
YOU DON'T UNDERSTAND...
SO MAKE ME.
THIS'S JUST SO WEIRD... I JUST REMEMBERED WHERE I HID THESE KEYS, BECAUSE I NEEDED SOMEPLACE SAFE TO CRASH.
BUT I NEVER THOUGHT I'D RUN INTO YOU! WE ALL THOUGHT--
WAIT-- WHAT DO YOU MEAN BY SAFE?
WHAT'S WRONG?
BUT, IF YOU'RE BACK...
... YOU MUST KNOW, SELINA...
... SOMEONE'S KILLING US OUT THERE.

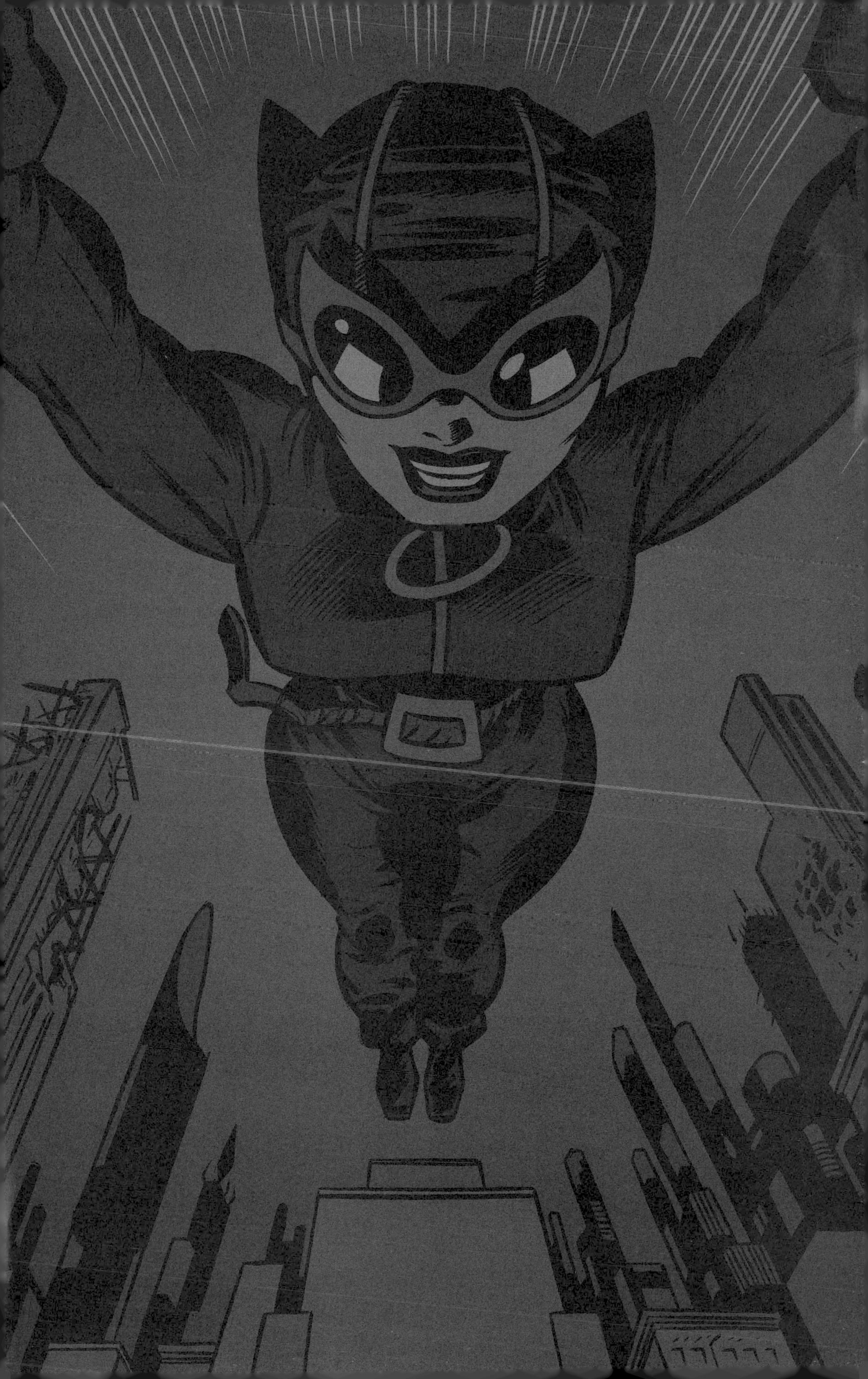

Catwoman 2 Cover by Darwyn Cooke

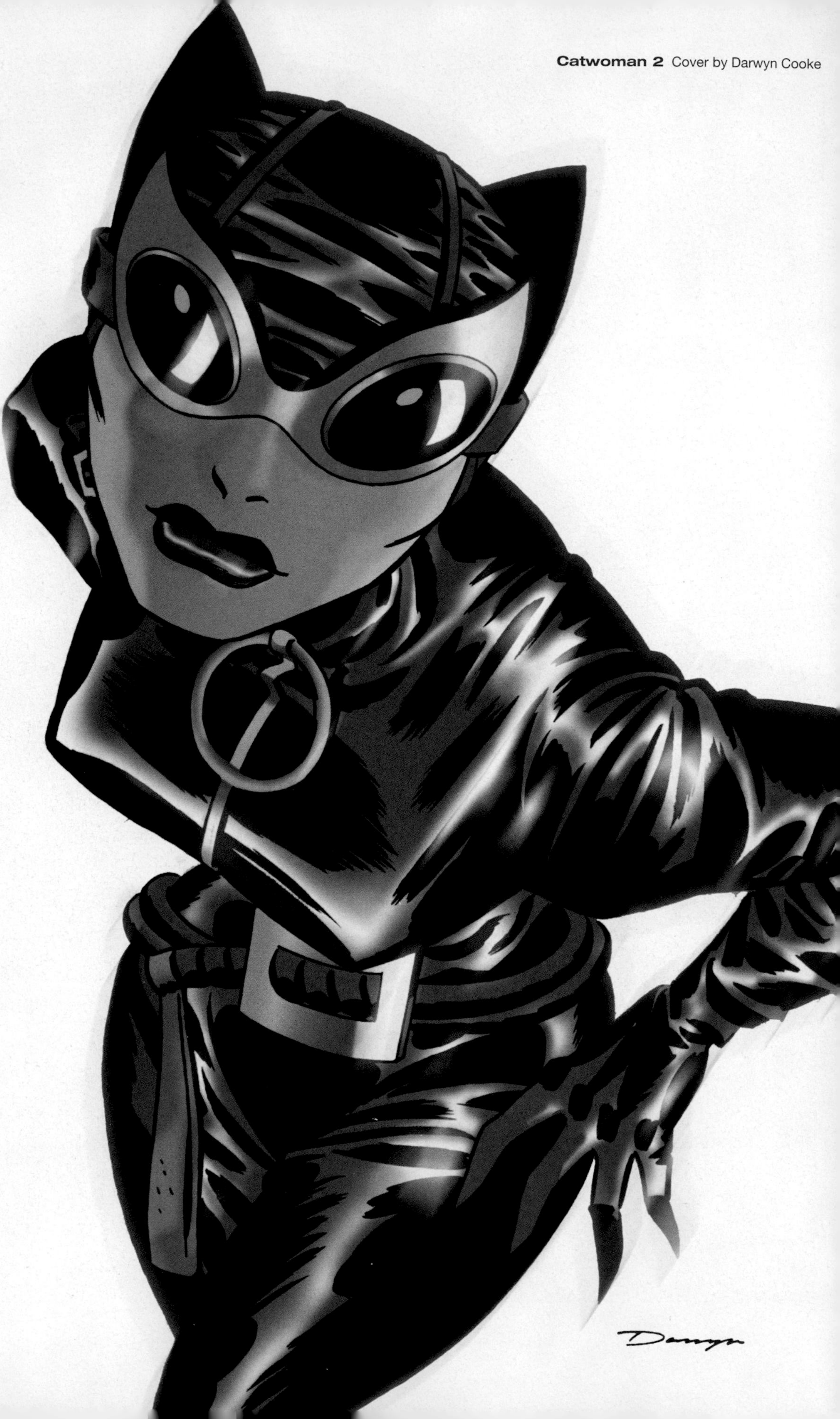
Darwyn

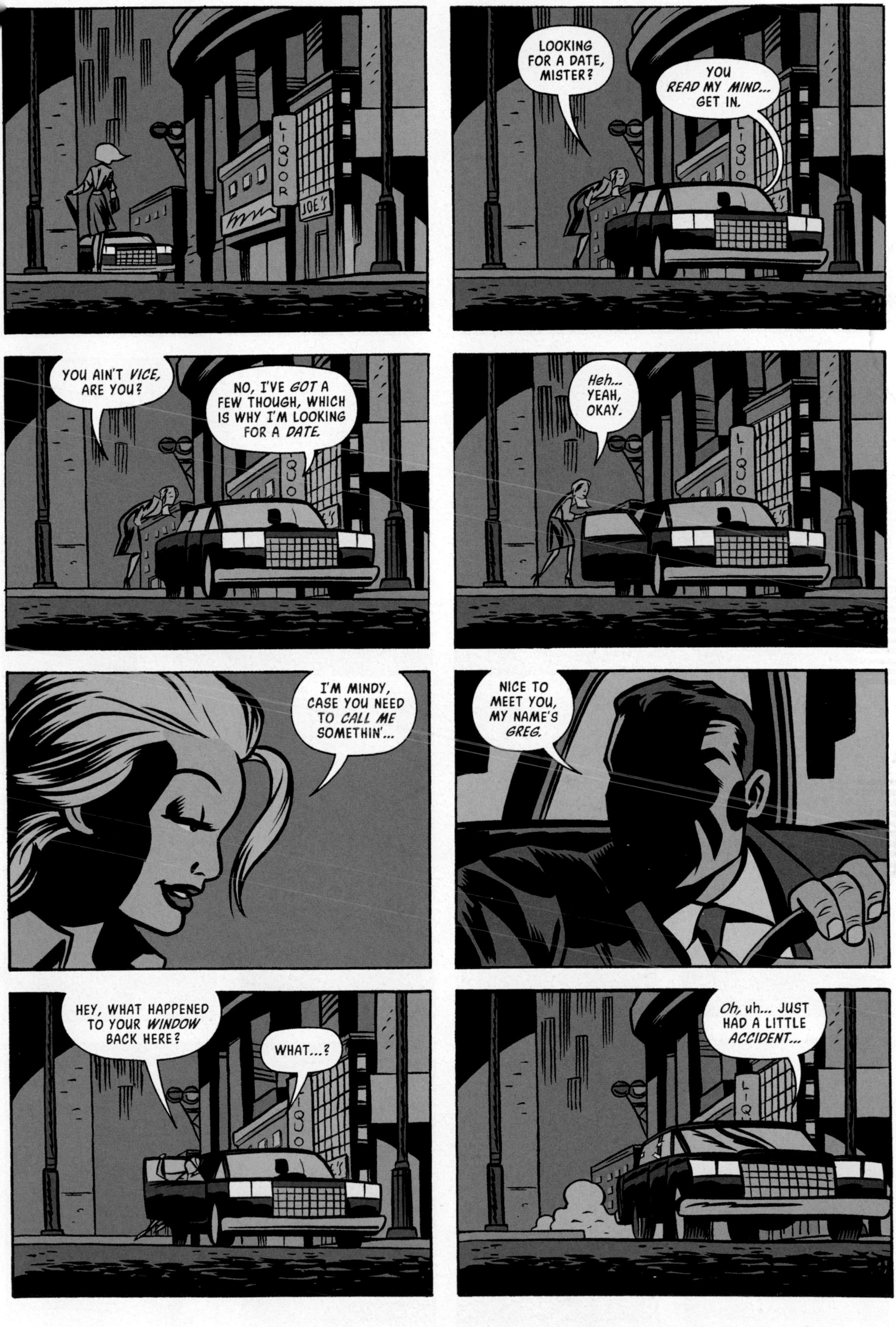
LOOKING FOR A DATE, MISTER?
YOU READ MY MIND... GET IN.
YOU AIN'T VICE, ARE YOU?
NO, I'VE GOT A FEW THOUGH, WHICH IS WHY I'M LOOKING FOR A DATE.
Heh... YEAH, OKAY.
I'M MINDY, CASE YOU NEED TO CALL ME SOMETHIN'...
NICE TO MEET YOU, MY NAME'S GREG.
HEY, WHAT HAPPENED TO YOUR WINDOW BACK HERE?
WHAT...?
Oh, uh... JUST HAD A LITTLE ACCIDENT...

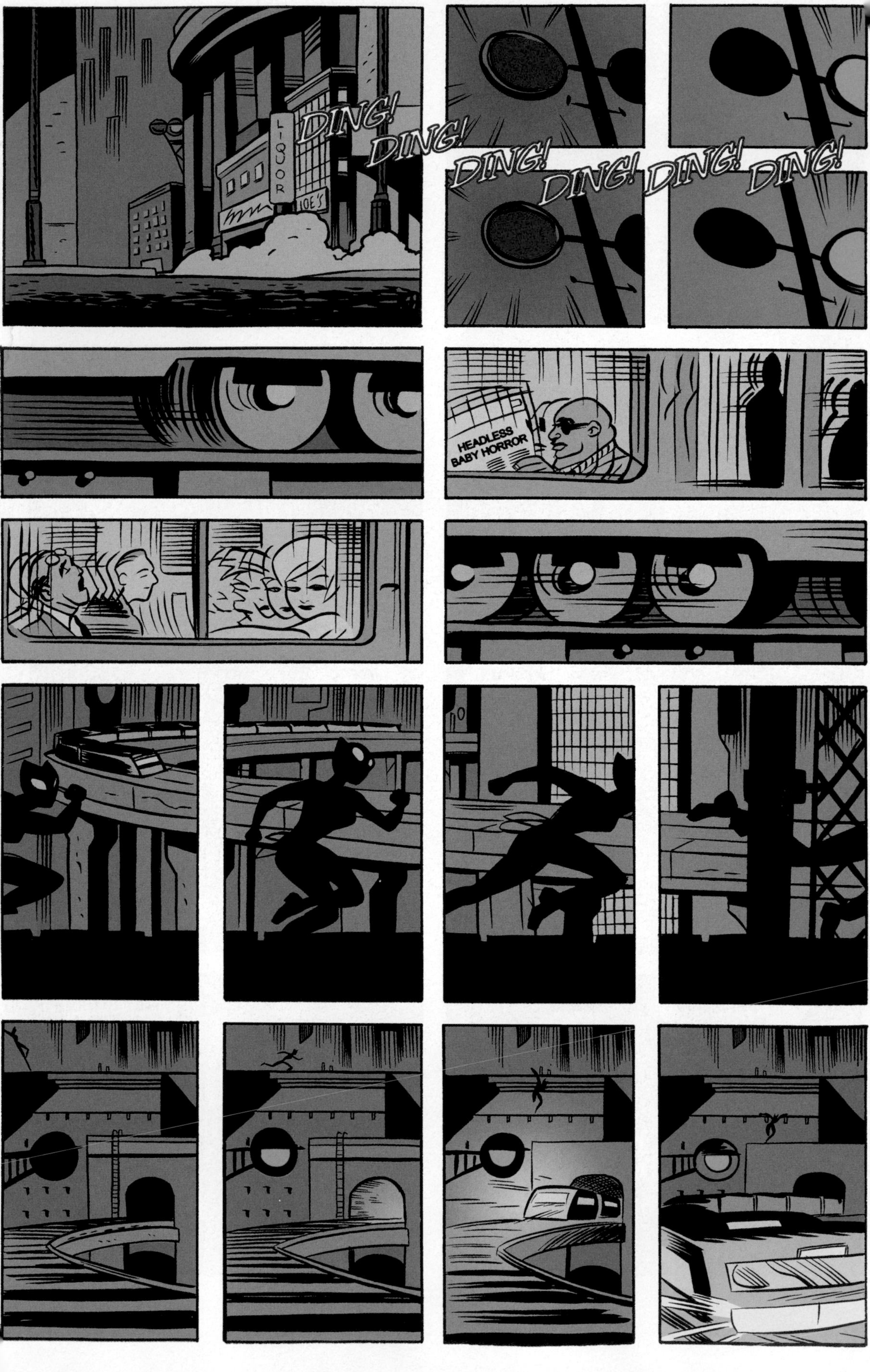
LIQUOR
JOE'S
DING!
DING!
DING!
DING!
DING!
DING!
HEADLESS BABY HORROR

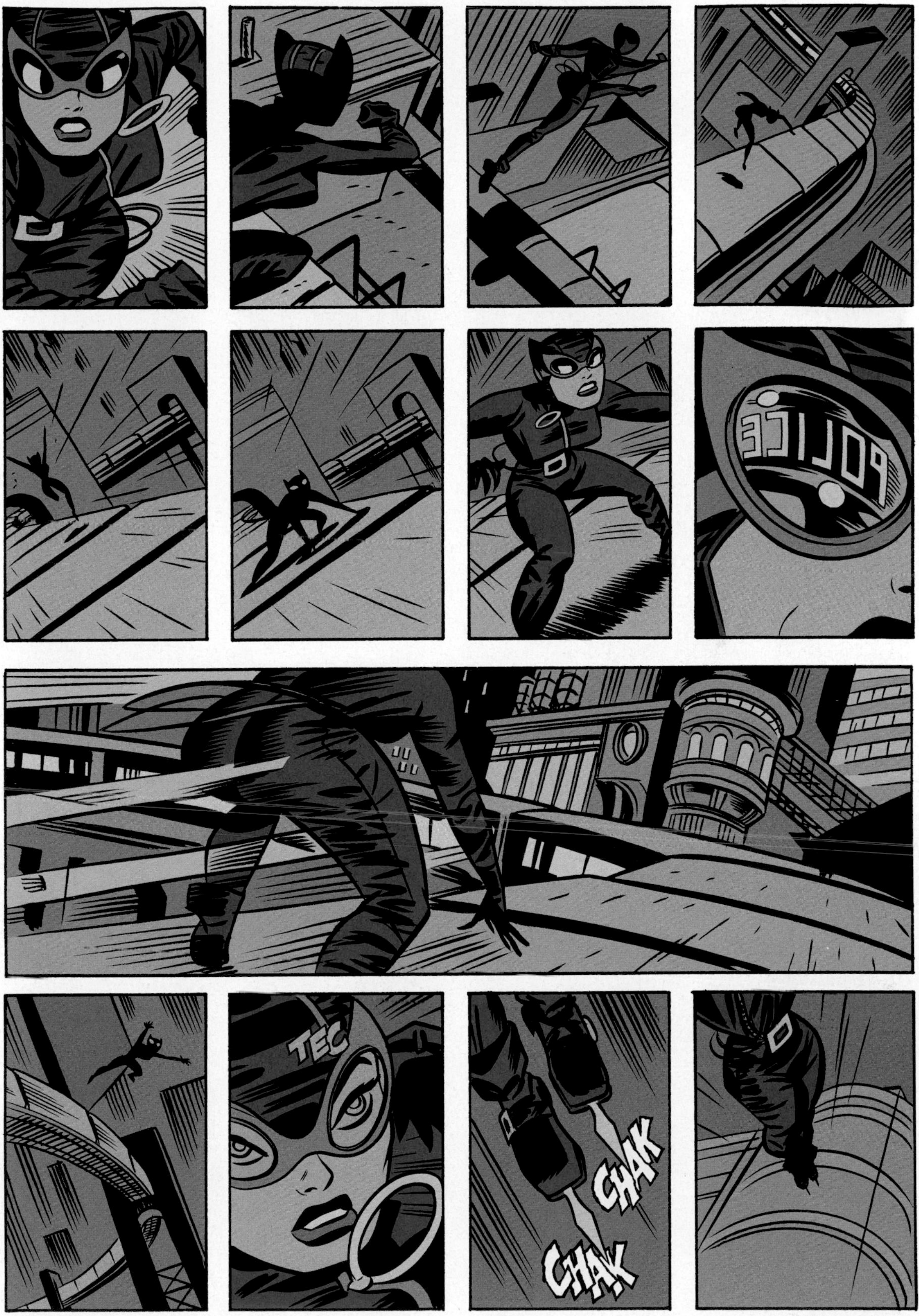
POLICE
TEC
CHAK
CHAK

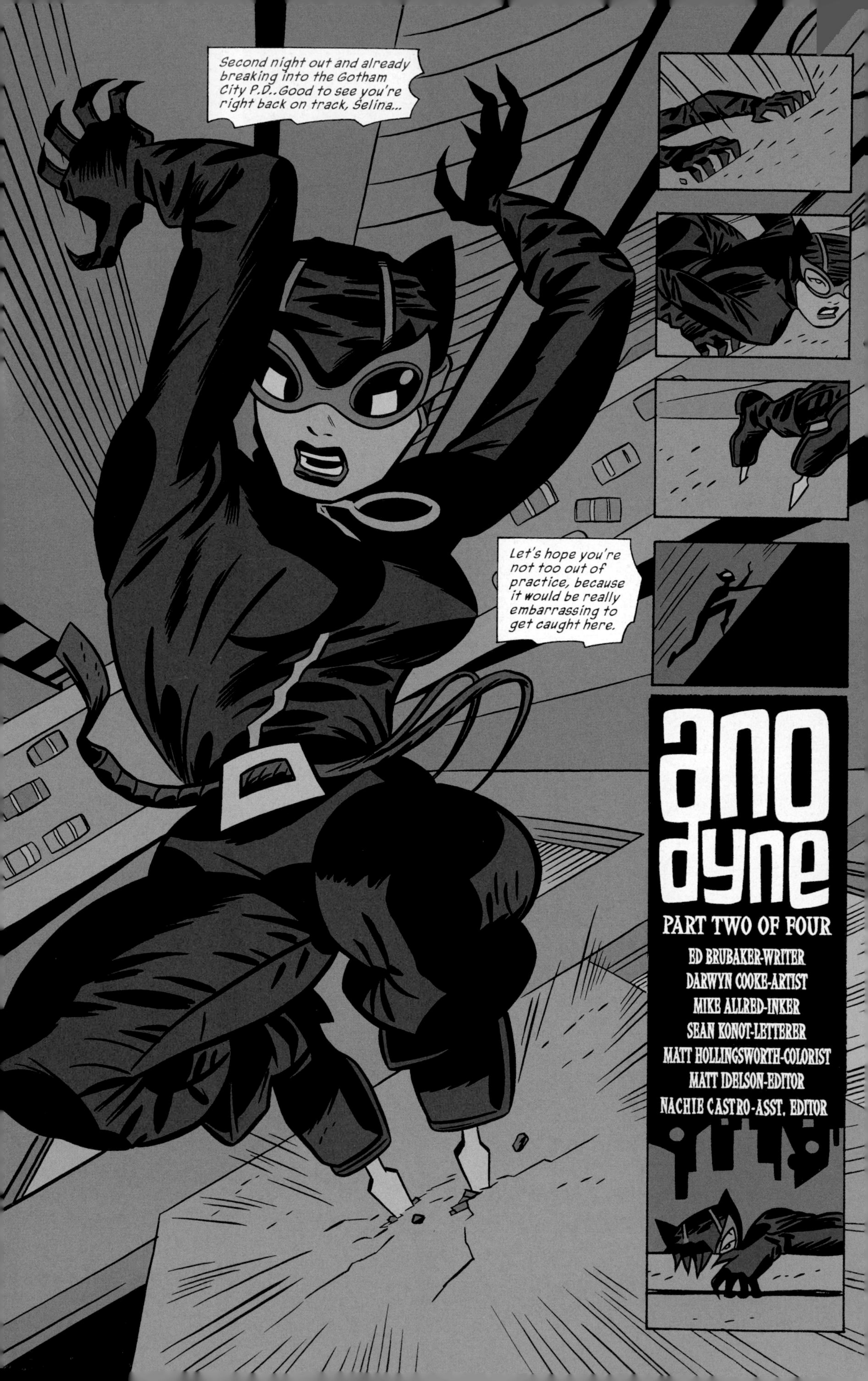
Second night out and already breaking into the Gotham City P.D..Good to see you're right back on track, Selina...
Let's hope you're not too out of practice, because it would be really embarrassing to get caught here.
ano dyne
PART TWO OF FOUR
ED BRUBAKER-WRITER
DARWYN COOKE-ARTIST
MIKE ALLRED-INKER
SEAN KONOT-LETTERER
MATT HOLLINGSWORTH-COLORIST
MATT IDELSON-EDITOR
NACHIE CASTRO-ASST. EDITOR

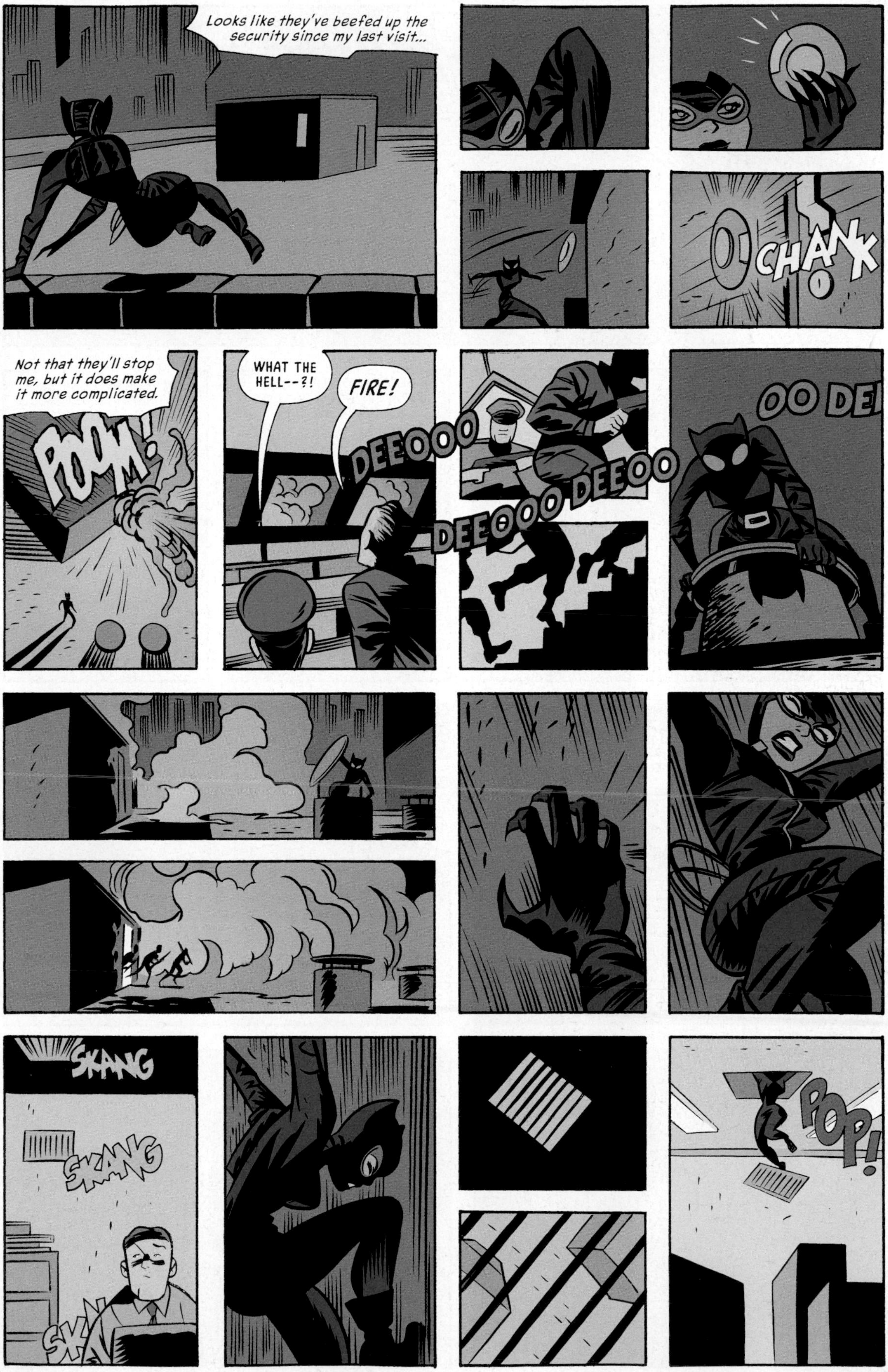

Looks like they've beefed up the security since my last visit...
CHANK
Not that they'll stop me, but it does make it more complicated.
POOM!
WHAT THE HELL--?!
FIRE!
DEEOOO
DEEOOO DEEOOO
OO DE
SKANG
SKANG

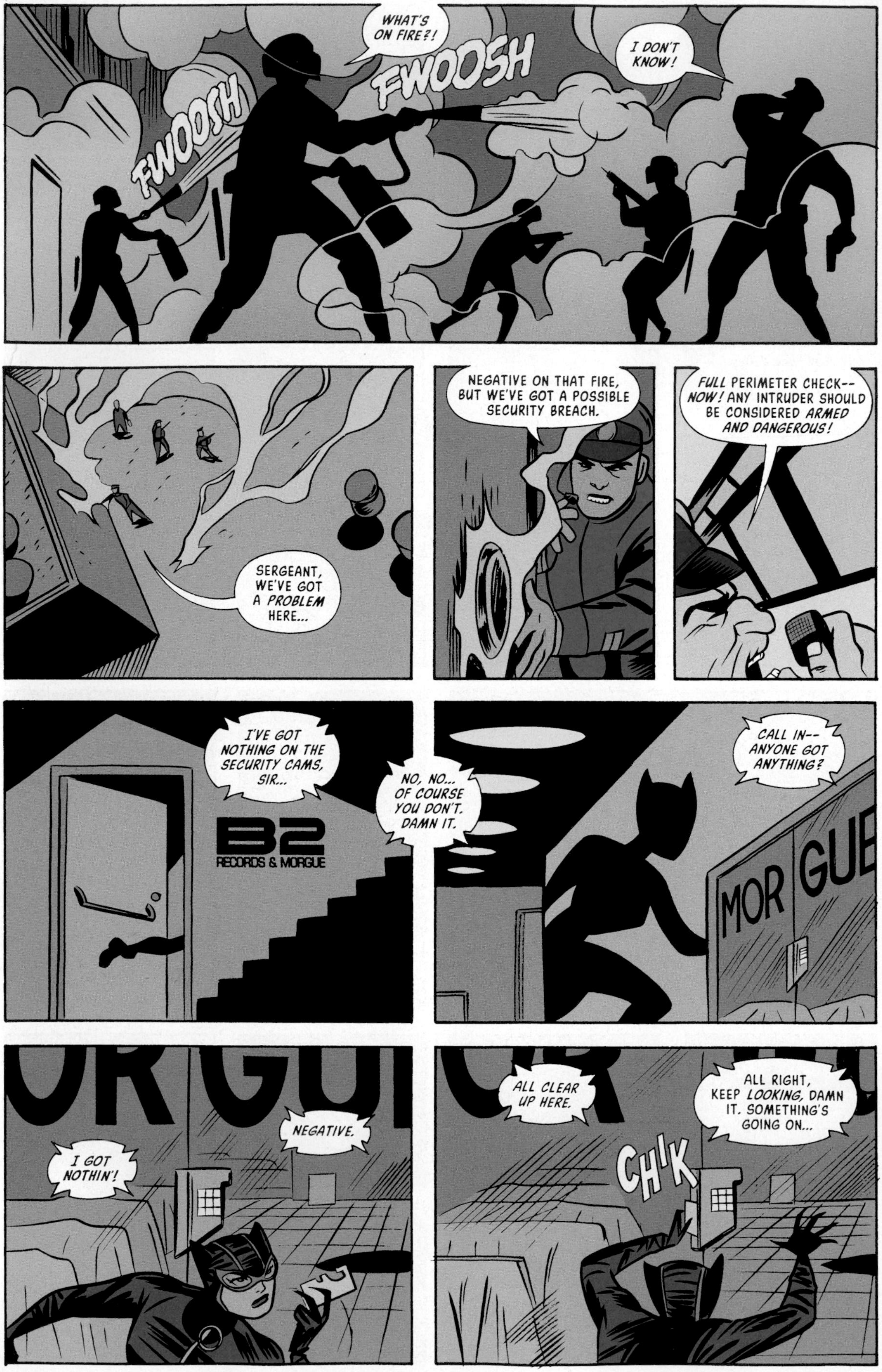
WHAT'S ON FIRE?!
FWOOSH
FWOOSH
I DON'T KNOW!
NEGATIVE ON THAT FIRE, BUT WE'VE GOT A POSSIBLE SECURITY BREACH.
FULL PERIMETER CHECK-- NOW! ANY INTRUDER SHOULD BE CONSIDERED ARMED AND DANGEROUS!
SERGEANT, WE'VE GOT A PROBLEM HERE...
I'VE GOT NOTHING ON THE SECURITY CAMS, SIR...
NO, NO... OF COURSE YOU DON'T. DAMN IT.
B2
RECORDS & MORGUE
CALL IN-- ANYONE GOT ANYTHING?
MOR GUE
NEGATIVE.
I GOT NOTHIN'!
ALL CLEAR UP HERE.
ALL RIGHT, KEEP LOOKING, DAMN IT. SOMETHING'S GOING ON...
CHIK

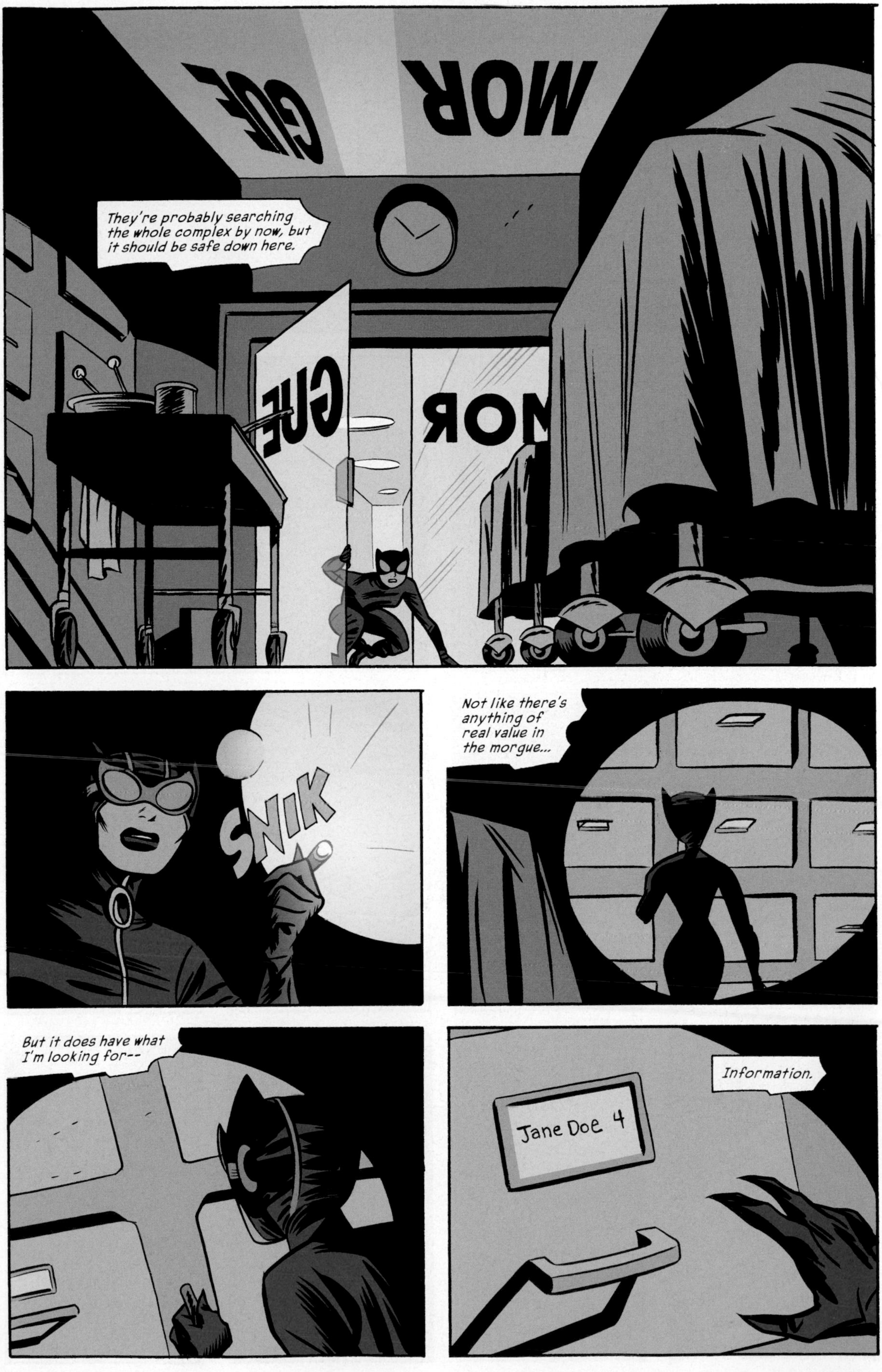

They're probably searching the whole complex by now, but it should be safe down here.
SNIK
Not like there's anything of real value in the morgue...
But it does have what I'm looking for--
Information.
Jane Doe 4

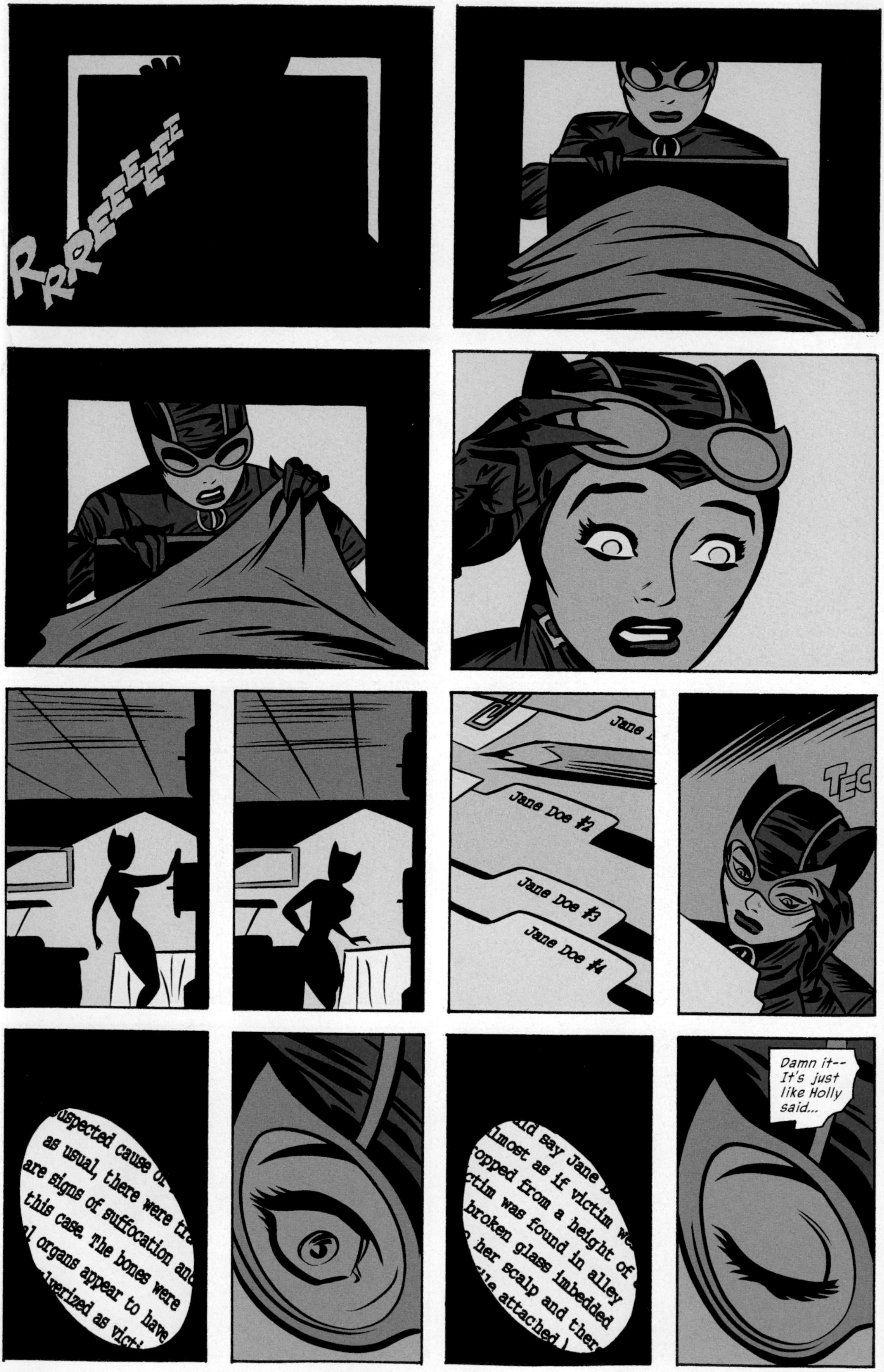

RREEEEEEEE
Jane Doe #2
Jane Doe #3
Jane Doe #4
TEC
suspected cause of
as usual, there were tr
are signs of suffocation and
this case. The bones were
l organs appear to have
lverized as victi
id say Jane
lmost as if victim we
ropped from a height of
ictim was found in alley
broken glass imbedded
o her scalp and ther
le attached.)
Damn it-- It's just like Holly said...

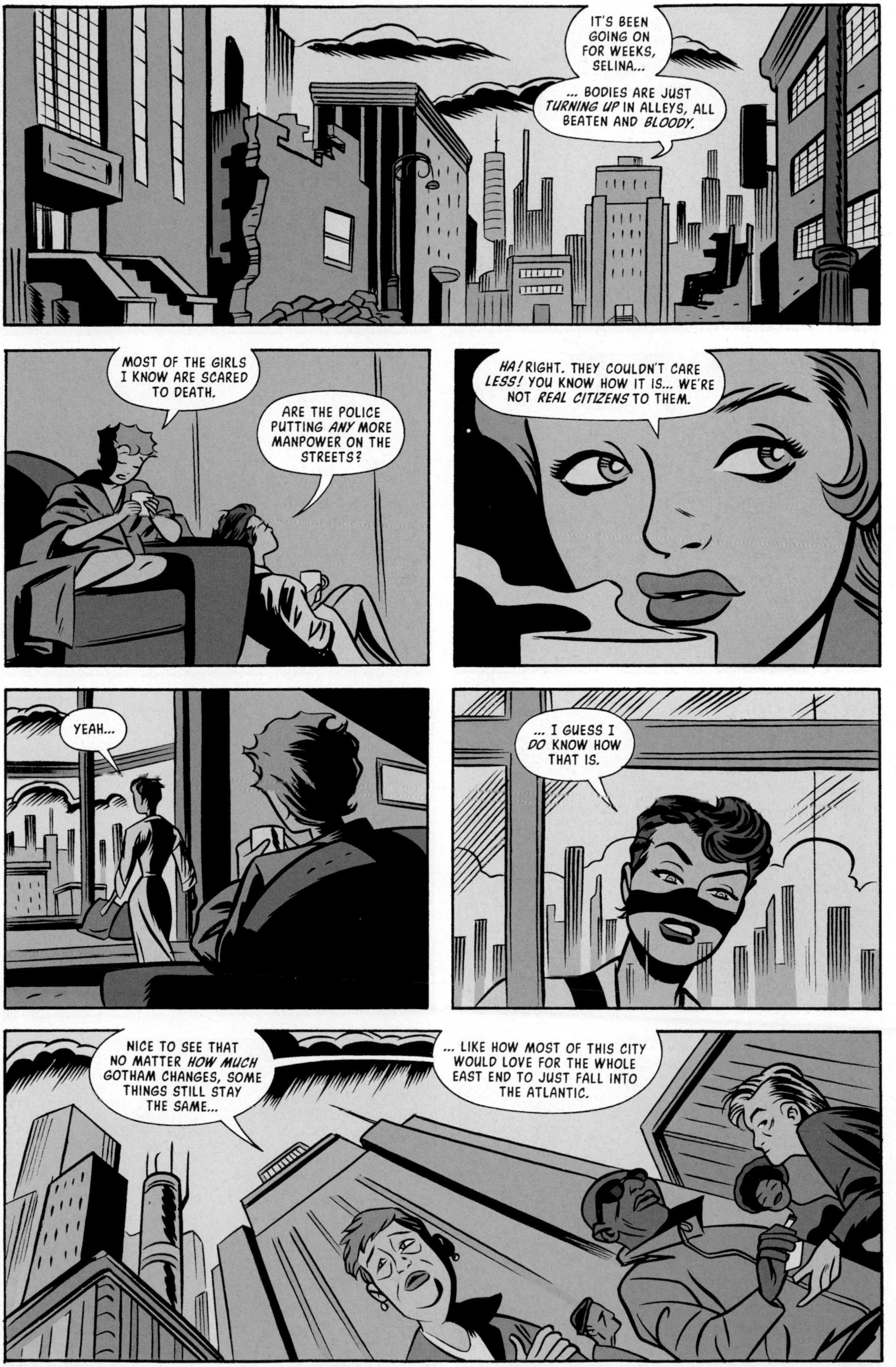
IT'S BEEN GOING ON FOR WEEKS, SELINA...
... BODIES ARE JUST TURNING UP IN ALLEYS, ALL BEATEN AND BLOODY.
MOST OF THE GIRLS I KNOW ARE SCARED TO DEATH.
ARE THE POLICE PUTTING ANY MORE MANPOWER ON THE STREETS?
HA! RIGHT. THEY COULDN'T CARE LESS! YOU KNOW HOW IT IS... WE'RE NOT REAL CITIZENS TO THEM.
YEAH...
... I GUESS I DO KNOW HOW THAT IS.
NICE TO SEE THAT NO MATTER HOW MUCH GOTHAM CHANGES, SOME THINGS STILL STAY THE SAME...
... LIKE HOW MOST OF THIS CITY WOULD LOVE FOR THE WHOLE EAST END TO JUST FALL INTO THE ATLANTIC.

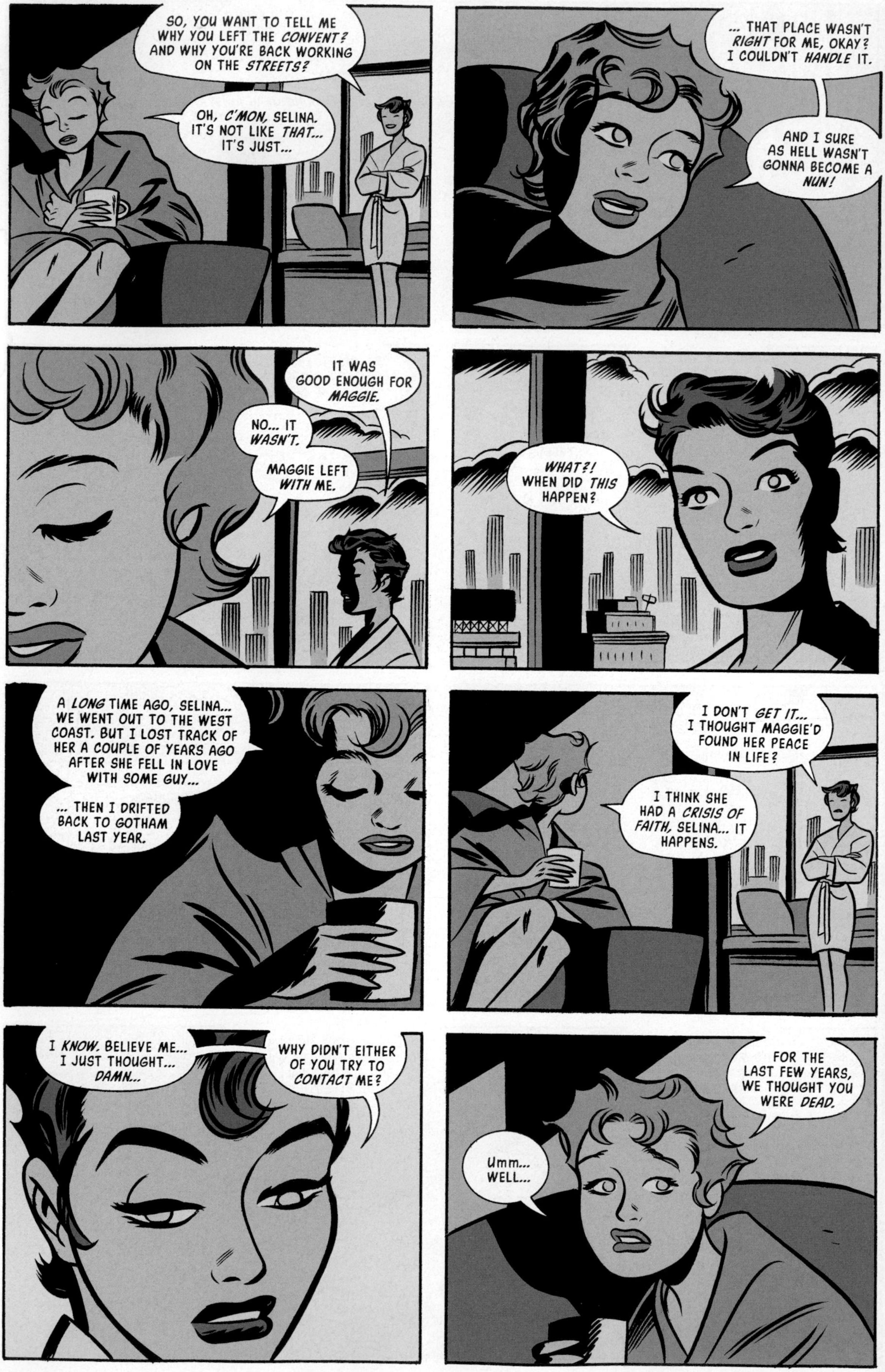
SO, YOU WANT TO TELL ME WHY YOU LEFT THE CONVENT? AND WHY YOU'RE BACK WORKING ON THE STREETS?
OH, C'MON, SELINA. IT'S NOT LIKE THAT... IT'S JUST...
... THAT PLACE WASN'T RIGHT FOR ME, OKAY? I COULDN'T HANDLE IT.
AND I SURE AS HELL WASN'T GONNA BECOME A NUN!
IT WAS GOOD ENOUGH FOR MAGGIE.
NO... IT WASN'T.
MAGGIE LEFT WITH ME.
WHAT?! WHEN DID THIS HAPPEN?
A LONG TIME AGO, SELINA... WE WENT OUT TO THE WEST COAST. BUT I LOST TRACK OF HER A COUPLE OF YEARS AGO AFTER SHE FELL IN LOVE WITH SOME GUY...
... THEN I DRIFTED BACK TO GOTHAM LAST YEAR.
I DON'T GET IT... I THOUGHT MAGGIE'D FOUND HER PEACE IN LIFE?
I THINK SHE HAD A CRISIS OF FAITH, SELINA... IT HAPPENS.
I KNOW. BELIEVE ME... I JUST THOUGHT... DAMN...
WHY DIDN'T EITHER OF YOU TRY TO CONTACT ME?
FOR THE LAST FEW YEARS, WE THOUGHT YOU WERE DEAD.
Umm... WELL...

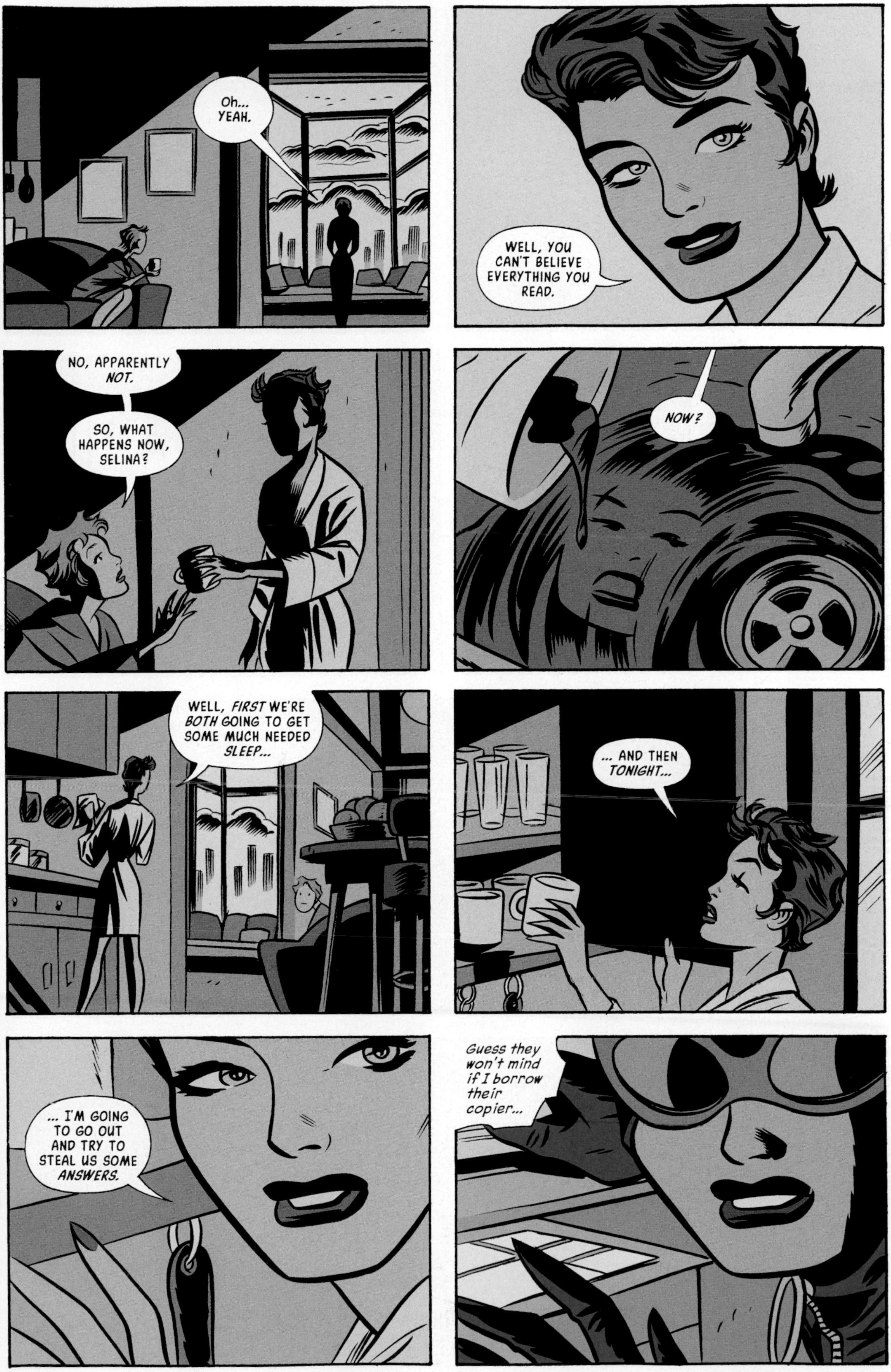
Oh... YEAH.
WELL, YOU CAN'T BELIEVE EVERYTHING YOU READ.
NO, APPARENTLY NOT.
SO, WHAT HAPPENS NOW, SELINA?
NOW?
WELL, FIRST WE'RE BOTH GOING TO GET SOME MUCH NEEDED SLEEP...
... AND THEN TONIGHT...
... I'M GOING TO GO OUT AND TRY TO STEAL US SOME ANSWERS.
Guess they won't mind if I borrow their copier...

I'd rather not just take this report, on the off-chance the cops decide to get off their butts and actually do something.

B2
RECORDS & MORGUE

WHIIRRR-CHK-WHIIIRR-

WHIIIRRR-CHK-WHIIIRRR-CHK-

WHIIRRR-CHK-

WHIIIRRR-CHK-WHIIIRR-

HELLO?

IS SOMEONE THERE?

WHIIRRR-CHK-WHIIIRR-CHK-WHIIIRR-

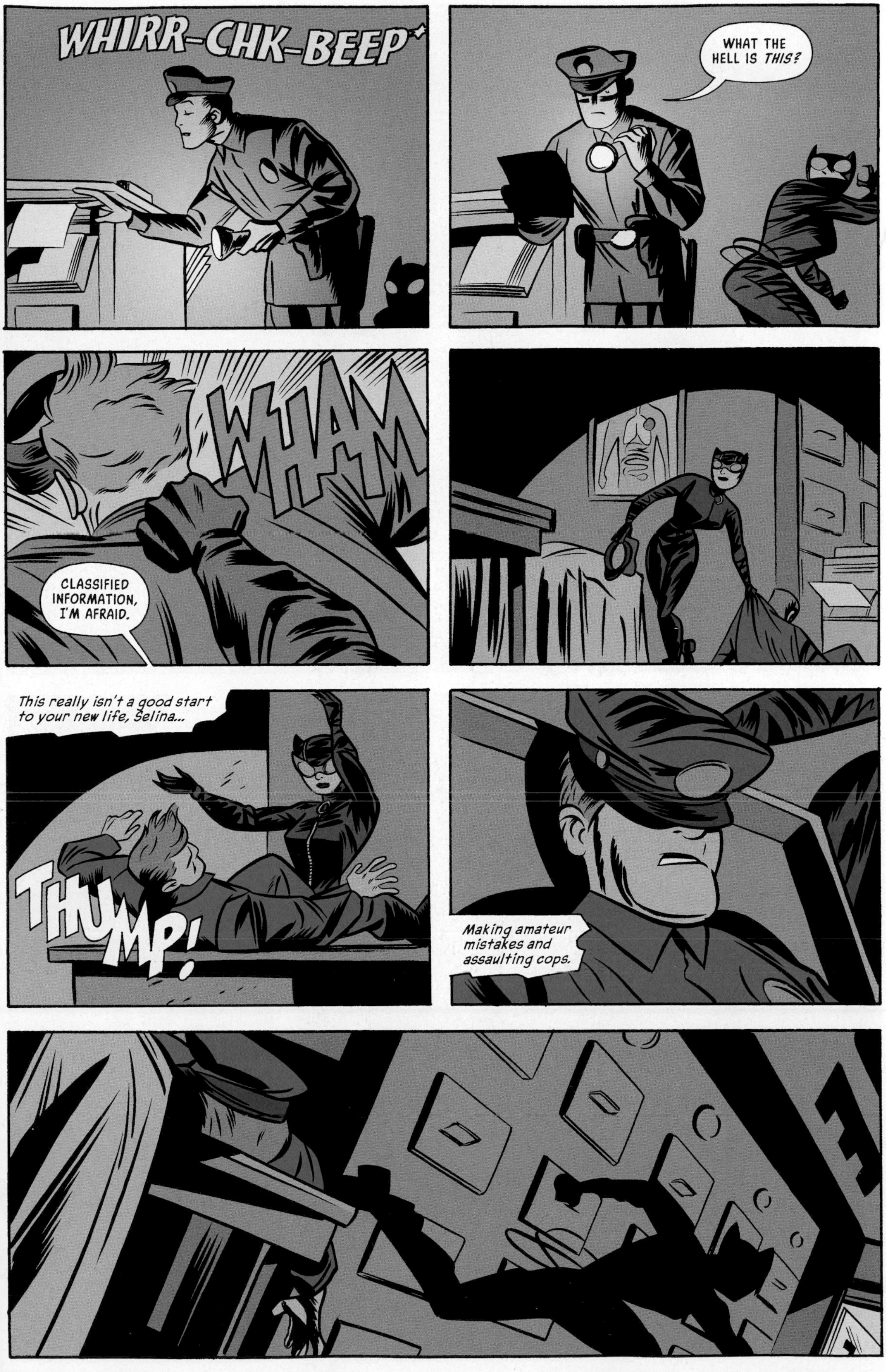

WHIRR-CHK-BEEP
WHAT THE HELL IS THIS?
WHAM
CLASSIFIED INFORMATION, I'M AFRAID.
This really isn't a good start to your new life, Selina...
THUMP!
Making amateur mistakes and assaulting cops.

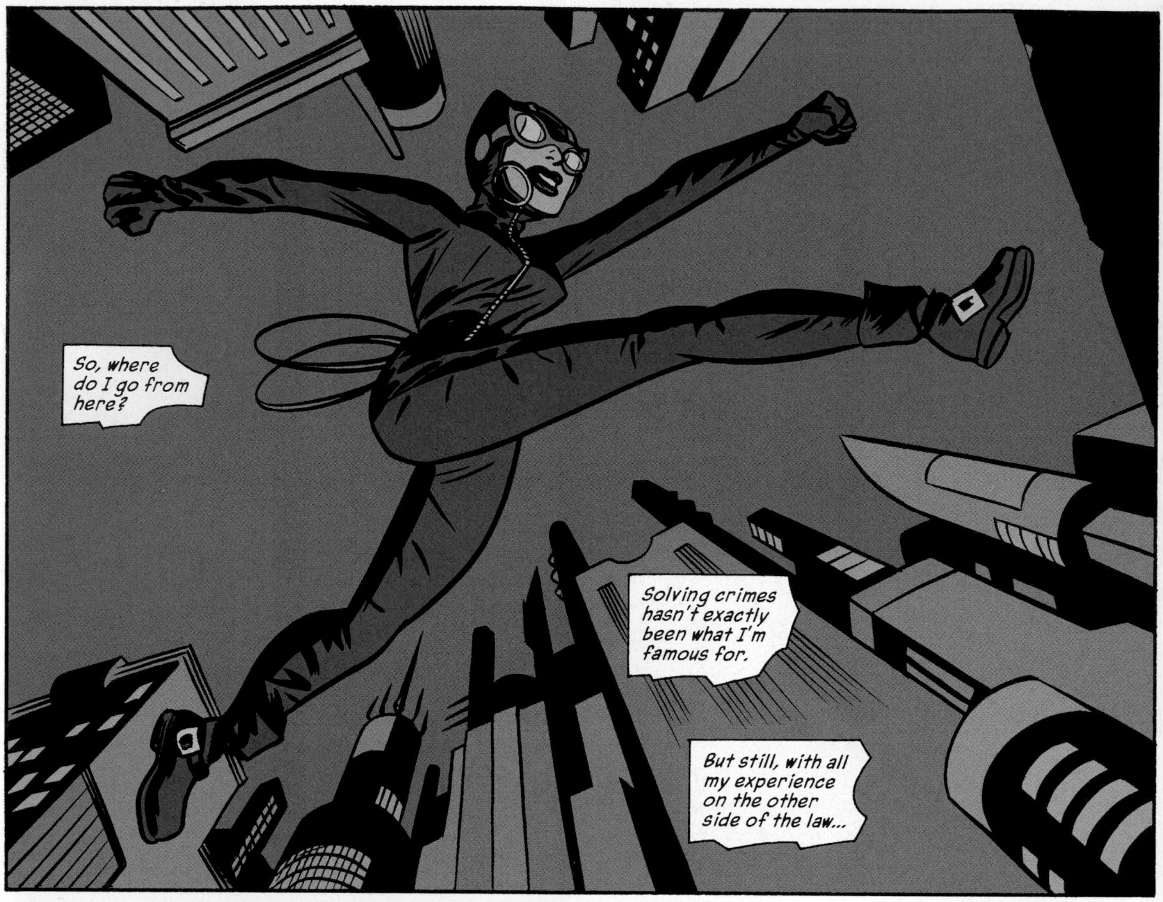
So, where do I go from here?
Solving crimes hasn't exactly been what I'm famous for.
But still, with all my experience on the other side of the law...

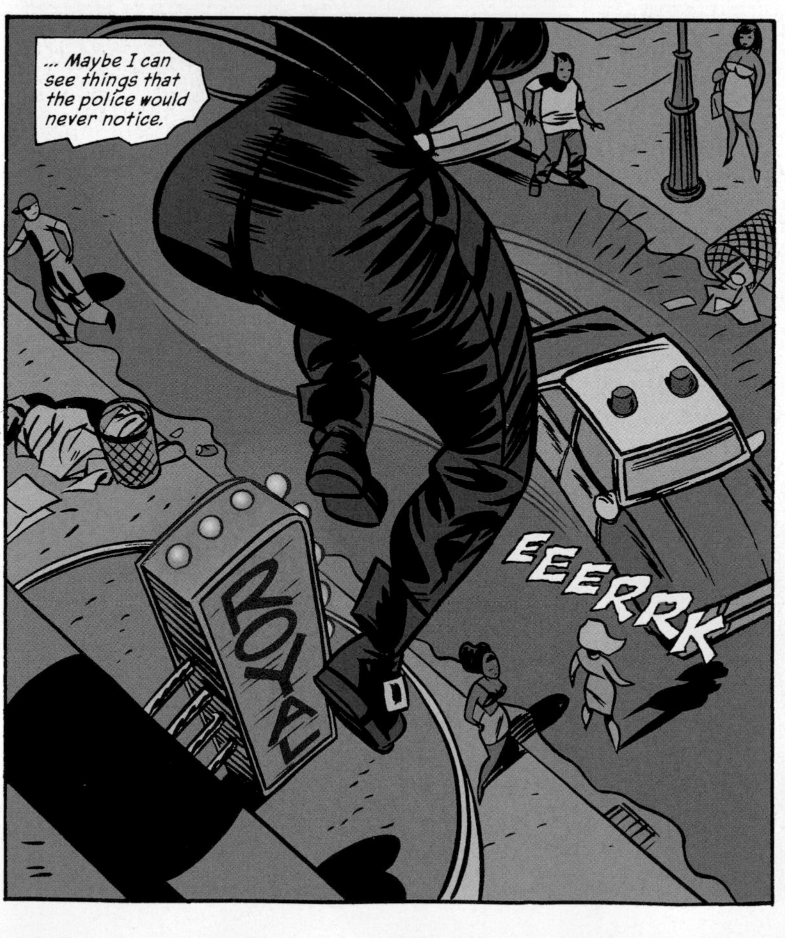
... Maybe I can see things that the police would never notice.
ROYAL
EEERRRK

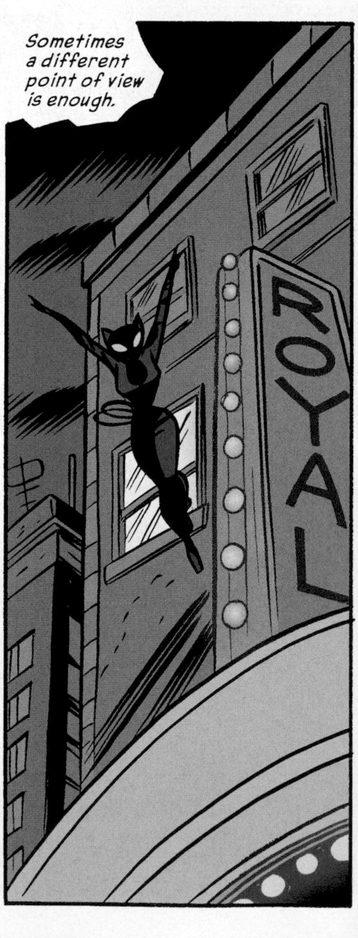
Sometimes a different point of view is enough.
ROYAL

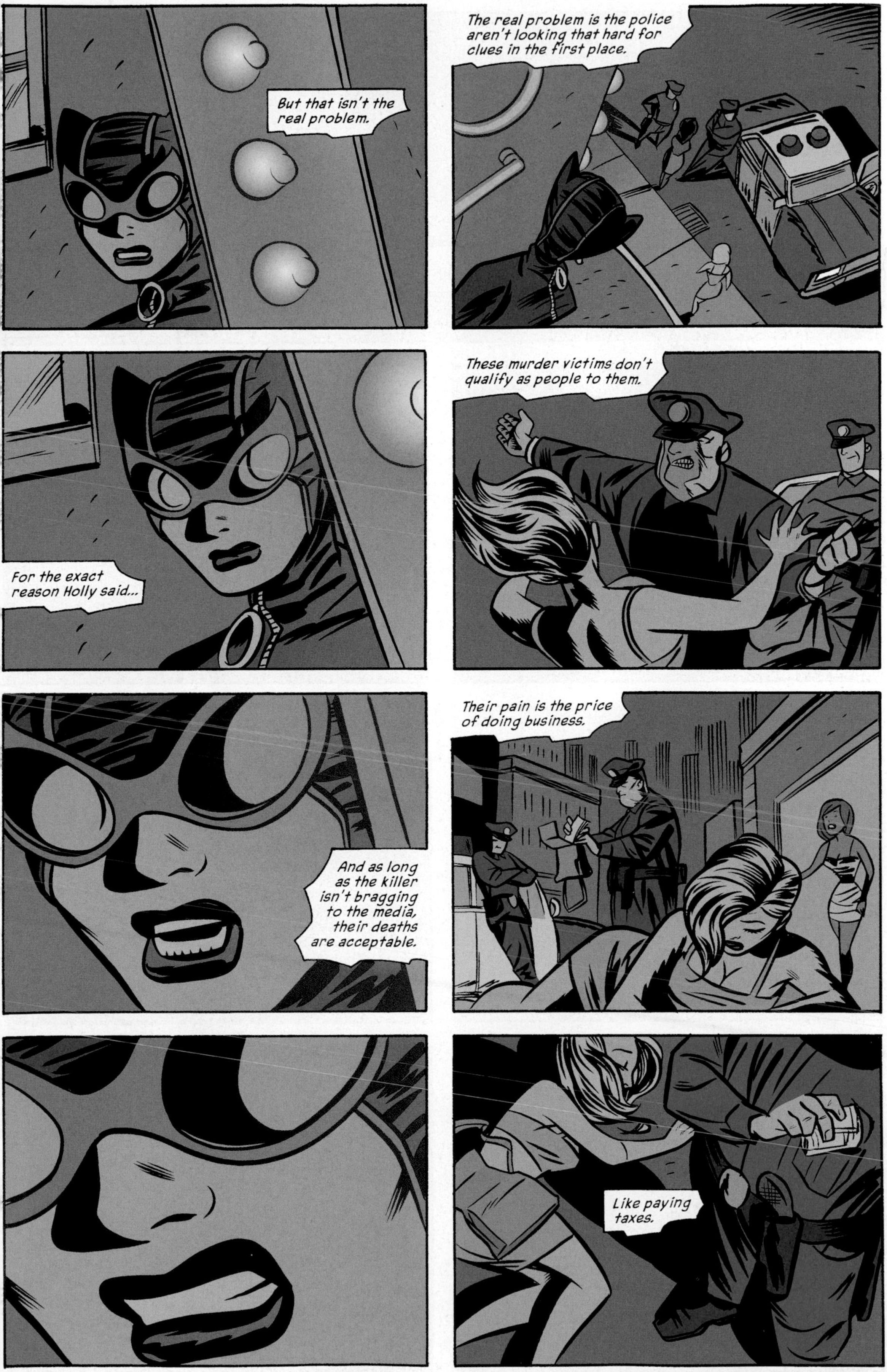
But that isn't the real problem.
The real problem is the police aren't looking that hard for clues in the first place.
For the exact reason Holly said...
These murder victims don't qualify as people to them.
And as long as the killer isn't bragging to the media, their deaths are acceptable.
Their pain is the price of doing business.
Like paying taxes.

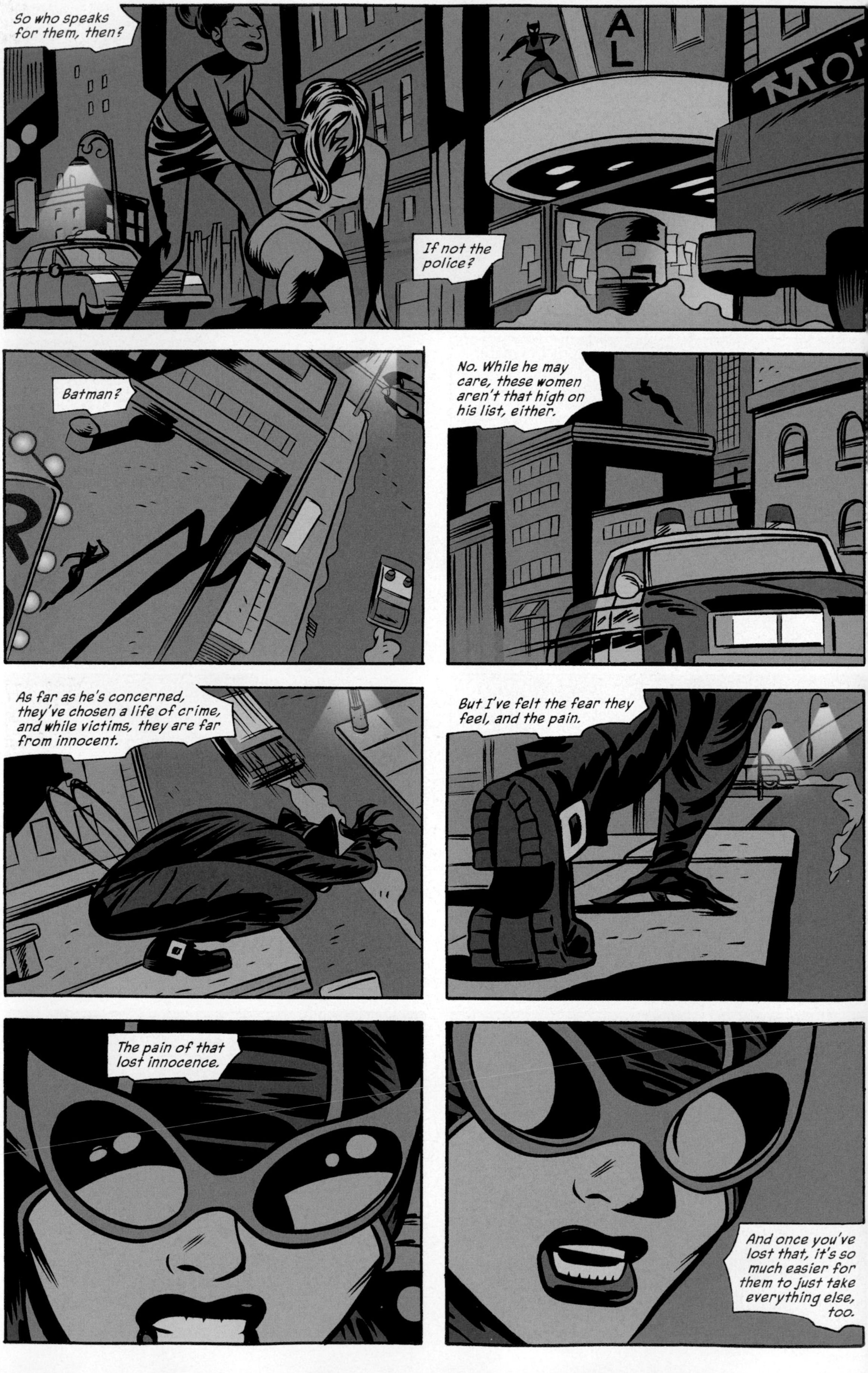
So who speaks for them, then?
If not the police?
Batman?
No. While he may care, these women aren't that high on his list, either.
As far as he's concerned, they've chosen a life of crime, and while victims, they are far from innocent.
But I've felt the fear they feel, and the pain.
The pain of that lost innocence.
And once you've lost that, it's so much easier for them to just take everything else, too.

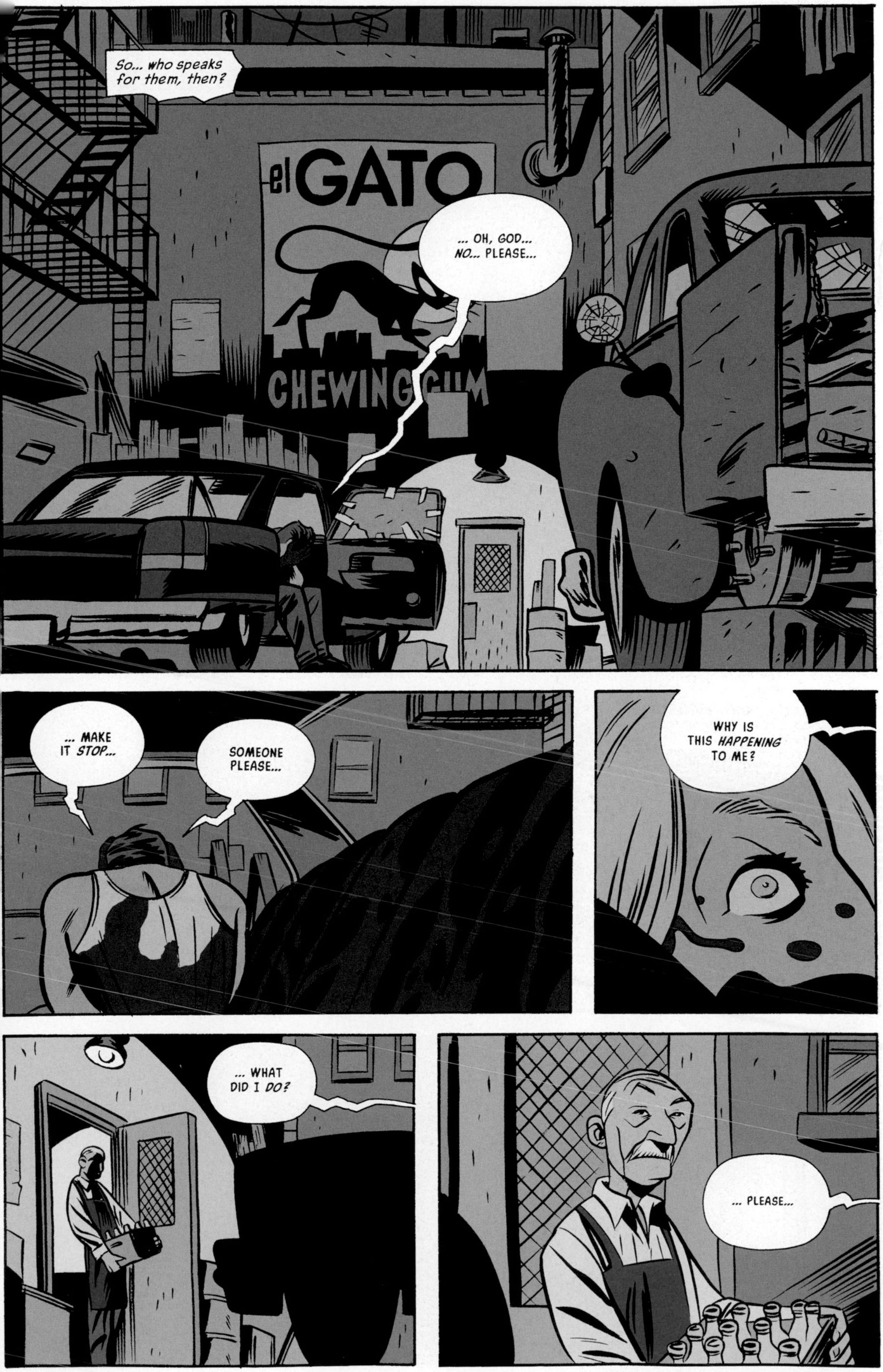
So... who speaks for them, then?
el GATO
CHEWING GUM
... OH, GOD... NO... PLEASE...
... MAKE IT STOP...
SOMEONE PLEASE...
WHY IS THIS HAPPENING TO ME?
... WHAT DID I DO?
... PLEASE...

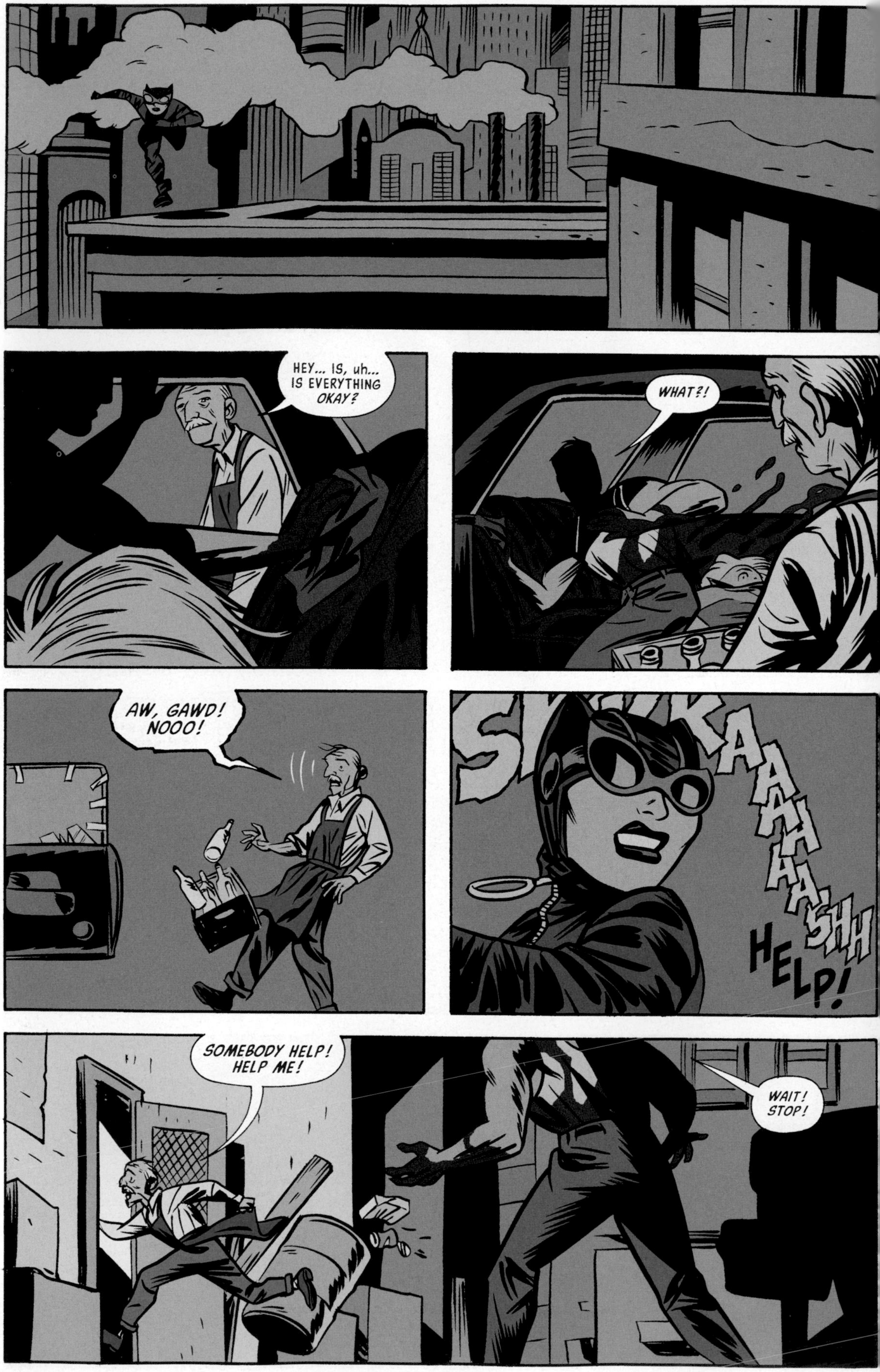
HEY... IS, uh... IS EVERYTHING OKAY?
WHAT?!
AW, GAWD! NOOO!
HELP!
SOMEBODY HELP! HELP ME!
WAIT! STOP!

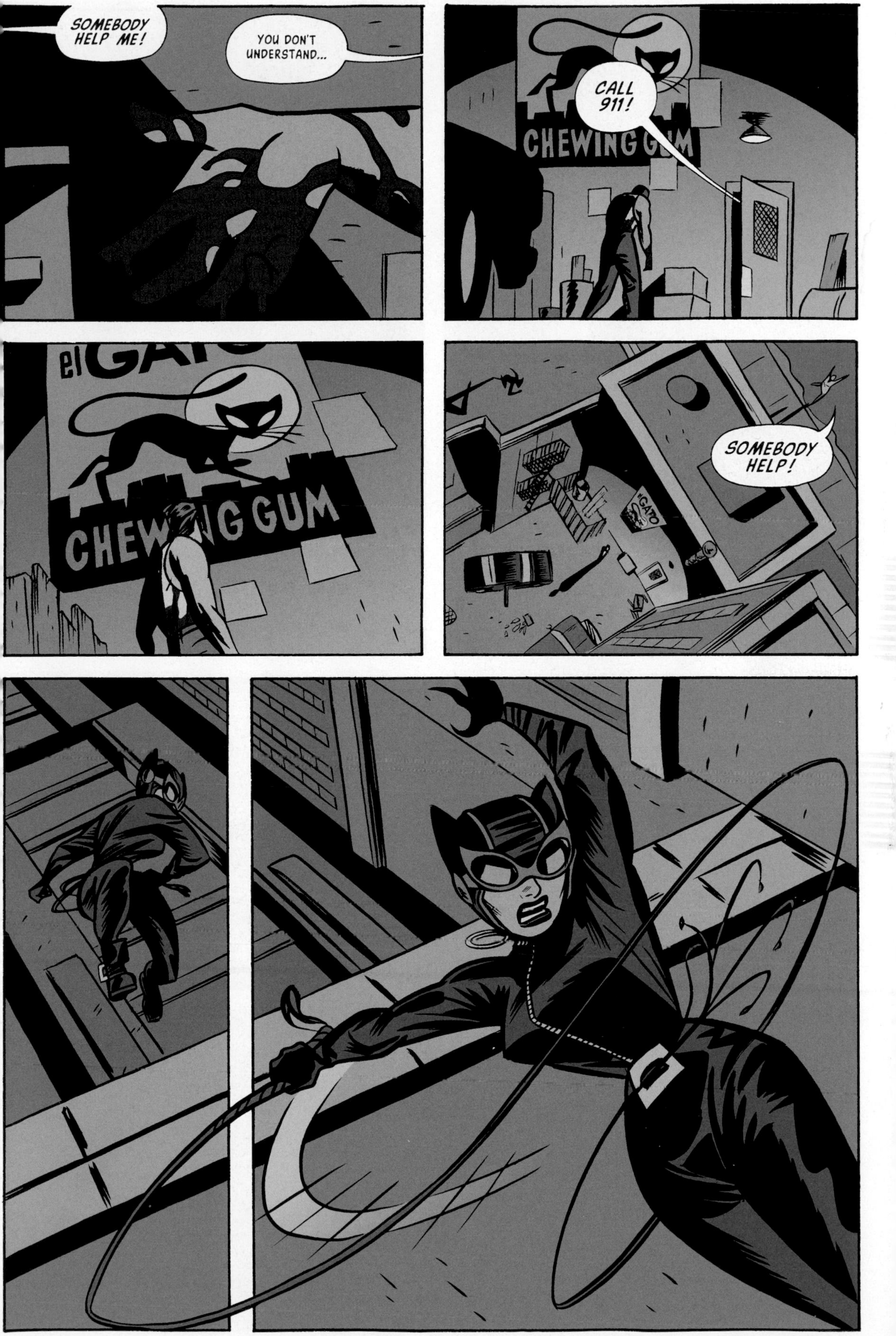
SOMEBODY HELP ME!
YOU DON'T UNDERSTAND...
el GATO
CHEWING GUM
CALL 911!
el GATO
CHEWING GUM
SOMEBODY HELP!

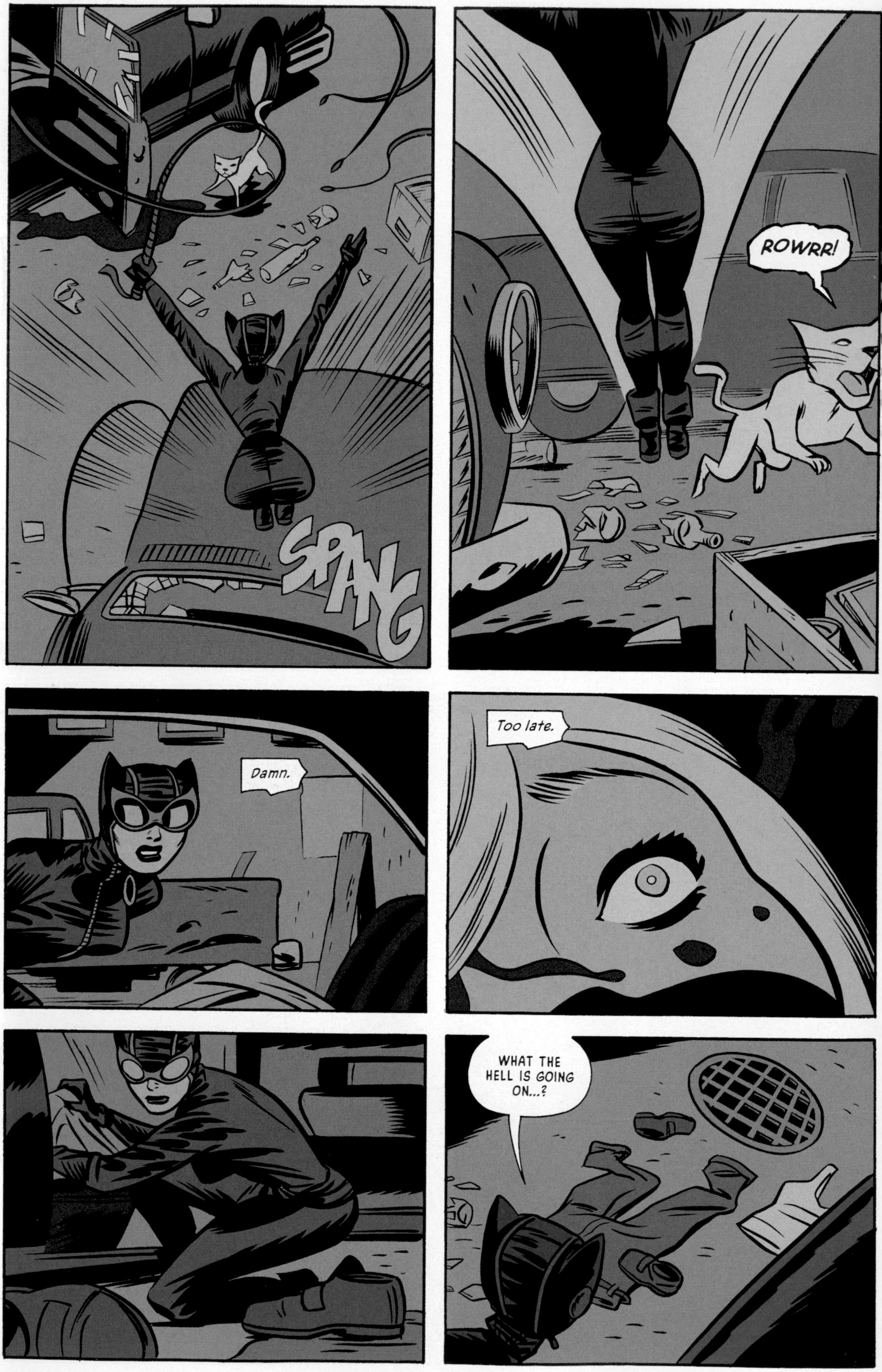
SPANG
ROWRR!
Damn.
Too late.
WHAT THE HELL IS GOING ON...?

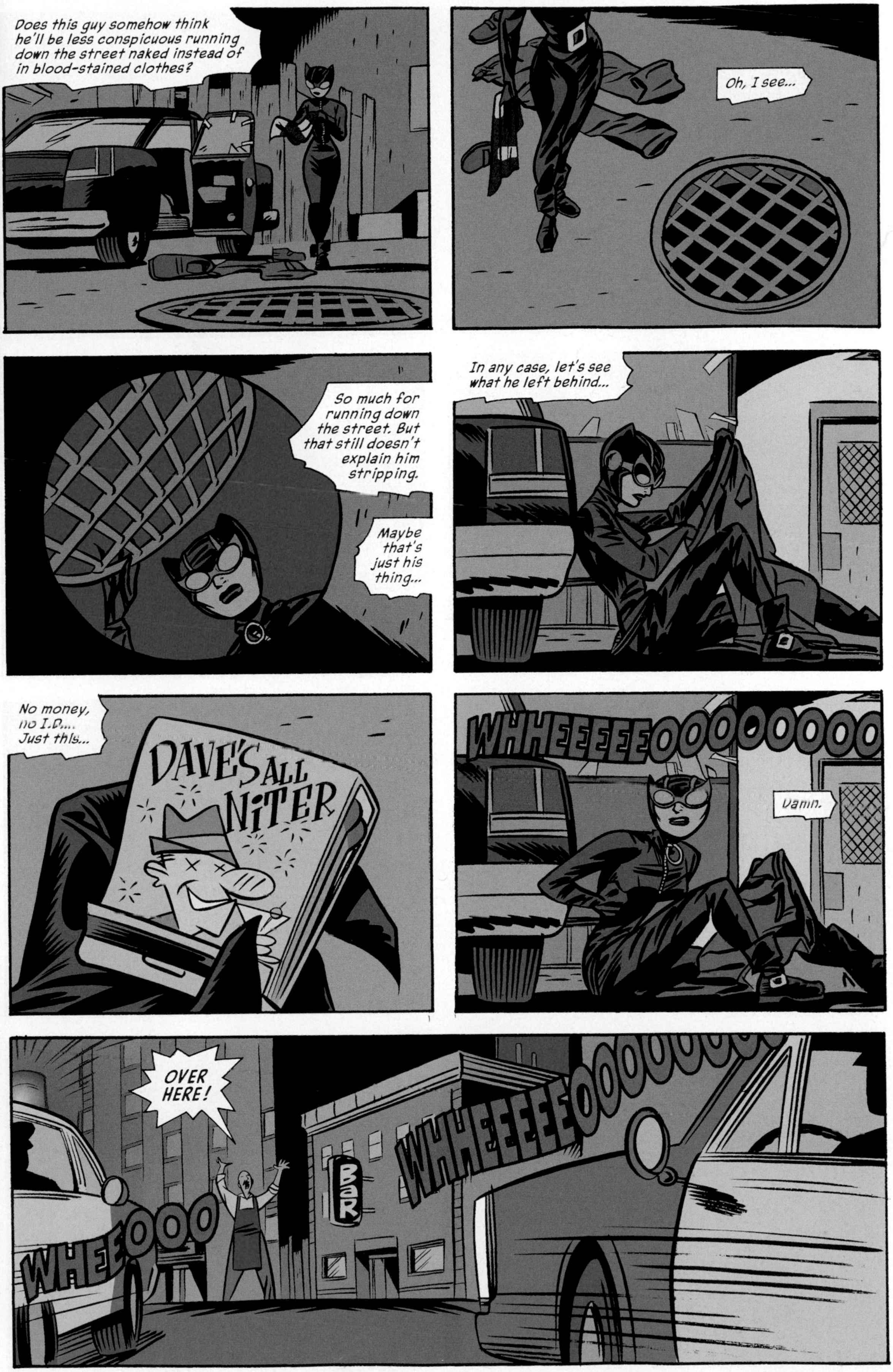
Does this guy somehow think he'll be less conspicuous running down the street naked instead of in blood-stained clothes?
Oh, I see...
So much for running down the street. But that still doesn't explain him stripping.
Maybe that's just his thing...
In any case, let's see what he left behind...
No money, no I.D.... Just this...
DAVE'S ALL NITER
WHHEEEEEOOOOOOOO
Damn.
OVER HERE!
BAR
WHEEOOO
WHHEEEEEOOOOOOO

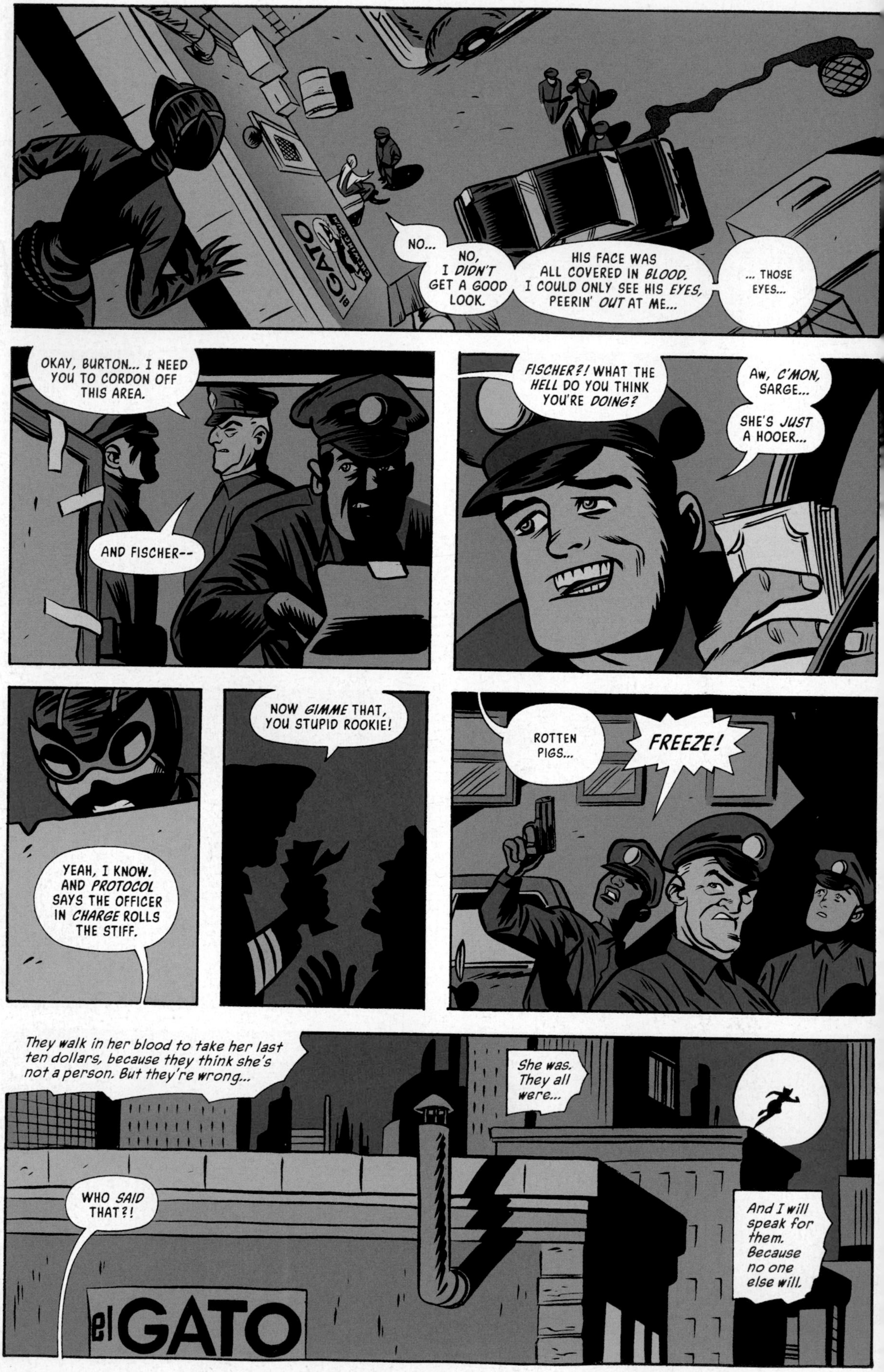
NO...
NO, I DIDN'T GET A GOOD LOOK.
HIS FACE WAS ALL COVERED IN BLOOD. I COULD ONLY SEE HIS EYES, PEERIN' OUT AT ME...
... THOSE EYES...
el GATO
OKAY, BURTON... I NEED YOU TO CORDON OFF THIS AREA.
AND FISCHER--
FISCHER?! WHAT THE HELL DO YOU THINK YOU'RE DOING?
Aw, C'MON, SARGE...
SHE'S JUST A HOOER...
YEAH, I KNOW. AND PROTOCOL SAYS THE OFFICER IN CHARGE ROLLS THE STIFF.
NOW GIMME THAT, YOU STUPID ROOKIE!
ROTTEN PIGS...
FREEZE!
They walk in her blood to take her last ten dollars, because they think she's not a person. But they're wrong...
She was. They all were...
WHO SAID THAT?!
And I will speak for them. Because no one else will.
el GATO

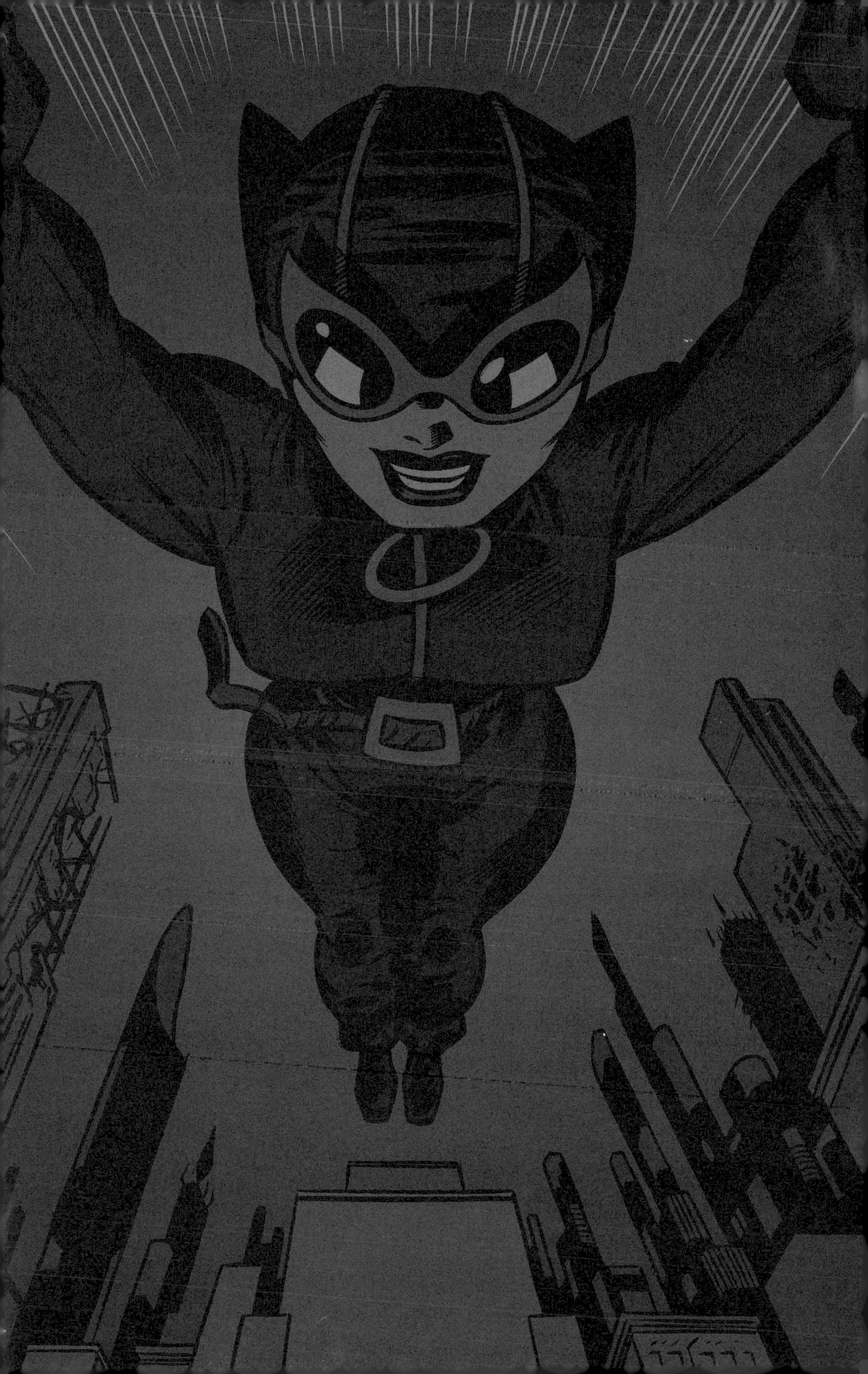

Catwoman 3 Cover by Darwyn Cooke

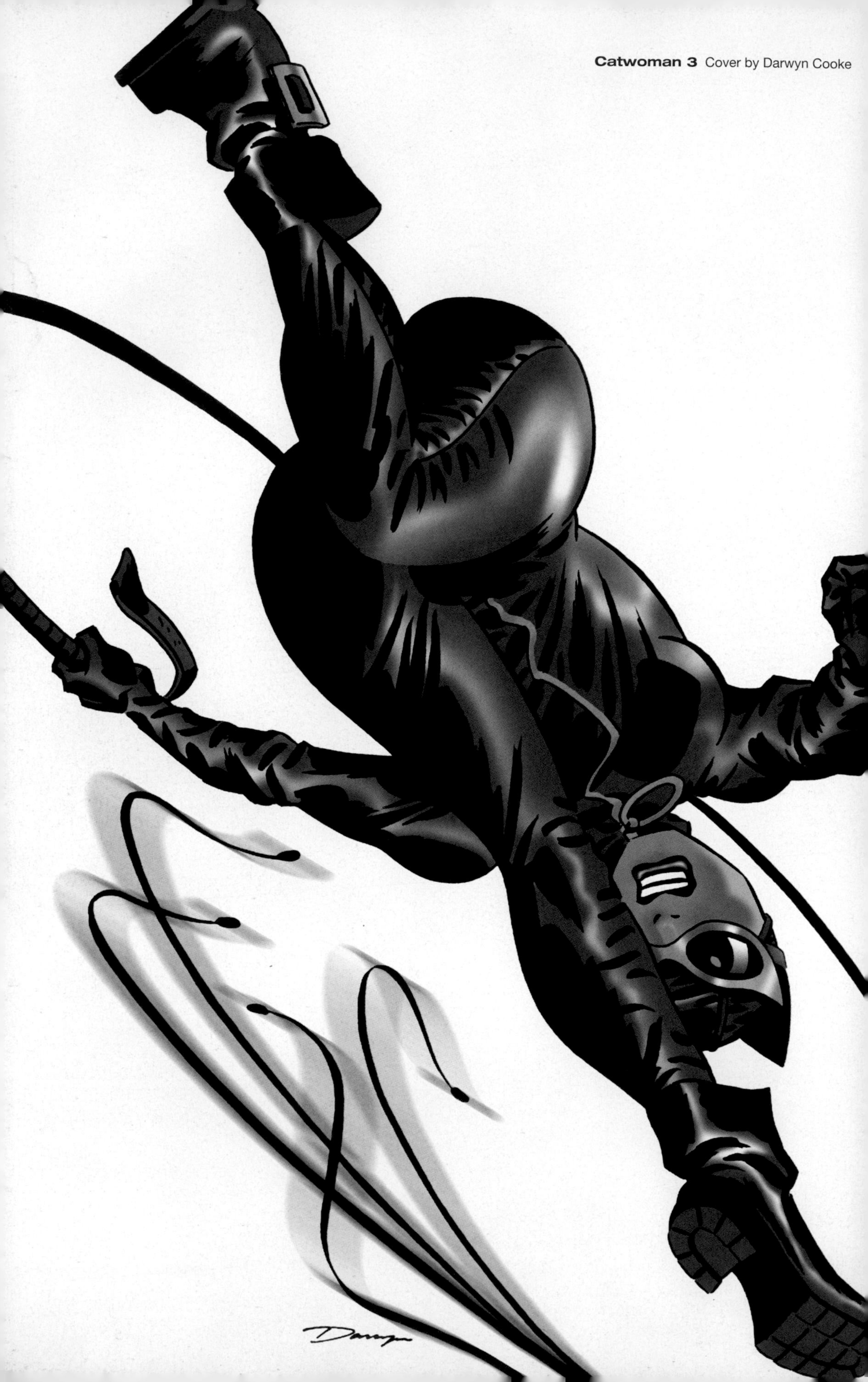

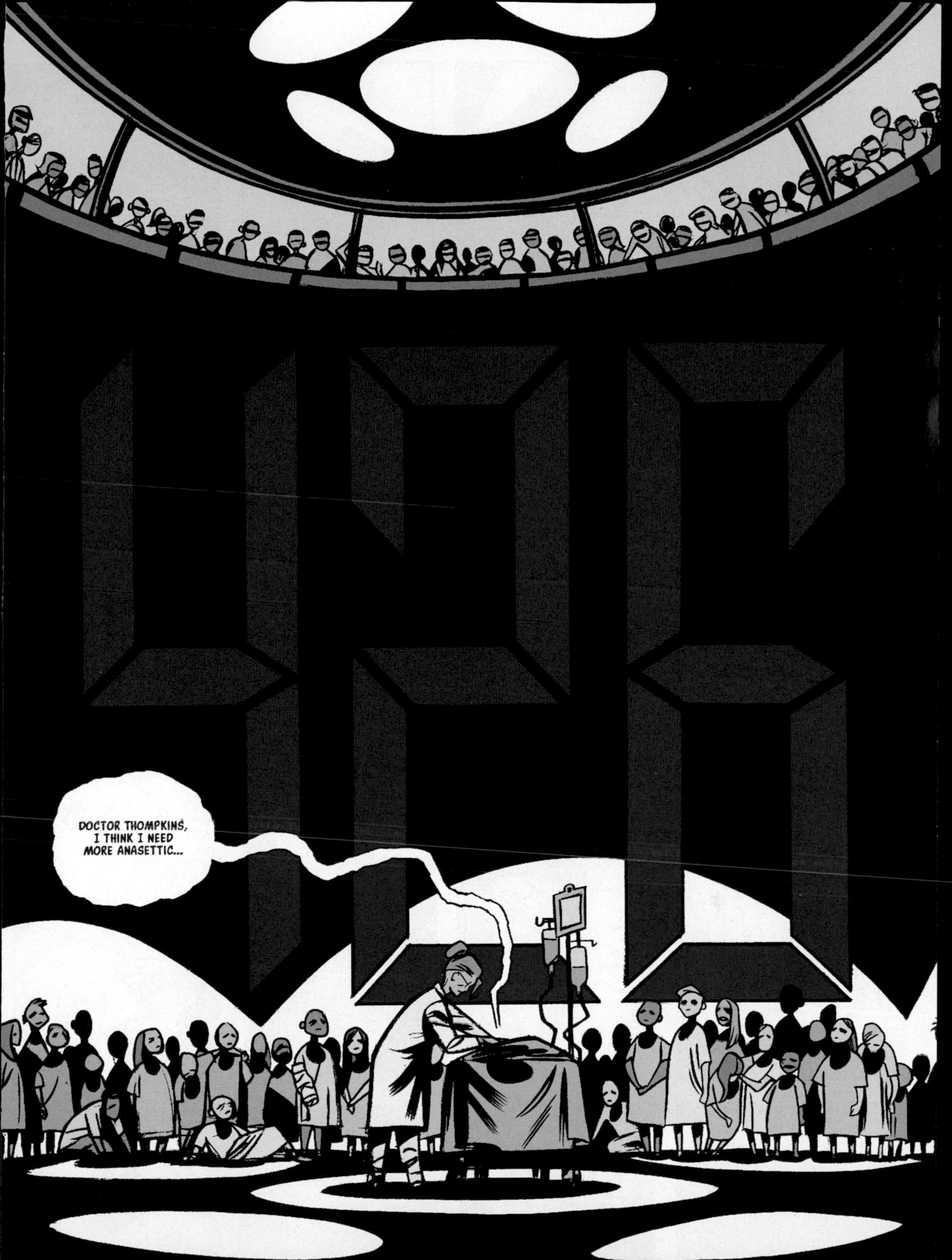
0:09
DOCTOR THOMPKINS, I THINK I NEED MORE ANASETTIC...

NO, IT'S GOING TO BE *ALL RIGHT*... JUST *RELAX*.

AM I GONNA *DIE*, DOCTOR THOMPKINS?

OF *COURSE* NOT...

TAP

'CAUSE I DON'T *FEEL* SO *GOOD*... I THINK I SHOT MYSELF...

DANNY SAID IT WASN'T LOADED, THOUGH...

TAP TAP TAP

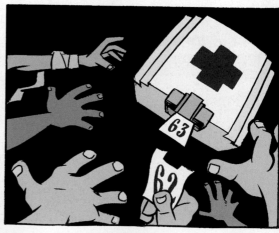

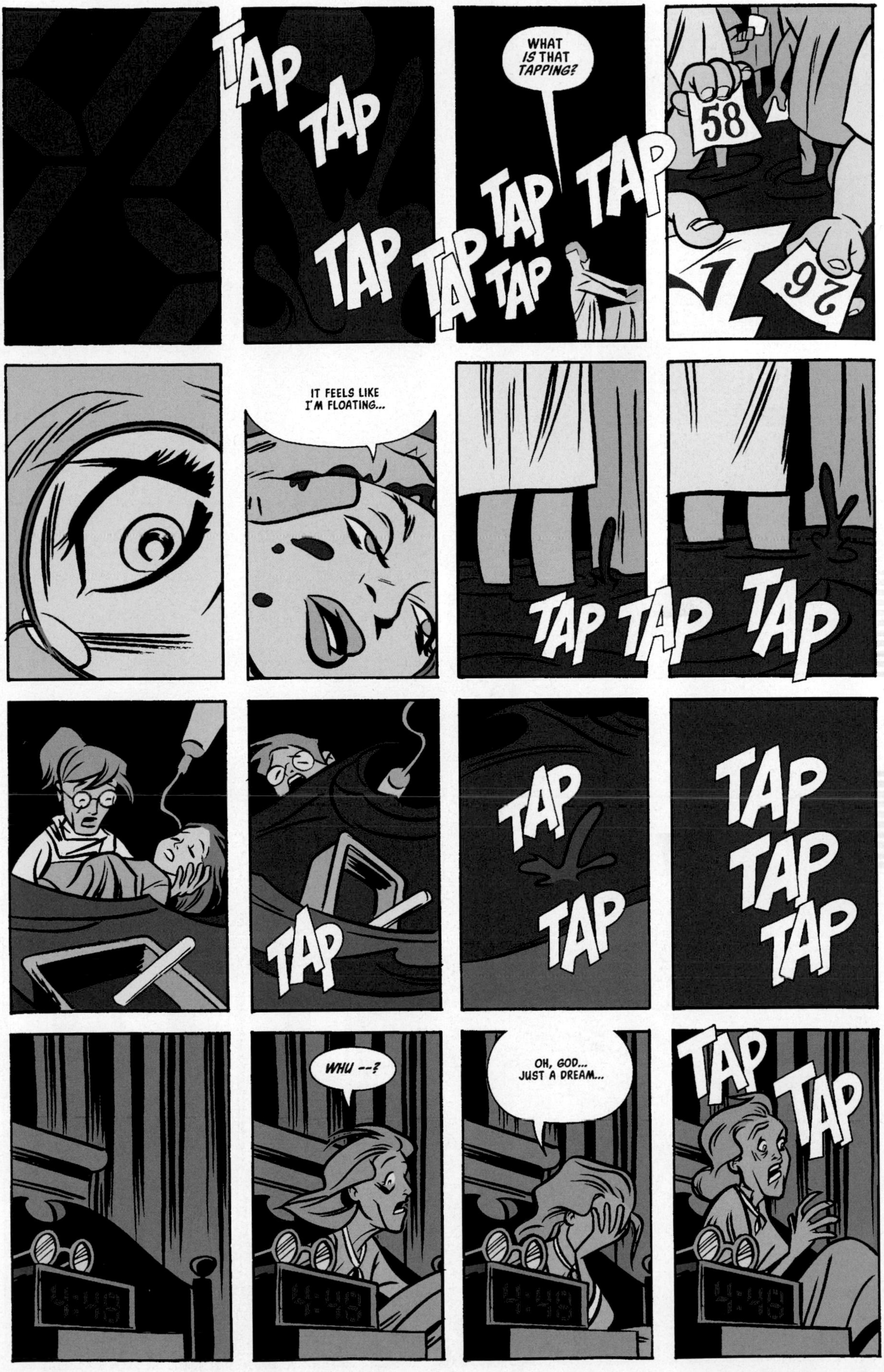
TAP
TAP
TAP
TAP TA
WHAT IS THAT TAPPING?
TAP TAP TAP
58
1
26
IT FEELS LIKE I'M FLOATING...
TAP TAP TAP
TAP
TAP
TAP
TAP TAP TAP
4:48
WHU --?
4:48
OH, GOD... JUST A DREAM...
4:48
TAP TAP
4:48

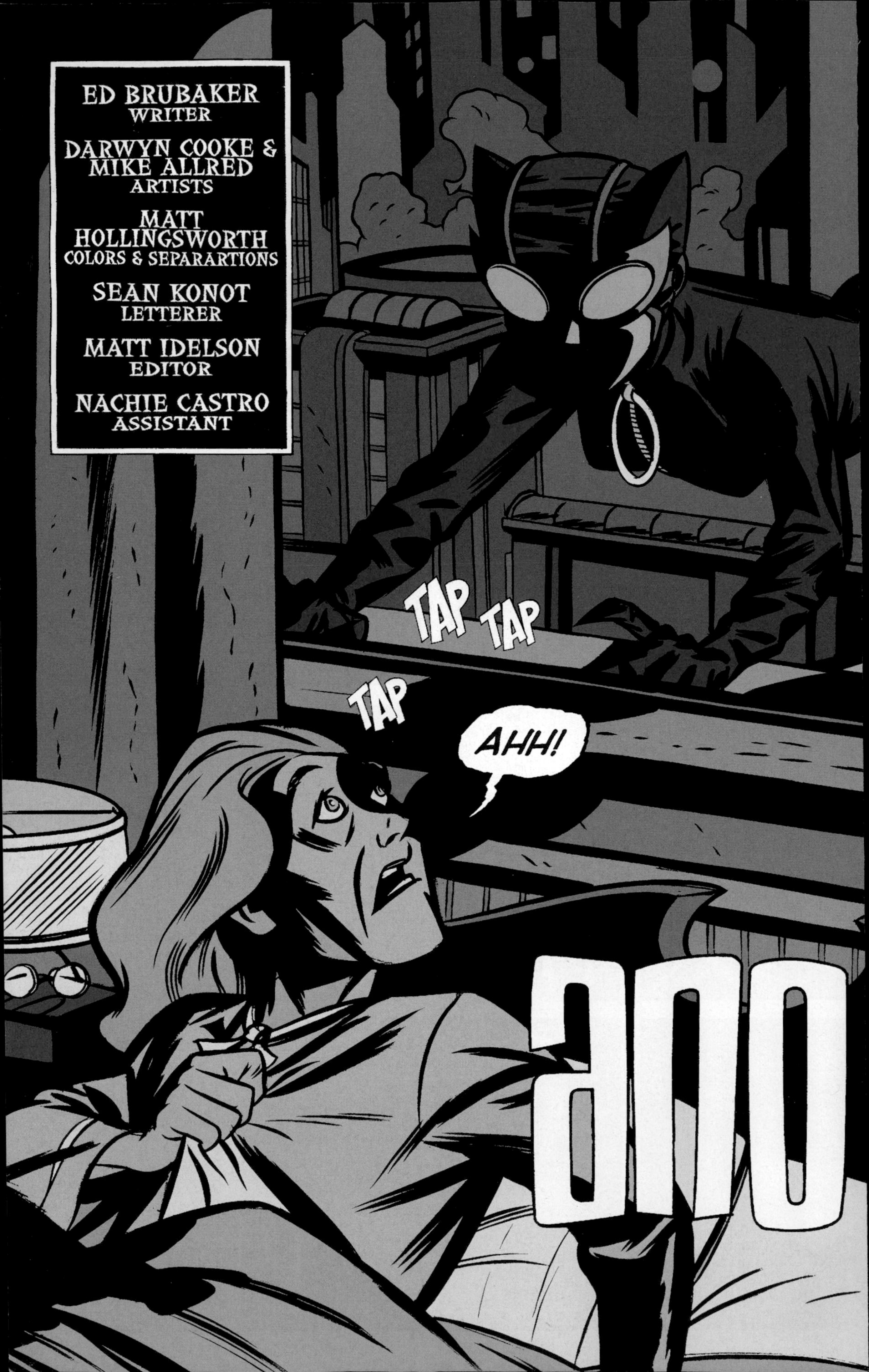
ED BRUBAKER
WRITER
DARWYN COOKE &
MIKE ALLRED
ARTISTS
MATT
HOLLINGSWORTH
COLORS & SEPARARTIONS
SEAN KONOT
LETTERER
MATT IDELSON
EDITOR
NACHIE CASTRO
ASSISTANT
TAP TAP
TAP
AHH!
one

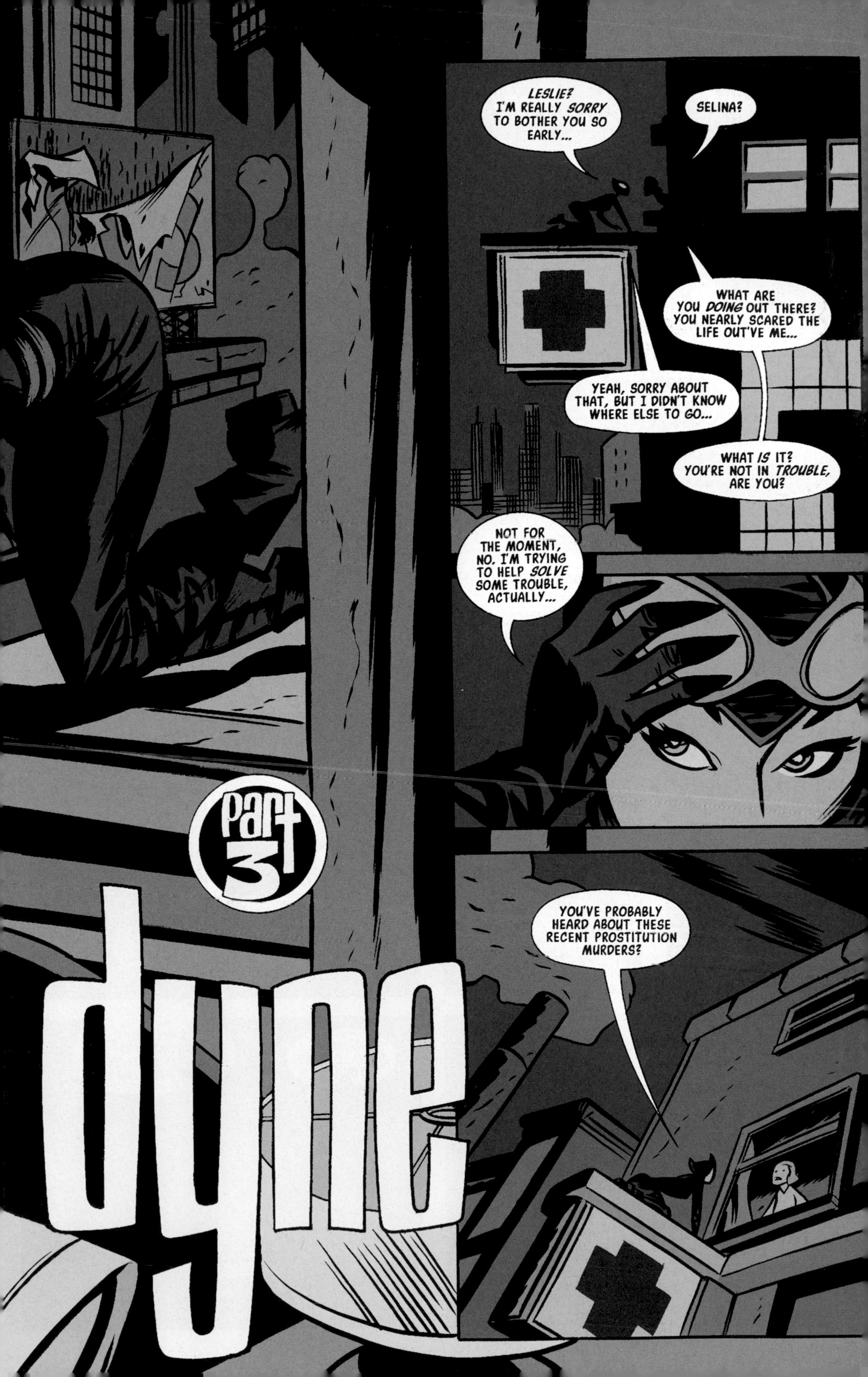
LESLIE? I'M REALLY SORRY TO BOTHER YOU SO EARLY...
SELINA?
WHAT ARE YOU DOING OUT THERE? YOU NEARLY SCARED THE LIFE OUT'VE ME...
YEAH, SORRY ABOUT THAT, BUT I DIDN'T KNOW WHERE ELSE TO GO...
WHAT IS IT? YOU'RE NOT IN TROUBLE, ARE YOU?
NOT FOR THE MOMENT, NO. I'M TRYING TO HELP SOLVE SOME TROUBLE, ACTUALLY...
part 3
dyne
YOU'VE PROBABLY HEARD ABOUT THESE RECENT PROSTITUTION MURDERS?

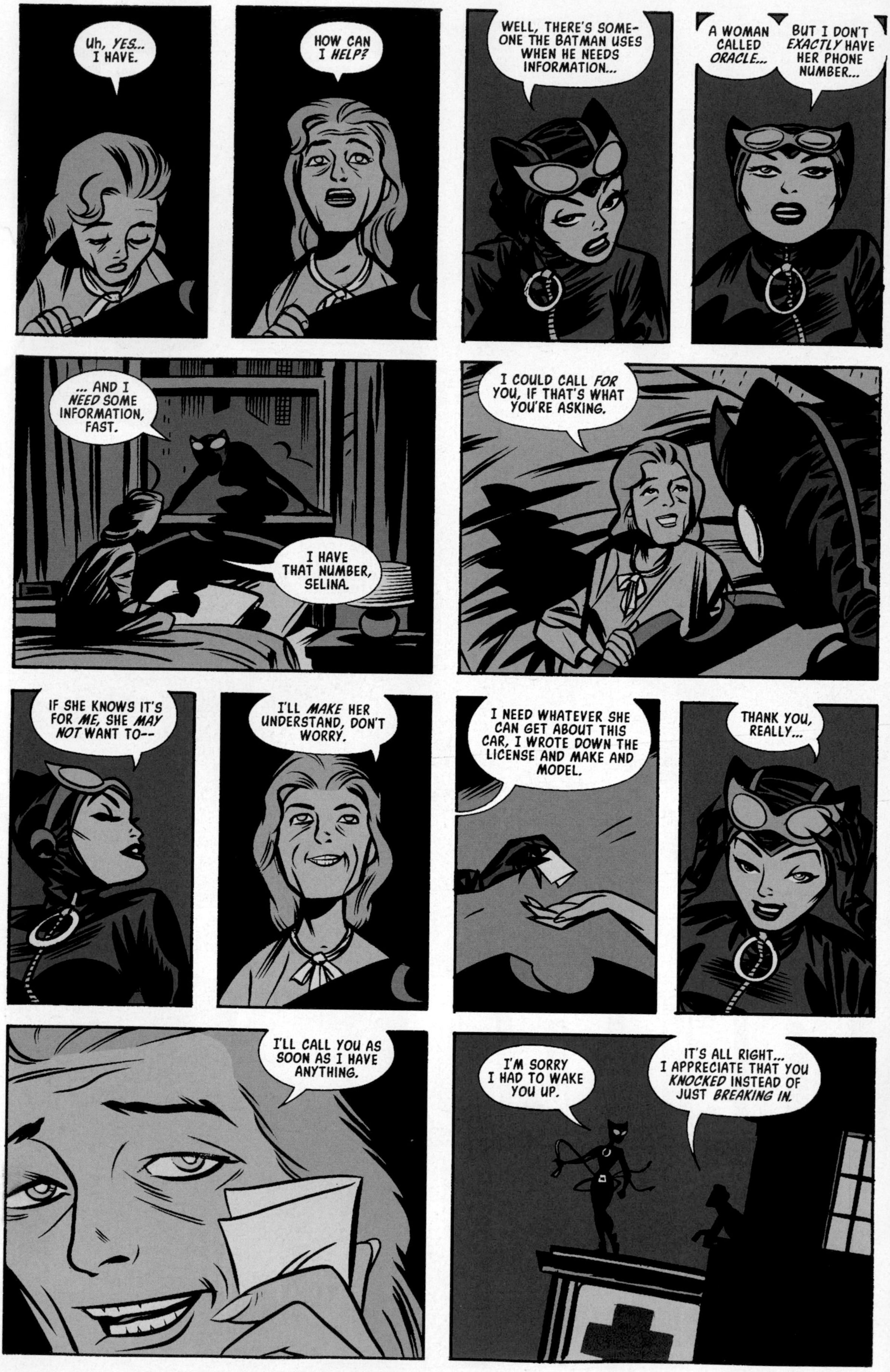
Uh, YES... I HAVE.
HOW CAN I HELP?
WELL, THERE'S SOME-ONE THE BATMAN USES WHEN HE NEEDS INFORMATION...
A WOMAN CALLED ORACLE...
BUT I DON'T EXACTLY HAVE HER PHONE NUMBER...
... AND I NEED SOME INFORMATION, FAST.
I HAVE THAT NUMBER, SELINA.
I COULD CALL FOR YOU, IF THAT'S WHAT YOU'RE ASKING.
IF SHE KNOWS IT'S FOR ME, SHE MAY NOT WANT TO--
I'LL MAKE HER UNDERSTAND, DON'T WORRY.
I NEED WHATEVER SHE CAN GET ABOUT THIS CAR, I WROTE DOWN THE LICENSE AND MAKE AND MODEL.
THANK YOU, REALLY...
I'LL CALL YOU AS SOON AS I HAVE ANYTHING.
I'M SORRY I HAD TO WAKE YOU UP.
IT'S ALL RIGHT... I APPRECIATE THAT YOU KNOCKED INSTEAD OF JUST BREAKING IN.

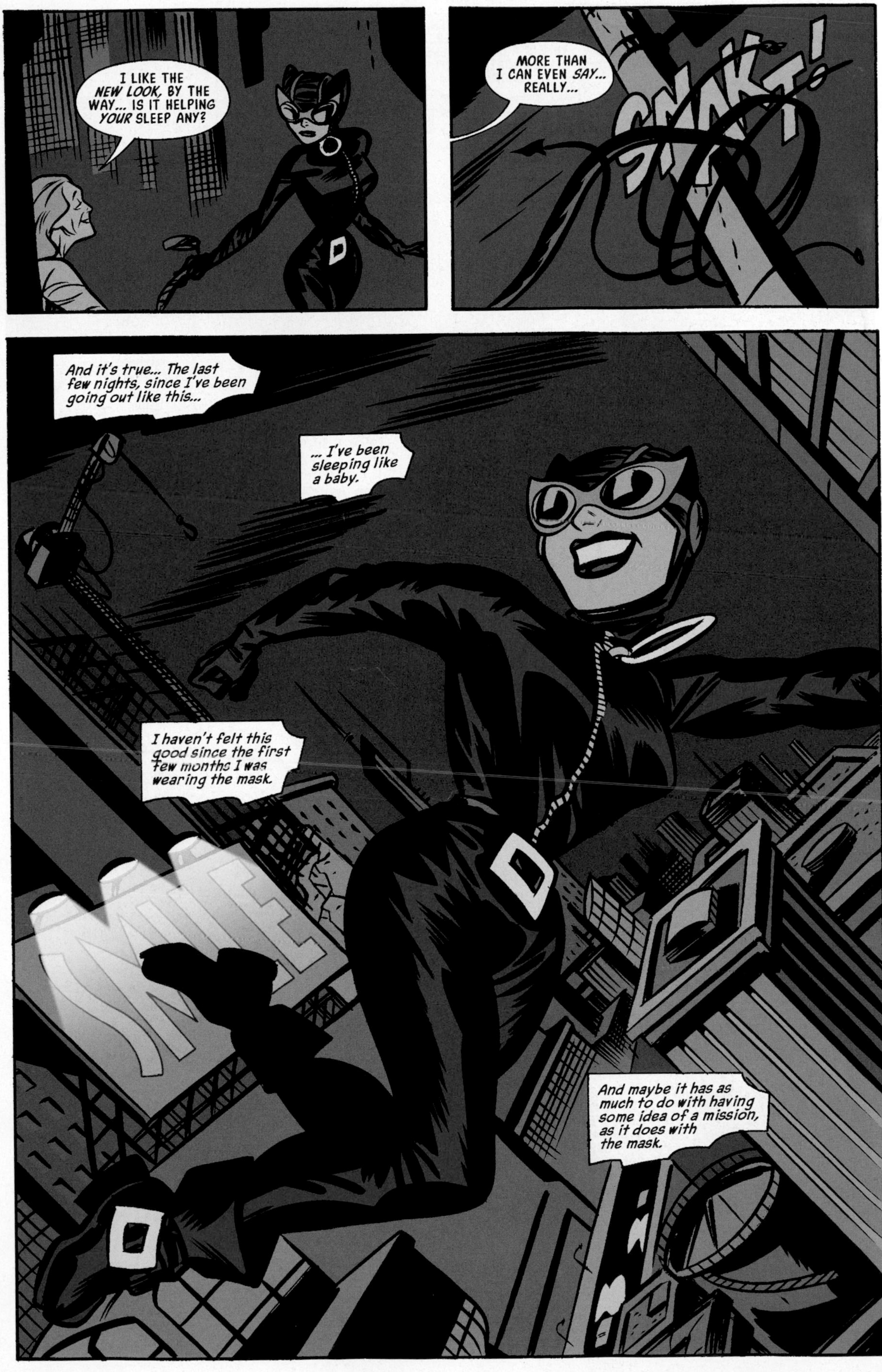
I LIKE THE *NEW LOOK,* BY THE WAY... IS IT HELPING *YOUR* SLEEP ANY?
MORE THAN I CAN EVEN *SAY...* REALLY...
SNAKT!
And it's true... The last few nights, since I've been going out like this...
... I've been sleeping like a baby.
I haven't felt this good since the first few months I was wearing the mask.
And maybe it has as much to do with having some idea of a mission, as it does with the mask.

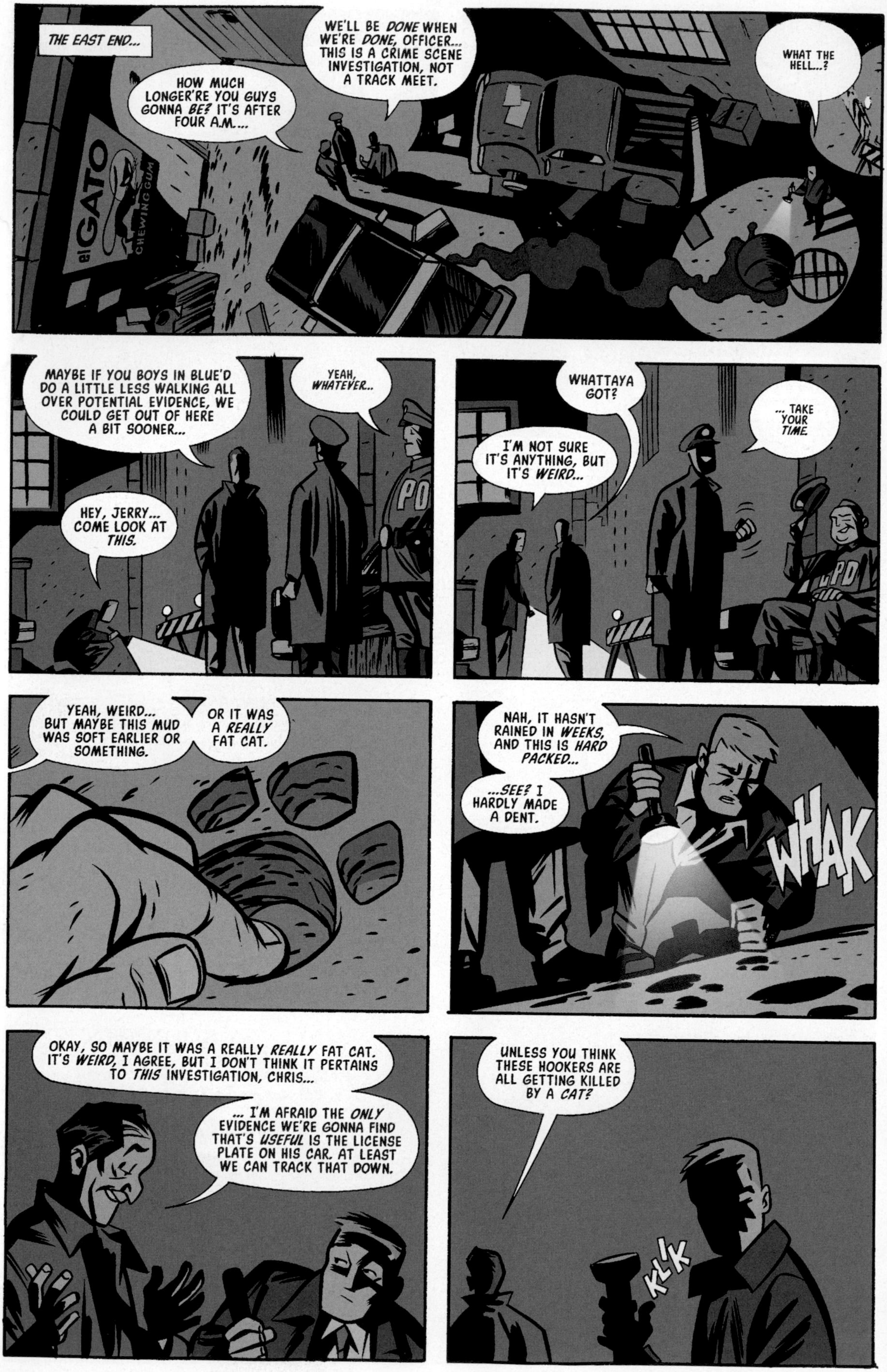
THE EAST END...
HOW MUCH LONGER'RE YOU GUYS GONNA BE? IT'S AFTER FOUR A.M....
WE'LL BE DONE WHEN WE'RE DONE, OFFICER... THIS IS A CRIME SCENE INVESTIGATION, NOT A TRACK MEET.
WHAT THE HELL...?
EL GATO CHEWING GUM
MAYBE IF YOU BOYS IN BLUE'D DO A LITTLE LESS WALKING ALL OVER POTENTIAL EVIDENCE, WE COULD GET OUT OF HERE A BIT SOONER...
YEAH, WHATEVER...
HEY, JERRY... COME LOOK AT THIS.
WHATTAYA GOT?
... TAKE YOUR TIME.
I'M NOT SURE IT'S ANYTHING, BUT IT'S WEIRD...
YEAH, WEIRD... BUT MAYBE THIS MUD WAS SOFT EARLIER OR SOMETHING.
OR IT WAS A REALLY FAT CAT.
NAH, IT HASN'T RAINED IN WEEKS, AND THIS IS HARD PACKED...
...SEE? I HARDLY MADE A DENT.
WHAK
OKAY, SO MAYBE IT WAS A REALLY REALLY FAT CAT. IT'S WEIRD, I AGREE, BUT I DON'T THINK IT PERTAINS TO THIS INVESTIGATION, CHRIS...
... I'M AFRAID THE ONLY EVIDENCE WE'RE GONNA FIND THAT'S USEFUL IS THE LICENSE PLATE ON HIS CAR. AT LEAST WE CAN TRACK THAT DOWN.
UNLESS YOU THINK THESE HOOKERS ARE ALL GETTING KILLED BY A CAT?
KLIK

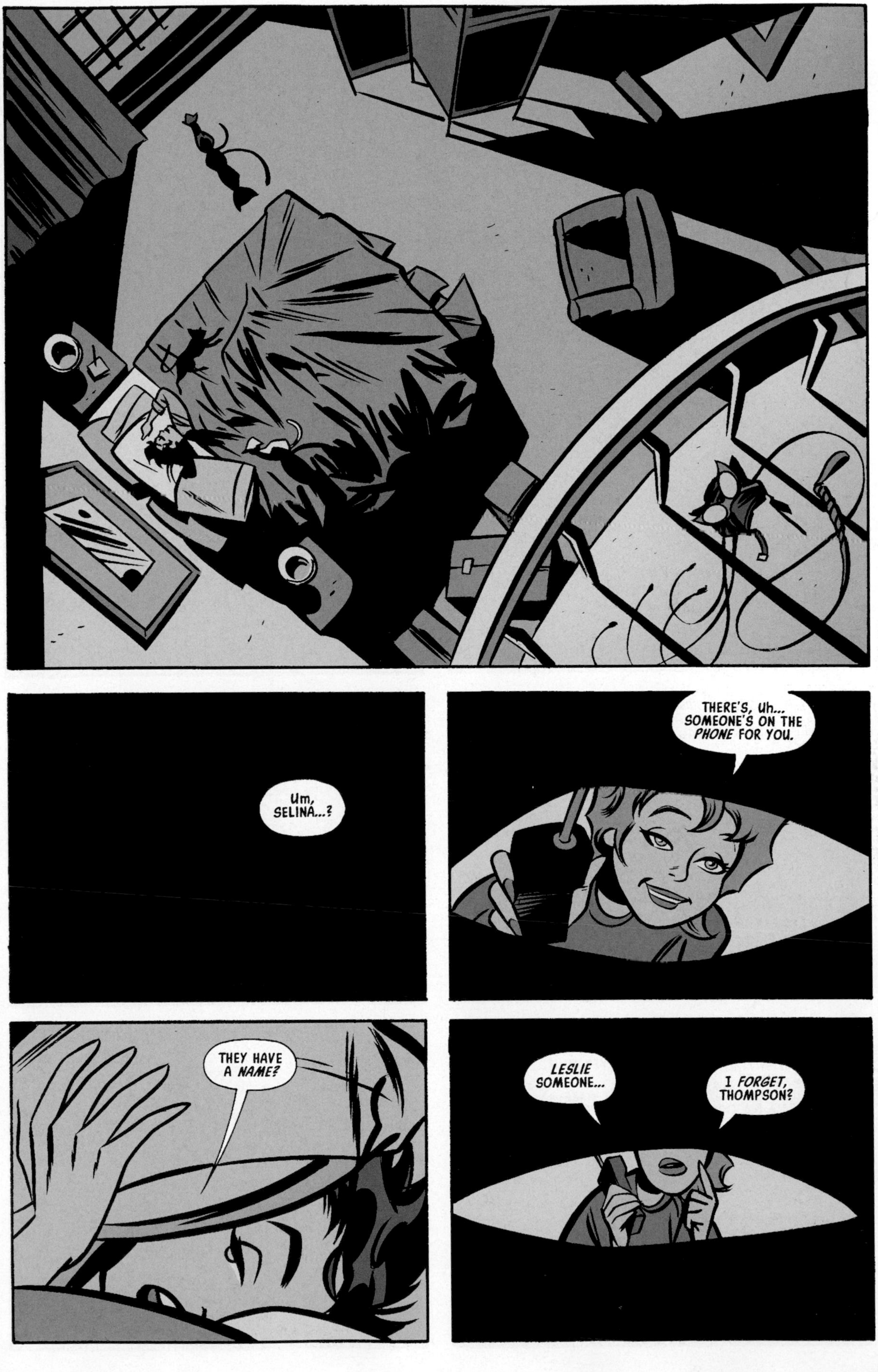
Um, SELINA...?
THERE'S, Uh... SOMEONE'S ON THE PHONE FOR YOU.
THEY HAVE A NAME?
LESLIE SOMEONE...
I FORGET, THOMPSON?

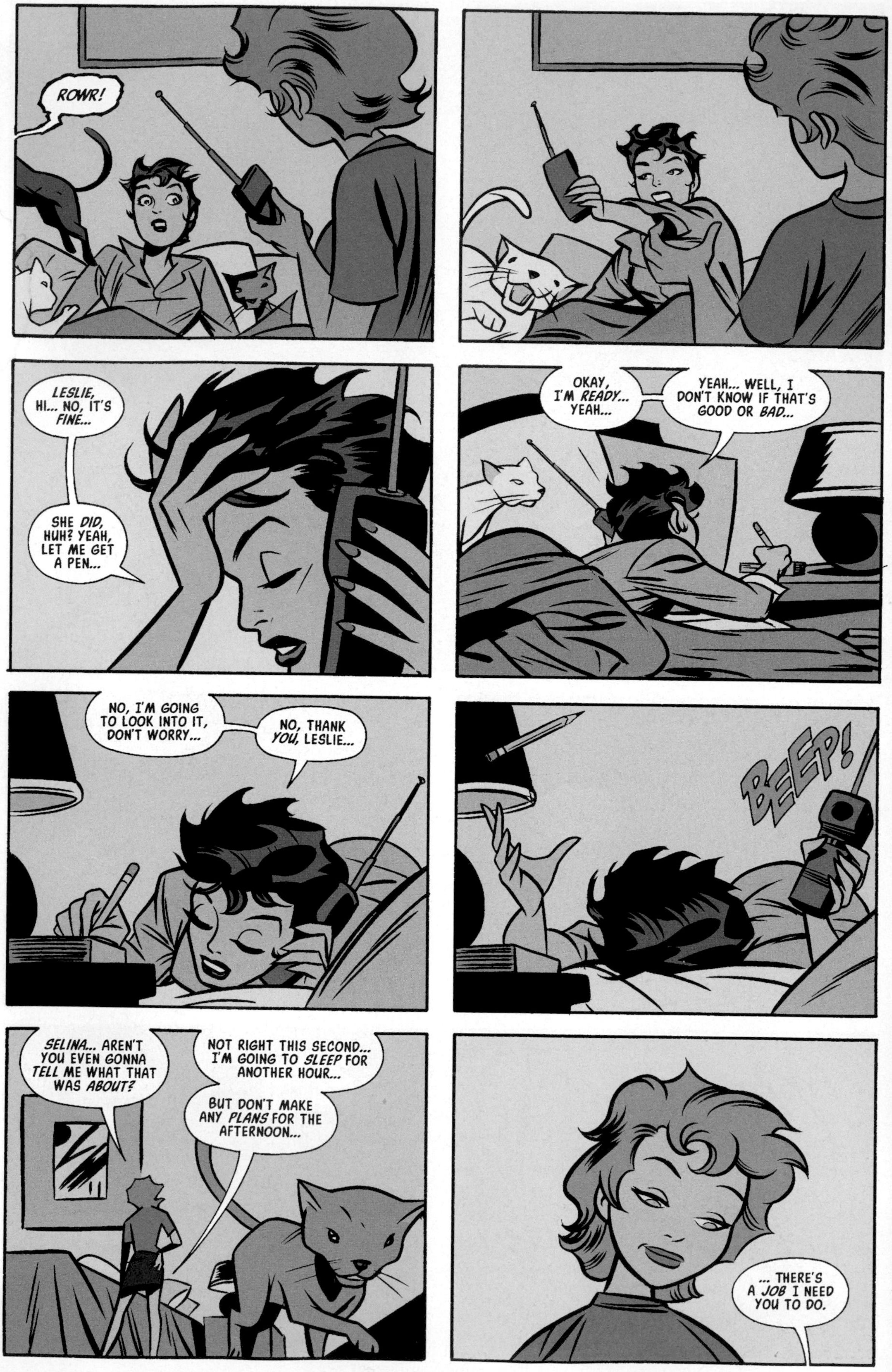
ROWR!
LESLIE, HI... NO, IT'S FINE...
SHE DID, HUH? YEAH, LET ME GET A PEN...
OKAY, I'M READY... YEAH...
YEAH... WELL, I DON'T KNOW IF THAT'S GOOD OR BAD...
NO, I'M GOING TO LOOK INTO IT, DON'T WORRY...
NO, THANK YOU, LESLIE...
BEEP!
SELINA... AREN'T YOU EVEN GONNA TELL ME WHAT THAT WAS ABOUT?
NOT RIGHT THIS SECOND... I'M GOING TO SLEEP FOR ANOTHER HOUR...
BUT DON'T MAKE ANY PLANS FOR THE AFTERNOON...
... THERE'S A JOB I NEED YOU TO DO.

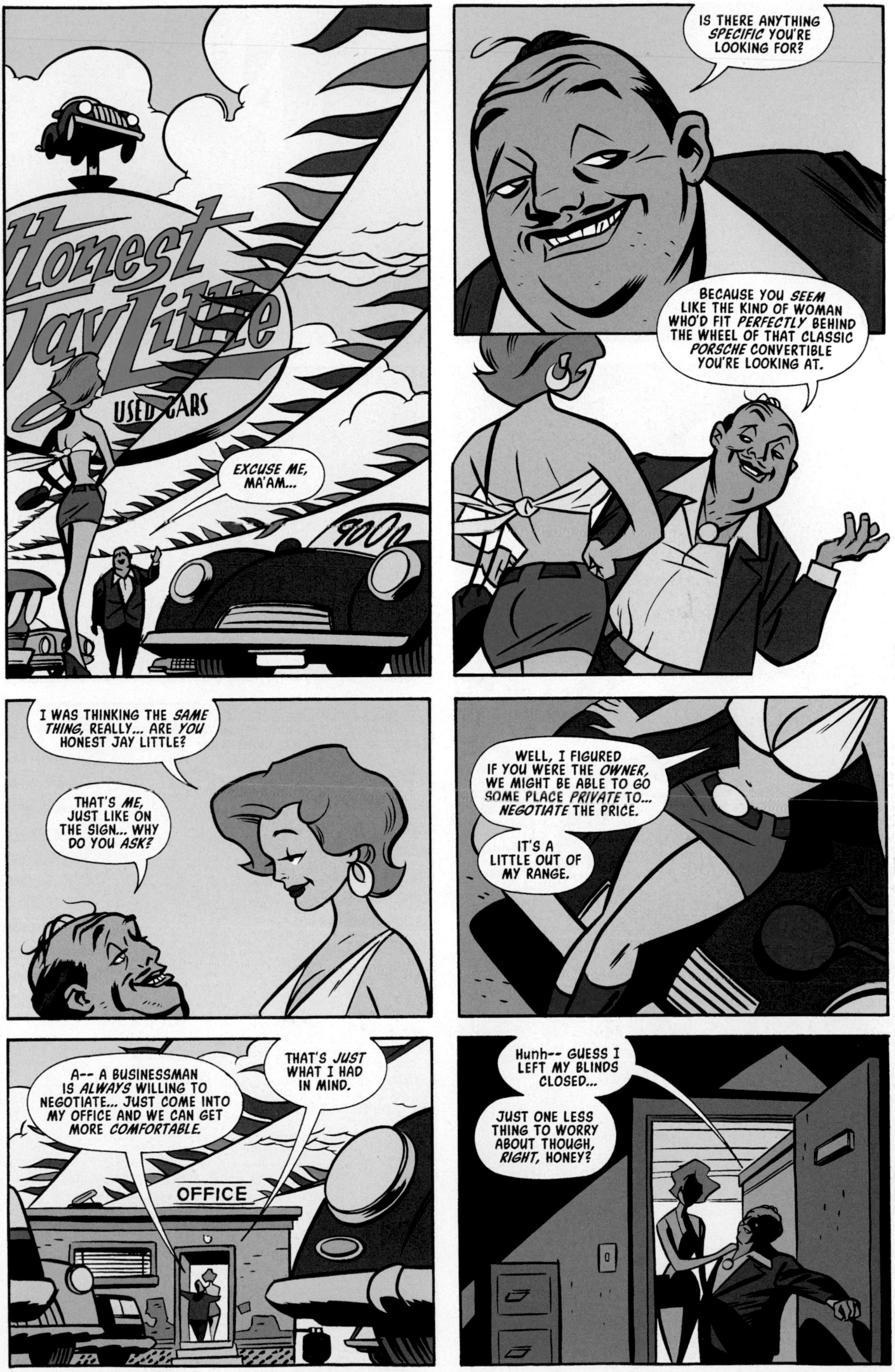
Honest Jay Little
USED CARS
EXCUSE ME, MA'AM...
IS THERE ANYTHING SPECIFIC YOU'RE LOOKING FOR?
BECAUSE YOU SEEM LIKE THE KIND OF WOMAN WHO'D FIT PERFECTLY BEHIND THE WHEEL OF THAT CLASSIC PORSCHE CONVERTIBLE YOU'RE LOOKING AT.
I WAS THINKING THE SAME THING, REALLY... ARE YOU HONEST JAY LITTLE?
THAT'S ME, JUST LIKE ON THE SIGN... WHY DO YOU ASK?
WELL, I FIGURED IF YOU WERE THE OWNER, WE MIGHT BE ABLE TO GO SOME PLACE PRIVATE TO... NEGOTIATE THE PRICE.
IT'S A LITTLE OUT OF MY RANGE.
A-- A BUSINESSMAN IS ALWAYS WILLING TO NEGOTIATE... JUST COME INTO MY OFFICE AND WE CAN GET MORE COMFORTABLE.
THAT'S JUST WHAT I HAD IN MIND.
OFFICE
Hunh-- GUESS I LEFT MY BLINDS CLOSED...
JUST ONE LESS THING TO WORRY ABOUT THOUGH, RIGHT, HONEY?

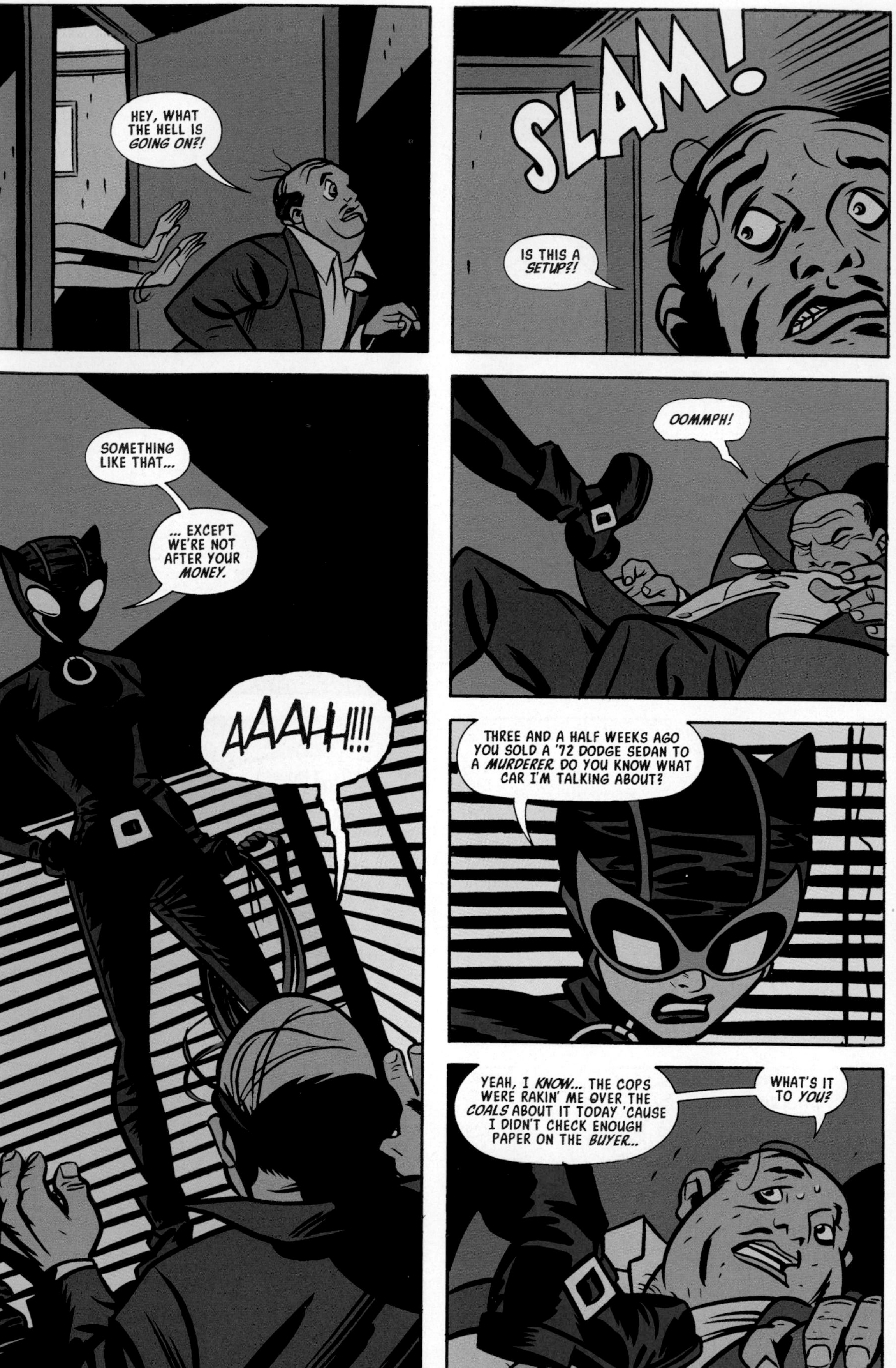
HEY, WHAT THE HELL IS GOING ON?!
SLAM!
IS THIS A SETUP?!
SOMETHING LIKE THAT...
... EXCEPT WE'RE NOT AFTER YOUR MONEY.
AAAHH!!!
OOMMPH!
THREE AND A HALF WEEKS AGO YOU SOLD A '72 DODGE SEDAN TO A MURDERER. DO YOU KNOW WHAT CAR I'M TALKING ABOUT?
YEAH, I KNOW... THE COPS WERE RAKIN' ME OVER THE COALS ABOUT IT TODAY 'CAUSE I DIDN'T CHECK ENOUGH PAPER ON THE BUYER...
WHAT'S IT TO YOU?

I'M ASKING THE QUESTIONS, HONEST JAY...

WHO WAS THE BUYER?

I DON'T *KNOW*-- HE JUST HAD A CHECK CASHING I.D., BUT IT DIDN'T REALLY *LOOK* LIKE HIM.

WHAT *DID* HE LOOK LIKE, THEN?

SERIOUSLY? HE LOOKED A HELLUVA LOT LIKE *TODD RUSSELL,* THE ACTOR. I KID YOU NOT...

I DIDN'T TELL THE *COPS* THAT, THOUGH-- OR ABOUT HIS I.D. BEIN' FAKE.

ARE YOU TRYING TO TELL ME A *FAMOUS ACTOR* IS MURDERING THESE WOMEN?

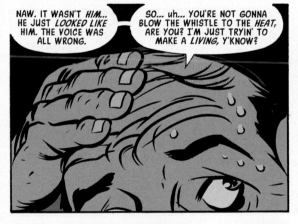

NAW. IT WASN'T *HIM*... HE JUST *LOOKED LIKE* HIM. THE VOICE WAS ALL WRONG.

SO... UH... YOU'RE NOT GONNA BLOW THE WHISTLE TO THE *HEAT,* ARE YOU? I'M JUST TRYIN' TO MAKE A *LIVING,* Y'KNOW?

I GOT A WIFE AND KIDS.

I'M NOT INTERESTED IN HOW YOU CHEAT THE *I.R.S.,* HONEST JAY...

BUT YOUR LACK OF RESPECT FOR YOUR *WIFE*...

NOW, *THAT'S* A DIFFERENT STORY ALTOGETHER.

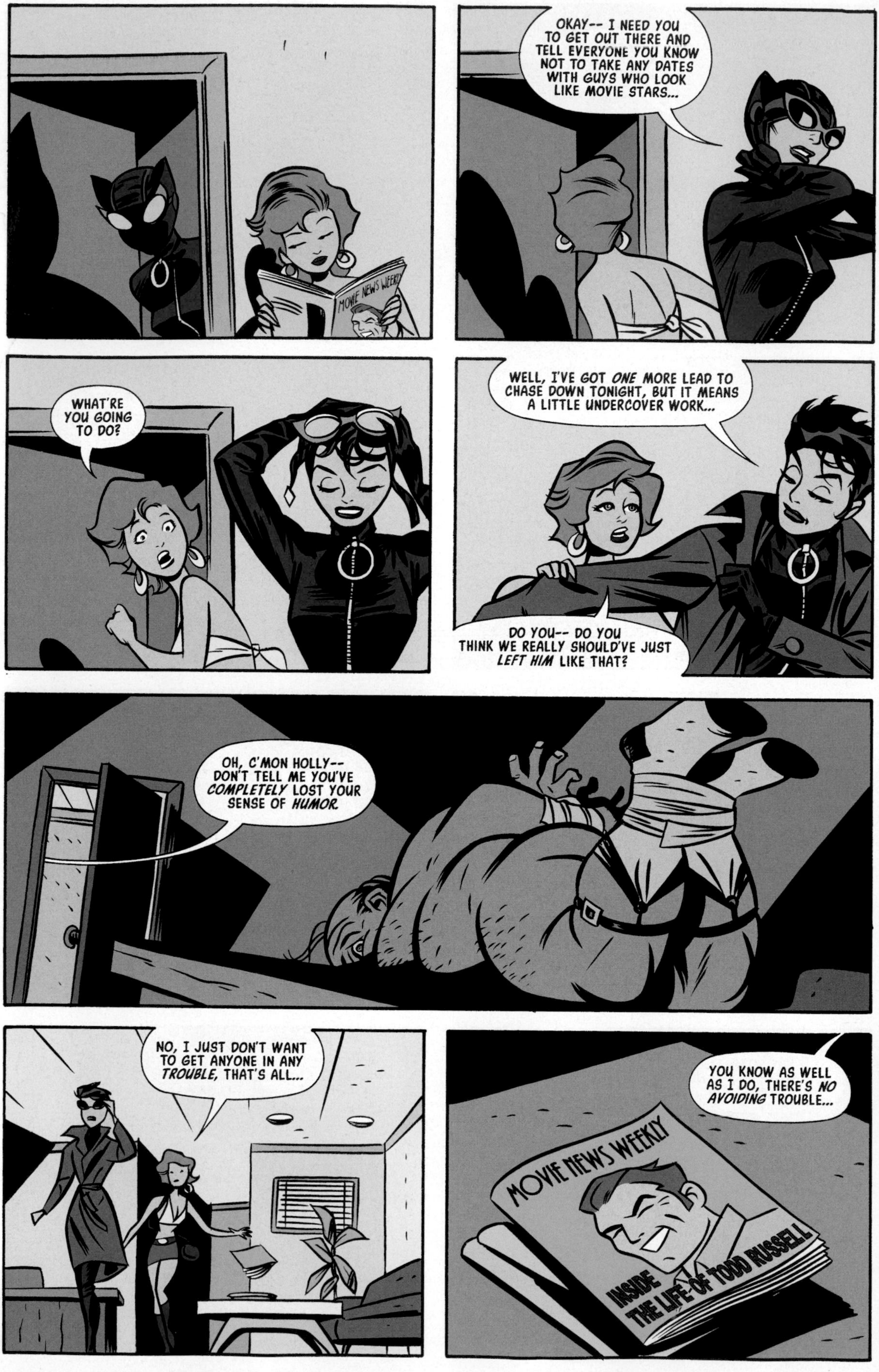
MOVIE NEWS WEEKLY
OKAY-- I NEED YOU TO GET OUT THERE AND TELL EVERYONE YOU KNOW NOT TO TAKE ANY DATES WITH GUYS WHO LOOK LIKE MOVIE STARS...
WHAT'RE YOU GOING TO DO?
WELL, I'VE GOT *ONE* MORE LEAD TO CHASE DOWN TONIGHT, BUT IT MEANS A LITTLE UNDERCOVER WORK...
DO YOU-- DO YOU THINK WE REALLY SHOULD'VE JUST *LEFT HIM* LIKE THAT?
OH, C'MON HOLLY-- DON'T TELL ME YOU'VE *COMPLETELY* LOST YOUR SENSE OF *HUMOR.*
NO, I JUST DON'T WANT TO GET ANYONE IN ANY *TROUBLE,* THAT'S ALL...
YOU KNOW AS WELL AS I DO, THERE'S *NO AVOIDING* TROUBLE...
MOVIE NEWS WEEKLY
INSIDE THE LIFE OF TODD RUSSELL

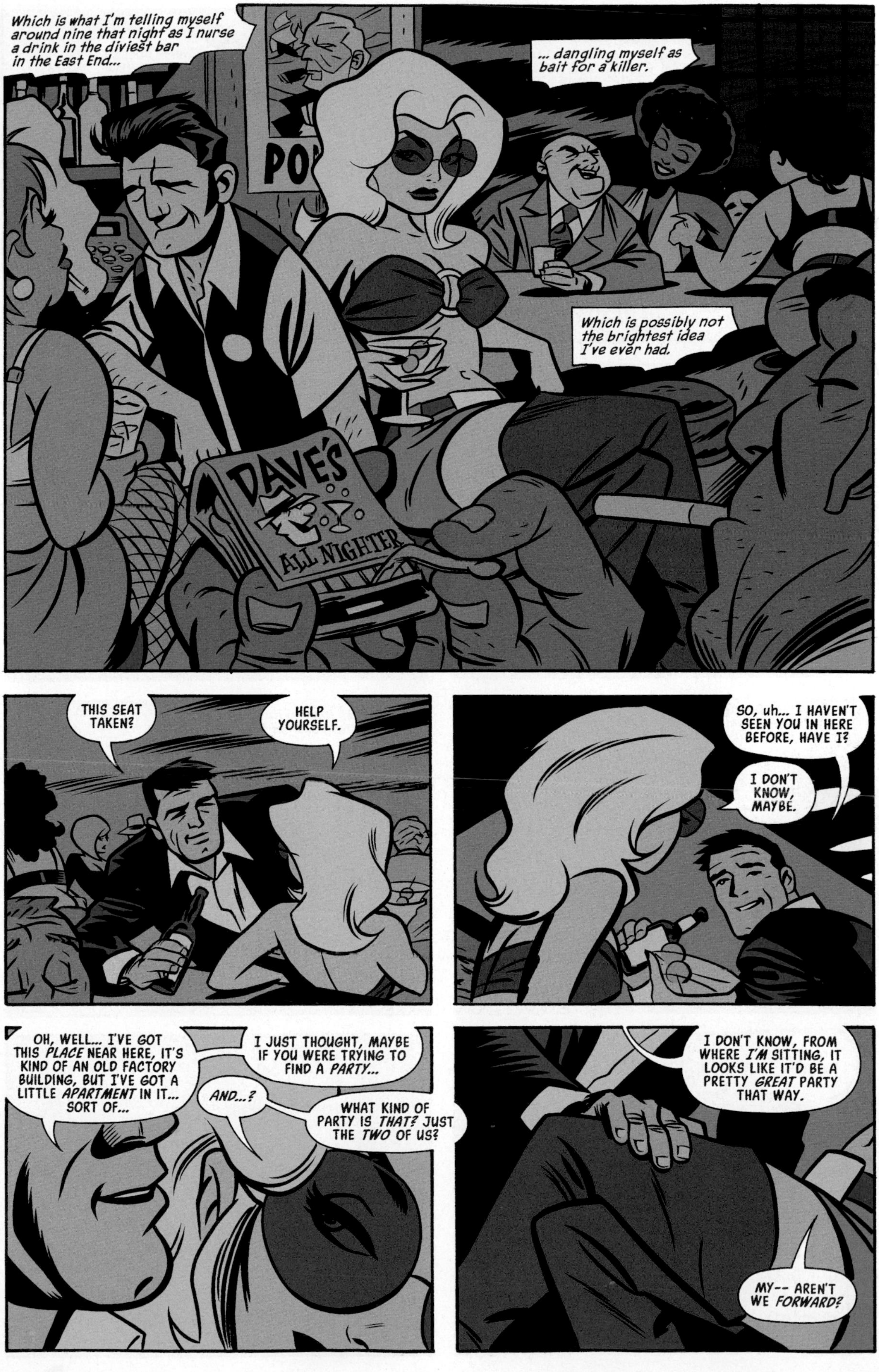

Which is what I'm telling myself around nine that night as I nurse a drink in the diviest bar in the East End...
... dangling myself as bait for a killer.
Which is possibly not the brightest idea I've ever had.
DAVE'S ALL NIGHTER
THIS SEAT TAKEN?
HELP YOURSELF.
SO, uh... I HAVEN'T SEEN YOU IN HERE BEFORE, HAVE I?
I DON'T KNOW, MAYBE.
OH, WELL... I'VE GOT THIS PLACE NEAR HERE, IT'S KIND OF AN OLD FACTORY BUILDING, BUT I'VE GOT A LITTLE APARTMENT IN IT... SORT OF...
I JUST THOUGHT, MAYBE IF YOU WERE TRYING TO FIND A PARTY...
AND...?
WHAT KIND OF PARTY IS THAT? JUST THE TWO OF US?
I DON'T KNOW, FROM WHERE I'M SITTING, IT LOOKS LIKE IT'D BE A PRETTY GREAT PARTY THAT WAY.
MY-- AREN'T WE FORWARD?

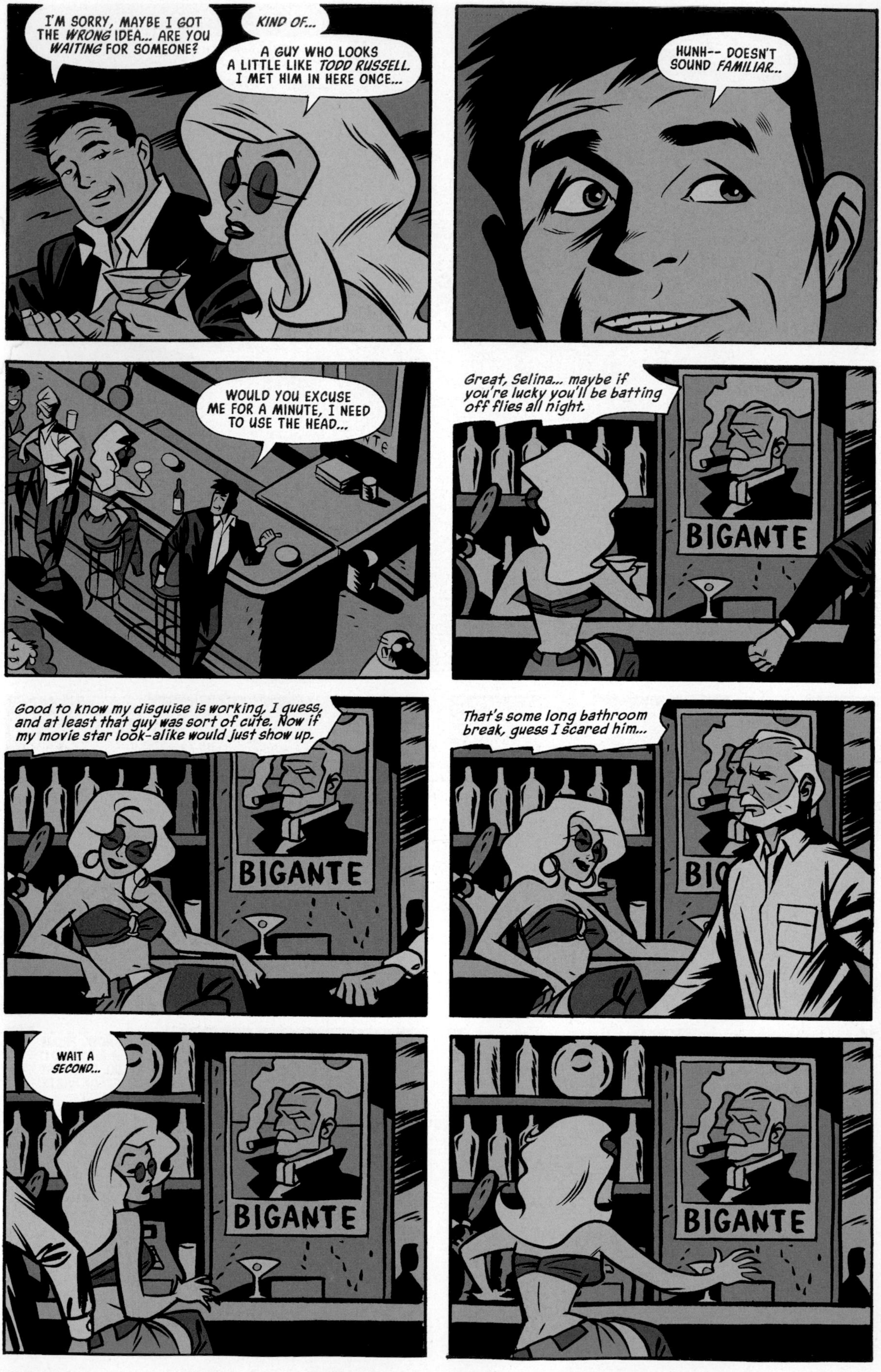
I'M SORRY, MAYBE I GOT THE WRONG IDEA... ARE YOU WAITING FOR SOMEONE?
KIND OF...
A GUY WHO LOOKS A LITTLE LIKE TODD RUSSELL. I MET HIM IN HERE ONCE...
HUNH-- DOESN'T SOUND FAMILIAR...
WOULD YOU EXCUSE ME FOR A MINUTE, I NEED TO USE THE HEAD...
Great, Selina... maybe if you're lucky you'll be batting off flies all night.
BIGANTE
Good to know my disguise is working, I guess, and at least that guy was sort of cute. Now if my movie star look-alike would just show up.
BIGANTE
That's some long bathroom break, guess I scared him...
WAIT A SECOND...
BIGANTE
BIGANTE

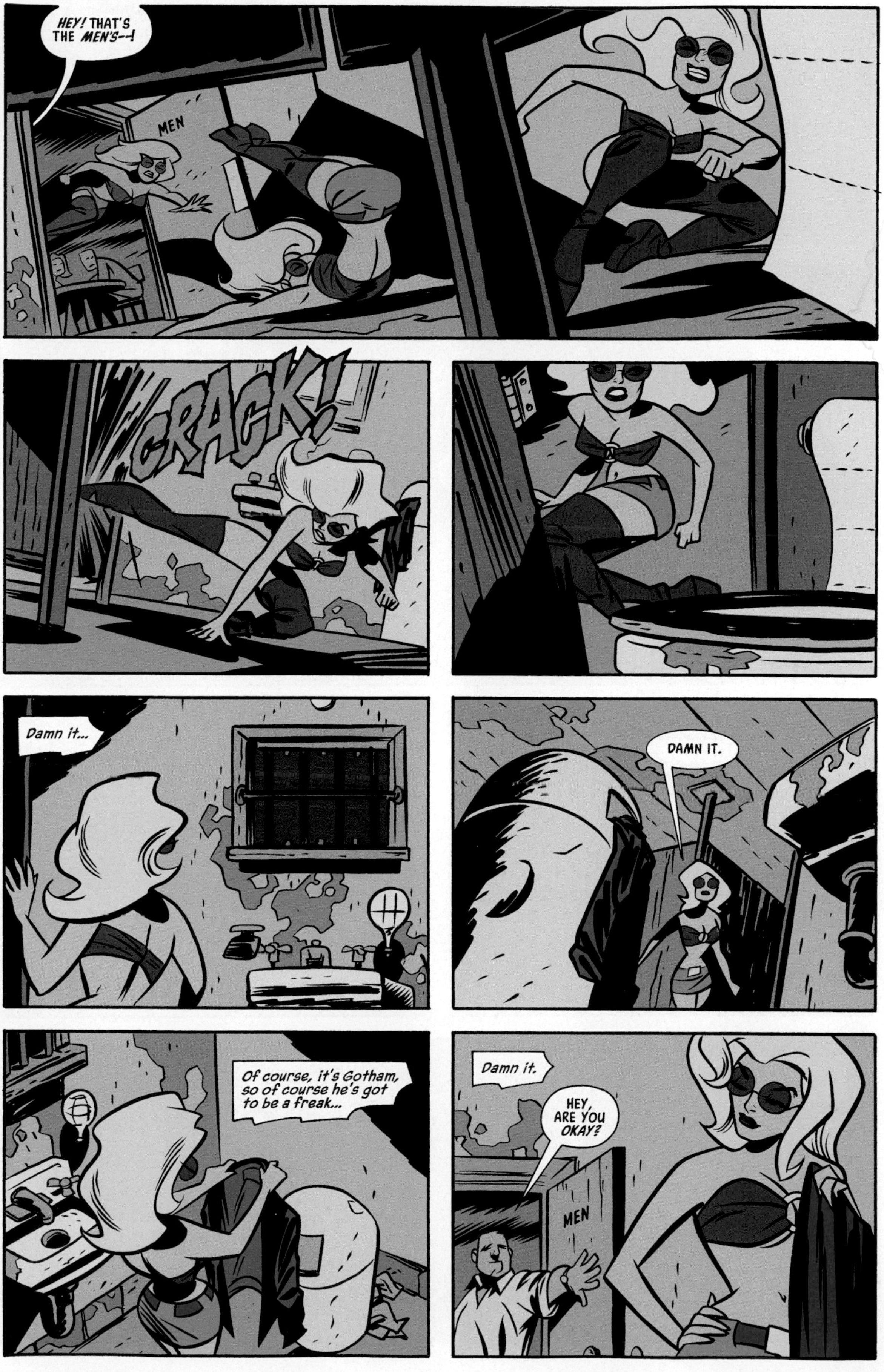

HEY! THAT'S THE MEN'S--!
MEN
CRACK!
Damn it...
DAMN IT.
Of course, it's Gotham, so of course he's got to be a freak...
Damn it.
HEY, ARE YOU OKAY?
MEN

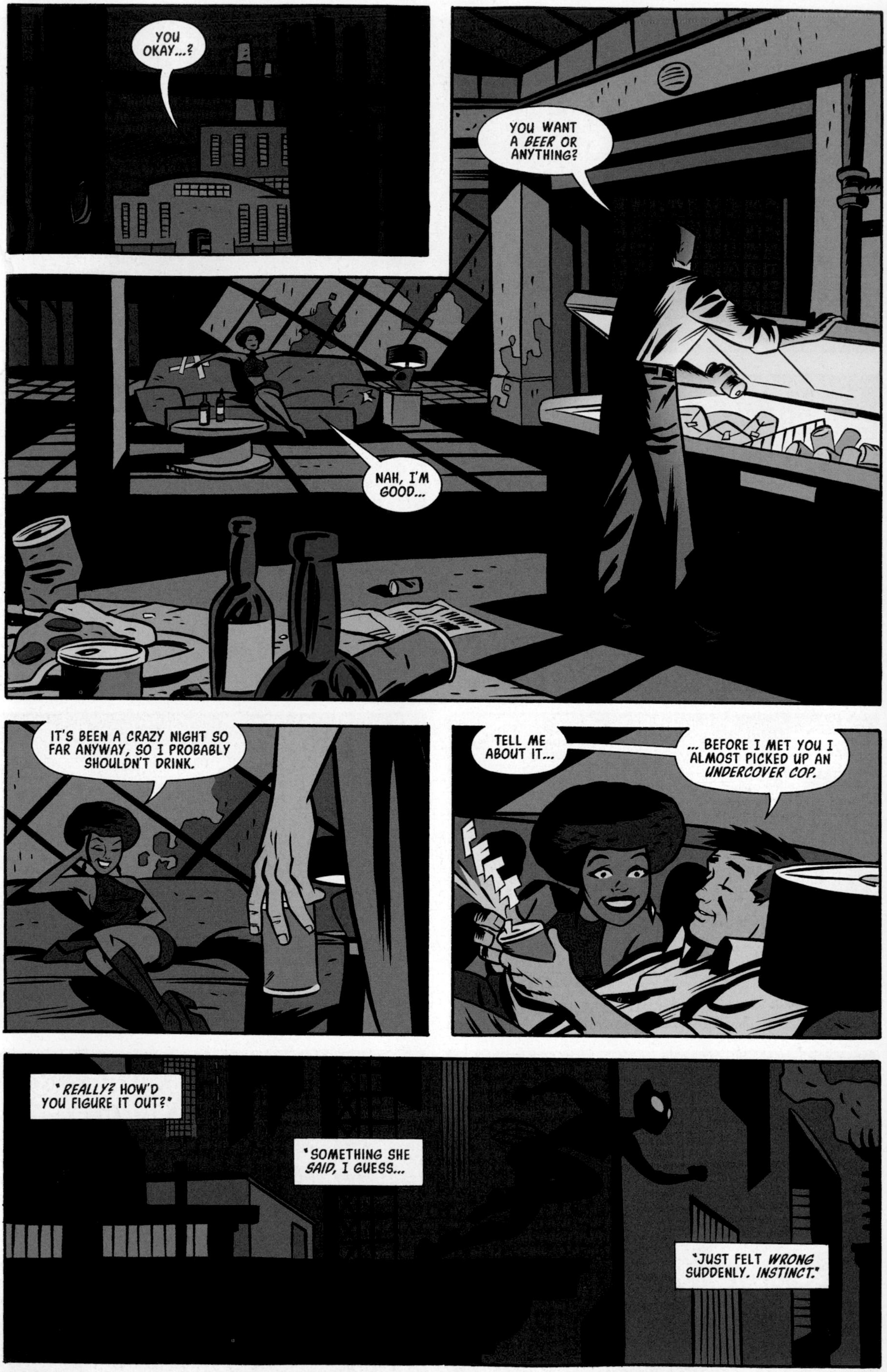
YOU OKAY...?
YOU WANT A BEER OR ANYTHING?
NAH, I'M GOOD...
IT'S BEEN A CRAZY NIGHT SO FAR ANYWAY, SO I PROBABLY SHOULDN'T DRINK.
TELL ME ABOUT IT...
... BEFORE I MET YOU I ALMOST PICKED UP AN UNDERCOVER COP.
FFFTT
"REALLY? HOW'D YOU FIGURE IT OUT?"
"SOMETHING SHE SAID, I GUESS...
"JUST FELT WRONG SUDDENLY. INSTINCT."

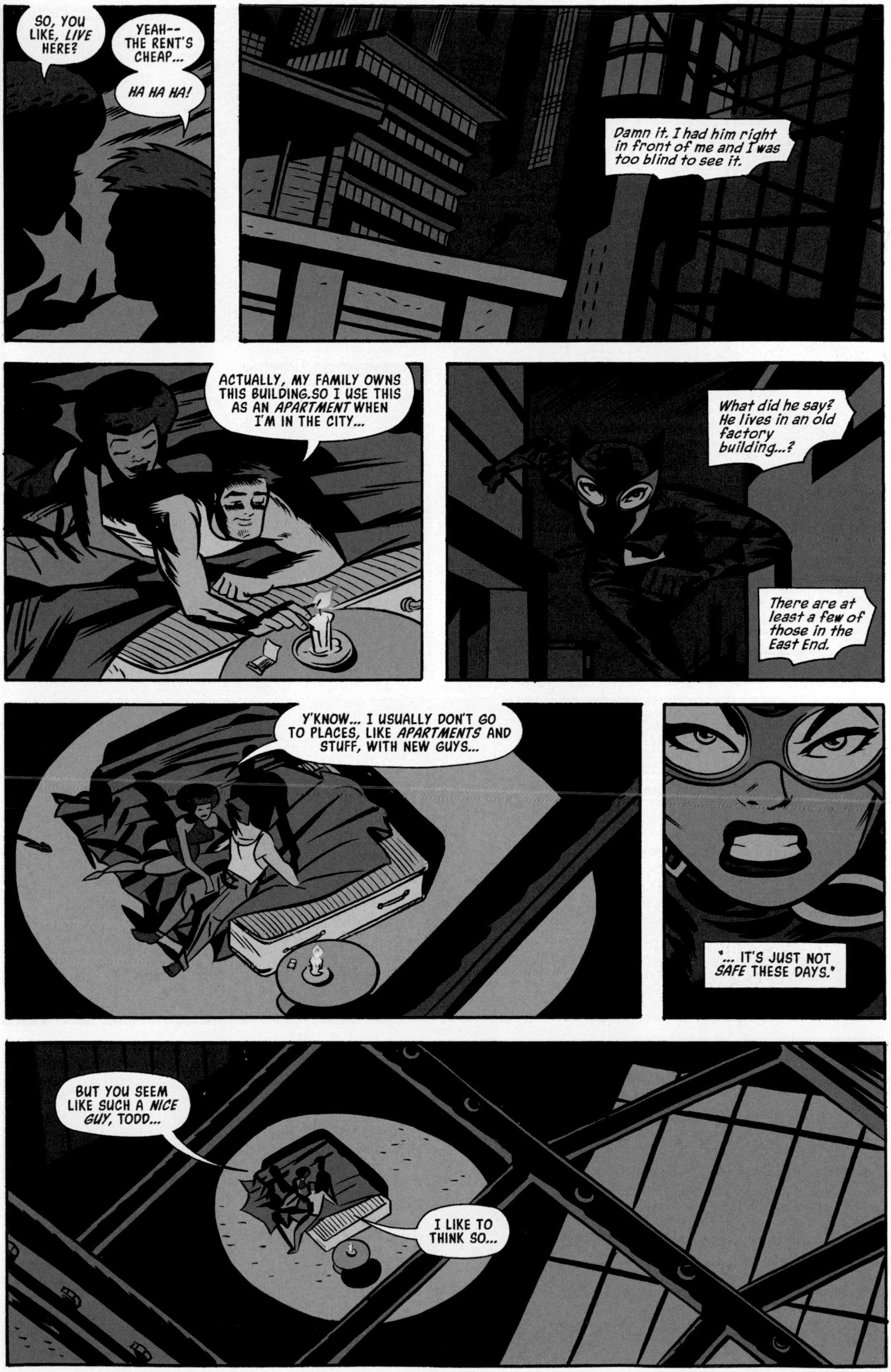
SO, YOU LIKE, LIVE HERE?
YEAH-- THE RENT'S CHEAP...
HA HA HA!
Damn it. I had him right in front of me and I was too blind to see it.
ACTUALLY, MY FAMILY OWNS THIS BUILDING.SO I USE THIS AS AN APARTMENT WHEN I'M IN THE CITY...
What did he say? He lives in an old factory building...?
There are at least a few of those in the East End.
Y'KNOW... I USUALLY DON'T GO TO PLACES, LIKE APARTMENTS AND STUFF, WITH NEW GUYS...
"... IT'S JUST NOT SAFE THESE DAYS."
BUT YOU SEEM LIKE SUCH A NICE GUY, TODD...
I LIKE TO THINK SO...

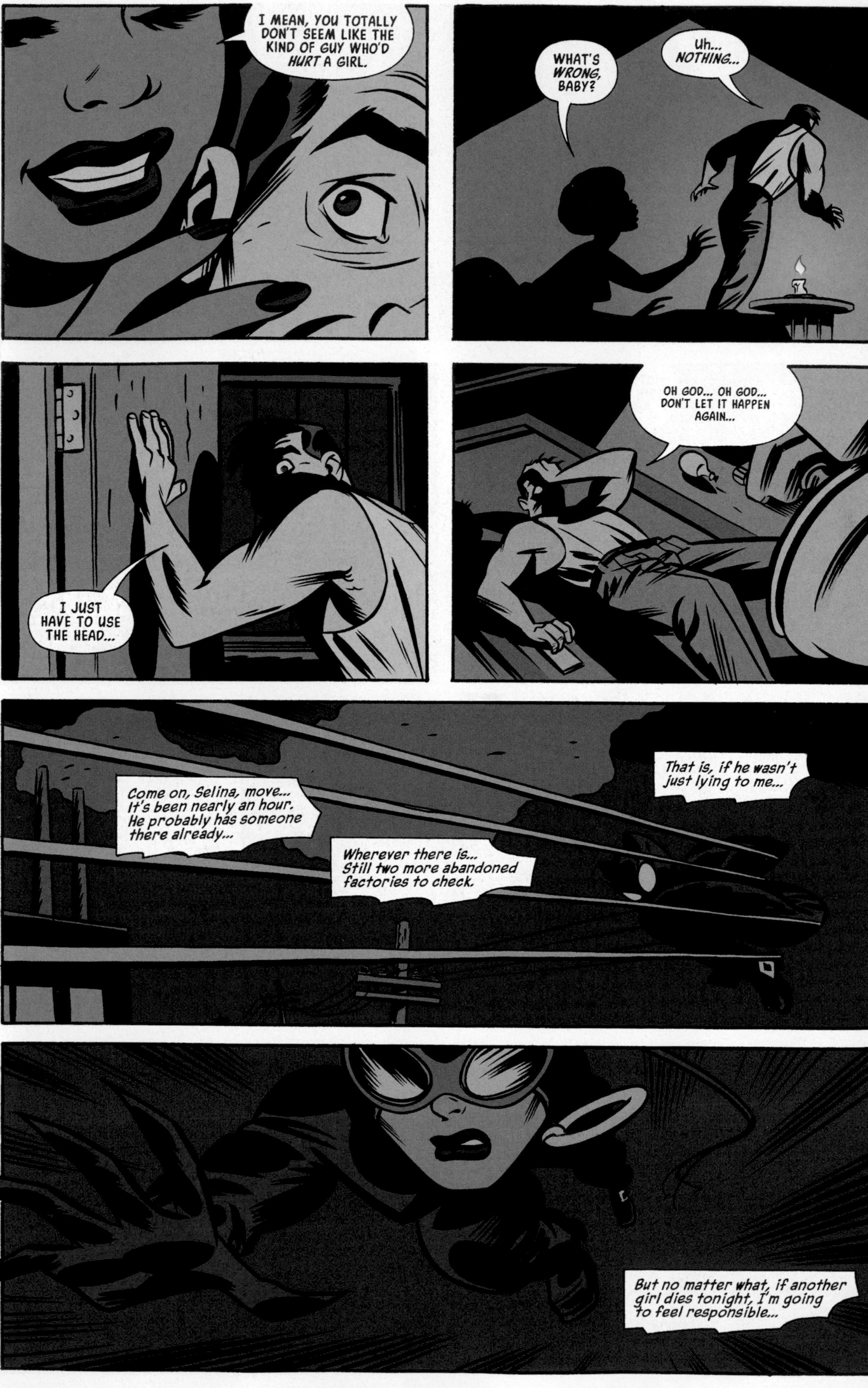
I MEAN, YOU TOTALLY DON'T SEEM LIKE THE KIND OF GUY WHO'D *HURT* A GIRL.
WHAT'S *WRONG*, BABY?
Uh... *NOTHING*...
I JUST HAVE TO USE THE HEAD...
OH GOD... OH GOD... DON'T LET IT HAPPEN AGAIN...
Come on, Selina, move... It's been nearly an hour. He probably has someone there already...
Wherever there is... Still two more abandoned factories to check.
That is, if he wasn't just lying to me...
But no matter what, if another girl dies tonight, I'm going to feel responsible...

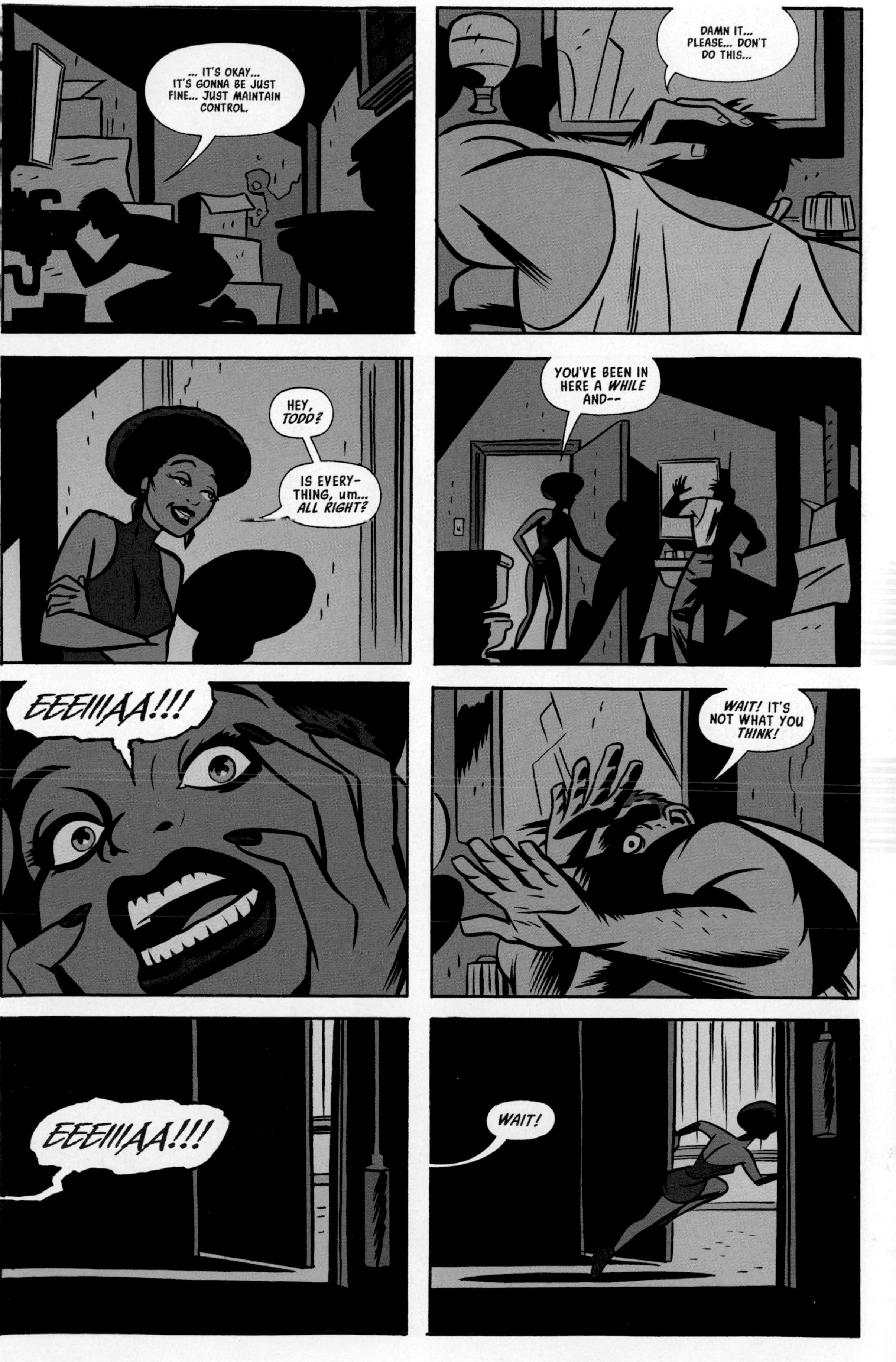
... IT'S OKAY... IT'S GONNA BE JUST FINE... JUST MAINTAIN CONTROL.
DAMN IT... PLEASE... DON'T DO THIS...
HEY, TODD?
IS EVERY-THING, um... ALL RIGHT?
YOU'VE BEEN IN HERE A WHILE AND--
EEEIII!AA!!!
WAIT! IT'S NOT WHAT YOU THINK!
EEEIII!AA!!!
WAIT!

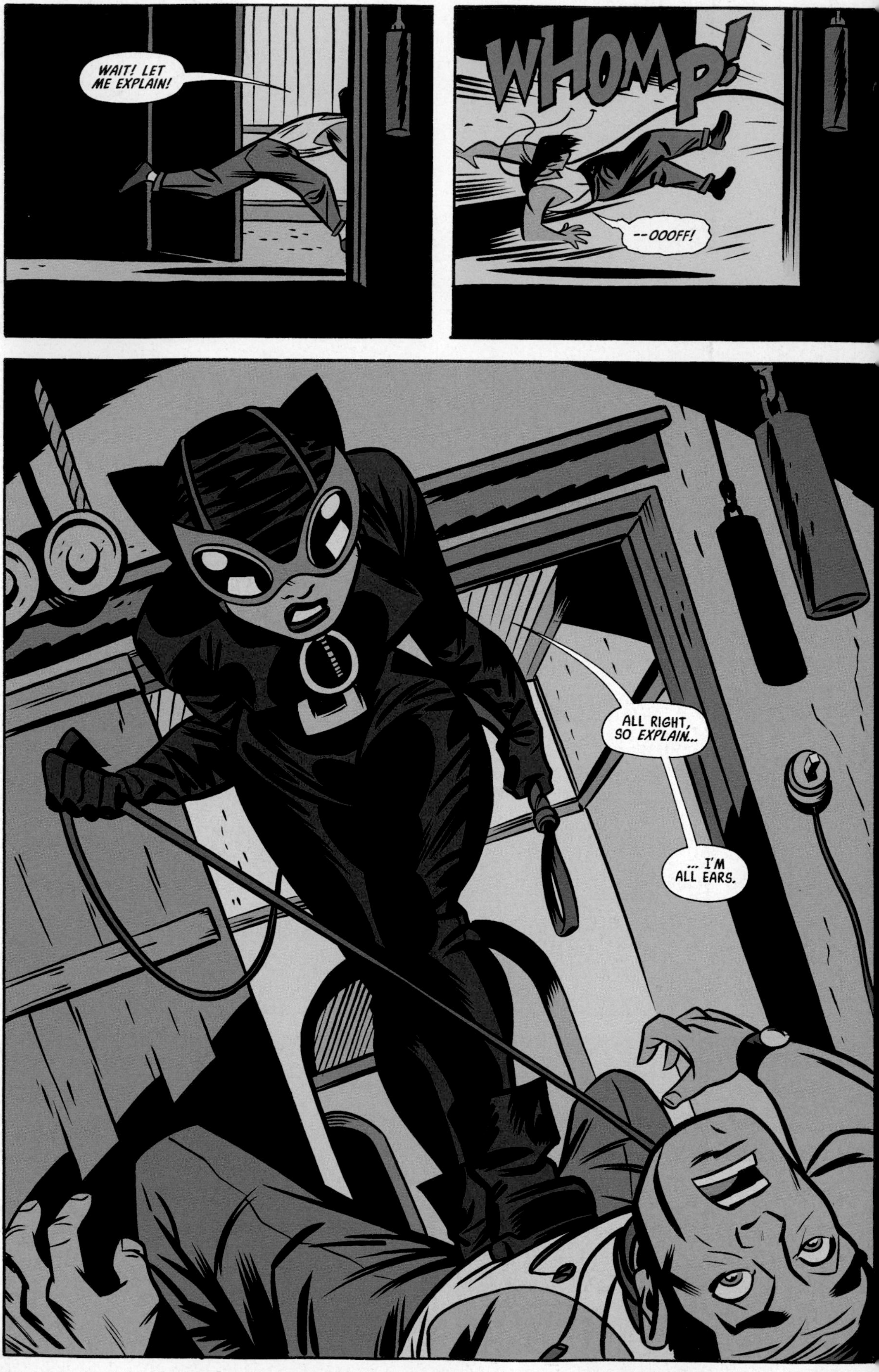
WAIT! LET ME EXPLAIN!
WHOMP!
--OOOFF!
ALL RIGHT, SO EXPLAIN...
... I'M ALL EARS.

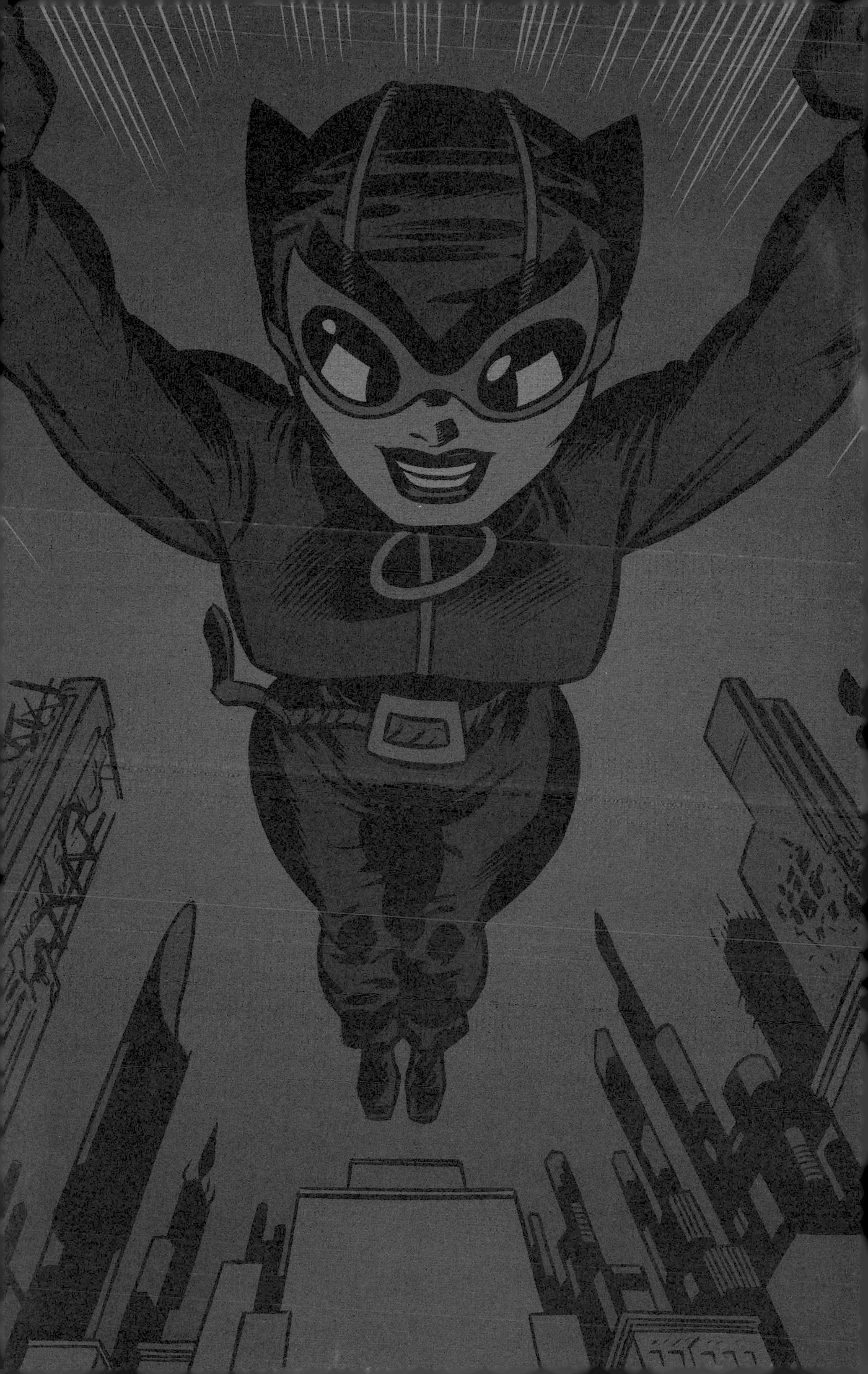

Catwoman 4 Cover by Darwyn Cooke

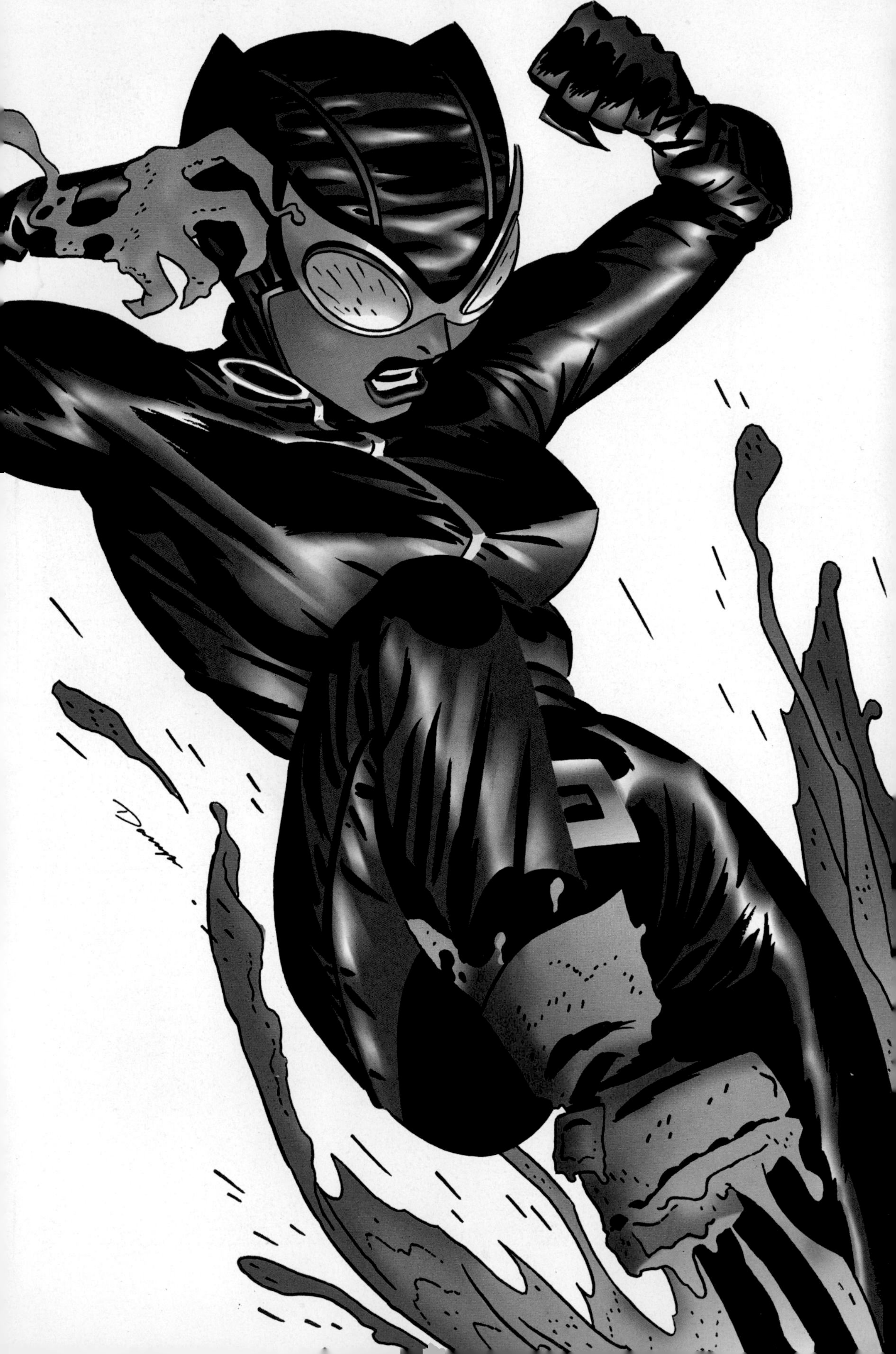

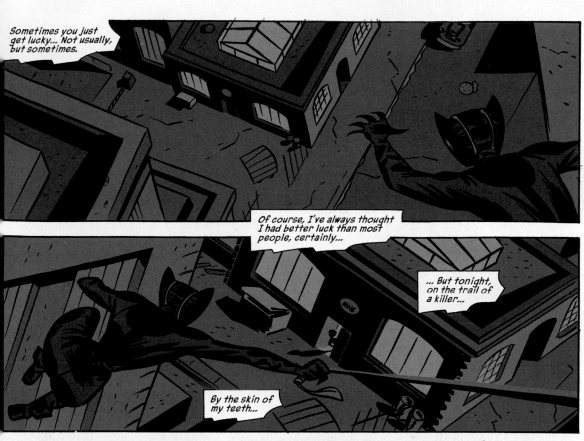

Sometimes you just get lucky... Not usually, but sometimes.

Of course, I've always thought I had better luck than most people, certainly...

... But tonight, on the trail of a killer...

By the skin of my teeth...

EEIIAAA!

... I literally arrived in the nick of time.

And if that's not luck, I don't know what is.

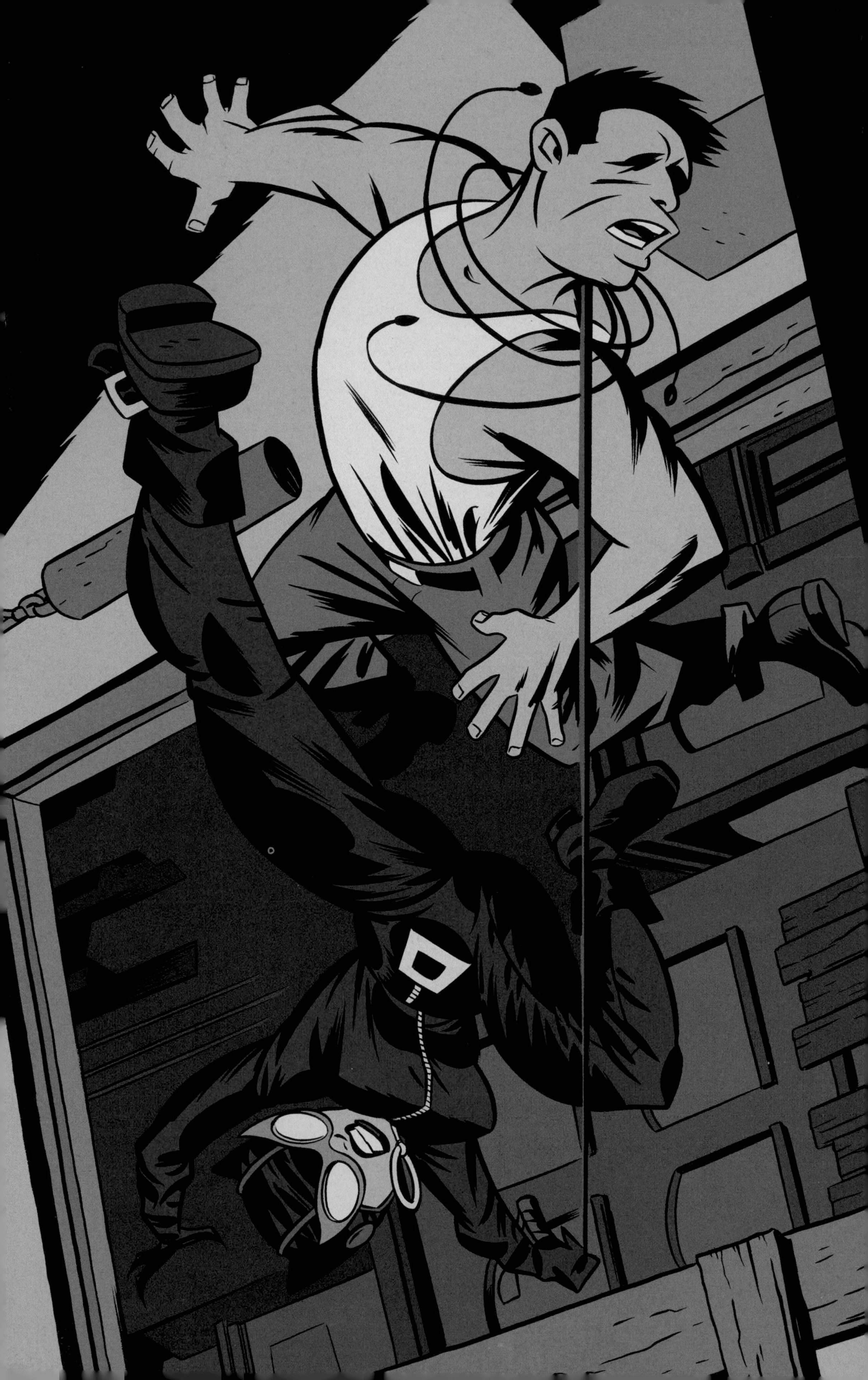

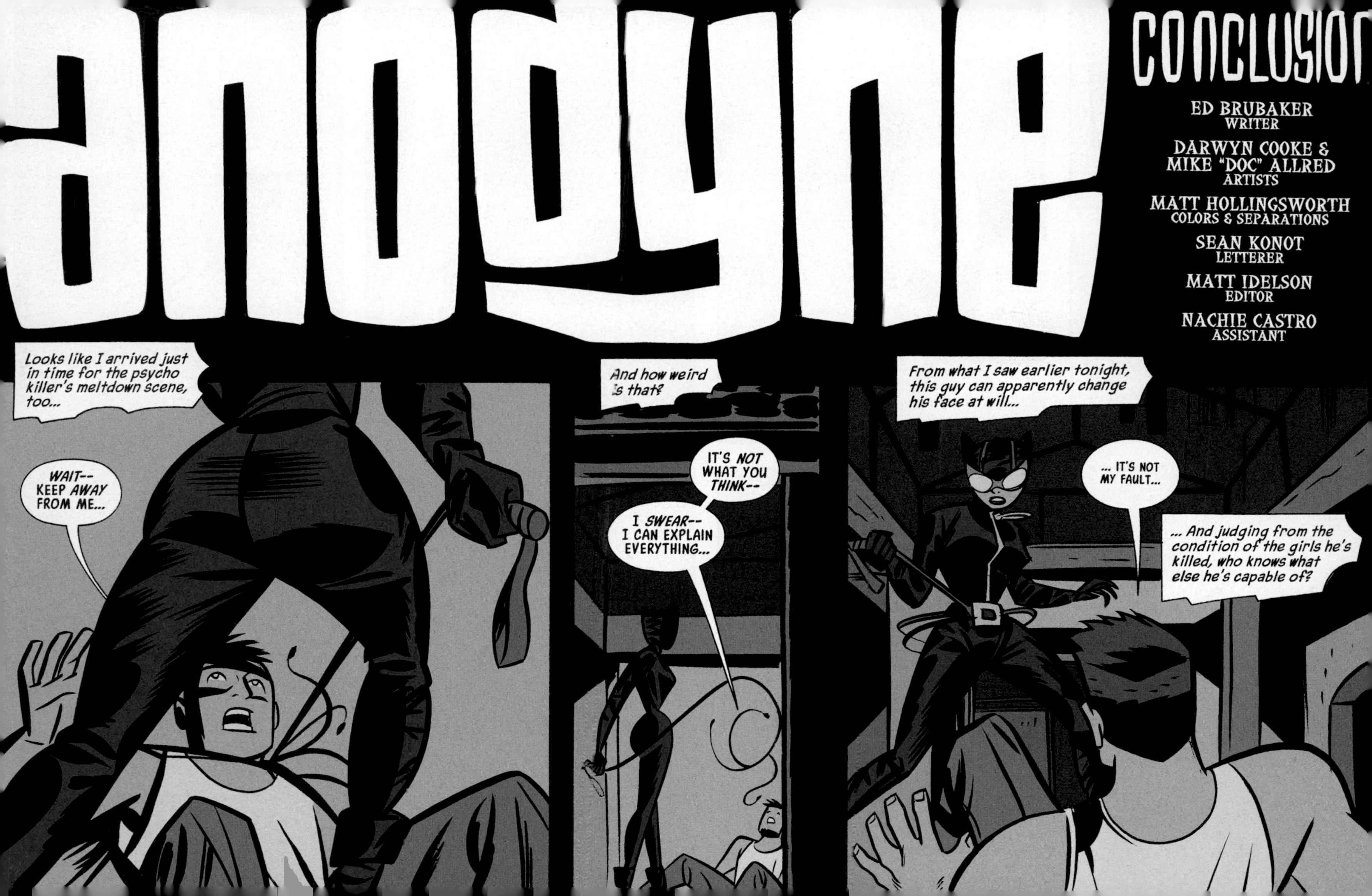
anodyne
CONCLUSION
ED BRUBAKER
WRITER
DARWYN COOKE &
MIKE "DOC" ALLRED
ARTISTS
MATT HOLLINGSWORTH
COLORS & SEPARATIONS
SEAN KONOT
LETTERER
MATT IDELSON
EDITOR
NACHIE CASTRO
ASSISTANT
Looks like I arrived just in time for the psycho killer's meltdown scene, too...
WAIT-- KEEP AWAY FROM ME...
And how weird is that?
IT'S NOT WHAT YOU THINK--
I SWEAR-- I CAN EXPLAIN EVERYTHING...
From what I saw earlier tonight, this guy can apparently change his face at will...
... IT'S NOT MY FAULT...
... And judging from the condition of the girls he's killed, who knows what else he's capable of?

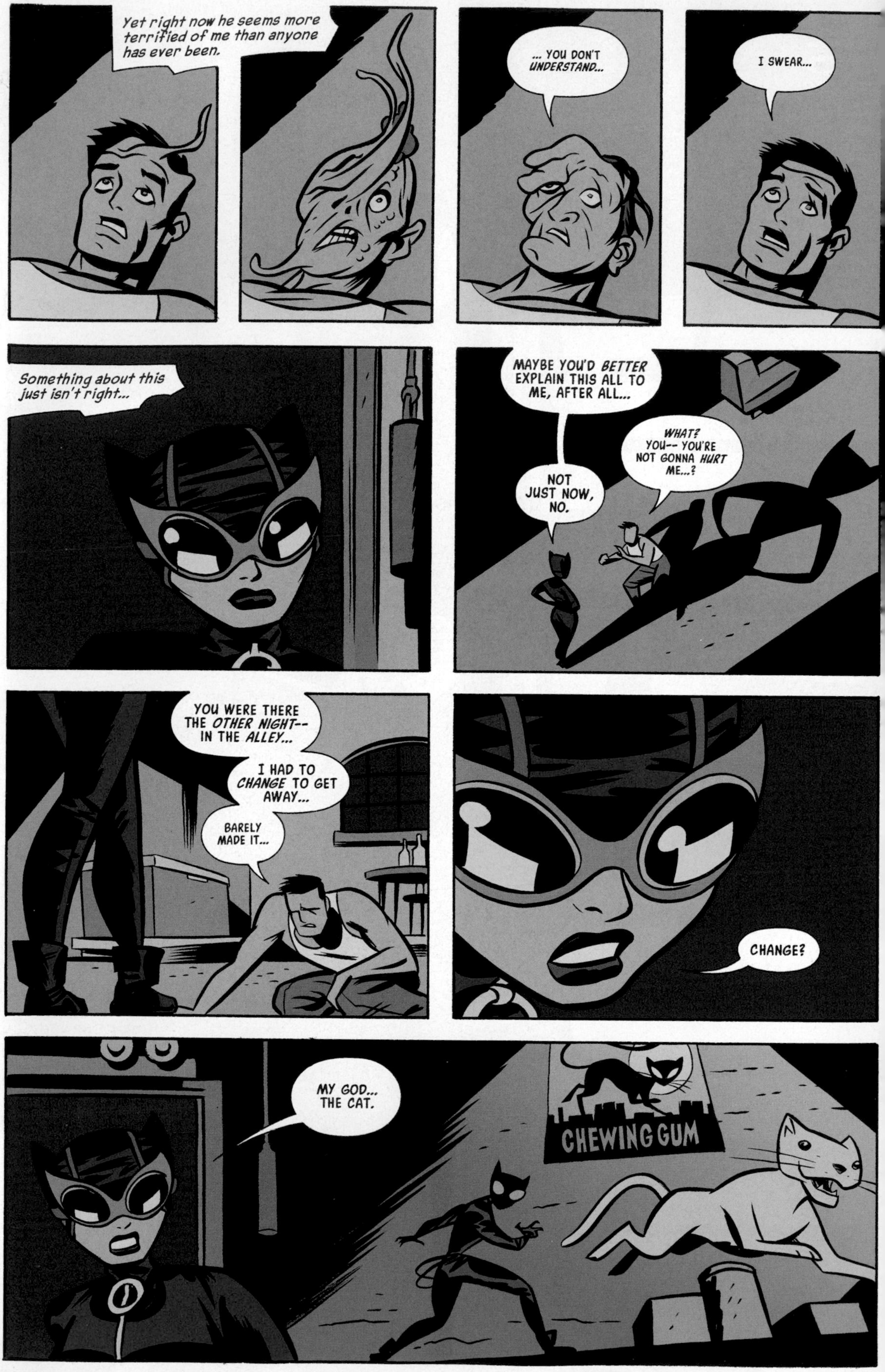
Yet right now he seems more terrified of me than anyone has ever been.
... YOU DON'T UNDERSTAND...
I SWEAR...
Something about this just isn't right...
MAYBE YOU'D BETTER EXPLAIN THIS ALL TO ME, AFTER ALL...
WHAT? YOU-- YOU'RE NOT GONNA HURT ME...?
NOT JUST NOW, NO.
YOU WERE THERE THE OTHER NIGHT-- IN THE ALLEY...
I HAD TO CHANGE TO GET AWAY...
BARELY MADE IT...
CHANGE?
MY GOD... THE CAT.
CHEWING GUM

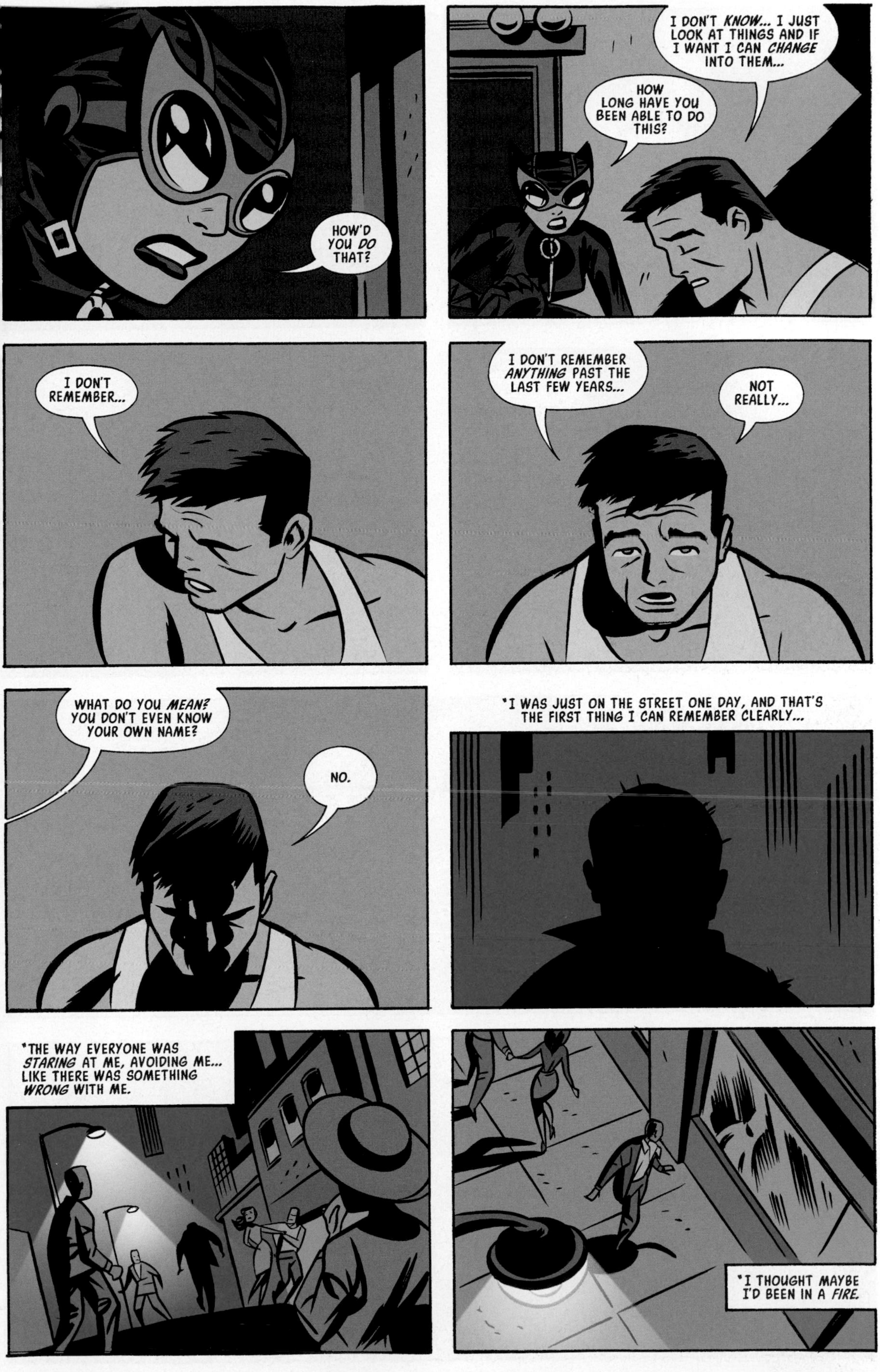
HOW'D YOU DO THAT?
HOW LONG HAVE YOU BEEN ABLE TO DO THIS?
I DON'T KNOW... I JUST LOOK AT THINGS AND IF I WANT I CAN CHANGE INTO THEM...
I DON'T REMEMBER...
I DON'T REMEMBER ANYTHING PAST THE LAST FEW YEARS...
NOT REALLY...
WHAT DO YOU MEAN? YOU DON'T EVEN KNOW YOUR OWN NAME?
NO.
"I WAS JUST ON THE STREET ONE DAY, AND THAT'S THE FIRST THING I CAN REMEMBER CLEARLY...
"THE WAY EVERYONE WAS STARING AT ME, AVOIDING ME... LIKE THERE WAS SOMETHING WRONG WITH ME.
"I THOUGHT MAYBE I'D BEEN IN A FIRE.

"MY FACE DIDN'T LOOK RIGHT... I WASN'T SUPPOSED TO BE *UGLY*...

"SO I *FIXED* IT."

YOU COULD JUST *DO* THAT? HOW DID YOU KNOW?

I *DIDN'T* KNOW... I JUST *WISHED* IT, I GUESS...

WHAT ABOUT *BEFORE* THAT DAY, DO YOU REMEMBER ANYTHING *AT ALL* BEFORE THEN?

JUST LITTLE *FLASHES*...

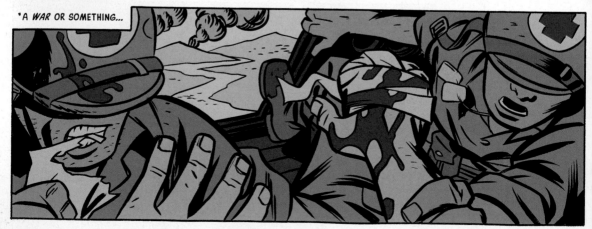

"A *WAR* OR SOMETHING...

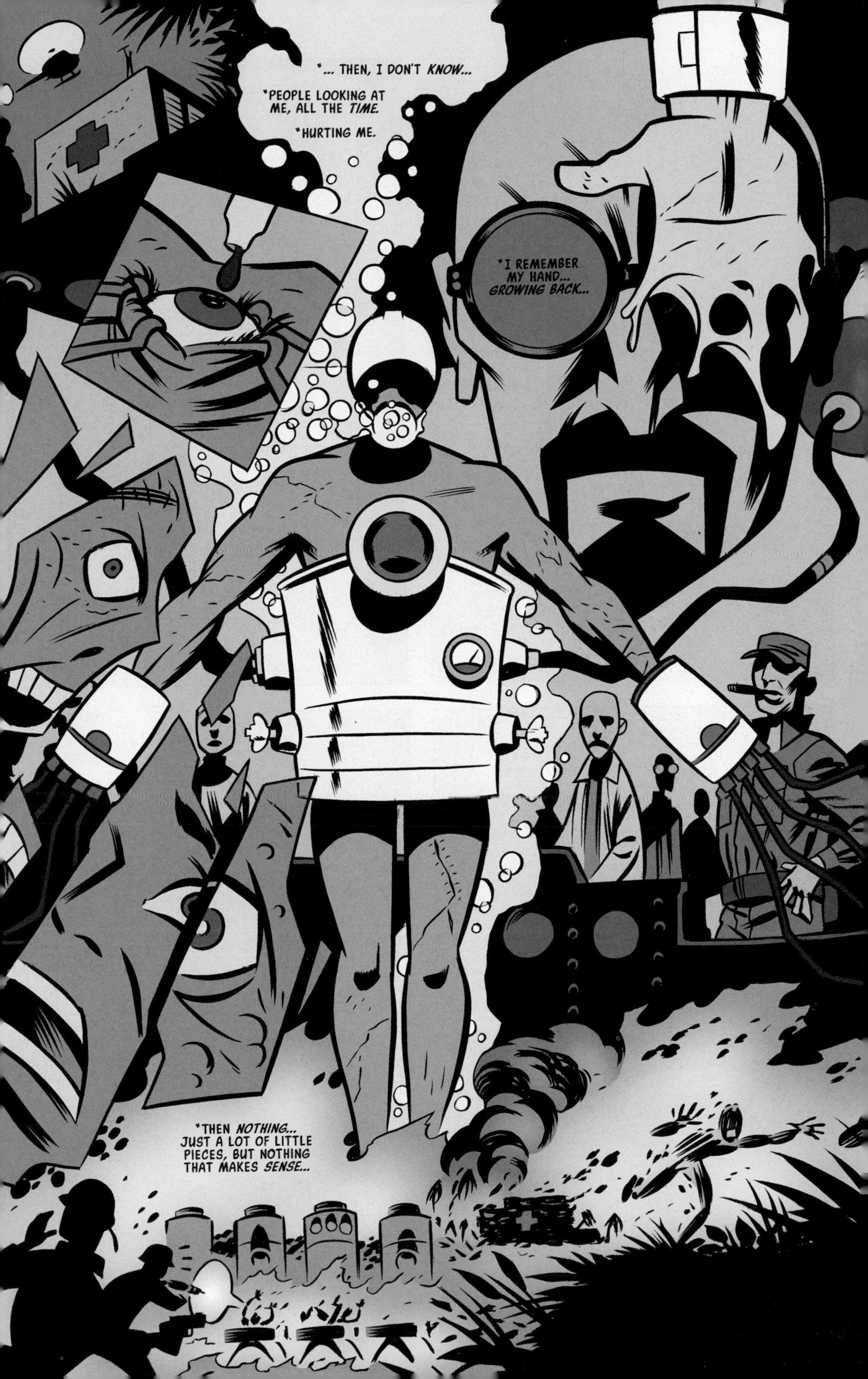
"... THEN, I DON'T KNOW...
"PEOPLE LOOKING AT ME, ALL THE TIME.
"HURTING ME.
"I REMEMBER MY HAND... GROWING BACK...
"THEN NOTHING... JUST A LOT OF LITTLE PIECES, BUT NOTHING THAT MAKES SENSE...

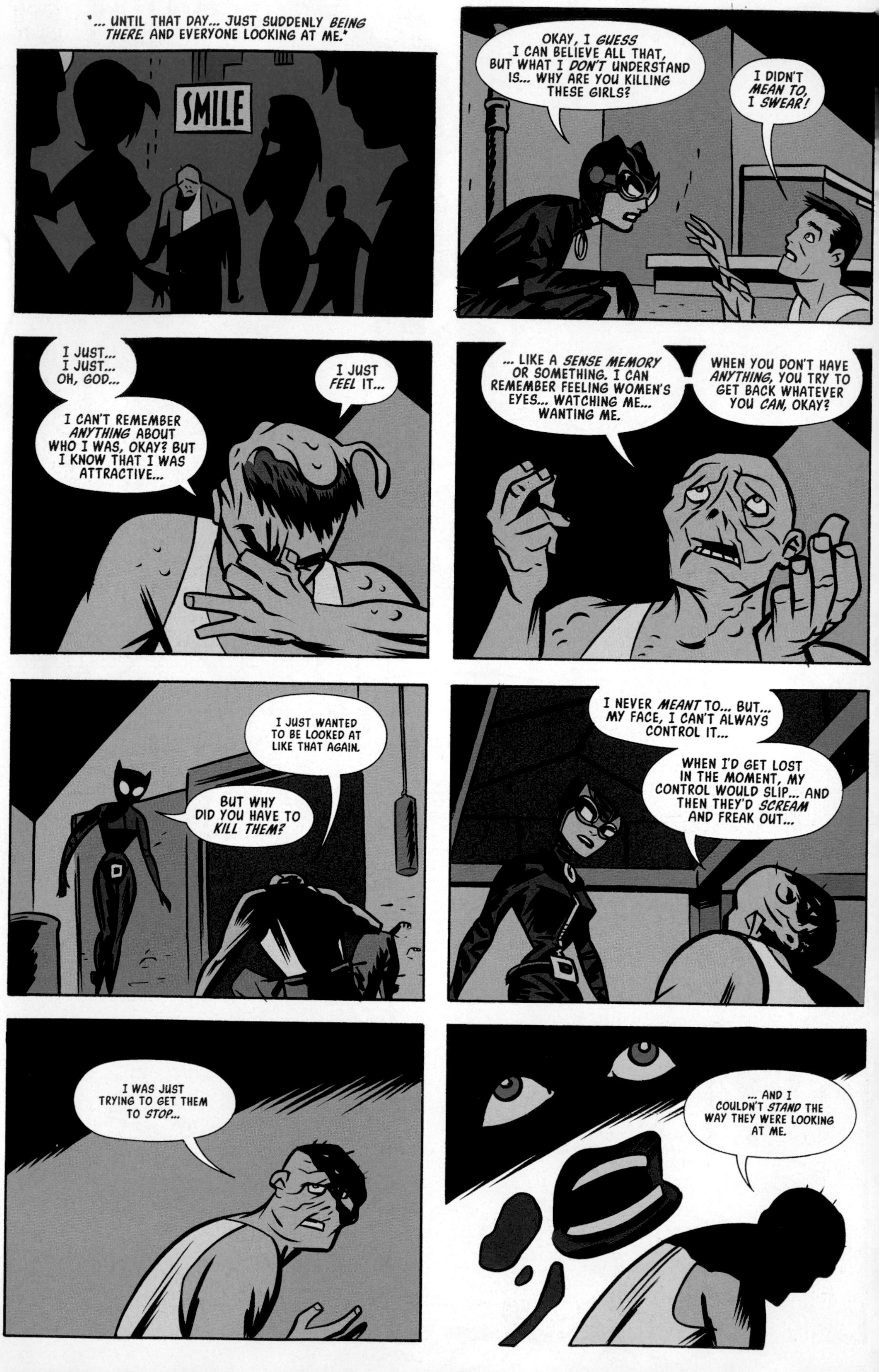
"... UNTIL THAT DAY... JUST SUDDENLY BEING THERE. AND EVERYONE LOOKING AT ME."
SMILE
OKAY, I GUESS I CAN BELIEVE ALL THAT, BUT WHAT I DON'T UNDERSTAND IS... WHY ARE YOU KILLING THESE GIRLS?
I DIDN'T MEAN TO, I SWEAR!
I JUST... I JUST... OH, GOD...
I CAN'T REMEMBER ANYTHING ABOUT WHO I WAS, OKAY? BUT I KNOW THAT I WAS ATTRACTIVE...
I JUST FEEL IT...
... LIKE A SENSE MEMORY OR SOMETHING. I CAN REMEMBER FEELING WOMEN'S EYES... WATCHING ME... WANTING ME.
WHEN YOU DON'T HAVE ANYTHING, YOU TRY TO GET BACK WHATEVER YOU CAN, OKAY?
I JUST WANTED TO BE LOOKED AT LIKE THAT AGAIN.
BUT WHY DID YOU HAVE TO KILL THEM?
I NEVER MEANT TO... BUT... MY FACE, I CAN'T ALWAYS CONTROL IT...
WHEN I'D GET LOST IN THE MOMENT, MY CONTROL WOULD SLIP... AND THEN THEY'D SCREAM AND FREAK OUT...
I WAS JUST TRYING TO GET THEM TO STOP...
... AND I COULDN'T STAND THE WAY THEY WERE LOOKING AT ME.

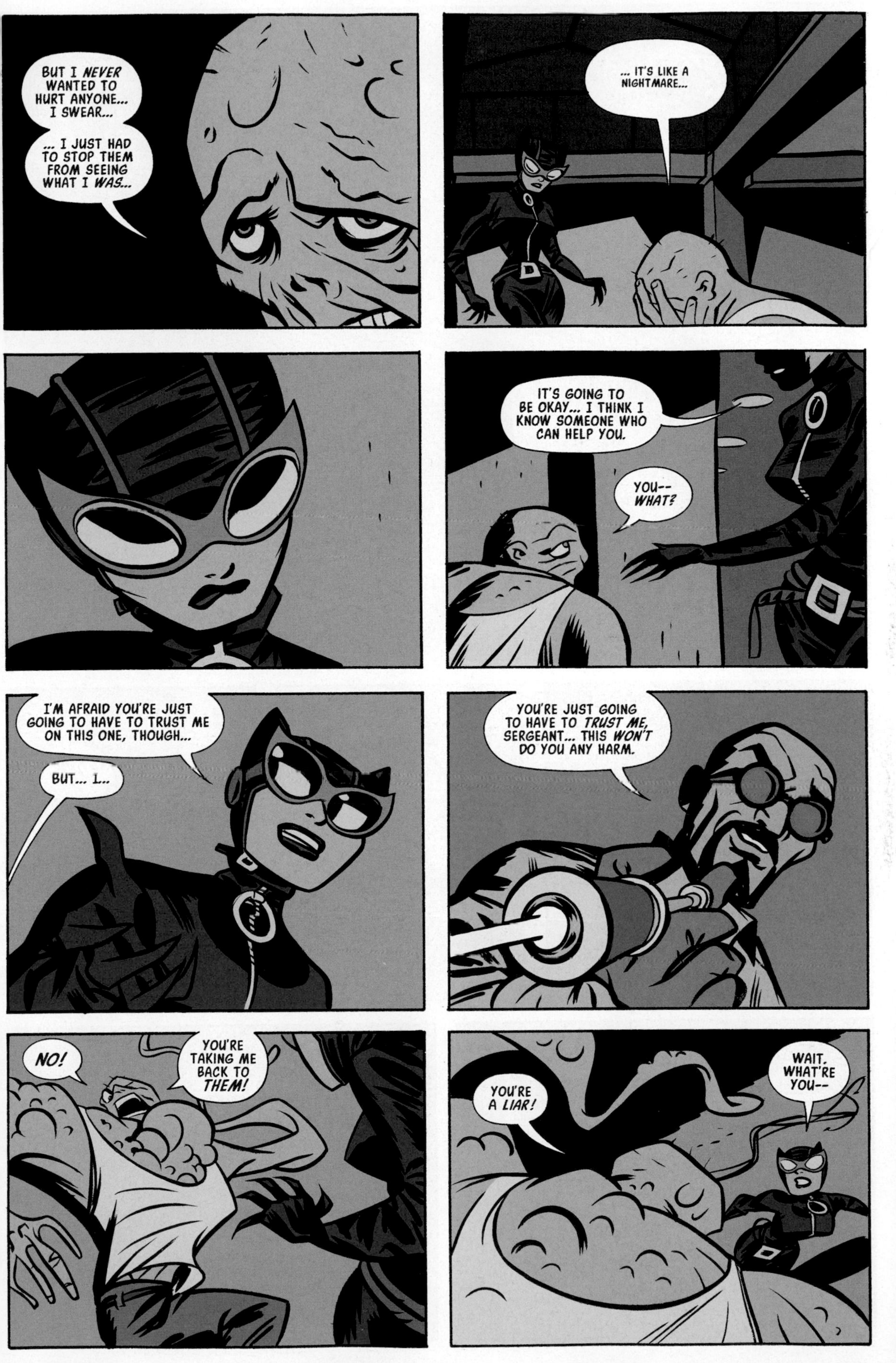
BUT I *NEVER* WANTED TO HURT ANYONE... I SWEAR...
... I JUST HAD TO STOP THEM FROM SEEING WHAT I *WAS*...
... IT'S LIKE A NIGHTMARE...
IT'S GOING TO BE OKAY... I THINK I KNOW SOMEONE WHO CAN HELP YOU.
YOU-- *WHAT?*
I'M AFRAID YOU'RE JUST GOING TO HAVE TO TRUST ME ON THIS ONE, THOUGH...
BUT... I...
YOU'RE JUST GOING TO HAVE TO *TRUST ME,* SERGEANT... THIS *WON'T* DO YOU ANY HARM.
NO!
YOU'RE TAKING ME BACK TO *THEM!*
YOU'RE A *LIAR!*
WAIT. WHAT'RE YOU--

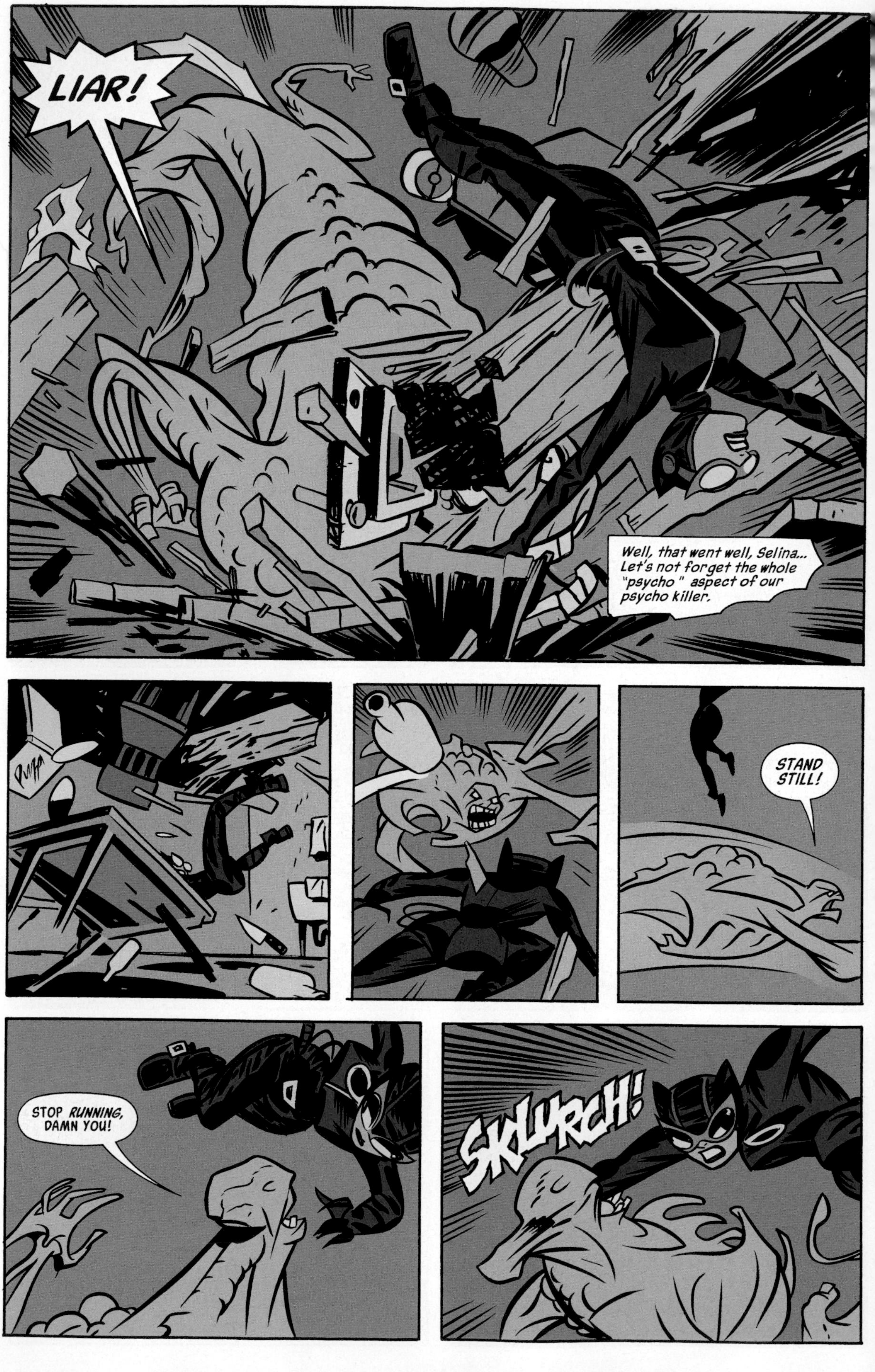
LIAR!
Well, that went well, Selina... Let's not forget the whole "psycho" aspect of our psycho killer.
STAND STILL!
STOP RUNNING, DAMN YOU!
SKLURCH!

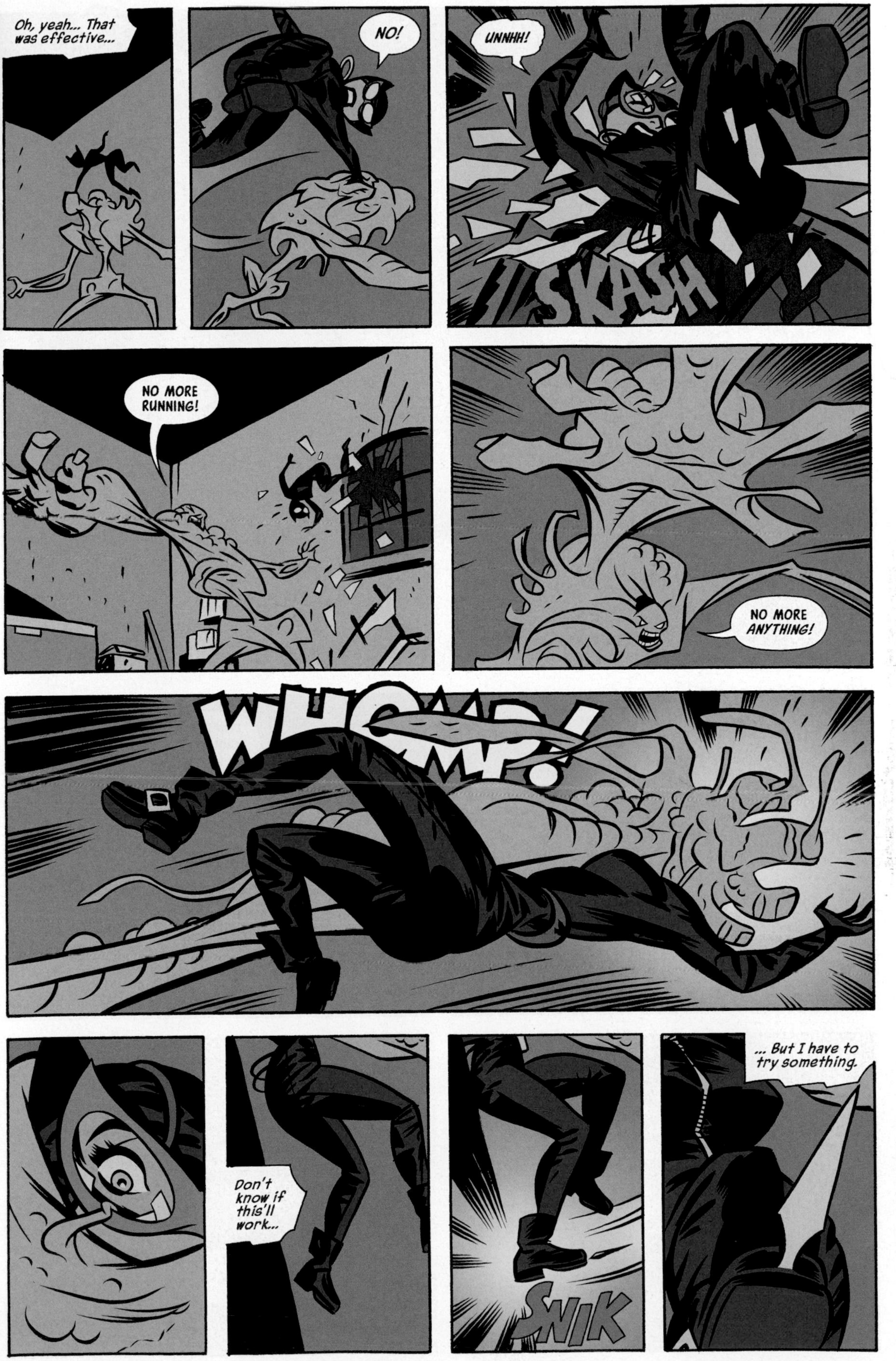
Oh, yeah... That was effective...
NO!
UNNHH!
SKASH
NO MORE RUNNING!
NO MORE ANYTHING!
WHOMP!
Don't know if this'll work...
SNIK
... But I have to try something.

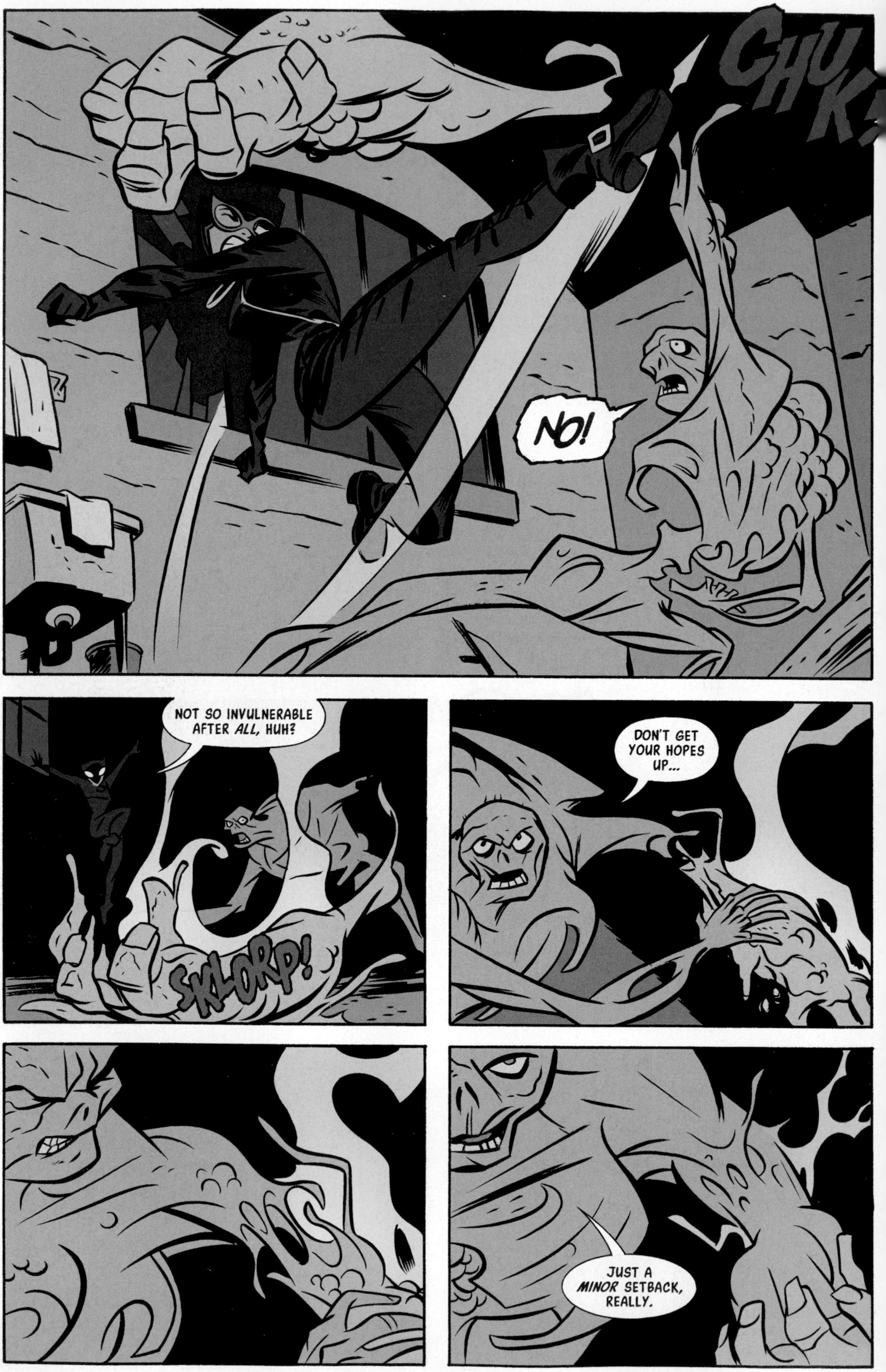
CHUK!
NO!
NOT SO INVULNERABLE AFTER ALL, HUH?
SKLORP!
DON'T GET YOUR HOPES UP...
JUST A MINOR SETBACK, REALLY.

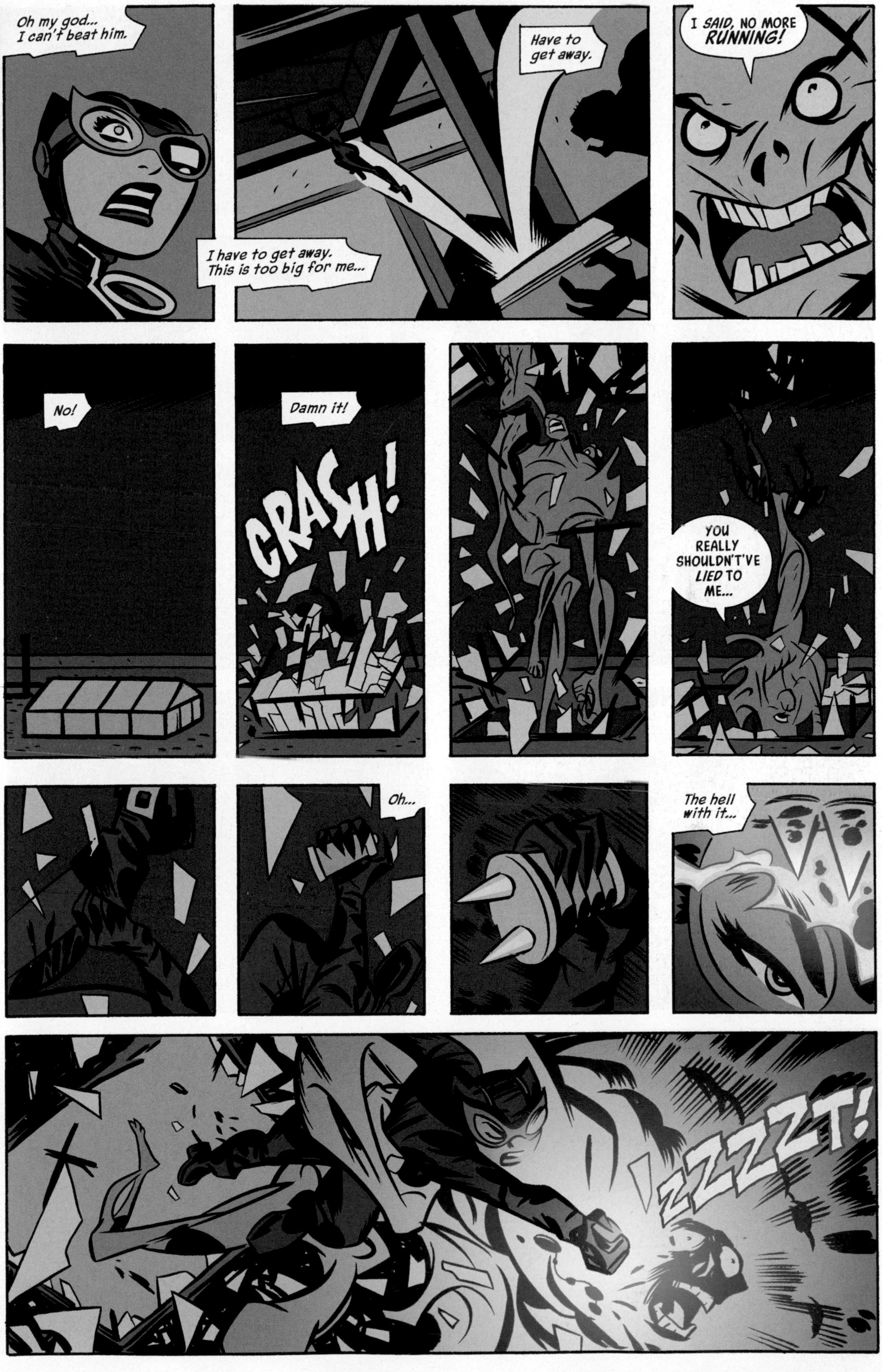

Oh my god...
I can't beat him.
Have to get away.
I have to get away. This is too big for me...
I SAID, NO MORE RUNNING!
No!
Damn it!
CRASH!
YOU REALLY SHOULDN'T'VE LIED TO ME...
Oh...
The hell with it...
ZZZZZT!

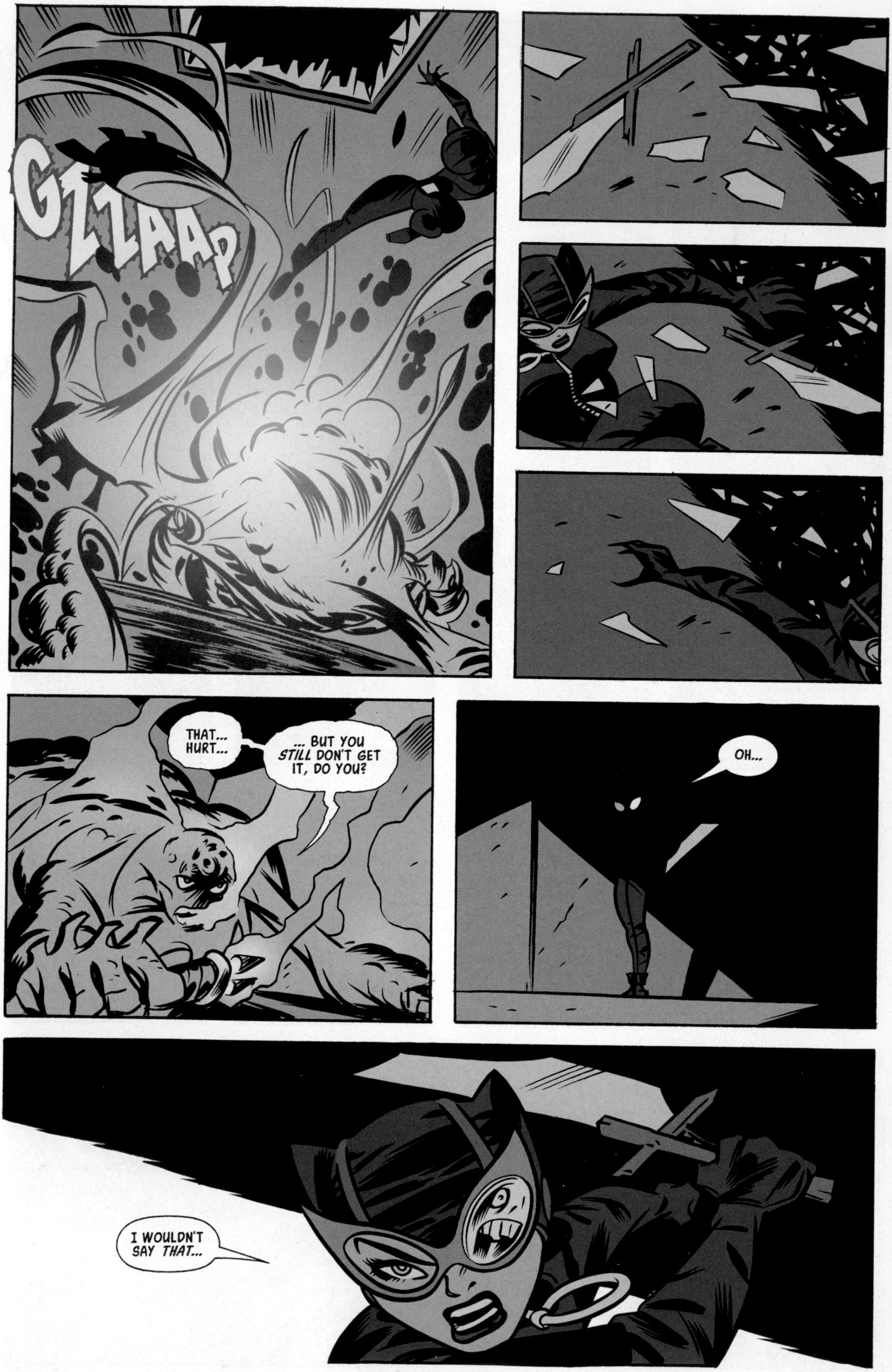
GZZAAP
THAT... HURT...
... BUT YOU STILL DON'T GET IT, DO YOU?
OH...
I WOULDN'T SAY THAT...

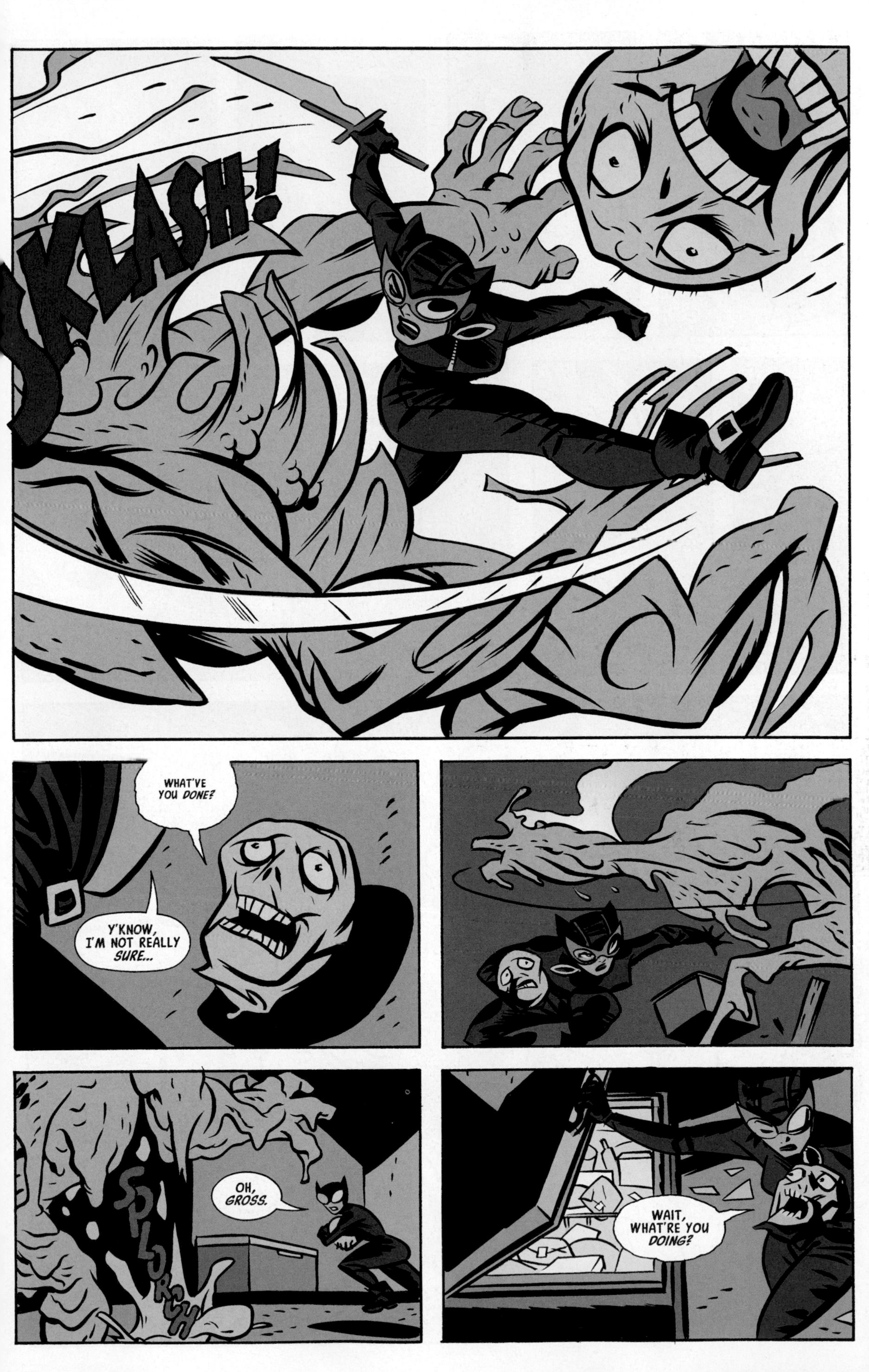
SKLASH!
WHAT'VE YOU DONE?
Y'KNOW, I'M NOT REALLY SURE...
SPLORCH
OH, GROSS.
WAIT, WHAT'RE YOU DOING?

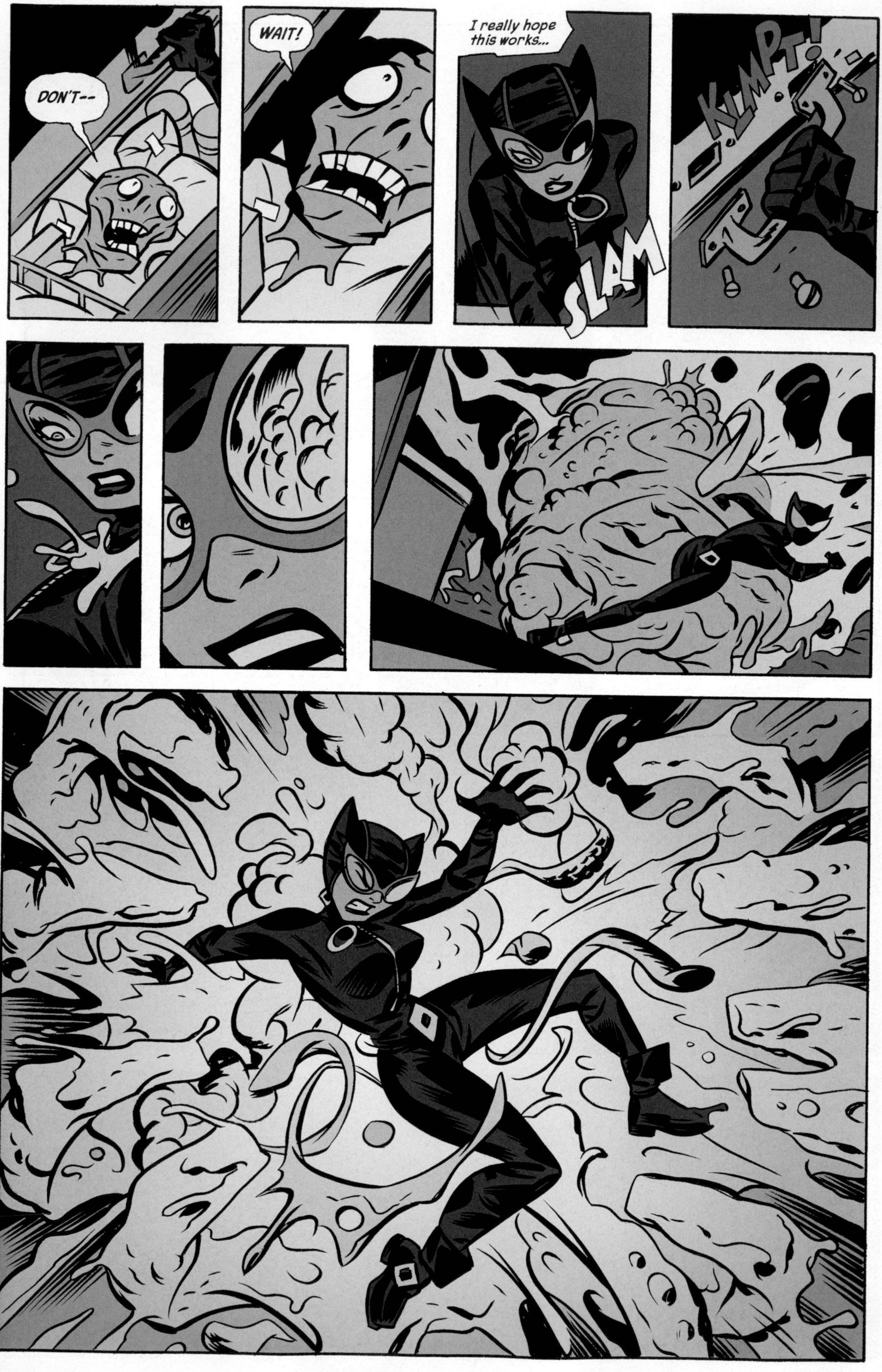
DON'T--
WAIT!
I really hope this works...
SLAM
KLMPT!

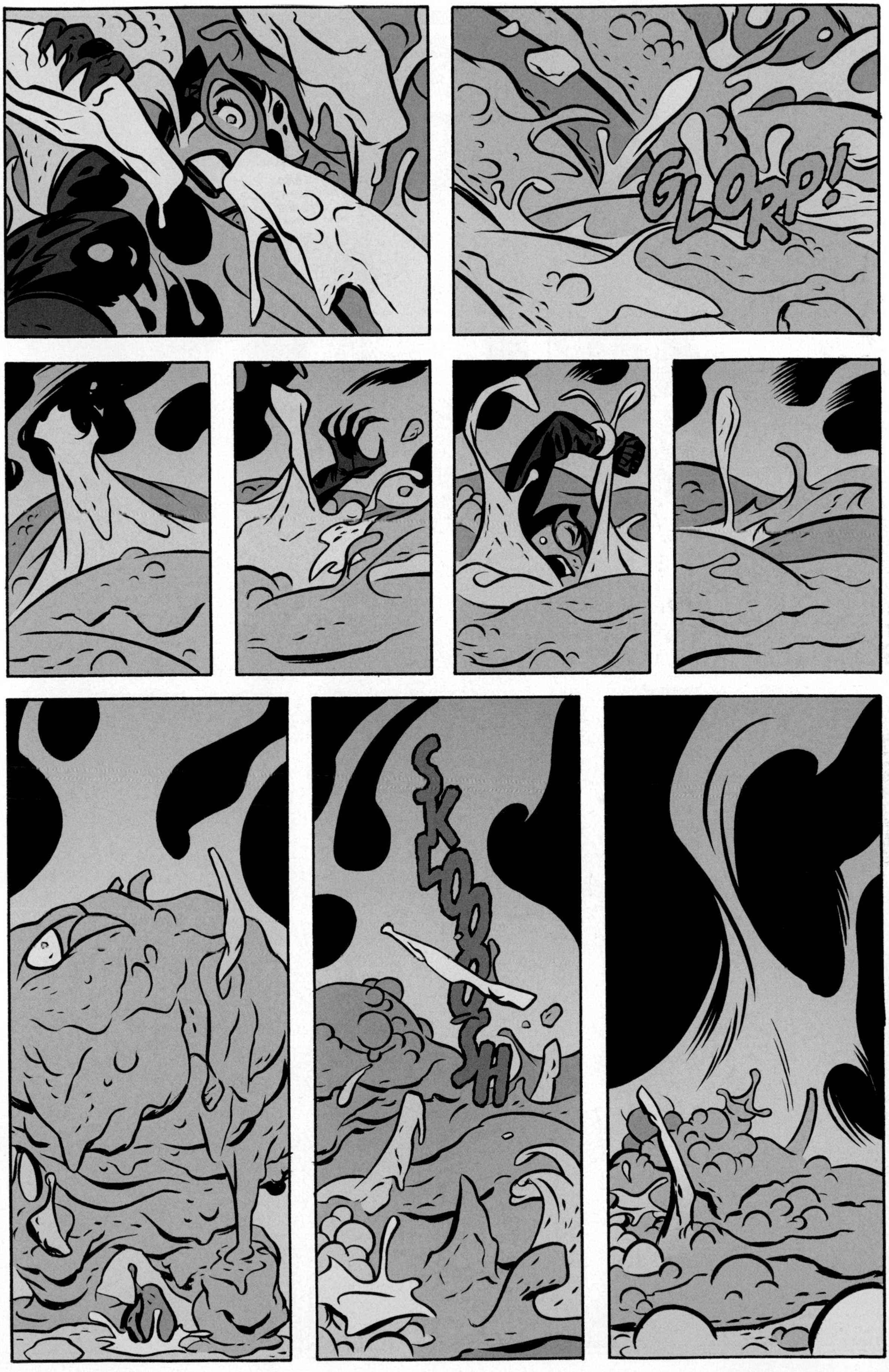
GLORP!
SKLOOOOSH

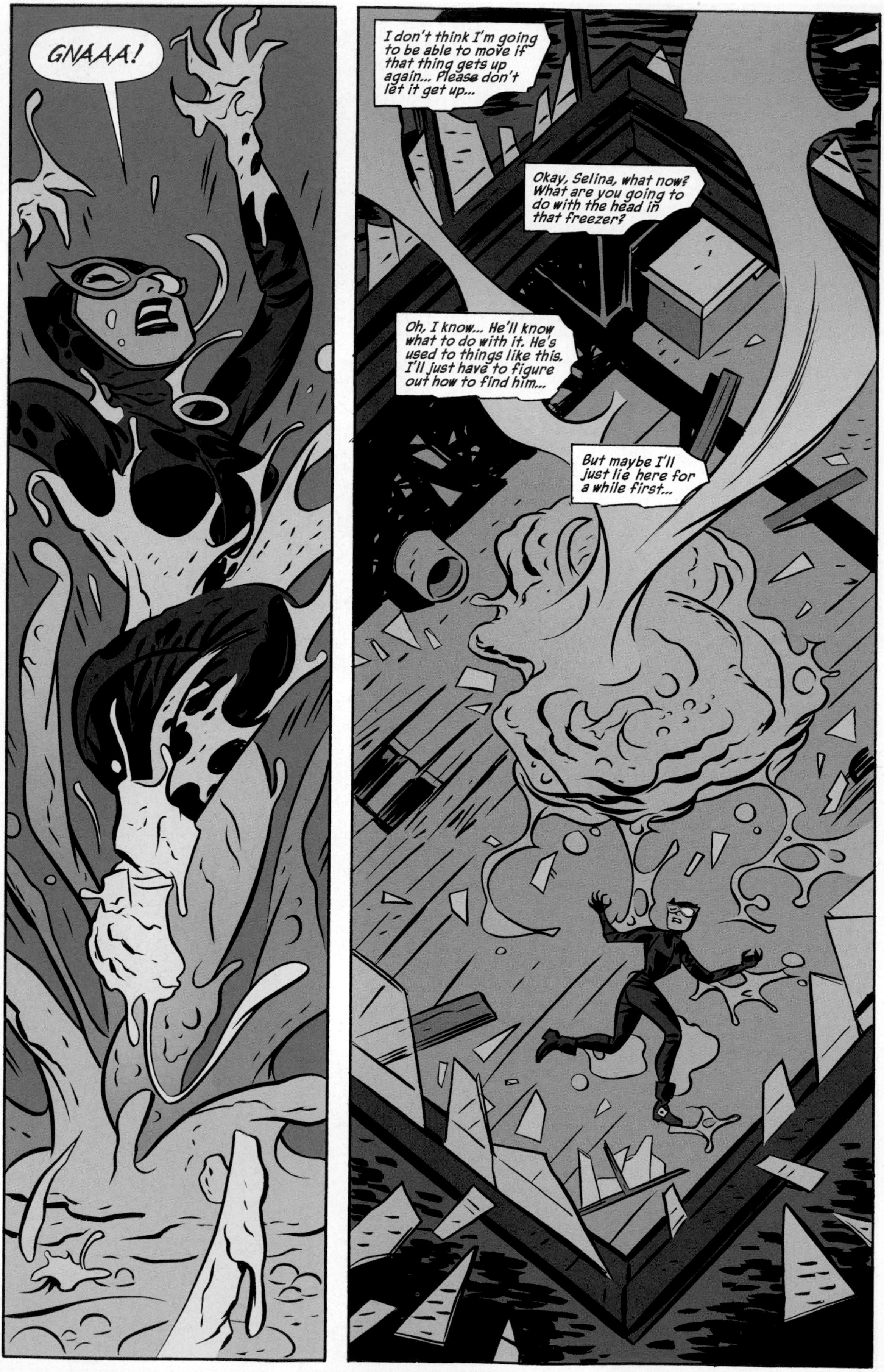
GNAAA!
I don't think I'm going to be able to move if that thing gets up again... Please don't let it get up...
Okay, Selina, what now? What are you going to do with the head in that freezer?
Oh, I know... He'll know what to do with it. He's used to things like this. I'll just have to figure out how to find him...
But maybe I'll just lie here for a while first...

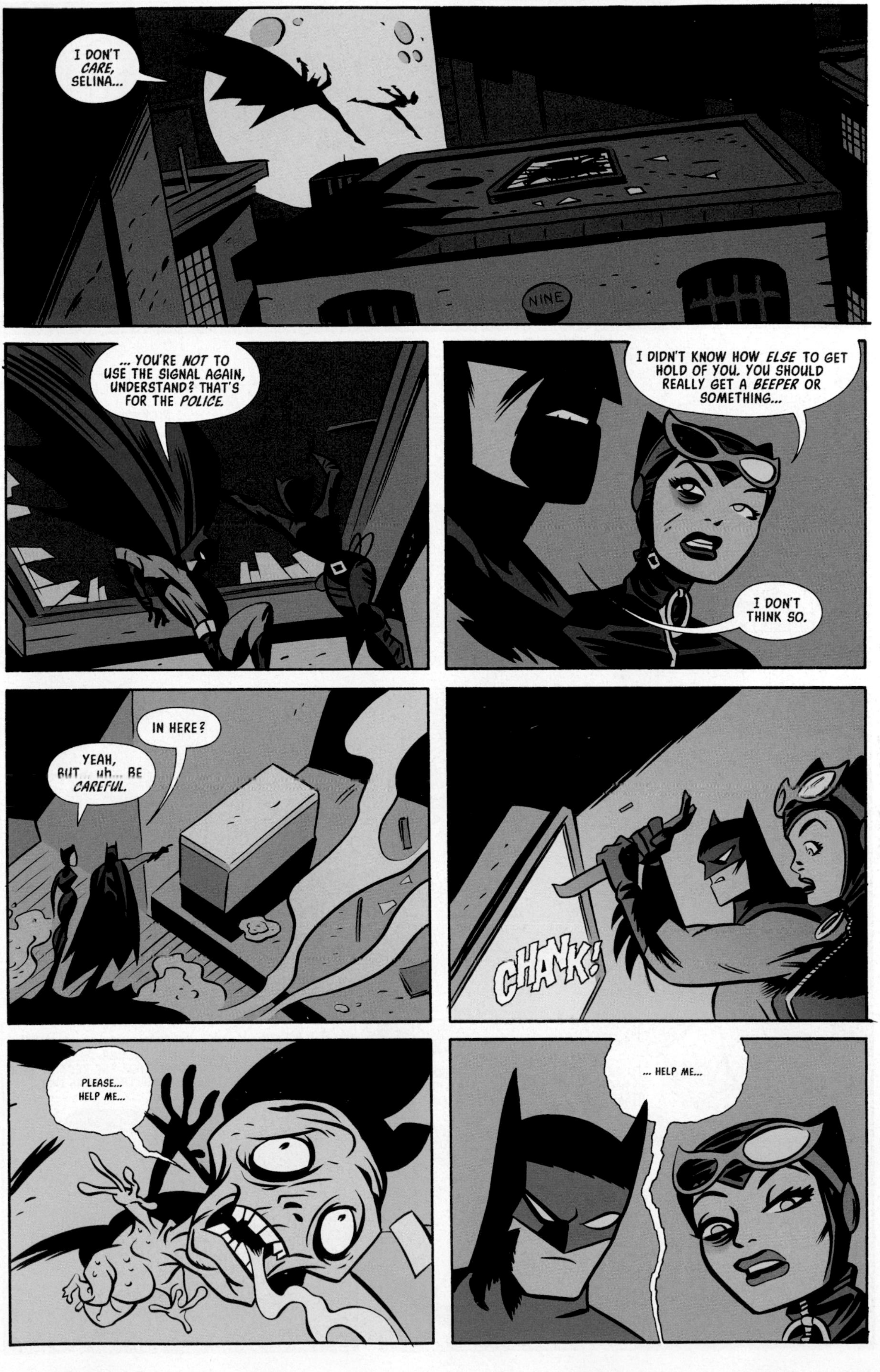

I DON'T CARE, SELINA...
... YOU'RE NOT TO USE THE SIGNAL AGAIN, UNDERSTAND? THAT'S FOR THE POLICE.
I DIDN'T KNOW HOW ELSE TO GET HOLD OF YOU. YOU SHOULD REALLY GET A BEEPER OR SOMETHING...
I DON'T THINK SO.
IN HERE?
YEAH, BUT uh... BE CAREFUL.
CHANK!
PLEASE... HELP ME...
... HELP ME...

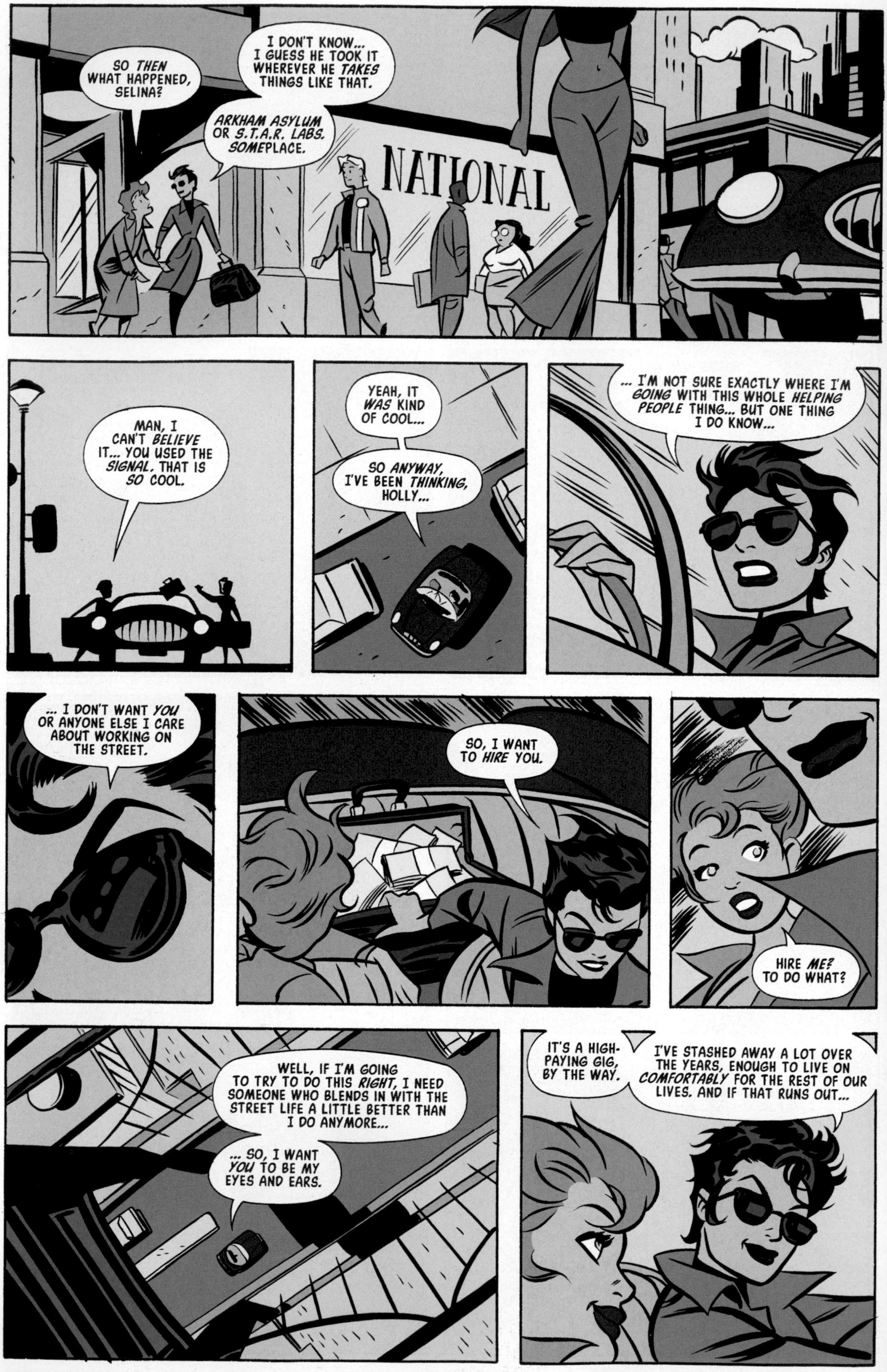
SO THEN WHAT HAPPENED, SELINA?
I DON'T KNOW... I GUESS HE TOOK IT WHEREVER HE TAKES THINGS LIKE THAT.
ARKHAM ASYLUM OR S.T.A.R. LABS. SOMEPLACE.
NATIONAL
MAN, I CAN'T BELIEVE IT... YOU USED THE SIGNAL. THAT IS SO COOL.
YEAH, IT WAS KIND OF COOL...
SO ANYWAY, I'VE BEEN THINKING, HOLLY...
... I'M NOT SURE EXACTLY WHERE I'M GOING WITH THIS WHOLE HELPING PEOPLE THING... BUT ONE THING I DO KNOW...
... I DON'T WANT YOU OR ANYONE ELSE I CARE ABOUT WORKING ON THE STREET.
SO, I WANT TO HIRE YOU.
HIRE ME? TO DO WHAT?
WELL, IF I'M GOING TO TRY TO DO THIS RIGHT, I NEED SOMEONE WHO BLENDS IN WITH THE STREET LIFE A LITTLE BETTER THAN I DO ANYMORE...
... SO, I WANT YOU TO BE MY EYES AND EARS.
IT'S A HIGH-PAYING GIG, BY THE WAY.
I'VE STASHED AWAY A LOT OVER THE YEARS, ENOUGH TO LIVE ON COMFORTABLY FOR THE REST OF OUR LIVES. AND IF THAT RUNS OUT...

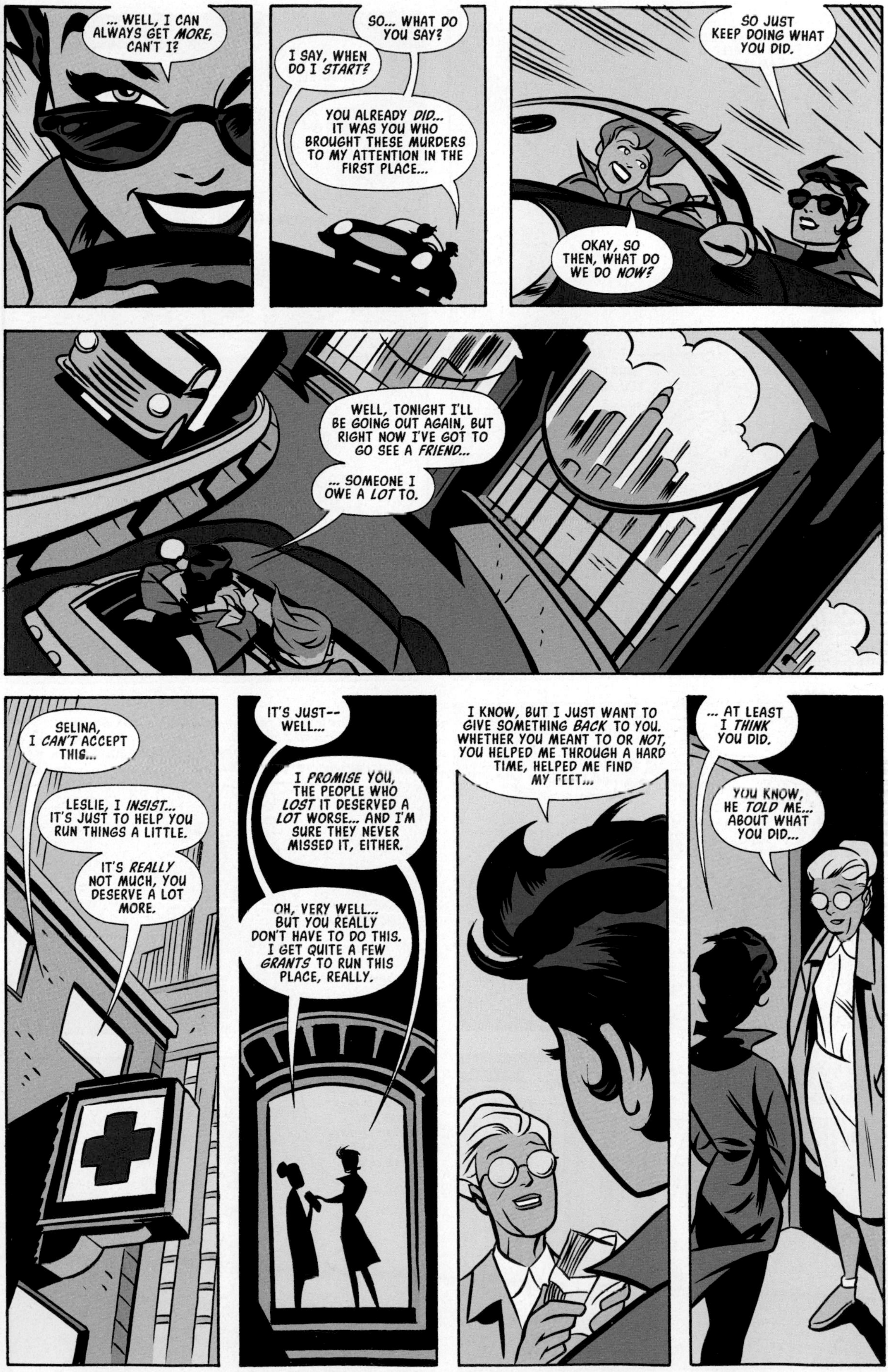

... WELL, I CAN ALWAYS GET MORE, CAN'T I?
SO... WHAT DO YOU SAY?
I SAY, WHEN DO I START?
YOU ALREADY DID... IT WAS YOU WHO BROUGHT THESE MURDERS TO MY ATTENTION IN THE FIRST PLACE...
SO JUST KEEP DOING WHAT YOU DID.
OKAY, SO THEN, WHAT DO WE DO NOW?
WELL, TONIGHT I'LL BE GOING OUT AGAIN, BUT RIGHT NOW I'VE GOT TO GO SEE A FRIEND...
... SOMEONE I OWE A LOT TO.
SELINA, I CAN'T ACCEPT THIS...
LESLIE, I INSIST... IT'S JUST TO HELP YOU RUN THINGS A LITTLE.
IT'S REALLY NOT MUCH, YOU DESERVE A LOT MORE.
IT'S JUST-- WELL...
I PROMISE YOU, THE PEOPLE WHO LOST IT DESERVED A LOT WORSE... AND I'M SURE THEY NEVER MISSED IT, EITHER.
OH, VERY WELL... BUT YOU REALLY DON'T HAVE TO DO THIS. I GET QUITE A FEW GRANTS TO RUN THIS PLACE, REALLY.
I KNOW, BUT I JUST WANT TO GIVE SOMETHING BACK TO YOU. WHETHER YOU MEANT TO OR NOT, YOU HELPED ME THROUGH A HARD TIME, HELPED ME FIND MY FEET...
... AT LEAST I THINK YOU DID.
YOU KNOW, HE TOLD ME... ABOUT WHAT YOU DID...

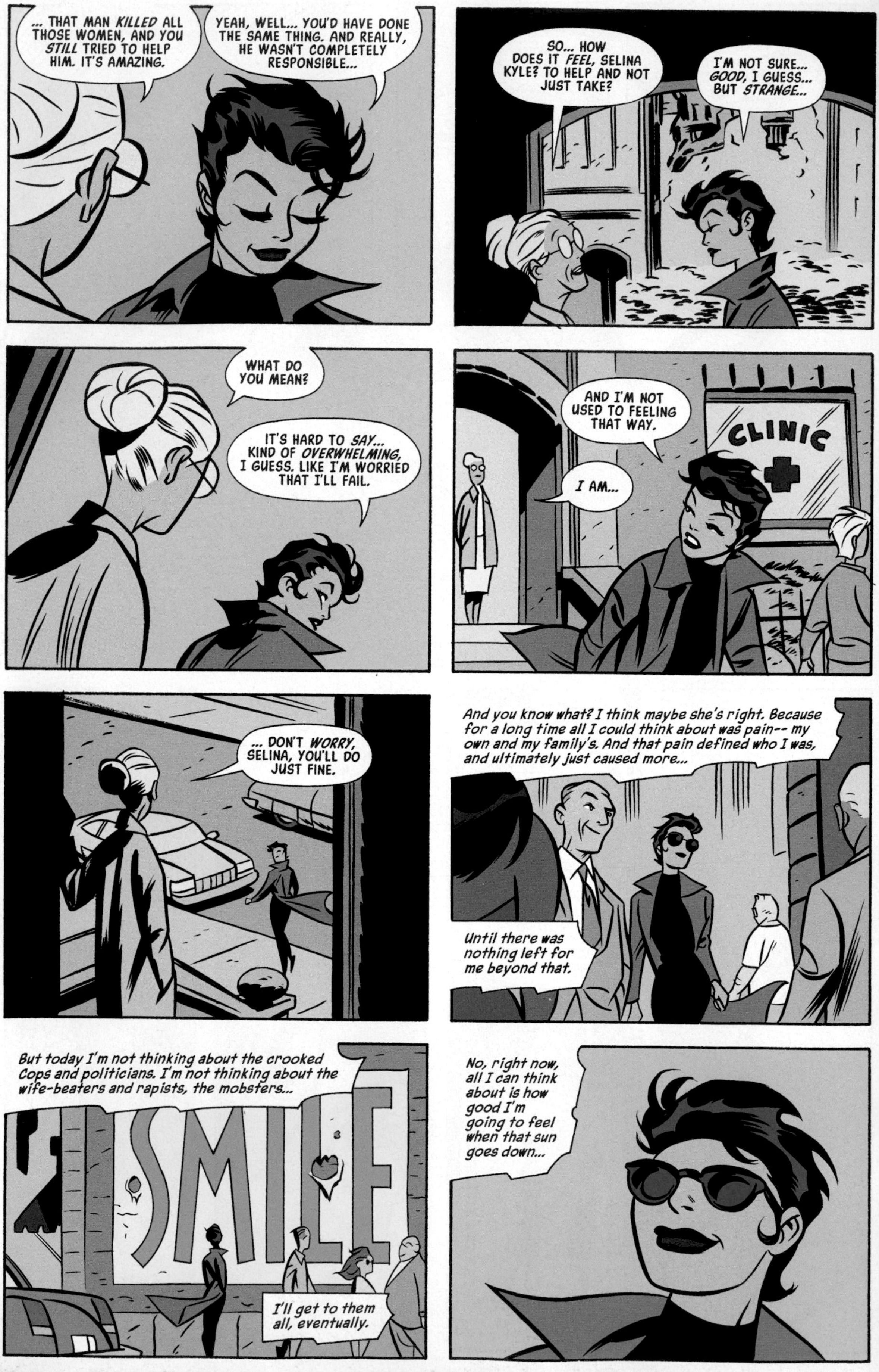
... THAT MAN *KILLED* ALL THOSE WOMEN, AND YOU *STILL* TRIED TO HELP HIM. IT'S AMAZING.
YEAH, WELL... YOU'D HAVE DONE THE SAME THING. AND REALLY, HE WASN'T COMPLETELY RESPONSIBLE...
SO... HOW DOES IT *FEEL*, SELINA KYLE? TO HELP AND NOT JUST TAKE?
I'M NOT SURE... *GOOD*, I GUESS... BUT *STRANGE*...
WHAT DO YOU MEAN?
IT'S HARD TO *SAY*... KIND OF *OVERWHELMING*, I GUESS. LIKE I'M WORRIED THAT I'LL FAIL.
AND I'M NOT USED TO FEELING THAT WAY.
CLINIC
I AM...
... DON'T *WORRY*, SELINA, YOU'LL DO JUST FINE.
And you know what? I think maybe she's right. Because for a long time all I could think about was pain-- my own and my family's. And that pain defined who I was, and ultimately just caused more...
Until there was nothing left for me beyond that.
But today I'm not thinking about the crooked Cops and politicians. I'm not thinking about the wife-beaters and rapists, the mobsters...
SMILE
I'll get to them all, eventually.
No, right now, all I can think about is how good I'm going to feel when that sun goes down...

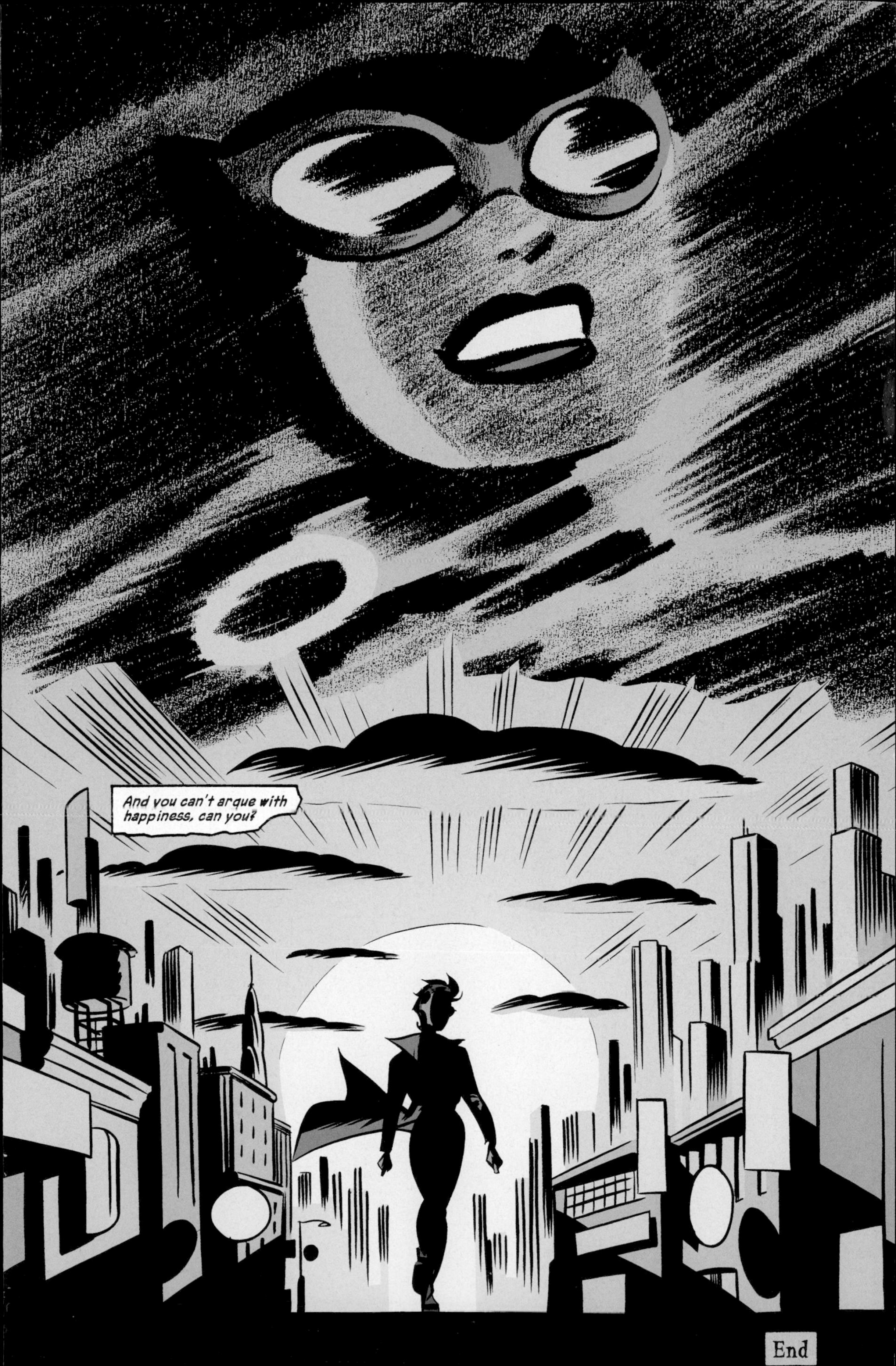
And you can't argue with happiness, can you?
End

Catwoman 5 Cover by Paul Pope

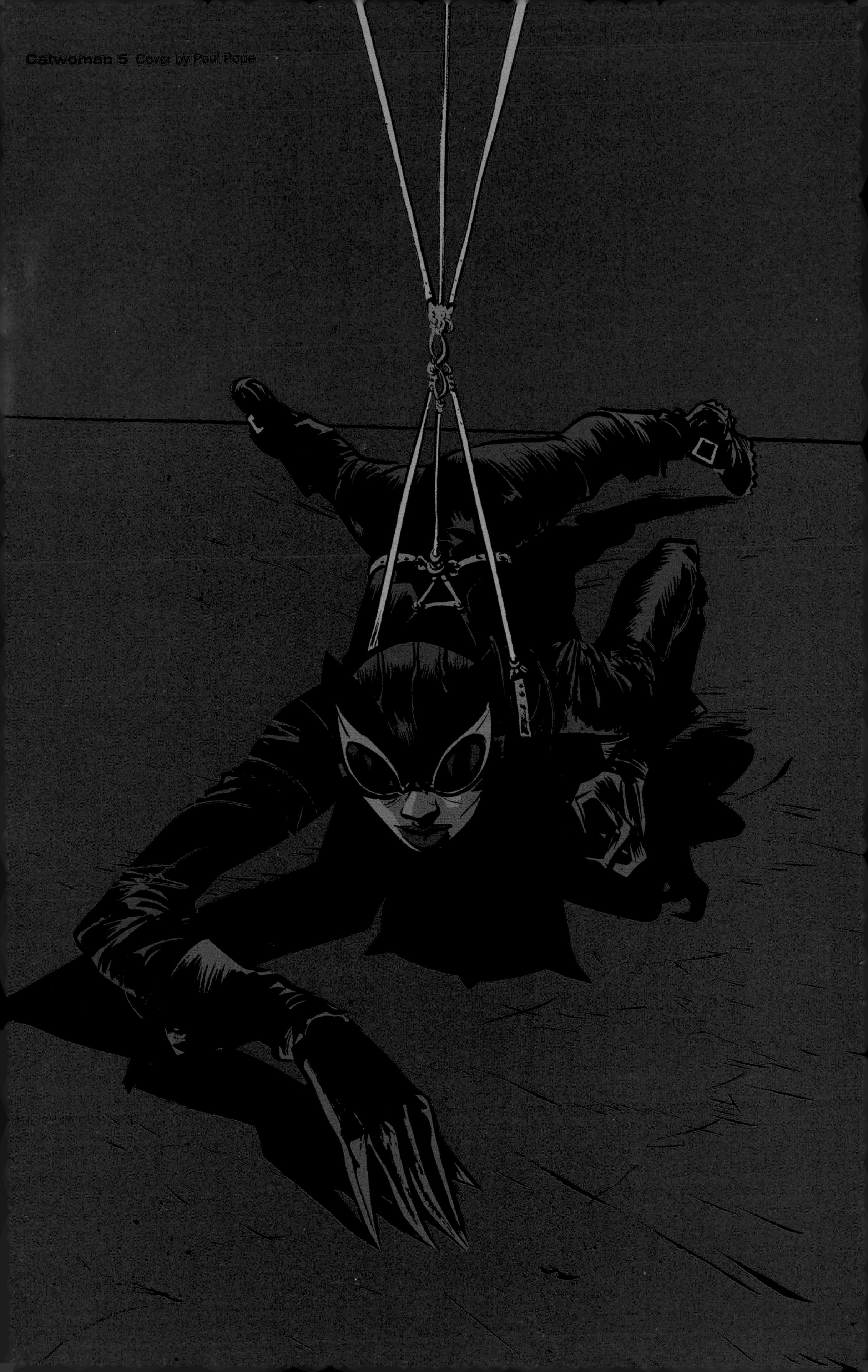

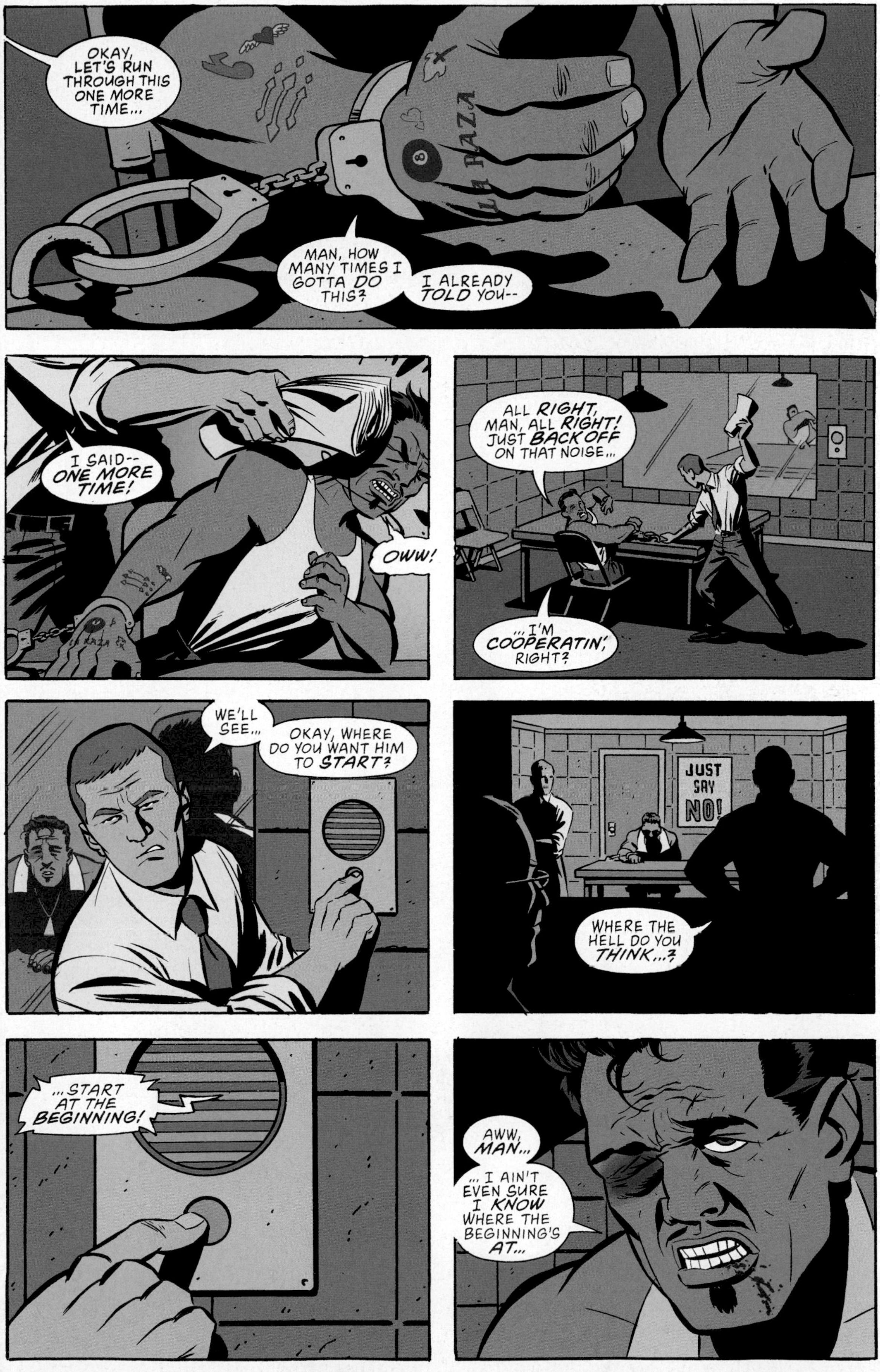
OKAY, LET'S RUN THROUGH THIS ONE MORE TIME...
LA RAZA
MAN, HOW MANY TIMES I GOTTA DO THIS?
I ALREADY TOLD YOU--
I SAID-- ONE MORE TIME!
OWW!
ALL RIGHT, MAN, ALL RIGHT! JUST BACK OFF ON THAT NOISE...
...I'M COOPERATIN', RIGHT?
WE'LL SEE...
OKAY, WHERE DO YOU WANT HIM TO START?
JUST SAY NO!
WHERE THE HELL DO YOU THINK...?
...START AT THE BEGINNING!
AWW, MAN...
...I AIN'T EVEN SURE I KNOW WHERE THE BEGINNING'S AT...

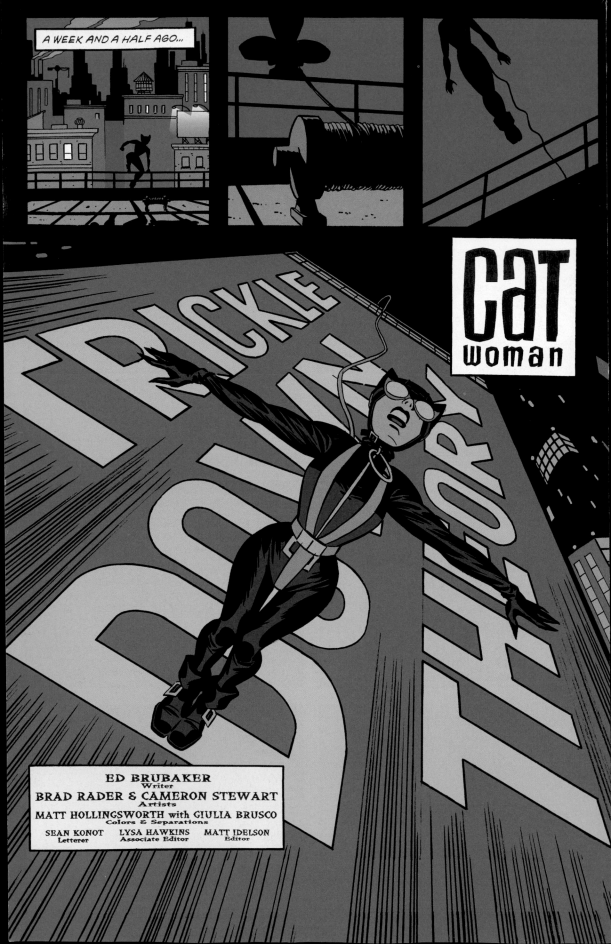

A WEEK AND A HALF AGO...

CAT
woman

ED BRUBAKER
Writer

BRAD RADER & CAMERON STEWART
Artists

MATT HOLLINGSWORTH with GIULIA BRUSCO
Colors & Separations

SEAN KONOT   LYSA HAWKINS   MATT IDELSON
Letterer   Associate Editor   Editor

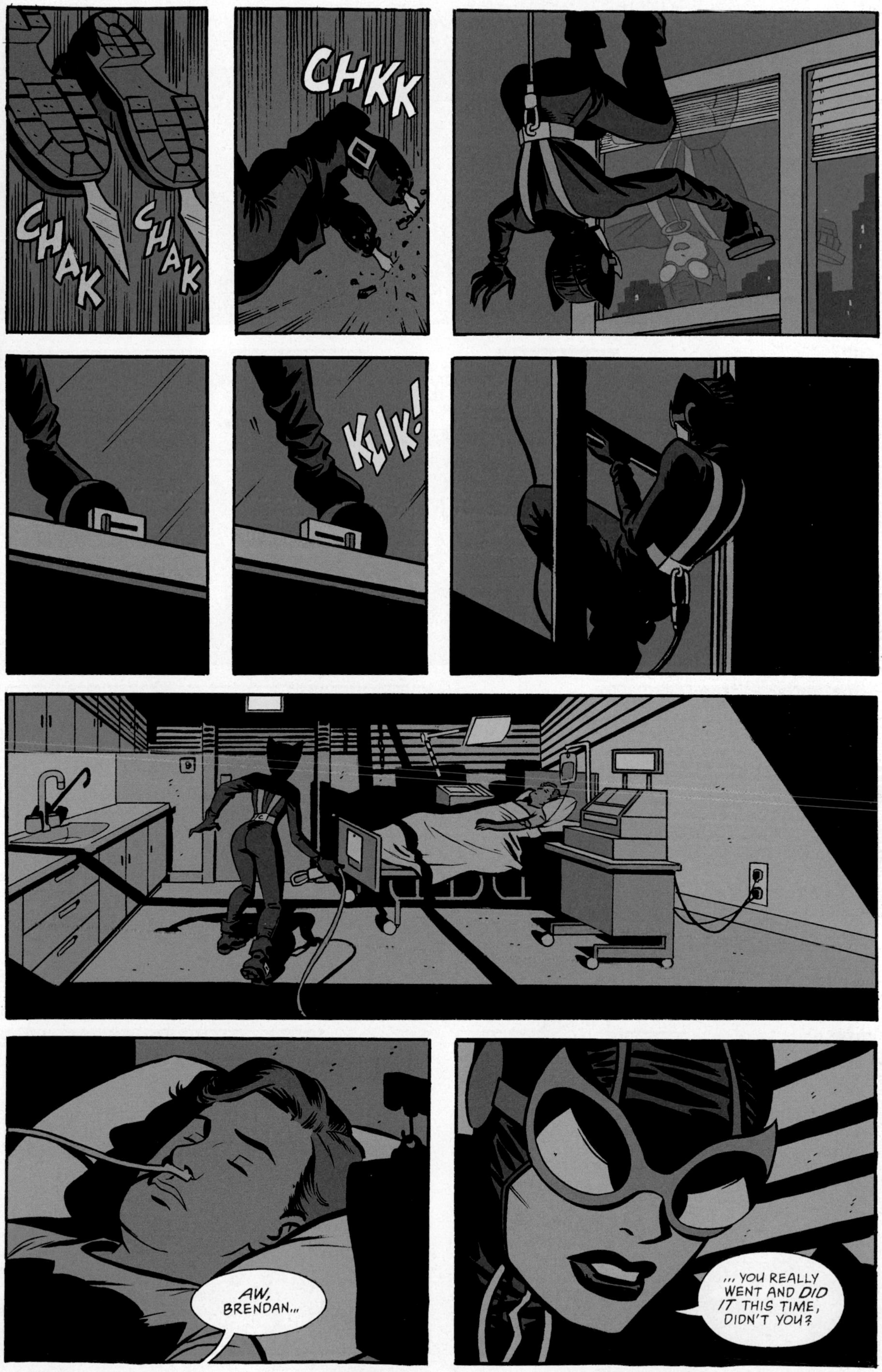
CHAK
CHAK
CHKK
KLIK!
AW, BRENDAN...
...YOU REALLY WENT AND DID IT THIS TIME, DIDN'T YOU?

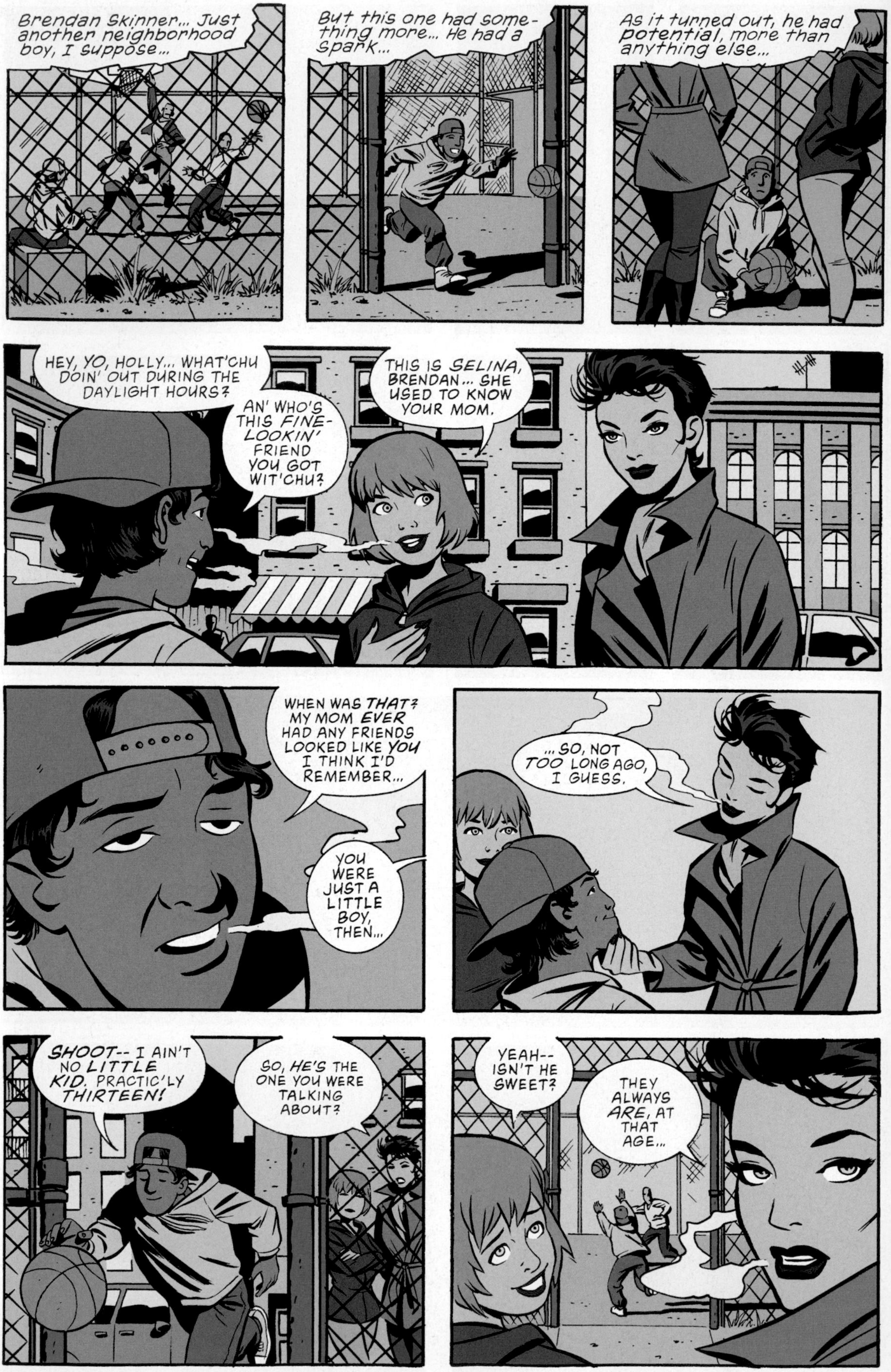
Brendan Skinner... Just another neighborhood boy, I suppose...
But this one had something more... He had a Spark...
As it turned out, he had potential, more than anything else...
HEY, YO, HOLLY... WHAT'CHU DOIN' OUT DURING THE DAYLIGHT HOURS?
AN' WHO'S THIS FINE-LOOKIN' FRIEND YOU GOT WIT'CHU?
THIS IS SELINA, BRENDAN... SHE USED TO KNOW YOUR MOM.
WHEN WAS THAT? MY MOM EVER HAD ANY FRIENDS LOOKED LIKE YOU I THINK I'D REMEMBER...
YOU WERE JUST A LITTLE BOY, THEN...
...SO, NOT TOO LONG AGO, I GUESS.
SHOOT-- I AIN'T NO LITTLE KID. PRACTIC'LY THIRTEEN!
SO, HE'S THE ONE YOU WERE TALKING ABOUT?
YEAH-- ISN'T HE SWEET?
THEY ALWAYS ARE, AT THAT AGE...

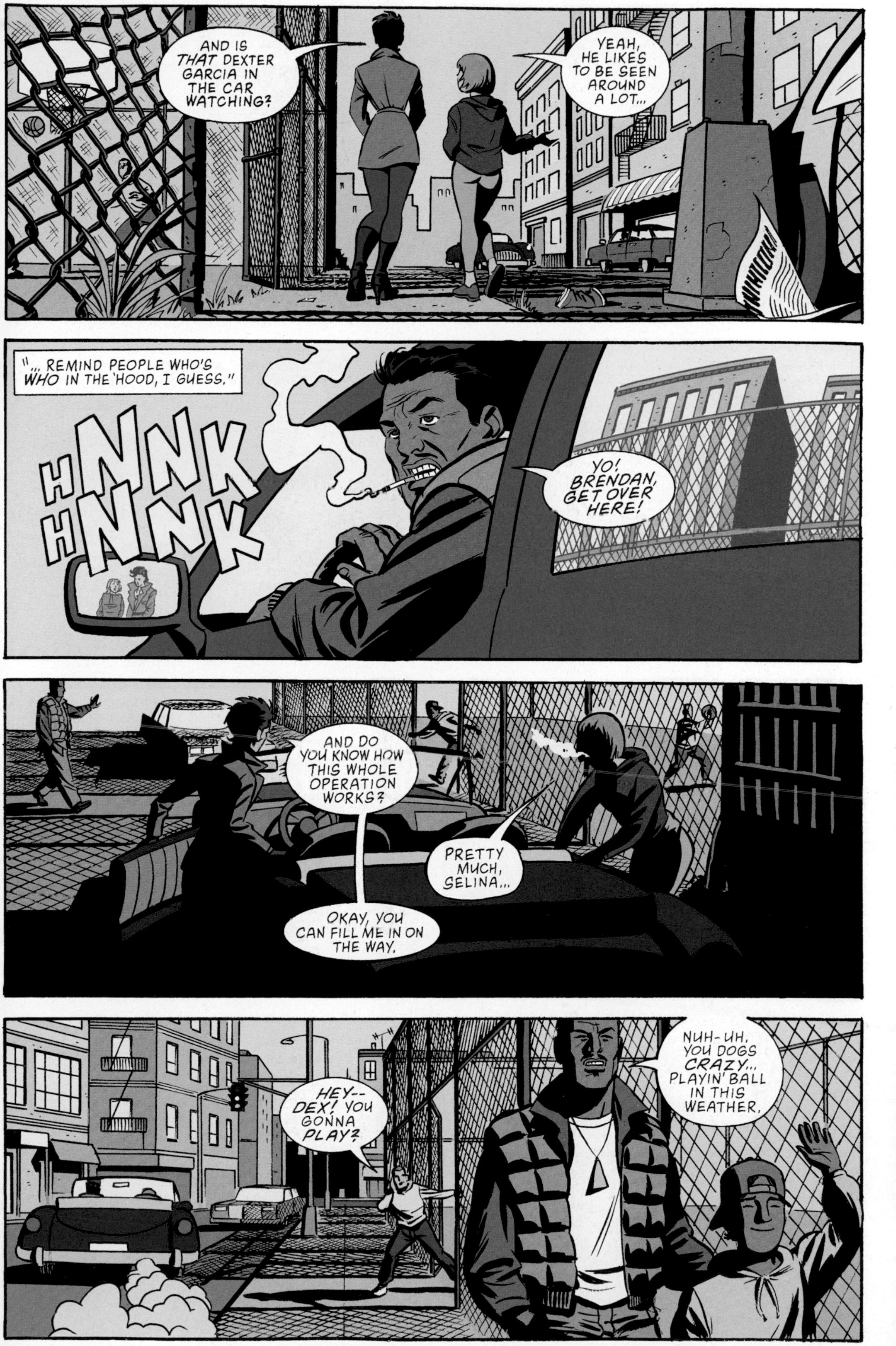
AND IS THAT DEXTER GARCIA IN THE CAR WATCHING?
YEAH, HE LIKES TO BE SEEN AROUND A LOT...
"...REMIND PEOPLE WHO'S WHO IN THE 'HOOD, I GUESS."
HNNK HNNK
YO! BRENDAN, GET OVER HERE!
AND DO YOU KNOW HOW THIS WHOLE OPERATION WORKS?
PRETTY MUCH, SELINA...
OKAY, YOU CAN FILL ME IN ON THE WAY.
HEY-- DEX! YOU GONNA PLAY?
NUH-UH, YOU DOGS CRAZY... PLAYIN' BALL IN THIS WEATHER.

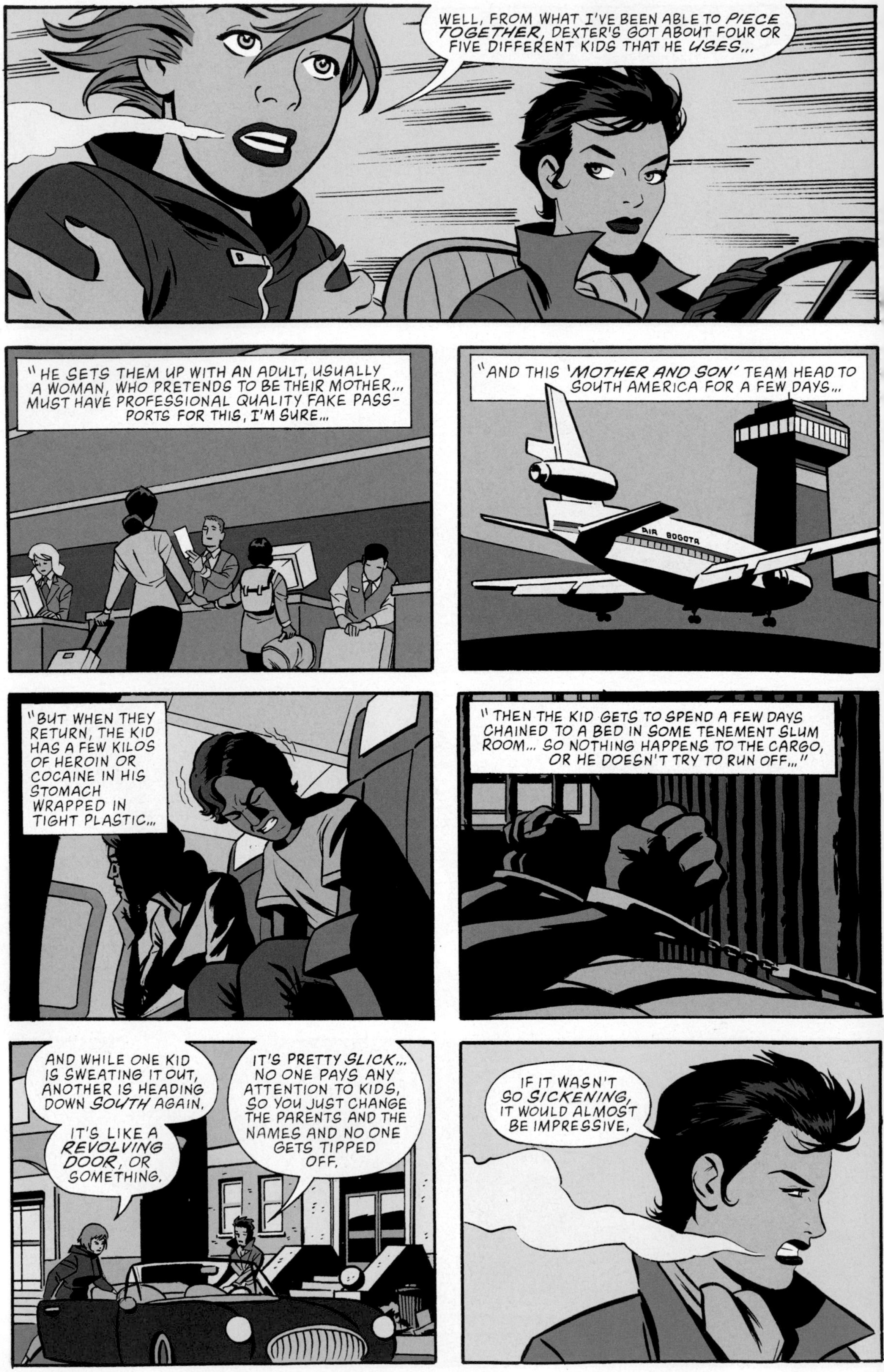
WELL, FROM WHAT I'VE BEEN ABLE TO PIECE TOGETHER, DEXTER'S GOT ABOUT FOUR OR FIVE DIFFERENT KIDS THAT HE USES...
"HE SETS THEM UP WITH AN ADULT, USUALLY A WOMAN, WHO PRETENDS TO BE THEIR MOTHER... MUST HAVE PROFESSIONAL QUALITY FAKE PASS-PORTS FOR THIS, I'M SURE...
"AND THIS 'MOTHER AND SON' TEAM HEAD TO SOUTH AMERICA FOR A FEW DAYS...
AIR BOGOTA
"BUT WHEN THEY RETURN, THE KID HAS A FEW KILOS OF HEROIN OR COCAINE IN HIS STOMACH WRAPPED IN TIGHT PLASTIC...
"THEN THE KID GETS TO SPEND A FEW DAYS CHAINED TO A BED IN SOME TENEMENT SLUM ROOM... SO NOTHING HAPPENS TO THE CARGO, OR HE DOESN'T TRY TO RUN OFF..."
AND WHILE ONE KID IS SWEATING IT OUT, ANOTHER IS HEADING DOWN SOUTH AGAIN.
IT'S LIKE A REVOLVING DOOR, OR SOMETHING.
IT'S PRETTY SLICK... NO ONE PAYS ANY ATTENTION TO KIDS, SO YOU JUST CHANGE THE PARENTS AND THE NAMES AND NO ONE GETS TIPPED OFF.
IF IT WASN'T SO SICKENING, IT WOULD ALMOST BE IMPRESSIVE.

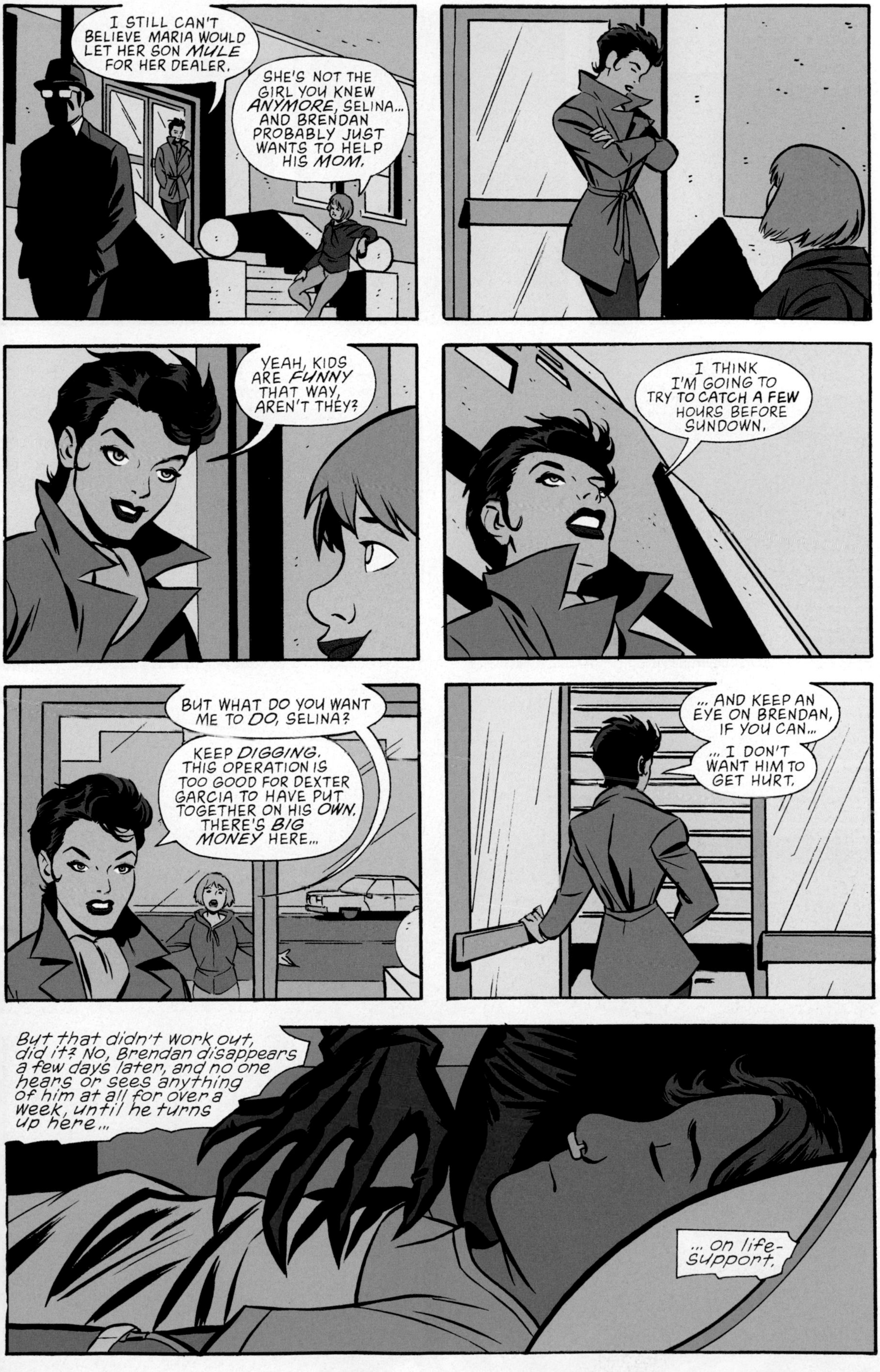
I STILL CAN'T BELIEVE MARIA WOULD LET HER SON MULE FOR HER DEALER.
SHE'S NOT THE GIRL YOU KNEW ANYMORE, SELINA... AND BRENDAN PROBABLY JUST WANTS TO HELP HIS MOM.
YEAH, KIDS ARE FUNNY THAT WAY, AREN'T THEY?
I THINK I'M GOING TO TRY TO CATCH A FEW HOURS BEFORE SUNDOWN.
BUT WHAT DO YOU WANT ME TO DO, SELINA?
KEEP DIGGING. THIS OPERATION IS TOO GOOD FOR DEXTER GARCIA TO HAVE PUT TOGETHER ON HIS OWN. THERE'S BIG MONEY HERE...
...AND KEEP AN EYE ON BRENDAN, IF YOU CAN...
...I DON'T WANT HIM TO GET HURT.
But that didn't work out, did it? No, Brendan disappears a few days later, and no one hears or sees anything of him at all for over a week, until he turns up here...
...on life-support.

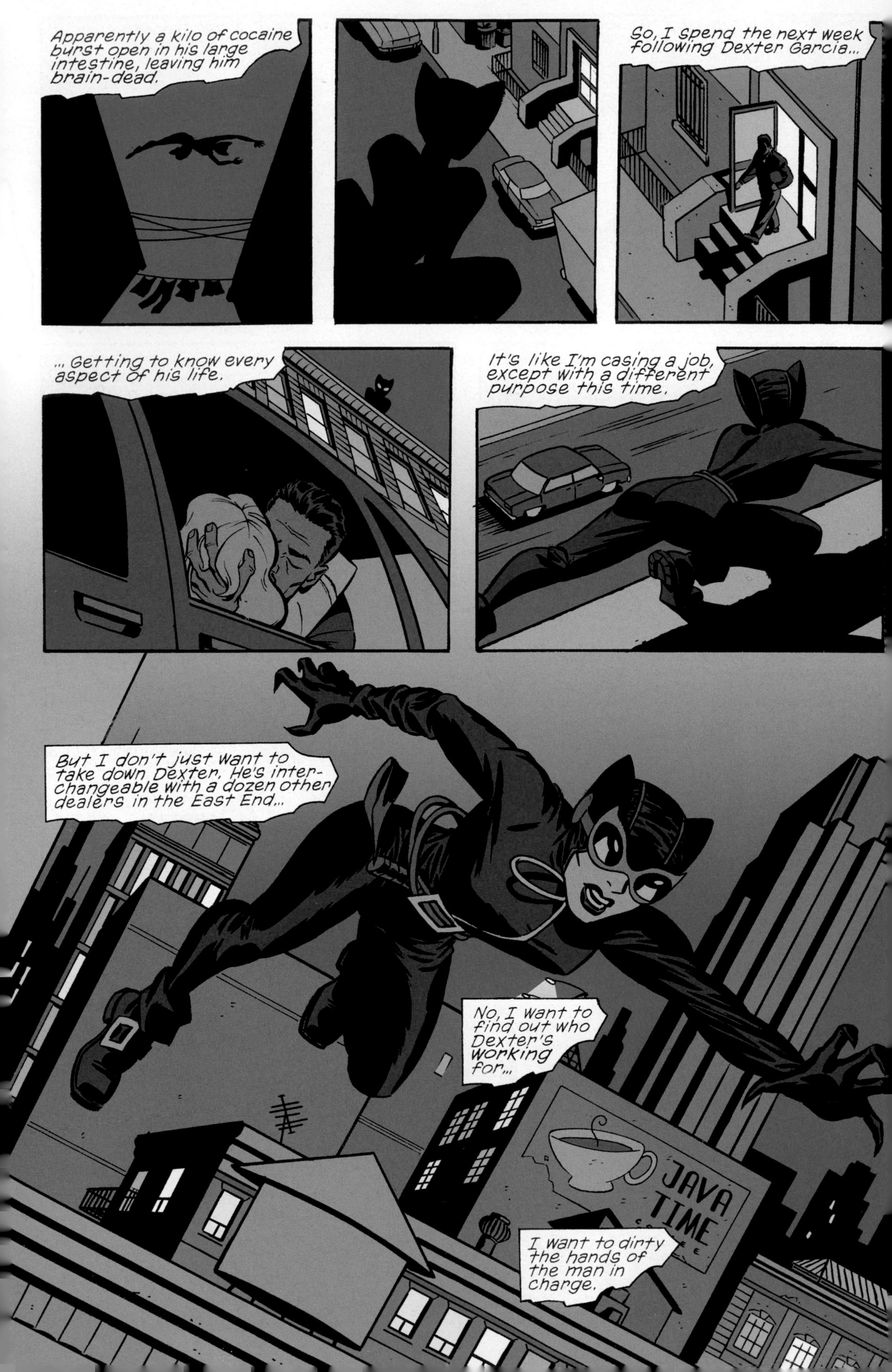
Apparently a kilo of cocaine burst open in his large intestine, leaving him brain-dead.
So, I spend the next week following Dexter Garcia...
... Getting to know every aspect of his life.
It's like I'm casing a job, except with a different purpose this time.
But I don't just want to take down Dexter. He's interchangeable with a dozen other dealers in the East End...
No, I want to find out who Dexter's working for...
JAVA TIME
I want to dirty the hands of the man in charge.

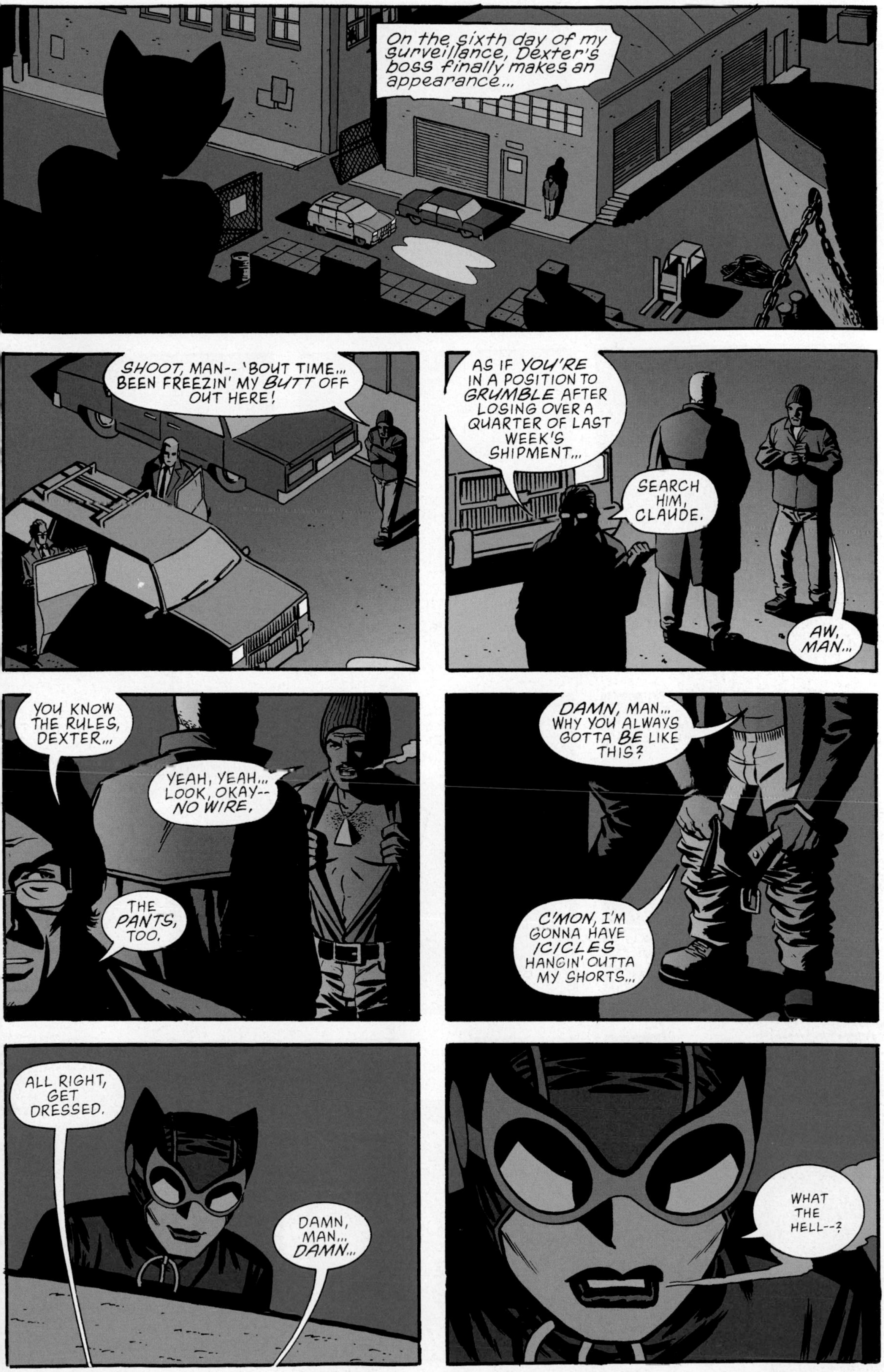
On the sixth day of my surveillance, Dexter's boss finally makes an appearance...
SHOOT, MAN-- 'BOUT TIME... BEEN FREEZIN' MY BUTT OFF OUT HERE!
AS IF YOU'RE IN A POSITION TO GRUMBLE AFTER LOSING OVER A QUARTER OF LAST WEEK'S SHIPMENT...
SEARCH HIM, CLAUDE.
AW, MAN...
YOU KNOW THE RULES, DEXTER...
YEAH, YEAH... LOOK, OKAY-- NO WIRE.
THE PANTS, TOO.
DAMN, MAN... WHY YOU ALWAYS GOTTA BE LIKE THIS?
C'MON, I'M GONNA HAVE ICICLES HANGIN' OUTTA MY SHORTS...
ALL RIGHT, GET DRESSED.
DAMN, MAN... DAMN...
WHAT THE HELL--?

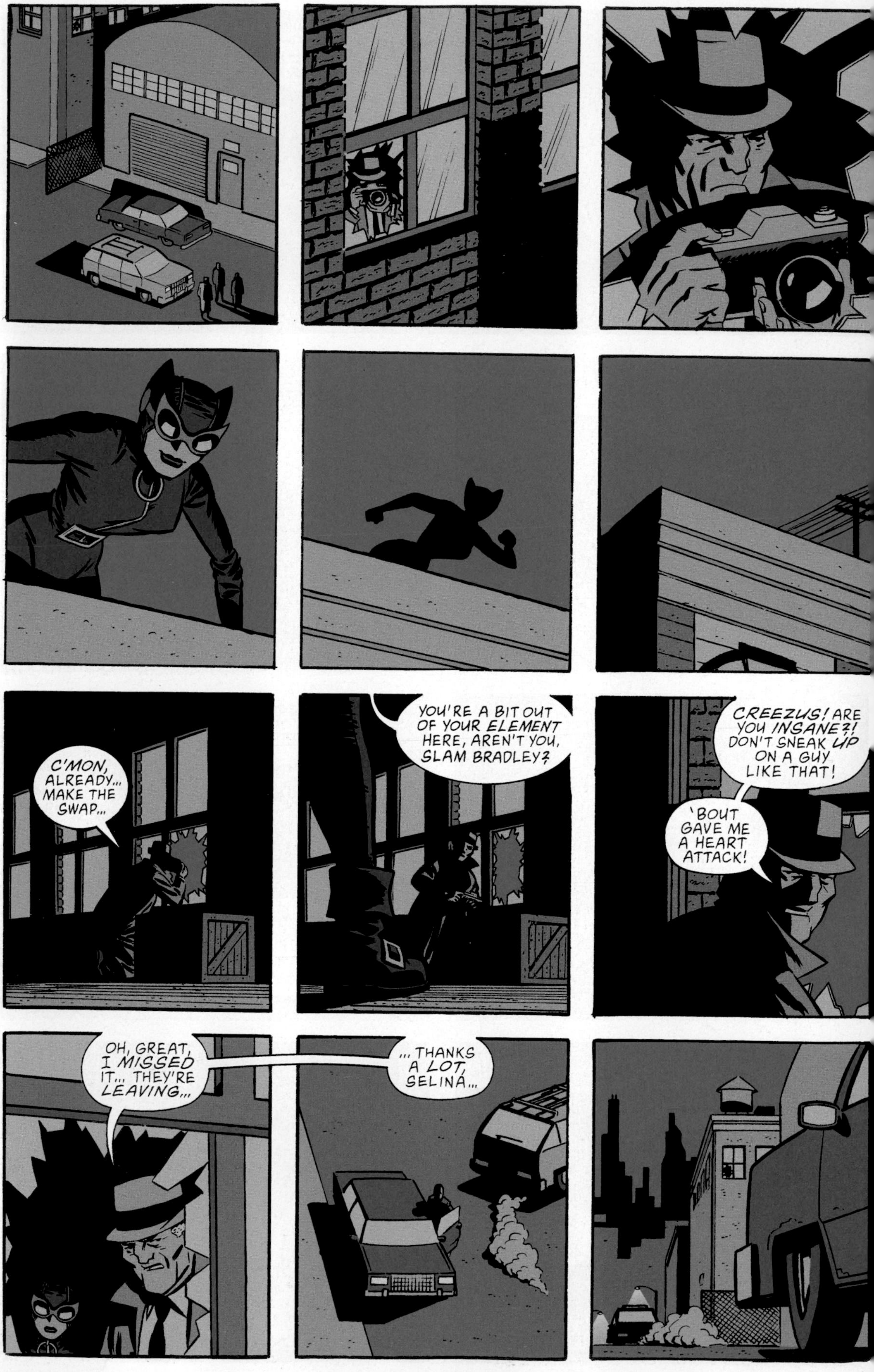
C'MON, ALREADY... MAKE THE SWAP...
YOU'RE A BIT OUT OF YOUR ELEMENT HERE, AREN'T YOU, SLAM BRADLEY?
CREEZUS! ARE YOU INSANE?! DON'T SNEAK UP ON A GUY LIKE THAT!
'BOUT GAVE ME A HEART ATTACK!
OH, GREAT, I MISSED IT... THEY'RE LEAVING...
...THANKS A LOT, SELINA...

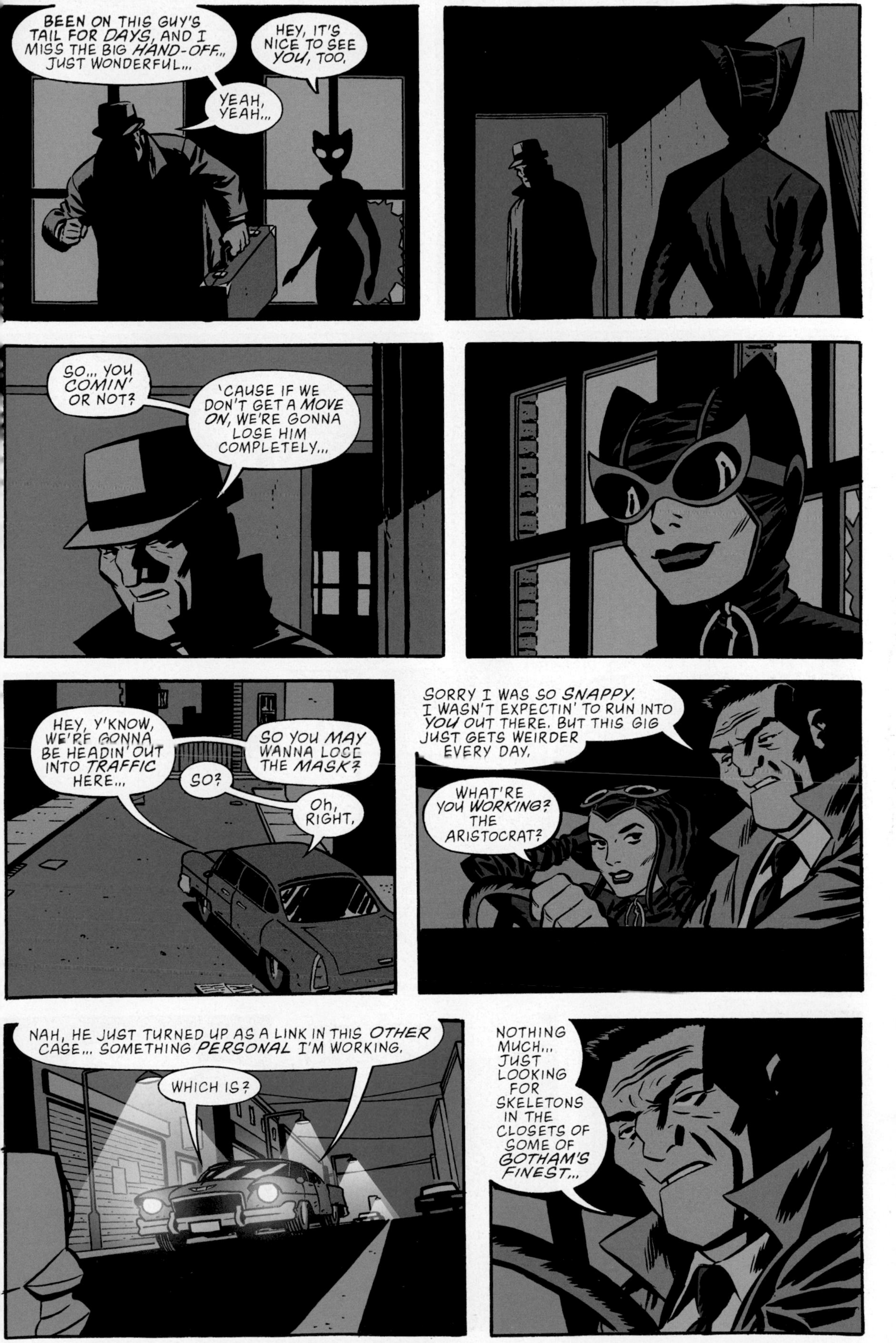
BEEN ON THIS GUY'S TAIL FOR DAYS, AND I MISS THE BIG HAND-OFF... JUST WONDERFUL...
HEY, IT'S NICE TO SEE YOU, TOO.
YEAH, YEAH...
SO... YOU COMIN' OR NOT?
'CAUSE IF WE DON'T GET A MOVE ON, WE'RE GONNA LOSE HIM COMPLETELY...
HEY, Y'KNOW, WE'RE GONNA BE HEADIN' OUT INTO TRAFFIC HERE...
SO?
SO YOU MAY WANNA LOSE THE MASK?
Oh, RIGHT.
SORRY I WAS SO SNAPPY. I WASN'T EXPECTIN' TO RUN INTO YOU OUT THERE. BUT THIS GIG JUST GETS WEIRDER EVERY DAY.
WHAT'RE YOU WORKING? THE ARISTOCRAT?
NAH, HE JUST TURNED UP AS A LINK IN THIS OTHER CASE... SOMETHING PERSONAL I'M WORKING.
WHICH IS?
NOTHING MUCH... JUST LOOKING FOR SKELETONS IN THE CLOSETS OF SOME OF GOTHAM'S FINEST...

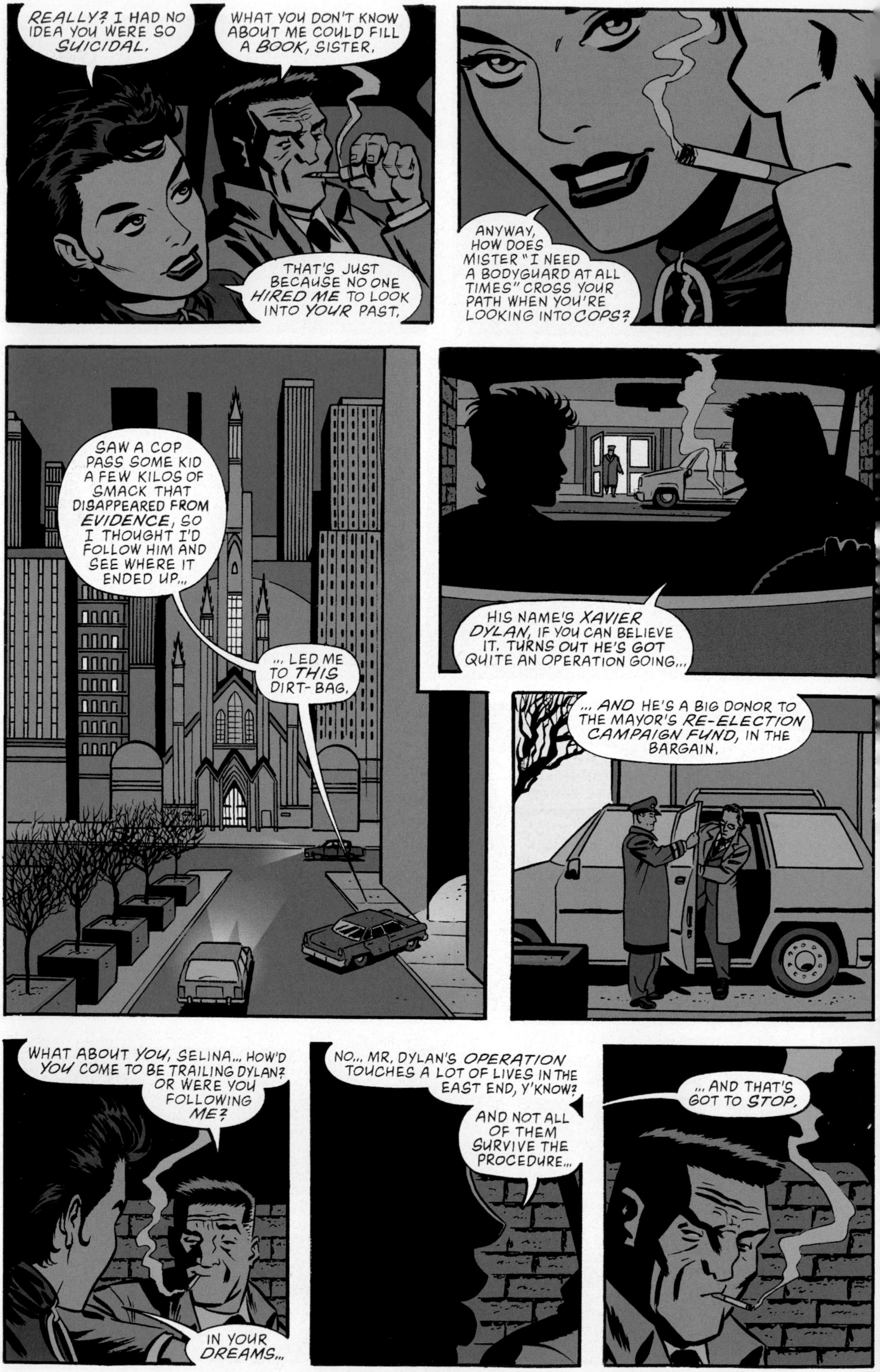

REALLY? I HAD NO IDEA YOU WERE SO SUICIDAL.
WHAT YOU DON'T KNOW ABOUT ME COULD FILL A BOOK, SISTER.
THAT'S JUST BECAUSE NO ONE HIRED ME TO LOOK INTO YOUR PAST.
ANYWAY, HOW DOES MISTER "I NEED A BODYGUARD AT ALL TIMES" CROSS YOUR PATH WHEN YOU'RE LOOKING INTO COPS?
SAW A COP PASS SOME KID A FEW KILOS OF SMACK THAT DISAPPEARED FROM EVIDENCE, SO I THOUGHT I'D FOLLOW HIM AND SEE WHERE IT ENDED UP...
... LED ME TO THIS DIRT-BAG.
HIS NAME'S XAVIER DYLAN, IF YOU CAN BELIEVE IT. TURNS OUT HE'S GOT QUITE AN OPERATION GOING...
... AND HE'S A BIG DONOR TO THE MAYOR'S RE-ELECTION CAMPAIGN FUND, IN THE BARGAIN.
WHAT ABOUT YOU, SELINA... HOW'D YOU COME TO BE TRAILING DYLAN? OR WERE YOU FOLLOWING ME?
IN YOUR DREAMS...
NO... MR. DYLAN'S OPERATION TOUCHES A LOT OF LIVES IN THE EAST END, Y'KNOW?
AND NOT ALL OF THEM SURVIVE THE PROCEDURE...
... AND THAT'S GOT TO STOP.

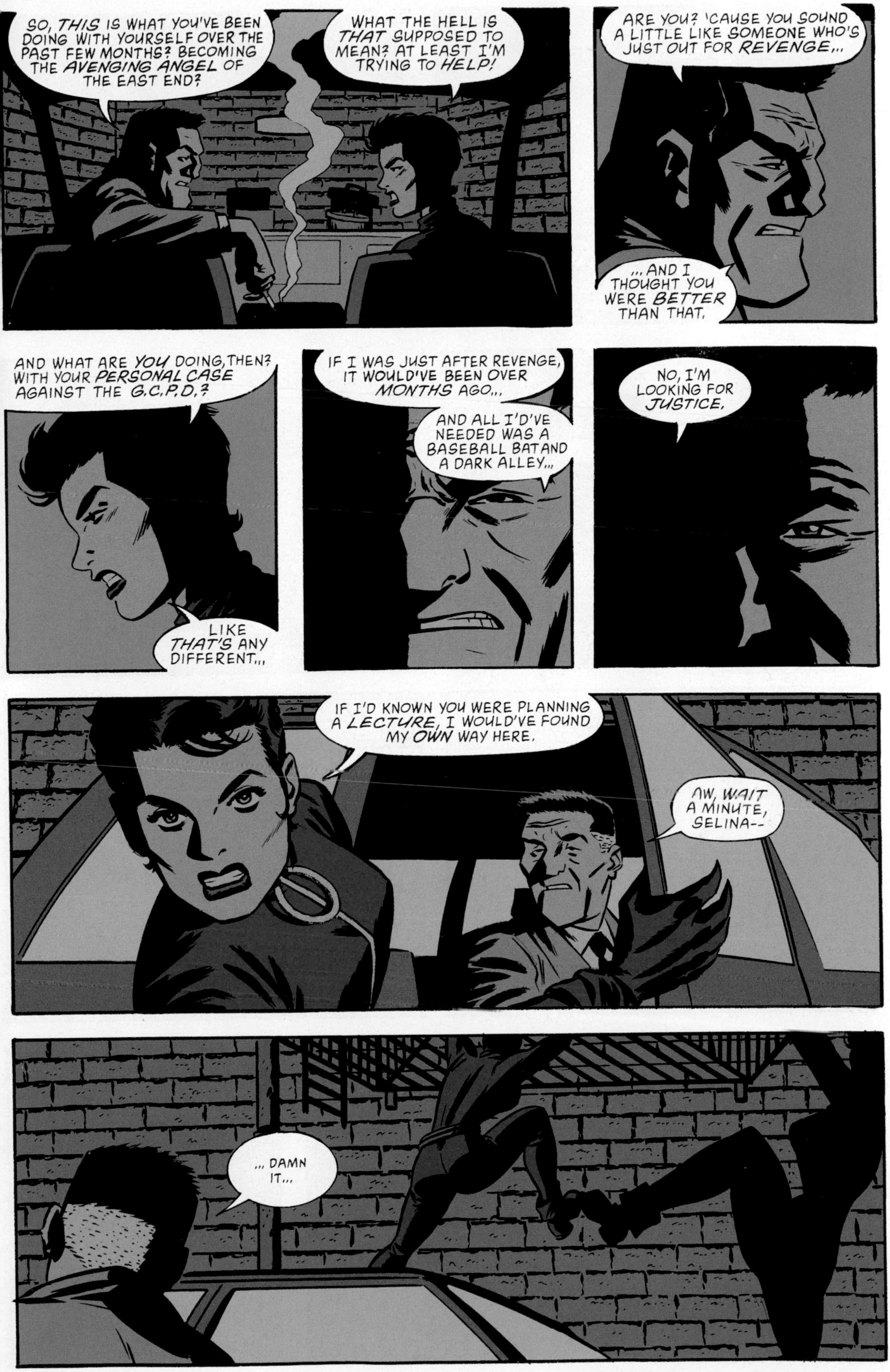
SO, THIS IS WHAT YOU'VE BEEN DOING WITH YOURSELF OVER THE PAST FEW MONTHS? BECOMING THE AVENGING ANGEL OF THE EAST END?
WHAT THE HELL IS THAT SUPPOSED TO MEAN? AT LEAST I'M TRYING TO HELP!
ARE YOU? 'CAUSE YOU SOUND A LITTLE LIKE SOMEONE WHO'S JUST OUT FOR REVENGE...
...AND I THOUGHT YOU WERE BETTER THAN THAT.
AND WHAT ARE YOU DOING, THEN? WITH YOUR PERSONAL CASE AGAINST THE G.C.P.D.?
LIKE THAT'S ANY DIFFERENT...
IF I WAS JUST AFTER REVENGE, IT WOULD'VE BEEN OVER MONTHS AGO...
AND ALL I'D'VE NEEDED WAS A BASEBALL BAT AND A DARK ALLEY...
NO, I'M LOOKING FOR JUSTICE.
IF I'D KNOWN YOU WERE PLANNING A LECTURE, I WOULD'VE FOUND MY OWN WAY HERE.
AW, WAIT A MINUTE, SELINA--
...DAMN IT...

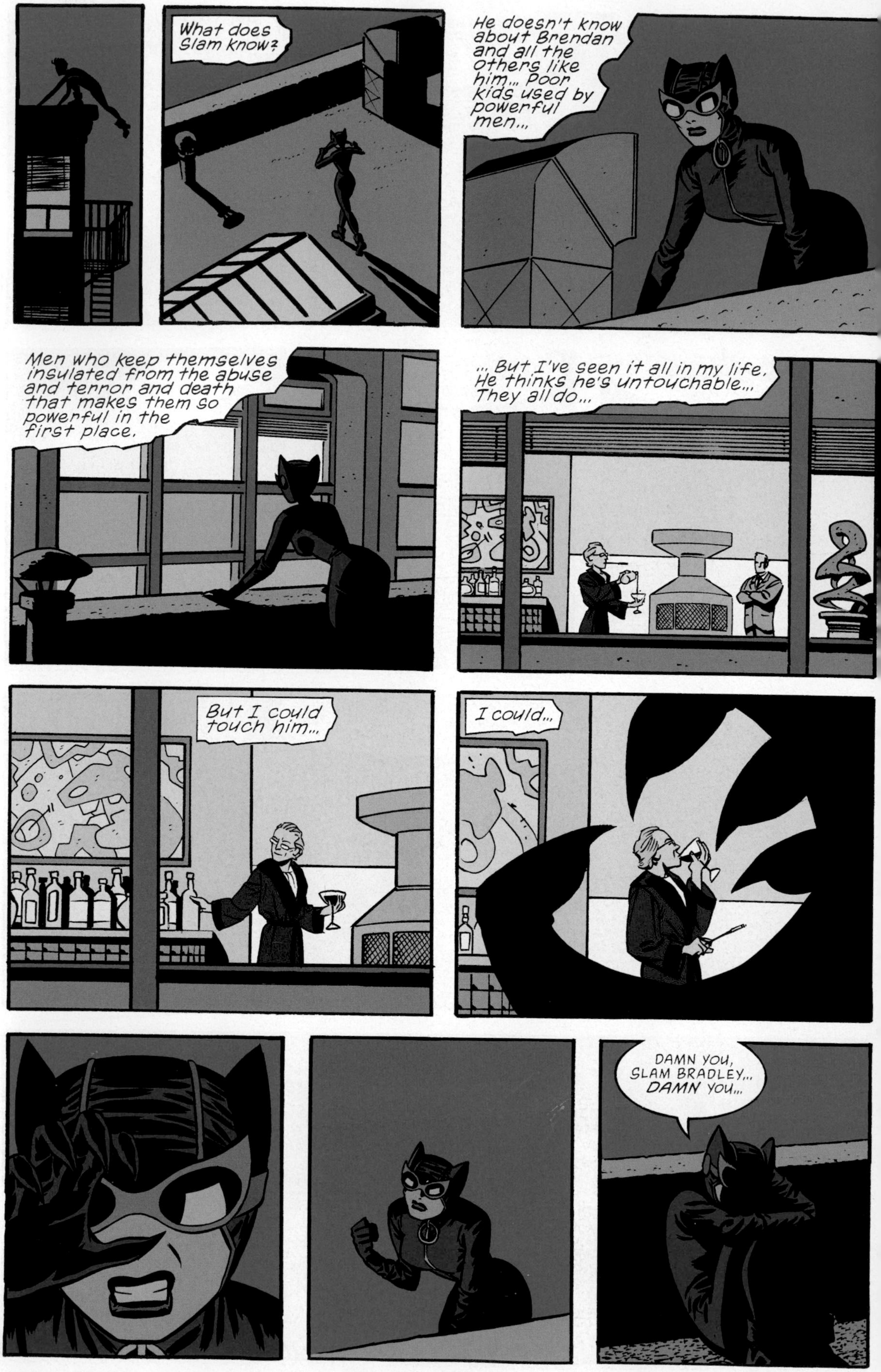
What does Slam know?
He doesn't know about Brendan and all the others like him... Poor kids used by powerful men...
Men who keep themselves insulated from the abuse and terror and death that makes them so powerful in the first place.
...But I've seen it all in my life. He thinks he's untouchable... They all do...
But I could touch him...
I could...
DAMN YOU, SLAM BRADLEY... DAMN YOU...

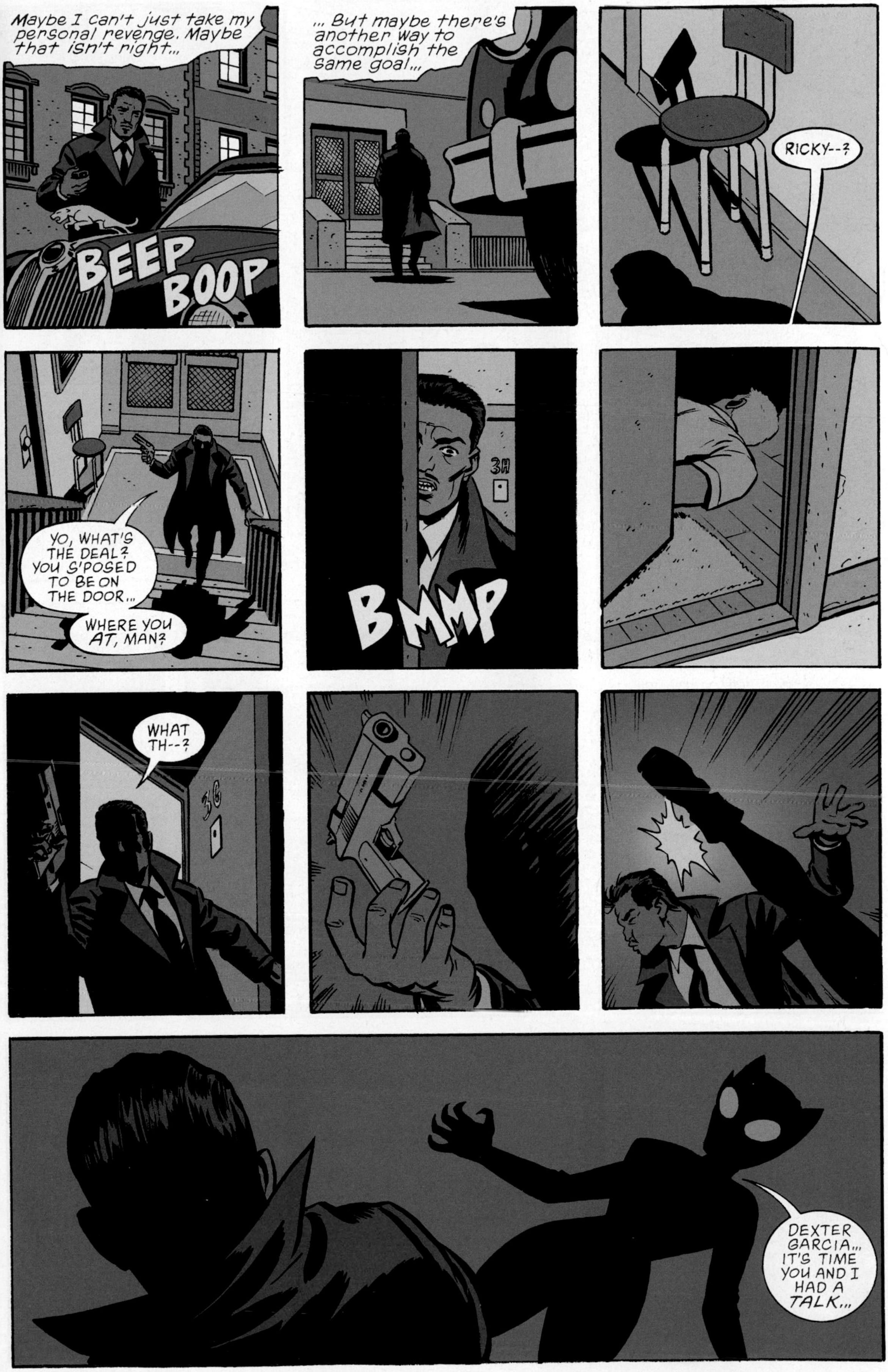
Maybe I can't just take my personal revenge. Maybe that isn't right...
BEEP
BOOP
... But maybe there's another way to accomplish the same goal...
RICKY--?
YO, WHAT'S THE DEAL? YOU S'POSED TO BE ON THE DOOR...
WHERE YOU AT, MAN?
3H
BMMP
WHAT TH--?
3G
DEXTER GARCIA... IT'S TIME YOU AND I HAD A TALK...

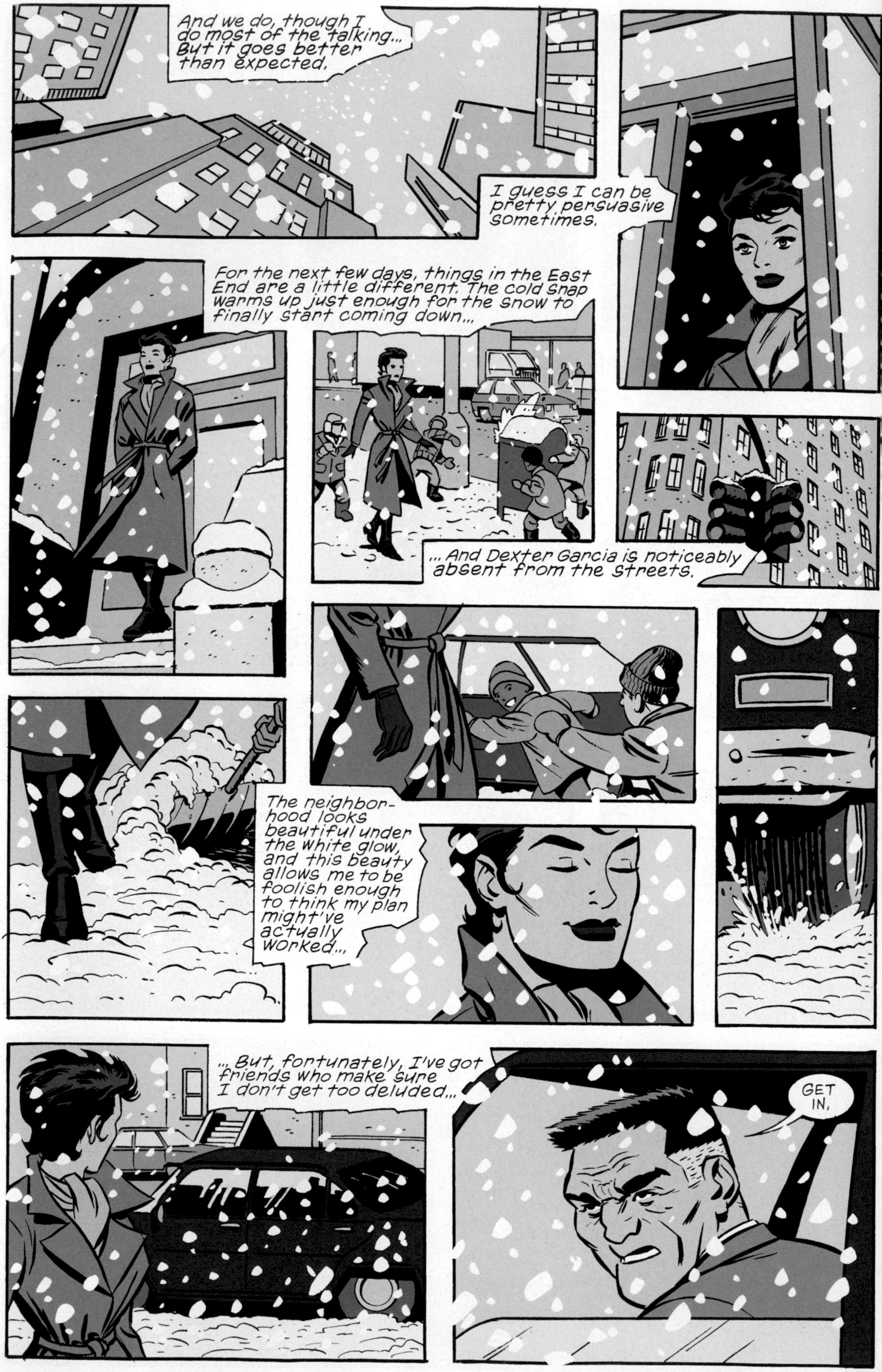
And we do, though I do most of the talking... But it goes better than expected.
I guess I can be pretty persuasive sometimes.
For the next few days, things in the East End are a little different. The cold snap warms up just enough for the snow to finally start coming down...
...And Dexter Garcia is noticeably absent from the streets.
The neighbor-hood looks beautiful under the white glow, and this beauty allows me to be foolish enough to think my plan might've actually worked...
...But, fortunately, I've got friends who make sure I don't get too deluded...
GET IN.

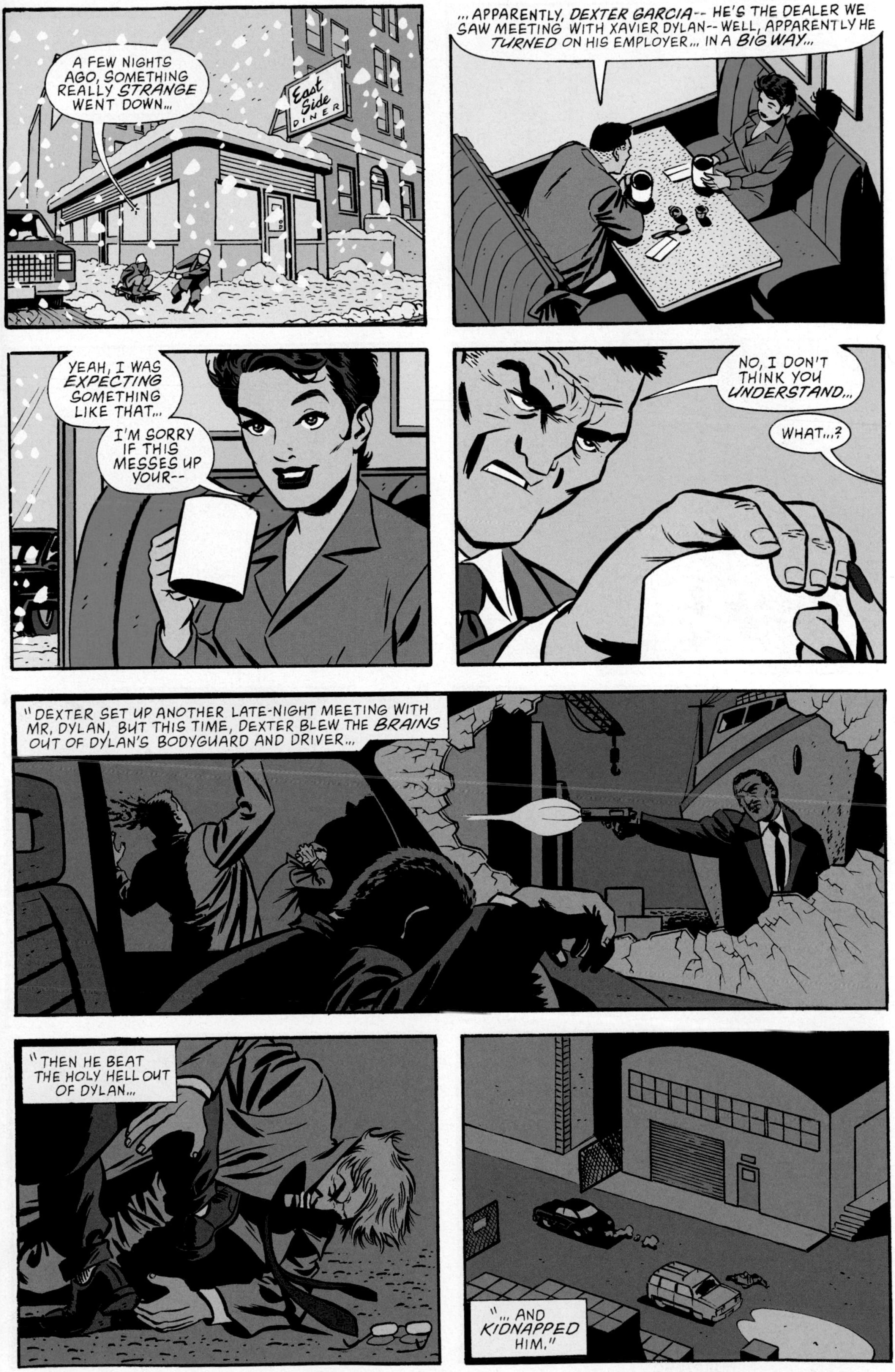
A FEW NIGHTS AGO, SOMETHING REALLY STRANGE WENT DOWN...
East Side DINER
... APPARENTLY, DEXTER GARCIA-- HE'S THE DEALER WE SAW MEETING WITH XAVIER DYLAN-- WELL, APPARENTLY HE TURNED ON HIS EMPLOYER... IN A BIG WAY...
YEAH, I WAS EXPECTING SOMETHING LIKE THAT...
I'M SORRY IF THIS MESSES UP YOUR--
NO, I DON'T THINK YOU UNDERSTAND...
WHAT...?
"DEXTER SET UP ANOTHER LATE-NIGHT MEETING WITH MR. DYLAN, BUT THIS TIME, DEXTER BLEW THE BRAINS OUT OF DYLAN'S BODYGUARD AND DRIVER...
"THEN HE BEAT THE HOLY HELL OUT OF DYLAN...
"... AND KIDNAPPED HIM."

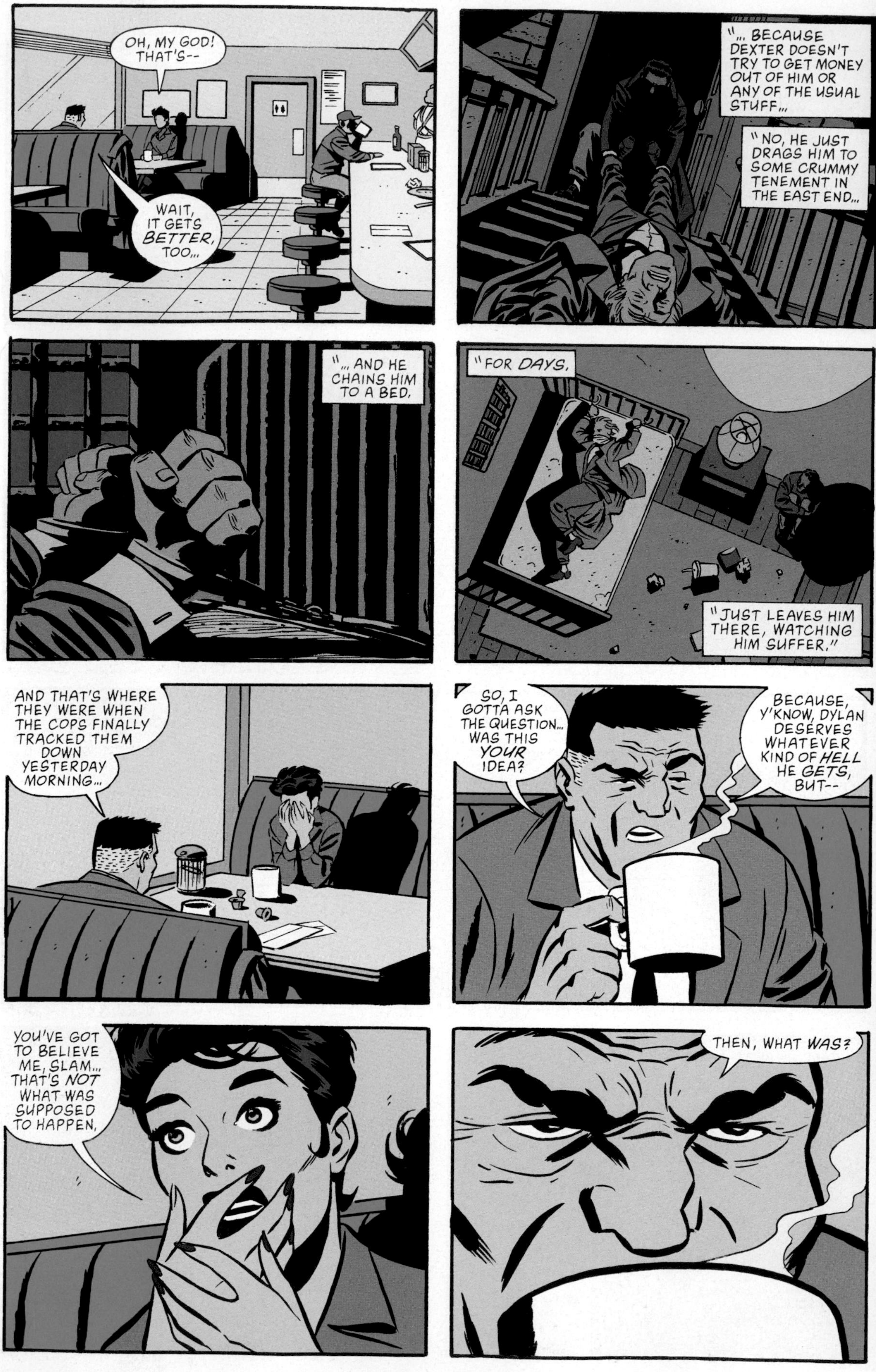
OH, MY GOD! THAT'S--
WAIT, IT GETS BETTER, TOO...
"... BECAUSE DEXTER DOESN'T TRY TO GET MONEY OUT OF HIM OR ANY OF THE USUAL STUFF...
"NO, HE JUST DRAGS HIM TO SOME CRUMMY TENEMENT IN THE EAST END...
"... AND HE CHAINS HIM TO A BED.
"FOR DAYS.
"JUST LEAVES HIM THERE, WATCHING HIM SUFFER."
AND THAT'S WHERE THEY WERE WHEN THE COPS FINALLY TRACKED THEM DOWN YESTERDAY MORNING...
SO, I GOTTA ASK THE QUESTION... WAS THIS YOUR IDEA?
BECAUSE, Y'KNOW, DYLAN DESERVES WHATEVER KIND OF HELL HE GETS, BUT--
YOU'VE GOT TO BELIEVE ME, SLAM... THAT'S NOT WHAT WAS SUPPOSED TO HAPPEN.
THEN, WHAT WAS?

SO, IT WAS *HER* IDEA, THEN... CATWOMAN, IS THAT IT...?

NAW, MAN, NAW... I THOUGHT THAT PART UP ALL ON MY *OWN*...

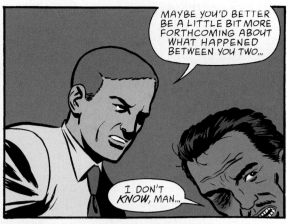

MAYBE YOU'D BETTER BE A LITTLE BIT MORE FORTHCOMING ABOUT WHAT HAPPENED BETWEEN YOU TWO...

I DON'T *KNOW*, MAN...

"...SHE JUST BUSTED LOOSE WITH THE *KNOWLEDGE*, Y'KNOW?"

I AIN'T DONE *NUTHIN'* TO YOU, WOMAN! WHAT'CHU WANT WITH *ME*?!

IT'S NOT ABOUT YOU AND ME, *DEXTER*...

IT'S MUCH *LARGER* THAN THAT.

SEE, YOU'RE JUST A *TOOL*... YOU BRING THIS GARBAGE IN AND DISTRIBUTE IT, BUT YOU PAY MOST OF YOUR PROFIT OUT TO *XAVIER DYLAN*, DON'T YOU?

WHAT-- YOU WANT A *CUT* 'ZAT IT? YOU GOTTA TALK TO THE *MAN*, NOT ME...

YOU *IDIOT*...

...YOU THINK YOU'RE A *BIG MAN*, BUT YOU'RE JUST A *PAWN* FOR SOME RICH WHITE MAN WHO GOT YOU TO *TURN* ON YOUR OWN KIND,

YOU DID IT SO *EASILY*, TOO.

AND YOU DON'T EVEN GET ANY *RESPECT* FROM YOUR BOSS...

...BECAUSE JUST LIKE *ME*, HE KNOWS IF *YOU* FALL, TEN MORE CREEPS JUST *LIKE YOU* WILL TAKE YOUR PLACE,

SHOOT, WOMAN... IT AIN'T *LIKE THAT!* YOU DON'T *KNOW--*

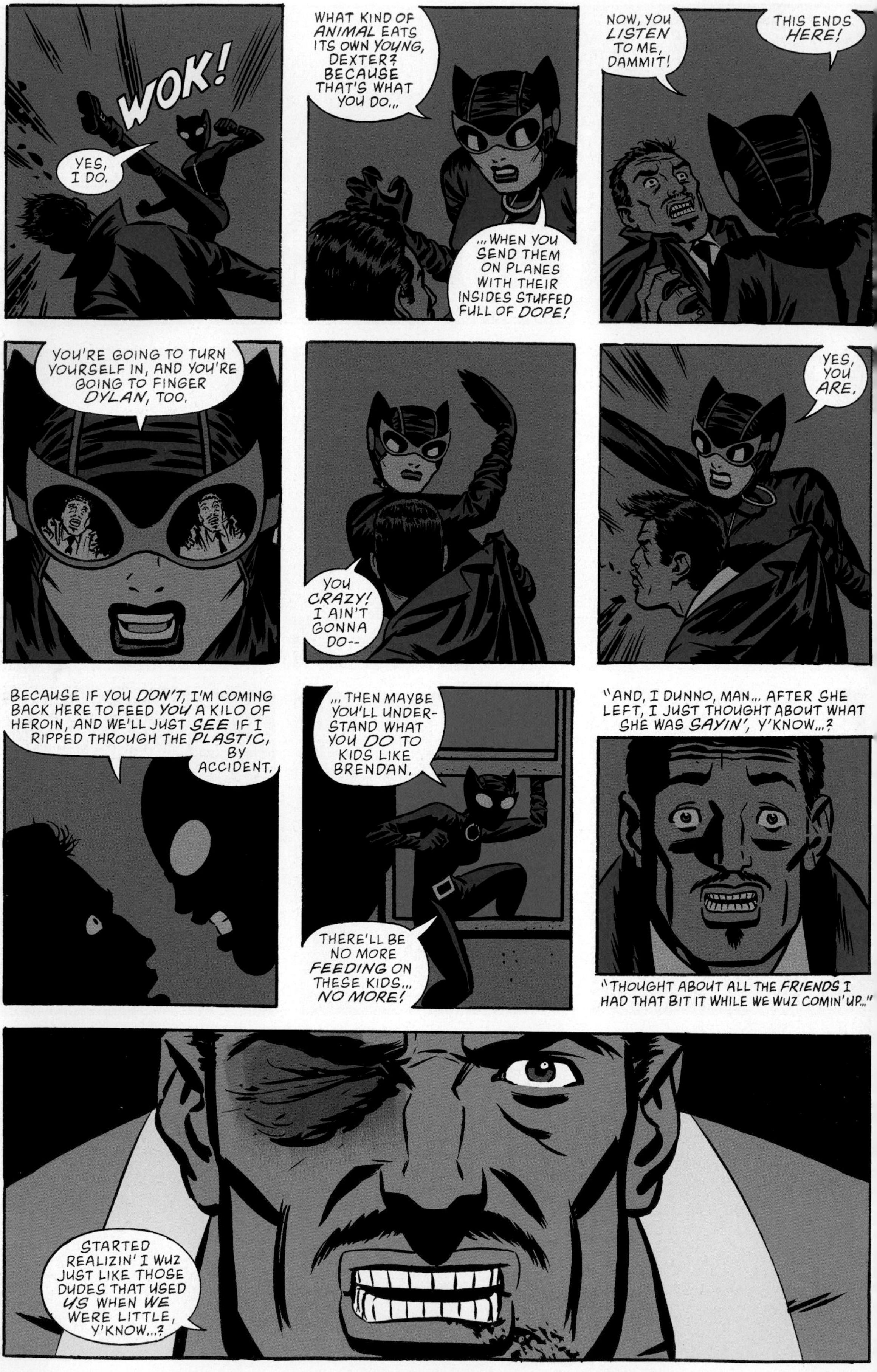
WOK!
YES, I DO.
WHAT KIND OF ANIMAL EATS ITS OWN YOUNG, DEXTER? BECAUSE THAT'S WHAT YOU DO...
...WHEN YOU SEND THEM ON PLANES WITH THEIR INSIDES STUFFED FULL OF DOPE!
NOW, YOU LISTEN TO ME, DAMMIT!
THIS ENDS HERE!
YOU'RE GOING TO TURN YOURSELF IN, AND YOU'RE GOING TO FINGER DYLAN, TOO.
YOU CRAZY! I AIN'T GONNA DO--
YES, YOU ARE.
BECAUSE IF YOU DON'T, I'M COMING BACK HERE TO FEED YOU A KILO OF HEROIN, AND WE'LL JUST SEE IF I RIPPED THROUGH THE PLASTIC, BY ACCIDENT.
...THEN MAYBE YOU'LL UNDERSTAND WHAT YOU DO TO KIDS LIKE BRENDAN.
THERE'LL BE NO MORE FEEDING ON THESE KIDS... NO MORE!
"AND, I DUNNO, MAN... AFTER SHE LEFT, I JUST THOUGHT ABOUT WHAT SHE WAS SAYIN', Y'KNOW...?
"THOUGHT ABOUT ALL THE FRIENDS I HAD THAT BIT IT WHILE WE WUZ COMIN' UP..."
STARTED REALIZIN' I WUZ JUST LIKE THOSE DUDES THAT USED US WHEN WE WERE LITTLE, Y'KNOW...?

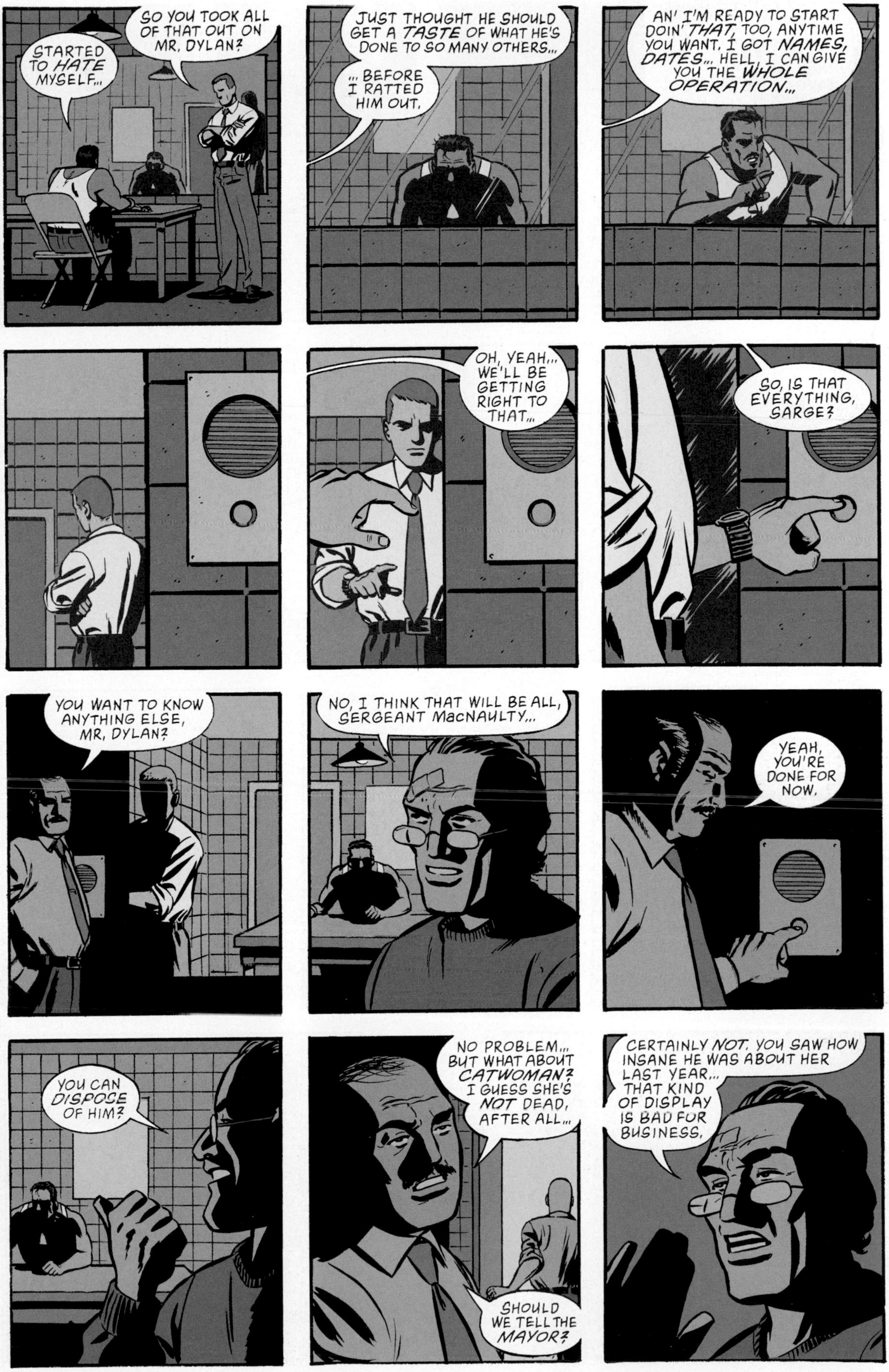
STARTED TO HATE MYSELF...
SO YOU TOOK ALL OF THAT OUT ON MR. DYLAN?
JUST THOUGHT HE SHOULD GET A TASTE OF WHAT HE'S DONE TO SO MANY OTHERS...
...BEFORE I RATTED HIM OUT.
AN' I'M READY TO START DOIN' THAT, TOO, ANYTIME YOU WANT. I GOT NAMES, DATES... HELL, I CAN GIVE YOU THE WHOLE OPERATION...
OH, YEAH... WE'LL BE GETTING RIGHT TO THAT...
SO, IS THAT EVERYTHING, SARGE?
YOU WANT TO KNOW ANYTHING ELSE, MR. DYLAN?
NO, I THINK THAT WILL BE ALL, SERGEANT MacNAULTY...
YEAH, YOU'RE DONE FOR NOW.
YOU CAN DISPOSE OF HIM?
NO PROBLEM... BUT WHAT ABOUT CATWOMAN? I GUESS SHE'S NOT DEAD, AFTER ALL...
SHOULD WE TELL THE MAYOR?
CERTAINLY NOT. YOU SAW HOW INSANE HE WAS ABOUT HER LAST YEAR... THAT KIND OF DISPLAY IS BAD FOR BUSINESS.

NO, IF CATWOMAN BECOMES A *PERSISTENT* NUISANCE, I'LL TAKE CARE OF HER MYSELF...

...IF YOU UNDERSTAND MY MEANING.

UH... YO, AIN'T ANYBODY GONNA TAKE MY *STATEMENT?*

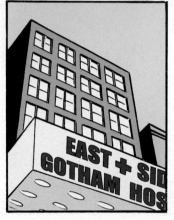

EAST + SID GOTHAM HOS

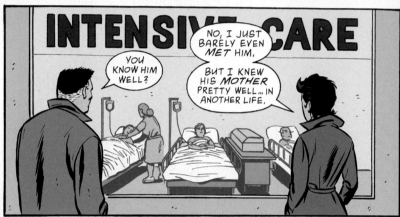

INTENSIVE CARE

YOU KNOW HIM WELL?

NO, I JUST BARELY EVEN *MET* HIM,

BUT I KNEW HIS *MOTHER* PRETTY WELL... IN ANOTHER LIFE.

YEAH... IT'S *ROUGH*, SEEING WHAT THIS WORLD DOES TO KIDS...

Y'KNOW, YOU CAN ONLY DO YOUR *BEST*. NOT MUCH WORKS OUT HOW YOU WANT IT TO...

BUT, AT LEAST YOU *TRIED*, RIGHT?

I GUESS SO...

C'MON, LET'S GET OUT OF HERE... THIS PLACE IS DEPRESSING.

THE END

Catwoman 6 Cover by Paul Pope

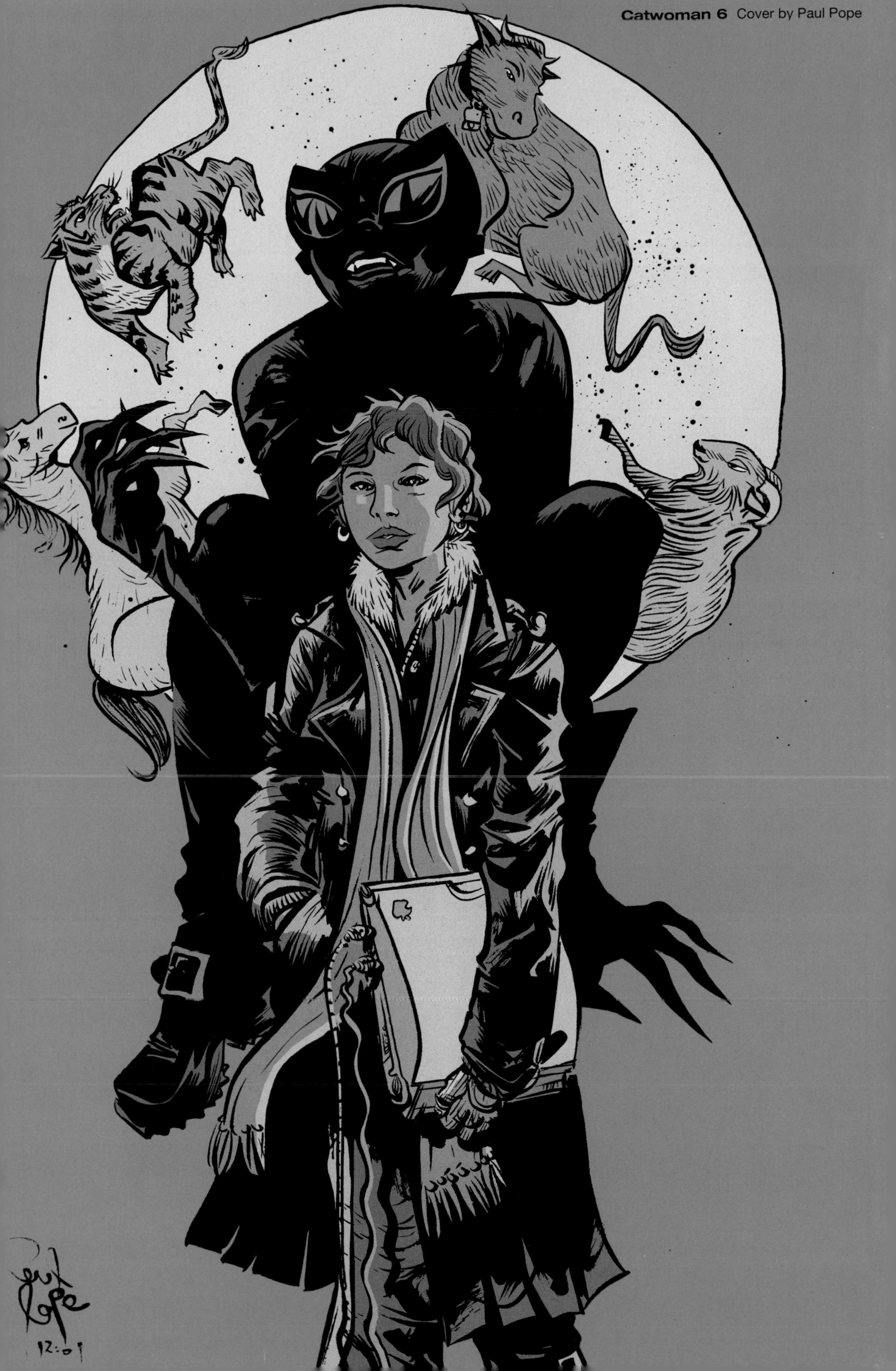
Paul Pope
12.01

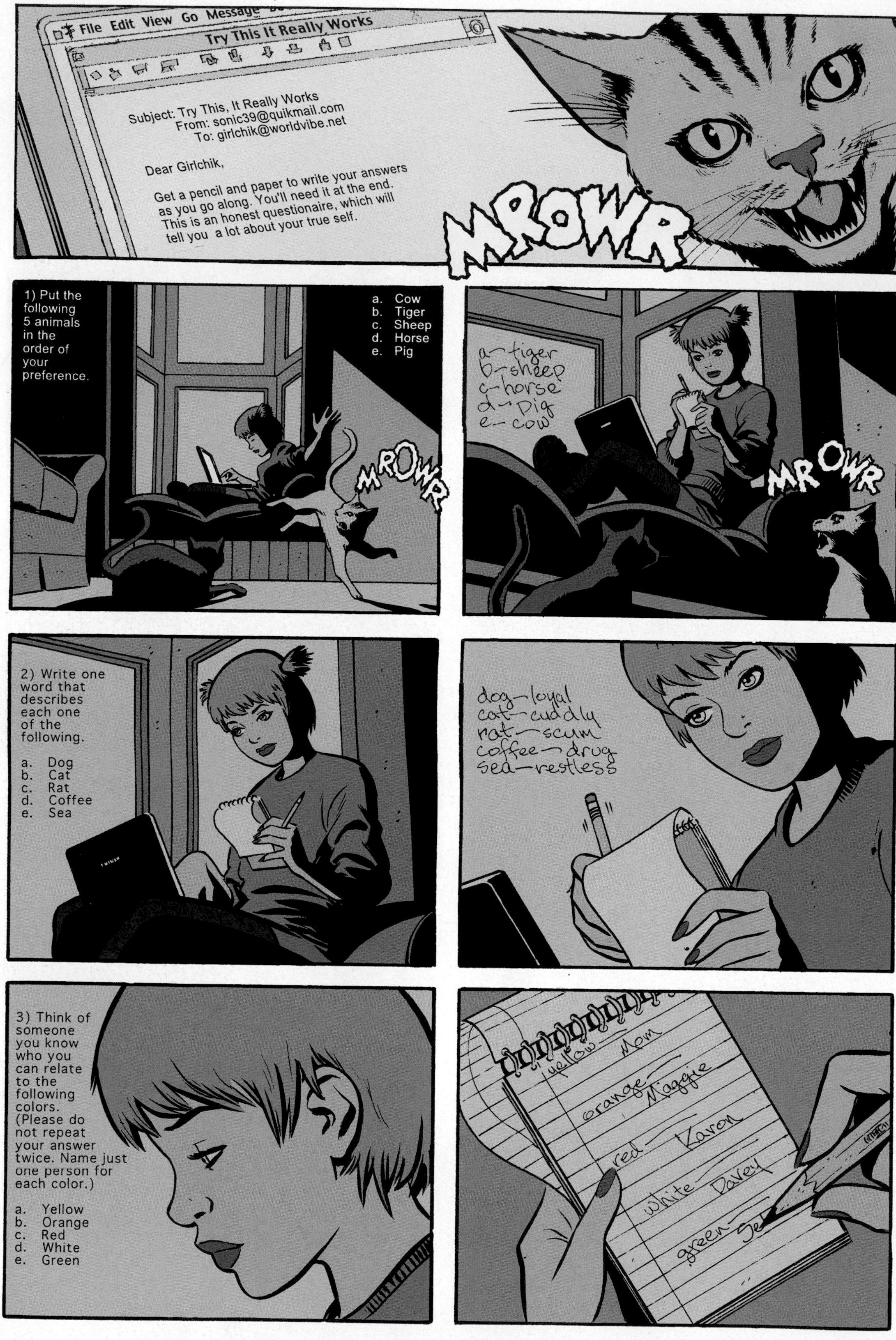
File Edit View Go Message
Try This It Really Works
Subject: Try This, It Really Works
From: sonic39@quikmail.com
To: girlchik@worldvibe.net
Dear Girlchik,
Get a pencil and paper to write your answers as you go along. You'll need it at the end. This is an honest questionaire, which will tell you a lot about your true self.
MROWR
1) Put the following 5 animals in the order of your preference.
a. Cow
b. Tiger
c. Sheep
d. Horse
e. Pig
MROWR
a—tiger
b—sheep
c—horse
d—pig
e—cow
MROWR
2) Write one word that describes each one of the following.
a. Dog
b. Cat
c. Rat
d. Coffee
e. Sea
dog—loyal
cat—cuddly
rat—scum
coffee—drug
sea—restless
3) Think of someone you know who you can relate to the following colors. (Please do not repeat your answer twice. Name just one person for each color.)
a. Yellow
b. Orange
c. Red
d. White
e. Green
yellow Mom
orange Maggie
red Karon
white Davey
green Se

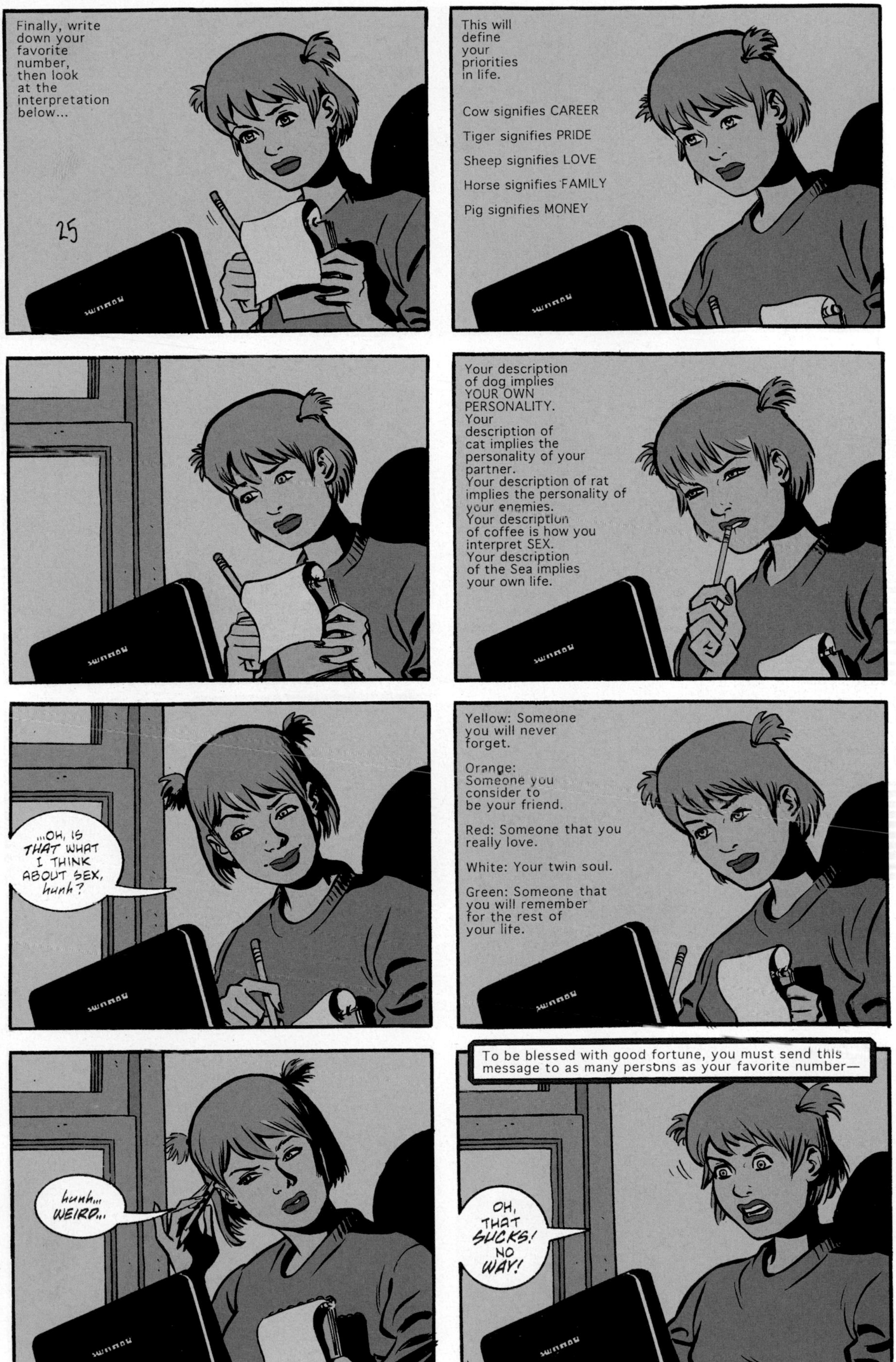
Finally, write down your favorite number, then look at the interpretation below...
25
This will define your priorities in life.
Cow signifies CAREER
Tiger signifies PRIDE
Sheep signifies LOVE
Horse signifies FAMILY
Pig signifies MONEY
Your description of dog implies YOUR OWN PERSONALITY.
Your description of cat implies the personality of your partner.
Your description of rat implies the personality of your enemies.
Your description of coffee is how you interpret SEX.
Your description of the Sea implies your own life.
...OH, IS THAT WHAT I THINK ABOUT SEX, hunh?
Yellow: Someone you will never forget.
Orange: Someone you consider to be your friend.
Red: Someone that you really love.
White: Your twin soul.
Green: Someone that you will remember for the rest of your life.
hunh... WEIRD...
To be blessed with good fortune, you must send this message to as many persons as your favorite number—
OH, THAT SUCKS! NO WAY!

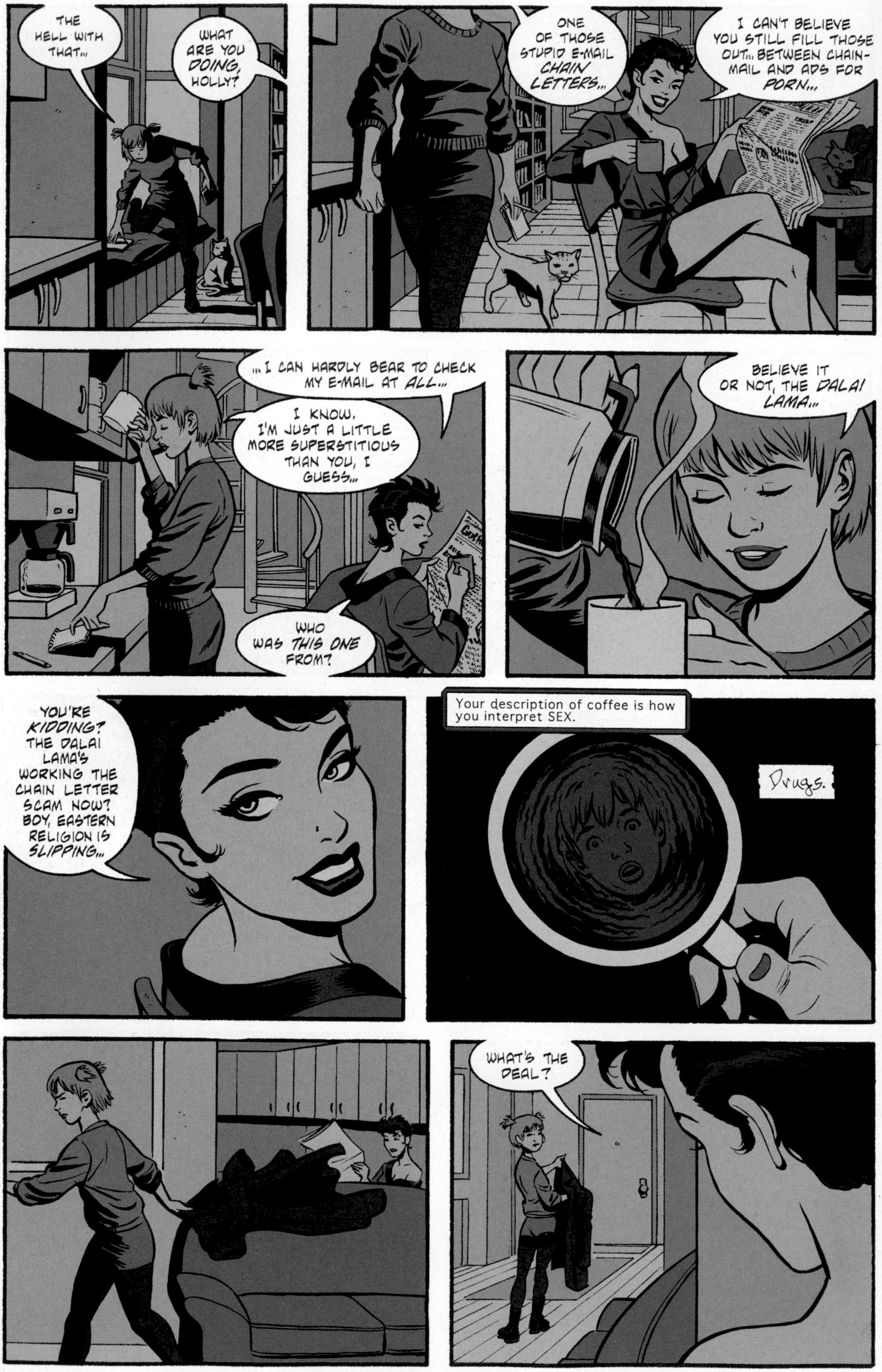
THE HELL WITH THAT...
WHAT ARE YOU DOING, HOLLY?
ONE OF THOSE STUPID E-MAIL CHAIN LETTERS...
I CAN'T BELIEVE YOU STILL FILL THOSE OUT... BETWEEN CHAIN-MAIL AND ADS FOR PORN...
...I CAN HARDLY BEAR TO CHECK MY E-MAIL AT ALL...
I KNOW. I'M JUST A LITTLE MORE SUPERSTITIOUS THAN YOU, I GUESS...
WHO WAS THIS ONE FROM?
BELIEVE IT OR NOT, THE DALAI LAMA...
YOU'RE KIDDING? THE DALAI LAMA'S WORKING THE CHAIN LETTER SCAM NOW? BOY, EASTERN RELIGION IS SLIPPING...
Your description of coffee is how you interpret SEX.
Drugs.
WHAT'S THE DEAL?

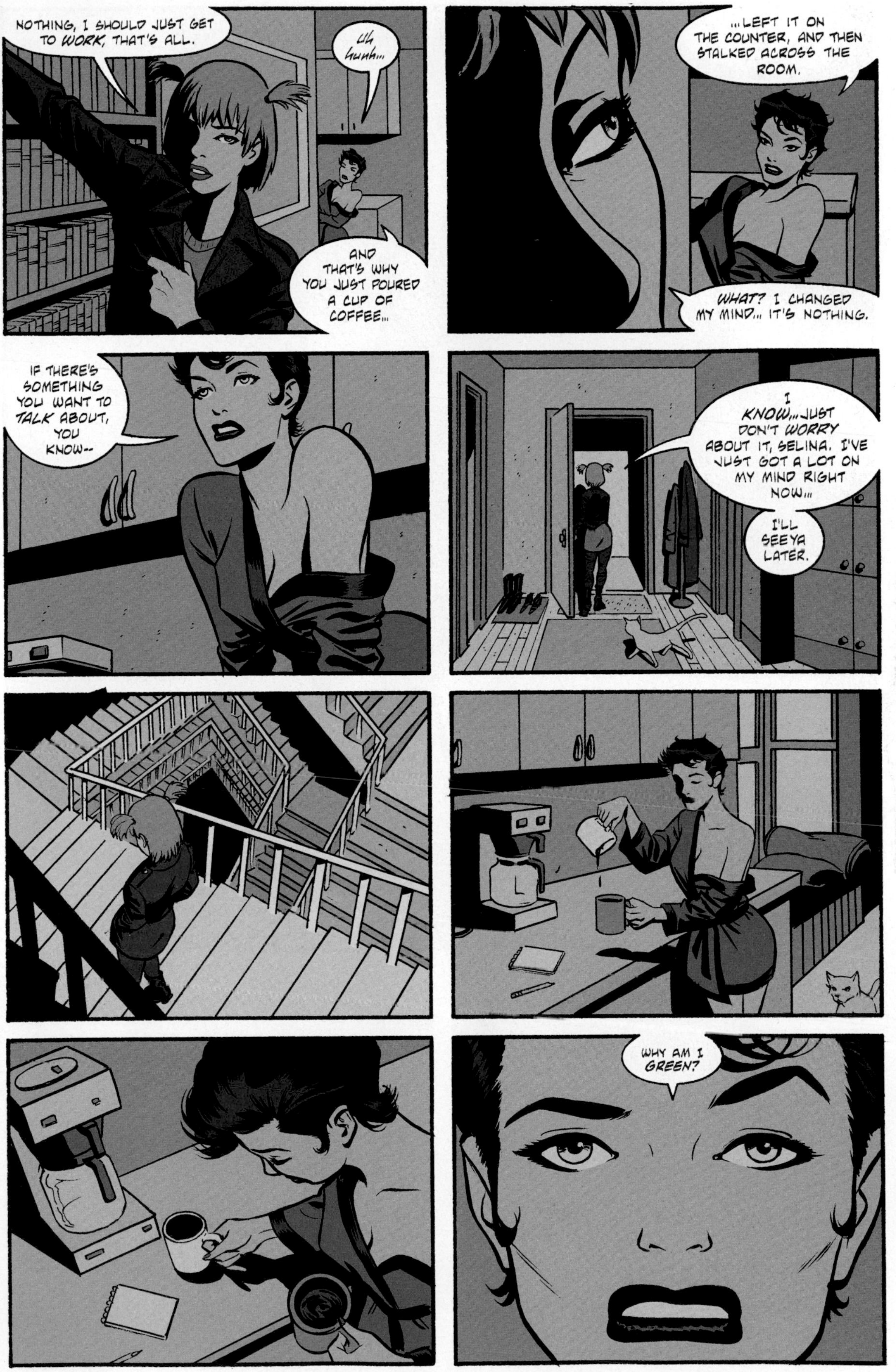
NOTHING, I SHOULD JUST GET TO WORK, THAT'S ALL.
Uh huh...
AND THAT'S WHY YOU JUST POURED A CUP OF COFFEE...
...LEFT IT ON THE COUNTER, AND THEN STALKED ACROSS THE ROOM.
WHAT? I CHANGED MY MIND... IT'S NOTHING.
IF THERE'S SOMETHING YOU WANT TO TALK ABOUT, YOU KNOW--
I KNOW... JUST DON'T WORRY ABOUT IT, SELINA. I'VE JUST GOT A LOT ON MY MIND RIGHT NOW...
I'LL SEEYA LATER.
WHY AM I GREEN?

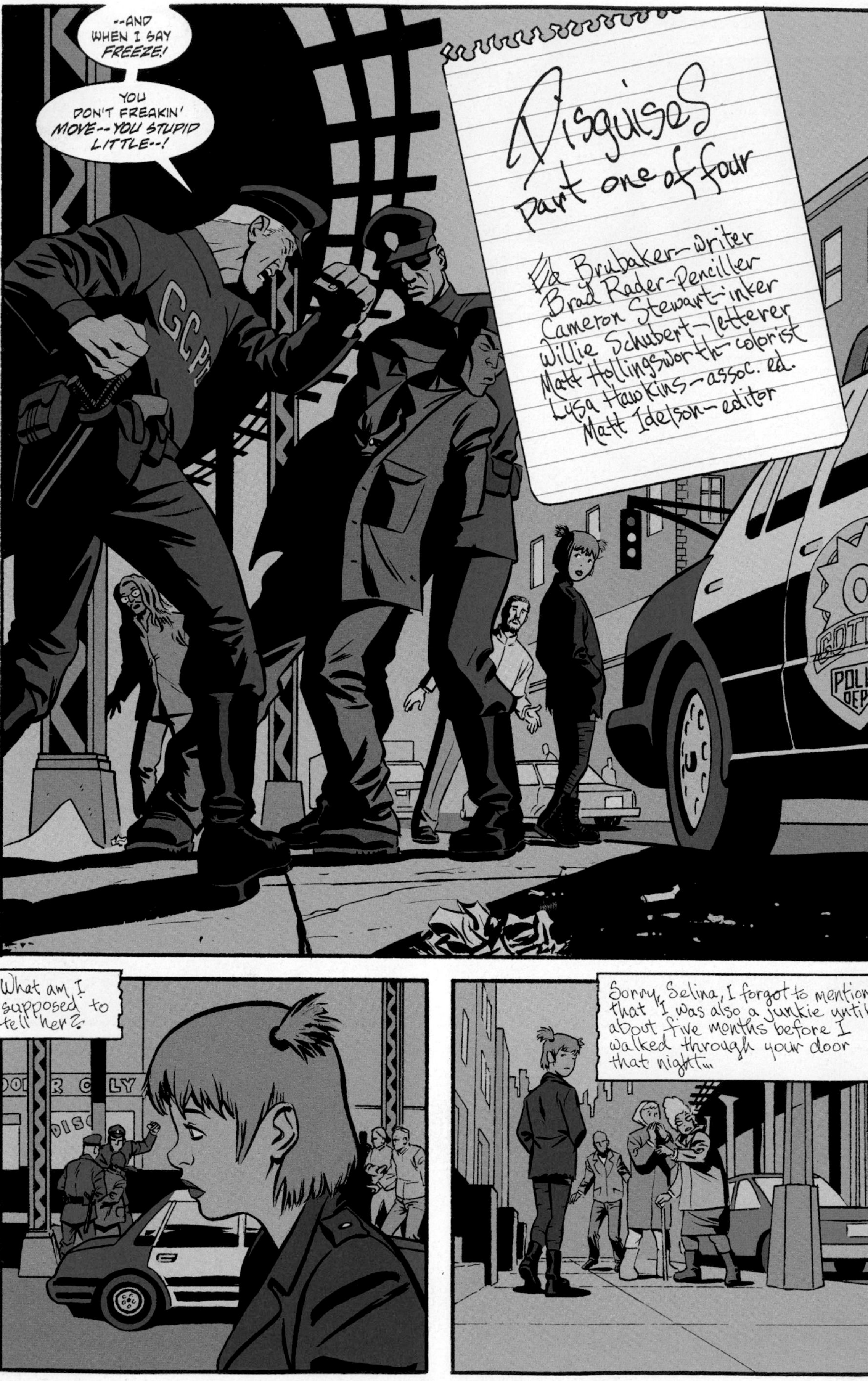
--AND WHEN I SAY FREEZE!
YOU DON'T FREAKIN' MOVE--YOU STUPID LITTLE--!
Disguises
part one of four
Ed Brubaker-writer
Brad Rader-Penciller
Cameron Stewart-inker
Willie Schubert-letterer
Matt Hollingsworth-colorist
Lysa Hawkins-assoc. ed.
Matt Idelson-editor
What am I supposed to tell her?
Sorry, Selina, I forgot to mention that I was also a junkie until about five months before I walked through your door that night...

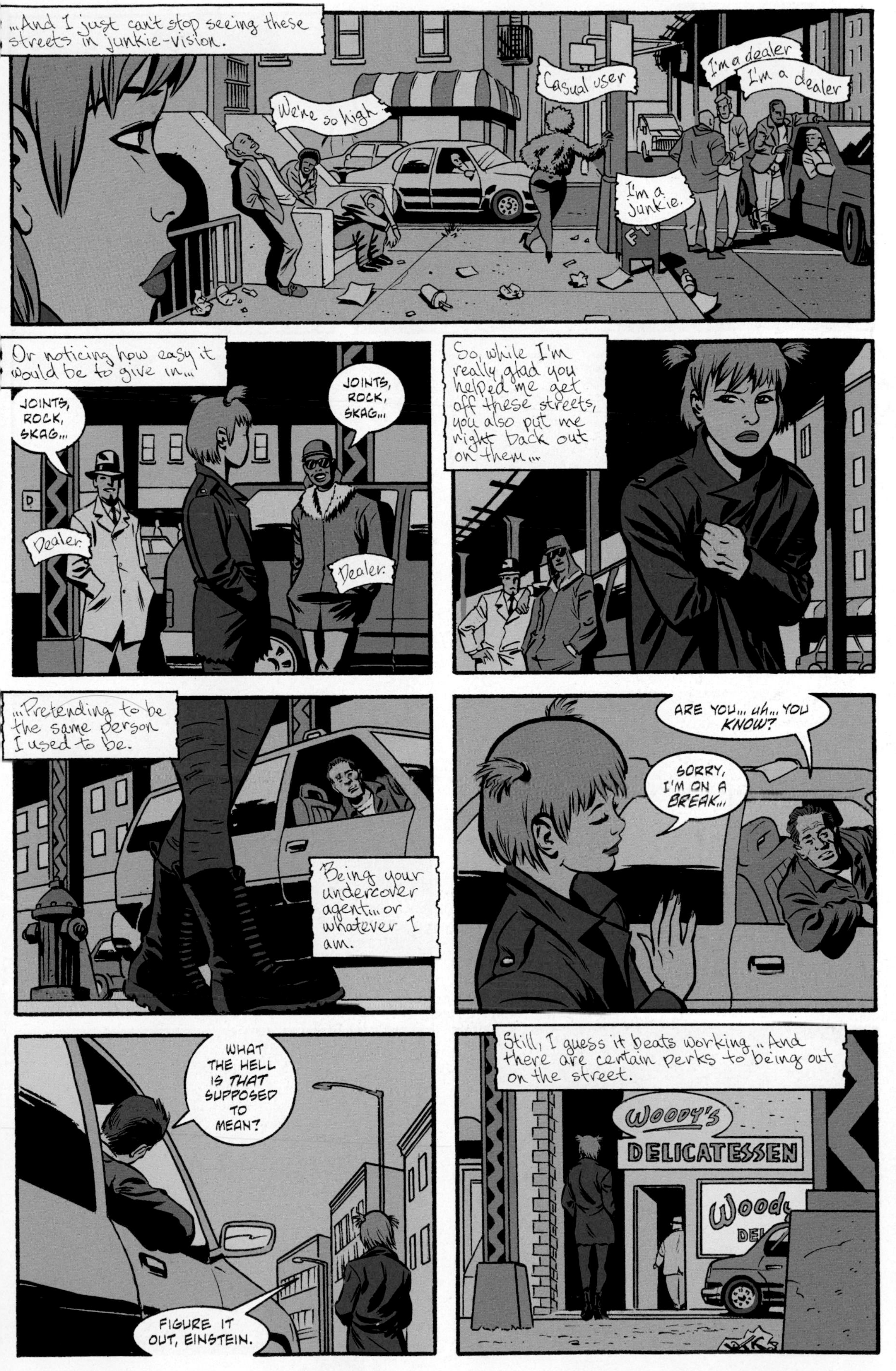

...And I just can't stop seeing these streets in junkie-vision.
We're so high
Casual user
I'm a dealer
I'm a dealer
I'm a junkie.
Or noticing how easy it would be to give in...
JOINTS, ROCK, SKAG...
JOINTS, ROCK, SKAG...
Dealer.
Dealer.
So, while I'm really glad you helped me get off these streets, you also put me right back out on them...
...Pretending to be the same person I used to be.
Being your undercover agent... or whatever I am.
ARE YOU... uh... YOU KNOW?
SORRY, I'M ON A BREAK...
WHAT THE HELL IS THAT SUPPOSED TO MEAN?
FIGURE IT OUT, EINSTEIN.
Still, I guess it beats working... And there are certain perks to being out on the street.
WOODY'S
DELICATESSEN

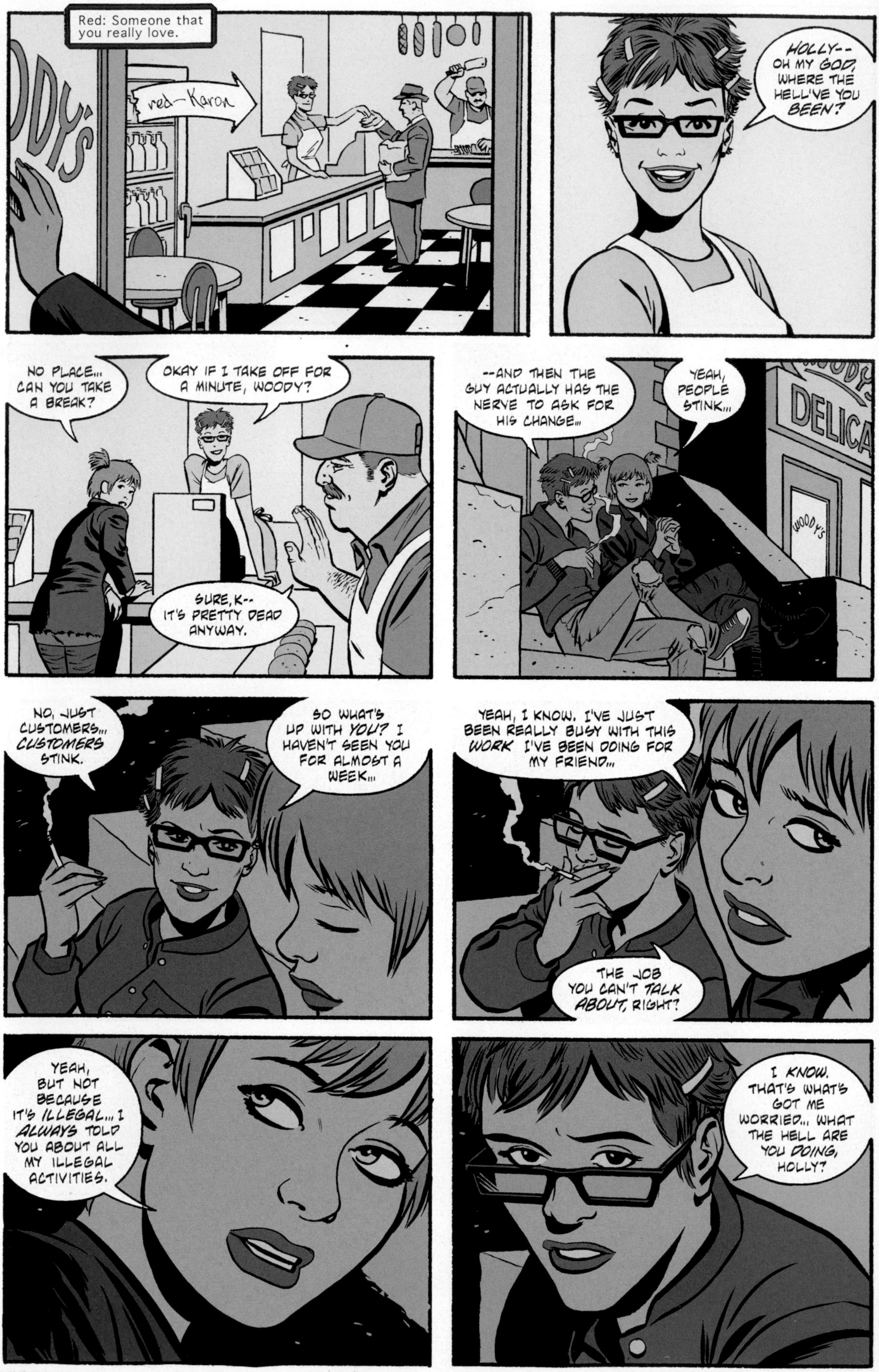
Red: Someone that you really love.
ODY'S
red—Karon
HOLLY-- OH MY GOD, WHERE THE HELL'VE YOU BEEN?
NO PLACE... CAN YOU TAKE A BREAK?
OKAY IF I TAKE OFF FOR A MINUTE, WOODY?
SURE, K-- IT'S PRETTY DEAD ANYWAY.
--AND THEN THE GUY ACTUALLY HAS THE NERVE TO ASK FOR HIS CHANGE...
YEAH, PEOPLE STINK...
DELICA
WOODY'S
NO, JUST CUSTOMERS... CUSTOMERS STINK.
SO WHAT'S UP WITH YOU? I HAVEN'T SEEN YOU FOR ALMOST A WEEK...
YEAH, I KNOW. I'VE JUST BEEN REALLY BUSY WITH THIS WORK I'VE BEEN DOING FOR MY FRIEND...
THE JOB YOU CAN'T TALK ABOUT, RIGHT?
YEAH, BUT NOT BECAUSE IT'S ILLEGAL... I ALWAYS TOLD YOU ABOUT ALL MY ILLEGAL ACTIVITIES.
I KNOW. THAT'S WHAT'S GOT ME WORRIED... WHAT THE HELL ARE YOU DOING, HOLLY?

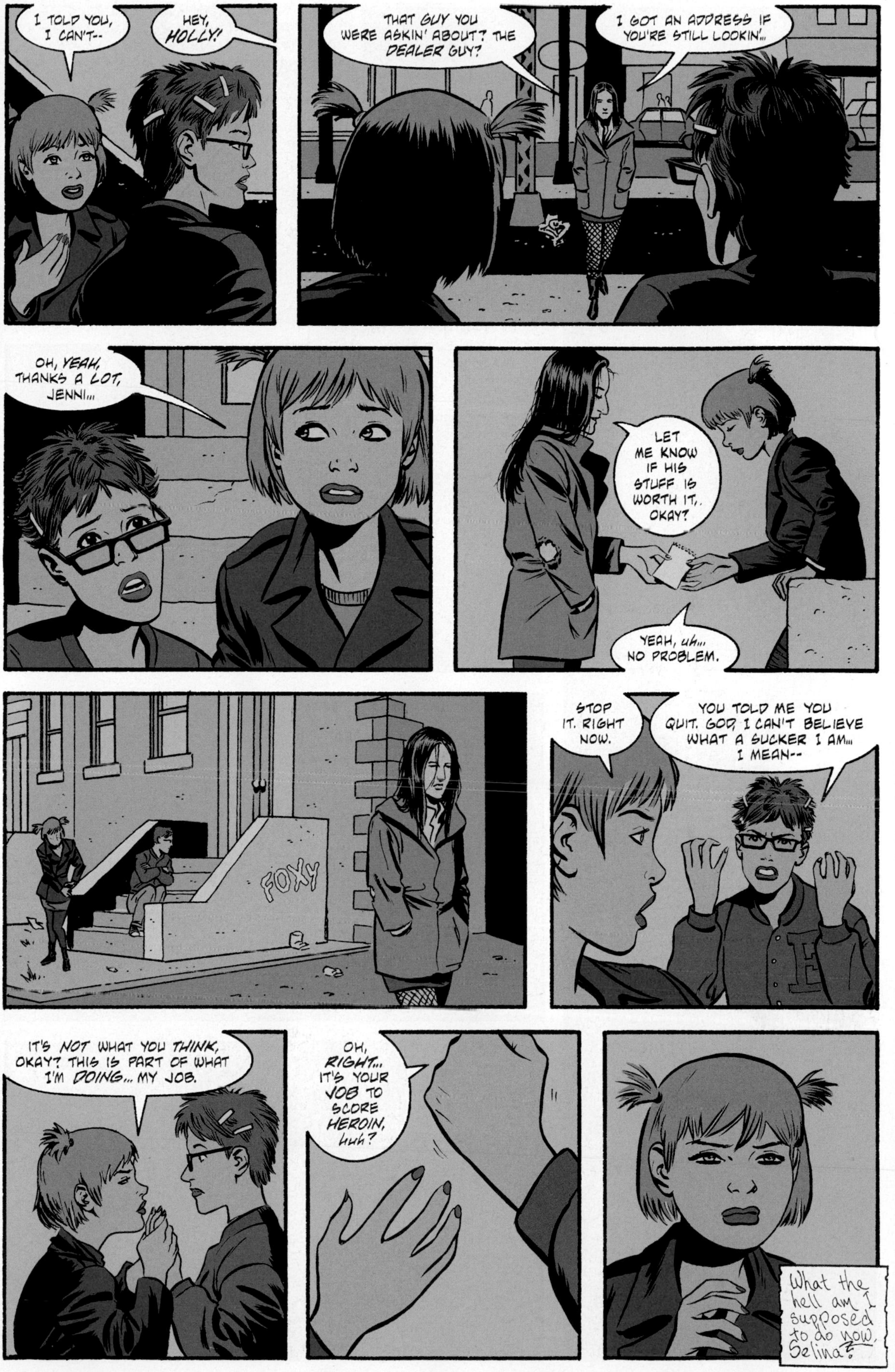

I TOLD YOU, I CAN'T--
HEY, HOLLY!
THAT GUY YOU WERE ASKIN' ABOUT? THE DEALER GUY?
I GOT AN ADDRESS IF YOU'RE STILL LOOKIN'...
OH, YEAH, THANKS A LOT, JENNI...
LET ME KNOW IF HIS STUFF IS WORTH IT, OKAY?
YEAH, UH... NO PROBLEM.
FOXY
STOP IT. RIGHT NOW.
YOU TOLD ME YOU QUIT. GOD, I CAN'T BELIEVE WHAT A SUCKER I AM... I MEAN--
IT'S NOT WHAT YOU THINK, OKAY? THIS IS PART OF WHAT I'M DOING... MY JOB.
OH, RIGHT... IT'S YOUR JOB TO SCORE HEROIN, HUH?
What the hell am I supposed to do now, Selina?

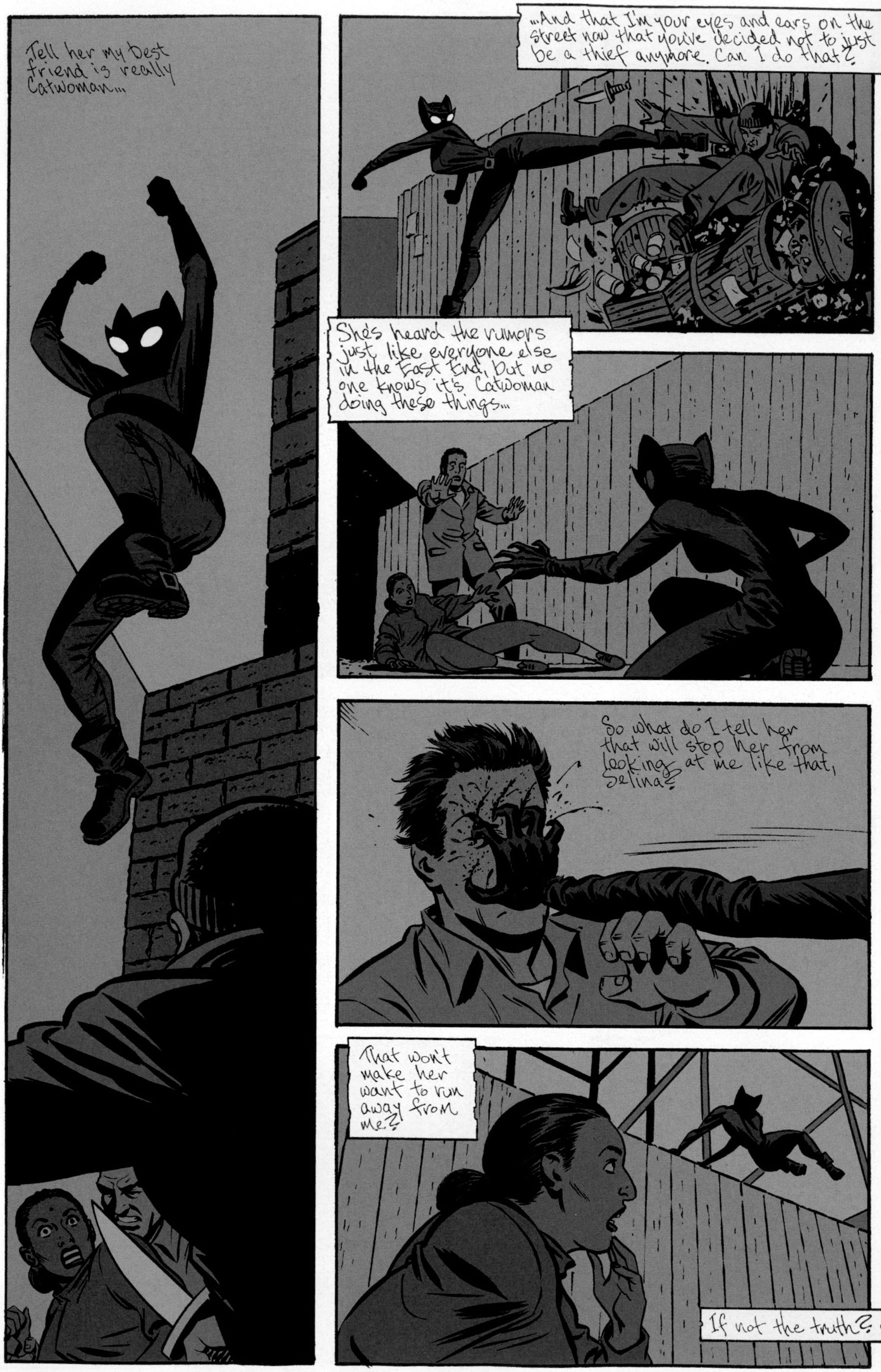

Tell her my best friend is really Catwoman...
...And that I'm your eyes and ears on the street now that you've decided not to just be a thief anymore. Can I do that?
She's heard the rumors just like everyone else in the East End, but no one knows it's Catwoman doing these things...
So what do I tell her that will stop her from looking at me like that, Selina?
That won't make her want to run away from me?
If not the truth?

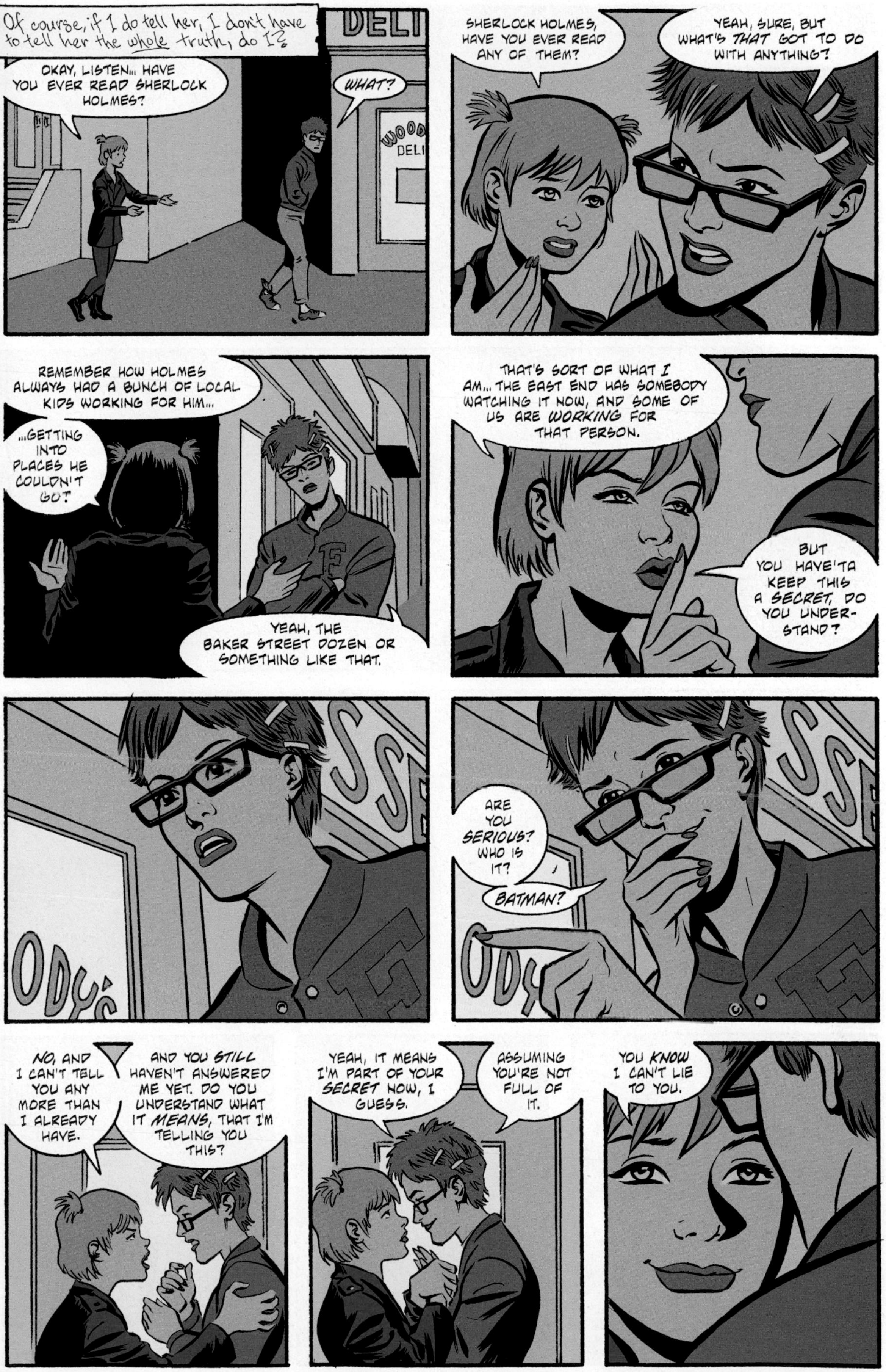
Of course, if I do tell her, I don't have to tell her the whole truth, do I?
DELI
OKAY, LISTEN... HAVE YOU EVER READ SHERLOCK HOLMES?
WHAT?
WOOD
DELI
SHERLOCK HOLMES, HAVE YOU EVER READ ANY OF THEM?
YEAH, SURE, BUT WHAT'S THAT GOT TO DO WITH ANYTHING?
REMEMBER HOW HOLMES ALWAYS HAD A BUNCH OF LOCAL KIDS WORKING FOR HIM...
...GETTING INTO PLACES HE COULDN'T GO?
YEAH, THE BAKER STREET DOZEN OR SOMETHING LIKE THAT.
THAT'S SORT OF WHAT I AM... THE EAST END HAS SOMEBODY WATCHING IT NOW, AND SOME OF US ARE WORKING FOR THAT PERSON.
BUT YOU HAVE'TA KEEP THIS A SECRET, DO YOU UNDER-STAND?
ARE YOU SERIOUS? WHO IS IT?
BATMAN?
NO, AND I CAN'T TELL YOU ANY MORE THAN I ALREADY HAVE.
AND YOU STILL HAVEN'T ANSWERED ME YET. DO YOU UNDERSTAND WHAT IT MEANS, THAT I'M TELLING YOU THIS?
YEAH, IT MEANS I'M PART OF YOUR SECRET NOW, I GUESS.
ASSUMING YOU'RE NOT FULL OF IT.
YOU KNOW I CAN'T LIE TO YOU.

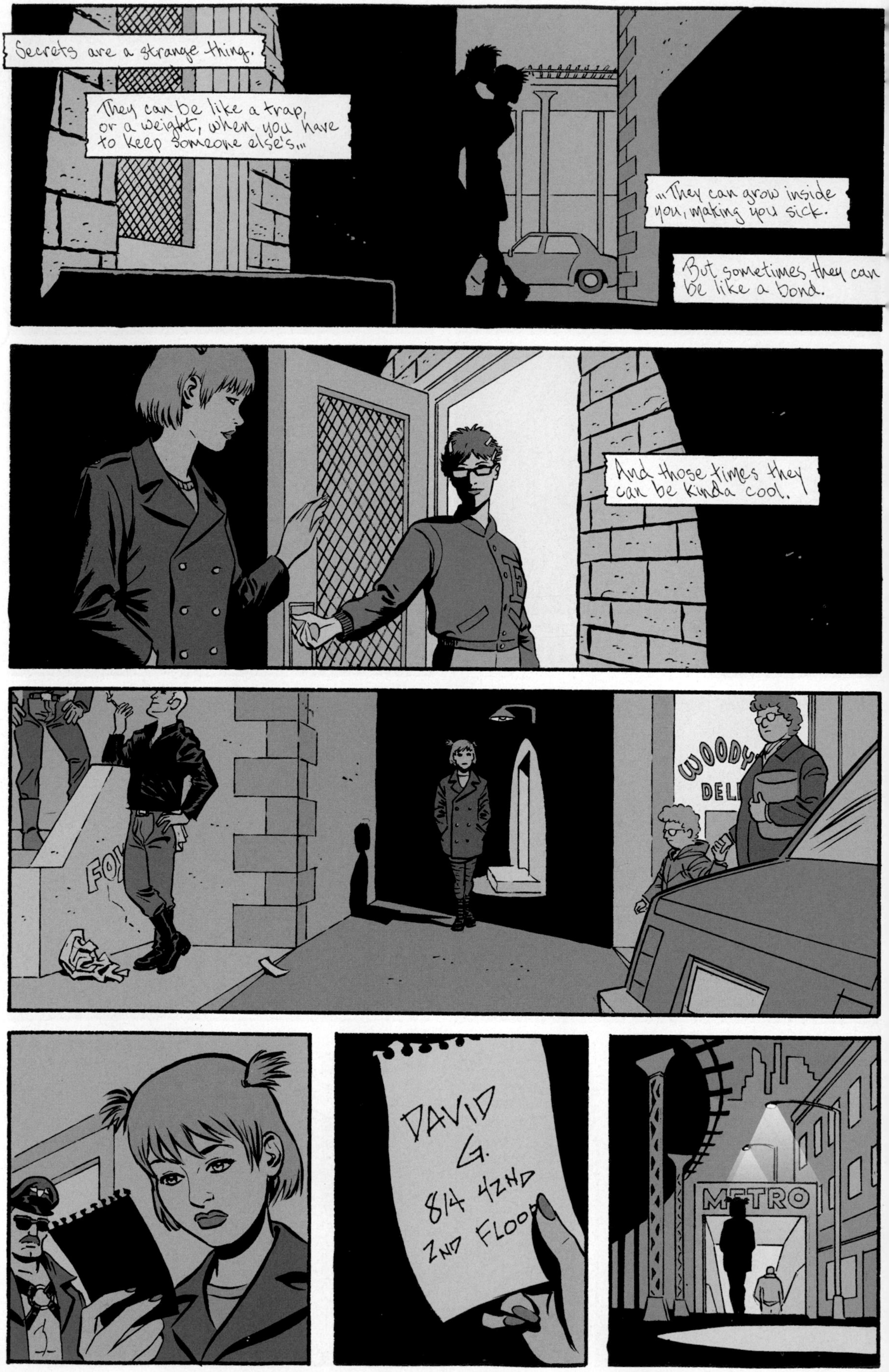
Secrets are a strange thing.
They can be like a trap, or a weight, when you have to keep someone else's...
...They can grow inside you, making you sick.
But sometimes they can be like a bond.
And those times they can be kinda cool.
WOODY'S
DELI
FOX
DAVID G. 814 42ND 2ND FLOOR
METRO

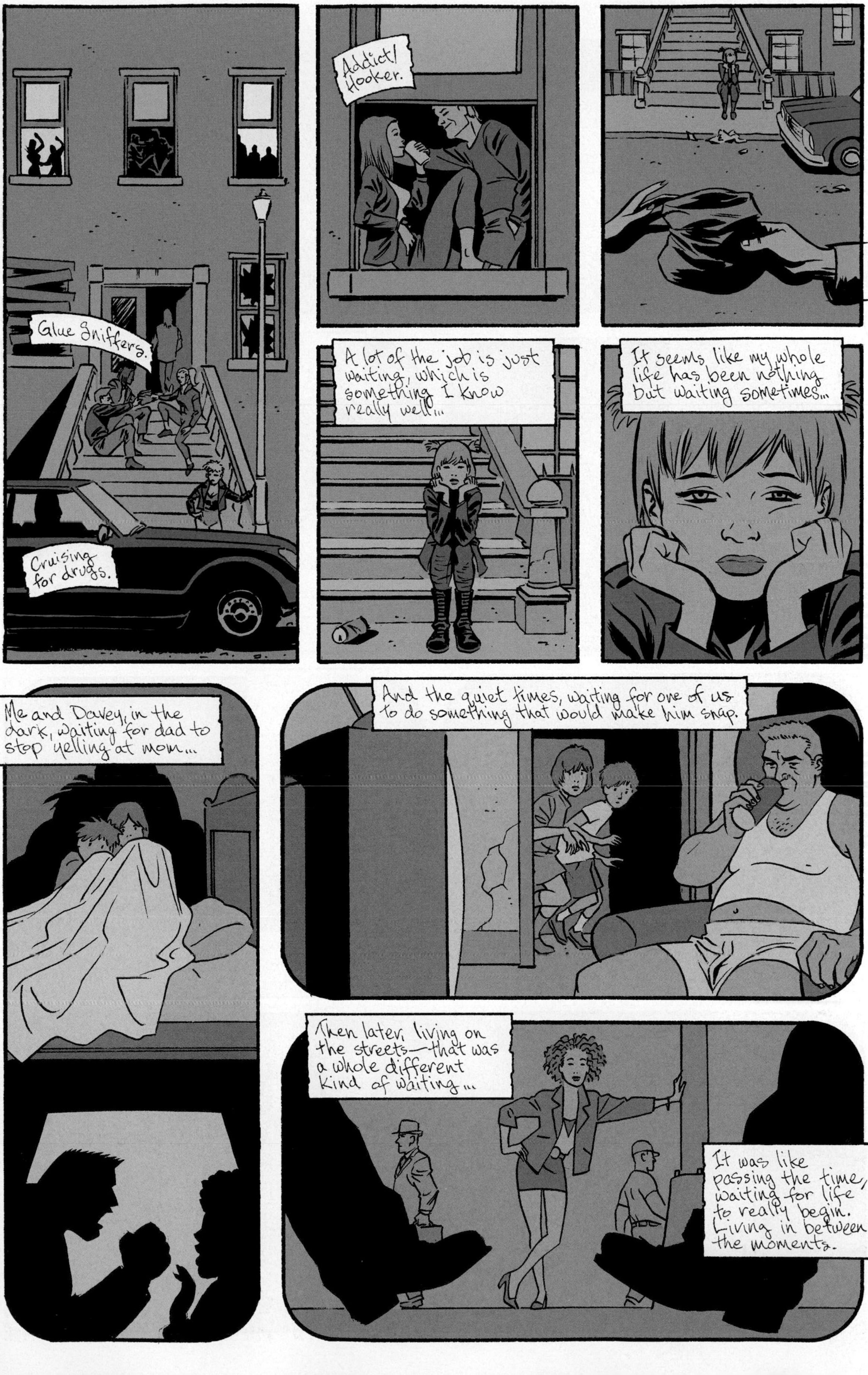

Glue Sniffers.
Cruising for drugs.
Addict/Hooker.
A lot of the job is just waiting, which is something I know really well...
It seems like my whole life has been nothing but waiting sometimes...
Me and Davey, in the dark, waiting for dad to stop yelling at mom...
And the quiet times, waiting for one of us to do something that would make him snap.
Then later, living on the streets—that was a whole different kind of waiting...
It was like passing the time, waiting for life to really begin. Living in between the moments.

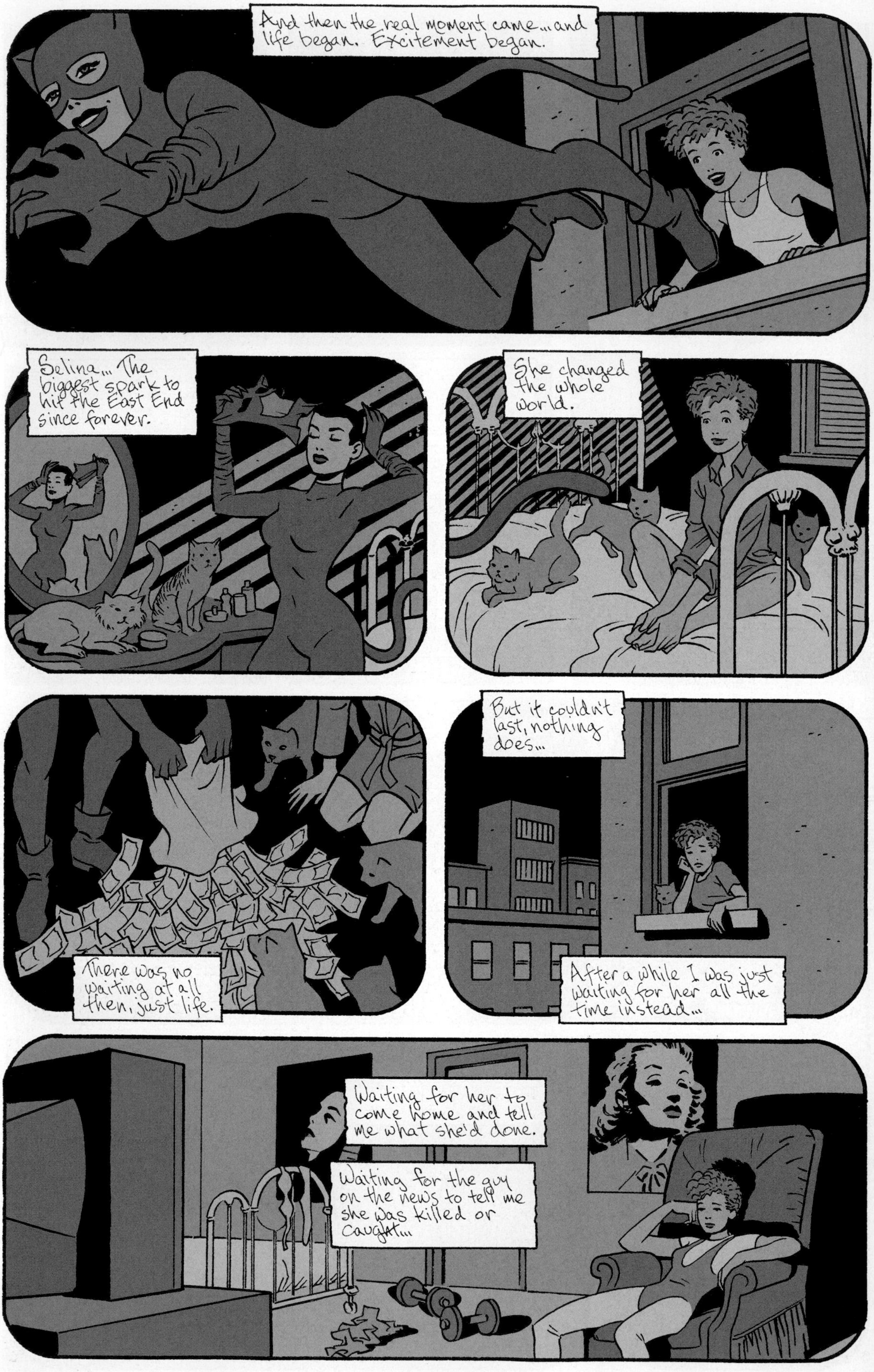
And then the real moment came... and life began. Excitement began.
Selina... The biggest spark to hit the East End since forever.
She changed the whole world.
There was no waiting at all then, just life.
But it couldn't last, nothing does...
After a while I was just waiting for her all the time instead...
Waiting for her to come home and tell me what she'd done.
Waiting for the guy on the news to tell me she was killed or caught...

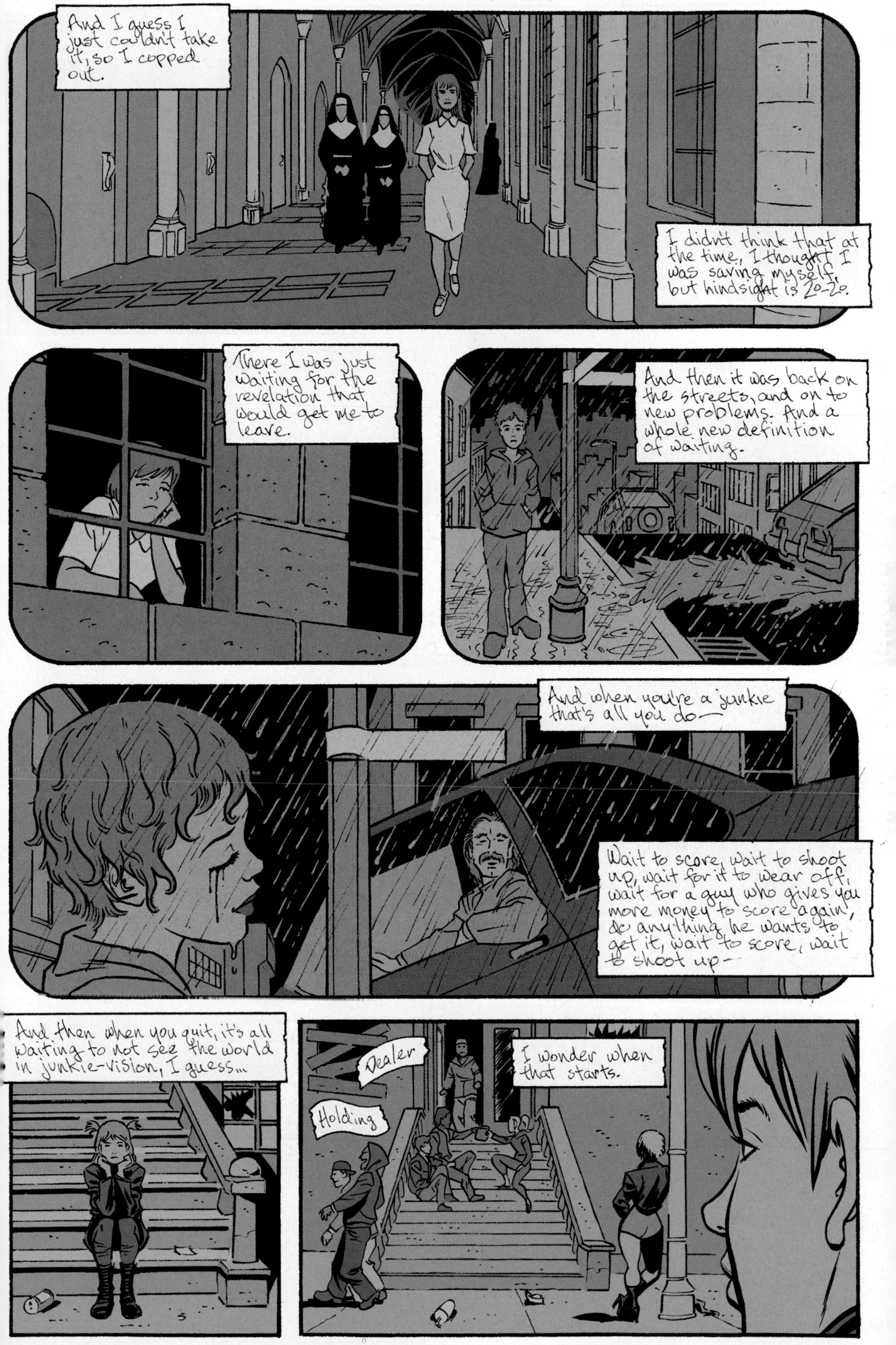
And I guess I just couldn't take it, so I copped out.
I didn't think that at the time, I thought I was saving myself, but hindsight is 20-20.
There I was just waiting for the revelation that would get me to leave.
And then it was back on the streets, and on to new problems. And a whole new definition of waiting.
And when you're a junkie that's all you do—
Wait to score, wait to shoot up, wait for it to wear off, wait for a guy who gives you more money to score again, do anything he wants to get it, wait to score, wait to shoot up—
And then when you quit, it's all waiting to not see the world in junkie-vision, I guess...
Dealer
Holding
I wonder when that starts.

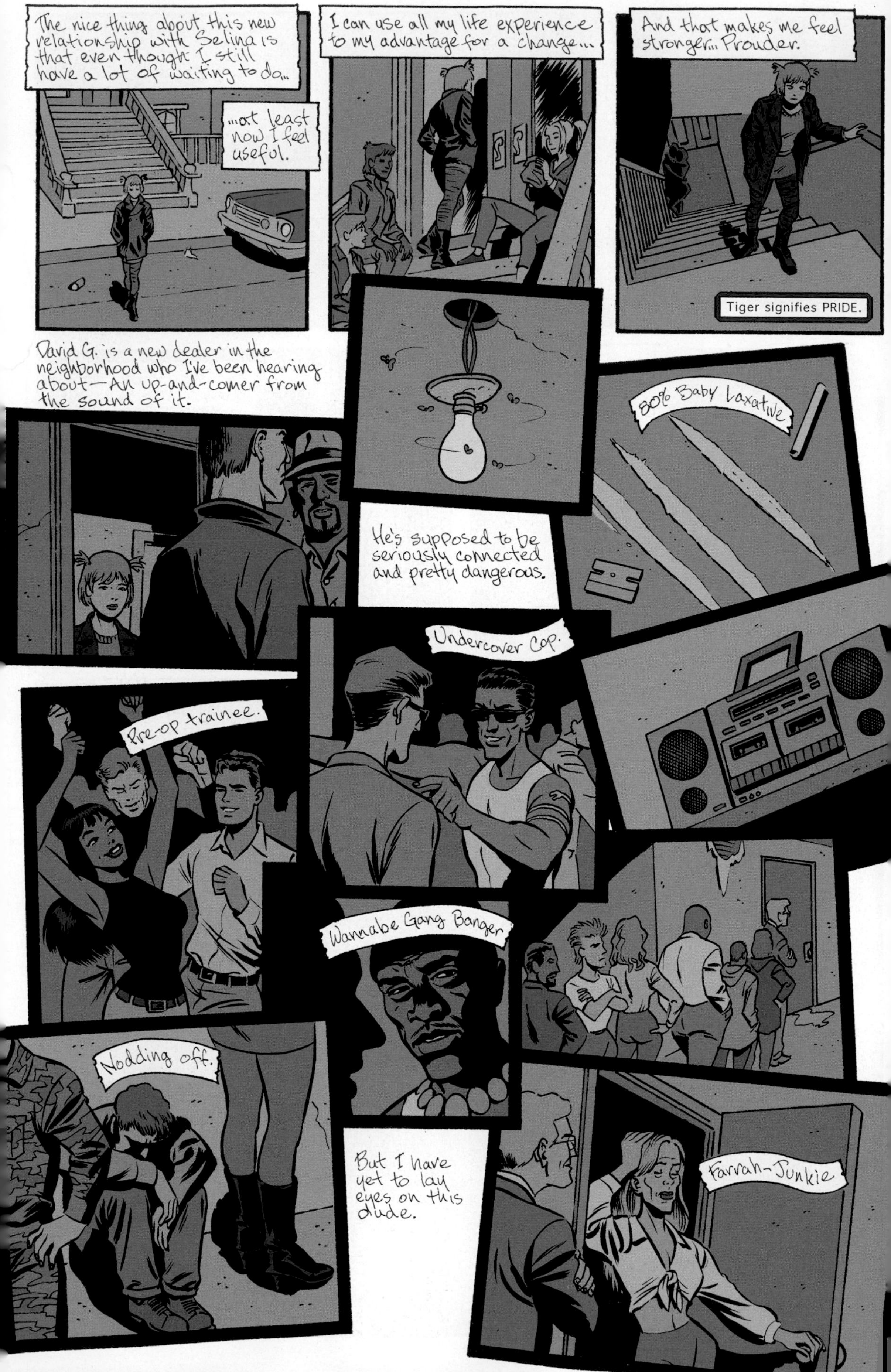
The nice thing about this new relationship with Selina is that even though I still have a lot of waiting to do...
...at least now I feel useful.
I can use all my life experience to my advantage for a change...
And that makes me feel stronger... Prouder.
Tiger signifies PRIDE.
David G. is a new dealer in the neighborhood who I've been hearing about— An up-and-comer from the sound of it.
80% Baby Laxative
He's supposed to be seriously connected and pretty dangerous.
Undercover Cop.
Pre-op trainee.
Wannabe Gang Banger
Nodding off.
But I have yet to lay eyes on this dude.
Farrah-Junkie

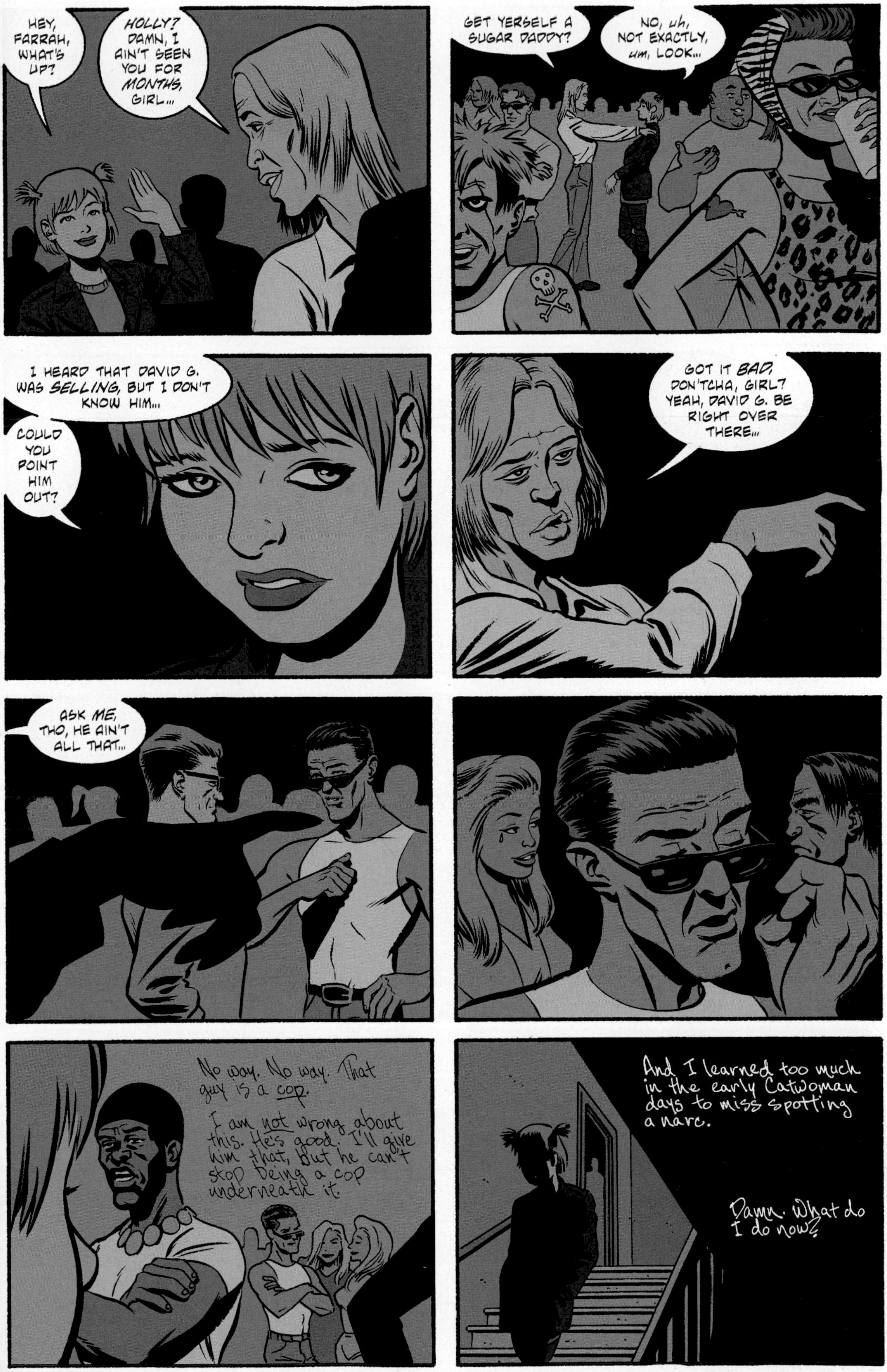

HEY, FARRAH, WHAT'S UP?
HOLLY? DAMN, I AIN'T SEEN YOU FOR MONTHS, GIRL...
GET YERSELF A SUGAR DADDY?
NO, uh, NOT EXACTLY, um, LOOK...
I HEARD THAT DAVID G. WAS SELLING, BUT I DON'T KNOW HIM...
COULD YOU POINT HIM OUT?
GOT IT BAD, DON'TCHA, GIRL? YEAH, DAVID G. BE RIGHT OVER THERE...
ASK ME, THO, HE AIN'T ALL THAT...
No way. No way. That guy is a cop.
I am not wrong about this. He's good. I'll give him that, but he can't stop being a cop underneath it.
And I learned too much in the early Catwoman days to miss spotting a narc.
Damn. What do I do now?

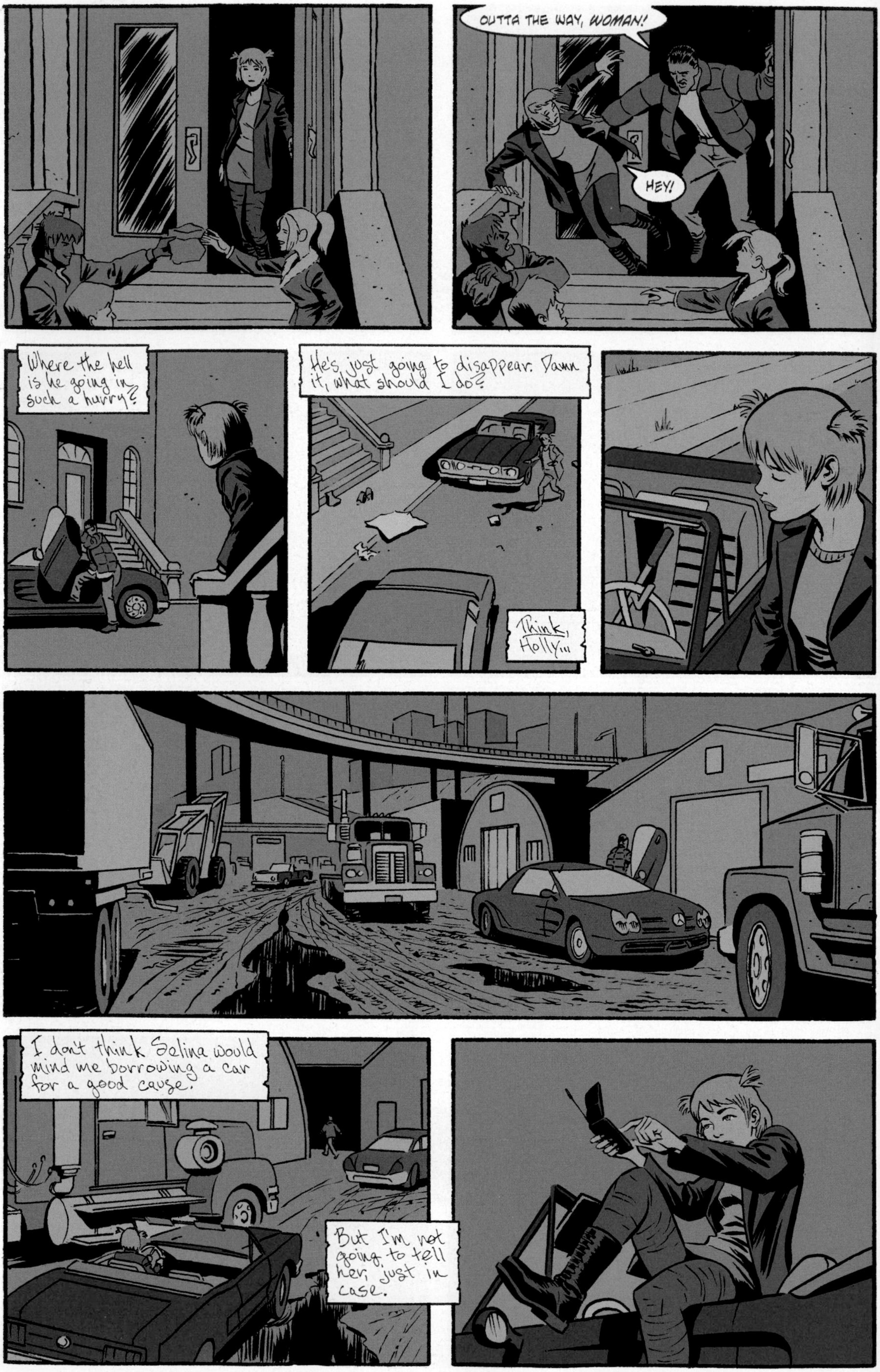
OUTTA THE WAY, WOMAN!
HEY!
Where the hell is he going in such a hurry?
He's just going to disappear. Damn it, what should I do?
Think, Holly...
I don't think Selina would mind me borrowing a car for a good cause.
But I'm not going to tell her, just in case.

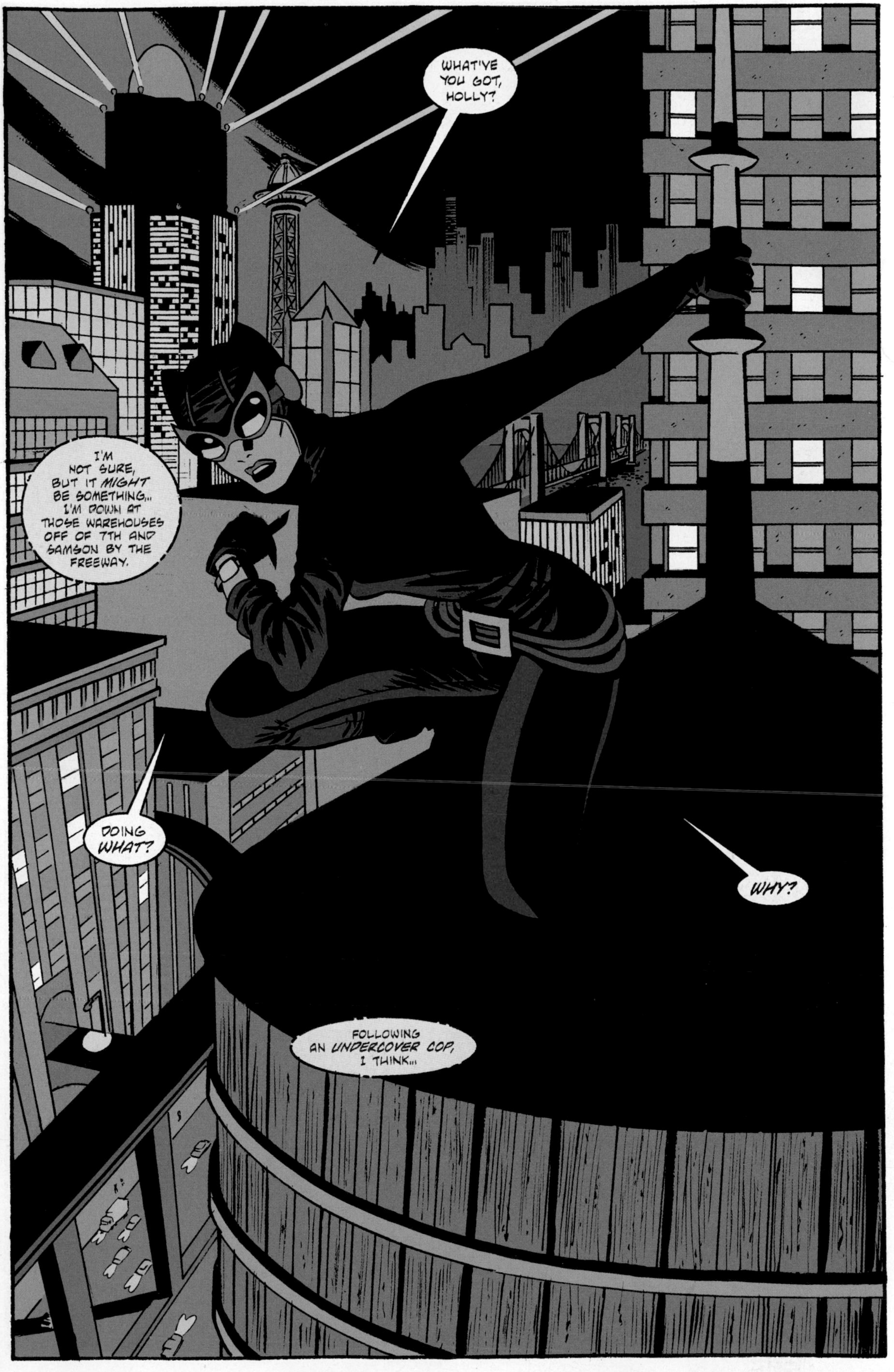
WHAT'VE YOU GOT, HOLLY?
I'M NOT SURE, BUT IT MIGHT BE SOMETHING... I'M DOWN AT THOSE WAREHOUSES OFF OF 7TH AND SAMSON BY THE FREEWAY.
DOING WHAT?
WHY?
FOLLOWING AN UNDERCOVER COP, I THINK...

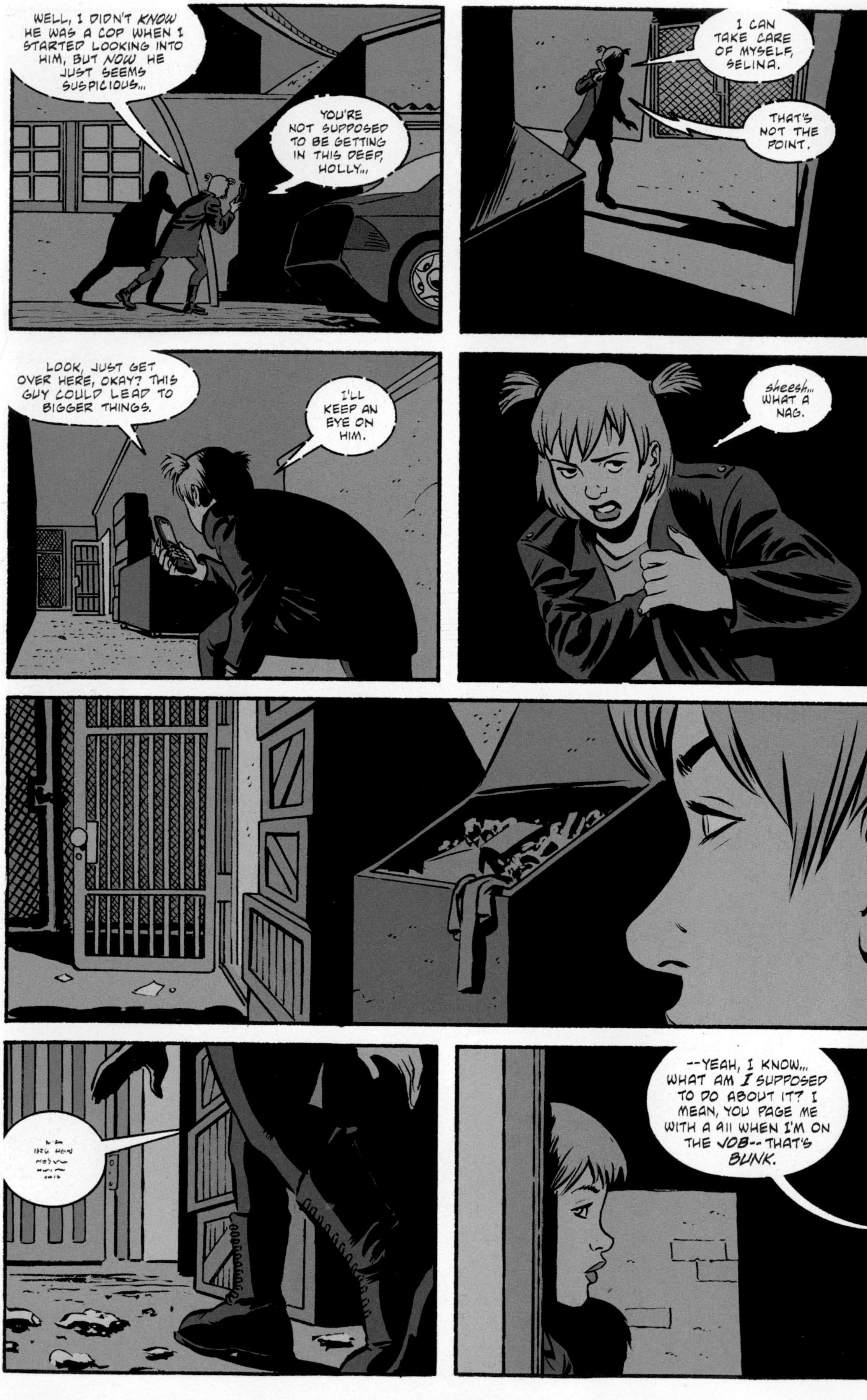
WELL, I DIDN'T KNOW HE WAS A COP WHEN I STARTED LOOKING INTO HIM, BUT NOW HE JUST SEEMS SUSPICIOUS...
YOU'RE NOT SUPPOSED TO BE GETTING IN THIS DEEP, HOLLY...
I CAN TAKE CARE OF MYSELF, SELINA.
THAT'S NOT THE POINT.
LOOK, JUST GET OVER HERE, OKAY? THIS GUY COULD LEAD TO BIGGER THINGS.
I'LL KEEP AN EYE ON HIM.
sheesh... WHAT A NAG.
--YEAH, I KNOW... WHAT AM I SUPPOSED TO DO ABOUT IT? I MEAN, YOU PAGE ME WITH A 911 WHEN I'M ON THE JOB--THAT'S BUNK.

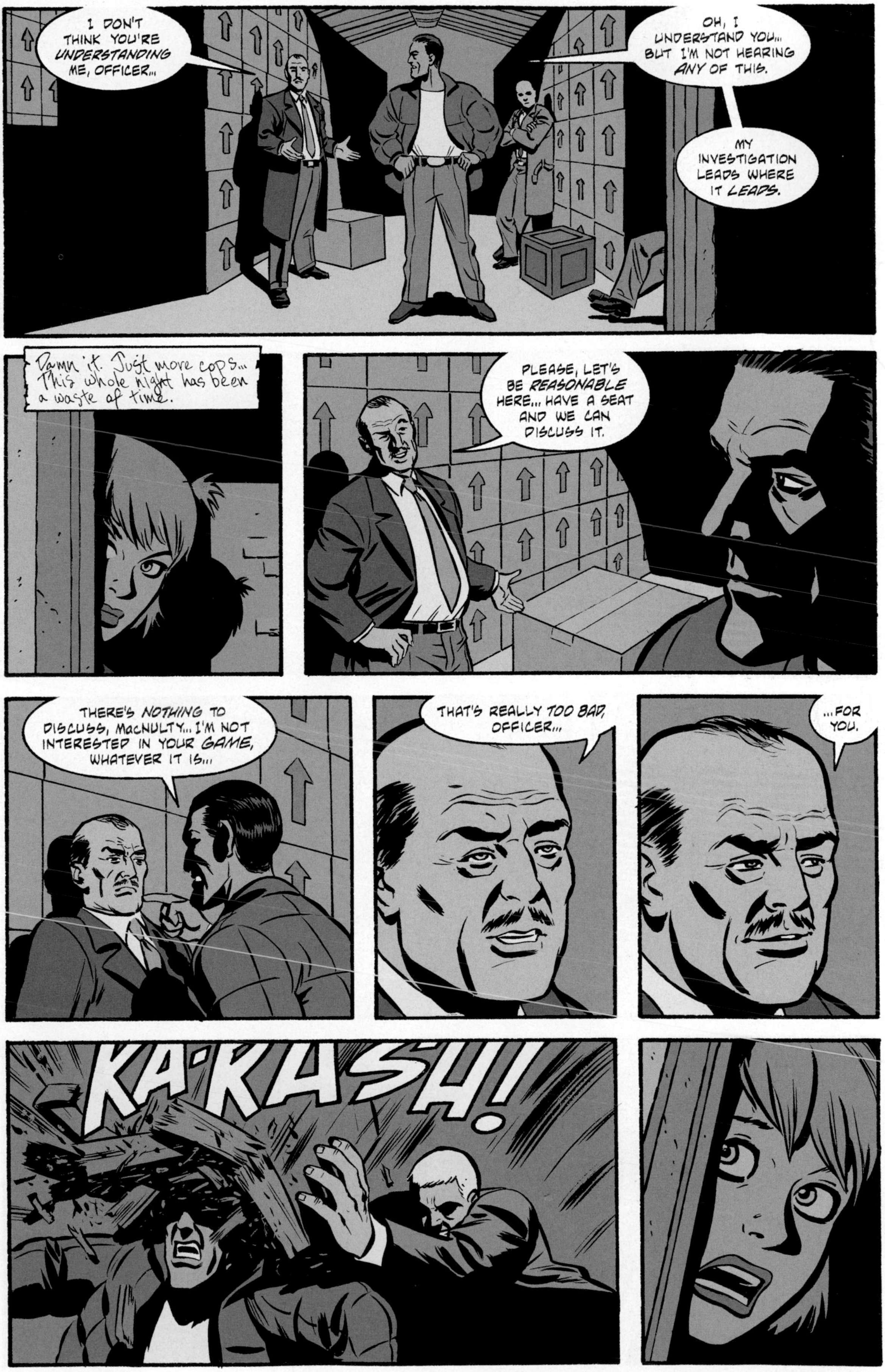
I DON'T THINK YOU'RE UNDERSTANDING ME, OFFICER...
OH, I UNDERSTAND YOU... BUT I'M NOT HEARING ANY OF THIS.
MY INVESTIGATION LEADS WHERE IT LEADS.
Damn it. Just more cops... This whole night has been a waste of time.
PLEASE, LET'S BE REASONABLE HERE... HAVE A SEAT AND WE CAN DISCUSS IT.
THERE'S NOTHING TO DISCUSS, MacNULTY... I'M NOT INTERESTED IN YOUR GAME, WHATEVER IT IS...
THAT'S REALLY TOO BAD, OFFICER...
...FOR YOU.
KA-RASH!

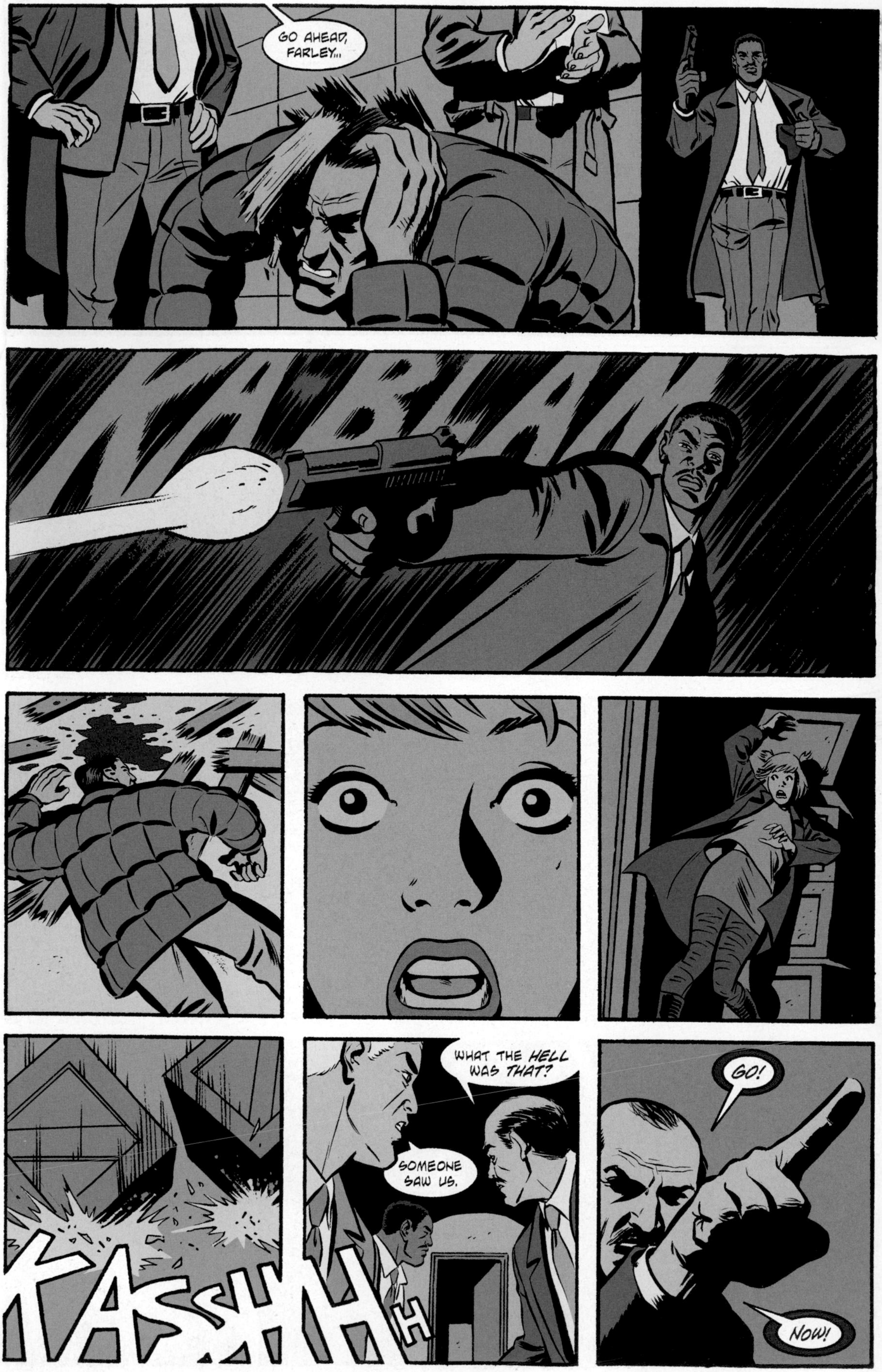
GO AHEAD, FARLEY...
KABLAM
KASHHH
WHAT THE HELL WAS THAT?
SOMEONE SAW US.
GO!
NOW!

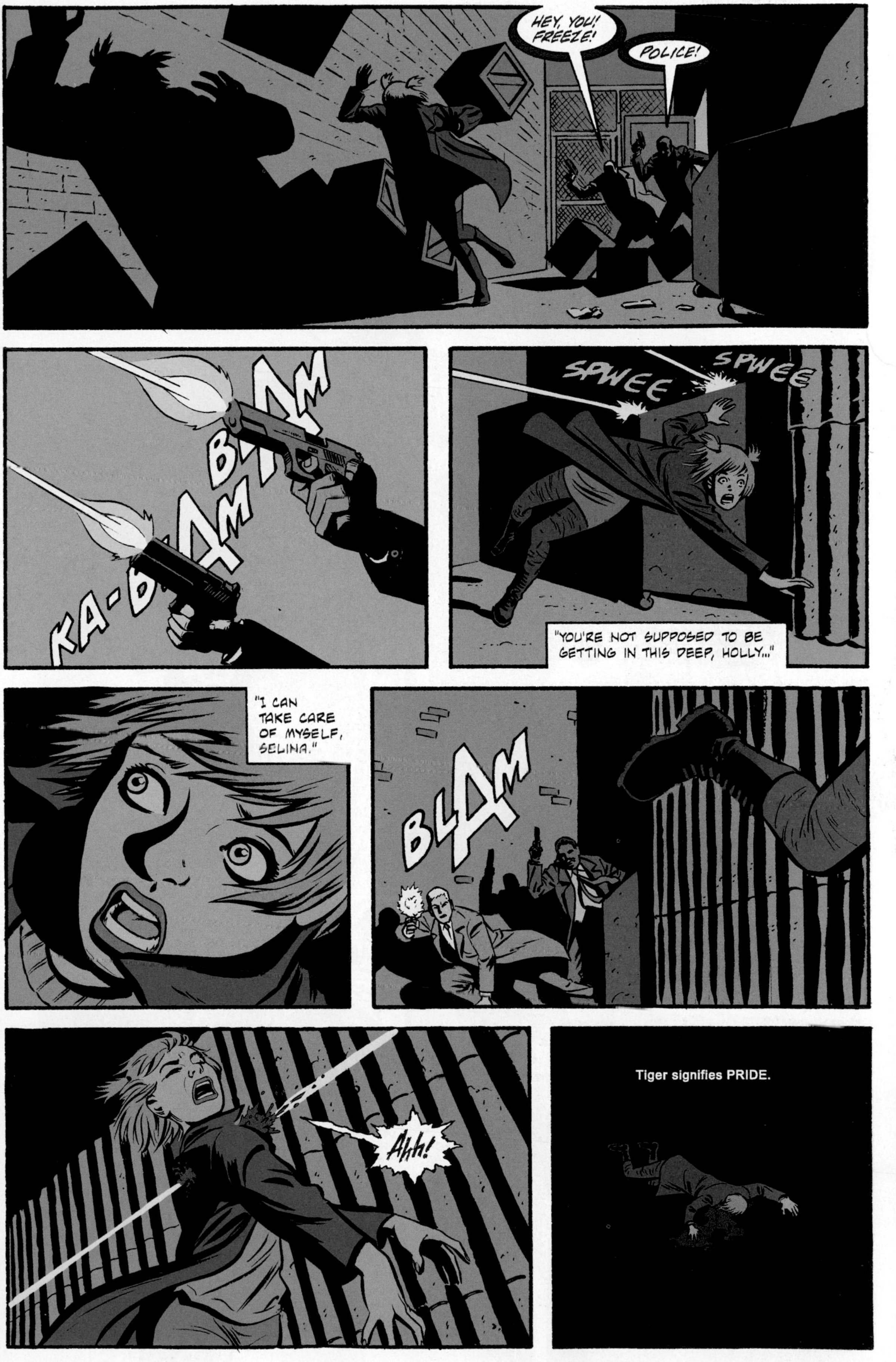
HEY, YOU! FREEZE!
POLICE!
KA-BLAM BLAM
SPWEE
SPWEE
"YOU'RE NOT SUPPOSED TO BE GETTING IN THIS DEEP, HOLLY..."
"I CAN TAKE CARE OF MYSELF, SELINA."
BLAM
Ahh!
Tiger signifies PRIDE.

Catwoman 7 Cover by Paul Pope

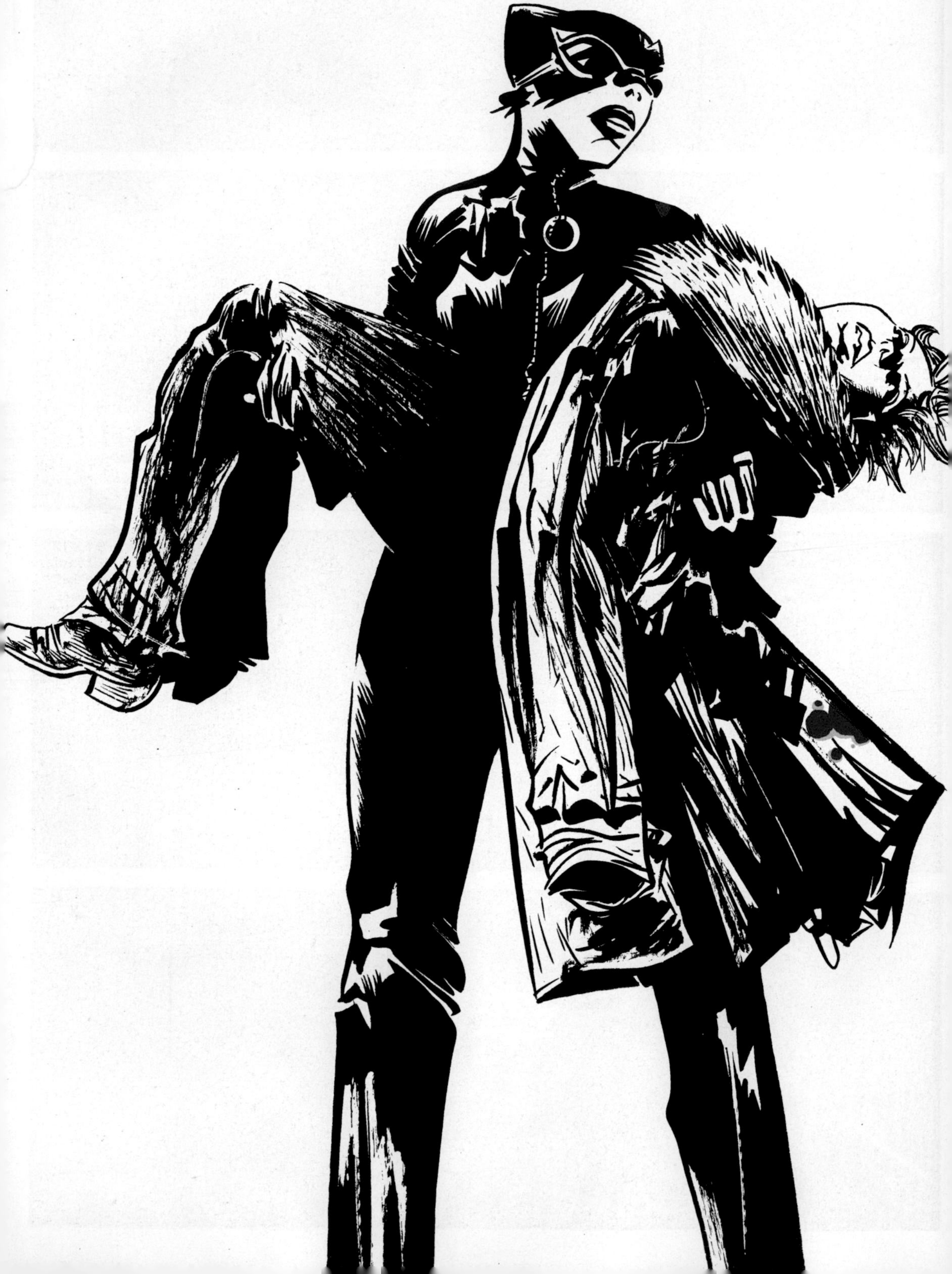

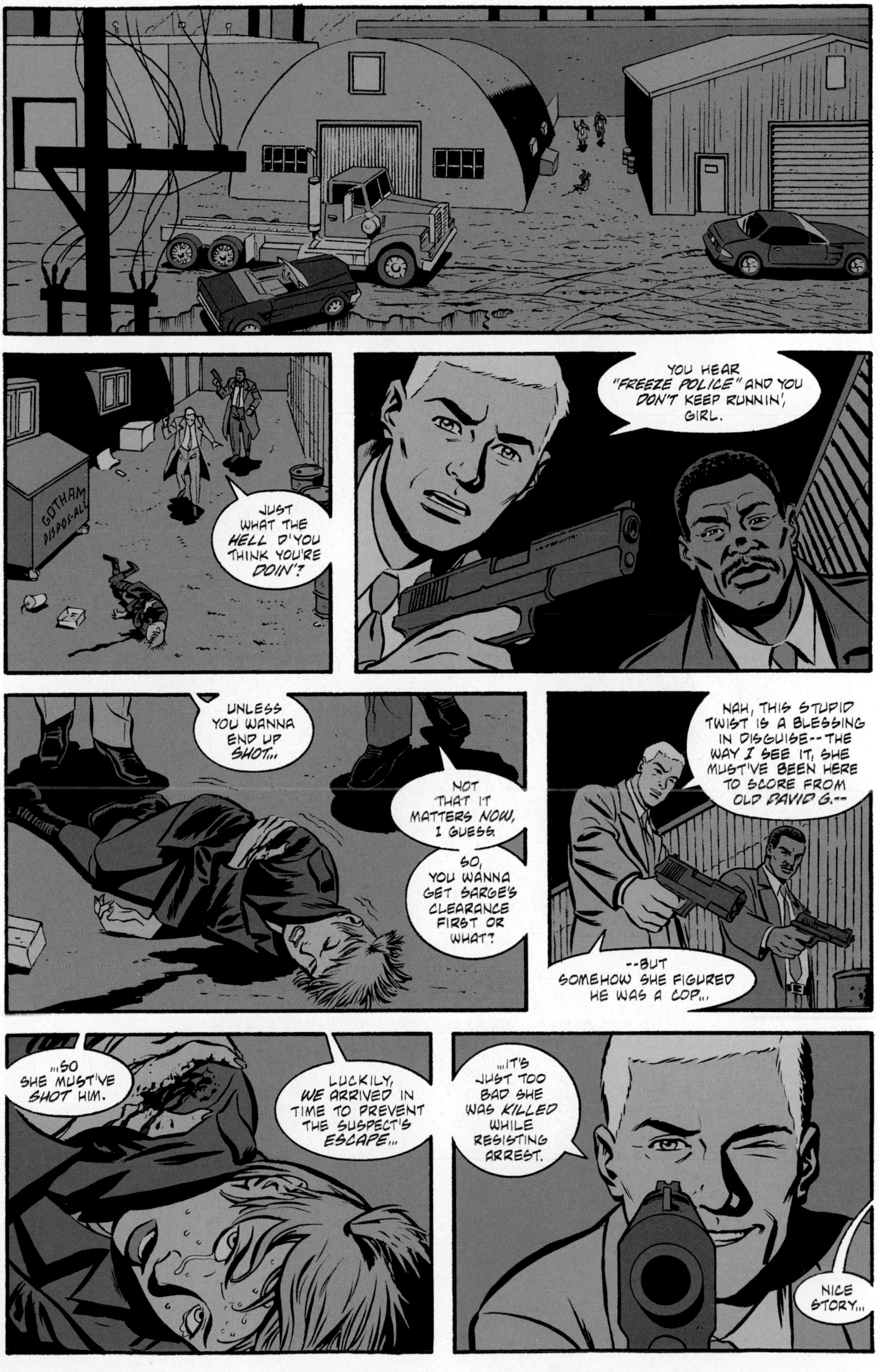
GOTHAM DISPOS-ALL
JUST WHAT THE HELL D'YOU THINK YOU'RE DOIN'?
YOU HEAR "FREEZE POLICE" AND YOU DON'T KEEP RUNNIN', GIRL.
UNLESS YOU WANNA END UP SHOT...
NOT THAT IT MATTERS NOW, I GUESS.
SO, YOU WANNA GET SARGE'S CLEARANCE FIRST OR WHAT?
NAH, THIS STUPID TWIST IS A BLESSING IN DISGUISE--THE WAY I SEE IT, SHE MUST'VE BEEN HERE TO SCORE FROM OLD DAVID G.--
--BUT SOMEHOW SHE FIGURED HE WAS A COP...
...SO SHE MUST'VE SHOT HIM.
LUCKILY, WE ARRIVED IN TIME TO PREVENT THE SUSPECT'S ESCAPE...
...IT'S JUST TOO BAD SHE WAS KILLED WHILE RESISTING ARREST.
NICE STORY...

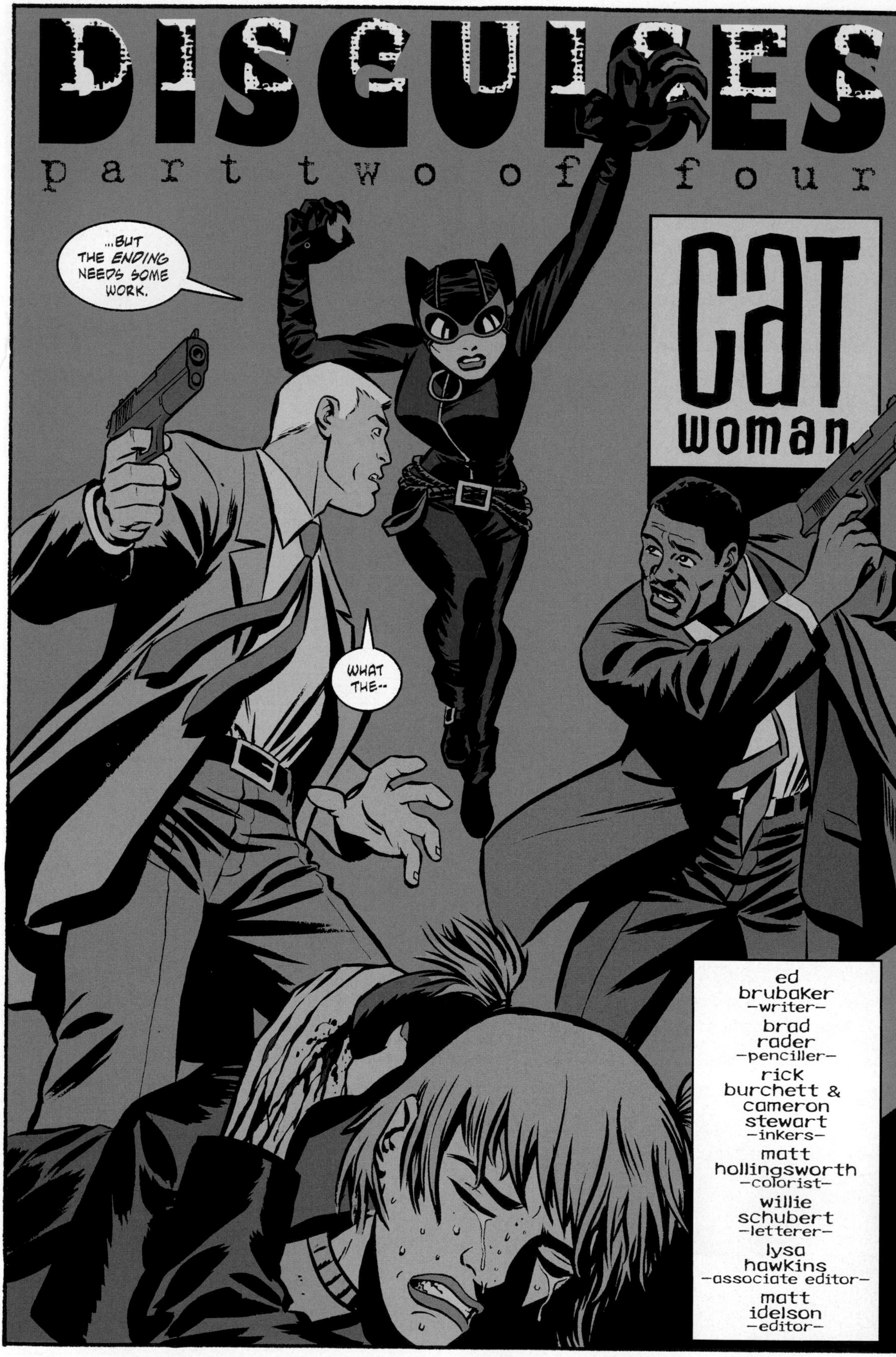
DISGUISES
part two of four
...BUT THE ENDING NEEDS SOME WORK.
CAT WOMAN
WHAT THE--
ed brubaker -writer-
brad rader -penciller-
rick burchett & cameron stewart -inkers-
matt hollingsworth -colorist-
willie schubert -letterer-
lysa hawkins -associate editor-
matt idelson -editor-

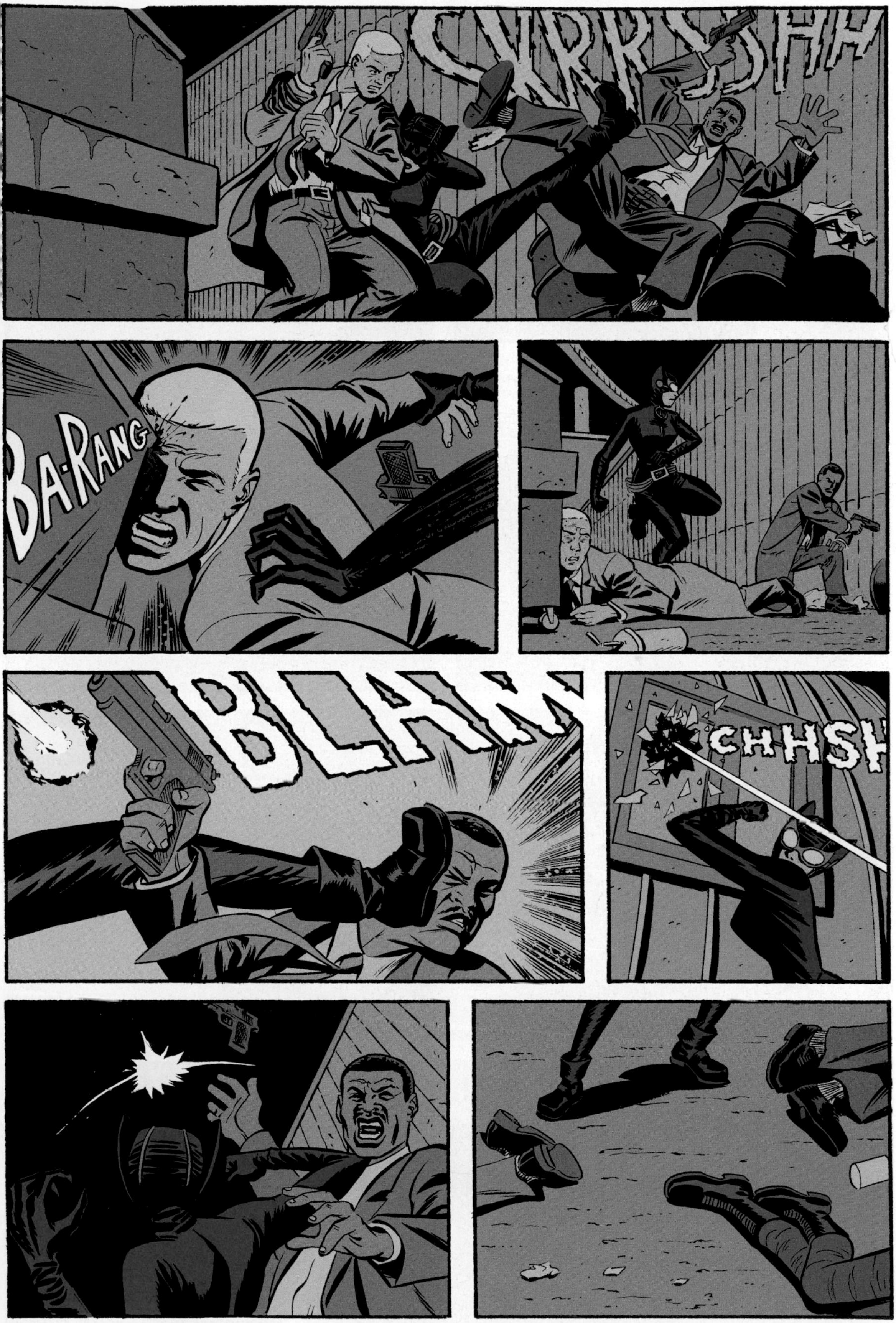
CVRRSSHH
BA-RANG
BLAM
CHHSH

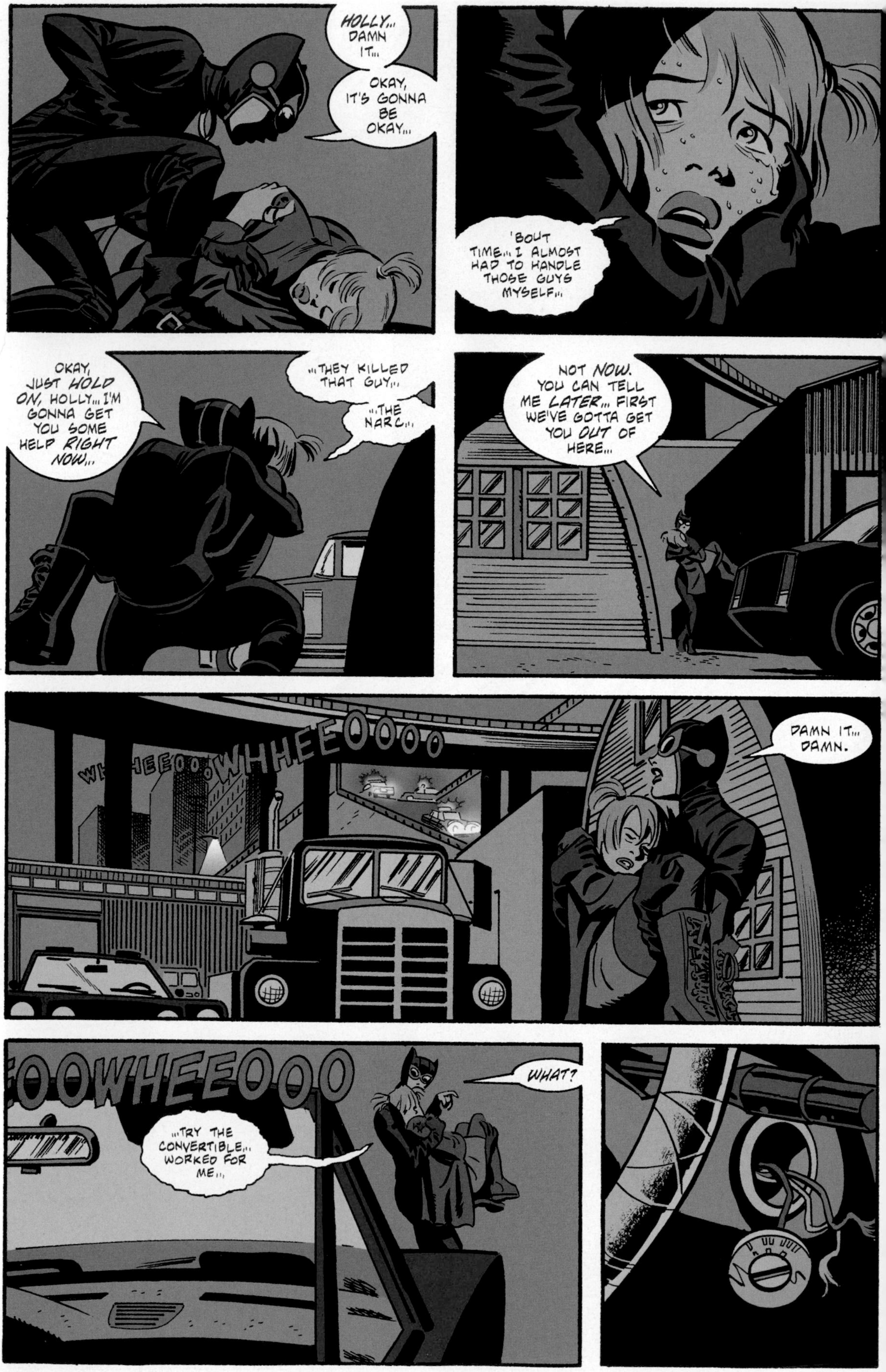
HOLLY... DAMN IT...
OKAY, IT'S GONNA BE OKAY...
'BOUT TIME... I ALMOST HAD TO HANDLE THOSE GUYS MYSELF...
OKAY, JUST HOLD ON, HOLLY... I'M GONNA GET YOU SOME HELP RIGHT NOW...
...THEY KILLED THAT GUY...
...THE NARC...
NOT NOW. YOU CAN TELL ME LATER... FIRST WE'VE GOTTA GET YOU OUT OF HERE...
WHHEEOOO WHHEEOOOO
DAMN IT... DAMN.
EOOWHEEOOO
WHAT?
...TRY THE CONVERTIBLE... WORKED FOR ME...

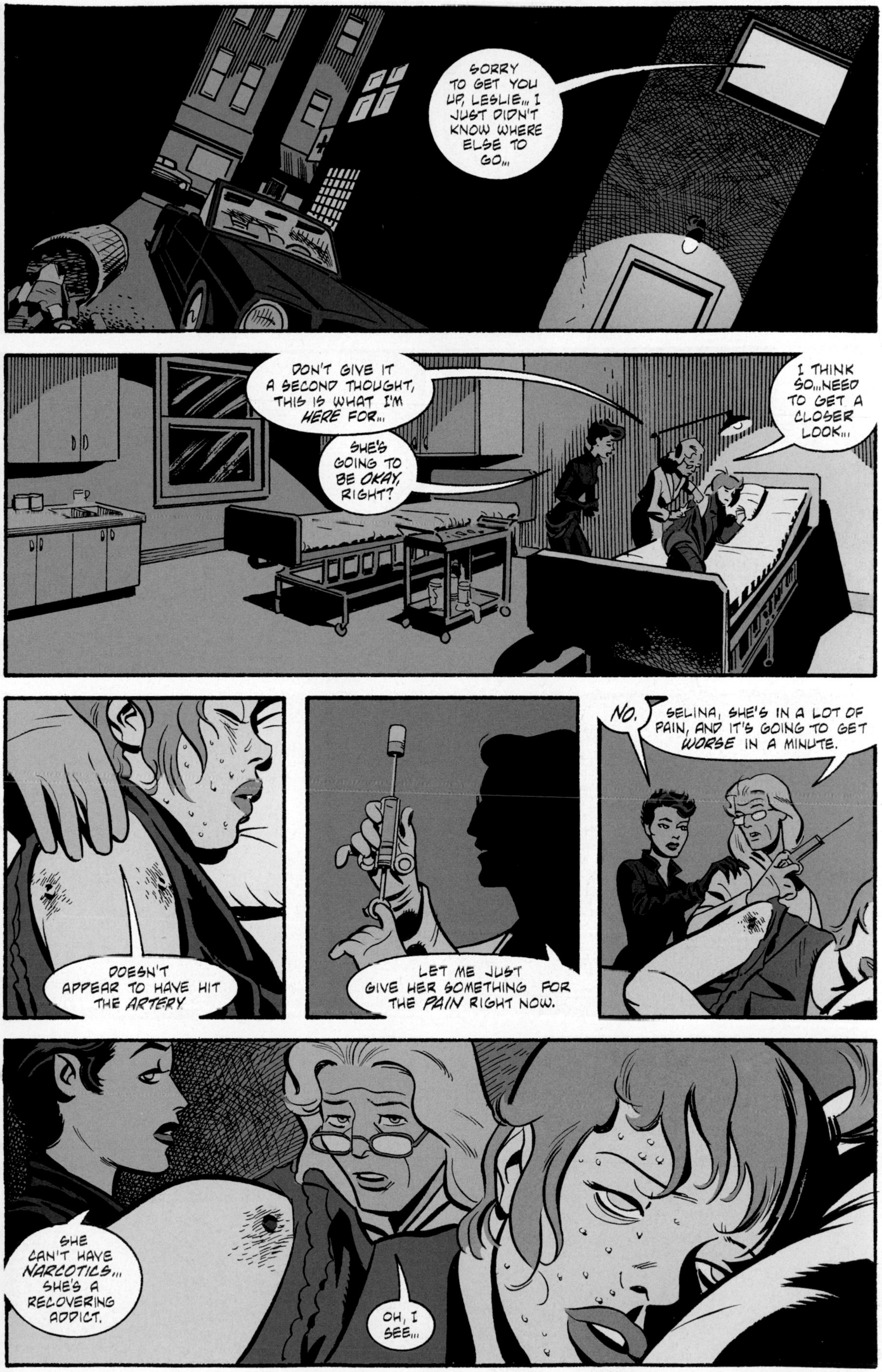
SORRY TO GET YOU UP, LESLIE... I JUST DIDN'T KNOW WHERE ELSE TO GO...
DON'T GIVE IT A SECOND THOUGHT, THIS IS WHAT I'M *HERE* FOR...
SHE'S GOING TO BE *OKAY*, RIGHT?
I THINK SO...NEED TO GET A CLOSER LOOK...
DOESN'T APPEAR TO HAVE HIT THE *ARTERY*
LET ME JUST GIVE HER SOMETHING FOR THE *PAIN* RIGHT NOW.
NO.
SELINA, SHE'S IN A LOT OF PAIN, AND IT'S GOING TO GET *WORSE* IN A MINUTE.
SHE CAN'T HAVE *NARCOTICS*... SHE'S A RECOVERING ADDICT.
OH, I SEE...

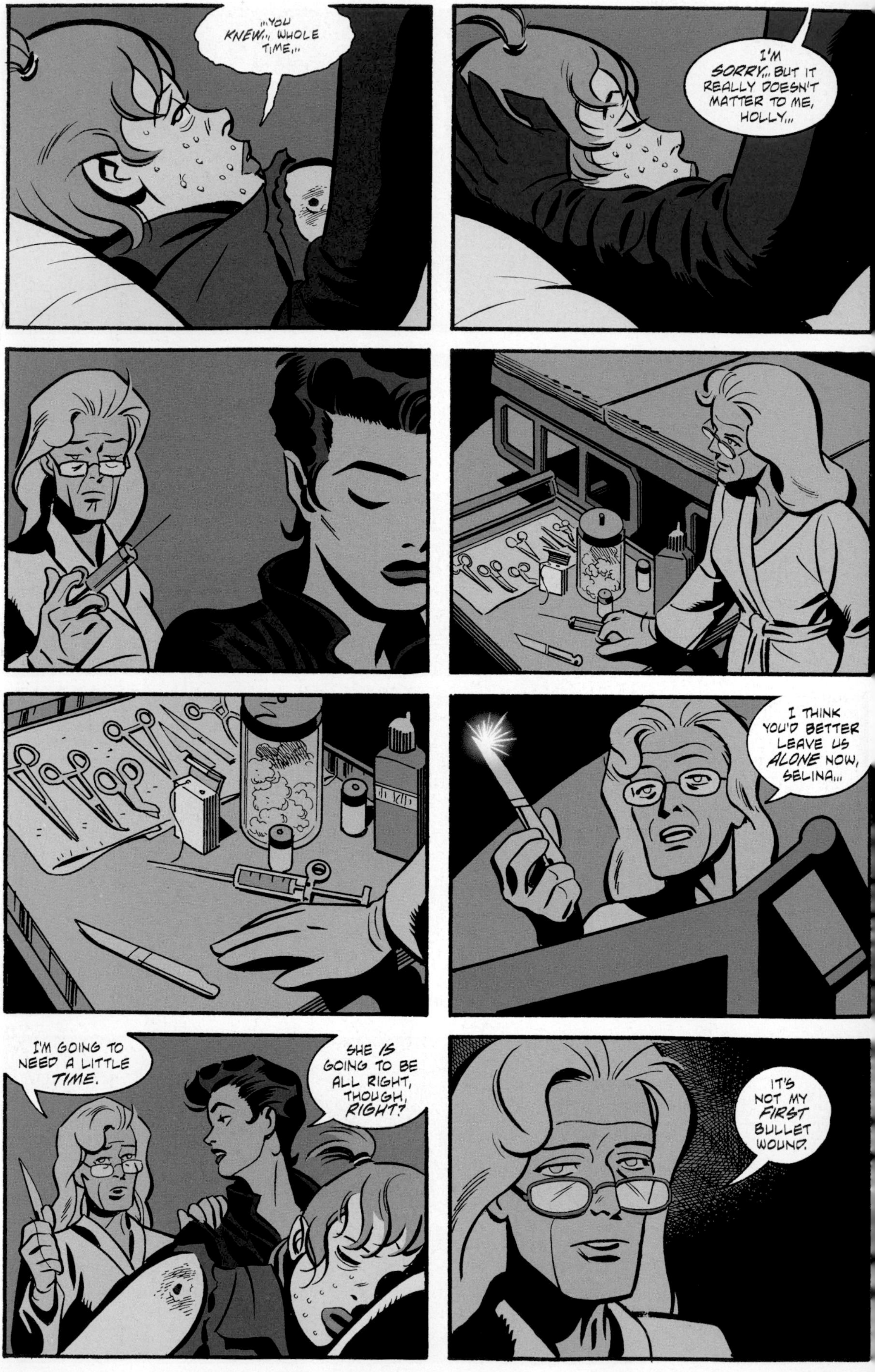
...YOU KNEW... WHOLE TIME...
I'M SORRY... BUT IT REALLY DOESN'T MATTER TO ME, HOLLY...
I THINK YOU'D BETTER LEAVE US ALONE NOW, SELINA...
I'M GOING TO NEED A LITTLE TIME.
SHE IS GOING TO BE ALL RIGHT, THOUGH, RIGHT?
IT'S NOT MY FIRST BULLET WOUND.

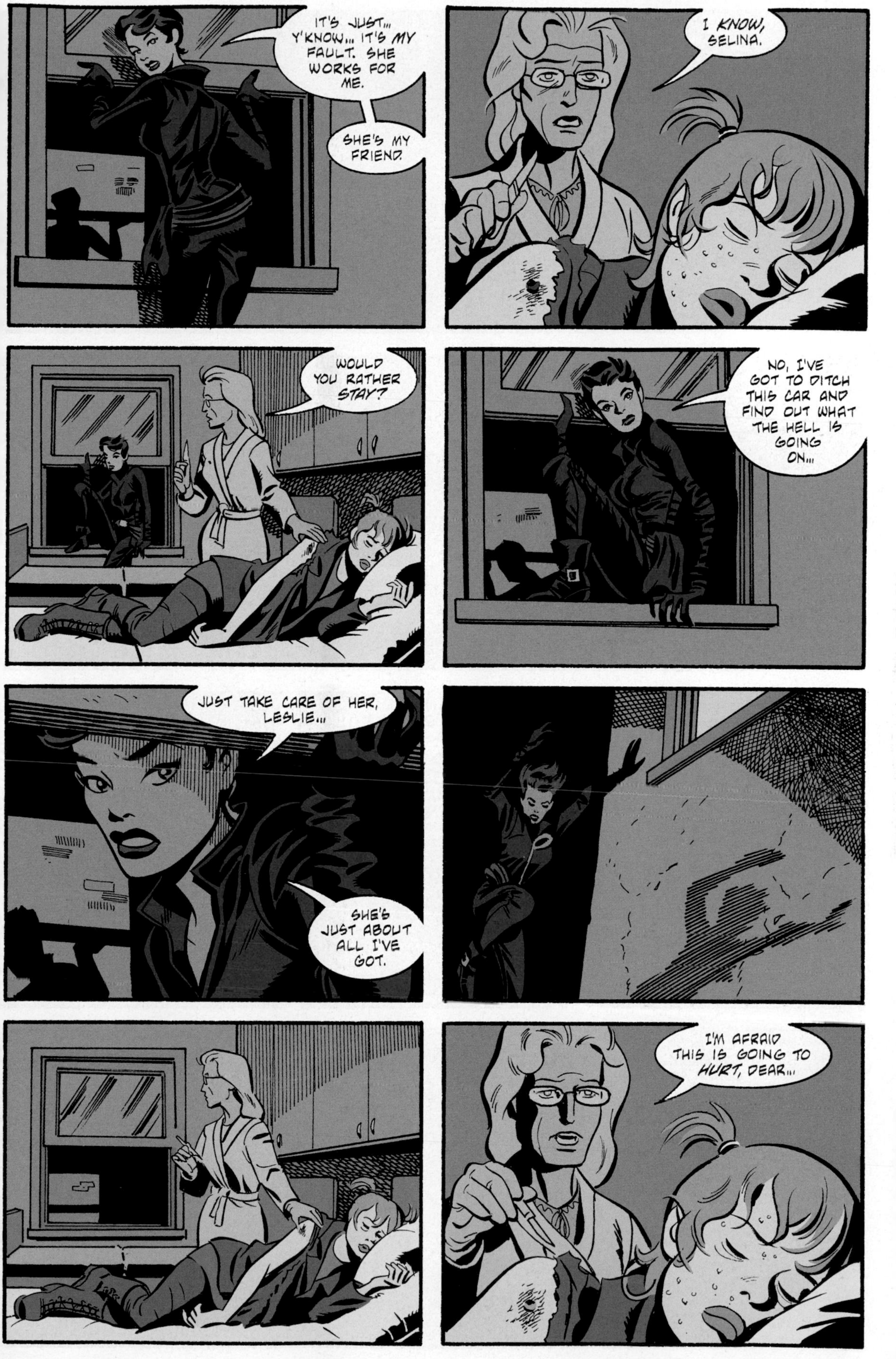
IT'S JUST... Y'KNOW... IT'S MY FAULT. SHE WORKS FOR ME.
SHE'S MY FRIEND.
I KNOW, SELINA.
WOULD YOU RATHER STAY?
NO, I'VE GOT TO DITCH THIS CAR AND FIND OUT WHAT THE HELL IS GOING ON...
JUST TAKE CARE OF HER, LESLIE...
SHE'S JUST ABOUT ALL I'VE GOT.
I'M AFRAID THIS IS GOING TO HURT, DEAR...

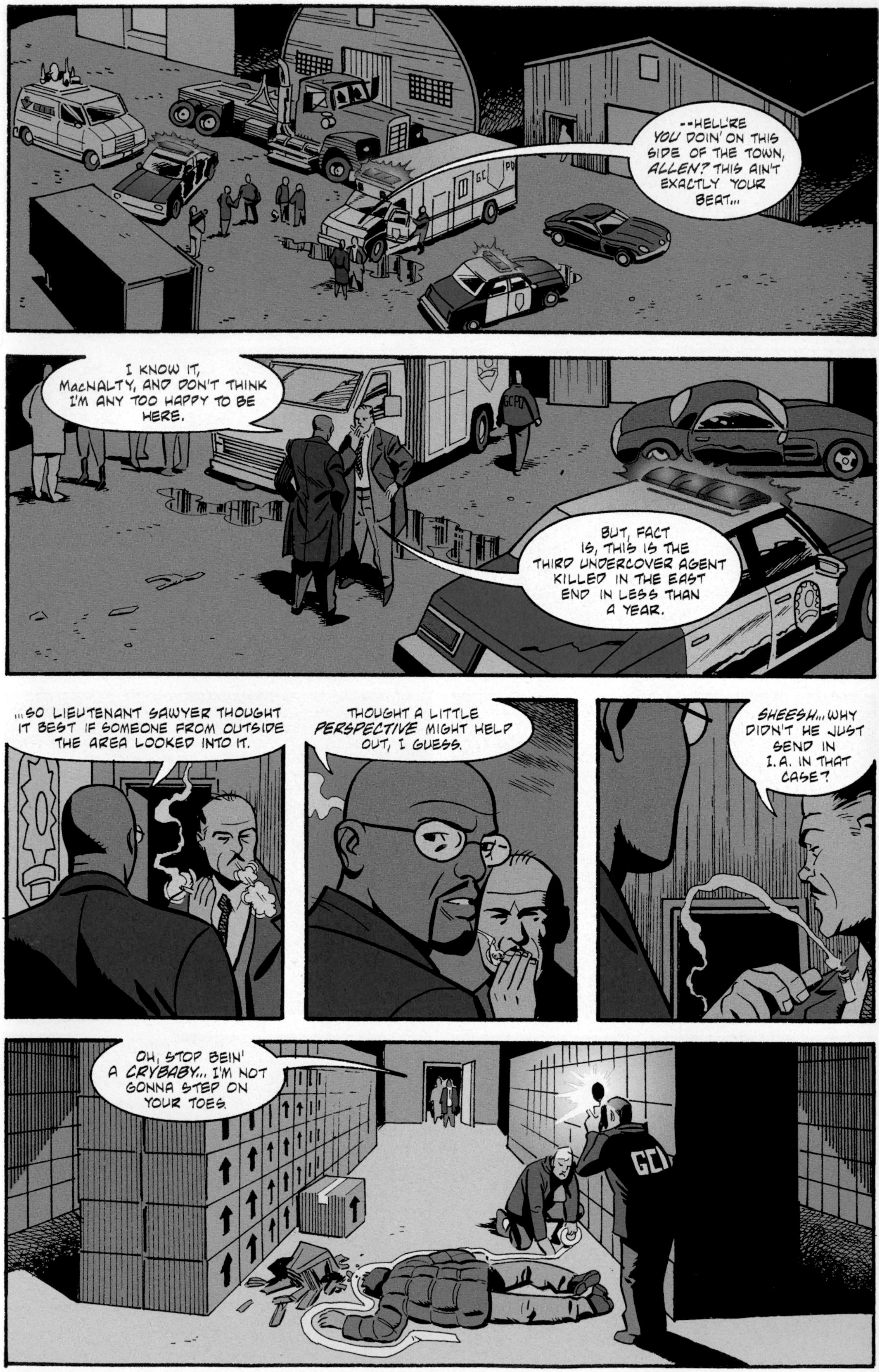
--HELL'RE YOU DOIN' ON THIS SIDE OF THE TOWN, ALLEN? THIS AIN'T EXACTLY YOUR BEAT...
I KNOW IT, MacNALTY, AND DON'T THINK I'M ANY TOO HAPPY TO BE HERE.
BUT, FACT IS, THIS IS THE THIRD UNDERCOVER AGENT KILLED IN THE EAST END IN LESS THAN A YEAR.
...SO LIEUTENANT SAWYER THOUGHT IT BEST IF SOMEONE FROM OUTSIDE THE AREA LOOKED INTO IT.
THOUGHT A LITTLE PERSPECTIVE MIGHT HELP OUT, I GUESS.
SHEESH... WHY DIDN'T HE JUST SEND IN I.A. IN THAT CASE?
OH, STOP BEIN' A CRYBABY... I'M NOT GONNA STEP ON YOUR TOES.

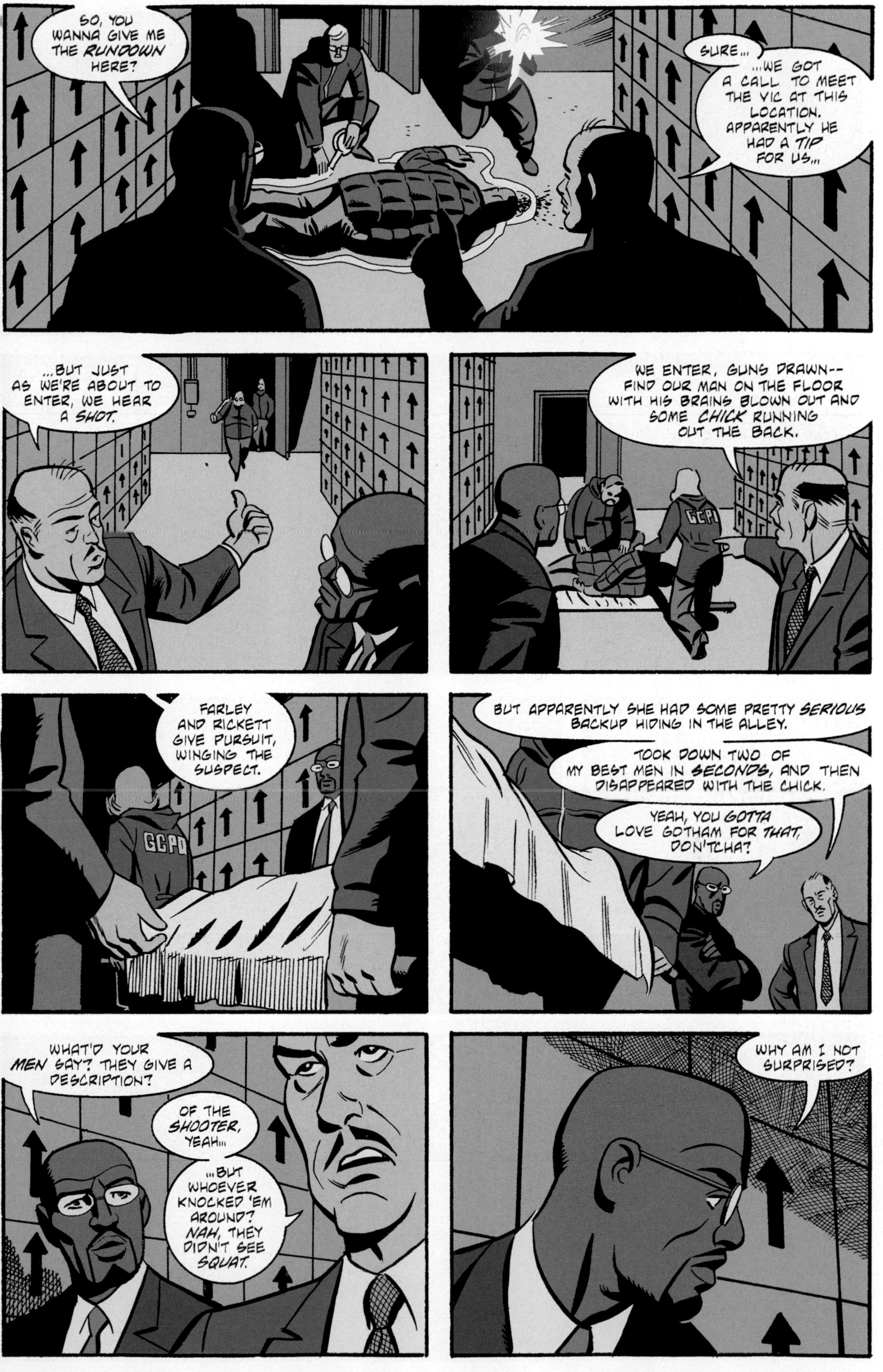
SO, YOU WANNA GIVE ME THE RUNDOWN HERE?
SURE...
...WE GOT A CALL TO MEET THE VIC AT THIS LOCATION. APPARENTLY HE HAD A TIP FOR US...
...BUT JUST AS WE'RE ABOUT TO ENTER, WE HEAR A SHOT.
WE ENTER, GUNS DRAWN-- FIND OUR MAN ON THE FLOOR WITH HIS BRAINS BLOWN OUT AND SOME CHICK RUNNING OUT THE BACK.
FARLEY AND RICKETT GIVE PURSUIT, WINGING THE SUSPECT.
BUT APPARENTLY SHE HAD SOME PRETTY SERIOUS BACKUP HIDING IN THE ALLEY.
TOOK DOWN TWO OF MY BEST MEN IN SECONDS, AND THEN DISAPPEARED WITH THE CHICK.
YEAH, YOU GOTTA LOVE GOTHAM FOR THAT, DON'TCHA?
WHAT'D YOUR MEN SAY? THEY GIVE A DESCRIPTION?
OF THE SHOOTER, YEAH...
...BUT WHOEVER KNOCKED 'EM AROUND? NAH, THEY DIDN'T SEE SQUAT.
WHY AM I NOT SURPRISED?

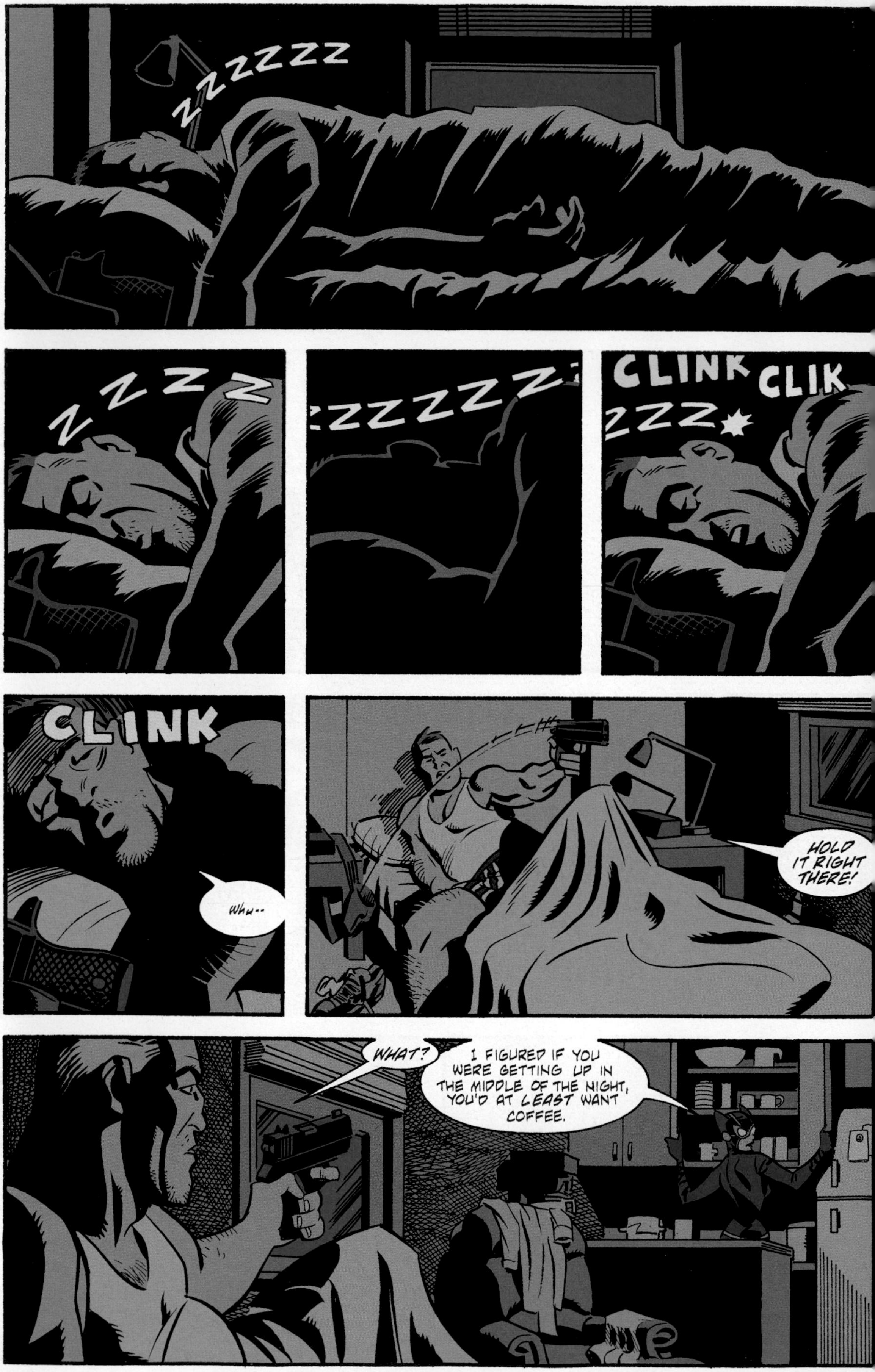

ZZZZZZ
ZZZZ
ZZZZZZZ
CLINK CLIK
ZZZ
CLINK
Whw--
HOLD IT RIGHT THERE!
WHAT?
I FIGURED IF YOU WERE GETTING UP IN THE MIDDLE OF THE NIGHT, YOU'D AT LEAST WANT COFFEE.

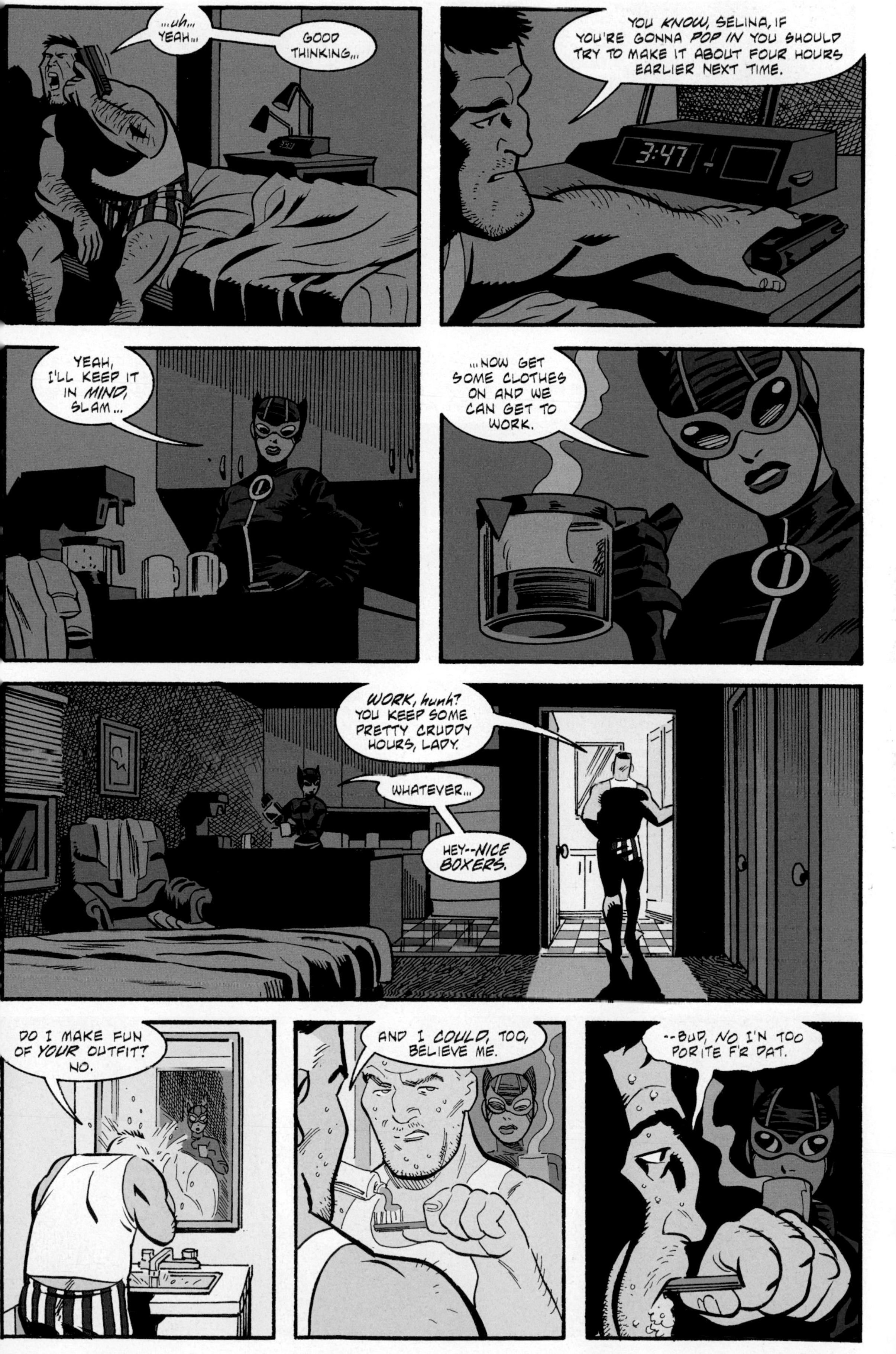

...uh... YEAH...
GOOD THINKING...
YOU KNOW, SELINA, IF YOU'RE GONNA POP IN YOU SHOULD TRY TO MAKE IT ABOUT FOUR HOURS EARLIER NEXT TIME.
3:47
YEAH, I'LL KEEP IT IN MIND, SLAM...
...NOW GET SOME CLOTHES ON AND WE CAN GET TO WORK.
WORK, hunh? YOU KEEP SOME PRETTY CRUDDY HOURS, LADY.
WHATEVER...
HEY--NICE BOXERS.
DO I MAKE FUN OF YOUR OUTFIT? NO.
AND I COULD, TOO, BELIEVE ME.
--BUD, NO I'N TOO PORITE F'R DAT.

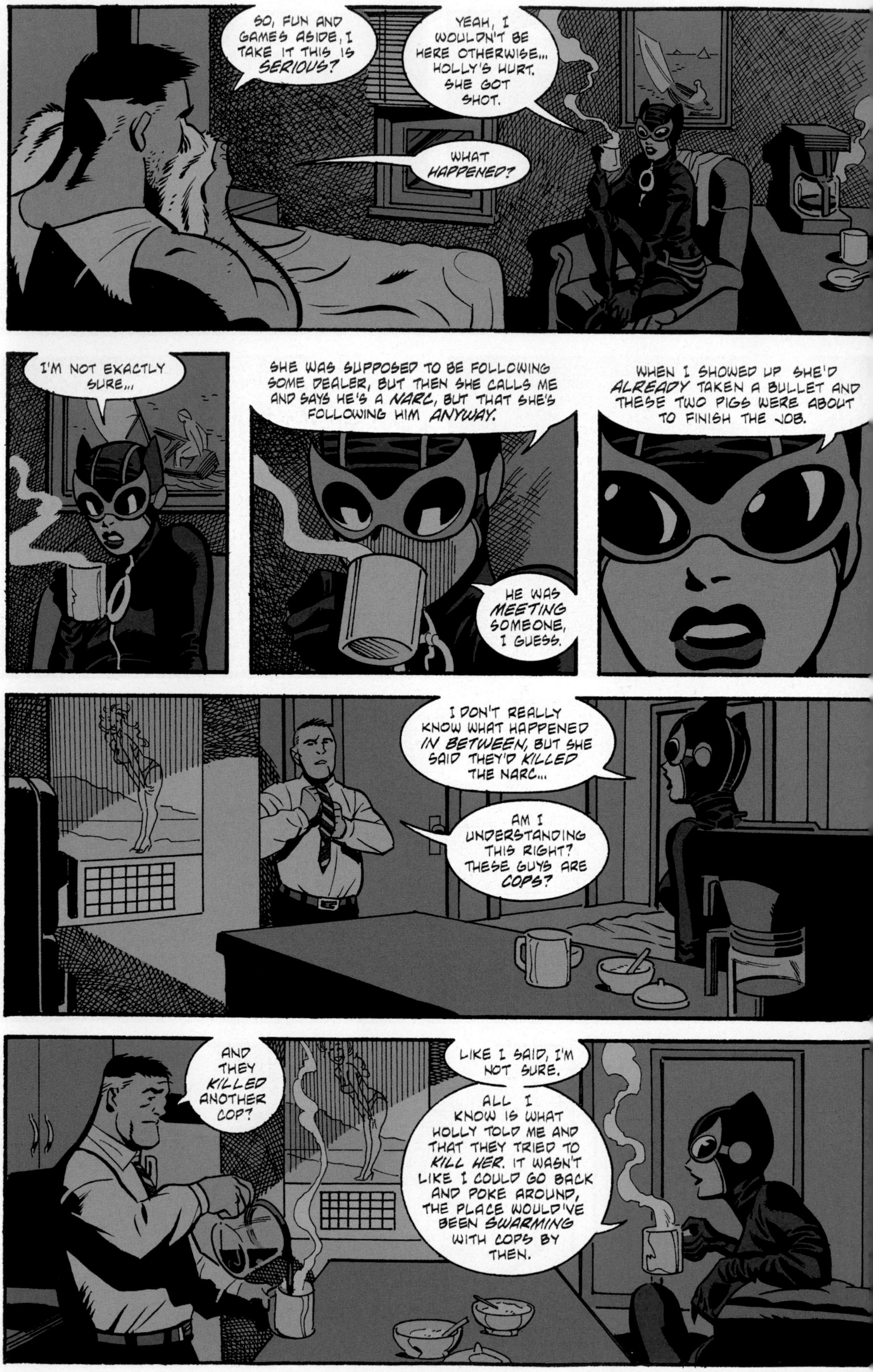
SO, FUN AND GAMES ASIDE, I TAKE IT THIS IS SERIOUS?
YEAH, I WOULDN'T BE HERE OTHERWISE... HOLLY'S HURT. SHE GOT SHOT.
WHAT HAPPENED?
I'M NOT EXACTLY SURE...
SHE WAS SUPPOSED TO BE FOLLOWING SOME DEALER, BUT THEN SHE CALLS ME AND SAYS HE'S A NARC, BUT THAT SHE'S FOLLOWING HIM ANYWAY.
HE WAS MEETING SOMEONE, I GUESS.
WHEN I SHOWED UP SHE'D ALREADY TAKEN A BULLET AND THESE TWO PIGS WERE ABOUT TO FINISH THE JOB.
I DON'T REALLY KNOW WHAT HAPPENED IN BETWEEN, BUT SHE SAID THEY'D KILLED THE NARC...
AM I UNDERSTANDING THIS RIGHT? THESE GUYS ARE COPS?
AND THEY KILLED ANOTHER COP?
LIKE I SAID, I'M NOT SURE.
ALL I KNOW IS WHAT HOLLY TOLD ME AND THAT THEY TRIED TO KILL HER. IT WASN'T LIKE I COULD GO BACK AND POKE AROUND, THE PLACE WOULD'VE BEEN SWARMING WITH COPS BY THEN.

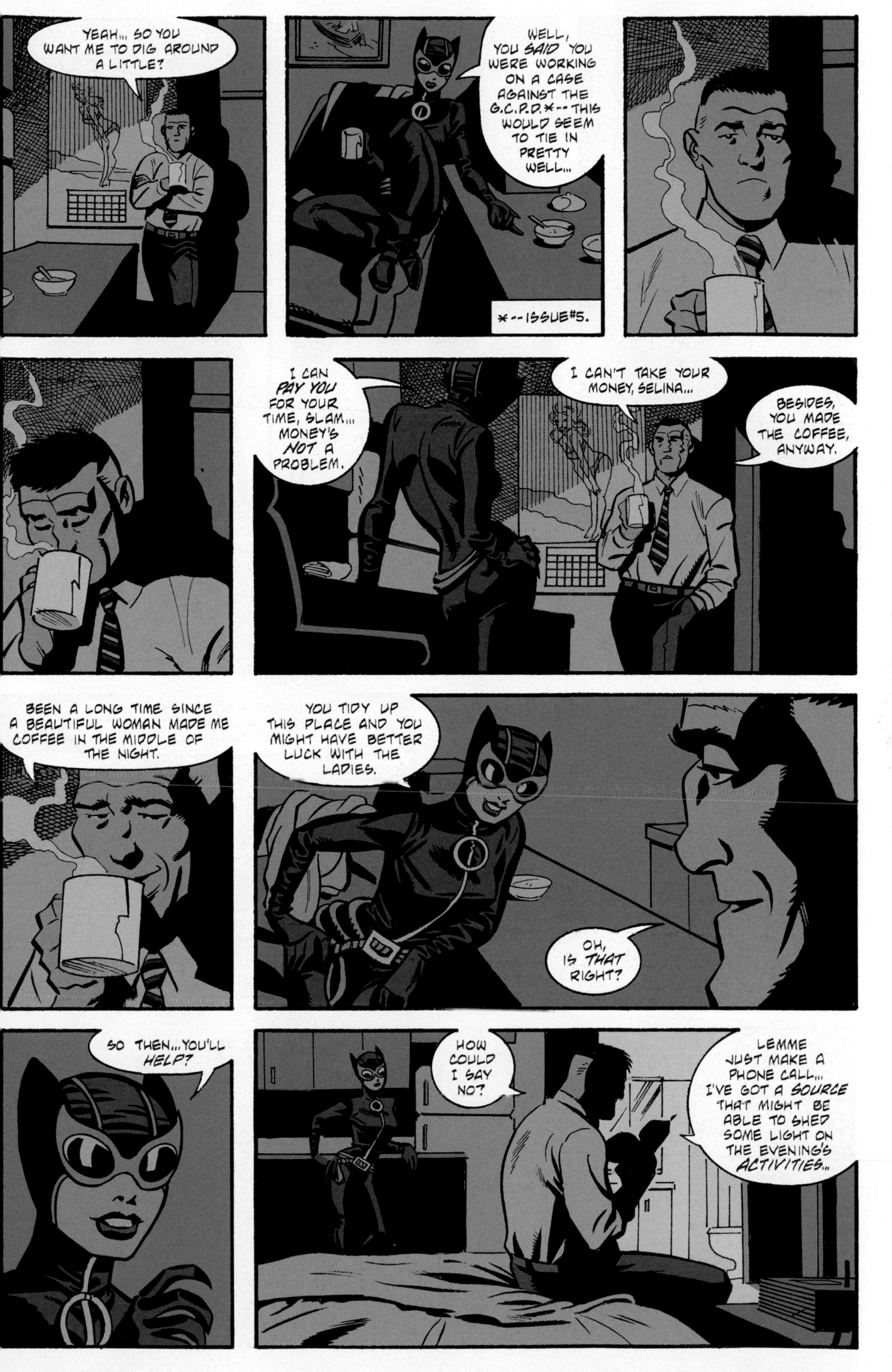
YEAH... SO YOU WANT ME TO DIG AROUND A LITTLE?
WELL, YOU SAID YOU WERE WORKING ON A CASE AGAINST THE G.C.P.D.* -- THIS WOULD SEEM TO TIE IN PRETTY WELL...
*--ISSUE#5.
I CAN PAY YOU FOR YOUR TIME, SLAM... MONEY'S NOT A PROBLEM.
I CAN'T TAKE YOUR MONEY, SELINA...
BESIDES, YOU MADE THE COFFEE, ANYWAY.
BEEN A LONG TIME SINCE A BEAUTIFUL WOMAN MADE ME COFFEE IN THE MIDDLE OF THE NIGHT.
YOU TIDY UP THIS PLACE AND YOU MIGHT HAVE BETTER LUCK WITH THE LADIES.
OH, IS THAT RIGHT?
SO THEN... YOU'LL HELP?
HOW COULD I SAY NO?
LEMME JUST MAKE A PHONE CALL... I'VE GOT A SOURCE THAT MIGHT BE ABLE TO SHED SOME LIGHT ON THE EVENING'S ACTIVITIES...

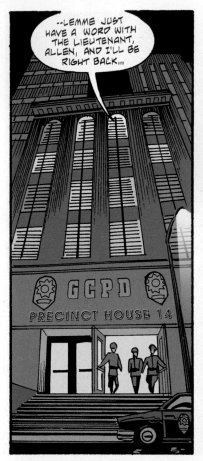

--LEMME JUST HAVE A WORD WITH THE LIEUTENANT, ALLEN, AND I'LL BE RIGHT BACK...

GCPD

PRECINCT HOUSE 14

TAKE YOUR TIME, SERGEANT.

RING RING

DETECTIVES, FARRUCCI HERE.

OH, GIVE ME A BREAK, IT'S THE MIDDLE OF THE DAMN NIGHT...

...YEAH YEAH... ALL RIGHT. GIMME A HALF HOUR.

UNBELIEVABLE, MY MOTHER-IN-LAW NEEDS ME TO PICK UP HER PRESCRIPTION AT THIS HOUR.

YEAH, IT'S ALWAYS SOMETHING, ISN'T IT?

WITH THIS WOMAN IT IS...

DON'T LET MacNALTY YANK YOUR CHAIN TOO MUCH, ALLEN.

NOT TO WORRY, DETECTIVE FARRUCCI, I'VE HANDLED HIS TYPE BEFORE.

-- I MEAN HOW AM I SUPPOSED TO DO ANYTHING WITH THIS M.C.U. INTERLOPER NOSING AROUND?

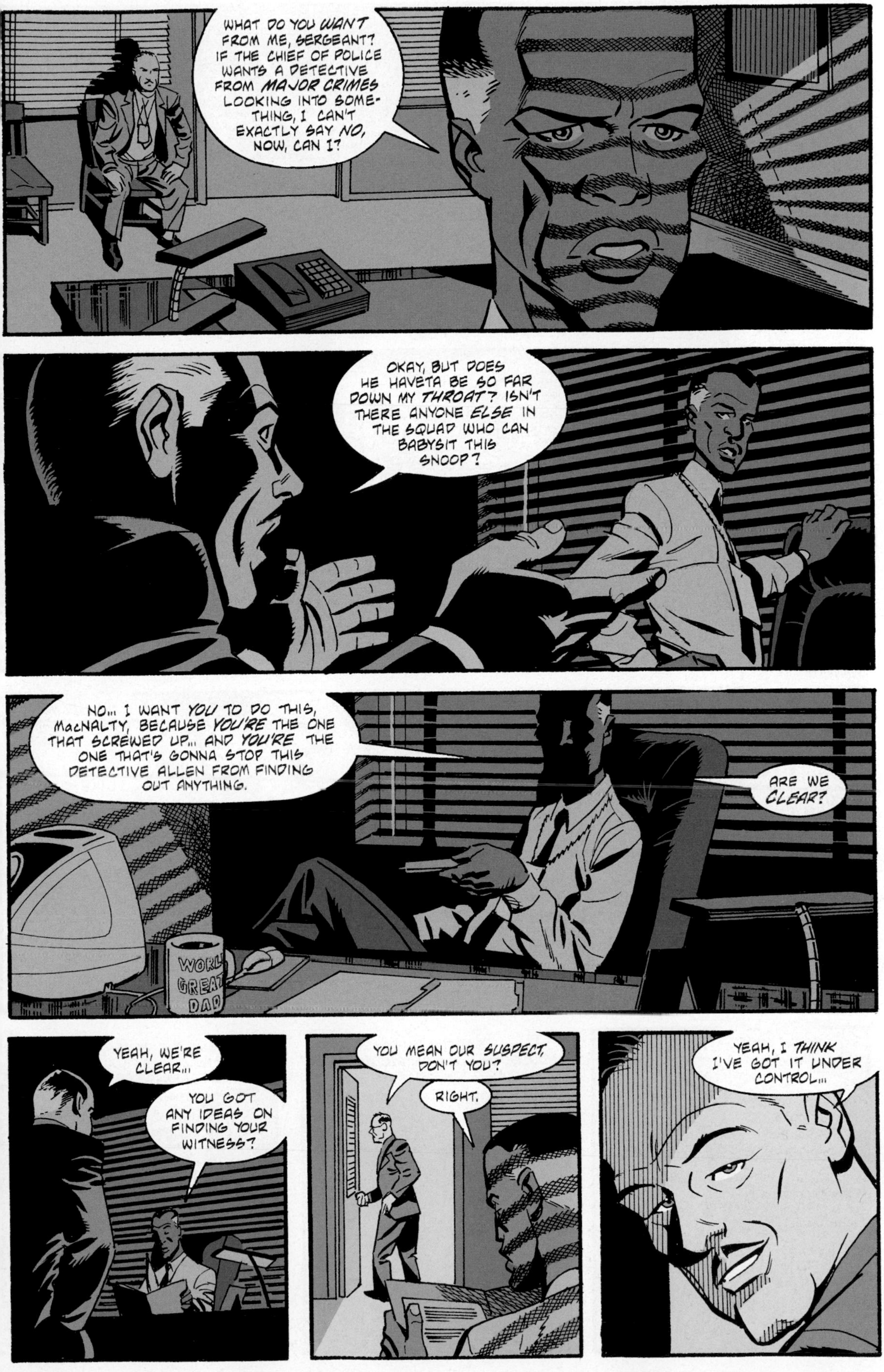
WHAT DO YOU WANT FROM ME, SERGEANT? IF THE CHIEF OF POLICE WANTS A DETECTIVE FROM MAJOR CRIMES LOOKING INTO SOME-THING, I CAN'T EXACTLY SAY NO, NOW, CAN I?
OKAY, BUT DOES HE HAVETA BE SO FAR DOWN MY THROAT? ISN'T THERE ANYONE ELSE IN THE SQUAD WHO CAN BABYSIT THIS SNOOP?
NO... I WANT YOU TO DO THIS, MacNALTY, BECAUSE YOU'RE THE ONE THAT SCREWED UP... AND YOU'RE THE ONE THAT'S GONNA STOP THIS DETECTIVE ALLEN FROM FINDING OUT ANYTHING.
ARE WE CLEAR?
WORLD'S GREATEST DAD
YEAH, WE'RE CLEAR...
YOU GOT ANY IDEAS ON FINDING YOUR WITNESS?
YOU MEAN OUR SUSPECT, DON'T YOU?
RIGHT.
YEAH, I THINK I'VE GOT IT UNDER CONTROL...

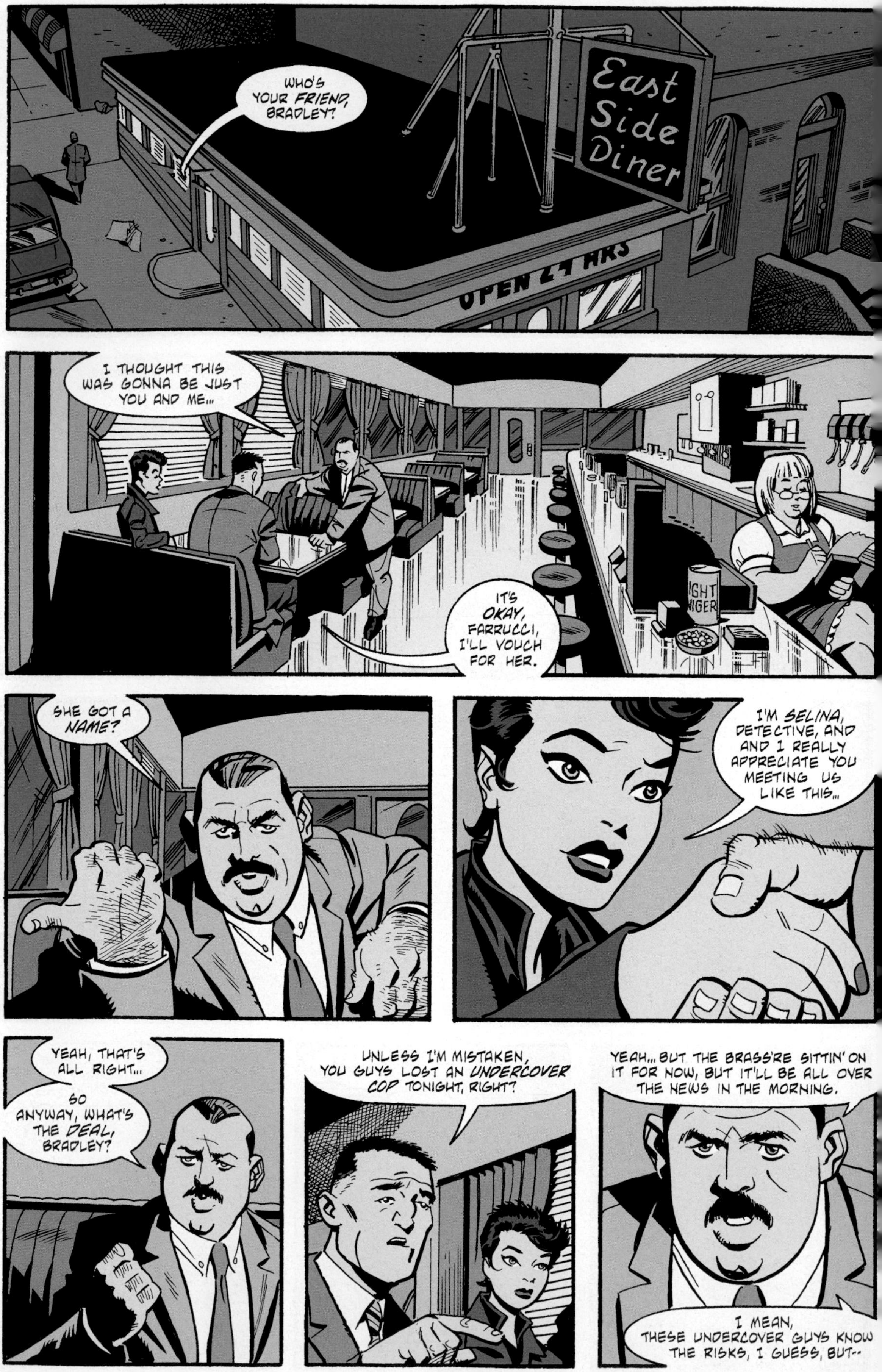

East Side Diner
OPEN 24 HRS
WHO'S YOUR FRIEND, BRADLEY?
I THOUGHT THIS WAS GONNA BE JUST YOU AND ME...
IT'S OKAY, FARRUCCI, I'LL VOUCH FOR HER.
SHE GOT A NAME?
I'M SELINA, DETECTIVE, AND AND I REALLY APPRECIATE YOU MEETING US LIKE THIS...
YEAH, THAT'S ALL RIGHT...
SO ANYWAY, WHAT'S THE DEAL, BRADLEY?
UNLESS I'M MISTAKEN, YOU GUYS LOST AN UNDERCOVER COP TONIGHT, RIGHT?
YEAH... BUT THE BRASS'RE SITTIN' ON IT FOR NOW, BUT IT'LL BE ALL OVER THE NEWS IN THE MORNING.
I MEAN, THESE UNDERCOVER GUYS KNOW THE RISKS, I GUESS, BUT--

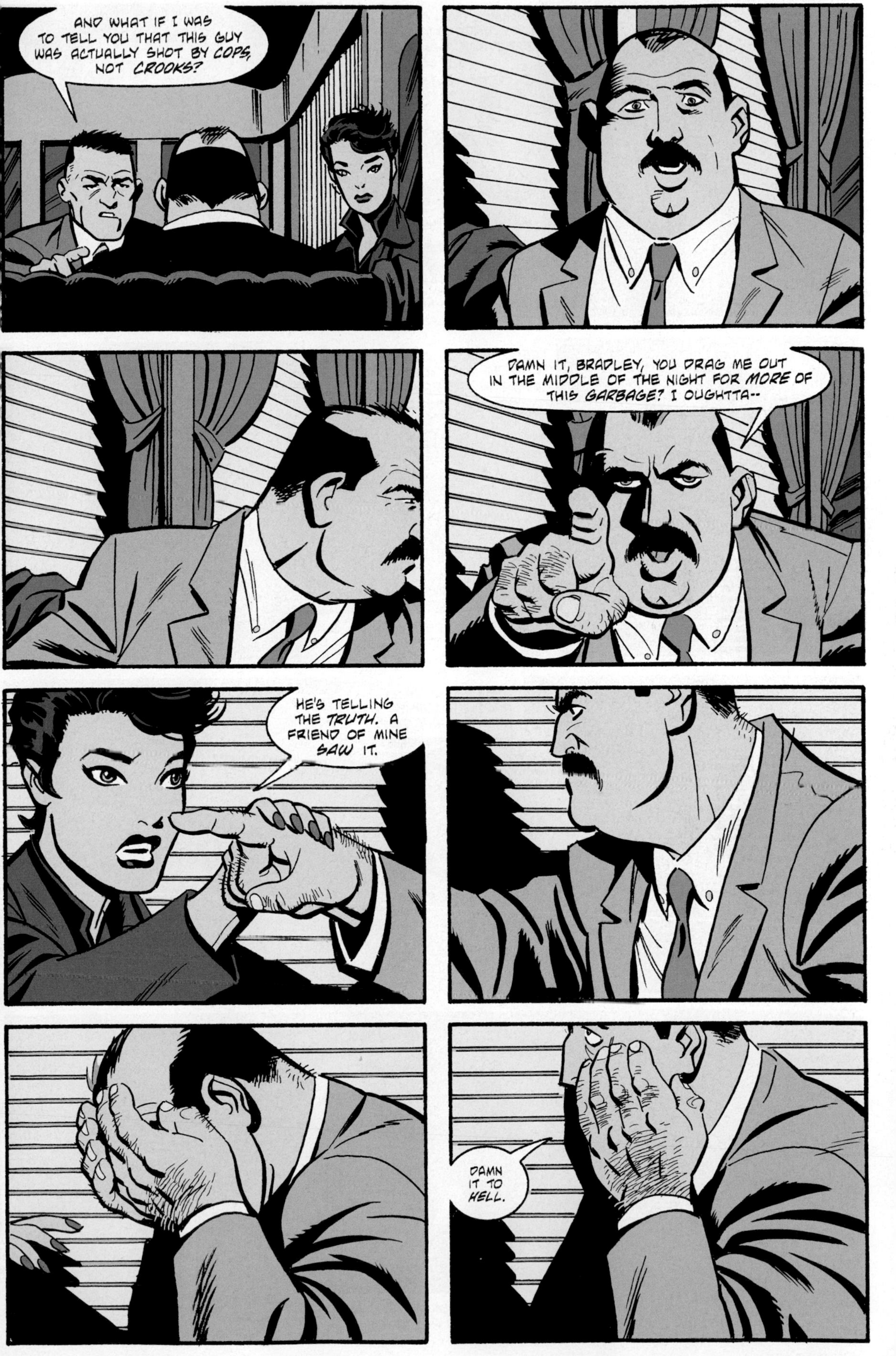
AND WHAT IF I WAS TO TELL YOU THAT THIS GUY WAS ACTUALLY SHOT BY *COPS*, NOT *CROOKS*?
DAMN IT, BRADLEY, YOU DRAG ME OUT IN THE MIDDLE OF THE NIGHT FOR *MORE* OF THIS *GARBAGE*? I OUGHTTA--
HE'S TELLING THE *TRUTH*. A FRIEND OF MINE *SAW* IT.
DAMN IT TO *HELL*.

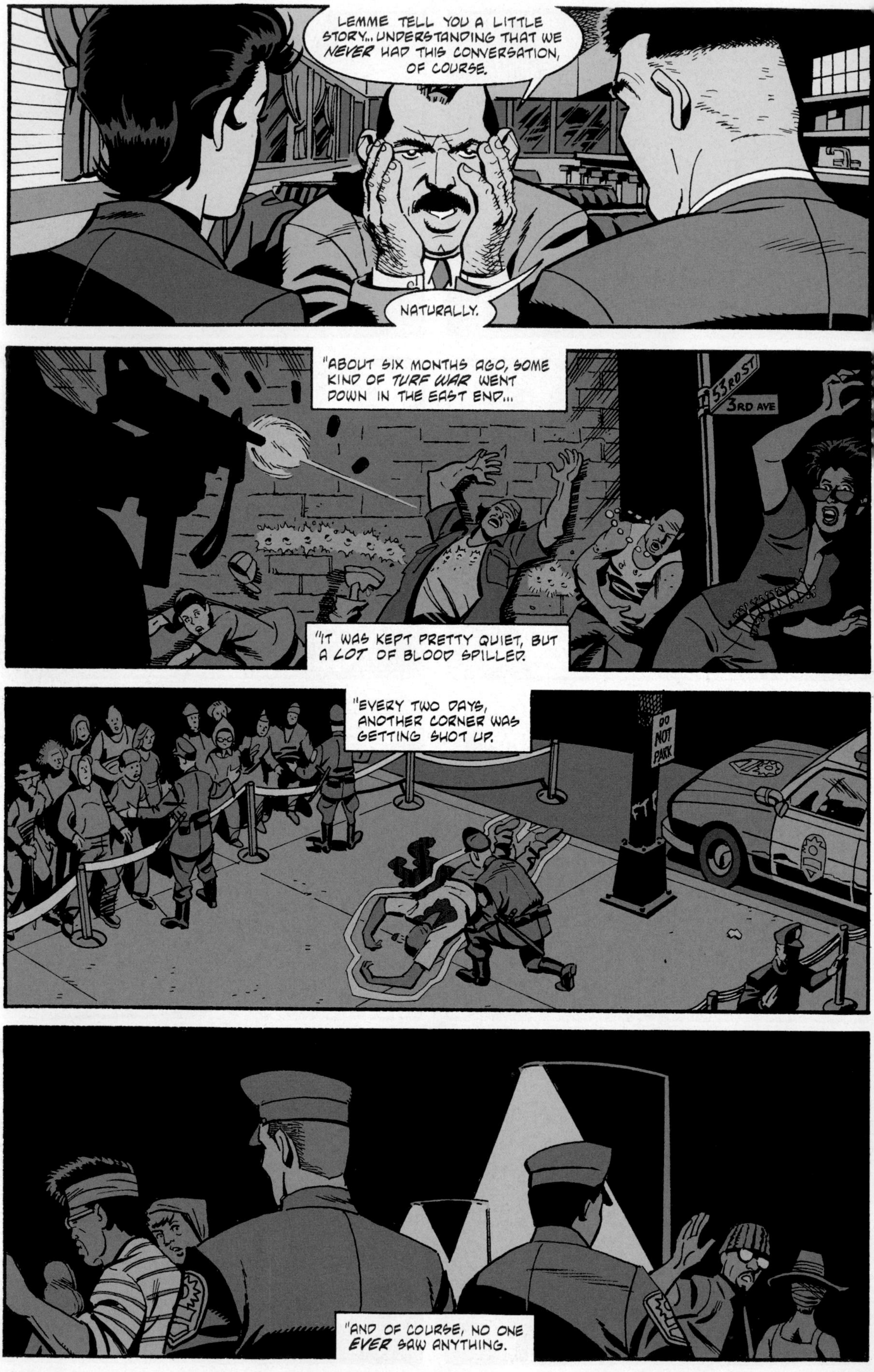
LEMME TELL YOU A LITTLE STORY... UNDERSTANDING THAT WE NEVER HAD THIS CONVERSATION, OF COURSE.
NATURALLY.
"ABOUT SIX MONTHS AGO, SOME KIND OF TURF WAR WENT DOWN IN THE EAST END...
53RD ST
3RD AVE
"IT WAS KEPT PRETTY QUIET, BUT A LOT OF BLOOD SPILLED.
"EVERY TWO DAYS, ANOTHER CORNER WAS GETTING SHOT UP.
DO NOT PARK
"AND OF COURSE, NO ONE EVER SAW ANYTHING.

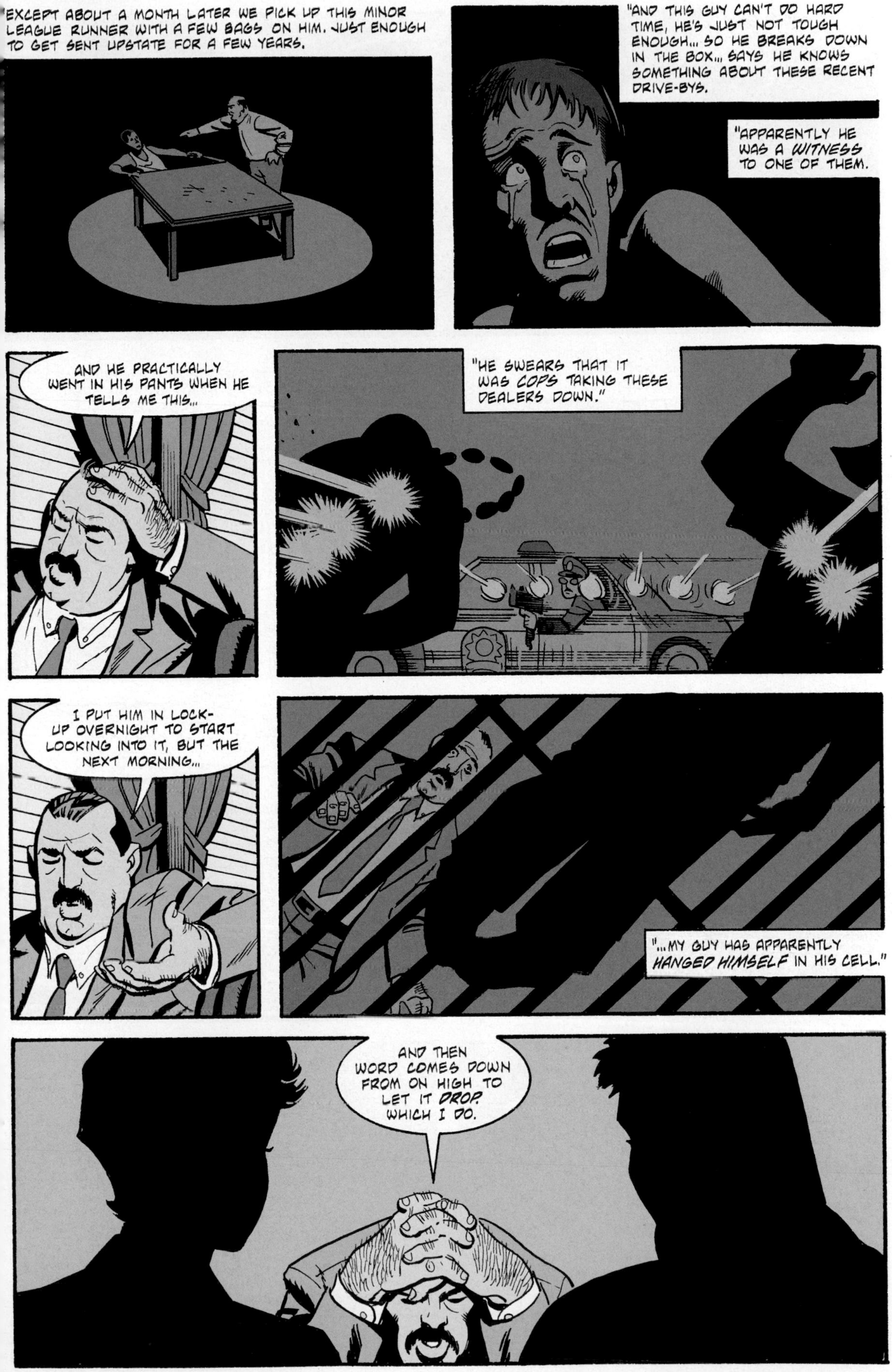
"EXCEPT ABOUT A MONTH LATER WE PICK UP THIS MINOR LEAGUE RUNNER WITH A FEW BAGS ON HIM. JUST ENOUGH TO GET SENT UPSTATE FOR A FEW YEARS.
"AND THIS GUY CAN'T DO HARD TIME, HE'S JUST NOT TOUGH ENOUGH... SO HE BREAKS DOWN IN THE BOX... SAYS HE KNOWS SOMETHING ABOUT THESE RECENT DRIVE-BYS.
"APPARENTLY HE WAS A *WITNESS* TO ONE OF THEM.
AND HE PRACTICALLY WENT IN HIS PANTS WHEN HE TELLS ME THIS...
"HE SWEARS THAT IT WAS *COPS* TAKING THESE DEALERS DOWN."
I PUT HIM IN LOCK-UP OVERNIGHT TO START LOOKING INTO IT, BUT THE NEXT MORNING...
"...MY GUY HAS APPARENTLY *HANGED HIMSELF* IN HIS CELL."
AND THEN WORD COMES DOWN FROM ON HIGH TO LET IT *DROP.* WHICH I DO.

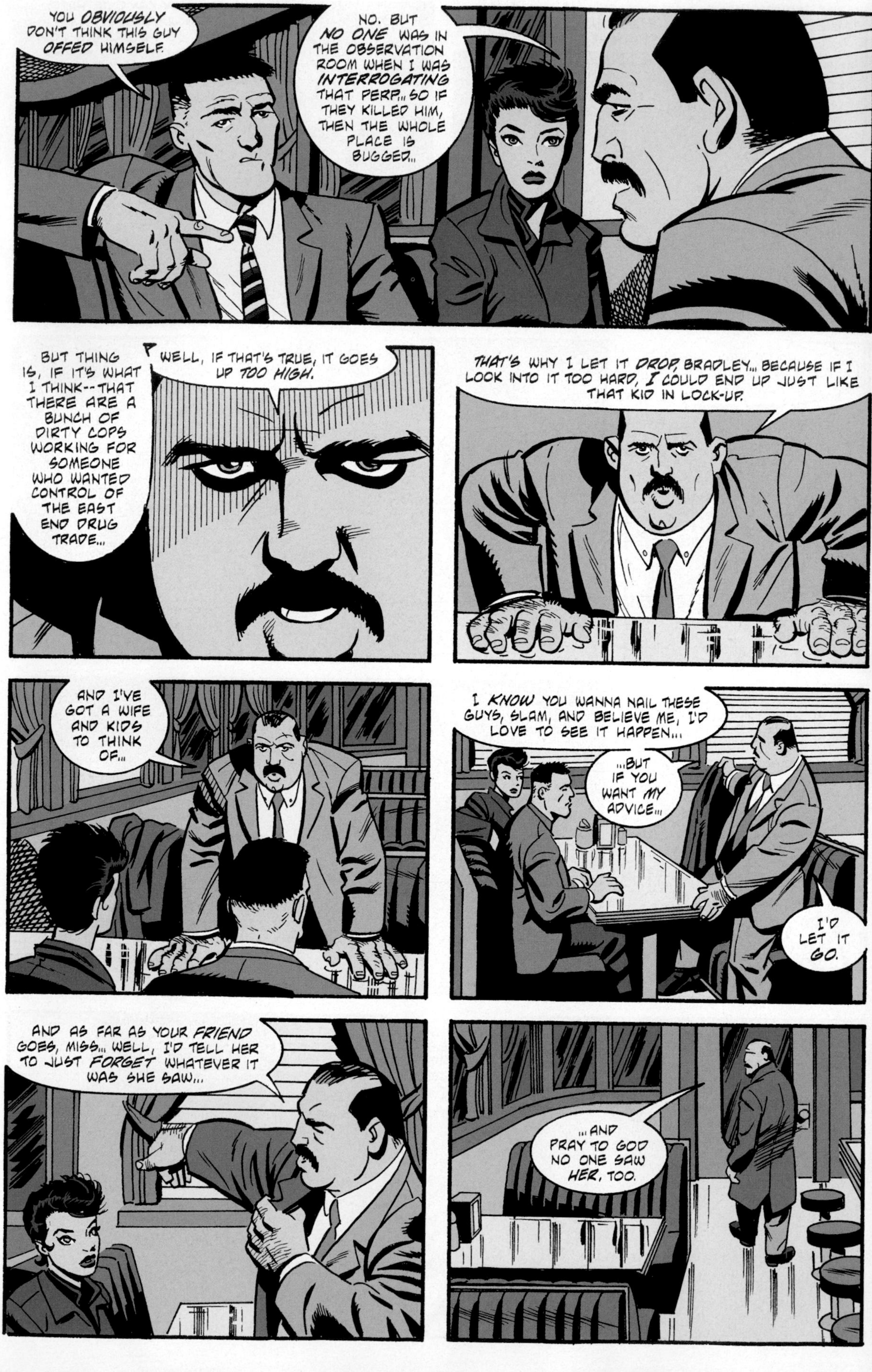
YOU OBVIOUSLY DON'T THINK THIS GUY OFFED HIMSELF.
NO. BUT NO ONE WAS IN THE OBSERVATION ROOM WHEN I WAS INTERROGATING THAT PERP... SO IF THEY KILLED HIM, THEN THE WHOLE PLACE IS BUGGED...
BUT THING IS, IF IT'S WHAT I THINK--THAT THERE ARE A BUNCH OF DIRTY COPS WORKING FOR SOMEONE WHO WANTED CONTROL OF THE EAST END DRUG TRADE...
WELL, IF THAT'S TRUE, IT GOES UP TOO HIGH.
THAT'S WHY I LET IT DROP, BRADLEY... BECAUSE IF I LOOK INTO IT TOO HARD, I COULD END UP JUST LIKE THAT KID IN LOCK-UP.
AND I'VE GOT A WIFE AND KIDS TO THINK OF...
I KNOW YOU WANNA NAIL THESE GUYS, SLAM, AND BELIEVE ME, I'D LOVE TO SEE IT HAPPEN...
...BUT IF YOU WANT MY ADVICE...
I'D LET IT GO.
AND AS FAR AS YOUR FRIEND GOES, MISS... WELL, I'D TELL HER TO JUST FORGET WHATEVER IT WAS SHE SAW...
...AND PRAY TO GOD NO ONE SAW HER, TOO.

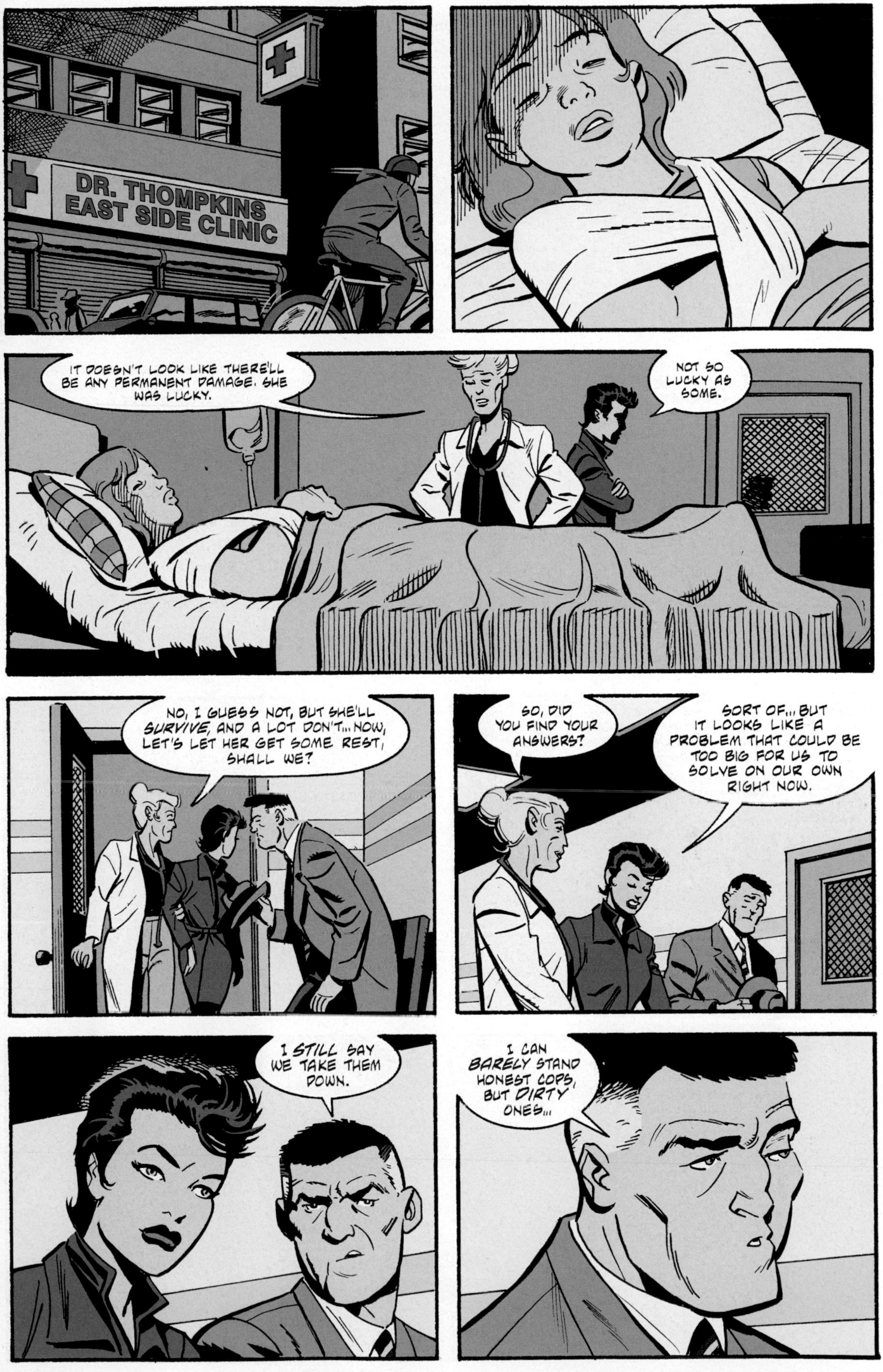
DR. THOMPKINS
EAST SIDE CLINIC
IT DOESN'T LOOK LIKE THERE'LL BE ANY PERMANENT DAMAGE. SHE WAS LUCKY.
NOT SO LUCKY AS SOME.
NO, I GUESS NOT, BUT SHE'LL *SURVIVE*, AND A LOT DON'T... NOW, LET'S LET HER GET SOME REST, SHALL WE?
SO, DID YOU FIND YOUR ANSWERS?
SORT OF... BUT IT LOOKS LIKE A PROBLEM THAT COULD BE TOO BIG FOR US TO SOLVE ON OUR OWN RIGHT NOW.
I *STILL* SAY WE TAKE THEM DOWN.
I CAN *BARELY* STAND HONEST COPS, BUT *DIRTY* ONES...

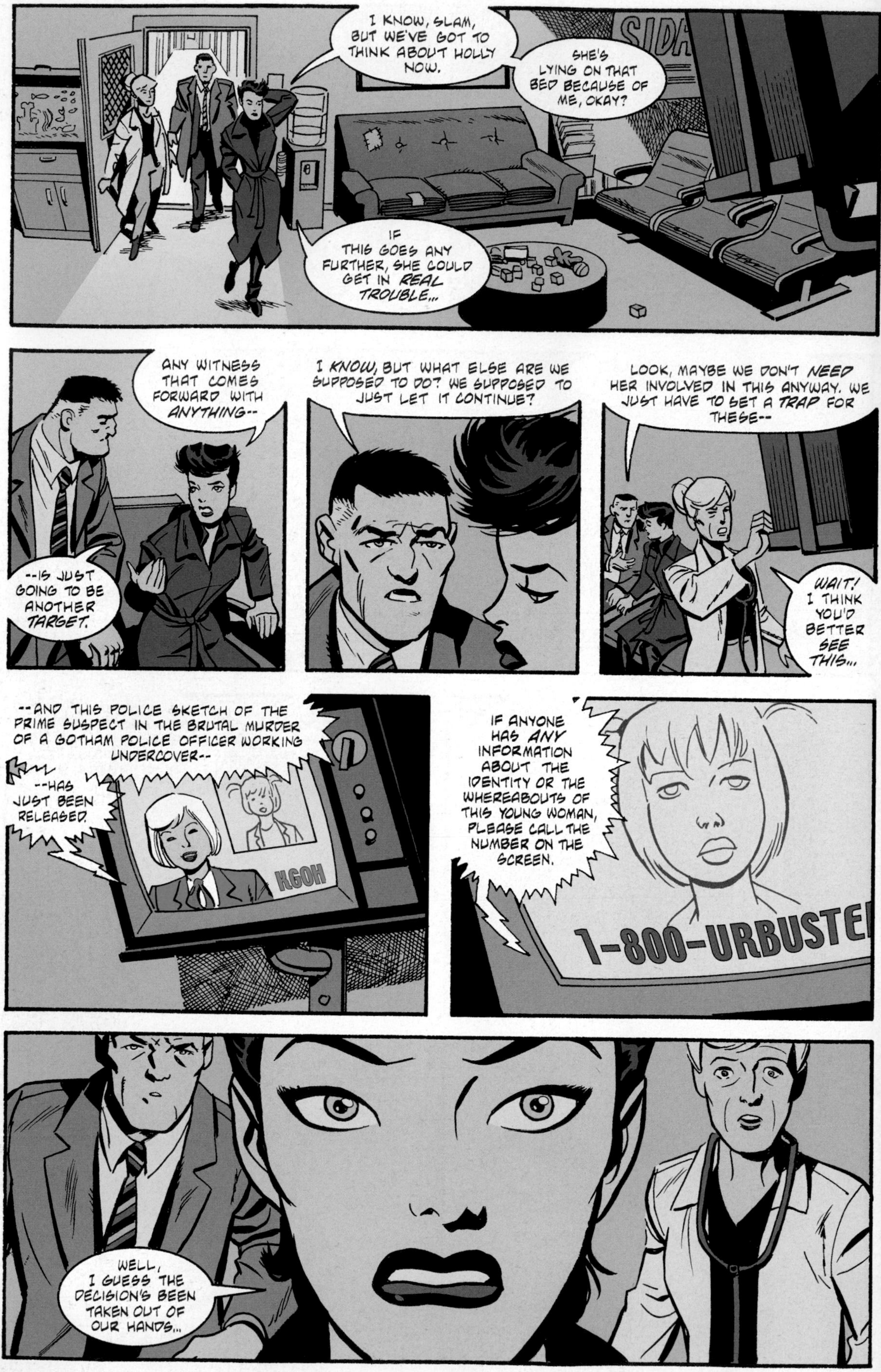
I KNOW, SLAM, BUT WE'VE GOT TO THINK ABOUT HOLLY NOW.
SHE'S LYING ON THAT BED BECAUSE OF ME, OKAY?
IF THIS GOES ANY FURTHER, SHE COULD GET IN REAL TROUBLE...
ANY WITNESS THAT COMES FORWARD WITH ANYTHING--
--IS JUST GOING TO BE ANOTHER TARGET.
I KNOW, BUT WHAT ELSE ARE WE SUPPOSED TO DO? WE SUPPOSED TO JUST LET IT CONTINUE?
LOOK, MAYBE WE DON'T NEED HER INVOLVED IN THIS ANYWAY. WE JUST HAVE TO SET A TRAP FOR THESE--
WAIT! I THINK YOU'D BETTER SEE THIS...
--AND THIS POLICE SKETCH OF THE PRIME SUSPECT IN THE BRUTAL MURDER OF A GOTHAM POLICE OFFICER WORKING UNDERCOVER--
--HAS JUST BEEN RELEASED.
KGOH
IF ANYONE HAS ANY INFORMATION ABOUT THE IDENTITY OR THE WHEREABOUTS OF THIS YOUNG WOMAN, PLEASE CALL THE NUMBER ON THE SCREEN.
1-800-URBUSTE
WELL, I GUESS THE DECISION'S BEEN TAKEN OUT OF OUR HANDS...

Catwoman 8
Cover by Paul Pope

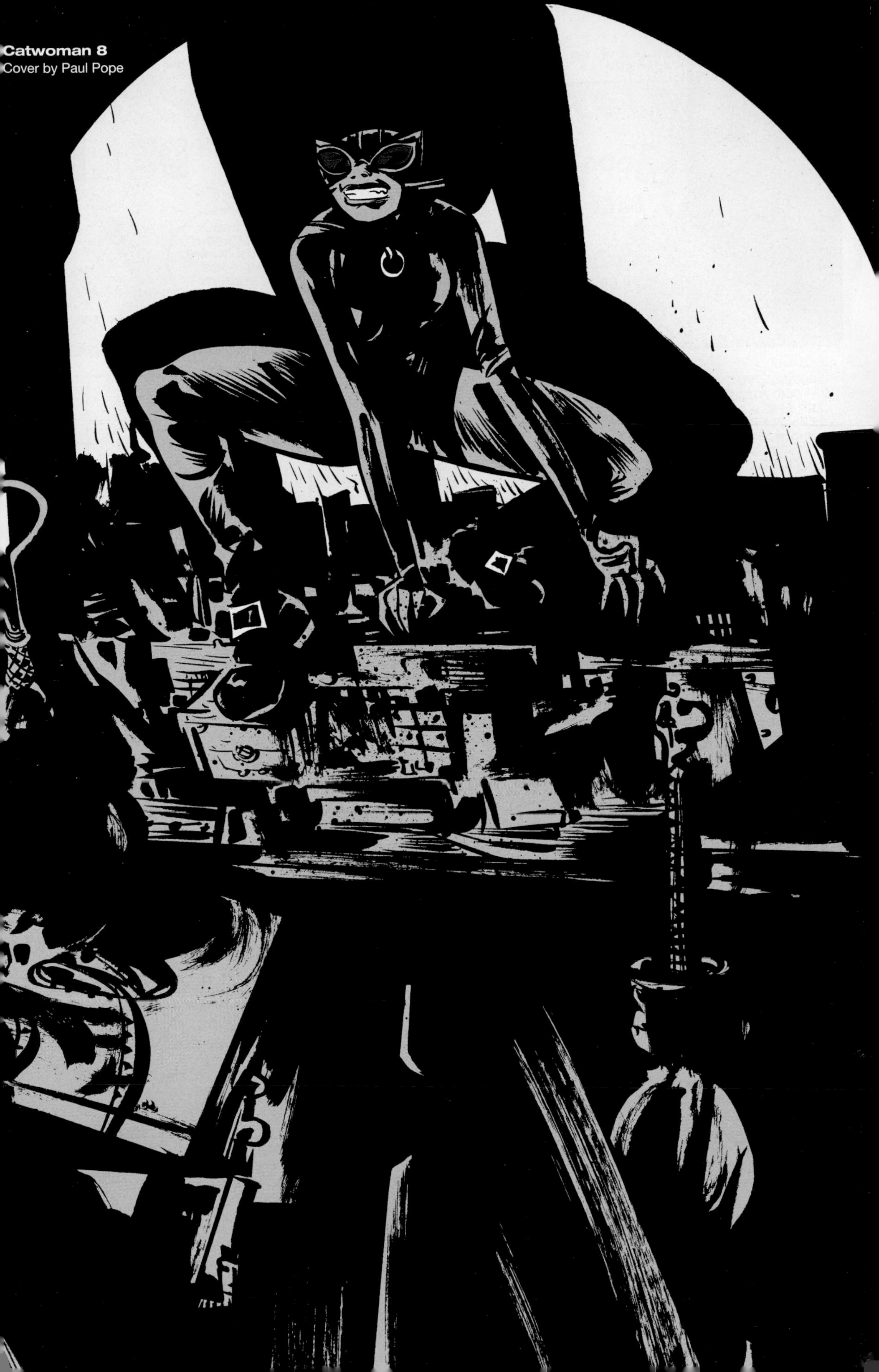

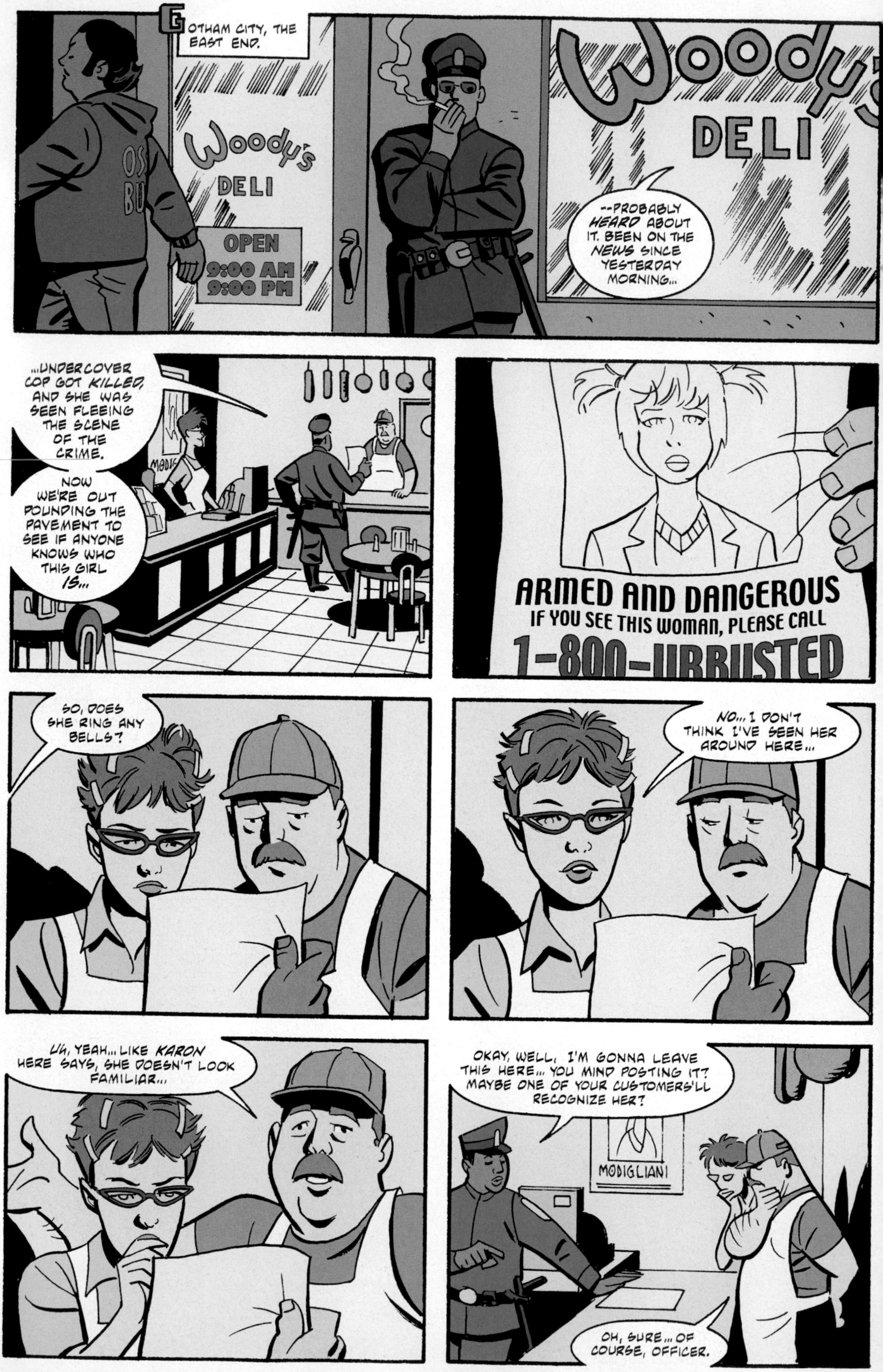
GOTHAM CITY, THE EAST END.
WOODY'S DELI
OPEN 9:00 AM 9:00 PM
WOODY'S DELI
--PROBABLY HEARD ABOUT IT. BEEN ON THE NEWS SINCE YESTERDAY MORNING...
...UNDERCOVER COP GOT KILLED, AND SHE WAS SEEN FLEEING THE SCENE OF THE CRIME.
NOW WE'RE OUT POUNDING THE PAVEMENT TO SEE IF ANYONE KNOWS WHO THIS GIRL IS...
ARMED AND DANGEROUS
IF YOU SEE THIS WOMAN, PLEASE CALL
1-800-URBUSTED
SO, DOES SHE RING ANY BELLS?
NO... I DON'T THINK I'VE SEEN HER AROUND HERE...
UH, YEAH... LIKE KARON HERE SAYS, SHE DOESN'T LOOK FAMILIAR...
OKAY, WELL, I'M GONNA LEAVE THIS HERE... YOU MIND POSTING IT? MAYBE ONE OF YOUR CUSTOMERS'LL RECOGNIZE HER?
MODIGLIANI
OH, SURE... OF COURSE, OFFICER.

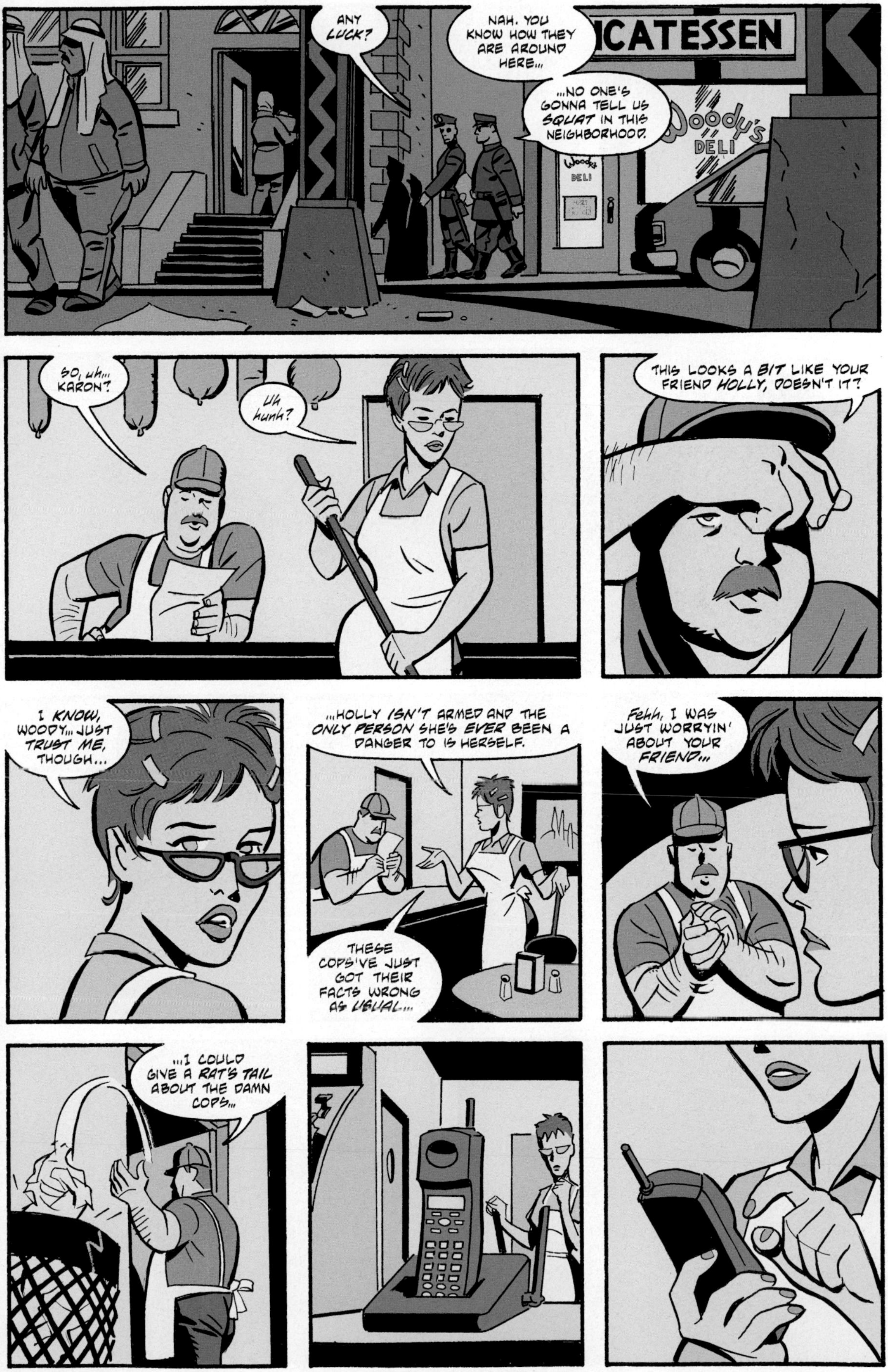
CATESSEN
ANY LUCK?
NAH. YOU KNOW HOW THEY ARE AROUND HERE...
...NO ONE'S GONNA TELL US SQUAT IN THIS NEIGHBORHOOD.
Woody's DELI
SO, UH... KARON?
Uh hunh?
THIS LOOKS A BIT LIKE YOUR FRIEND HOLLY, DOESN'T IT?
I KNOW, WOODY... JUST TRUST ME, THOUGH...
...HOLLY ISN'T ARMED AND THE ONLY PERSON SHE'S EVER BEEN A DANGER TO IS HERSELF.
THESE COPS'VE JUST GOT THEIR FACTS WRONG AS USUAL...
Fehh, I WAS JUST WORRYIN' ABOUT YOUR FRIEND...
...I COULD GIVE A RAT'S TAIL ABOUT THE DAMN COPS...

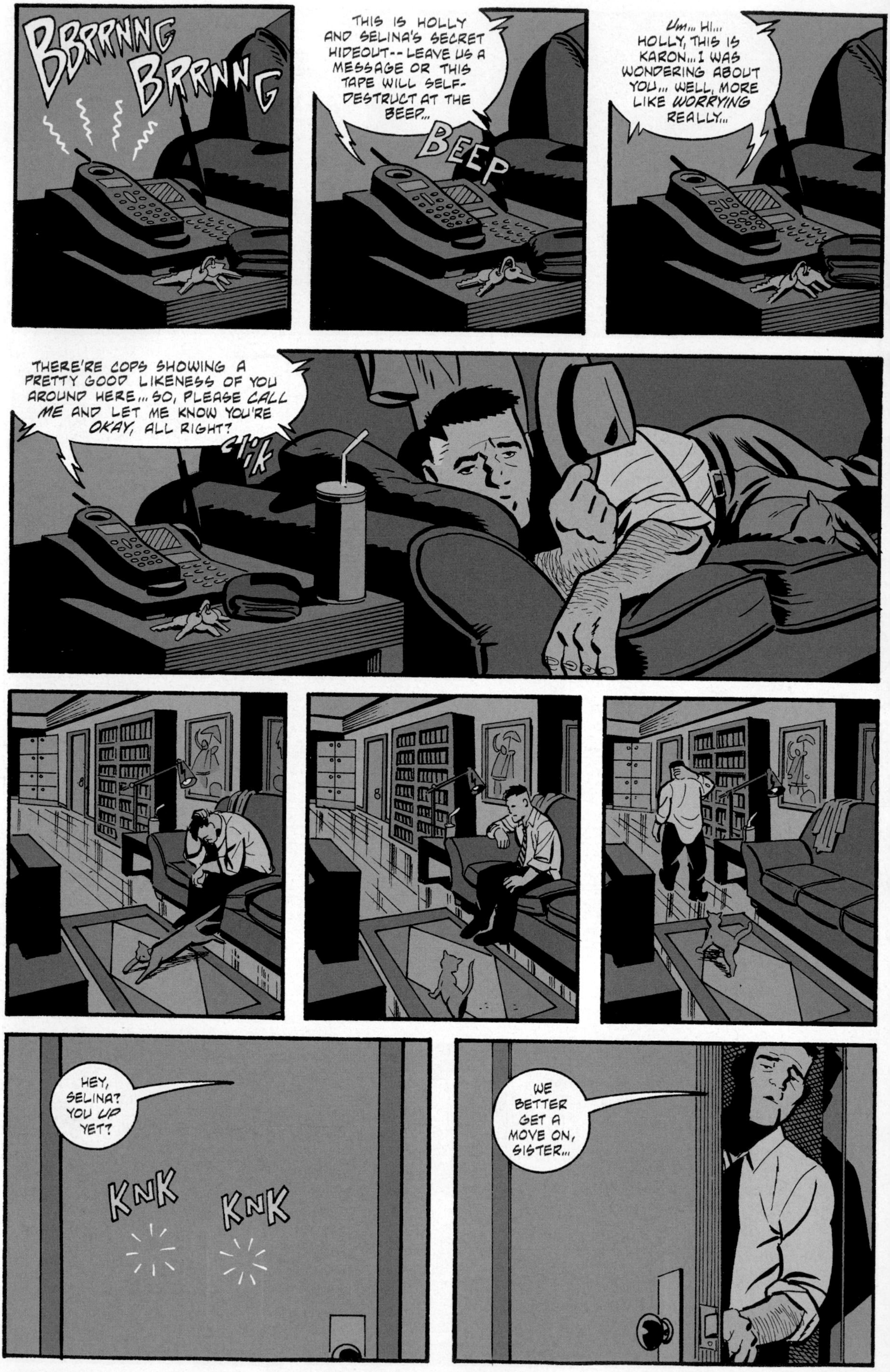
BBRRNNG BRRNNG
THIS IS HOLLY AND SELINA'S SECRET HIDEOUT-- LEAVE US A MESSAGE OR THIS TAPE WILL SELF-DESTRUCT AT THE BEEP...
BEEP
UM... HI... HOLLY, THIS IS KARON... I WAS WONDERING ABOUT YOU... WELL, MORE LIKE WORRYING REALLY...
THERE'RE COPS SHOWING A PRETTY GOOD LIKENESS OF YOU AROUND HERE... SO, PLEASE CALL ME AND LET ME KNOW YOU'RE OKAY, ALL RIGHT?
CLIK
HEY, SELINA? YOU UP YET?
KNK
KNK
WE BETTER GET A MOVE ON, SISTER...

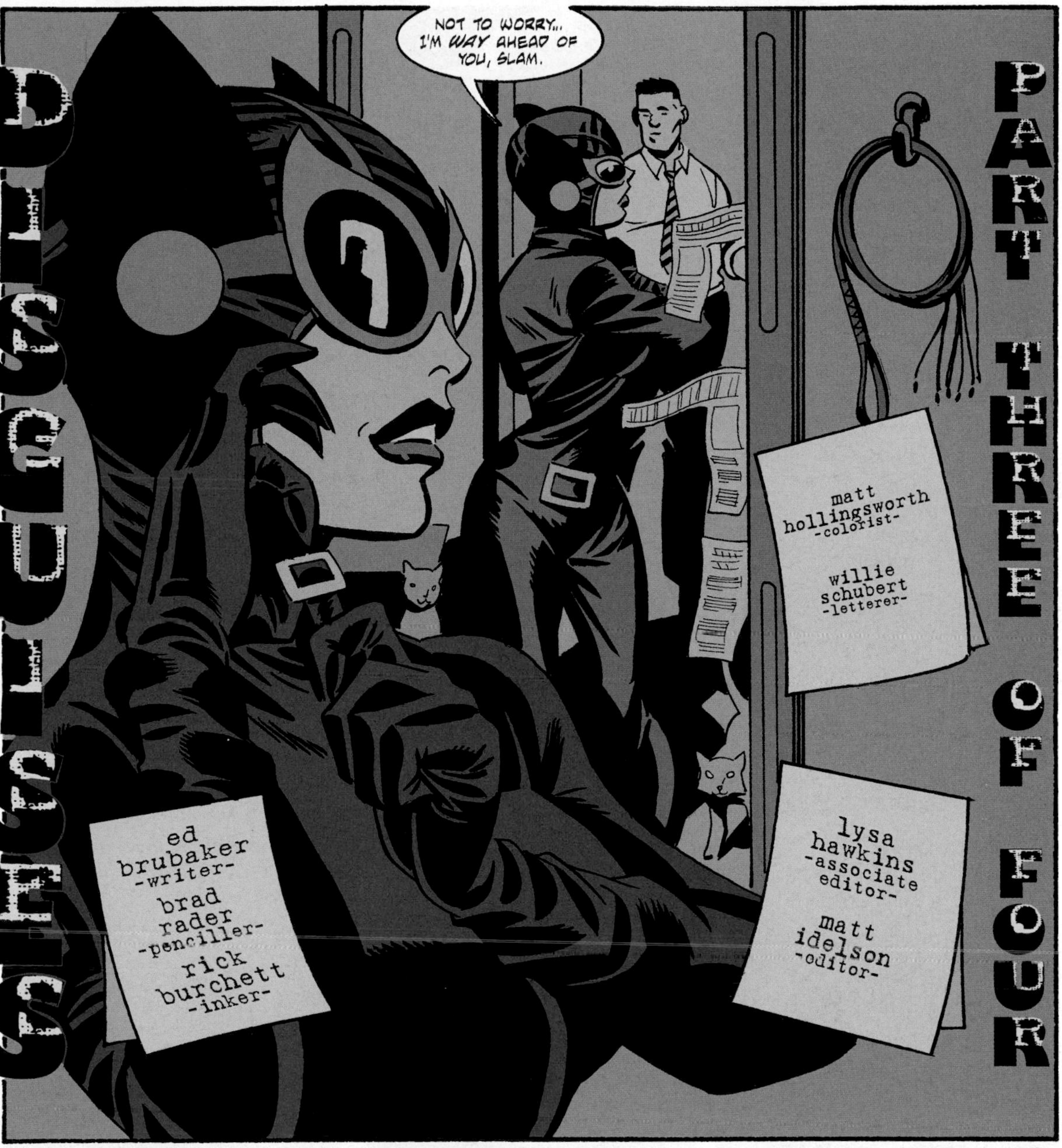
DISGUISES
NOT TO WORRY... I'M WAY AHEAD OF YOU, SLAM.
PART THREE OF FOUR
matt hollingsworth -colorist-
willie schubert -letterer-
ed brubaker -writer-
brad rader -penciller-
rick burchett -inker-
lysa hawkins -associate editor-
matt idelson -editor-

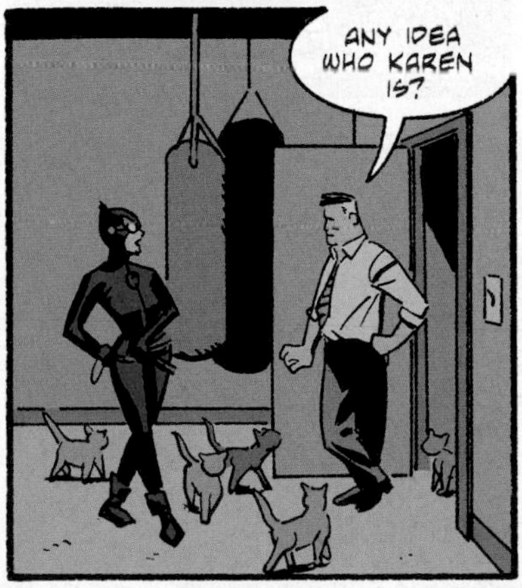
ANY IDEA WHO KAREN IS?

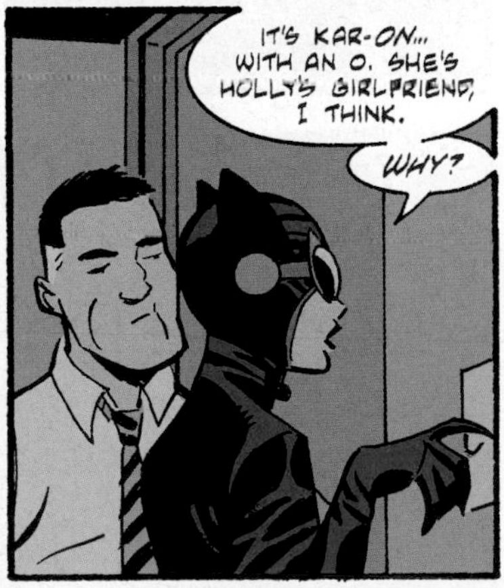
IT'S KAR-ON... WITH AN O. SHE'S HOLLY'S GIRLFRIEND, I THINK.
WHY?

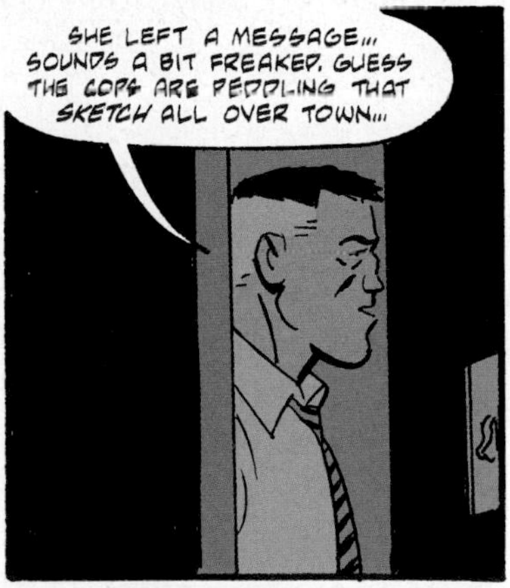
SHE LEFT A MESSAGE... SOUNDS A BIT FREAKED. GUESS THE COPS ARE PEDDLING THAT SKETCH ALL OVER TOWN...

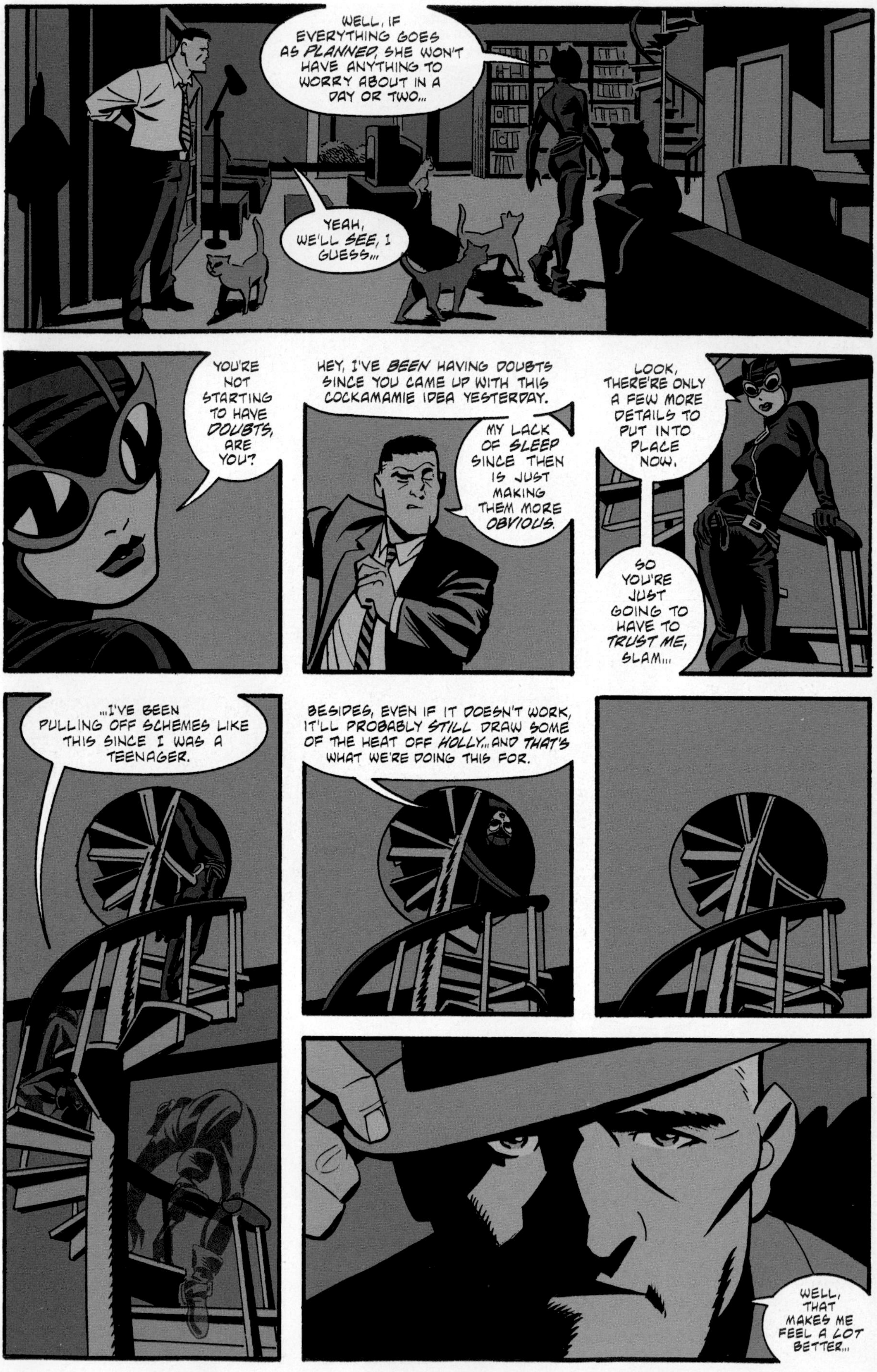
WELL, IF EVERYTHING GOES AS PLANNED, SHE WON'T HAVE ANYTHING TO WORRY ABOUT IN A DAY OR TWO...
YEAH, WE'LL SEE, I GUESS...
YOU'RE NOT STARTING TO HAVE DOUBTS, ARE YOU?
HEY, I'VE BEEN HAVING DOUBTS SINCE YOU CAME UP WITH THIS COCKAMAMIE IDEA YESTERDAY.
MY LACK OF SLEEP SINCE THEN IS JUST MAKING THEM MORE OBVIOUS.
LOOK, THERE'RE ONLY A FEW MORE DETAILS TO PUT INTO PLACE NOW.
SO YOU'RE JUST GOING TO HAVE TO TRUST ME, SLAM...
...I'VE BEEN PULLING OFF SCHEMES LIKE THIS SINCE I WAS A TEENAGER.
BESIDES, EVEN IF IT DOESN'T WORK, IT'LL PROBABLY STILL DRAW SOME OF THE HEAT OFF HOLLY... AND THAT'S WHAT WE'RE DOING THIS FOR.
WELL, THAT MAKES ME FEEL A LOT BETTER...

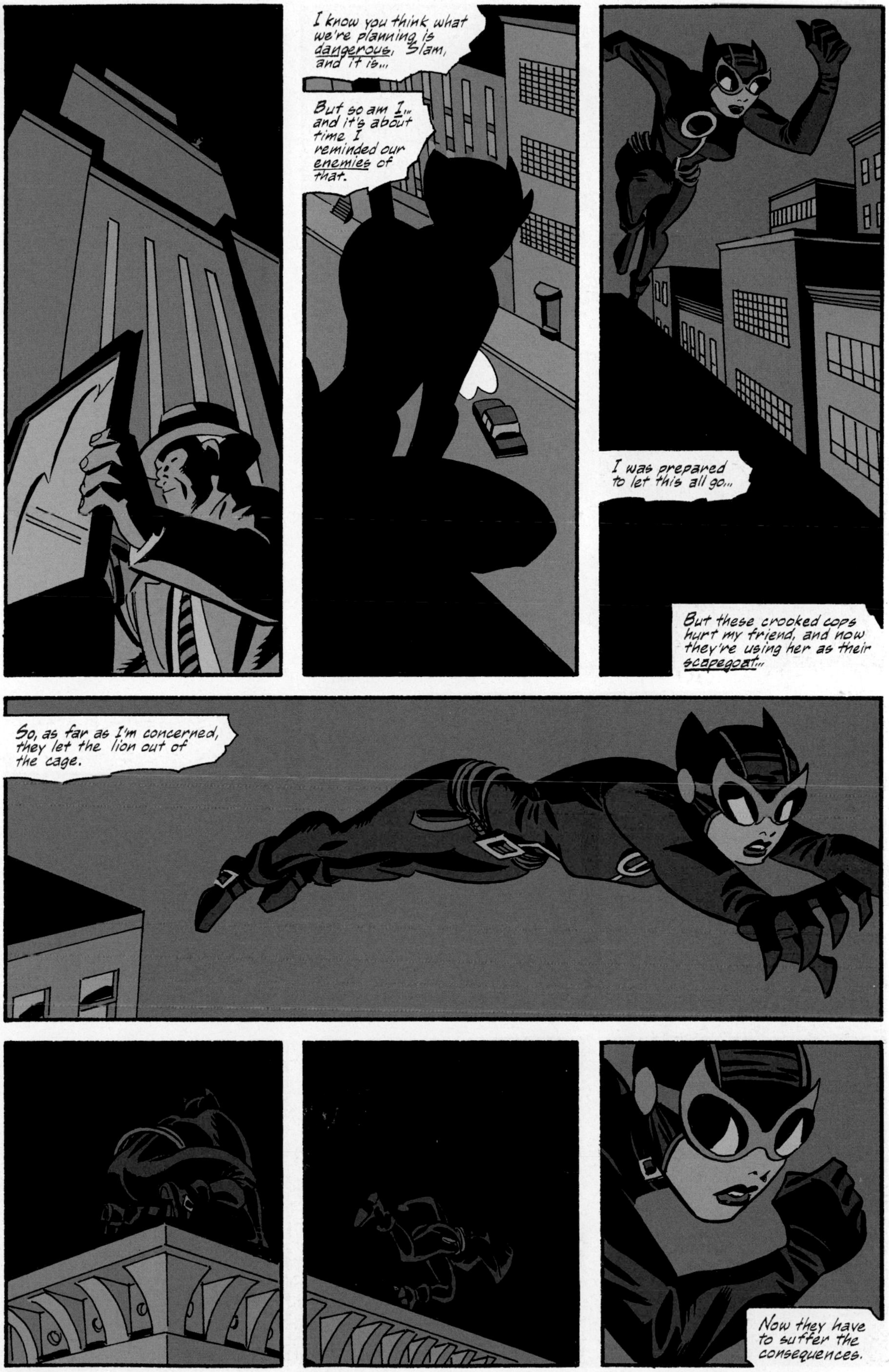

I know you think what we're planning is dangerous, Slam, and it is...
But so am I... and it's about time I reminded our enemies of that.
I was prepared to let this all go...
But these crooked cops hurt my friend, and now they're using her as their scapegoat...
So, as far as I'm concerned, they let the lion out of the cage.
Now they have to suffer the consequences.

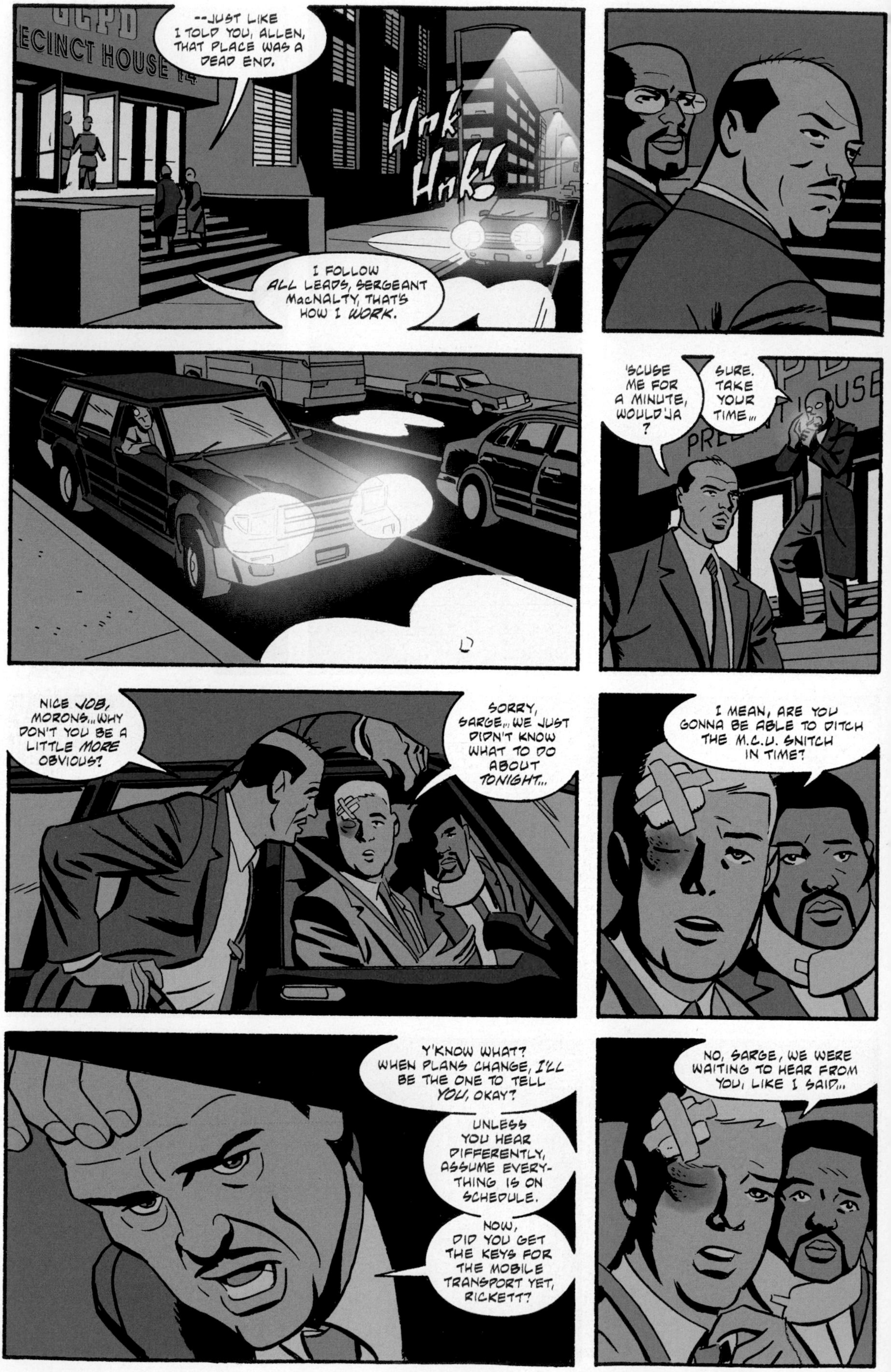
GCPD
PRECINCT HOUSE 14
--JUST LIKE I TOLD YOU, ALLEN, THAT PLACE WAS A DEAD END.
Hnk Hnk!
I FOLLOW ALL LEADS, SERGEANT MacNALTY, THAT'S HOW I WORK.
'SCUSE ME FOR A MINUTE, WOULD'JA?
SURE. TAKE YOUR TIME...
NICE JOB, MORONS... WHY DON'T YOU BE A LITTLE MORE OBVIOUS?
SORRY, SARGE... WE JUST DIDN'T KNOW WHAT TO DO ABOUT TONIGHT...
I MEAN, ARE YOU GONNA BE ABLE TO DITCH THE M.C.U. SNITCH IN TIME?
Y'KNOW WHAT? WHEN PLANS CHANGE, I'LL BE THE ONE TO TELL YOU, OKAY?
UNLESS YOU HEAR DIFFERENTLY, ASSUME EVERY-THING IS ON SCHEDULE.
NOW, DID YOU GET THE KEYS FOR THE MOBILE TRANSPORT YET, RICKETT?
NO, SARGE, WE WERE WAITING TO HEAR FROM YOU, LIKE I SAID...

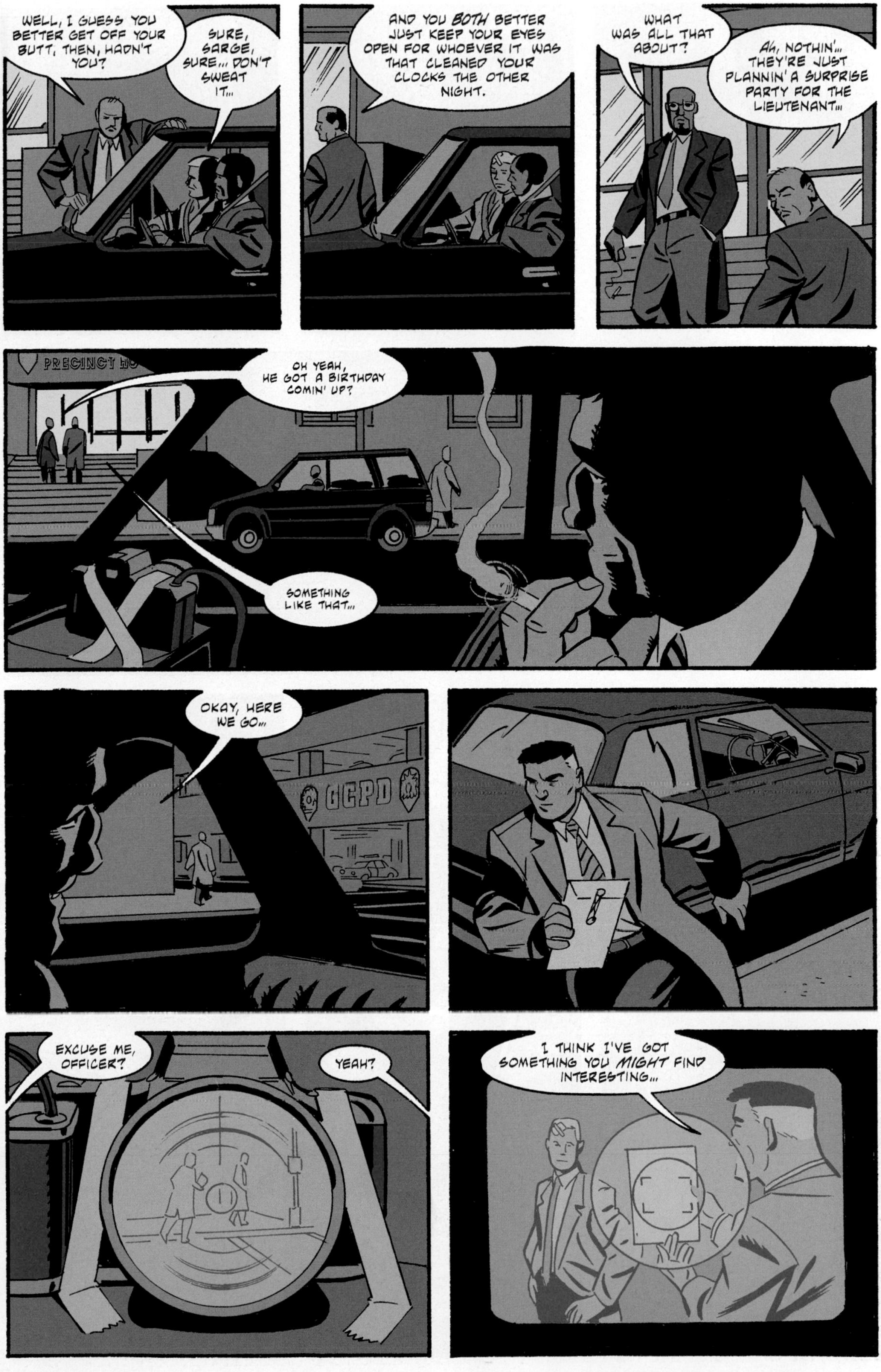
WELL, I GUESS YOU BETTER GET OFF YOUR BUTT, THEN, HADN'T YOU?
SURE, SARGE, SURE... DON'T SWEAT IT...
AND YOU BOTH BETTER JUST KEEP YOUR EYES OPEN FOR WHOEVER IT WAS THAT CLEANED YOUR CLOCKS THE OTHER NIGHT.
WHAT WAS ALL THAT ABOUT?
AH, NOTHIN'... THEY'RE JUST PLANNIN' A SURPRISE PARTY FOR THE LIEUTENANT...
PRECINCT HO
OH YEAH, HE GOT A BIRTHDAY COMIN' UP?
SOMETHING LIKE THAT...
OKAY, HERE WE GO...
GCPD
EXCUSE ME, OFFICER?
YEAH?
I THINK I'VE GOT SOMETHING YOU MIGHT FIND INTERESTING...

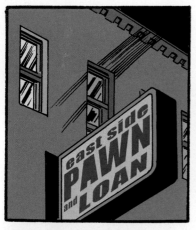

SNIKT

SMAK!

...JEEZ, I REALLY GOTTA START TAKIN' A BIGGER STINKIN' CUT OF 'SOMMA THIS ACTION...

"...THESE SUCKERS'R TAKIN' ADVANTAGE OF MY GENEROUS NATURE..."

WELL, I HOPE YOU SAVED UP SOME OF THAT GENEROSITY FOR ME, JEFFO...

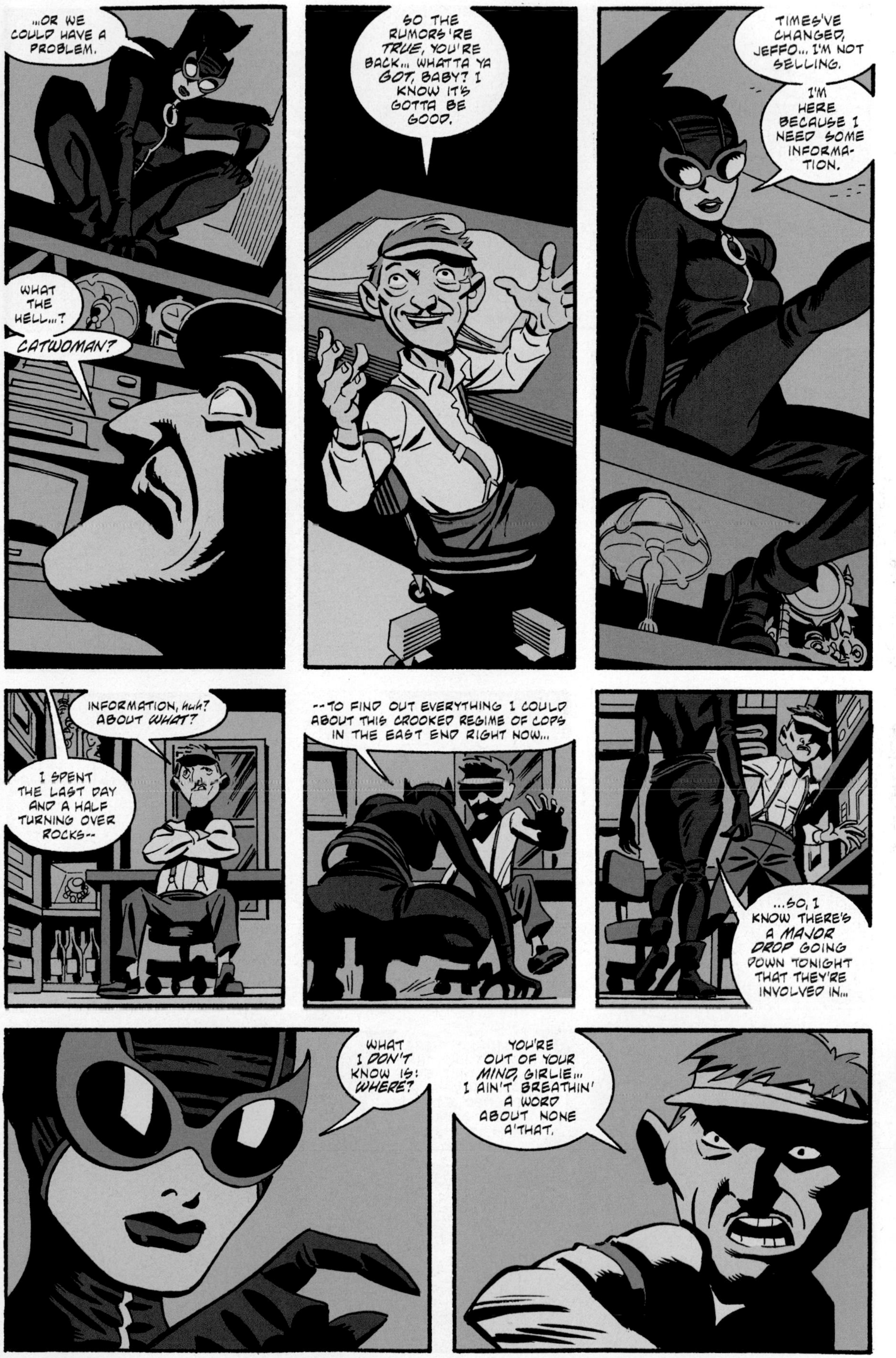

...OR WE COULD HAVE A PROBLEM.
WHAT THE HELL...? CATWOMAN?
SO THE RUMORS'RE TRUE, YOU'RE BACK... WHATTA YA GOT, BABY? I KNOW IT'S GOTTA BE GOOD.
TIMES'VE CHANGED, JEFFO... I'M NOT SELLING.
I'M HERE BECAUSE I NEED SOME INFORMATION.
INFORMATION, huh? ABOUT WHAT?
I SPENT THE LAST DAY AND A HALF TURNING OVER ROCKS--
--TO FIND OUT EVERYTHING I COULD ABOUT THIS CROOKED REGIME OF COPS IN THE EAST END RIGHT NOW...
...SO, I KNOW THERE'S A MAJOR DROP GOING DOWN TONIGHT THAT THEY'RE INVOLVED IN...
WHAT I DON'T KNOW IS: WHERE?
YOU'RE OUT OF YOUR MIND, GIRLIE... I AIN'T BREATHIN' A WORD ABOUT NONE A'THAT.

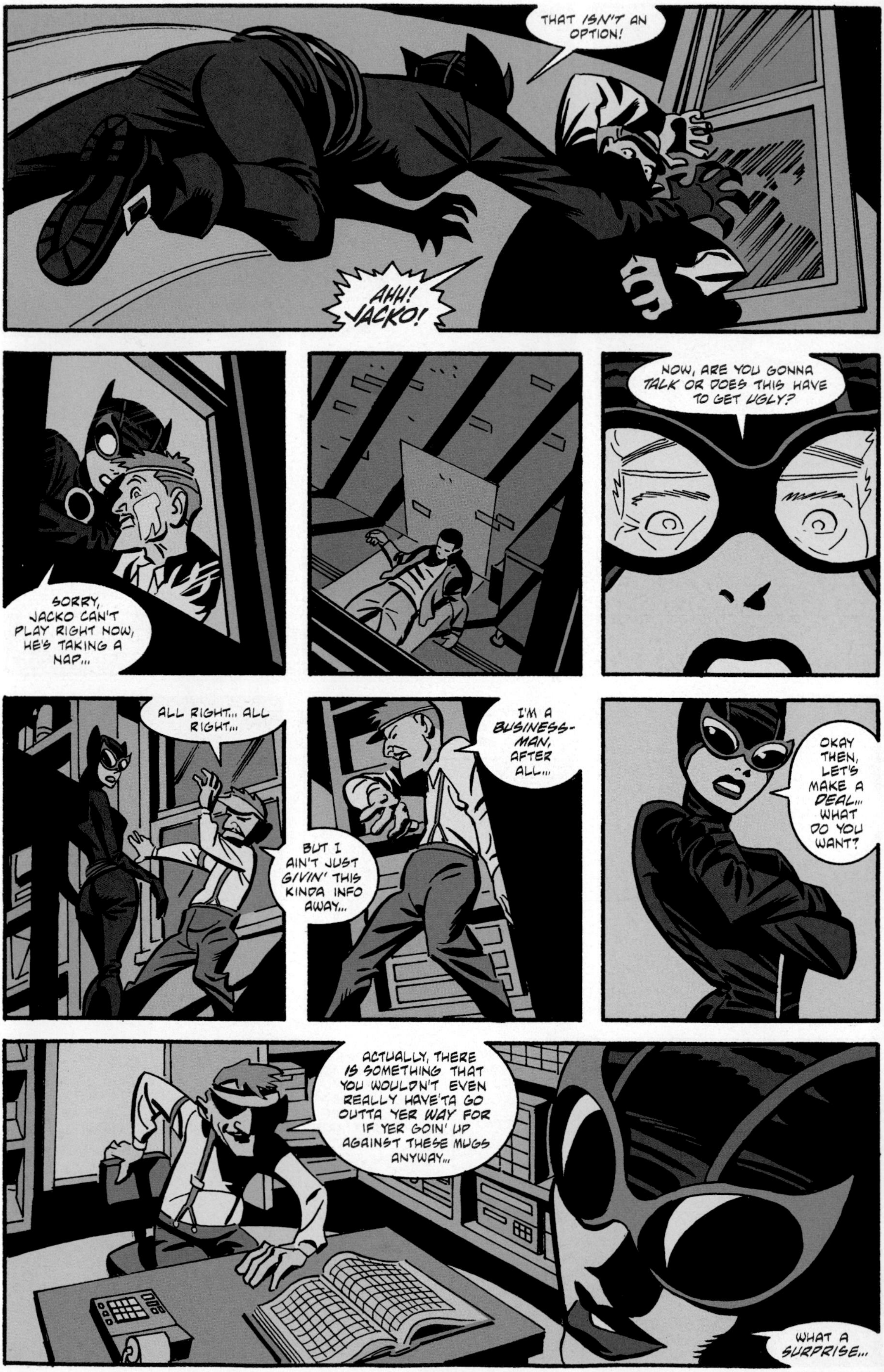

THAT ISN'T AN OPTION!
AHH! JACKO!
SORRY, JACKO CAN'T PLAY RIGHT NOW, HE'S TAKING A NAP...
NOW, ARE YOU GONNA TALK OR DOES THIS HAVE TO GET UGLY?
ALL RIGHT... ALL RIGHT...
BUT I AIN'T JUST GIVIN' THIS KINDA INFO AWAY...
I'M A BUSINESS-MAN, AFTER ALL...
OKAY THEN, LET'S MAKE A DEAL... WHAT DO YOU WANT?
ACTUALLY, THERE IS SOMETHING THAT YOU WOULDN'T EVEN REALLY HAVE'TA GO OUTTA YER WAY FOR IF YER GOIN' UP AGAINST THESE MUGS ANYWAY...
WHAT A SURPRISE...

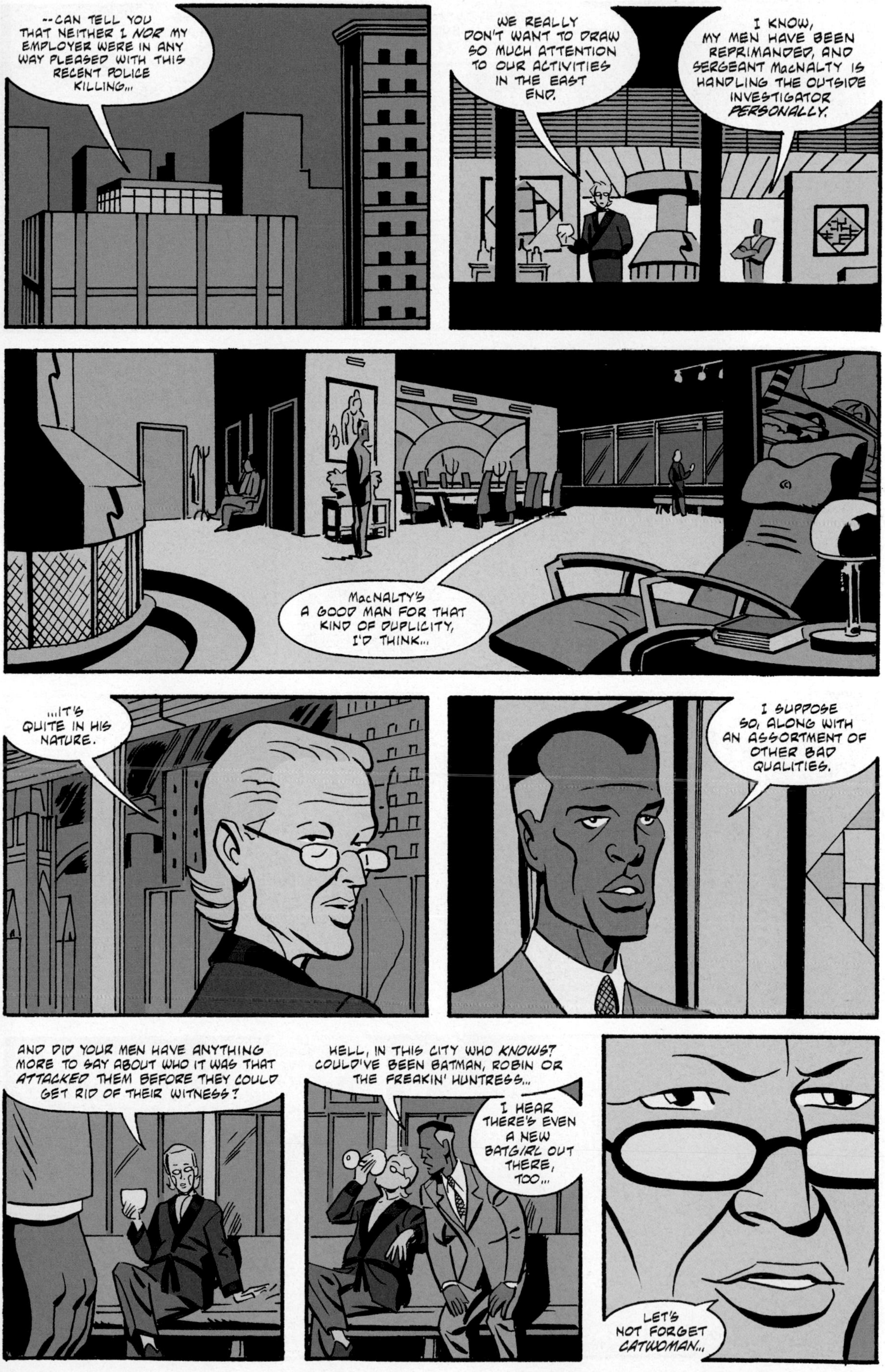
--CAN TELL YOU THAT NEITHER I NOR MY EMPLOYER WERE IN ANY WAY PLEASED WITH THIS RECENT POLICE KILLING...
WE REALLY DON'T WANT TO DRAW SO MUCH ATTENTION TO OUR ACTIVITIES IN THE EAST END.
I KNOW, MY MEN HAVE BEEN REPRIMANDED, AND SERGEANT MacNALTY IS HANDLING THE OUTSIDE INVESTIGATOR PERSONALLY.
MacNALTY'S A GOOD MAN FOR THAT KIND OF DUPLICITY, I'D THINK...
...IT'S QUITE IN HIS NATURE.
I SUPPOSE SO, ALONG WITH AN ASSORTMENT OF OTHER BAD QUALITIES.
AND DID YOUR MEN HAVE ANYTHING MORE TO SAY ABOUT WHO IT WAS THAT ATTACKED THEM BEFORE THEY COULD GET RID OF THEIR WITNESS?
HELL, IN THIS CITY WHO KNOWS? COULD'VE BEEN BATMAN, ROBIN OR THE FREAKIN' HUNTRESS...
I HEAR THERE'S EVEN A NEW BATGIRL OUT THERE, TOO...
LET'S NOT FORGET CATWOMAN...

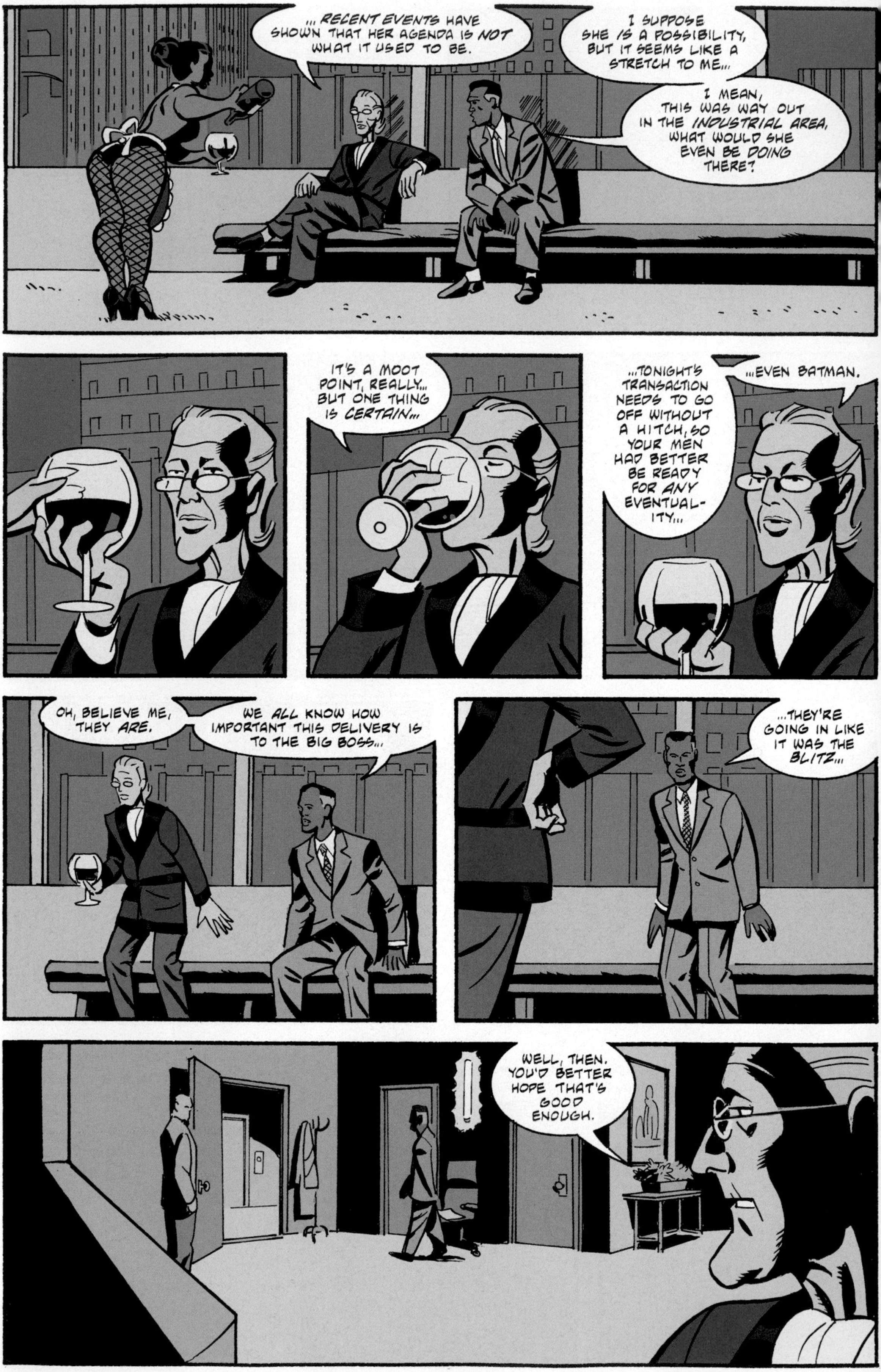
...RECENT EVENTS HAVE SHOWN THAT HER AGENDA IS NOT WHAT IT USED TO BE.
I SUPPOSE SHE IS A POSSIBILITY, BUT IT SEEMS LIKE A STRETCH TO ME...
I MEAN, THIS WAS WAY OUT IN THE INDUSTRIAL AREA. WHAT WOULD SHE EVEN BE DOING THERE?
IT'S A MOOT POINT, REALLY... BUT ONE THING IS CERTAIN...
...TONIGHT'S TRANSACTION NEEDS TO GO OFF WITHOUT A HITCH, SO YOUR MEN HAD BETTER BE READY FOR ANY EVENTUAL-ITY...
...EVEN BATMAN.
OH, BELIEVE ME, THEY ARE.
WE ALL KNOW HOW IMPORTANT THIS DELIVERY IS TO THE BIG BOSS...
...THEY'RE GOING IN LIKE IT WAS THE BLITZ...
WELL, THEN. YOU'D BETTER HOPE THAT'S GOOD ENOUGH.

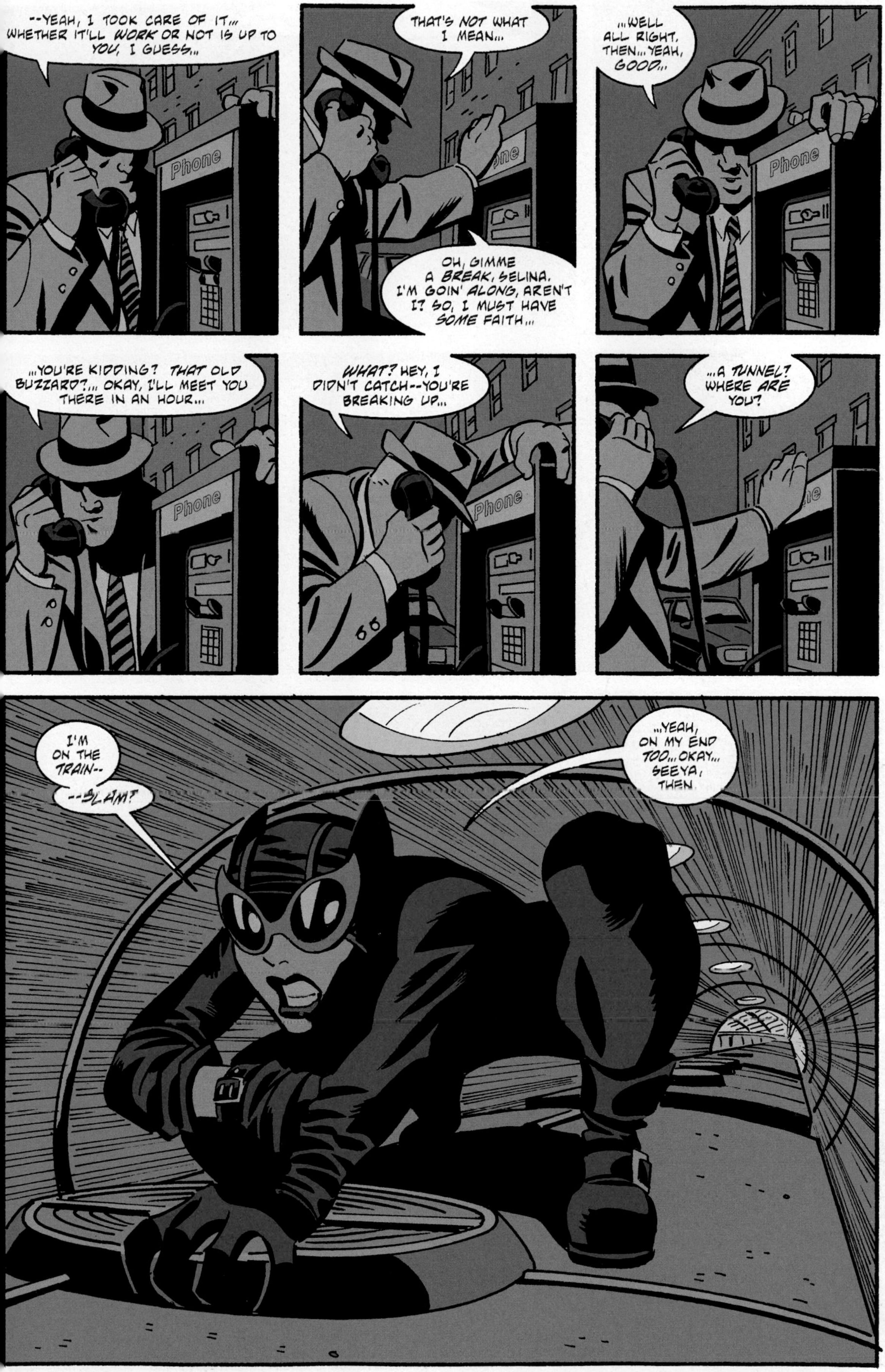
--YEAH, I TOOK CARE OF IT... WHETHER IT'LL WORK OR NOT IS UP TO YOU, I GUESS...
Phone
THAT'S NOT WHAT I MEAN...
OH, GIMME A BREAK, SELINA. I'M GOIN' ALONG, AREN'T I? SO, I MUST HAVE SOME FAITH...
...WELL ALL RIGHT, THEN... YEAH, GOOD...
Phone
...YOU'RE KIDDING? THAT OLD BUZZARD?... OKAY, I'LL MEET YOU THERE IN AN HOUR...
Phone
WHAT? HEY, I DIDN'T CATCH--YOU'RE BREAKING UP...
Phone
...A TUNNEL? WHERE ARE YOU?
I'M ON THE TRAIN--
--SLAM!
...YEAH, ON MY END TOO... OKAY... SEEYA, THEN.

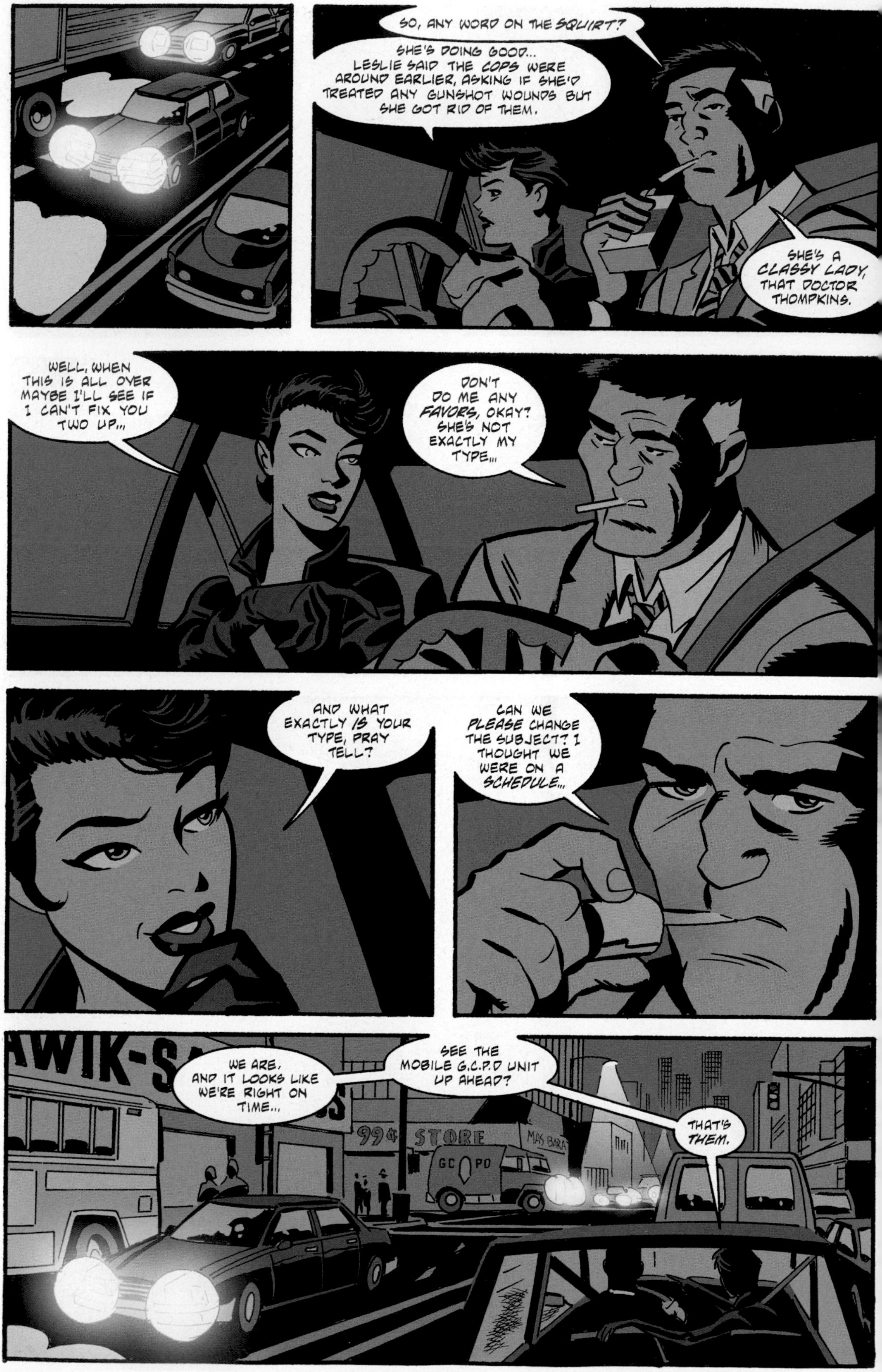

SO, ANY WORD ON THE SQUIRT?
SHE'S DOING GOOD... LESLIE SAID THE COPS WERE AROUND EARLIER, ASKING IF SHE'D TREATED ANY GUNSHOT WOUNDS BUT SHE GOT RID OF THEM.
SHE'S A CLASSY LADY, THAT DOCTOR THOMPKINS.
WELL, WHEN THIS IS ALL OVER MAYBE I'LL SEE IF I CAN'T FIX YOU TWO UP...
DON'T DO ME ANY FAVORS, OKAY? SHE'S NOT EXACTLY MY TYPE...
AND WHAT EXACTLY IS YOUR TYPE, PRAY TELL?
CAN WE PLEASE CHANGE THE SUBJECT? I THOUGHT WE WERE ON A SCHEDULE...
WE ARE. AND IT LOOKS LIKE WE'RE RIGHT ON TIME...
SEE THE MOBILE G.C.P.D UNIT UP AHEAD?
THAT'S THEM.
99¢ STORE
GCPD

JEFFO *DIDN'T* KNOW THE *EXACT* LOCATION OF THE SWAP, BUT HE KNEW ABOUT THE TRANSPORT VAN, WHICH WAS GOOD ENOUGH.

OH *MAN,* THESE GUYS'VE GOT *BRASS ONES,* I'M TELLIN' YA...

TRUE, BUT AFTER TONIGHT, THEY'LL BE *LUCKY* IF THEY HAVE *ANY* AT ALL.

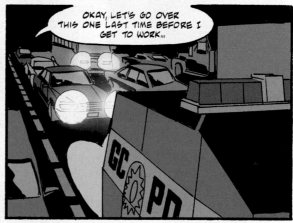

OKAY, LET'S GO OVER THIS ONE LAST TIME BEFORE I GET TO *WORK...*

THEY STILL BACK THERE?

YEAH, JUST LIKE HE *SAID...*

...*ONE* CAR LENGTH BEHIND, JUST IN CASE.

YEAH, LIKE *ANYONE'S* GONNA BE STUPID ENOUGH TO TAKE ON A *POLICE* VAN...

...EVEN WHEN IT'S CARRYING *200 POUNDS* OF PURE GRADE *SMACK.*

YOU THINK WHAT YOU *WANT,* FARLEY--

--I'LL STOP WORRYING WHEN WE DROP THIS *JUNK* OFF AND GET THE *PACKAGE.*

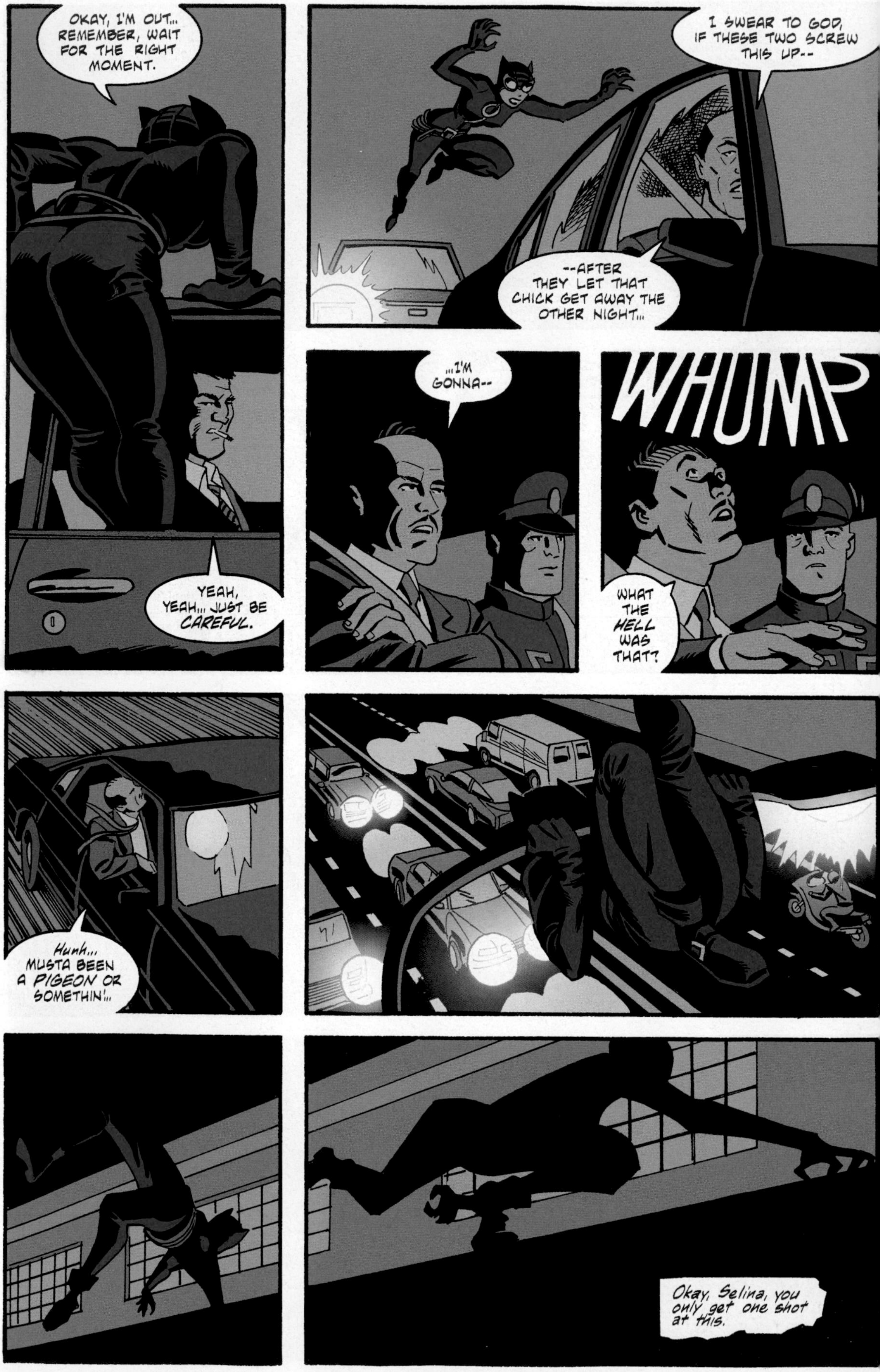
OKAY, I'M OUT... REMEMBER, WAIT FOR THE RIGHT MOMENT.
YEAH, YEAH... JUST BE CAREFUL.
I SWEAR TO GOD, IF THESE TWO SCREW THIS UP--
--AFTER THEY LET THAT CHICK GET AWAY THE OTHER NIGHT...
...I'M GONNA--
WHUMP
WHAT THE HELL WAS THAT?
Hunh... MUSTA BEEN A PIGEON OR SOMETHIN'...
Okay, Selina, you only get one shot at this.

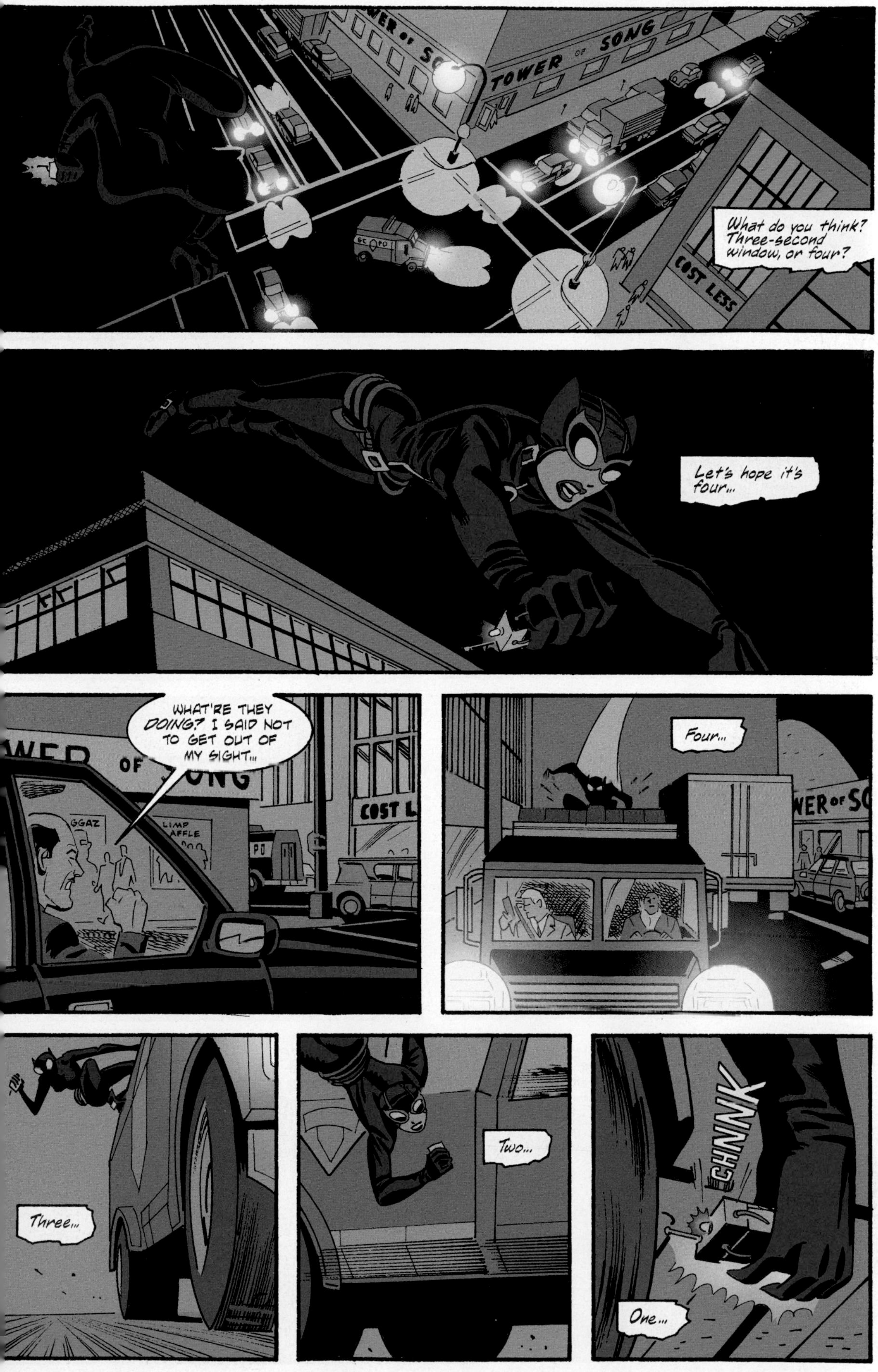
TOWER OF SONG
What do you think? Three-second window, or four?
COST LESS
Let's hope it's four...
WHAT'RE THEY DOING? I SAID NOT TO GET OUT OF MY SIGHT...
COST L
Four...
Three...
Two...
CHNNK
One...

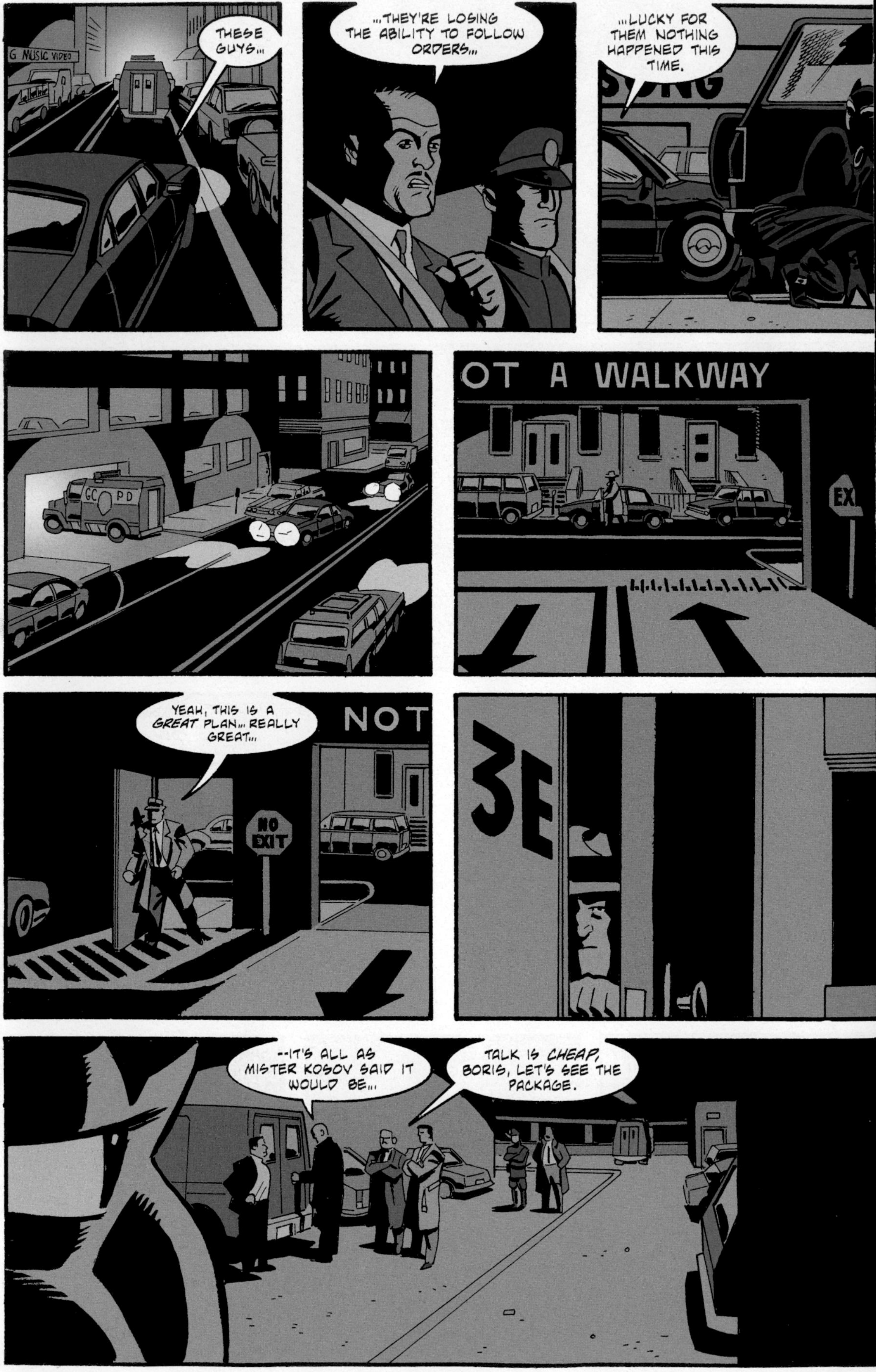
THESE GUYS...
...THEY'RE LOSING THE ABILITY TO FOLLOW ORDERS...
...LUCKY FOR THEM NOTHING HAPPENED THIS TIME.
G MUSIC VIDEO
SONG
GC PD
OT A WALKWAY
EX
YEAH, THIS IS A GREAT PLAN... REALLY GREAT...
NOT
NO EXIT
3E
--IT'S ALL AS MISTER KOSOV SAID IT WOULD BE...
TALK IS CHEAP, BORIS, LET'S SEE THE PACKAGE.

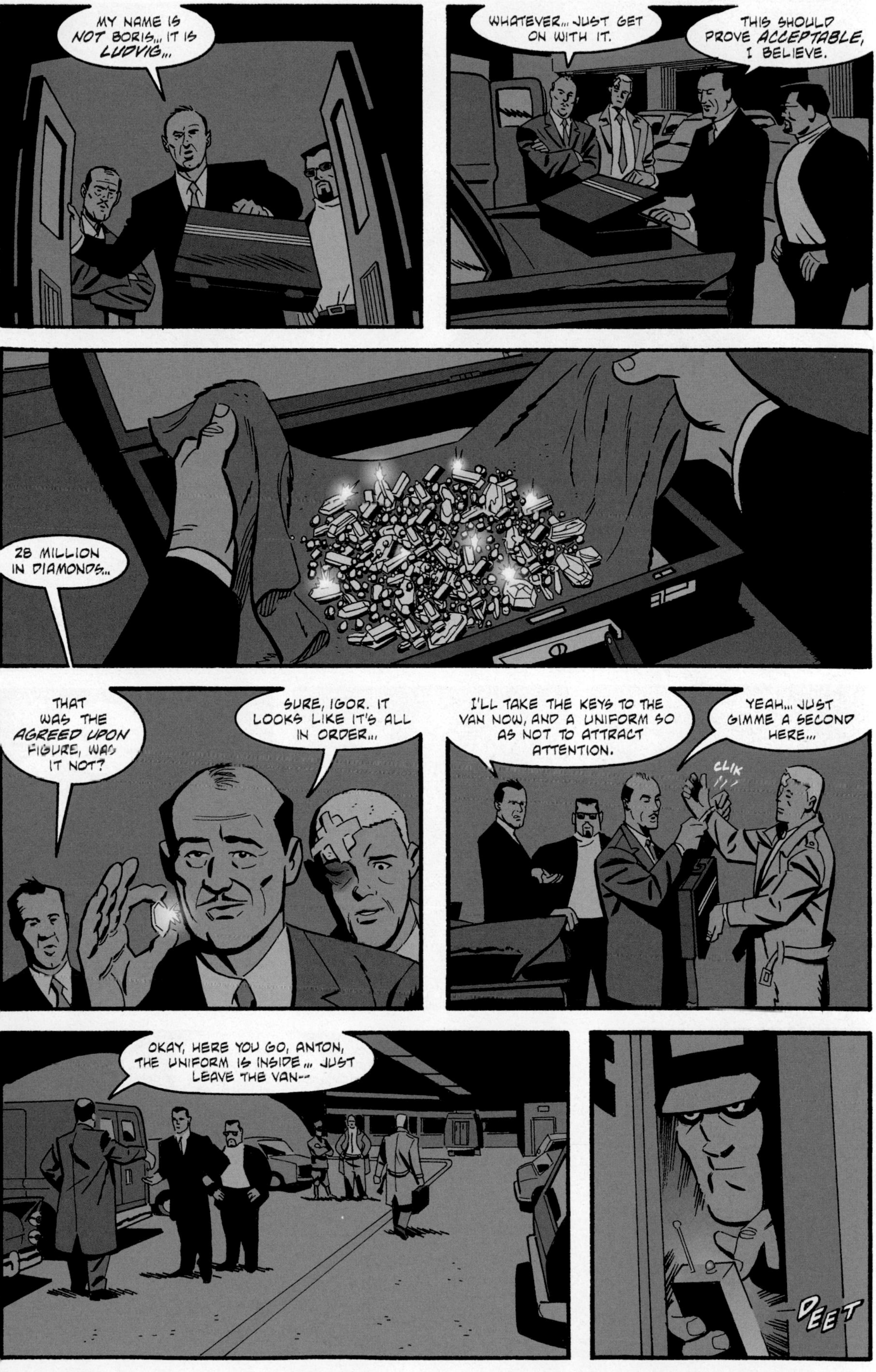
MY NAME IS NOT BORIS... IT IS LUDVIG...
WHATEVER... JUST GET ON WITH IT.
THIS SHOULD PROVE ACCEPTABLE, I BELIEVE.
28 MILLION IN DIAMONDS...
THAT WAS THE AGREED UPON FIGURE, WAS IT NOT?
SURE, IGOR. IT LOOKS LIKE IT'S ALL IN ORDER...
I'LL TAKE THE KEYS TO THE VAN NOW, AND A UNIFORM SO AS NOT TO ATTRACT ATTENTION.
YEAH... JUST GIMME A SECOND HERE...
CLIK
OKAY, HERE YOU GO, ANTON, THE UNIFORM IS INSIDE... JUST LEAVE THE VAN--
DEET

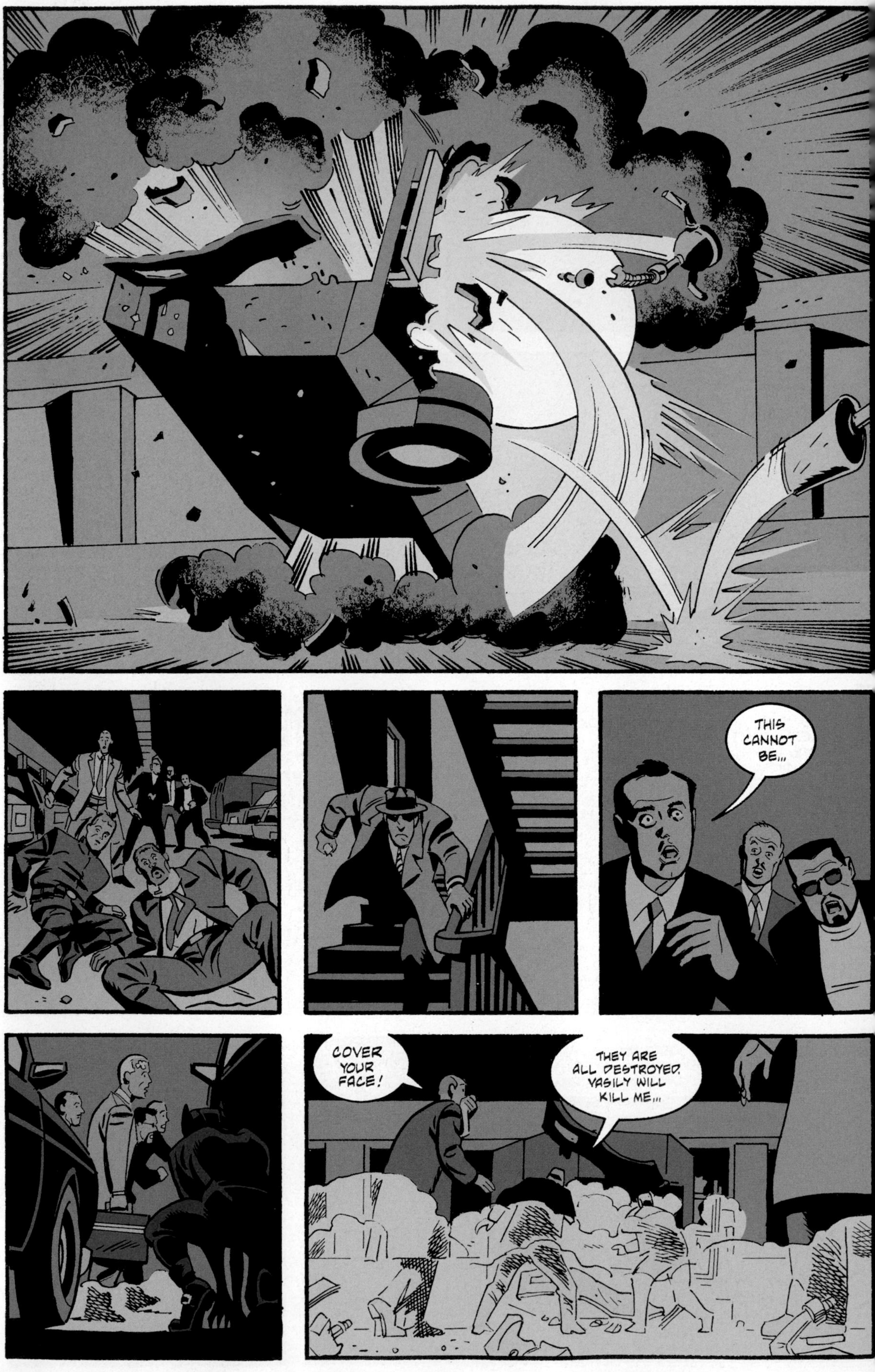
THIS CANNOT BE...
COVER YOUR FACE!
THEY ARE ALL DESTROYED. VASILY WILL KILL ME...

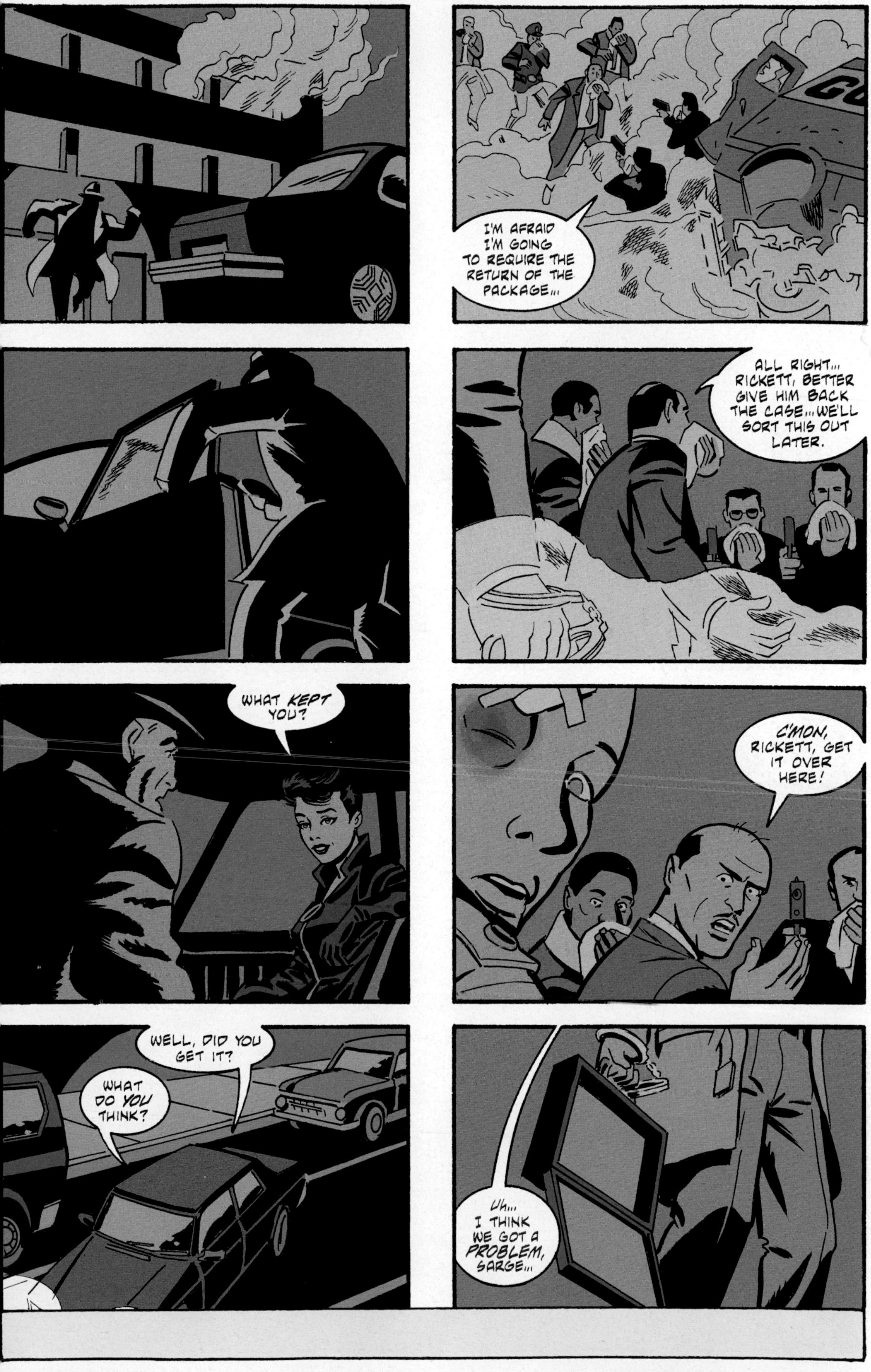
I'M AFRAID I'M GOING TO REQUIRE THE RETURN OF THE PACKAGE...
ALL RIGHT... RICKETT, BETTER GIVE HIM BACK THE CASE... WE'LL SORT THIS OUT LATER.
WHAT KEPT YOU?
C'MON, RICKETT, GET IT OVER HERE!
WELL, DID YOU GET IT?
WHAT DO YOU THINK?
Uh... I THINK WE GOT A PROBLEM, SARGE...

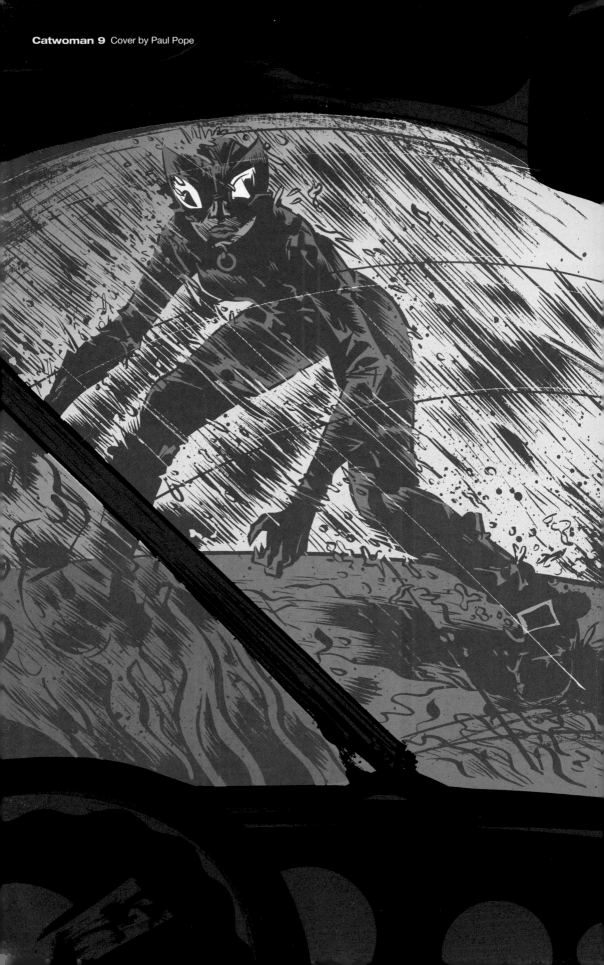

Catwoman 9 Cover by Paul Pope

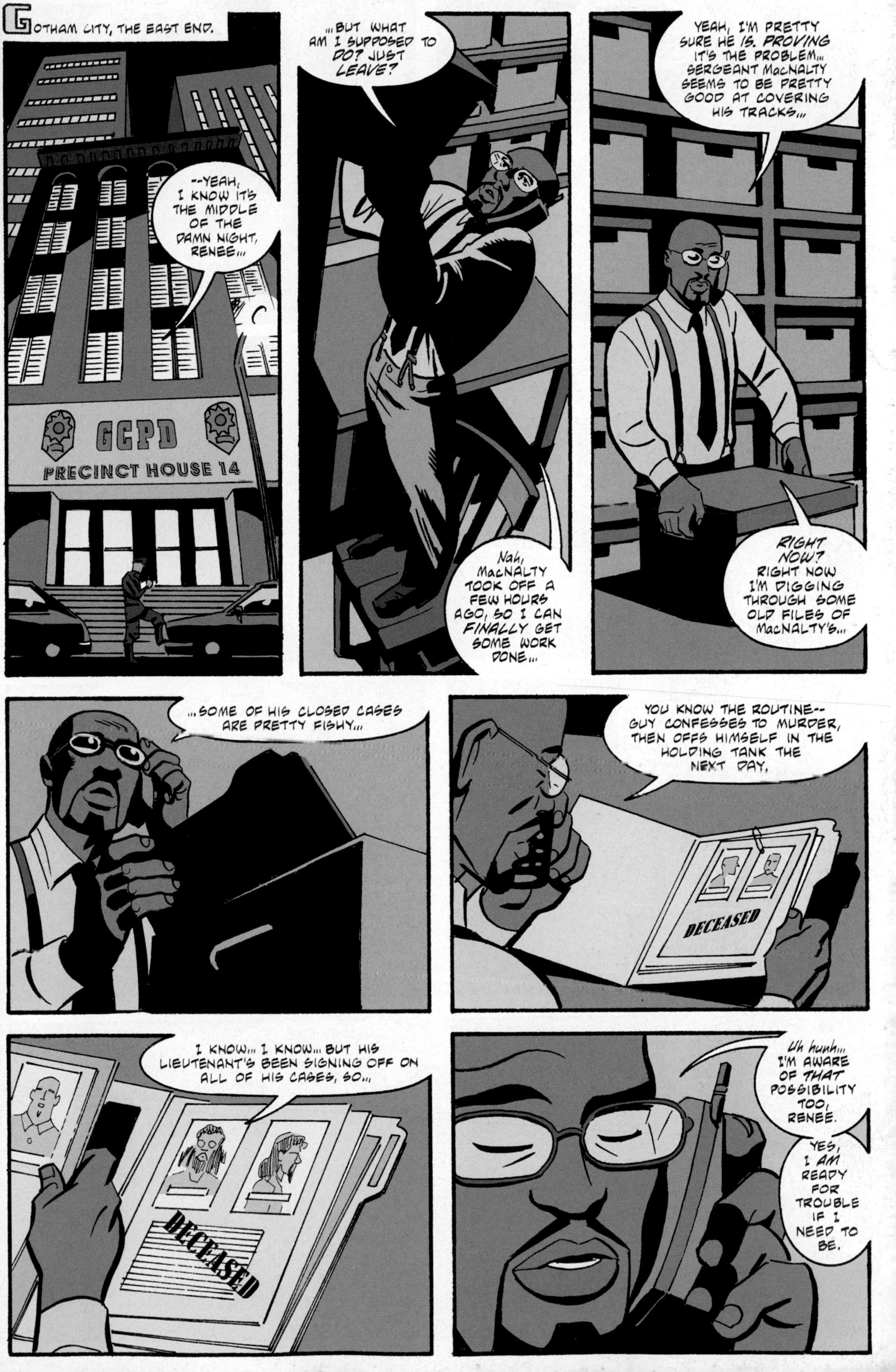
GOTHAM CITY, THE EAST END.
--YEAH, I KNOW IT'S THE MIDDLE OF THE DAMN NIGHT, RENEE...
GCPD
PRECINCT HOUSE 14
...BUT WHAT AM I SUPPOSED TO DO? JUST LEAVE?
Nah, MacNALTY TOOK OFF A FEW HOURS AGO, SO I CAN FINALLY GET SOME WORK DONE...
YEAH, I'M PRETTY SURE HE IS. PROVING IT'S THE PROBLEM... SERGEANT MacNALTY SEEMS TO BE PRETTY GOOD AT COVERING HIS TRACKS...
RIGHT NOW? RIGHT NOW I'M DIGGING THROUGH SOME OLD FILES OF MacNALTY'S...
...SOME OF HIS CLOSED CASES ARE PRETTY FISHY...
YOU KNOW THE ROUTINE-- GUY CONFESSES TO MURDER, THEN OFFS HIMSELF IN THE HOLDING TANK THE NEXT DAY.
DECEASED
I KNOW... I KNOW... BUT HIS LIEUTENANT'S BEEN SIGNING OFF ON ALL OF HIS CASES, SO...
DECEASED
Uh hunh... I'M AWARE OF THAT POSSIBILITY TOO, RENEE.
YES, I AM READY FOR TROUBLE IF I NEED TO BE.

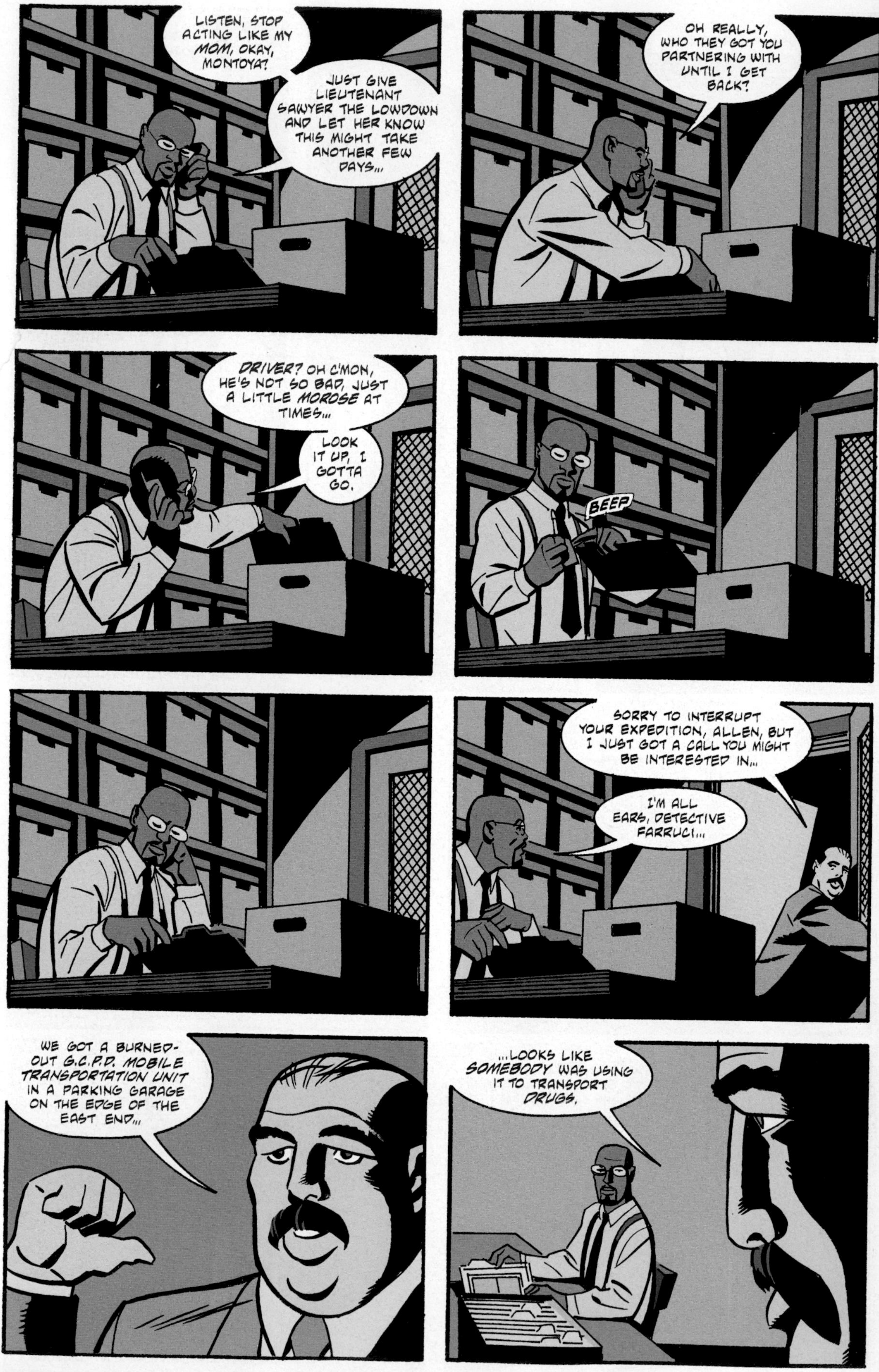
LISTEN, STOP ACTING LIKE MY MOM, OKAY, MONTOYA?
JUST GIVE LIEUTENANT SAWYER THE LOWDOWN AND LET HER KNOW THIS MIGHT TAKE ANOTHER FEW DAYS...
OH REALLY, WHO THEY GOT YOU PARTNERING WITH UNTIL I GET BACK?
DRIVER? OH C'MON, HE'S NOT SO BAD, JUST A LITTLE MOROSE AT TIMES...
LOOK IT UP, I GOTTA GO.
BEEP
SORRY TO INTERRUPT YOUR EXPEDITION, ALLEN, BUT I JUST GOT A CALL YOU MIGHT BE INTERESTED IN...
I'M ALL EARS, DETECTIVE FARRUCI...
WE GOT A BURNED-OUT G.C.P.D. MOBILE TRANSPORTATION UNIT IN A PARKING GARAGE ON THE EDGE OF THE EAST END...
...LOOKS LIKE SOMEBODY WAS USING IT TO TRANSPORT DRUGS.

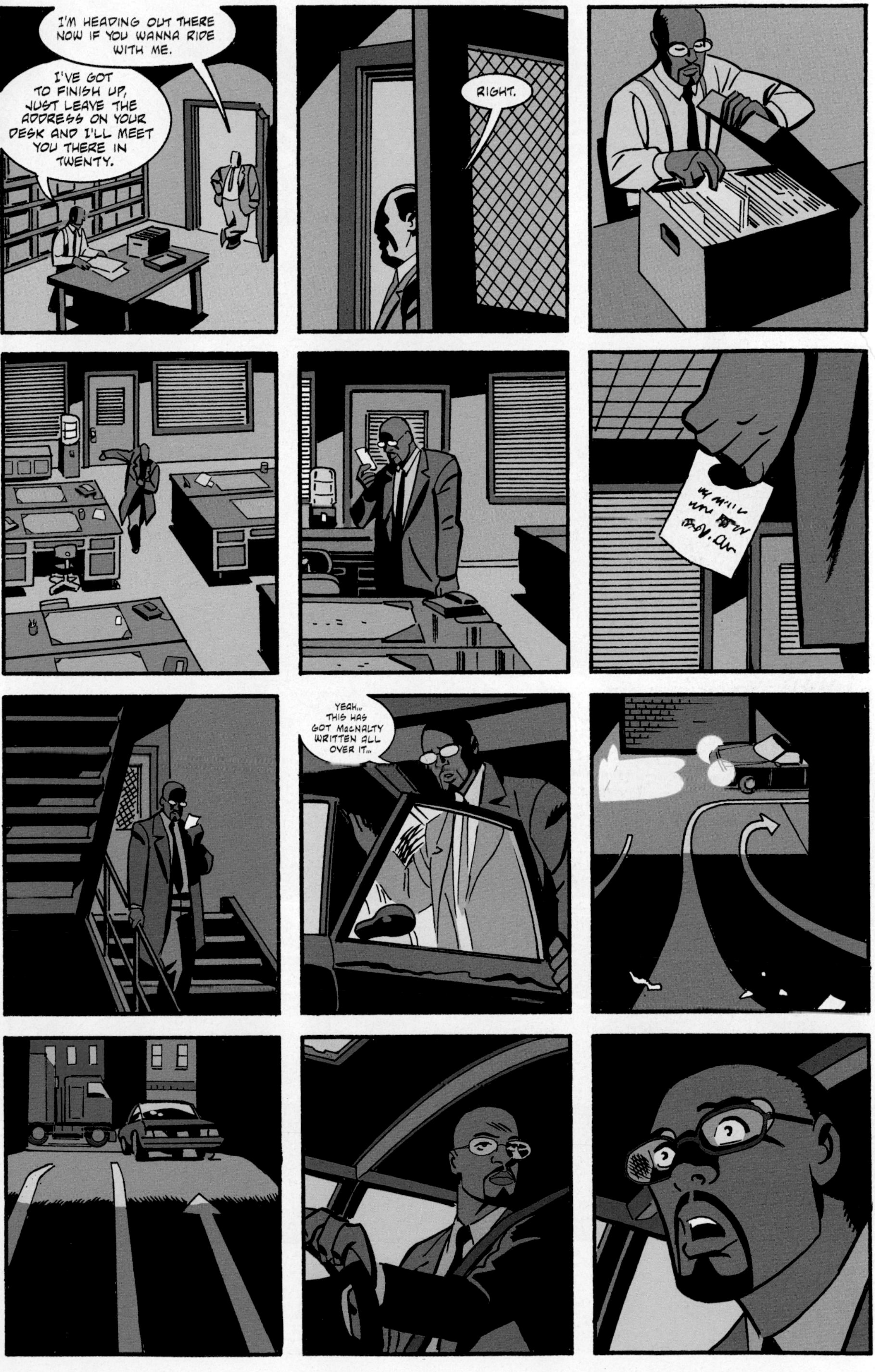
I'M HEADING OUT THERE NOW IF YOU WANNA RIDE WITH ME.
I'VE GOT TO FINISH UP, JUST LEAVE THE ADDRESS ON YOUR DESK AND I'LL MEET YOU THERE IN TWENTY.
RIGHT.
YEAH... THIS HAS GOT MacNALTY WRITTEN ALL OVER IT...

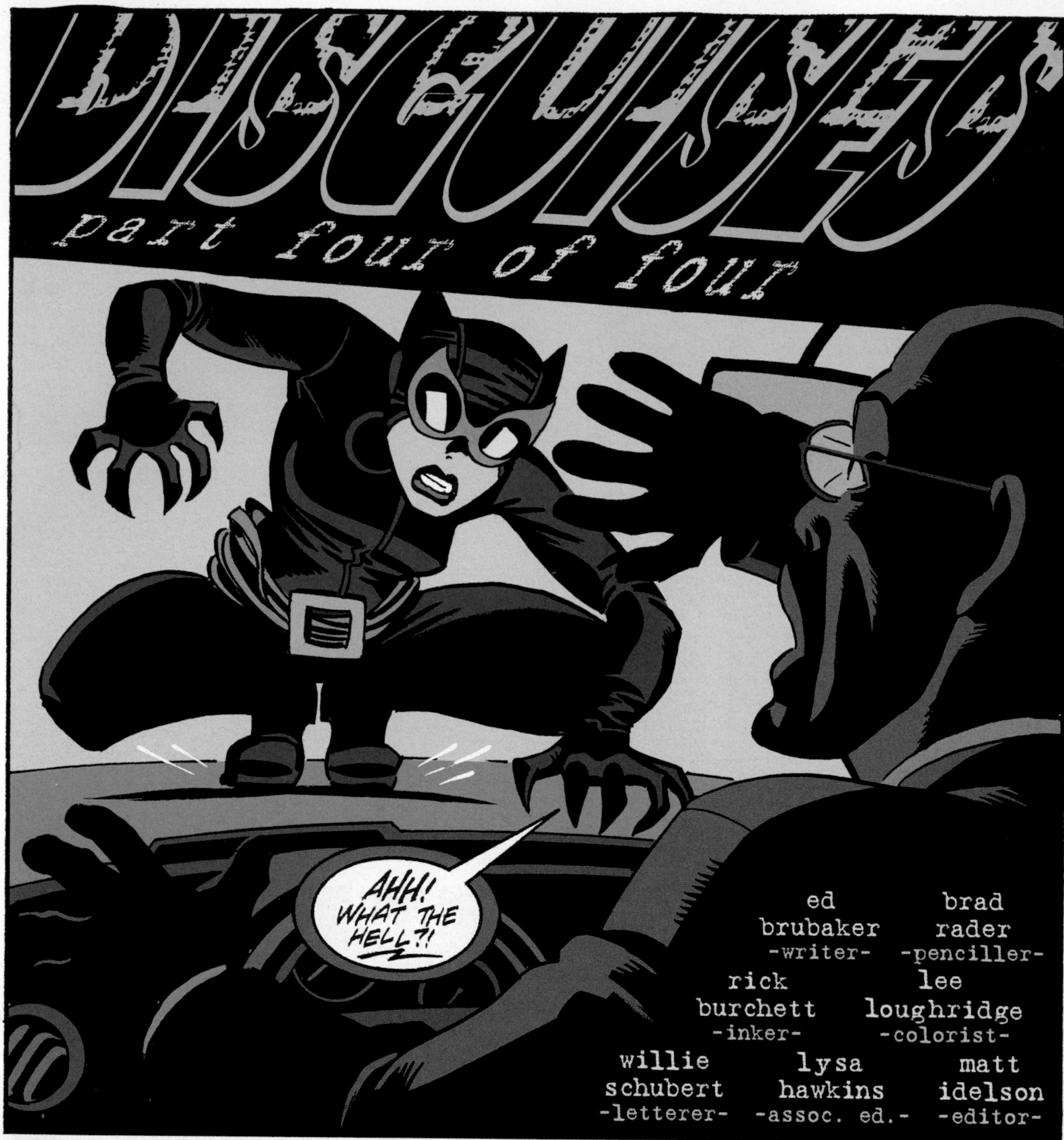
DISGUISES
part four of four
AHH! WHAT THE HELL?!
ed brubaker -writer-
brad rader -penciller-
rick burchett -inker-
lee loughridge -colorist-
willie schubert -letterer-
lysa hawkins -assoc. ed.-
matt idelson -editor-

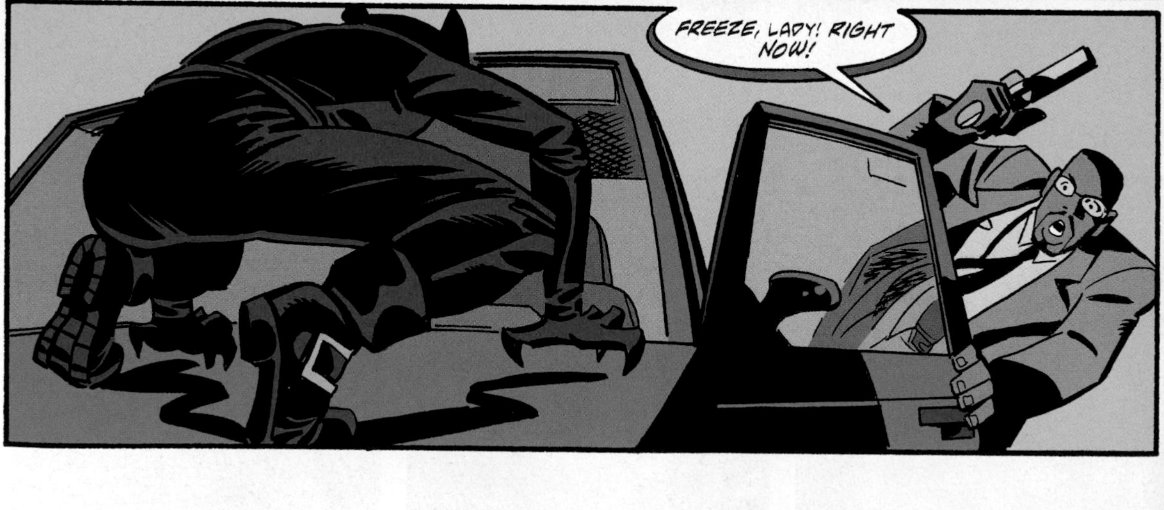
FREEZE, LADY! RIGHT NOW!

DO YOU COPS *ALWAYS* HAVE TO BE SUCH *TOTAL* CLICHÉS?

PUT THAT STUPID THING AWAY...

NOT A CHANCE. GIVE ME ONE *REASON* I SHOULDN'T SHOOT YOU RIGHT HERE...

WELL, BECAUSE THERE'RE *NO BULLETS* IN YOUR GUN, DETECTIVE ALLEN.

WHAT? HOW DID YOU--?

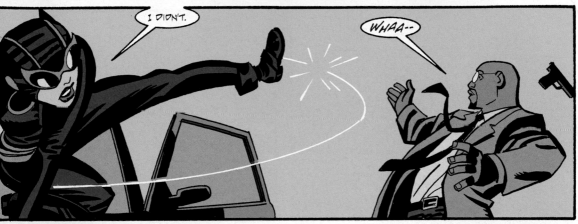

I DIDN'T.

WHAA--

NOW, IF YOU CAN STOP YOURSELF FROM PULLING YOUR BACKUP PIECE ON ME FOR A MINUTE--

--I'D LIKE TO TALK...

WHAT ABOUT?

I THINK YOU AND I ARE WORKING TOWARDS THE SAME GOAL HERE, DETECTIVE, SO I THOUGHT MAYBE WE COULD MAKE A *DEAL*...

OH, *REALLY?*

YEAH, I GIVE YOU MacNALTY AND A BUNCH OF OTHER BAD COPS...

...AND YOU MAKE SURE MY *FRIEND,* THE GIRL WHO'S BEING ACCUSED OF KILLING THAT UNDERCOVER GUY, GETS CLEARED OF ALL CHARGES.

TELL ME ABOUT THIS GIRL...

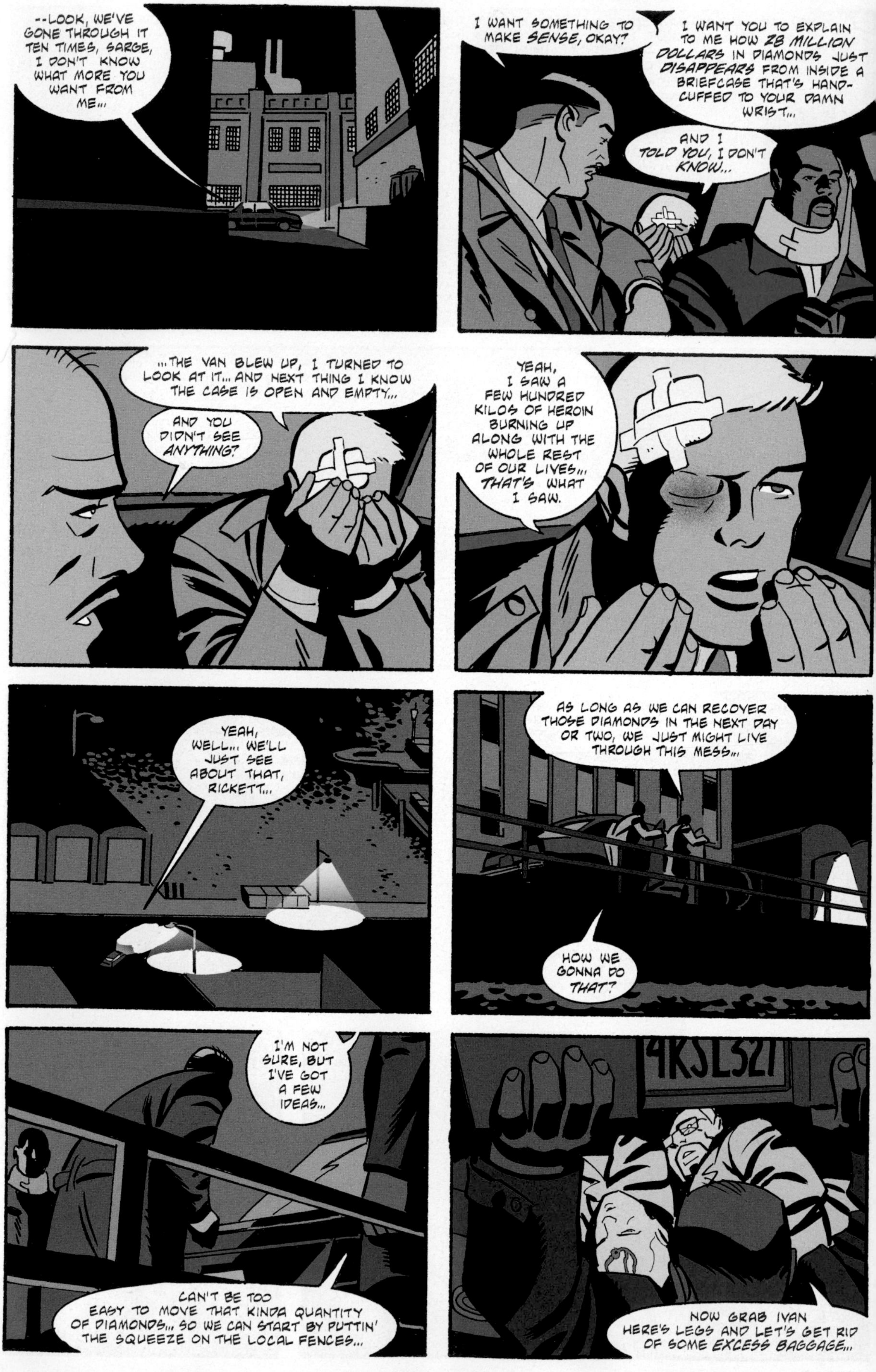
--LOOK, WE'VE GONE THROUGH IT TEN TIMES, SARGE, I DON'T KNOW WHAT MORE YOU WANT FROM ME...
I WANT SOMETHING TO MAKE SENSE, OKAY?
I WANT YOU TO EXPLAIN TO ME HOW 28 MILLION DOLLARS IN DIAMONDS JUST DISAPPEARS FROM INSIDE A BRIEFCASE THAT'S HANDCUFFED TO YOUR DAMN WRIST...
AND I TOLD YOU, I DON'T KNOW...
...THE VAN BLEW UP, I TURNED TO LOOK AT IT... AND NEXT THING I KNOW THE CASE IS OPEN AND EMPTY...
AND YOU DIDN'T SEE ANYTHING?
YEAH, I SAW A FEW HUNDRED KILOS OF HEROIN BURNING UP ALONG WITH THE WHOLE REST OF OUR LIVES... THAT'S WHAT I SAW.
YEAH, WELL... WE'LL JUST SEE ABOUT THAT, RICKETT...
AS LONG AS WE CAN RECOVER THOSE DIAMONDS IN THE NEXT DAY OR TWO, WE JUST MIGHT LIVE THROUGH THIS MESS...
HOW WE GONNA DO THAT?
I'M NOT SURE, BUT I'VE GOT A FEW IDEAS...
CAN'T BE TOO EASY TO MOVE THAT KINDA QUANTITY OF DIAMONDS... SO WE CAN START BY PUTTIN' THE SQUEEZE ON THE LOCAL FENCES...
4KSL527
NOW GRAB IVAN HERE'S LEGS AND LET'S GET RID OF SOME EXCESS BAGGAGE...

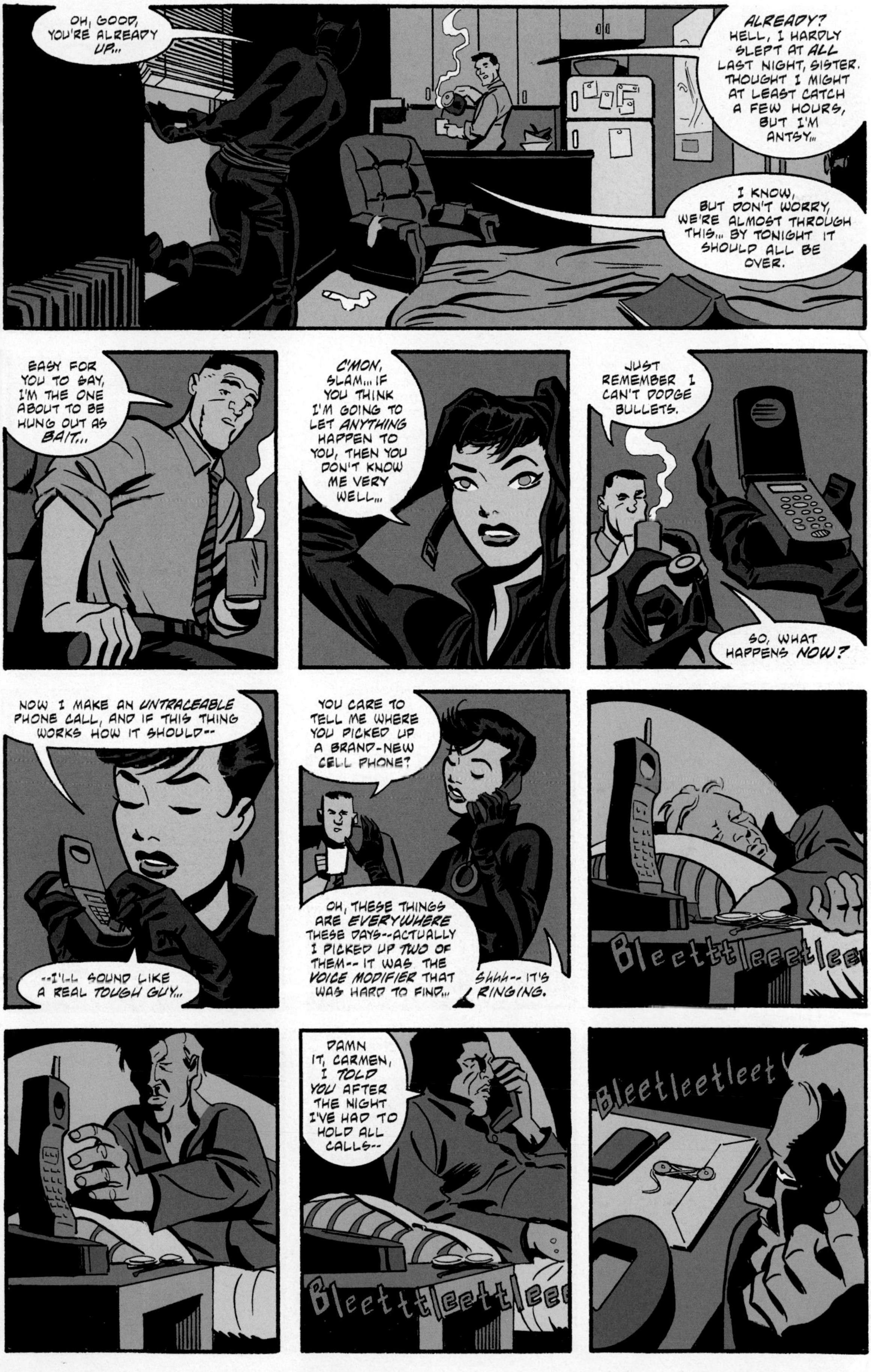
OH, GOOD, YOU'RE ALREADY UP...
ALREADY? HELL, I HARDLY SLEPT AT ALL LAST NIGHT, SISTER. THOUGHT I MIGHT AT LEAST CATCH A FEW HOURS, BUT I'M ANTSY...
I KNOW, BUT DON'T WORRY, WE'RE ALMOST THROUGH THIS... BY TONIGHT IT SHOULD ALL BE OVER.
EASY FOR YOU TO SAY, I'M THE ONE ABOUT TO BE HUNG OUT AS BAIT...
C'MON, SLAM... IF YOU THINK I'M GOING TO LET ANYTHING HAPPEN TO YOU, THEN YOU DON'T KNOW ME VERY WELL...
JUST REMEMBER I CAN'T DODGE BULLETS.
SO, WHAT HAPPENS NOW?
NOW I MAKE AN UNTRACEABLE PHONE CALL, AND IF THIS THING WORKS HOW IT SHOULD--
--I'LL SOUND LIKE A REAL TOUGH GUY...
YOU CARE TO TELL ME WHERE YOU PICKED UP A BRAND-NEW CELL PHONE?
OH, THESE THINGS ARE EVERYWHERE THESE DAYS--ACTUALLY I PICKED UP TWO OF THEM-- IT WAS THE VOICE MODIFIER THAT WAS HARD TO FIND...
Shhh-- IT'S RINGING.
Bleetttleeetleee
Bleetttleettleee
DAMN IT, CARMEN, I TOLD YOU AFTER THE NIGHT I'VE HAD TO HOLD ALL CALLS--
Bleetleetleet

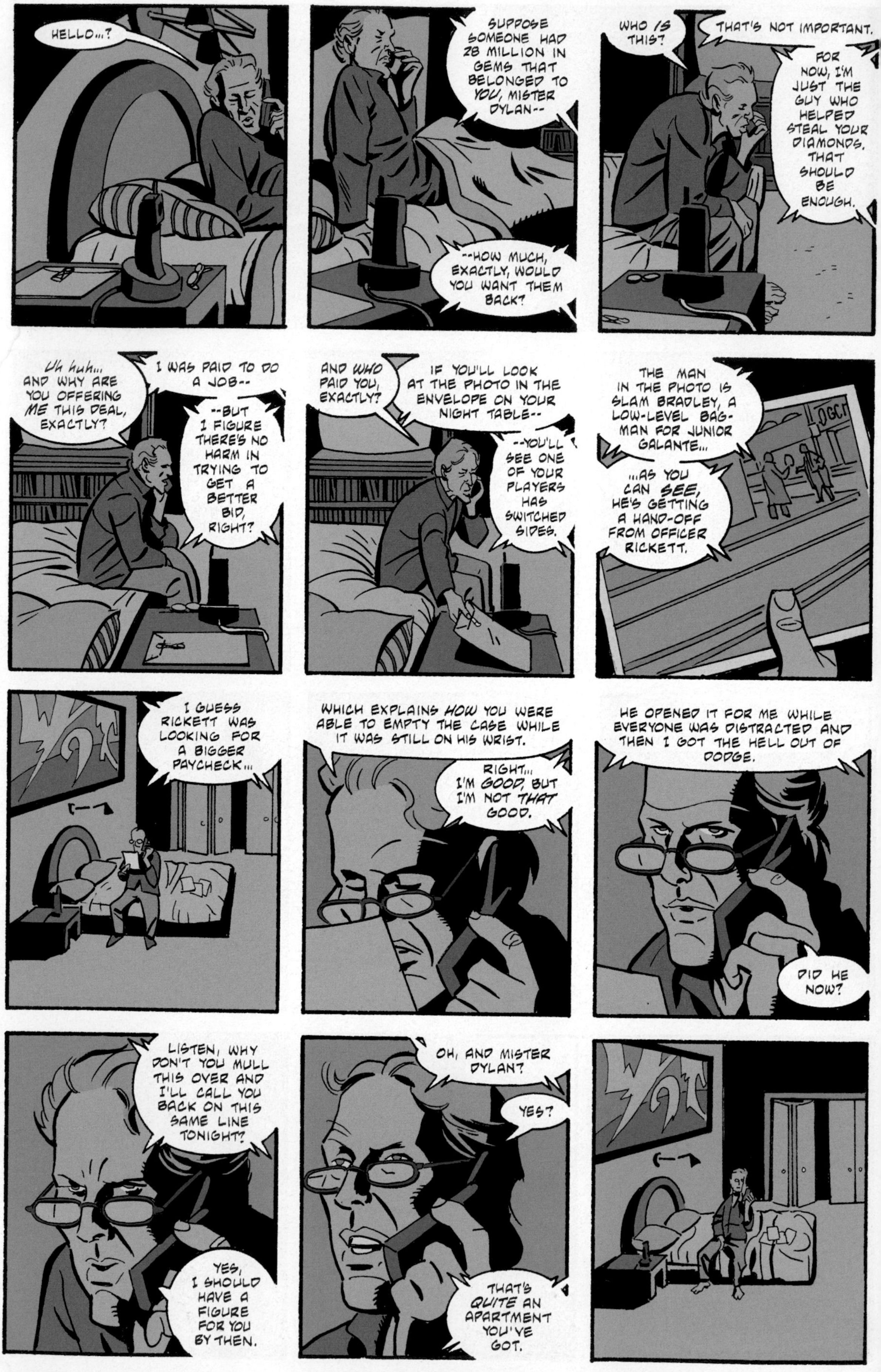
HELLO...?
SUPPOSE SOMEONE HAD 28 MILLION IN GEMS THAT BELONGED TO YOU, MISTER DYLAN--
--HOW MUCH, EXACTLY, WOULD YOU WANT THEM BACK?
WHO IS THIS?
THAT'S NOT IMPORTANT.
FOR NOW, I'M JUST THE GUY WHO HELPED STEAL YOUR DIAMONDS. THAT SHOULD BE ENOUGH.
Uh huh... AND WHY ARE YOU OFFERING ME THIS DEAL, EXACTLY?
I WAS PAID TO DO A JOB--
--BUT I FIGURE THERE'S NO HARM IN TRYING TO GET A BETTER BID, RIGHT?
AND WHO PAID YOU, EXACTLY?
IF YOU'LL LOOK AT THE PHOTO IN THE ENVELOPE ON YOUR NIGHT TABLE--
--YOU'LL SEE ONE OF YOUR PLAYERS HAS SWITCHED SIDES.
THE MAN IN THE PHOTO IS SLAM BRADLEY, A LOW-LEVEL BAG-MAN FOR JUNIOR GALANTE...
...AS YOU CAN SEE, HE'S GETTING A HAND-OFF FROM OFFICER RICKETT.
I GUESS RICKETT WAS LOOKING FOR A BIGGER PAYCHECK...
WHICH EXPLAINS HOW YOU WERE ABLE TO EMPTY THE CASE WHILE IT WAS STILL ON HIS WRIST.
RIGHT... I'M GOOD, BUT I'M NOT THAT GOOD.
HE OPENED IT FOR ME WHILE EVERYONE WAS DISTRACTED AND THEN I GOT THE HELL OUT OF DODGE.
DID HE NOW?
LISTEN, WHY DON'T YOU MULL THIS OVER AND I'LL CALL YOU BACK ON THIS SAME LINE TONIGHT?
YES, I SHOULD HAVE A FIGURE FOR YOU BY THEN.
OH, AND MISTER DYLAN?
YES?
THAT'S QUITE AN APARTMENT YOU'VE GOT.

Wootlootloot Wootlootloot

SORRY, I GOTTA TAKE THIS...

MORNIN', SIR. I DIDN'T THINK I'D BE HEARING FROM YOU THIS SOON. I THOUGHT WE'D HAVE A FEW DAYS TO--

YOU'RE *KIDDING*, RIGHT?

WELL, IT'S GOTTA BE SOME KINDA SCAM OR SOMETHING...

WHO? *SLAM BRADLEY?*

NO, THAT'S *BUNK*... I KNOW WHO THAT GUY IS, HE'S JUST A *SHAMUS*... HE DON'T--

OKAY, ALL RIGHT... LET ME LOOK INTO IT AND I'LL CALL YOU BACK.

HOLD ON, LEMME CHECK...

HEY, LOUIE, YOU GOT A FAX MACHINE I CAN USE?

UH... SURE, MacNALTY... IT'S IN THE BACK...

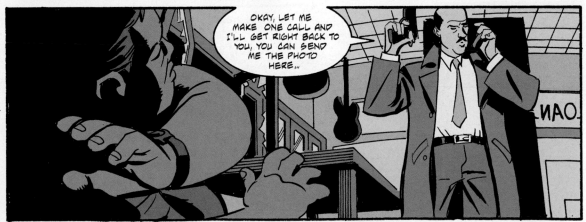

OKAY, LET ME MAKE ONE CALL AND I'LL GET RIGHT BACK TO YOU, YOU CAN SEND ME THE PHOTO HERE...

OAN

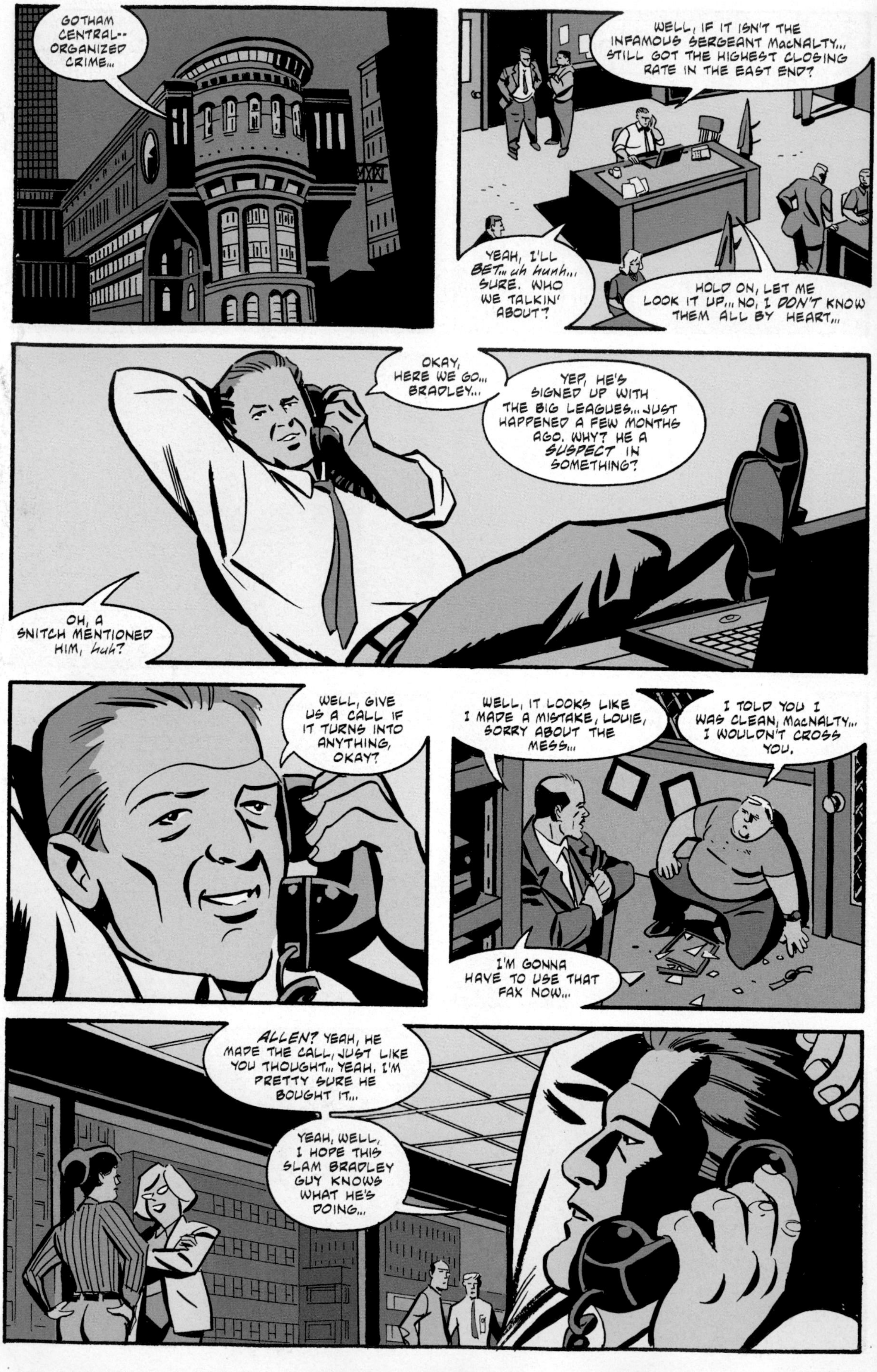
GOTHAM CENTRAL-- ORGANIZED CRIME...
WELL, IF IT ISN'T THE INFAMOUS SERGEANT MacNALTY... STILL GOT THE HIGHEST CLOSING RATE IN THE EAST END?
YEAH, I'LL BET... uh hunh... SURE. WHO WE TALKIN' ABOUT?
HOLD ON, LET ME LOOK IT UP... NO, I DON'T KNOW THEM ALL BY HEART...
OKAY, HERE WE GO... BRADLEY...
YEP, HE'S SIGNED UP WITH THE BIG LEAGUES... JUST HAPPENED A FEW MONTHS AGO. WHY? HE A SUSPECT IN SOMETHING?
OH, A SNITCH MENTIONED HIM, huh?
WELL, GIVE US A CALL IF IT TURNS INTO ANYTHING, OKAY?
WELL, IT LOOKS LIKE I MADE A MISTAKE, LOUIE, SORRY ABOUT THE MESS...
I TOLD YOU I WAS CLEAN, MacNALTY... I WOULDN'T CROSS YOU.
I'M GONNA HAVE TO USE THAT FAX NOW...
ALLEN? YEAH, HE MADE THE CALL, JUST LIKE YOU THOUGHT... YEAH, I'M PRETTY SURE HE BOUGHT IT...
YEAH, WELL, I HOPE THIS SLAM BRADLEY GUY KNOWS WHAT HE'S DOING...

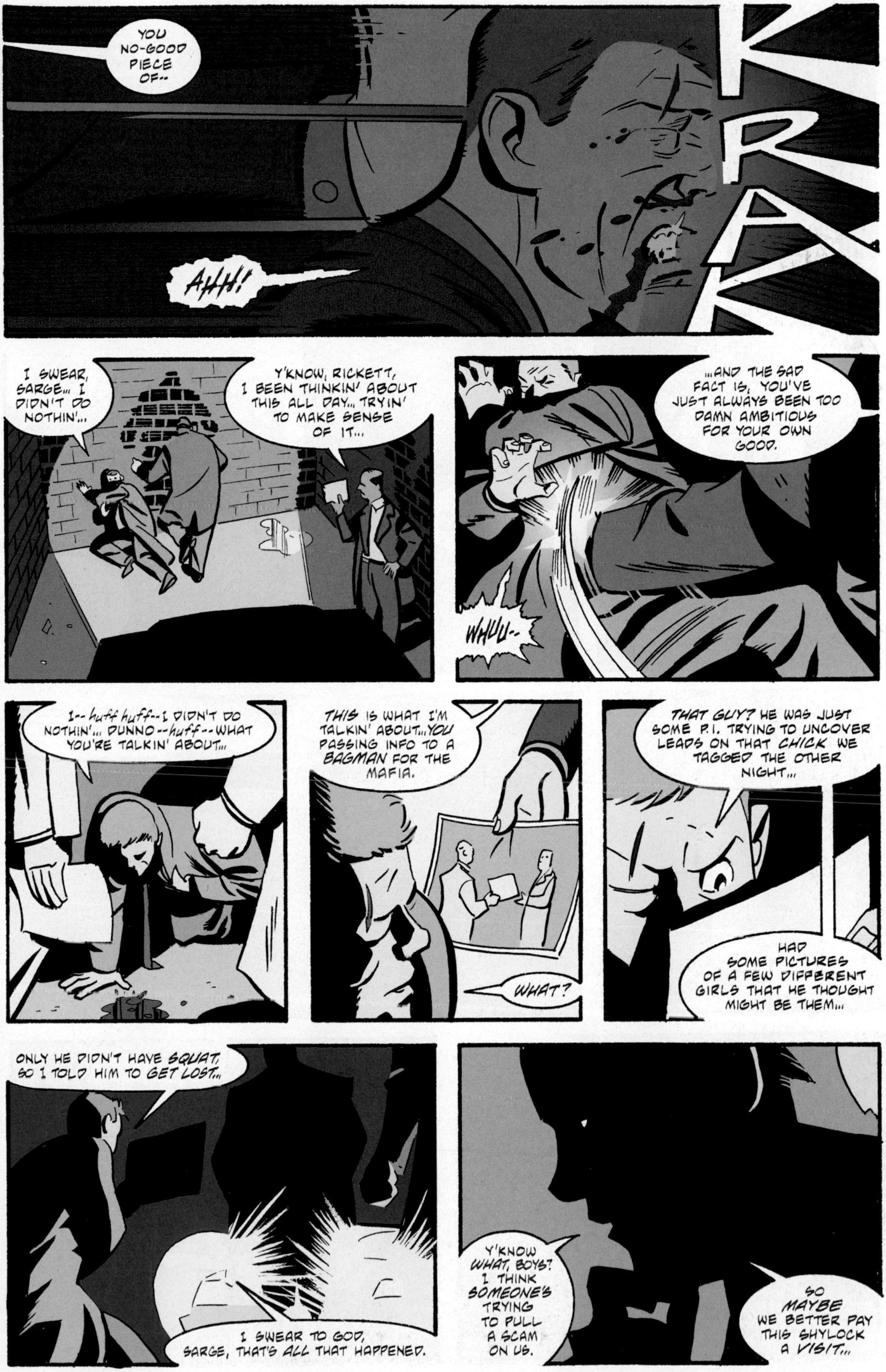
YOU NO-GOOD PIECE OF--
KRAK
AHH!
I SWEAR, SARGE... I DIDN'T DO NOTHIN'...
Y'KNOW, RICKETT, I BEEN THINKIN' ABOUT THIS ALL DAY... TRYIN' TO MAKE SENSE OF IT...
...AND THE SAD FACT IS, YOU'VE JUST ALWAYS BEEN TOO DAMN AMBITIOUS FOR YOUR OWN GOOD.
WHUU--
I-- huff huff-- I DIDN'T DO NOTHIN'... DUNNO-- huff-- WHAT YOU'RE TALKIN' ABOUT...
THIS IS WHAT I'M TALKIN' ABOUT... YOU PASSING INFO TO A BAGMAN FOR THE MAFIA.
WHAT?
THAT GUY? HE WAS JUST SOME P.I. TRYING TO UNCOVER LEADS ON THAT CHICK WE TAGGED THE OTHER NIGHT...
HAD SOME PICTURES OF A FEW DIFFERENT GIRLS THAT HE THOUGHT MIGHT BE THEM...
ONLY HE DIDN'T HAVE SQUAT, SO I TOLD HIM TO GET LOST...
I SWEAR TO GOD, SARGE, THAT'S ALL THAT HAPPENED.
Y'KNOW WHAT, BOYS? I THINK SOMEONE'S TRYING TO PULL A SCAM ON US.
SO MAYBE WE BETTER PAY THIS SHYLOCK A VISIT...

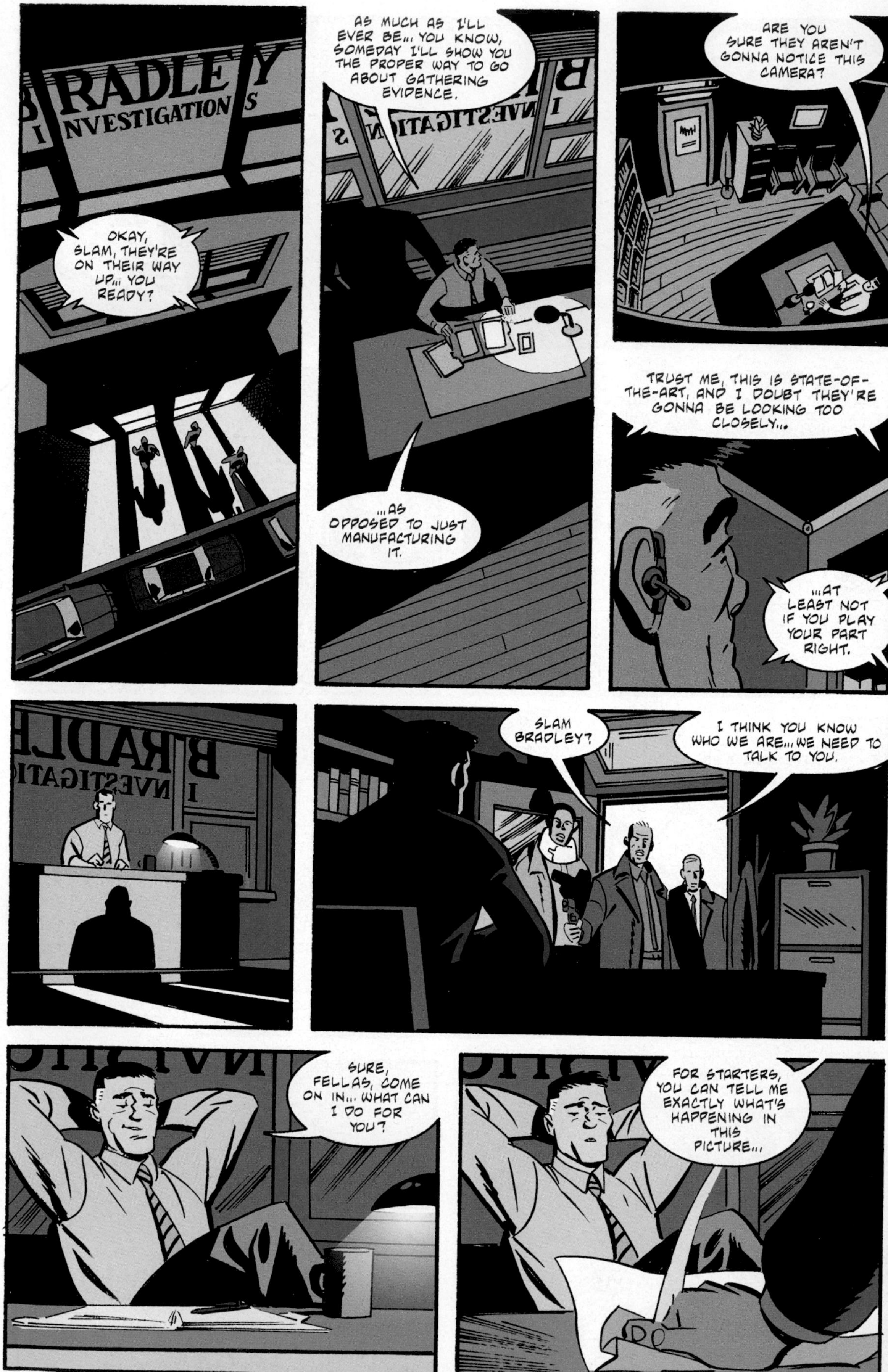
BRADLEY INVESTIGATIONS
OKAY, SLAM, THEY'RE ON THEIR WAY UP... YOU READY?
AS MUCH AS I'LL EVER BE... YOU KNOW, SOMEDAY I'LL SHOW YOU THE PROPER WAY TO GO ABOUT GATHERING EVIDENCE.
...AS OPPOSED TO JUST MANUFACTURING IT.
ARE YOU SURE THEY AREN'T GONNA NOTICE THIS CAMERA?
TRUST ME, THIS IS STATE-OF-THE-ART, AND I DOUBT THEY'RE GONNA BE LOOKING TOO CLOSELY...
...AT LEAST NOT IF YOU PLAY YOUR PART RIGHT.
SLAM BRADLEY?
I THINK YOU KNOW WHO WE ARE... WE NEED TO TALK TO YOU.
SURE, FELLAS, COME ON IN... WHAT CAN I DO FOR YOU?
FOR STARTERS, YOU CAN TELL ME EXACTLY WHAT'S HAPPENING IN THIS PICTURE...

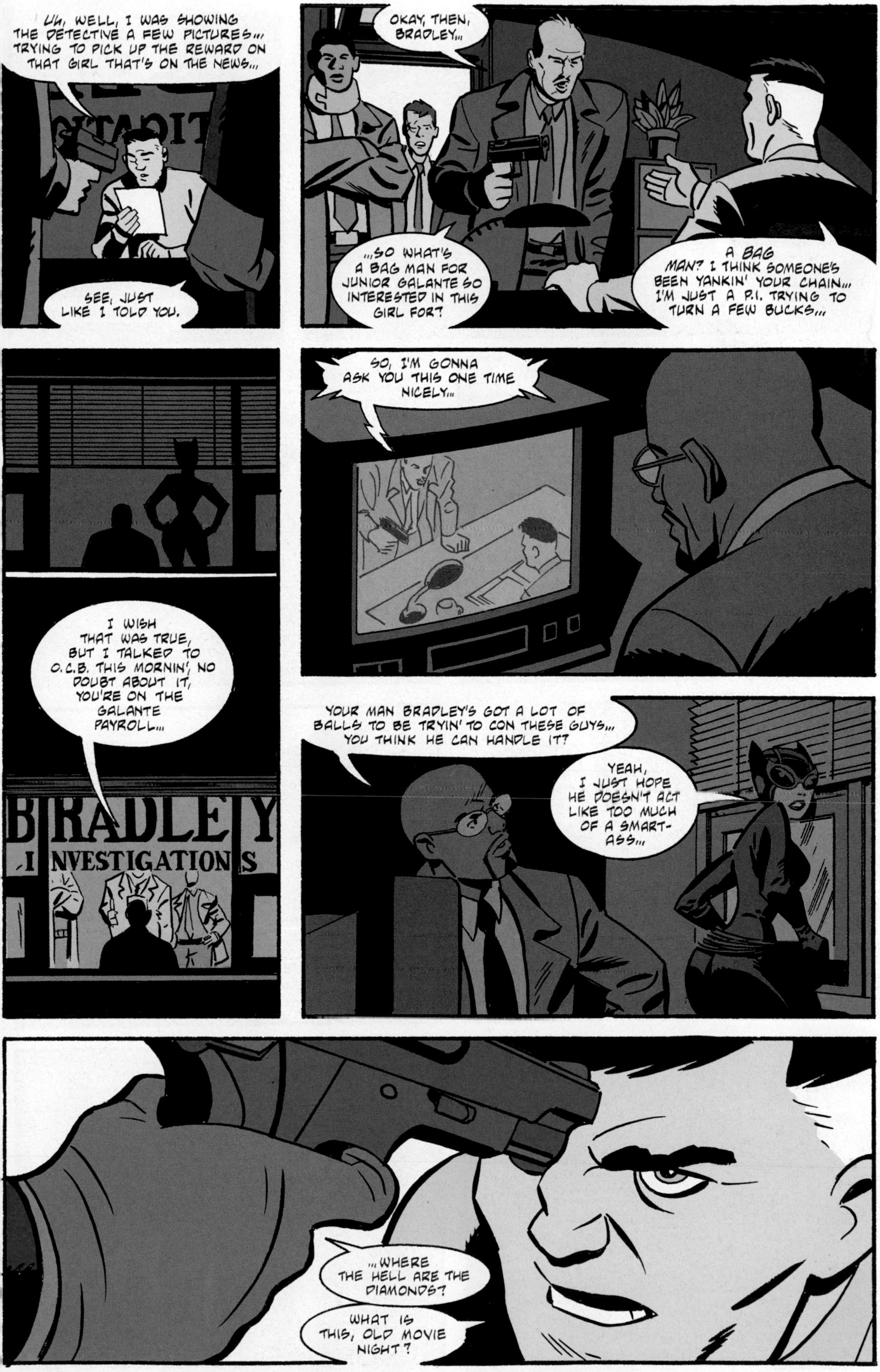
UH, WELL, I WAS SHOWING THE DETECTIVE A FEW PICTURES... TRYING TO PICK UP THE REWARD ON THAT GIRL THAT'S ON THE NEWS...
SEE, JUST LIKE I TOLD YOU.
OKAY, THEN, BRADLEY...
...SO WHAT'S A BAG MAN FOR JUNIOR GALANTE SO INTERESTED IN THIS GIRL FOR?
A BAG MAN? I THINK SOMEONE'S BEEN YANKIN' YOUR CHAIN... I'M JUST A P.I. TRYING TO TURN A FEW BUCKS...
I WISH THAT WAS TRUE, BUT I TALKED TO O.C.B. THIS MORNIN', NO DOUBT ABOUT IT, YOU'RE ON THE GALANTE PAYROLL...
BRADLEY INVESTIGATIONS
SO, I'M GONNA ASK YOU THIS ONE TIME NICELY...
YOUR MAN BRADLEY'S GOT A LOT OF BALLS TO BE TRYIN' TO CON THESE GUYS... YOU THINK HE CAN HANDLE IT?
YEAH, I JUST HOPE HE DOESN'T ACT LIKE TOO MUCH OF A SMART-ASS...
...WHERE THE HELL ARE THE DIAMONDS?
WHAT IS THIS, OLD MOVIE NIGHT?

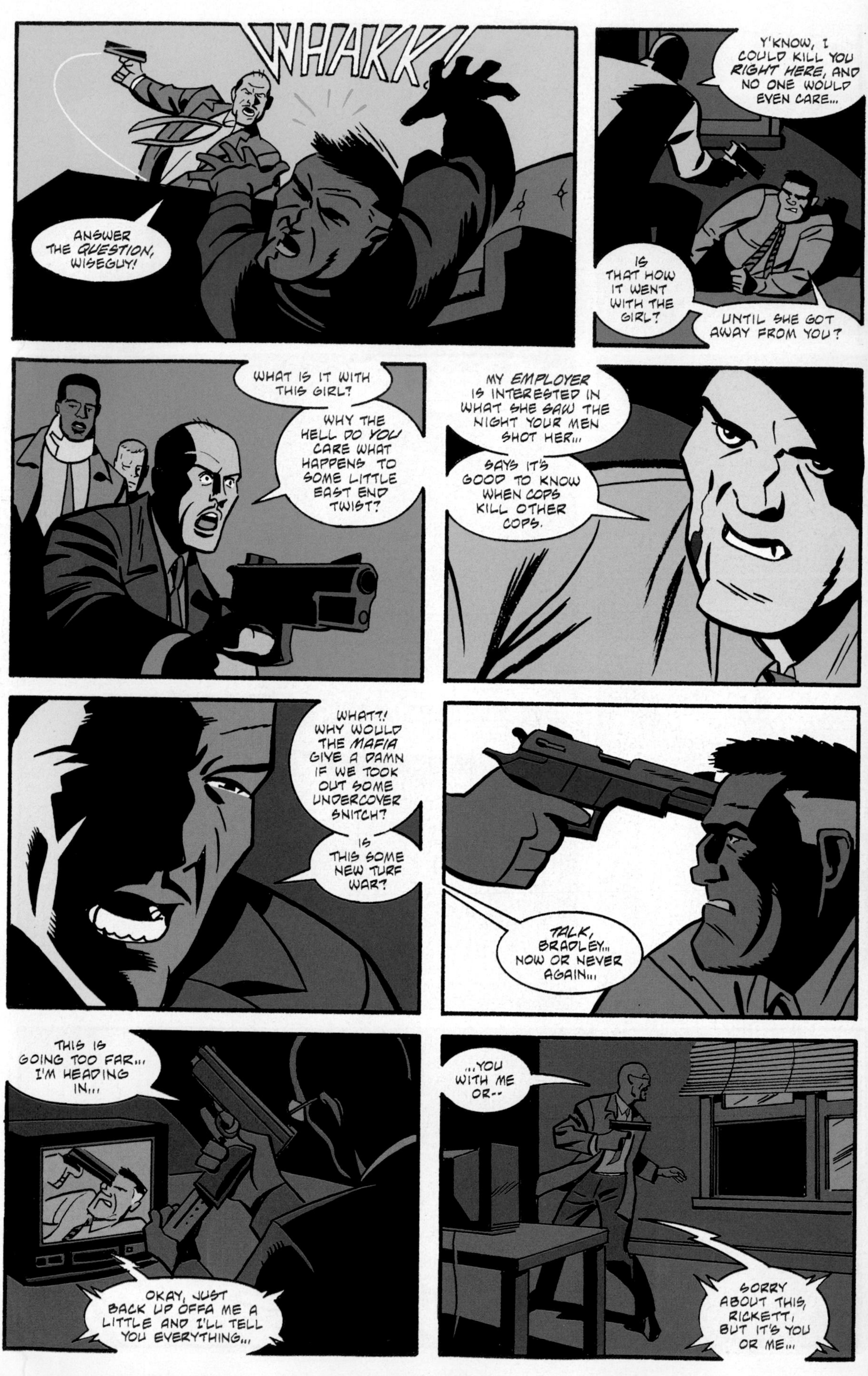
WHAKK!
ANSWER THE QUESTION, WISEGUY!
Y'KNOW, I COULD KILL YOU RIGHT HERE, AND NO ONE WOULD EVEN CARE...
IS THAT HOW IT WENT WITH THE GIRL?
UNTIL SHE GOT AWAY FROM YOU?
WHAT IS IT WITH THIS GIRL?
WHY THE HELL DO YOU CARE WHAT HAPPENS TO SOME LITTLE EAST END TWIST?
MY EMPLOYER IS INTERESTED IN WHAT SHE SAW THE NIGHT YOUR MEN SHOT HER...
SAYS IT'S GOOD TO KNOW WHEN COPS KILL OTHER COPS.
WHAT?! WHY WOULD THE MAFIA GIVE A DAMN IF WE TOOK OUT SOME UNDERCOVER SNITCH?
IS THIS SOME NEW TURF WAR?
TALK, BRADLEY... NOW OR NEVER AGAIN...
THIS IS GOING TOO FAR... I'M HEADING IN...
OKAY, JUST BACK UP OFFA ME A LITTLE AND I'LL TELL YOU EVERYTHING...
...YOU WITH ME OR--
SORRY ABOUT THIS, RICKETT, BUT IT'S YOU OR ME...

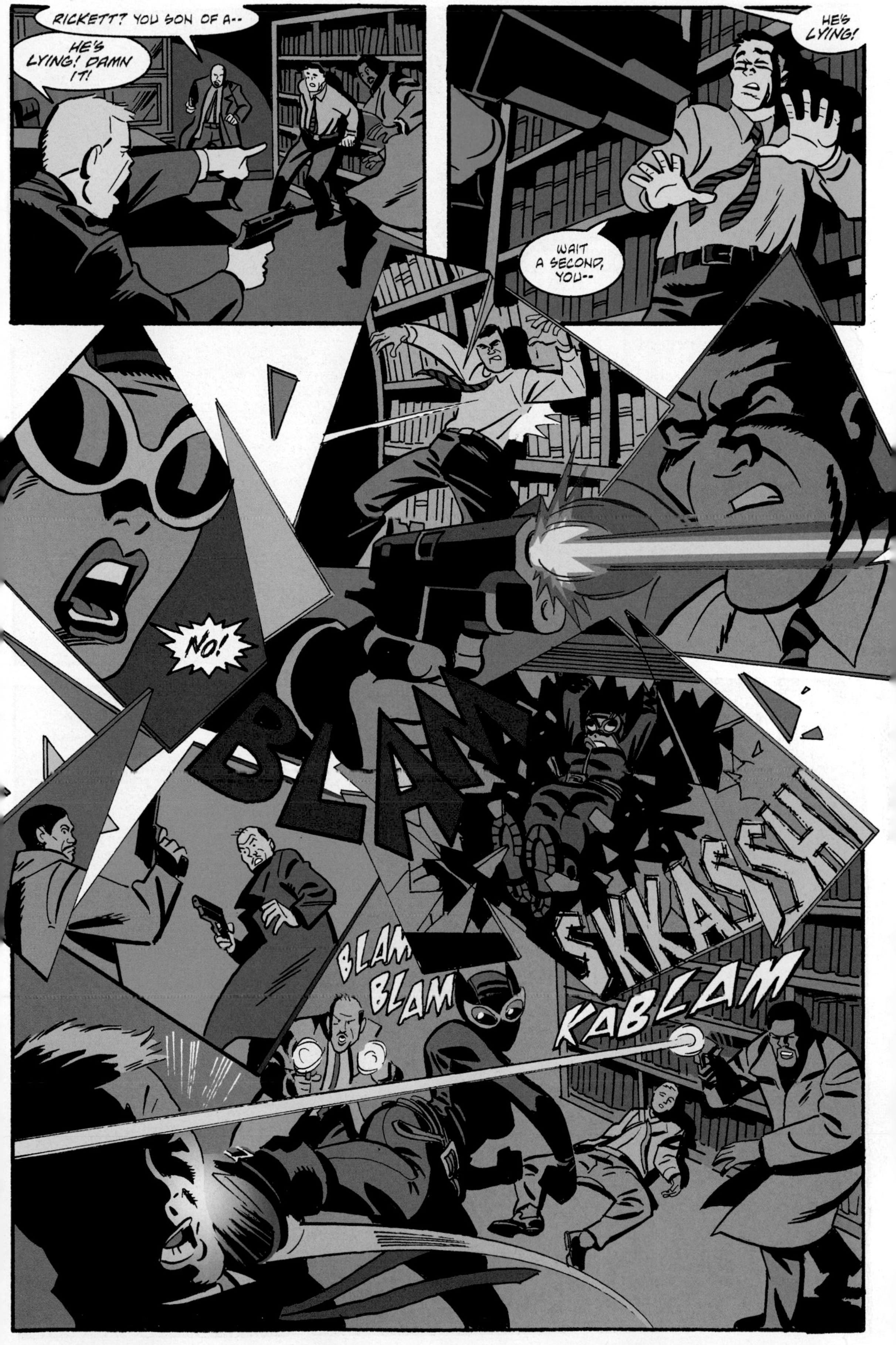
RICKETT? YOU SON OF A--
HE'S LYING! DAMN IT!
HE'S LYING!
WAIT A SECOND, YOU--
NO!
BLAM
SKKASSH
BLAM
BLAM
KABLAM

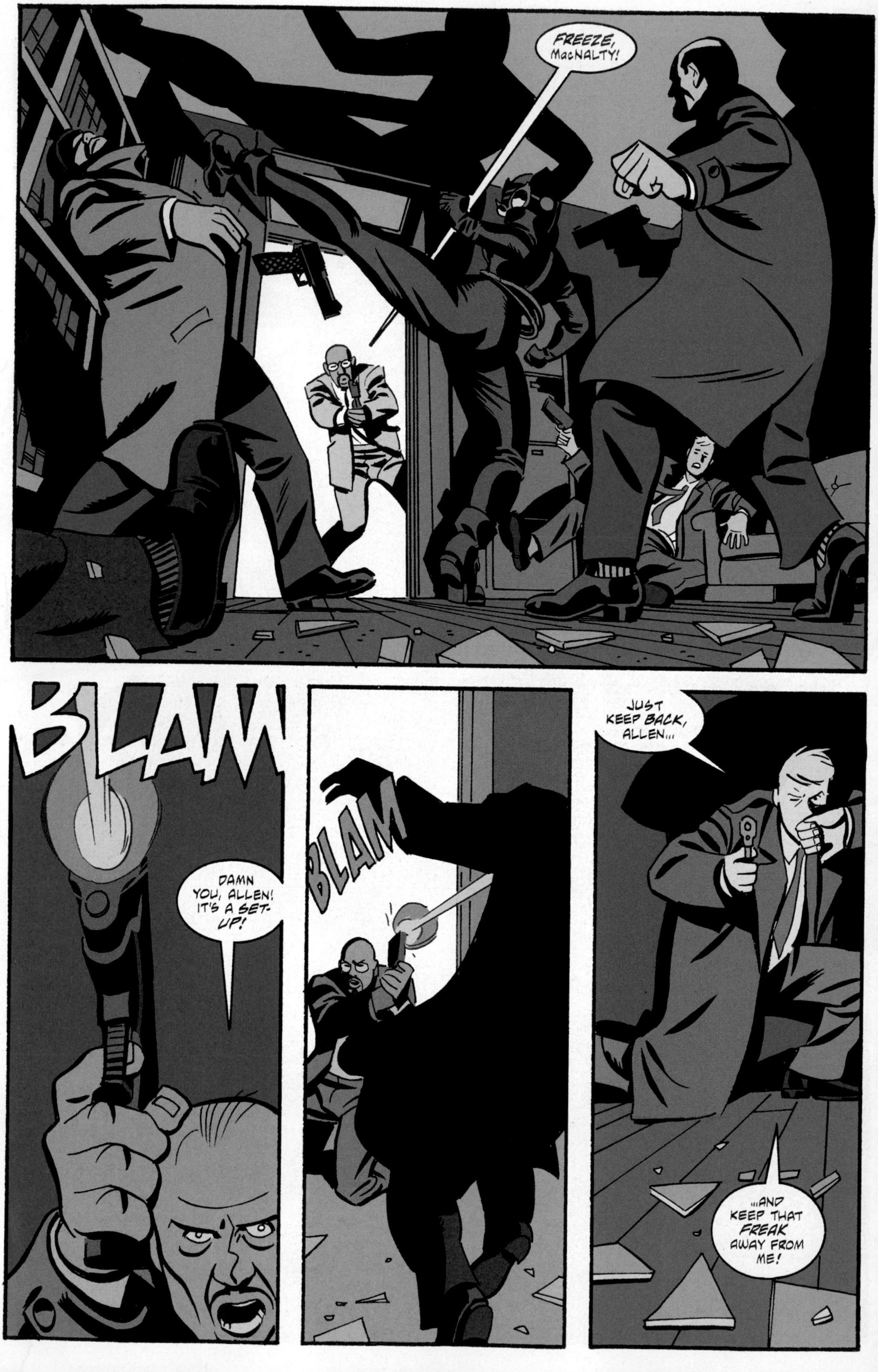
FREEZE, MacNALTY!
BLAM
DAMN YOU, ALLEN! IT'S A SET-UP!
BLAM
JUST KEEP BACK, ALLEN...
...AND KEEP THAT FREAK AWAY FROM ME!

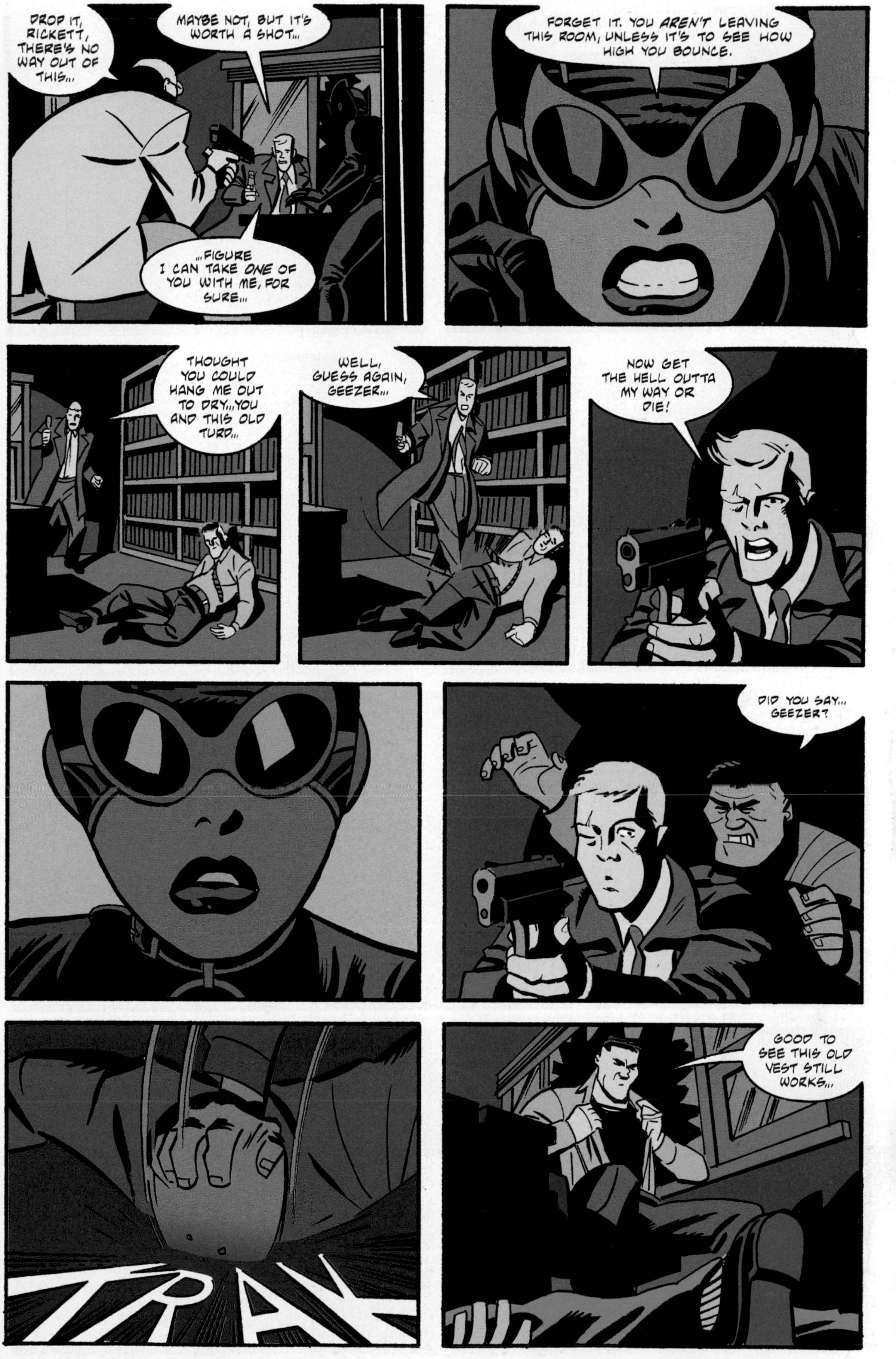
DROP IT, RICKETT, THERE'S NO WAY OUT OF THIS...
MAYBE NOT, BUT IT'S WORTH A SHOT...
...FIGURE I CAN TAKE ONE OF YOU WITH ME, FOR SURE...
FORGET IT. YOU AREN'T LEAVING THIS ROOM, UNLESS IT'S TO SEE HOW HIGH YOU BOUNCE.
THOUGHT YOU COULD HANG ME OUT TO DRY...YOU AND THIS OLD TURD...
WELL, GUESS AGAIN, GEEZER...
NOW GET THE HELL OUTTA MY WAY OR DIE!
DID YOU SAY... GEEZER?
TRAK
GOOD TO SEE THIS OLD VEST STILL WORKS...

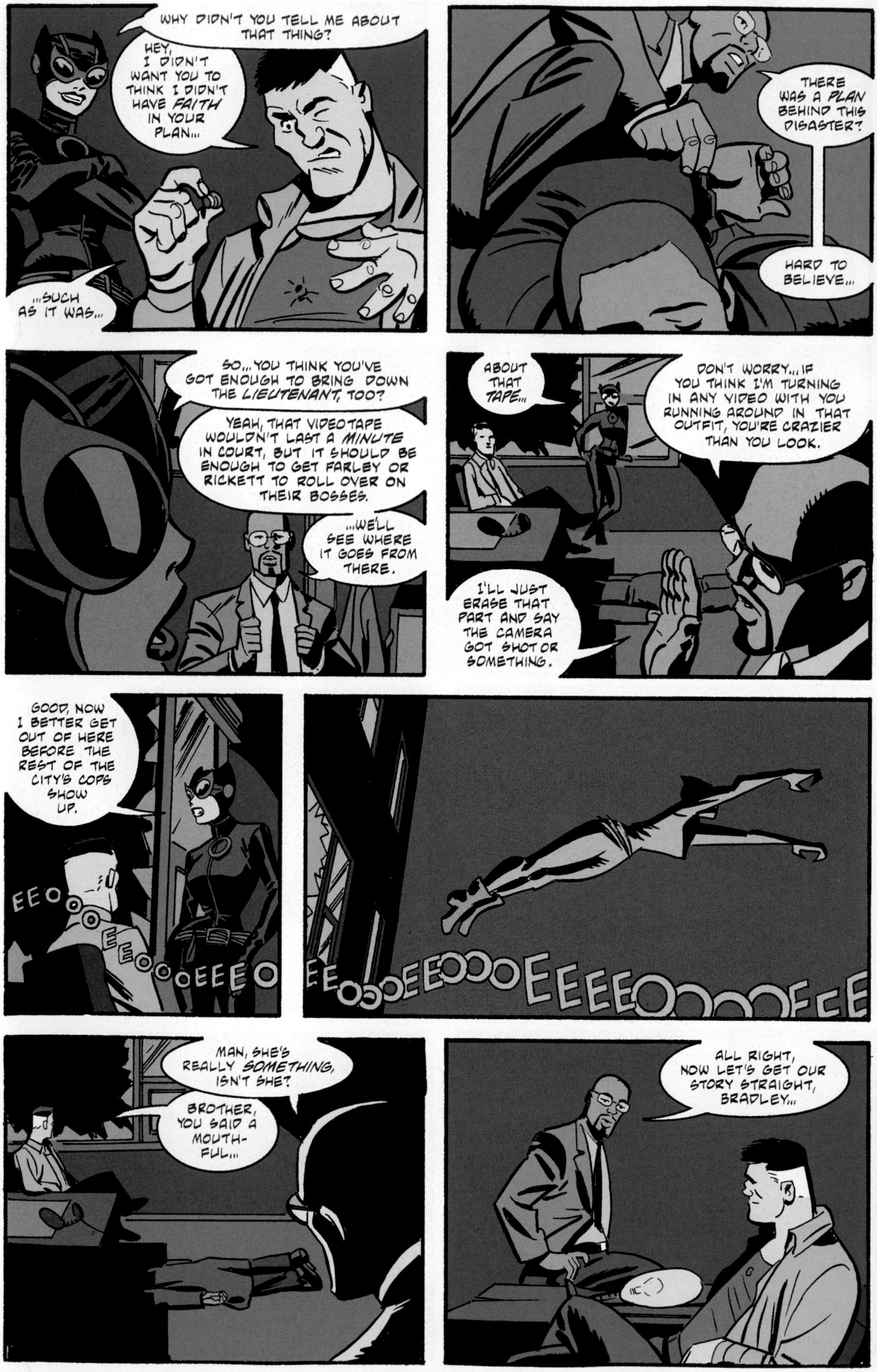

WHY DIDN'T YOU TELL ME ABOUT THAT THING?
HEY, I DIDN'T WANT YOU TO THINK I DIDN'T HAVE FAITH IN YOUR PLAN...
...SUCH AS IT WAS...
THERE WAS A PLAN BEHIND THIS DISASTER?
HARD TO BELIEVE...
SO... YOU THINK YOU'VE GOT ENOUGH TO BRING DOWN THE LIEUTENANT, TOO?
YEAH, THAT VIDEOTAPE WOULDN'T LAST A MINUTE IN COURT, BUT IT SHOULD BE ENOUGH TO GET FARLEY OR RICKETT TO ROLL OVER ON THEIR BOSSES.
...WE'LL SEE WHERE IT GOES FROM THERE.
ABOUT THAT TAPE...
DON'T WORRY... IF YOU THINK I'M TURNING IN ANY VIDEO WITH YOU RUNNING AROUND IN THAT OUTFIT, YOU'RE CRAZIER THAN YOU LOOK.
I'LL JUST ERASE THAT PART AND SAY THE CAMERA GOT SHOT OR SOMETHING.
GOOD, NOW I BETTER GET OUT OF HERE BEFORE THE REST OF THE CITY'S COPS SHOW UP.
EEOOOOEEOOOEEEEO
EEOOOEEOOOEEEEOOOOEEE
MAN, SHE'S REALLY SOMETHING, ISN'T SHE?
BROTHER, YOU SAID A MOUTH-FUL...
ALL RIGHT, NOW LET'S GET OUR STORY STRAIGHT, BRADLEY...

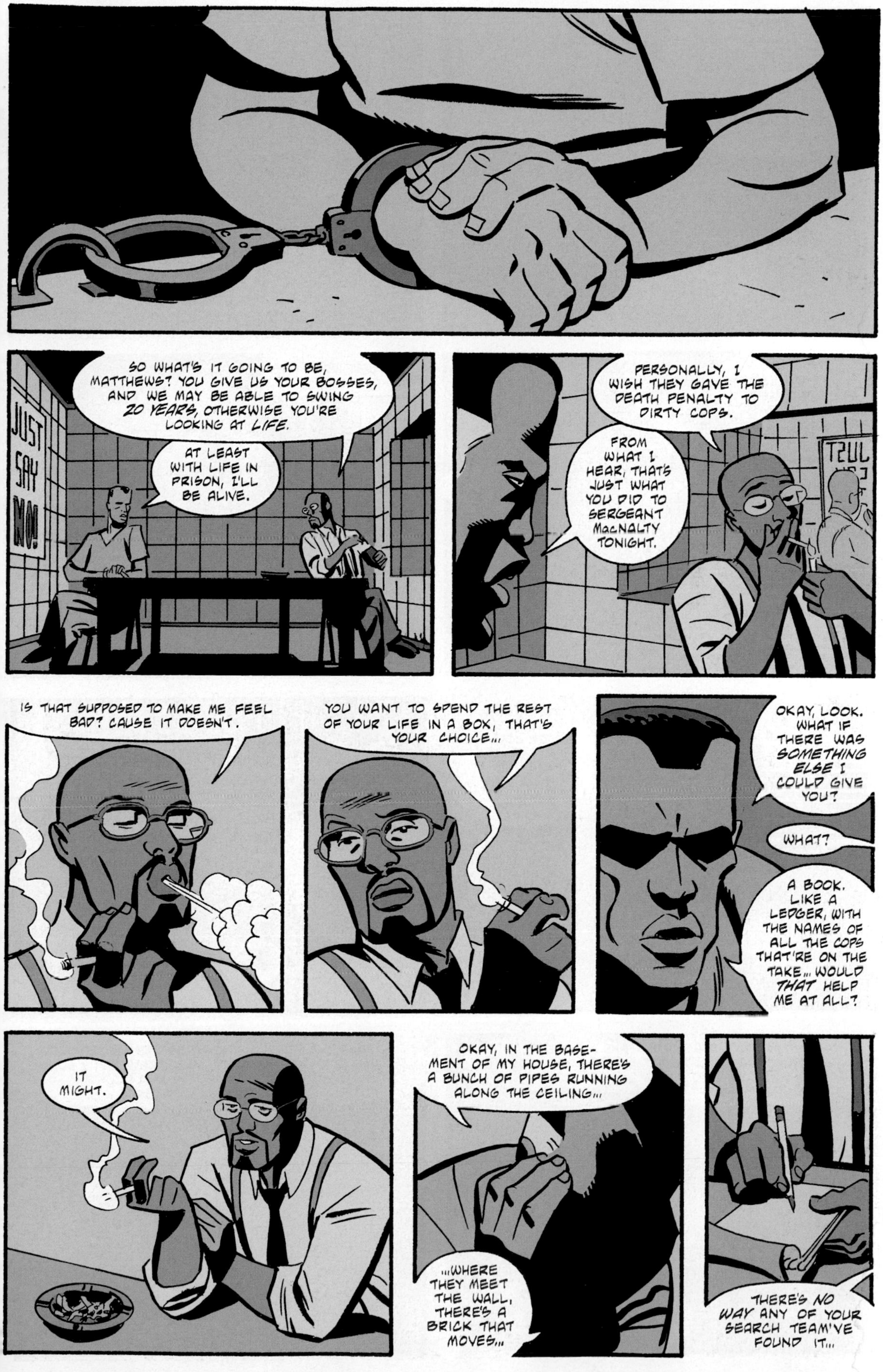
SO WHAT'S IT GOING TO BE, MATTHEWS? YOU GIVE US YOUR BOSSES, AND WE MAY BE ABLE TO SWING *20 YEARS*, OTHERWISE YOU'RE LOOKING AT *LIFE*.
AT LEAST WITH LIFE IN PRISON, I'LL BE ALIVE.
JUST SAY NO!
PERSONALLY, I WISH THEY GAVE THE DEATH PENALTY TO DIRTY COPS.
FROM WHAT I HEAR, THAT'S JUST WHAT YOU DID TO SERGEANT MacNALTY TONIGHT.
IS THAT SUPPOSED TO MAKE ME FEEL BAD? CAUSE IT DOESN'T.
YOU WANT TO SPEND THE REST OF YOUR LIFE IN A BOX, THAT'S YOUR CHOICE...
OKAY, LOOK. WHAT IF THERE WAS *SOMETHING ELSE* I COULD GIVE YOU?
WHAT?
A BOOK. LIKE A LEDGER, WITH THE NAMES OF ALL THE COPS THAT'RE ON THE TAKE... WOULD *THAT* HELP ME AT ALL?
IT MIGHT.
OKAY, IN THE BASEMENT OF MY HOUSE, THERE'S A BUNCH OF PIPES RUNNING ALONG THE CEILING...
...WHERE THEY MEET THE WALL, THERE'S A BRICK THAT MOVES...
THERE'S *NO WAY* ANY OF YOUR SEARCH TEAM'VE FOUND IT...

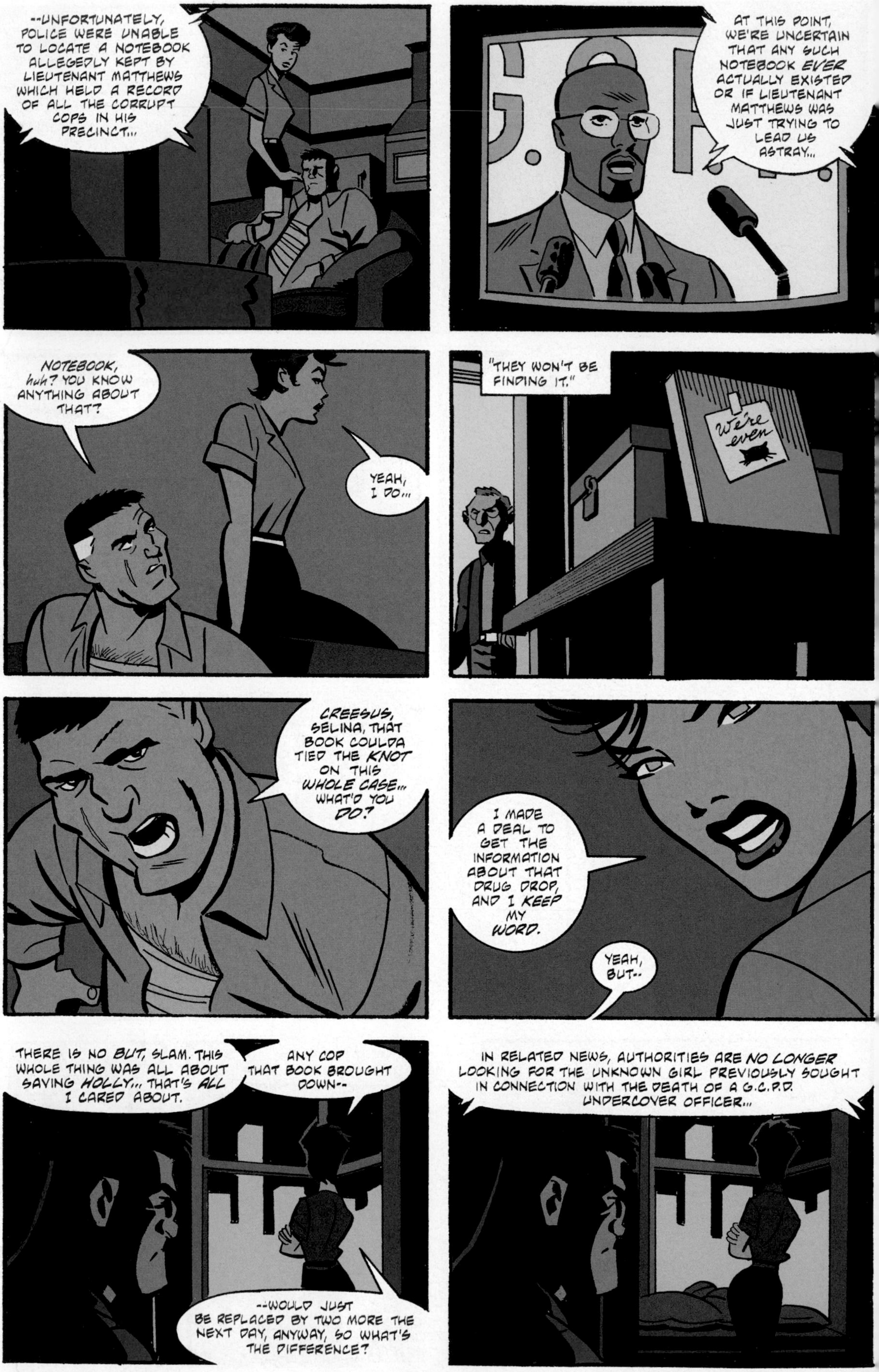
--UNFORTUNATELY, POLICE WERE UNABLE TO LOCATE A NOTEBOOK ALLEGEDLY KEPT BY LIEUTENANT MATTHEWS WHICH HELD A RECORD OF ALL THE CORRUPT COPS IN HIS PRECINCT...
AT THIS POINT, WE'RE UNCERTAIN THAT ANY SUCH NOTEBOOK EVER ACTUALLY EXISTED OR IF LIEUTENANT MATTHEWS WAS JUST TRYING TO LEAD US ASTRAY...
NOTEBOOK, huh? YOU KNOW ANYTHING ABOUT THAT?
YEAH, I DO...
"THEY WON'T BE FINDING IT."
We're even
CREESUS, SELINA, THAT BOOK COULDA TIED THE KNOT ON THIS WHOLE CASE... WHAT'D YOU DO?
I MADE A DEAL TO GET THE INFORMATION ABOUT THAT DRUG DROP, AND I KEEP MY WORD.
YEAH, BUT--
THERE IS NO BUT, SLAM. THIS WHOLE THING WAS ALL ABOUT SAVING HOLLY... THAT'S ALL I CARED ABOUT.
ANY COP THAT BOOK BROUGHT DOWN--
--WOULD JUST BE REPLACED BY TWO MORE THE NEXT DAY, ANYWAY, SO WHAT'S THE DIFFERENCE?
IN RELATED NEWS, AUTHORITIES ARE NO LONGER LOOKING FOR THE UNKNOWN GIRL PREVIOUSLY SOUGHT IN CONNECTION WITH THE DEATH OF A G.C.P.D. UNDERCOVER OFFICER...

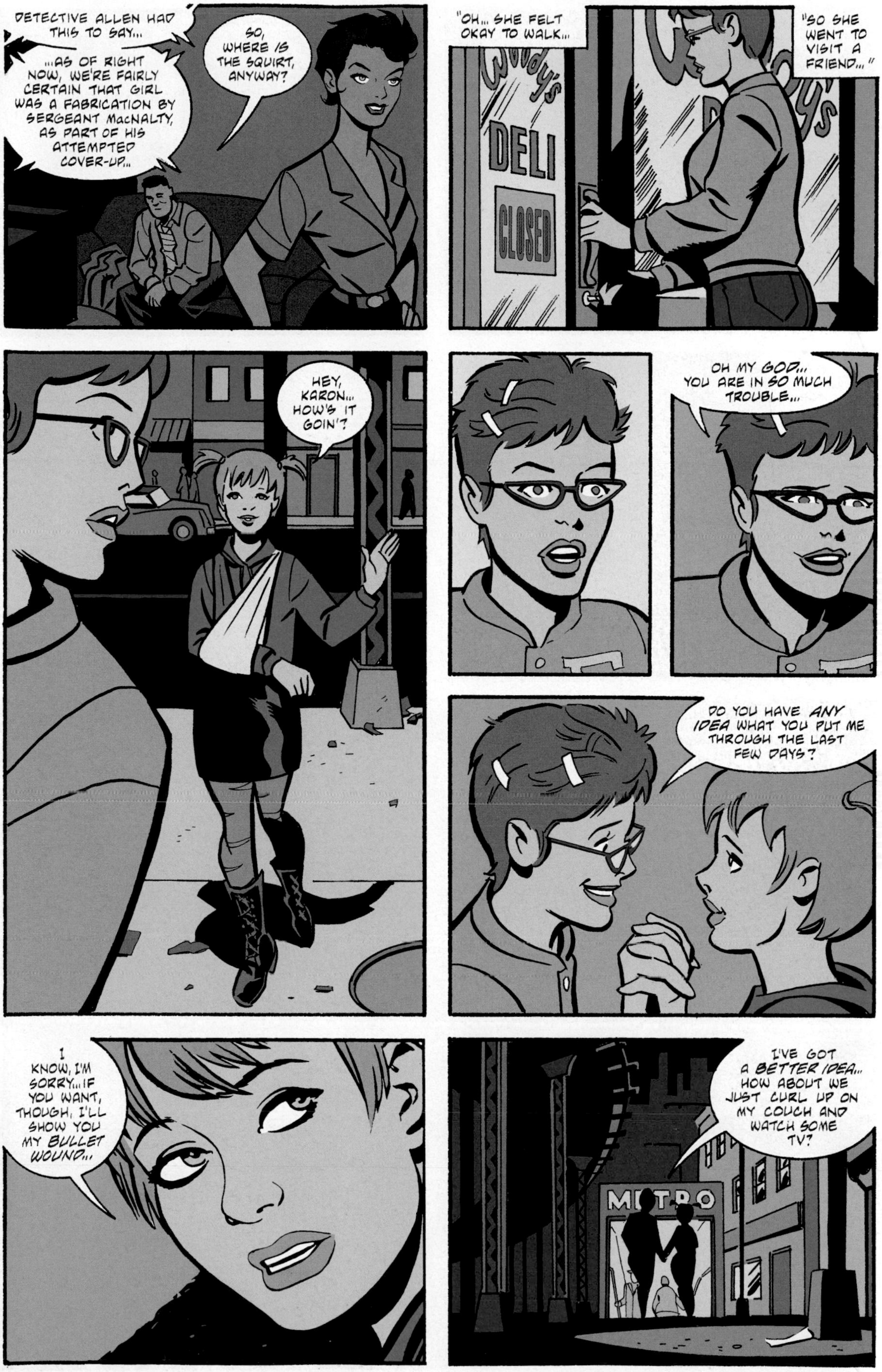
DETECTIVE ALLEN HAD THIS TO SAY... ...AS OF RIGHT NOW, WE'RE FAIRLY CERTAIN THAT GIRL WAS A FABRICATION BY SERGEANT MacNALTY, AS PART OF HIS ATTEMPTED COVER-UP...
SO, WHERE IS THE SQUIRT, ANYWAY?
"OH... SHE FELT OKAY TO WALK...
"SO SHE WENT TO VISIT A FRIEND..."
Woody's
DELI
CLOSED
HEY, KARON... HOW'S IT GOIN'?
OH MY GOD... YOU ARE IN SO MUCH TROUBLE...
DO YOU HAVE ANY IDEA WHAT YOU PUT ME THROUGH THE LAST FEW DAYS?
I KNOW, I'M SORRY... IF YOU WANT, THOUGH, I'LL SHOW YOU MY BULLET WOUND...
I'VE GOT A BETTER IDEA... HOW ABOUT WE JUST CURL UP ON MY COUCH AND WATCH SOME TV?
METRO

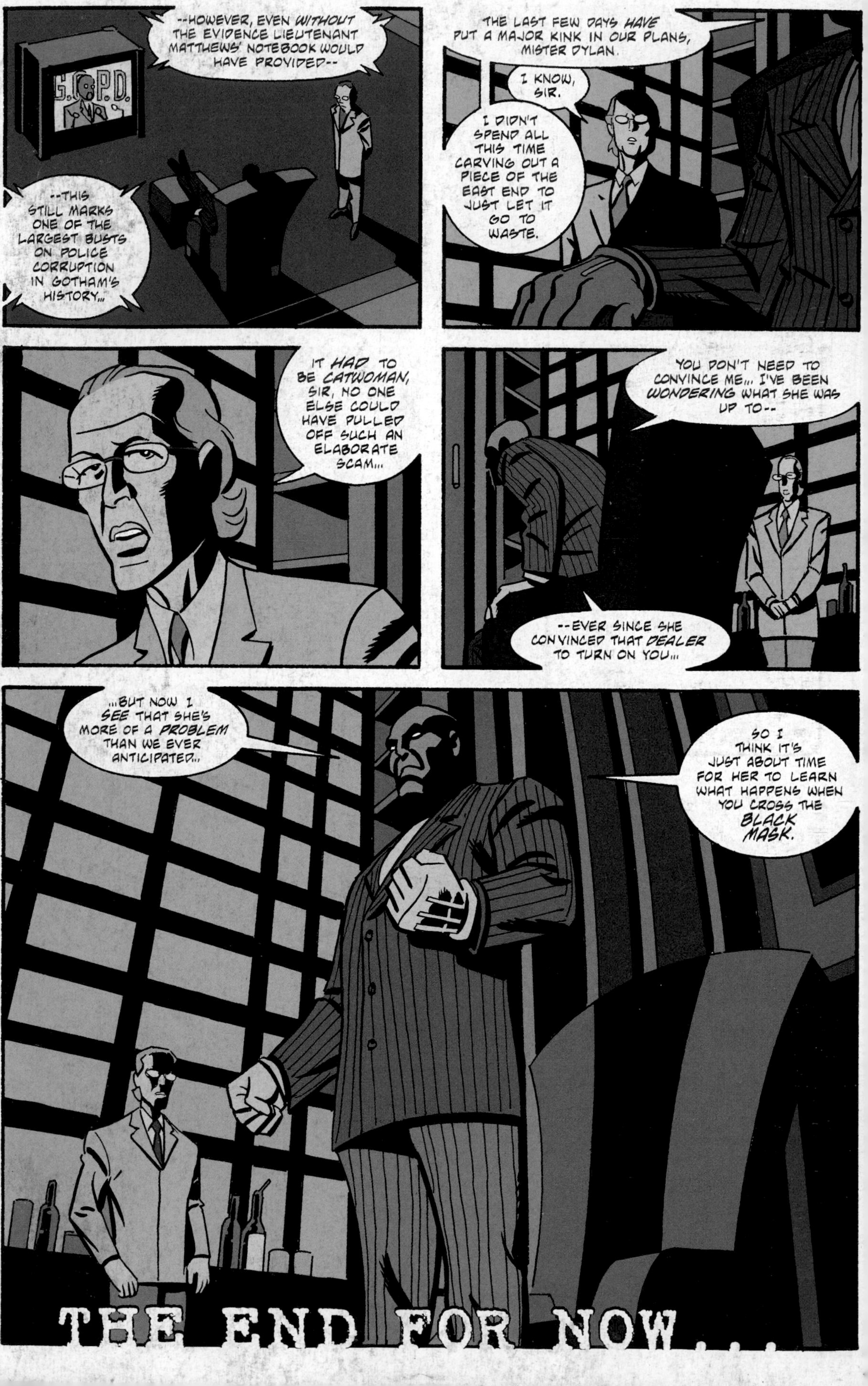

G.C.P.D.
--HOWEVER, EVEN WITHOUT THE EVIDENCE LIEUTENANT MATTHEWS' NOTEBOOK WOULD HAVE PROVIDED--
--THIS STILL MARKS ONE OF THE LARGEST BUSTS ON POLICE CORRUPTION IN GOTHAM'S HISTORY...
THE LAST FEW DAYS HAVE PUT A MAJOR KINK IN OUR PLANS, MISTER DYLAN.
I KNOW, SIR.
I DIDN'T SPEND ALL THIS TIME CARVING OUT A PIECE OF THE EAST END TO JUST LET IT GO TO WASTE.
IT HAD TO BE CATWOMAN, SIR, NO ONE ELSE COULD HAVE PULLED OFF SUCH AN ELABORATE SCAM...
YOU DON'T NEED TO CONVINCE ME... I'VE BEEN WONDERING WHAT SHE WAS UP TO--
--EVER SINCE SHE CONVINCED THAT DEALER TO TURN ON YOU...
...BUT NOW I SEE THAT SHE'S MORE OF A PROBLEM THAN WE EVER ANTICIPATED...
SO I THINK IT'S JUST ABOUT TIME FOR HER TO LEARN WHAT HAPPENS WHEN YOU CROSS THE BLACK MASK.
THE END FOR NOW...

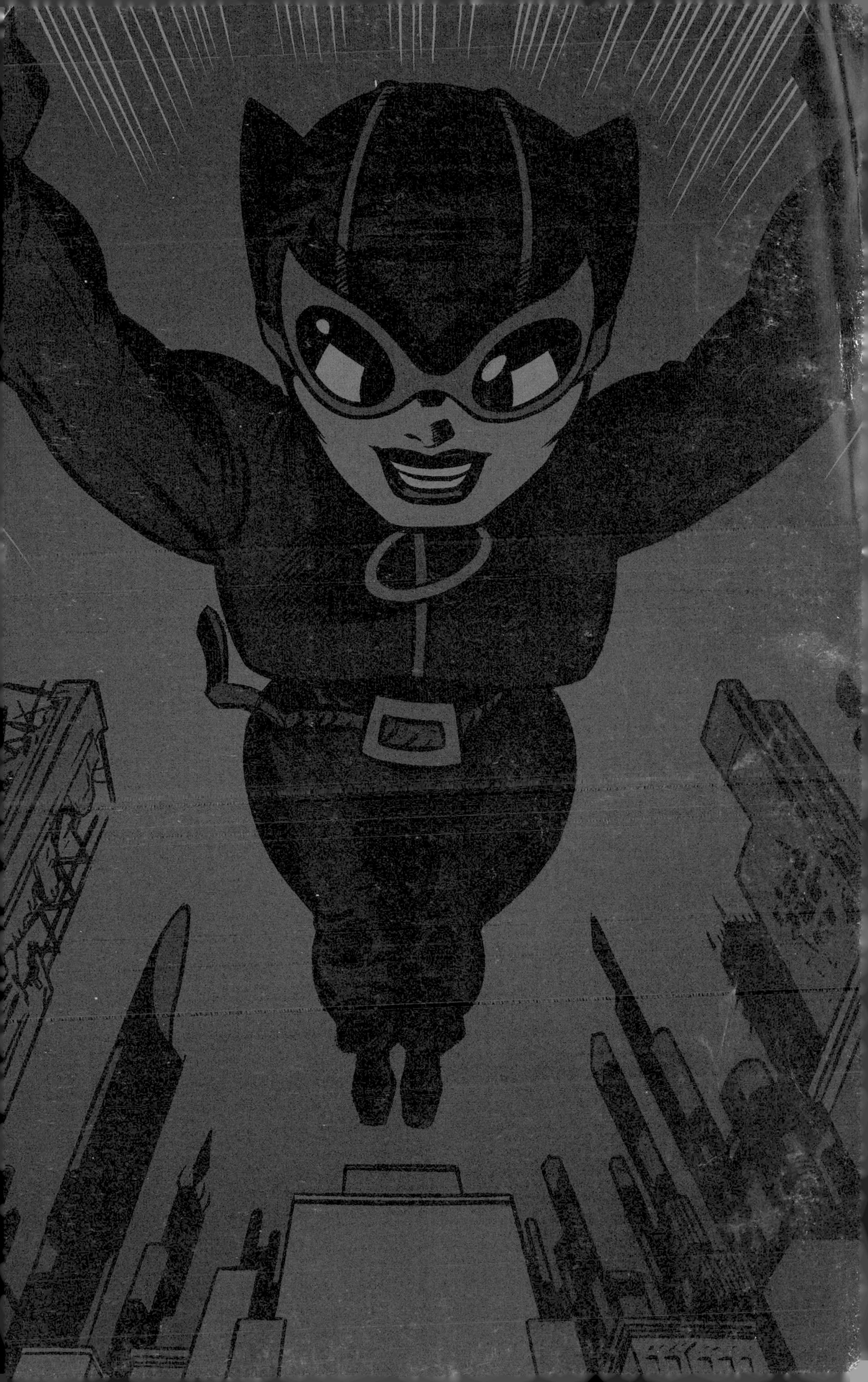

FROM THE WRITER OF
WONDER WOMAN & SECRET SIX

GAIL SIMONE

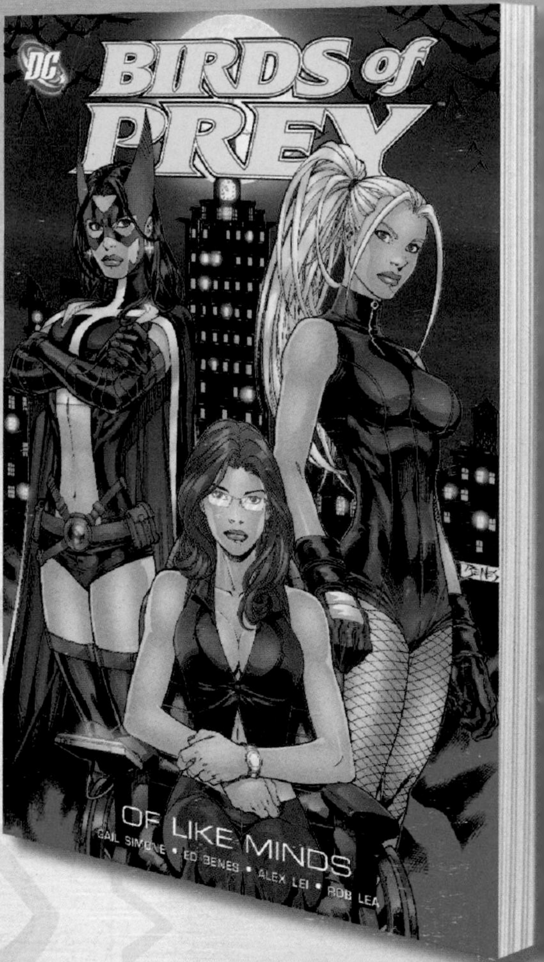
DC
BIRDS of PREY
OF LIKE MINDS
GAIL SIMONE • ED BENES • ALEX LEI • ROB LEA

"A well written guilty pleasure."
– ENTERTAINMENT WEEKLY

"Simone knows how to push her readers' buttons. There's something hugely entertaining happening on almost every page."
–THE BOSTON PHOENIX

"The art is gorgeous, the dialogue crisp, sharp and true. And the action and plotting should please any fan."
–ATLANTA JOURNAL-CONSTITUTION

SENSEI & STUDENT
BETWEEN DARK & DAWN
THE BATTLE WITHIN
PERFECT PITCH
BLOOD AND CIRCUITS
DEAD OF WINTER

BIRDS OF PREY:
SENSEI & STUDENT

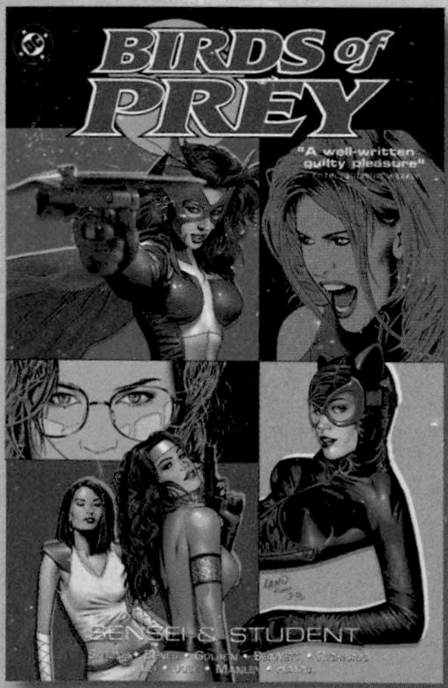
DC
BIRDS of PREY
"A well-written guilty pleasure"
SENSEI & STUDENT

with
ED BENES
& VARIOUS

BIRDS OF PREY:
BETWEEN DARK & DAWN

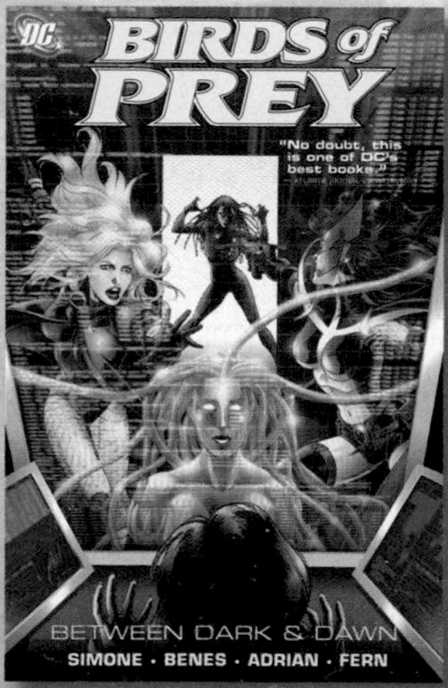
DC
BIRDS of PREY
"No doubt, this is one of DC's best books."
BETWEEN DARK & DAWN
SIMONE • BENES • ADRIAN • FERN

with
ED BENES
& VARIOUS

BIRDS OF PREY:
THE BATTLE WITHIN

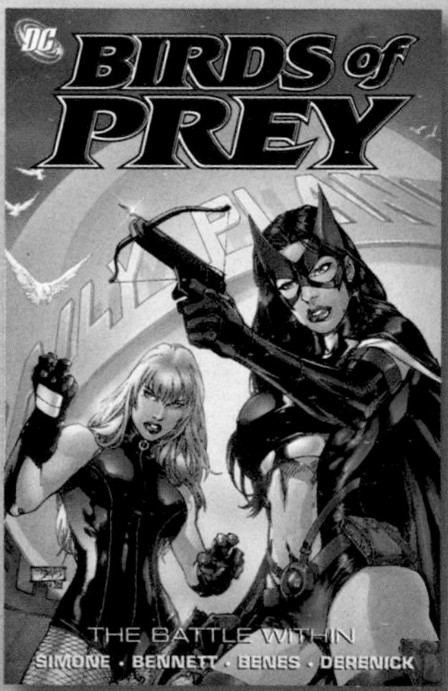
DC
BIRDS of PREY
THE BATTLE WITHIN
SIMONE • BENNETT • BENES • DERENICK

with
ED BENES
& VARIOUS

SEARCH THE GRAPHIC NOVELS SECTION OF
DCCOMICS.COM
FOR ART AND INFORMATION ON ALL OF OUR BOOKS!